Theory and Methods in Social Research

Education at SAGE

SAGE is a leading international publisher of journals, books, and electronic media for academic, educational, and professional markets.

Our education publishing includes:

- accessible and comprehensive texts for aspiring education professionals and practitioners looking to further their careers through continuing professional development

- inspirational advice and guidance for the classroom

- authoritative state of the art reference from the leading authors in the field

Find out more at: **www.sagepub.co.uk/education**

Theory and Methods in Social Research

SECOND EDITION

Edited by
Bridget Somekh and Cathy Lewin

Los Angeles | London | New Delhi
Singapore | Washington DC

First published in 2005
Reprinted 2006, 2007
Second edition published 2011
Reprinted 2012

SAGE Publications Ltd
1 Oliver's Yard
55 City Road
London EC1Y 1SP

SAGE Publications Inc.
2455 Teller Road
Thousand Oaks, California 91320

SAGE Publications India Pvt Ltd
B 1/I 1 Mohan Cooperative Industrial Area
Mathura Road
New Delhi 110 044

SAGE Publications Asia-Pacific Pte Ltd
3 Church Street
#10-04 Samsung Hub
Singapore 049483

Library of Congress Control Number: 2010926743

British Library Cataloguing in Publication data

A catalogue record for this book is available from the British Library

ISBN 978-1-84920-014-1
ISBN 978-1-84920-015-8 (pbk)

Production by Deer Park Productions, Tavistock, Devon
Typeset by TW Typesetting, Plymouth, Devon
Printed and bound by CPI Group (UK) Ltd, Croydon, CR0 4YY
Printed on paper from sustainable sources

FSC
www.fsc.org
MIX
Paper from
responsible sources
FSC® C013604

This book is dedicated to Robert, Jack, Poppy and Bill

CONTENTS

ACKNOWLEDGEMENTS

The editors would like to thank all the contributors who have made the production of this book so fascinating and enjoyable. Their scholarship and dedicated commitment to 'getting it right' are the keys to the book's quality, and we greatly appreciate their good nature over many months in the face of our editorial demands and draconian word limits. We would also like to thank Erica Burman and Julienne Meyer for their help in consolidating the interdisciplinarity of the book. We are also grateful to Martyn Hammersley and Daniel Muijs for their comments on the glossary. The editors, authors and publisher would like to thank the following for permission to use figures in the book:

Adams, Doig and Rosier, *Science Learning in Victorian Schools*, ACER Research Monograph No. 41 © 1990. Reproduced by permission of the Australian Council for Educational Research.

CONTRIBUTOR BIOGRAPHIES

Tineke A. Abma is Professor of Client Participation in Elderly Care and research director at the Department of Medical Humanities, and senior researcher at the EMGO Institute for Health and Care Research of VU University Medical Centre, Amsterdam. Abma has published on client participation, transdisciplinary research teams, qualitative research, narrative and responsive approaches to evaluation, learning communities, dialogical ethics, moral deliberation and ethics of chronic care (psychiatry and elderly care). She is a member of the *Editorial Board of Evaluation and Program Planning* and the *Quality of Higher Education*.

Dr John Ainley has extensive experience in longitudinal and survey research in different contexts and directed the Literacy Advance Research Project (LARP) (http://www.acer.edu.au/about/staffbios/ainleyjohn.html).

Herbert Altrichter is Professor of Education and Educational Psychology at Johannes Kepler University, Linz, Austria. His research interests include school improvement, governance of schooling, teacher education and research methodology (http://paedpsych.jku.at/).

Rosaline Barbour is a medical sociologist and Professor of Health and Social Care. Her research focuses on professionals' response to change and user perspectives, including the sociology of recovery. She has a particular interest in strengthening the rigour of qualitative research (http://dundee.academia.edu/RosalineBarbour).

Sally Barnes teaches statistics and quantitative research methods. Her area of research is how technol-ogy is integrated into teaching and learning (http://www.bristol.ac.uk/education/people/person.html?personKey=P7eSKTkVSiruSsvTcpZSmRVwRlWuuX).

Dr David Benzie both teaches on undergraduate and postgraduate courses and conducts research concerned with IT in education.

Professor Jill Blackmore's research interests include globalization, educational restructuring and reform, leadership and organizational change, feminist theory and equity issues.

Tony Brown is Professor of Mathematics Education, Educational and Social Research Institute, Manchester Metropolitan University, whose research interests span practitioner research and teacher education. His latest books are forthcoming: *Mathematics Education and Subjectivity* and *Becoming a Mathematics Teacher*.

Erica Burman is Professor of Psychology and Women's Studies. She researches intersections between gender, childhood and models of subjectivity in therapeutic and educational practices, integrating feminist critiques of psychology. She co-directs the Women's Studies Research Centre and Discourse Unit, and is co-founder of the Manchester Feminist Theory Network.

Diane Burns is an organizational psychologist and researcher at the University of East Anglia. Her interests are in relational approaches to (inter) organizational change and development, and in both participatory research and discourse analytic methods. She has undertaken projects into the organization of elder care and issues of elder institutional mistreatment (www.uea.ac.uk/foh/diane-burns).

Charlotte Chadderton is a researcher and lecturer. Her interests include social justice research, and issues around race and citizenship and their impact on secondary education and lifelong and informal learning.

Dr Khatidja Chantler is a lecturer and researcher in Social Work at the University of Manchester. She has undertaken a range of research projects at the intersections of gender/multiculturalism and violence against women in minoritized communities (http://www.nursing.manchester.ac.uk/staff/149484).

Juliet Corbin DNSc is an Adjunct Professor at the International Institute of Qualitative Research, University of Alberta, Canada. She has retired from formal teaching but occasionally presents international workshops and lectures on grounded theory and chronic illness.

Charles Crook is Reader in ICT and Education at the Learning Sciences Research Institute. His research takes a cultural psychological perspective on young people's use of new technology (http://dev europe.com/ckc).

Bronwyn Davies is an independent scholar and Professorial Fellow at Melbourne University, interested in poststructural discourse analysis, subjectivity/subjectification, gender, and body/landscape relations.

Brent Davis is Professor and Research Chair in Mathematics Education at the University of Calgary. His research focuses on the relevance of developments in the cognitive and complexity sciences for mathematics education and teacher education.

Sara Delamont is Reader in Sociology at Cardiff University. Since 2003 she has been doing an ethnography on how capoeira, the Brazilian martial art, is taught in the UK. Her publications focus mainly on qualitative methods and feminism.

Brian Doig lectures to undergraduates and postgraduates in primary mathematics education and quantitative methods, with an emphasis on quality assessment and reporting.

Gloria Filax is Associate Professor, Equality and Social Justice in the Master of Arts – Integrated Studies at Athabasca University. Her research interests are in the area of gender and sexuality, cultural studies and pedagogy, and youth studies (gloriaf@athabascau.ca).

Jo Frankham is Senior Fellow, CERES, Liverpool John Moores University and has wide experience in teaching and conducting interpretive research with particular experience in 'critical ethnography'. Studies have included HIV prevention initiatives, learning network communities and partnership approaches to research and public policy.

Susanne Gannon is a senior lecturer in secondary English education at the University of Western Sydney, Australia. She is interested in writing practices and how poststructural theory opens spaces for writing otherwise in academia (http://www.uws.edu.au/education/soe/key_people/academic_staff/dr_susanne_gannon).

Dr Dean Garratt is Reader in Education at the University of Chester. His interests span a broad range of social and educational issues, including a long-standing interest in the philosophy of social research, touching on phenomenology, hermeneutics and post-structural theorizing.

Scherto Gill is Senior Research Fellow at the Centre for Research in Human Development, Guerrand-Hermès Foundation. Her research focus is on personal narratives in relation to education, learning and transformation.

Ivor Goodson is Professor of Learning Theory at the University of Brighton. He is interested in key issues in narrative and education and has contributed many books and articles to the field.

Jennifer Greene is a scholar-practitioner of evaluation, committed to advancing evaluation as a vehicle for greater democratization in our societies.

Dan Heggs is a senior lecturer in Psychology, and is interested in varieties of discourse, subjectivity and media representations of risk.

Dawn Hobson has a PhD in nursing and is a Visiting Research Fellow at the School of Community and Health Sciences, City University London.

Mary Louise Holly researches learning and professional development in environmental education. She is director of the Faculty Professional Development Center and Professor in Teaching, Learning and Curriculum Studies at Kent State University, Ohio.

Nick Holt is an Associate Professor in the Faculty of Physical Education and Recreation at the University of Alberta. He directs the Child and Adolescent Sport and Activity Lab (http://www.ualberta.ca/nholt/index.html).

Kelvyn Jones is Professor of Geography and particularly interested in health. He regularly teaches multi-level modelling at the Essex Summer School (http://www.bris.ac.uk/geography/staff/?PersonKeyC4p9Iz RzmbklUsYM5dHhIyKO7ZX08U).

Liz Jones is Professor of Early Childhood Education at the Education and Social Research Institute, Manchester Metropolitan University and leads the Centre for Cultural Studies of Children and Childhood. She puts poststructural theory to work, opening up the ways in which we think of the child and her social world.

Professor Barbara Kamler has researched writing from early childhood to old age, in primary, secondary, university and community contexts. She currently mentors doctoral students and early career academics to develop authoritative writing for publication (www.writingdesigns.com.au).

Michele Knobel researches young people's literacy and digital technology practices, drawing principally on sociocultural theory (http://everydayliteracies.blog spot.com).

Holly Kreider is Director of Programs at the national office of Raising A Reader in Mountain View, California, where she oversees program quality, research and evaluation, training, and affiliate relations with local partners across the US. Her areas of interest include family engagement, early childhood development, program evaluation, and professional development.

Gunther Kress is Professor of Semiotics and Education at the Institute of Education, University of London. His research interests include social semiotics, multimodality, literacy, discourse analysis and learning theory.

Ines Langemeyer is a lecturer and researcher. She earned her doctoral degree in vocational education in Hamburg. Her research interests are the scientification and informatization of work, workplace learning and power relations.

Colin Lankshear researches literacy and social practices mediated by digital technologies drawing mainly on sociocultural and philosophical perspectives (http://www.everydayliteracies.net).

Professor Hugh Lauder has research interests in the political economy of skill formation and education, educational policy, and school effectiveness.

Kevin Leander researches youth literacy practices, drawing on sociocultural theory, critical and human geography, and social practice theories.

Alison Lee has undertaken discourse analytic research in higher education with a particular focus on doctoral education. Most recently she has been developing methods of analysing discourse in health, focusing on affect, practice and the body.

Cathy Lewin is a senior research fellow. Her research focuses on young people's ICT use at school and at home to support formal and informal learning. She teaches quantitative research methods (http://www.esri.mmu.ac.uk/resstaff/profile.php?surname=Lewin &%20name=Cathy).

Maggie MacLure is Professor of Education at the Education and Social Research Institute at Manchester Metropolitan University. She is interested in deconstruction and post-structuralism. She is the author of *Discourse in Educational and Social Research* (Open University Press) (http://www.esri.mmu.ac.uk/resstaff/profile.php?name=Maggie&%20sur-name=MacLure).

Christina MacRae is a researcher at Manchester Metropolitan University. Her recently completed PhD offers a critique of normative ways of interpreting children's representations in the early years classroom. She is also an artist interested in objects and the process of collection. Currently she is an artist-in-residence in an early years setting, undertaking a practice-led research project funded by the Arts and Humanities Research Council exploring and documenting children's collecting practices.

Diane Mavers is a lecturer in contemporary literacy at the Institute of Education, University of London. Her research interests include social semiotics, multimodality, literacy, drawing and digital technologies in the classroom.

Ellen Mayer is a sociologist interested in moving family educational involvement research into practice. She is developing research derived children's storybooks to help families support their children's learning.

Julienne Meyer is both a nurse and teacher. Her research focuses on improving care for older people through action research (http://www.city.ac.uk/sonm/adult/staff/j_meyer.html).

Morten Nissen PhD has studied theories of participation, and 'wild' social work projects, since 1990. He edits the journal *Outlines – Critical Practice Studies* (http://mnissen.psy.ku.dk).

Susan Noffke has written about and practised participatory action research in the field of social studies with a particular interest in anti-racist education.

Laurence Parker is a Professor in the Department of Educational Leadership and Policy, College of Education, University of Utah, Salt Lake City. His research and teaching interests are in the area of educational policy analysis and critical race theory and equity issues.

Malcolm Payne is Adviser, Policy and Development, St Christopher's Hospice, London and Visiting Professor at Opole University, Poland.

W.J. Pelgrum is a senior researcher and has research interests in international comparative assessments, educational monitoring, indicator development and innovative pedagogies for e-Learning.

Alan Petersen researches and teaches in the fields of the sociology of health and illness, and the body and society.

Professor Heather Piper is a researcher with interests spanning violence, touch, gender, ethnicity, in fact anything of anthropological intrigue (http://www.esri.mmu.ac.uk/resstaff/profile.php?surname = Piper&%20name = Heather).

Lorna Roberts is a research fellow in the Education and Social Research Institute, Manchester Metropolitan University. She has worked on a number of research projects exploring minority ethnic trainee teachers' experiences of initial teacher training.

John Schostak is a Research Professor of Education, at the Education and Social Research Institute, Manchester Metropolitan University. He is interested in radical and qualitative methodologies, postmodernism, post-structuralism, and posttheory (http://www.enquirylearning.net/schostak.html).

Thomas A. Schwandt's work is focused on the theory of evaluation and the application of practical philosophy to evaluation practice. He is Professor and Chair, Department of Educational Psychology, University of Illinois at Champaign-Urbana, USA.

Debra Shogan is a Professor Emeritus at the University of Alberta in Edmonton, Canada. Her most recent book is *Sport Ethics in Context* (2007). She resides with her partner and animal companions on Gabriola Island, BC.

Helen Simons is Professor Emeritus of Evaluation and Education at the University of Southampton. She has research interests in programme, policy and institutional evaluation, ethics and politics of research, qualitative methodology (including case study and narrative) and evaluation and the arts.

Bridget Somekh's research interests are in the process of innovation and the management of change, and in developing appropriate research methods (http://www.esri.mmu.ac.uk/resstaff/profile.php?name = Bridget&%20surname = Somekh).

Ian Stronach is Professor of Educational Research and Co-Director of the Centre for Research and Evaluation Services (CERES). Recent publications include *Don't Touch!* (2008), and *Globalizing Education, Educating the Local: How Method Made Us Mad* (2010).

Dennis Sumara is Professor and Dean of the Faculty of Education, University of Calgary. His research interests include curriculum theory, teacher education, and literacy education, as informed by hermeneutic phenomenology, literary response theory, and complexity science.

Richard Thorpe is Professor of Management Development at Leeds University Business School and Head of the Division of Management. He is a co-author of both *Management Research* (Sage), and *The SAGE Dictionary of Qualitative Management Research*.

Professor Angie Titchen has extensive experience in doing, facilitating and writing about practice development and research that is person-centred, critical, creative, transformative and action-oriented.

Pat Thomson is Professor of Education at the University of Nottingham. Her current research focuses on arts and creativity in school and community change (see www.artsandcreativeactivityresearch.org. uk).

Harry Torrance is Professor of Education and Director of the Education and Social Research Institute, Manchester Metropolitan University. He was formerly Professor of Education at the University of Sussex (http://www.esri.mmu.ac.uk/resstaff/profile.php?name = Harry&%20surname = Torrance).

Joanne 'Bob' Whalley and **Lee Miller** have collaborated on various performance projects since they met in 1992. In 2004 they completed the first joint practice-led PhD to be undertaken within a UK Higher Education Institution. Alongside their ongoing site-based performance practice, Bob works at University College, Falmouth incorporating Dartington College of Arts, as Senior Lecturer in Devised Theatre. Lee runs the MA Performance Practice at University of Plymouth.

FOREWORD

I dream of the intellectual destroyer of evidence and universities, the one who, in the inertias and constraints of the present, locates and marks the weak points, the openings, the lines of power, who incessantly displaces himself ... (Foucault, quoted in Peters and Besley, 2007: 159)

Research Methods can become a fetish, either a set of procedures that must be followed to achieve rigour or a second-order account of procedures to convince readers of the authenticity of research. For the new researcher methods can be simply about getting it right! And that is understandable to a degree; doing good research is a matter of confidence and experience more than anything else. This cannot be learnt from a textbook. Research is much more like an art than a science. It requires invention, imagination and creativity rather than slavish following of textbook bullet points. Or as Charles Wright Mills (Wright Mills, 1970) put it, 'to the individual social scientist who feels himself [sic] part of the classic tradition, social science is the practice of a craft' (p. 215). He goes on to talk about the researcher 'made impatient and weary by elaborate discussions of method-and-theory-in-general' (p. 215). His conception of what he calls 'intellectual craftmanship' is a process of constant revisions and one that rests on imagination and personal commitment. Research is a complex interplay between techniques, questions and reading, it usually evolves rather than following a fixed plan or formula and the elements cannot be separated out. Method only makes sense if it has some ontological grounding in the theoretical ideas with which the researcher is working and 'data' only makes sense in terms of the interpretive resources the research brings to bear. But this can also make the beginning researcher nervous, again understandably.

The point is that we need to understand and 'use' methods rather than follow them. We need to be adept, agile and responsive rather than procedural. We need to be aware of our limits rather than celebrate our purism. We need to be resourceful and tentative, at the same time. As Foucault constantly emphasised about his own work, his research and writing was about thinking differently, about being changed by intellectual practice rather than confirmed by it. 'When I write I do it above all to change myself and not to think the same thing as before' (Foucault, 'Remarks on Marx', 1991: 27).

This collection sensibly and artfully avoids being simply authoritative; there is plenty of contingency and thoughtful uncertainty. It offers a set of papers that frame method in the context of power, struggle and reflexivity. The title makes the point – *Theory and Methods* – they are indivisible. All of this is far removed from the 'research for dummies' approach of many contemporary method texts. The reader here is interlocutor, someone who must make decisions, who must think about what they do when they do research and challenge tired orthodoxies, and hopefully having read the book they will think differently.

Stephen J. Ball
London, 2010

References

Peters, M. and Besley, T. (eds) (2007) *Why Foucault? New Directions in Educational Research*. New York: Peter Lang.
Wright Mills, C. (1970) *The Sociological Imagination*. Harmondsworth: Penguin.

Introduction

An invitation to think afresh about social science research

In this book, the full spectrum of social science research methods is presented, rather than drawing on any particular paradigm. Readers are invited to explore the ideas in these chapters, seeking to learn with an open mind, and revisit and challenge previously held assumptions. Ideal researchers are, perhaps, in the words of one of the founders of scientific method:

> Mindes, that have not suffered themselves to fixe, but have kept themselves open and prepared to receive continual Amendment, which is exceeding Rare. (Francis Bacon, 1597, On Custome and Education)

What is special about this book?

This book, *Theory and Methods in Social Research*, is the second edition of a book that appeared in 2005 under the title *Research Methods in the Social Sciences*. The change of title clarifies that this is a research methods book with a difference, written *to guide and inspire high quality research practices* rather than as a prescriptive textbook. Most research methods books are written by one or two 'generalists' who are specialists in teaching research methods, but this book is written by practising researchers who are specialists in the particular theories and methods that they use for their own research.

This book welcomes readers into the community of social science researchers. It is aimed at both graduate students studying for masters and doctoral degrees, and practising researchers.

Social science research is concerned with people and their life contexts, and with philosophical questions relating to the nature of knowledge and truth (epistemology), values (axiology) and being (ontology) which underpin human judgements and activities. To carry out high quality research, it is important to work with a methodology and methods that are appropriate to both the area of enquiry and the researcher's own way of seeing the world. We are defining 'methodology' here as the theories and analytical framework for the research, and 'methods' as the specific means by which data are collected or analysed.

Starting out as a new researcher it is not easy to know where to begin: the area of enquiry may not yet be clear, and how 'one's way of seeing the world' affects choices of research methodologies is unlikely to be clear either. This book is designed to provide scholarly and readable introductions to a wide range of available methods and methodologies, so that new researchers can make their own choices.

This book does not employ the organizing device of presenting research methods grouped in three or four 'paradigms' since these are always over-simplifications. Instead, in this book each chapter contains a section entitled Implications for Research Design which shows how the particular methodology or method under discussion shapes the whole of the research process.

Paradigms (Kuhn, 1970) can, perhaps, be best understood as elaborate methodological fortresses in which particular understandings of epistemology, axiology and ontology set firm foundations for research design and provide defensive bulwarks against external criticism (including criticism from other academics). These paradigms, or ways of seeing the world, provide security in what Foucault (1972: 131) called a 'regime of truth' or set of values and beliefs expressed in a discourse that maps out what can – and cannot – be said. Specific aspects of the paradigm are, of course, continuously under debate, rather in the manner of small building work to improve the defensibility of a fortress. Whilst paradigms provide important frameworks of ideas for thinking about research methodology, their development has had the unfortunate effect of polarizing social science researchers. There is a tendency for oppositional groups to belittle the work of others, often by means of attaching grossly simplified (and therefore meaningless) epithets to their work such as 'positivist' (for quantitative and statistical methods) and 'subjective' (for interpretive methods). In this book there are chapters that celebrate a range of different perspectives.

How is this book different from the first edition?

The second edition contains a substantial amount of new material, including a new Introduction, six completely new chapters and 12 chapters extensively revised. The chapters carried forward from the first edition have all been revised and updated.

There are new content summaries at the start of each chapter.

All the chapters now have a separate section on Implications for Research Design. These play an important role in giving readers clear guidance on research practices: for example, on the extent to which each approach involves advanced planning or will evolve in the course of the research. Although there is too much variety between approaches to make a common format useful, all the authors have addressed the same checklist of questions when writing this section.

The Glossary has been extensively revised with a large amount of new material, doubling its length.

The companion website (www.sagepub.co.uk/somekh) has been revised and now includes free access to at least two peer-reviewed journal articles per chapter, recommended by the chapter authors (for copyright reasons, these are all drawn from journals published by Sage).

How is the book as a whole organized?

The book is divided into eight Parts which together illustrate the holistic nature of social science research.

The term *social science* is used inclusively to encompass all the research, from the multiple social science disciplines, which shares a common focus on people, their experiences, behaviours and life contexts.

Part I: Reading, Reviewing and Reflecting provides the cross-hatching that should be read with – and across – the other seven Parts. Our metaphor here is of a chart, or table, in which Part I sets out the broad themes which readers are asked to apply vertically to the specialist themes of the horizontals in Parts II–VIII. The contents of Part I should make this clear. It begins, in Chapter 1, with an introduction to social science research generally and six exemplar social science disciplines. Chapter 2 addresses the key research work of literature reviewing; it clarifies and illustrates how to go about the important but difficult business of reading oneself into a new field, and how to write critically, and with authority, about the literature that sets the scene for one's own research. Chapter 3 addresses ethical issues in generating public knowledge; it goes to the heart of social scientists' special responsibilities, towards the participants in the research, when gathering evidence and creating knowledge which gives them power in the community under study. Arguably, the importance of 'reflecting' is the most important message of Part I. Becoming a researcher requires focused thinking and the development of self-knowledge.

Part II: Listening, Exploring the Case and Theorizing provides the first set of specialist themes of the horizontal axis. Its four chapters deal with Ethnography and Case Study, and their core methods of Research Diaries and Interviewing.

Part III: Addressing Issues of Power and Researching for Impact contains five chapters that deal with theories and methods relating to research that confronts power and sets out to 'make a difference': Feminist Methodologies, Critical Theories of Race, Queer Theory, Action Research and the Evaluation of Social Programmes.

Part IV: Observing, Querying, Interpreting introduces a set of themes concerned with making meaning out of social interactions. Its five chapters deal with Grounded Theory and Phenomenology, Observation and Discourse Analysis. It also contains a chapter on Researching Online Practices. By now, of course, the reader will have realized that the metaphor of cross-hatching on a neatly structured table is becoming blurred, since grounded theory and phenomenology also use interviewing and diary writing as core methods, and ethnography and case study certainly use observation. Thus we intend that the book's structure should be seen as reflexive and fluid.

Part V: Identity, Community and Representation provides five chapters that focus on two broad themes that explore human experience in terms of 'texts' and 'communities'. It has chapters on Life History and Narrative Methods; Social Semiotics and Multimodal Texts; Communities of Practice; and Activity Theory. Its final chapter, on Researching Policy, turns our attention back to the power issues of Part III in looking at the relationship between policy-making and social action.

Part VI: Quantitative Methods: Theories and Perspectives explores the theories and terminology related to methods that focus on measurement and quantification. It starts with a chapter outlining the theories and principles underpinning contemporary quantitative methods, and this is followed by a chapter that explores how the quantitative methods of the discipline of psychology can be adapted for use within a framework of sociocultural theories. The other three chapters in this section present three approaches to the use of quantitative data and statistical analysis.

Part VII: Quantitative Methods in Action presents five Stories from the Field that take readers inside the process of designing and conducting quantitative research. Each chapter focuses on a research project which used a specific approach: for example, one is about a large-scale international comparative study, and a second is about an evaluation of the impact of a reform in the teaching of mathematics carried out for a State government. Part VII begins with a chapter that presents a research project with a 'mixed methods' design, using both quantitative and qualitative data.

Part VIII: Researching in Postmodern Contexts challenges the certainties that may have been suggested by the metaphor of the cross-hatched table and the apparently neat boundaries between themes. It is intentionally placed in contrast to the orderly quantitative methods presented in Parts VI and VII. These final four chapters deal with themes that blur one into another, and overlap across chapter boundaries: Deconstruction ~~as a Method of Research~~ (yes, the strikethrough is intentional); From Hermeneutics to Post-Structuralism to Psychoanalysis; From Structuralism to Post-Structuralism; and Feminism/Poststructuralism.

The book ends with a Glossary that explores the meanings of social science research terminology used in the chapters.

How are the chapters organized?

The great majority of chapters are co-authored and written to a common format so that each provides readers with a good balance between theoretical expositions, practical examples of methods and theories in use, and advice on further reading:

Key Concepts (approximately 2,000 words). This section provides a scholarly overview of the theories and methods under discussion. It tracks historical developments, key issues and principles, and areas where there is disagreement among researchers. The authors of these sections are all experienced researchers, most internationally recognized for their expertise in the field.

Implications for Research Design (approximately 500 words). This section clarifies how this particular approach determines the way the research is carried out – e.g. whether research questions are the starting point or emerge in the course of the work. It is interesting that the concept of 'designing' research is itself contentious, so that in one case (Chapter 35) the authors chose to re-title this section Implications for Research Practice.

Stories from the Field (approximately 2,000 words). This section presents a narrative, reflexive account of the research process in a particular project. The authors write from personal experience, tracking how they made decisions about the research process, any challenges that arose, and how they responded. The authors of these chapters vary in their length of experience. Some write about the research they lived and breathed over several years of doctoral study. Others write about research that was the culmination of a lifetime's work.

Annotated Bibliography (approximately 500 words). This section lists up to 10 publications that are recommended as the starting point for more in-depth study of the approach. Each is accompanied by a note explaining why the authors are recommending this publication.

Further References. In providing additional references we have struck a balance between breadth of scholarship and the need to keep as much as possible of the word allocation for the writing itself. The final decision on this balance has been left to the authors.

Chapters in Part I – our vertical cross-hatching themes – only follow this format where appropriate.

In Parts VI and VII this format has been adapted to enable the clearest possible presentation of quantitative methods, their underpinning theories, and exemplar projects. Hence, four of the five chapters in Part VI present expositions of Key Concepts only; and four of the five chapters in Part VII present Stories from the Field only. The latter – narrative, reflexive accounts of the research process in studies using quantitative methods – are one of the strengths of this book. Quantitative methods are usually reported in an 'objective' format which conceals the decision making and challenges of the research process. Yet, just as in other research paradigms, the quality of the research depends on the sensitivity and expertise of the researchers in their day to day experiences of carrying out the work.

How should this book be used?

Theory and Methods in Social Research invites readers to explore a wide range of possibilities and then make choices and focus, in depth, on their own chosen approach. It provides new researchers, and those wanting to enhance the quality of their work, with the knowledge necessary to make key decisions in planning their research. Its chapters encompass a very wide range of theories and methods – in order to enable readers to make informed choices about which theories and methods to focus upon. Good choices about how to carry out one's research can only be made on the basis of knowledge of the range of theories and methods available.

A good way of reading any one chapter, in Parts II–VI and Part VIII, might be to give the Key Concepts and Implications for Research Design sections an initial, quick reading, and then focus in depth on the Stories from the Field section. This could even be read aloud, or perhaps used as the focus for group discussion with peers. The Key Concepts section should then be re-visited for a careful reading, so that theoretical ideas can be understood more fully in the light of the narrative account of practice. At this stage the ideas set out in the Implications for Research Design section will also become much clearer. If the book is being used by a graduate class this pattern can be varied to enable the best possible use of the group's resources for learning (i.e. it can be incorporated into formal or informal teaching situations as the class teacher thinks best).

Once a choice has been made about the theories and methods to be used in the research, the chapters provide clear advice on moving beyond this book to more detailed study. In most research methods books, the reading lists provide no clues as to the contents of the publication and do little to inspire the curiosity of the reader. The Annotated Bibliographies in this book, on the contrary, contain notes explaining what each publication has to offer and why it is being recommended.

However, before embarking on reading chapters on the specific theories and methods of the 'horizontal themes', readers should familiarize themselves with the contents of the chapters in Part I. These provide an introduction to social science research traditions and key aspects of research that are of common concern, irrespective of which theories and methods are chosen. For example, many people reading this book will be simultaneously embarking on their own research for a higher degree, and it is a common experience to find it difficult to get started as the weeks and months begin, terrifyingly, to fly past. All research involves a set of activities that take place over time and have to be planned and carried through. This means that researchers need to make conscious use of a whole host of life skills that they may already have, such as:

- personal time management;
- enlisting others to work with you;
- organizational skills to assemble data and arrange it for easy retrieval;
- fascination with detail during the phase of immersion in data;
- curiosity and creativity to notice the meaning and patterns that emerge from it;
- synthesizing ideas and constructing and testing out theories;
- reflexive self-awareness to explore your own impact on the material you are analysing;
- critical reasoning to evaluate your interpretations in relation to others';
- presenting reports both in writing and orally which have sufficient persuasive power to command attention.

Becoming a good social science researcher

Social science research is an art as well as a science, and the skills and knowledge needed to be a researcher can only be acquired through experience over time. There are always judgements to be made and decisions to be taken about how best to go about research. It is always important to keep an open mind and expect the unexpected. Fundamental to the achievement of high quality is the preparedness and ability of social science researchers to critique their work and reflect on how it could have been done differently, and whether that might have changed the outcomes and, if so, how. Reflexivity, not recipes, is the hallmark of the good social science researcher.

References

Foucault, M. (1972) *The Archaeology of Knowledge*. London and New York: Tavistock Publications.

Kuhn, T. (1970) *The Structure of Scientific Revolutions*, 2nd edn. Chicago: University of Chicago Press.

READING, REVIEWING AND REFLECTING

Introduction

This part of the book is designed to provide a reference point to reading Parts II to VIII. The Introduction to this book is a 'must read' (unlike in many other books) because it answers key questions like, What is special about this book? How is the book as a whole organized? and How are the chapters organized? Coming immediately after the Introduction, Part I includes three chapters that provide essential information for every social science researcher.

The first chapter gives a readable but scholarly introduction to the history and development of social science research, including a general overview and six sub-sections focused on individual disciplines. As well as the 'core' disciplines of psychology and sociology, these include education, health, social work and business/management.

This is followed by a chapter on Literature Reviewing which places this daunting task – often the first that a new researcher embarks upon – in the context of mapping the field, and learning to identify the core texts in the area and engage in debate with them. This chapter provides examples of literature review draft texts and tracks their improvement after dialogue between graduate student and tutor. Rather than presenting literature reviewing as a monolith, the authors suggest that it can become identity work that moves a new researcher from the position of novice to that of an authority capable of working with texts reflexively.

The third chapter, on Ethical Issues in Generating Public Knowledge, should be read alongside whatever other chapters from Parts II – VIII readers choose as their special focus. All research methods and methodologies have ethical implications which have an impact on the quality of research data (e.g. interviewees are strongly influenced in what they say by the extent to which they trust the interviewer). In addition, these matters are covered by legislation, in most countries, with the result that seeking approval from an IRB (institutional review board) or ethics committee may be one of the first formal tasks that new researchers are asked to undertake.

1

Research in the Social Sciences

Bridget Somekh, Education and Social Research Institute,
Manchester Metropolitan University, UK, and the University of Canterbury, New Zealand

Erica Burman, Department of Psychology and Speech Pathology,
Manchester Metropolitan University, UK

Sara Delamont, Department of Sociology, University of Cardiff, UK

Julienne Meyer, School of Community & Health Sciences, City University London, UK

Malcolm Payne, St Christopher's Hospice, London, UK

Richard Thorpe, Leeds University Business School, UK

*The authors would like to thank Fazal Rizvi, Professor of Education at Melbourne University Graduate School of Education,
Australia and Emeritus Professor at the University of Illinois, USA,
for providing additional material to strengthen the international perspectives in this chapter.*

Summary

- Distinguishing features of social science research
- Variety of research traditions across disciplines
  - Diversification of methods
  - New theoretical understandings emerging from key theorists
  - History and current developments in six disciplines: psychology, sociology, education, health, social policy and management and business studies

Key features of research in the social sciences

Bridget Somekh

Social science research is concerned with people and their life contexts, and with philosophical questions relating to the nature of knowledge and truth (epistemology), values (axiology) and being (ontology) which underpin human judgements and activities. It differs from research in the natural sciences as a result of this focus on people – individuals and groups – and their behaviour within cultures and organizations that vary widely socially and historically. There is an unpredictability in the behaviour of human beings. Medical research is able to use probability theories to develop therapeutic drugs because bodily systems function relatively autonomously from the mind (though it is increasingly recognized that bodies do not all respond to treatment in identical ways). Social science research cannot develop similarly powerful solutions to social problems because people take decisions that vary, based on different cultural assumptions and purposes. Human experience is characterized by complexity, and social science researchers need to work with theories and methods that take account of this.

Empirical social science research – that is research which involves the collection of data about people

and their social contexts by a range of methods –
draws heavily upon the traditions and practices of
disciplines such as anthropology, sociology, psychology, history and the creative arts. Anthropology
contributes a tradition of participant observation and
interviews, field note-taking and heuristic interpretation of culture. For example, from Geertz we learn the
importance of reading the cultural meanings in details
of behaviour such as winks, and writing about research
using 'thick description' to give readers the experience
of 'being there' (Geertz, 1973). From sociology, we
learn how social relations are formed and reproduced.
Psychology provides us with an understanding of
human behaviour. History contributes a tradition of
document analysis (the weighing of evidence in the
light of the likely biases of the informant) and accords
importance to contemporary records including personal testimony in letters and note books. The creative
arts contribute a tradition of aesthetics (discernment
and judgement of worth) and accord importance to
creativity and imagination in interpretation. The notion of the social scientist creating knowledge by
bringing vision to the interpretation of evidence was
central to the work of Mills (1959) and more recently
researchers such as Eisner (1998: 63) have emphasized
the importance of the social scientist as a connoisseur,
who is able to 'appreciate' empirical data through a
process of 'artistry'.

The social science disciplines, which categorize and
operationalize social knowledge and its production,
have their origins in the emergence of the nation-state
with its political demands for the classification and
analysis of individuals and populations. Anthropology,
for example, emerged in the service of colonialism.
During the twentieth-century, the certainties of nineteenth century expansionism were challenged and
gave way to new ways of conceptualizing politics and
human identity. Social scientists such as Marx (1818–
83) and Freud (1856–1939) fundamentally influenced
the development of theoretical understandings of the
human condition and social formations. Marx's historical materialism turned attention to the oppressive
power of capitalism that appropriated and commodi-
tized the labour power of individuals; and to the
ideologies that privileged the upper classes and
created the false consciousness whereby working
people colluded in their own oppression (McLellen,
1977). These ideas provided analytical tools for
researching the processes of social class and economic
power. Freud's theory of psychoanalysis, although it
was highly contentious, was inspirational among

artists and stimulated the development of new ways
of exploring human consciousness in the social
sciences (Freud, 1986). Other specialist branches of
the social sciences have provided a range of concepts
and theories for the study of people. For example, in
anthropology Benedict (1935: 161–201) explored the
way in which individuals are shaped by their society,
while at the same time reconstructing and shaping
society itself. In cultural psychology, Wertsch (1998)
built on the work of Vygotsky to explore the ways
human activity is 'mediated' by cultural tools and
artefacts so that human agency is constantly enabled
or constrained by cultural and current contexts.

The very term social science indicates its emergence in relation to, sometimes in opposition to,
natural science. Early twentieth-century social scientists struggled to extricate themselves from the accu-
sations made by logical positivism that research which
lacked the solid foundation of measurement was no
better than fancy and invention. They sought to
develop methods which conformed to the methodology of the natural sciences, and researchers such as
Homans (1950) ('general theory') focused on seeking
generalizable laws governing the behaviour of human
groups. Today there is a strong tradition of social
science research using quantitative methods, such as
surveys which provide decision-makers with statistical
information on uptake of resources and the impact of
reforms. Sometimes these data are collected by the
researchers but often analysis is carried out on
large-scale databases already existing in the public
record. Research of this kind needs to be large scale
to provide a sufficient number of records to carry out
analyses of correlations between variables, for
example when using randomized controlled trials to
measure the impact of something new (a 'treatment').
It is in the use of quantification and statistical analysis
that social science methods come closest to natural
science methods and their strength lies in answering
What? How many? and When? questions. To use
these data to answer Why? and How? questions, it is
usually essential to collect additional qualitative data.

The early twentieth century was also the time when
social science was diversifying and growing in both
confidence and status. In the political turmoil of
Europe in the 1920s and 1930s, a group of philosophers and social scientists, known as 'The Frankfurt
School', developed an interdisciplinary social science
method, 'critical theory', that focused on critiquing
the assumptions springing from powerful ideologies.
Rather than seeking to confirm and strengthen the

existing order, for them social science should be concerned with critiquing and changing society. Influenced by Marx, they sought to understand the cultural factors that produced social conformity. They used a dialectic method to critique the assumptions of fashionable ideologies, including Marxism. During the period 1934–51, due to the political turmoil in Europe, the group were based in New York and California where their ideas were confronted by the celebrity culture of Hollywood. From 1956 onwards, after their return to Frankfurt, Habermas became a leading figure, focusing on ways in which language can empower and transform human interactions (Habermas, 1984). Another influential thinker of those years was the German Jewish political theorist, Arendt, who had escaped from Europe to New York in 1941. Much of her work focuses on human freedom and responsibility, challenging accepted orthodoxies, most famously in her book on the war trial of the Nazi war criminal, Eichmann, where she used the term 'the banality of evil' to describe the tendency in ordinary people to commit evil thoughtlessly because of a failure to think critically (Arendt, 1963). The work of Arendt and critical theorists, such as Habermas, illustrates the political dimension to being a social science researcher, pursuing knowledge and understanding of individuals, social groups and organizations, in a world where status is not accorded equally and researchers feel a responsibility to make a difference.

Since around 1970 social science research methods have considerably diversified, due largely to the influence of feminist theories that challenged many assumptions – such as the personal/political dichotomy – on the grounds that they derived from masculine hegemonies. The work of Harding (1987) was particularly important in challenging the concept of methodology as a set of theories, within a well-defined epistemology, with rules to which researchers must adhere. For Harding, a method is a technique or process for data collection, methodology incorporates both theory and the analytical process that guides the research, and epistemology incorporates 'strategies for justifying beliefs' (1987: 3). Partly due to Harding's concept of 'standpoint' theories, the period since 1970 has seen enormous growth in research into areas such as gender and race (Harding, 1991). Researchers working in areas where there is systemic disadvantage have a responsibility to adopt a standpoint that will counter the bias ingrained in society. Butler's work (1990) made another important contribution by challenging the notion that categories,

such as 'woman', can be used as stable or abiding terms, pointing out that the category 'woman' contains within it multiple variables, for example to name just three: 'black', 'lesbian' or 'abused'. Feminist research 'puts social construction of gender at the center of one's inquiry' (Lather, 1991: 71), reconstructing the process of research at all levels from the chosen focus of study, to relationships with participants, methods of data collection, choice of analytical concepts and approaches to reporting. In terms of research on race, the founding of the Du Bois Review in 2004 has provided a platform for scholars across the social sciences to share their work and cross-fertilize their ideas. It has also given a public voice to work that was previously silenced or marginalized (Bobo and Dawson, 2004).

As a result of its focus on people, ethical issues are centrally important in social science research. Knowledge confers power, so in collecting data researchers need to be sensitive to the possible ways in which participation in the research may have an impact on participants. Drawing on moral and ethical principles, social science researchers vary considerably in terms of the kinds of relationship they establish with participants, as indicated by the terms they use to describe them – 'subjects', 'informants' or 'co-researchers'. These different 'namings' all imply different ways of distributing power within the relationship, but whatever stance is adopted power differentials are never entirely within the researcher's control and can never be excised. This in turn has an impact on the quality and reliability of the data that can be collected. Social science researchers typically emphasize the need to establish a relationship of trust with the participants, as the necessary condition for carrying out high quality research. However, since relationships are organic rather than static, trust is a slippery concept, human beings (can) never reveal all that is in their minds and with this realization has come an increasing emphasis on the negotiation of the research contract, whether implicit or explicit.

Quality in social science research rests upon the persuasive power of its outcomes and therefore, fundamentally, upon how it uses language to construct and represent meaning. A key development in social science theory, that builds on the idea of the centrality of language in meaning making, is often referred to as 'the linguistic turn'. Since language can only ever be a representation, the 'meaning' of any statement is a linguistic construction. Using Foucault's concept of 'discourse' the focus of inquiry should, therefore, be on the relations of power contained in the language rather than an attempt to use reason to establish its meaning (Foucault, 1980: 114–15). For Derrida (1967), texts are 'fabrications' whose meanings cannot finally be pinned down. The focus of research is therefore to deconstruct: i.e. to uncover the workings of *différance* (both difference and deferral) through which truth and meaning are produced (see Burman and MacLure, in this volume).

Post-structuralists, building on the work of Foucault and Derrida, have challenged the whole idea that social science research should generate coherent meaning, accusing researchers of imposing an unwarranted order on data in order to present an – often formulaic – 'grand narrative'. Haraway (1991: 187) makes explicit the dilemmas that face social science researchers as a result of these new epistemologies, arguing that we need '*simultaneously* ... a critical practice for recognizing our own "semiotic technologies" for making meanings, *and* a no-nonsense commitment to faithful accounts of a "real" world'.

In recent years, globalization has raised new questions about the nature of identity, culture and social relations, as well as power configurations. Following both large-scale movement of people across the globe and the recognition of global interrelations, the issues of difference and diversity have come to occupy a central place within the social sciences, not only in anthropology and sociology but other disciplinary and policy fields as well. Thus, for example, theorists have begun to focus on global sociology, rather than national ones (Giddens, 2003). The issues of post-coloniality in a globalizing world raise a whole range of questions that can no longer be ignored. Appadurai (2001), drawing on his experience of working with researchers within an impoverished community in Mumbai, has called for 'the right to research' as a means of empowering the disadvantaged. In this way, his research supports the development of a counter-hegemonic movement that he calls 'globalization from below'.

Principles of research in six social science disciplines

The rest of Chapter 1, divided into six sub-sections, introduces the culture, values and politics that frame and influence research practice and underpinning methodologies within each of six disciplines of the social sciences. They are intended to illustrate the processes of history and tradition by which research in each discipline is shaped. There are, of course, a large number of social science disciplines from which these are only a selection. We have included the two major underpinning disciplines, Psychology and Sociology, from which we believe that all other social sciences draw models and theories. These are followed by four disciplines, Education, Health, Social policy, and Management and Business, which have been particularly strongly influenced by political fashions and ideologies in many countries during the last half century, and which are illustrative of the constraining and shaping processes of the sociology of knowledge. They have been chosen because of their fundamental importance in influencing social organization in a civil society. In choosing these six disciplines we have been influenced by the need to provide support and guidance for researchers working in fields in which the inter-relationship between theory and practice is critically important, and where there is often a need for researchers to become involved in researching the process of innovation and development. Many other social science disciplines, for example Anthropology and Economics, could make a stronger claim than some of these for their significance and impact in the social sciences as a whole, and we have ensured that many chapters of the book draw upon them for inspiration.

One: Psychology

Erica Burman

The origins of the modern psychology of western societies lie in political demands of the nation-state ranging from how the introduction of compulsory primary level schooling led to the 'need' to distinguish educational levels, to assessing the mental and physical 'abilities' of soldiers recruited for imperial wars. Hence notwithstanding its concern with the seemingly private or personal worlds of individual minds, family relationships and (usually small) group activity, psychology is far from being separate from broader social interests. The current popularity of psychology merely continues a longstanding strategy to shape appropriate forms of citizenship through interventions at the level of the individual.

Contemporary psychology has many sub-disciplinary divisions: for example, developmental, social, cognitive, educational, clinical – and more recently forensic, health and community, counselling and sports psychology. Some are now accorded distinct professional status, while others are considered more 'academic' specialisms. Most have been subject to shifting sets of methodological and theoretical paradigms: behaviourist, cognitive, humanist, deconstructionist. They all elaborate their own model of their subject as well as corresponding procedures for the investigation of its qualities.

Yet the early psychologists were both theoretical and applied in their concerns, and took an integrated approach to their investigations. Their methods combined observation, experimentation and interpretation. Notwithstanding the current focus of mainstream psychology on experimental techniques and statistical analyses, early key psychological studies were based on case studies with small sample sizes that were frequently accompanied by wide-ranging political, philosophical and social commentary and speculation.

Hence while psychology may have emerged to fulfil a political need for a science of the individual, its apparently specialist knowledge belies the ways it is imbued by its own cultural conditions. Its influence extends far beyond psychological 'laboratories' or elite academic settings. Psychological theories profoundly inflect a whole range of practices dealing with the assessment and evaluation of our lives: in schools, in work, in hospitals, in prisons – and even (or especially?) in our kitchens and bedrooms. Foucault (1981) aptly described psychoanalysis as a secular confessional and we increasingly look to psychological and psychotherapeutic ideas for advice. This 'psy complex' (Ingleby, 1985; Rose, 1985) invites us to construct a sense of interiority, or self-hood, through subscription to some – now secularized – authority. In this sense Foucault's analyses are particularly relevant as psychology plays a key role in forms of self-regulation or 'governmentality' by which liberal democracies define and limit 'normality', alongside informing how we experience ourselves as freely choosing the norms we live with and by (Rose, 1985, 1990).

The history of psychology is not a pretty one. Cyril Burt was the first person in Britain to be officially employed as a 'psychologist' – by London County Council in 1913. Other early psychologists were explicit advocates of eugenics (Richards, 1997), and their legacies remain in the statistical tests they invented. Burt's impact remains on the tripartite structure of the schooling system, as well as founding and editing the *British Journal of Statistical Psychology*. This is alongside having fabricated results (and research personnel!) to support his claims of the heritability of intelligence (Kamin, 1977). Despite

repudiating his 'data', the discipline of psychology has continued to benefit from his achievement in inscribing its place within social policy. In this, claims to 'science' were part of a legitimation strategy to build a credible arena of theory and practice.

Thus far from being 'scientific', in the usually accepted sense of being value-free or neutral, psychological research has from its inception been imbued with distinct policy (and personal) agendas. Psychology is the reflexive discipline par excellence – since it is about people studying people. Addressing this has made psychology rather a self-preoccupied discipline, endlessly exploring the methodological artefacts of its own (sometimes rather bizarre) interventions. Much psychological literature discusses conceptual devices that have been elaborated to try to describe and then screen out researcher effects: documenting how research participants (or 'subjects') are sensitive to particular contextual conditions (such as: primacy, recency or halo 'effects', and other demand and volunteer 'characteristics'). These analyses remain relevant within quantitative psychology, particularly experimental or survey design.

From the late 1970s the turn to qualitative and interpretive approaches ushered in more participative and humanist psychological research, positioning those who are studied as active constructors and expert interpreters of their own psychologies. Feminist critiques imported an attention to the ways social structural differences – such as gender – enter into research relationships and to more subtle ways that gendered representations and assumptions structure theoretical and methodological paradigms. Rather than being something to be screened out in the pursuit of accurate measurement, subjectivity – whether of the researcher or the researched – emerges as vital to include and address in generating rigorous and relevant analyses.

Hence psychology highlights starkly a key conundrum posed by power/knowledge relations within the social sciences. Is method theory? If it is not – or not only – this, what theory has psychology generated that is not merely recycled commonsense dressed up in jargon or poached from other disciplines? Rose (1985) persuasively argued that the emerging discipline of psychology gained its distinctive role through the generation of methods that masquerade as theory. That is, psychological expertise resides only in controlling and applying (i.e. the administration of) technologies of assessment: testing, measurement and classification. Linked to this interest in power/

knowledge relations, psychology has, in recent years, also witnessed a 'psychoanalytical turn', including an emphasis on clinical methods, designed to unearth fundamental assumptions in identity formations, underlining the importance of reflexivity.

Thus psychology's complicity within strategies of social regulation makes it a prime arena for the study of both oppression and resistance. Contemporary critical, constructionist and feminist researchers focus on psychological practices as a way of studying ideology in action (Parker, 2007). Here discursive and other critical interpretive frameworks work both to engage with psychological methods and theories, and to maintain some critical distance from them.

Two: Sociology

Sara Delamont

Sociology began in the nineteenth century, as thinkers in the industrializing countries puzzled over the social upheavals caused by the industrial revolution, the rapid growth of cities, and their accompanying social changes. Three internal disputes characterized sociology then, and continue to divide it today, about: (1) epistemologies and theories; (2) intellectual politics; and (3) methods. A more nuanced version of this very brief summary can be found in Delamont (2003).

One dispute is between those who prioritize thinking (theorizing) over empirical research. A second is between those who wish to harness sociology to political causes versus those who wish it to be a non-political academic discipline. The third, within the empiricists, is between those who want research to emulate the natural sciences (called positivists) and those who argue that because sociology investigates humans, who are reflexive beings, the methods must take account of that (called interpretivists). Positivists use both quantitative and qualitative methods, while interpretivists use only qualitative ones whether their data collection takes place in the 'real' world or in virtual worlds. This century all types of empirical research are regularly carried out in cyberspace (Robinson and Schulz, 2009).

The perennial debates between those who want sociological research to be scientific and objective, treating the humans studied as objects, and the interpretivists (Atkinson and Housley, 2004) – like the tensions between those who want sociology to be harnessed to political campaigns versus those who eschew causes – were central to the most famous sociology department of them all: Chicago in the

Golden Age (1893–1933) and in the Second Silver Age (1945–65) (Fine, 1995).

The leading figures in the development of sociology have been German, French and American. Many world leaders in sociology, such as Ulrich Beck and Anthony Giddens, are primarily desk-bound. Theorizing has higher status than empirical work. In the Anglophone world, theorists from continental Europe are often revered for their ideas (Foucault, Habermas and Bourdieu for example) but the agenda setters for empirical research (qualitative and quantitative) are mainly American (Scott, 2007). Advances in multi-dimensional scaling, in telephone interviewing, in CAQDAS, in autoethnography and in visual methods are led from the USA.

The second and third disputes are fundamental to empirical sociology, and are complicated by controversies over gender, race and sexuality. James Davis (1994: 188), for example, is a positivist who wants American sociology to eschew all political issues, and writes furiously that the discipline's 'weak immune system' has allowed it to be contaminated by 'humanistic sociology', 'critical theory', 'grounded theory', 'ethnomethodology', 'postmodernism', 'ethnic studies' and 'feminist methodology'. His objects of hatred are a mixture of interpretivist perspectives and explicitly politically engaged stances such as anti-racism and anti-sexism. The sociology Davis wants is, in essence, the discipline as it was in the USA before 1968. That sociology was predominantly quantitative, positivist and used functional theories. There were qualitative researchers, but they were relatively unfashionable. Then, when the USA and other capitalist countries went through political upheavals, sociology diversified. In the USA the anti-war movement, Black Power, and the rise of Women's movements and Gay Liberation disrupted social sciences. In Europe the events of May 1968, with working-class and student protest, had a similar effect. The overthrow of functionalist sociology was predicted by Gouldner (1971) in *The Coming Crisis of Western Sociology*. After 1968 four perspectives became briefly fashionable (Giddens, 1973): neo-Marxism, conflict theories, the sociology of knowledge, and interactionist approaches (symbolic interactionism, phenomenology, and ethnomethodology). None of these is still as influential in 2010 as the post-structuralism and postmodernism of Lyotard (1984) and Foucault (1979) and the social science ideas from the black, gay and women's movements, namely critical race theory, queer theory and feminism.

Sociology in the nineteenth century was male

dominated, although since the 1890s there were female sociologists, especially in empirical research. There have been, and are, women positivists and interpretivists, women opposed to politically engaged sociology and those who espouse it. Scott (2007) lists 10 women in his directory of key theorists. However, the work of women sociologists is frequently forgotten, and left out of the histories of the subject (Delamont, 2003).

It is easy to be misled by the high profile authors such as Denzin (2008) who are relentlessly innovative and passionate about the cultural turn and post post post modernism, and to think the whole discipline is suffused with wild ideas. In fact much of the research remains very conventional and is not at methodological frontiers. Most sociologists in the world, especially in America, are positivists in practice, who conduct traditional surveys by interview and questionnaire, analyse the data using statistical analysis software (SPSS/PASW), and present the results in journals and reports to sponsors written in a conventional hypothetical-deductive format and deploying essentially functionalist theories.

In research methods the biggest changes are due to more sophisticated computing, and the increased acceptability of qualitative methods. Analysis is more elaborate (Hardy and Bryman, 2004). Computing advances have revolutionized quantitative research: techniques that once took weeks now take seconds. The increased use of elaborate statistics makes much research hard to understand for a non-specialist. In qualitative research software to handle text (CAQDAS) has transformed analysis (Fielding, 2007). The distinction between academic and commercial research may change sociology in the next 50 years (Savage and Burrows, 2007). However, the core concerns of serious scholars have not changed over a century. Researchers need to pick sensible research questions, design their investigations carefully, collect data honestly, analyse them imaginatively, write them up accessibly, and generalize from them cautiously, all the time engaging in ruthless self-scrutiny to avoid bias, selective blindness and negligence, and to be their own toughest critics. Few sociologists live up to that ideal – but we should all strive to.

Three: Educational research

Bridget Somekh

There are differences of opinion about the purposes of education, based on ideological factors. Some see education as primarily for the benefit of the individual and others see it as the means of producing the human resources necessary to maintain the economy. Research has to work within and around these different conceptions of education. Inevitably, therefore, educational research has a political dimension. Key philosophers of education include Dewey (1944), who conceived of education as a child-centred process that underpinned democracy, and Greene (1988) who saw education as a means of personal growth.

An important and continuing struggle in educational research has been carried out between policymakers for national and state governments, on the one hand, who look to research to evaluate the impact of schooling, using quantitative measures, and those – often professional educators – on the other hand, who argue that research of this kind fails to take account of the complex variables in the social context of schooling (family, classroom, and the wider culture). Cronbach's work spans the best of both traditions. In 1951 he developed the 'Cronbach's alpha' statistical method for ensuring the consistency of test scores, but 30 years later was to demonstrate the unreliability of narrowly focused quantitative studies as the basis for decision-making: 'The evaluator [of an educational programme] should almost never sacrifice breadth of information for the sake of giving a definite answer to one narrow question' (Cronbach, 1982: xii).

Key organizing concepts for education are those of curriculum and pedagogy. These terms are not always used with the same meanings. For example, curriculum can be taken to mean the specified learning set out in policy documents, or the actual learning which results from students' experiences in the classroom. Stenhouse, who took the latter view, believed that curriculum specifications should be 'open to critical scrutiny and capable of effective translation into practice (Stenhouse, 1975: 4). Their worth should be judged in relation to what was actually enacted in the classroom. An important contribution to curriculum planning, not necessarily incompatible with the views of Stenhouse, was made by the educational philosopher Hirst (1974) who argued that there were seven forms of knowledge ('logically discrete forms of rational understanding') into which all students should be initiated by education. Pedagogy, rather than curriculum, has been the central focus of classroom research in recent years. Bruner (1996) describes how pedagogy is shaped by teachers' intuitive assumptions about students' learning, and argues for the importance of giving teachers deeper understanding of the learning process to take them beyond these 'folk pedagogies'. Alexander (2000), in a comparative study of classrooms in five countries, shows how pedagogy derives from national and local culture, which overlays the assumptions about classroom layout and the roles and behaviour of students and teachers that tend to be common to all cultures.

Learning theories are also contested. For example, Piaget suggests that learning is dependent upon the child's development through fairly well-recognized stages, whereas Vygotsky suggests that the key factor in the development of the mind is the process of interaction between the child and adults or peers. However, Bruner (1997) points to important commonalities between their theories. In the last 20 years there has been considerable consensus about the 'situated' nature of learning, which is consequently strongly influenced by the extent to which the context of learning is 'authentic' and therefore supports learning (e.g. Lave and Wenger, 1991).

Many educational researchers focus their attention on the processes whereby the power relations in society privilege some students at the expense of others. Bourdieu's (1977) theory of 'cultural capital' provides a framework for understanding how factors such as social class and parental education reproduce both social privilege and exclusion. Bowles and Gintis (1976) exemplified the operation of these theories in practice. Gilligan (1982) showed how social systems, including schooling and theory development, systematically discriminated against girls. Ladson-Billings (1995) has argued for the need to make the theories underpinning educational research explicit, especially when research is concerned with issues of race. Her theory of 'relevant pedagogy' takes account of the 'inherent subjectivity of educational research' and requires teachers to place questions about student culture (specifically urban poor African American culture) at the heart of their own classroom practice.

A considerable body of research, internationally, has focused on the means of improving schools, building on earlier school effectiveness research that sought to establish the features that characterized good schools. School improvement research always includes a central focus on teacher professional development and the ways that student learning can be supported by changes in teaching methods and school organization (Day and Sachs, 2005). A key problem in this work relates to how policies for action might emerge from empirical investigations, and even

more crucially how these might transform practice. Action research by teachers is recognized as a powerful strategy for bringing about improvements in teaching and learning and professional development (Elliott, 2007). This has been acknowledged and extended by policy-makers to include the larger notion of 'user involvement' of stakeholders in the implementation of research and – where possible – with its design. 'Systematic reviews' of research literature have been funded by the UK government to identify evidence of good practice and teachers have been encouraged to read this and other research and implement its findings.

Education research is often seen as *educational* in its processes as well as its effects. For example, researchers who acknowledge the educative nature of carrying out research are likely to adopt more participatory methods and may place less emphasis on seeking objective data and more on feeding back preliminary findings to enable practitioners to learn from research knowledge as it is generated. Constructing research as 'educative' has ethical implications and has effects in terms of the quality of outcomes, for example through its ability to fine-tune findings to the field of study and increase their impact on practice, perhaps with less emphasis on producing generalizable findings.

Four: Health research

Julienne Meyer

Health research is concerned with the health of individuals, the care they receive and the services that are delivered to them. The activity of health research is informed by a number of different disciplines, for example, medicine, nursing, allied health, social work, health economics, health management, medical sociology, health psychology, health and social care policy. However, historically health research has been dominated by the single discipline of medicine, which has tended to draw on positivist notions of science. In the past, medicine has held considerable power in shaping the research agenda, and its prestige continues to influence the practice and governance of research today. This can be seen in the disproportionate funding still spent on medical research, its dominant presence in funding bodies and research committees and the tendency, until more recently, for systems and paperwork (e.g. ethical approval) to primarily meet the needs of large-scale quantitative medical research (e.g. randomized control trials), as opposed to more in-depth smaller-scale qualitative studies. Researchers should be mindful of this historical legacy when applying for funding for health research, seeking ethical approval for their studies, dealing with gatekeepers to access research participants and seeking to publish their findings in more traditional academic journals.

More recently, medicine's authority over health research has been challenged. This is partly because the idea of health itself is a highly contested one, especially so in cross-cultural contexts. There is now more emphasis on involving actual and potential users of health services in research, in order to make research more responsive to and appropriate for the needs of the population. In the UK, this culture of being inclusive is being driven directly by government strategy, which is also encouraging use of a wider range of methods, a richer mix of multidisciplinary perspectives and better quality control mechanisms for research and its implementation. These changes are part of a wider societal shift towards replacing or reforming established research institutions, disciplines, practices and policies. Gibbons et al. (1994), focusing on research and development in science and technology, argue the need for a new mode of research that emphasizes reflexivity, transdisciplinarity and heterogeneity. They suggest that research should not be set within a particular disciplinary framework (e.g. medicine), but should be undertaken in the context of its application (e.g. health and social care settings) and involve the close interaction of many actors throughout the process of knowledge production (e.g. different academic disciplines, multidisciplinary practitioners and users of health services). These changes are further supported by the emphasis on 'impact' of the proposed Research Excellence Framework (HEFCE, 2009) which requires excellent research to deliver demonstrable benefits to the economy, society, public policy, culture and quality of life.

However, these developments need to be set in the context of the simultaneous emergence of evidence-based healthcare internationally. Evidence-based practice is concerned with the implementation of best available external clinical evidence from systematic research. International networks now exist to support the development of evidence-based medicine in the form of the Cochrane Collaboration, which has centres in the UK and continental Europe, North and South America, Africa, Asia and Australasia. To ensure better co-ordination from the centre, structures have been put in place to systematically review

the quality of research findings and to disseminate good practice across a variety of health and social care disciplines. Researchers are expected to produce the evidence for best practice and practitioners are required to implement it. This linear approach to research and development has been challenged over time (Trinder and Reynolds, 2000) and more recently, the importance of creating a Community of Practice as a means to deliver multidisciplinary evidence-based healthcare has been demonstrated (Kilbride, 2007; Kilbride et al., 2005). Kilbride (2007) argues that internationally, whilst much emphasis is placed on expert knowledge (in her example, evidence-based stroke guidelines), not enough attention is paid to the collaborative processes that lead to the delivery of good care.

In 2006, the British government introduced a new National Health Research Strategy 'Best Research for Best Health' (DH, 2006: 5) which aimed 'to create a health research system in which the NHS supports outstanding individuals, working in world-class facilities, conducting leading-edge research, focused on the needs of patients and the public'. Whilst laudable in its aims, this strategy continues to reinforce some of the pre-existing problems in health related research, namely the dominance of research by medicine and the continuing emphasis on traditional methods of research. For instance, linked to the National Research Strategy, the National Institute for Health Research (NIHR) has been established to commission and fund NHS and social care research. Their role is to develop research evidence to support decision-making by professionals, policy-makers and patients, make this evidence available, and encourage its uptake and use, for example, through 'NHS Evidence', which provides clinical and non-clinical evidence and best practice, so that informed decisions can be made. Other organizations in the UK, such as the National Institute for Health and Clinical Excellence, provide national guidance on promoting good health and preventing and treating ill health. However, NIHR funds research, not implementation or service development. This separation of research from action is not helpful, as it promotes an elitist model of research that assumes researchers are expert, a top-down linear model of evidence-based practice, and does not fund research that focuses on the learning that can be gained from attempts to improve practice in real-time contexts.

The split can also be seen in the NIHR-funded Clinical Academic Training Pathway for Nurses,

Midwives and Allied Health Professions. This research capacity-building scheme will only fund the more traditional PhD by research and not the Professional Doctorate, which enables practitioners to research their own practice thus linking research to action. The UKCRC Sub-committee for Nurses in Clinical Research (2007) in its Report *Developing the Best Research Professionals* clearly included both the PhD and the Professional Doctorate in its recommendations. However, it is interesting to note that following this report, the National Institute for Health Research (NIHR, 2008) went on to exclude the Professional Doctorate in its own recommendations to boost clinical academic training for nurses, midwives and allied health professionals. At the Royal College of Nursing International Research Conference, where this topic was debated, Meyer (2009) argued that research is inherently a political process and that the exclusion of Professional Doctorates from NIHR funding was due to medical dominance, suggesting that an opportunity had been missed to promote a more appropriate form of research training for clinical nurses: namely action research.

Hence, an interesting paradox has emerged in the early twenty-first century. As political forces encourage health researchers to become more inclusive and use a wider range of methods, the same forces have imposed structures (e.g. research funding bodies) which limit research training opportunities. The health researcher needs not only to be skilled, but also politically aware and prepared to challenge.

Five: Social policy research

Malcolm Payne

Social policy, in the British tradition, studies both the political and social debate within which policy is formed about the allocation outside the market of resources to develop citizens' well-being and local and interpersonal effects of policy implementation. In the USA, the focus of public policy studies is more directly on government policy-formation and work concerned with welfare policy is treated in many countries as an aspect of the academic study of social work. Comparative work on the effect of international trends in different systems of provision, from bodies such as OECD, UNICEF and UNESCO, has also had an impact on the limited assumptions of much nationally based research.

This wide range of research topics relies on many of the well-established techniques of social science

research such as attitude and opinion surveys or observational and interview studies. However, social policy has a particular focus on analysis of official data and documents, and placing official and informal policies in relation to how social resources are distributed in a broad historical, philosophical and social context.

For example, Jones's work (e.g. 1993) over 30 years on the history of mental health services in the UK involved detailed analysis of historical documents, government reports and contemporary research and comment to establish the importance of the continuing discourse between medical, legal and social conceptualizations of mental health. Martin's (1984) analysis of scandals in long-stay hospitals in the 1960s used detailed documentary and historical analysis to explore how scandals emerged and official investigations led to political action. Reith's (1998) study of the official reports on 28 community care scandals in the 1990s points to how the policy effects of the scandals studied by Martin led to the discharge of many long-stay patients into the community in the 1980s, and thus to failings in community services in the 1990s. She analyses the failings exposed in mental health inquiries to show how social work practice during the 1990s changed and draws lessons for future practice.

Social policy studies are often actively engaged in the political process, through the influence of 'think tanks' and government initiatives. Social policy researchers carry out studies of how policy is implemented, the impact of policy changes and the evaluation of possible alternative patterns of service. For example, a recent development in the UK is personalization policy in the social services. Experiments with providing disabled service users with budgets so that they could purchase and manage care services provided for them allowed them to have more control of their lives. Political support was strengthened by reports from a left-leaning think tank, Demos, with influence on the Labour government of the early twenty-first century (Leadbetter and Lownsbrough, 2005). A report on cross-government strategy for disabled people from the Prime Minister's Strategy Unit (DH, 2005) promoted the idea further, and the Department of Health (2005) made this a centrepiece in a programme for the transformation of adult social services. To understand the formation of policy, the interaction of a range of sources like this needs to be evaluated.

Any major service development is likely to be the product of research or to be evaluated. Experiments in personalization were developed in a number of local authorities and a process for exchanging information and sharing experience was managed by a specialist body. Alongside this, a major evaluation of the programme was undertaken on behalf of the Department of Health (Glendinning et al., 2008). Individual academics and practitioners also published research. Ellis (2007) for example, showed that there were a number of practical problems in managing payments, using the concept of the street-level bureaucrat who appears insignificant in policy-making but whose decisions can redirect policy initiatives. She found that some client groups, particularly older people, were less helped by the process. There were also academic discussions of theoretical and ideological problems, for example the loss of a sense of collective responsibility for people with social needs (Scourfield, 2007).

Such research has usually focused on a specific area of service or social problem, such as housing, health or poverty. However, social policy has also been concerned with generalizing about the process by which policy is formed. Levin (1997) identifies the three main processes to be researched as the formulation of policy, its adaptation in political and social processes and its implementation. Research may focus on powerful stakeholders, participants (such as politicians or service users), interests (such as the conflict between provider and consumer interests) and processes, such as participants' actions and decisions, and the outcomes of these.

Some examples illustrate the range of methods. Hall's (1976) study of the Seebohm reorganization of the social services and Nesbitt's (1995) account of the social security reforms of the 1980s used interviews with influential policy-makers, as well as documentary sources. Policy process analysis (Hill, 1997) looks at how services are managed and organized to implement policies. Sometimes, this is done by observational studies of organizations, such as Lipsky's (1980) work, the origins of the idea of street-level bureaucracy. Much of this work has links with management and public administration studies. Pithouse's (1998) ethnographic study of how workers managed child care work in a local social services office involved both observation and interviews with professionals to show how they interpreted and managed complex work implementing official policy.

Six: Research in management and business studies

Richard Thorpe

Social science as applied to management and industrial organization began from the 'scientific' approach adopted by managers such as F.W. Taylor, Gantt and Gilbreth (Lupton, 1983). Taylor (1947) maintained that the functions managers should perform were planning, organizing, co-ordinating, controlling, and standardizing. He stressed the systematic study of work, focusing on such aspects as poor tools, organization and management. The research methods of this early period were based on natural science principles and adopted experimental designs in order to investigate effectively management activities. After 1945 business schools sought greater academic respectability and disciplines such as finance, marketing, operations research and organizational behaviour strengthened greatly. During the 1960s a view developed that the key to effective management was the ability to take decisions, particularly under conditions of uncertainty (Cyert and March, 1992). As a consequence, the study of cognitive patterns associated with subjective judgement and decision-making, the use of quantitative methods of analysis, and model building still dominate the curricula of many business schools, especially in the USA.

However, in a parallel development, some researchers moved their attention to the psychological and sociological aspects of work. With this shift in focus came new and different methods, such as the study of groups and relationships at work using participant observers (Roethlisberger and Dickson, 1939). These studies demonstrated the importance of informal leaders and showed that satisfaction came from the quality of supervision and the social relationships formed as well as from monetary reward. This was in contrast to Taylor's solutions which essentially traded emotional and social welfare for supposed efficiency. Early contingency theorists, as they became known, undertook careful diagnosis of key variables on a case-by-case basis, focusing on a range of organizational issues, including the type of technology within a firm's organizational structure (Woodward, 1970) and the impact of market volatility on management systems (Burns and Stalker, 1994). Adopting a 'best fit' approach, the methods used in these investigations were both quantitative and qualitative. There was a gradual recognition that positivistic methods, with an emphasis on isolation and classification of elementary parts or variables and objectivity, were not always the most appropriate. As globalization increased, the focus shifted further to the ways in which management is practised from international and cross-cultural perspectives (Hofstede, 2001). It continues to be the case that different countries value different methodological approaches to research: these too are culturally bound.

During the last two decades 'classical' theory (namely Taylor) and 'decisions' theory (namely Cyert and March) have come under attack. Both are 'normative' theories which have implications for the questions that are worth researching and the methods to be employed. However, in both there is some confusion between what management is and what it ought to be. This has led to critiques which suggest that approaches to management research should adapt to meet the challenges of the future (French and Grey, 1996; Porter and McKibbin, 1988). There is also more or less universal recognition that managers need to be concerned with the application of theories in the workplace as opposed to simply the ideas themselves. The 1990s saw the emergence of a postmodern debate in management which queried beliefs in 'one world' with 'one truth', and began to develop a radical relativism that conceived of a world where no consensus exists and 'no rigorous evaluative criteria remain' (Holbrook and Hirschmann, 1982). Key assumptions concerning new forms of capitalism have also been a major strand in critical management studies.

Forms of research

The main classifications of research that have emerged from the management tradition described above are pure, applied and action research.

Pure research, which is sometimes referred to as domain driven, is intended to lead to theoretical development: there may, or may not, be any practical implications of this. Results are disseminated merely through academic media. Applied research is intended to lead to the solution of specific problems and usually involves working with clients who identify the problems. In these studies it is important, apart from reporting the specific problems, to try to explain what is happening. Phillips and Pugh (2005) stress that genuine research must include consideration of 'why' questions as well as 'what' questions.

Action research studies start from the view that research should converse with the researched in some way and should lead to change, and therefore that change should be incorporated into the research process itself. This questions the simplistic linear model of diffusion of findings into practice only after the completion of research, as traditionally found in management studies. Classical action research starts from the idea that if you want to understand something well you should try changing it, and this is most frequently adopted in organization development (French and Bell, 1999). The collaborative features of action research mean that participants are likely to learn a lot from the process itself by implementing the findings, and their interest may be on what happens next rather than on any formal account of research findings. Within the action research tradition, Gibbons et al. (1994) introduced an important debate on the nature of knowledge and approaches to knowledge generation in management. Mode 1 knowledge generation occurs within the context of existing institutions and academic disciplines. In contrast, mode 2 is transdisciplinary and created in context by those who combine their tacit/practitioner understandings with those of academics. The key aspect of mode 2 knowledge production is that it occurs as a result of the interaction that takes place between theory and practice. Management also requires both thought and action. Not only do most managers feel that research should lead to practical consequences, they are also quite capable of taking action themselves in the light of research results. As a result, the use of action research findings by managers needs to be undertaken with care, paying attention to how the research was conducted and whether new knowledge has been validated by testing it out in practice.

Further references

Alexander, R. (2000) *Culture and Pedagogy: International Comparisons in Primary Education*. Malden, MA and Oxford: Blackwell Publishing.

Appadurai, A. (2001) *Globalization*. Durham and London: Duke University Press.

Arendt, H. (1963) *Eichmann in Jerusalem: A Report on the Banality of Evil*. London: Faber and Faber.

Atkinson, P.A. and Housley, W. (2004) *Interactionism*. London: Sage.

Benedict, R. (1935) *Patterns of Culture*. London: Routledge and Kegan Paul.

Bobo, L.D. and Dawson, M.C. (2004) 'Scholarship above the veil: Statement from the editors', *Du Bois Review*, 1(1): 3–6.

Bourdieu, P. (1977) *Outline of a Theory of Practice*. Cambridge and New York: Cambridge University Press.

Bowles, S. and Gintis, H. (1976) *Schooling in Capitalist America*. New York: Basic Books.

Bruner, J. (1996) *The Culture of Education*. Cambridge, MA and London: Harvard University Press.

Bruner, J. (1997) 'Celebrating divergence: Piaget and Vygotsky', *Human Development*, 40: 63–73.

Burns, T. and Stalker, G. (1994) *The Management of Innovation*. New York and Oxford: Oxford University Press.

Butler, J. (1990) *Gender Trouble: Feminism and the Subversion of Identity*. New York and Oxford: Routledge.

Cronbach, L.J. (1982) *Designing Evaluations of Educational and Social Programs*. San Francisco, CA: Jossey-Bass.

Cyert, R.M. and March, J.G. (1992) *A Behavioural Theory of the Firm*. Cambridge, MA and Oxford: Blackwell Business.

Davis, J. (1994) 'What's wrong with sociology?' *Sociological Forum*, 9: 179–97.

Day, C. and Sachs, J. (2005) *International Handbook of Continuing Professional Development of Teachers*. Maidenhead: Open University Press.

Delamont, S. (2003) *Feminist Sociology*. London and Thousand Oaks, CA: Sage.

Denzin, N.K. (2008) *Searching for Yellowstone*. Walnut Creek, CA: Left Coast Press Ltd.

Derrida, J. (1967) *Writing and Difference*. London and New York: Routledge and Kegan Paul.

Dewey, J. (1944) *Democracy and Education*. New York: Free Press.

DH (2005) *Independence, Well-being and Choice: Our Vision for the Future of Social Care in England* (Cm 6499). London: TSO.

DH (2006) *Best Research for Best Health*. London: Department of Health.

Easterby-Smith, M., Thorpe, R. and Jackson, P. (2008) *Management Research*, 3rd edn. London: Sage.

Eisner, E.W. (1998) *The Enlightened Eye*, 1st revised edn. New York: Macmillan Publishing.

Elliott, J. (2007) *Reflecting Where the Action Is: The Selected Works of John Elliott*. London and New York: Routledge.

Ellis, K. (2007) 'Direct payments and social work practice: The significance of "street-level bureaucracy" in determining eligibility', *British Journal of Social Work*, 37(3): 405–22.

Fielding, N. (2007) 'Computer applications in qualitative research', in P. Atkinson et al. (eds), *Handbook of Ethnography*. London: Sage.

Fine, G.A. (ed.) (1995) *A Second Chicago School?* Chicago: University of Chicago Press.

Foucault, M. (1979) *Discipline and Punish*. New York: Vintage.

Foucault, M. (1980) *Power/Knowledge: Selected Interviews and Other Writings 1972–77*. Bury St Edmunds, UK: Harvester Press.

Foucault, M. (1981) *History of Sexuality 1: An Introduction*. Harmondsworth: Penguin.

French, R. and Grey, C. (1996) *Rethinking Management Education*. London: Sage.

French, W.L. and Bell, C.H. (1999) *Organizational Development*. Upper Saddle River, NJ: Prentice Hall.

Freud, S. (1986) *The Essentials of Psycho-Analysis*. London and New York: Penguin.

Geertz, C. (1973) *The Interpretation of Cultures*. London and New York: Fontana and Basic Books.

Gibbons, M., Limoges, C., Nowotny, H., Schwartzman, S., Scott, P. and Trow, M. (1994) *The New Production of Knowledge: The Dynamics of Science and Research in Contemporary Societies*. London: Sage.

Giddens, A. (1973) *The Class Structure of the Advanced Societies*. London: Heinemann.

Giddens, A. (2003) *Runaway World: How Globalization is Reshaping Our Lives*. New York: Routledge.

Gilligan, C. (1982) *In a Different Voice: Psychological Theory and Women's Development*. Harvard and London: Harvard University Press.

Glendinning, C., Challis, D., Fernandez, J., Jacobs, S., Jones, K., Knapp, M., Manthorpe, J., Moran, N., Netten, A., Stevens, M. and Wilberforce, M. (2008) *Evaluation of the Individual Budgets Pilot Programme: Final Report*. York: Social Policy Research Unit, University of York.

Gouldner, A. (1971) *The Coming Crisis of Western Sociology*. London: Heinemann.

Greene, M. (1988) *The Dialectic of Freedom*. New York: Teachers College Press.

Habermas, J. (1984) *The Theory of Communicative Action: Volume One: Reason and the Rationalization of Society*. London: Heinemann Educational Books.

Hall, P. (1976) *Reforming the Welfare*. London: Heinemann.

Haraway, D. (1991) *Simians, Cyborgs, and Women*. London: Free Association.

Harding, S. (1987) *Feminism and Methodology: Social Science Issues*. Bloomington, IN: Indiana University Press.

Harding, S. (1991) *Whose Science? Whose Knowledge?: Thinking From Women's Lives*. New York: Cornell University Press.

Hardy, M. and Bryman, A. (2004) (eds) *Handbook of Analysis*. London: Sage.

HEFCE (2009) *Research Excellence Framework, Second Consultation on the Assessment and Funding of Research*. Bristol: Higher Education Funding Council for England.

Hill, M. (1997) *The Policy Process in the Modern State*, 2nd edn. Harlow: Prentice Hall.

Hirst, P.H. (1974) *Knowledge and the Curriculum*. London: Routledge and Kegan Paul.

Hofstede, G. (2001) *Cultures Consequences: Comparing Values, Behaviors, Institution, and Organizations Across Nations*. Thousand Oaks, CA and London: Sage.

Holbrook, M.B. and Hirschmann, E.C. (1982) 'The experiential aspects of consumption', *Journal of Consumer Research*, 9: 132–40.

Homans, G.C. (1950) *The Human Group*. New York and London: Harcourt Brace Jovanovich.

Ingleby, D. (1985) 'Professionals as socialisers: The "psy complex"', *Research in Law, Deviance and Social Control*, 7: 79–109.

Jones, K. (1993) *Asylums and After: A Revised History of the Mental Health Services*. London: Athlone.

Kamin, L. (1977) *The Science and Politics of I.Q.* Harmondsworth: Penguin.

Kilbride, C., Meyer, J., Flatley, M. and Perry, L. (2005) 'Stroke units: The implementation of a complex intervention', *Educational Action Research Journal*, 13(4): 479–504.

Kilbride, C. (2007) 'Inside the black box: Creating excellence in stroke care through a community of practice'. Unpublished thesis, City University London.

Ladson-Billings, G.J. (1995) 'Toward a theory of culturally relevant pedagogy', *American Education Research Journal*, 35: 465–91.

Lather, P. (1991) *Getting Smart: Feminist Research and Pedagogy with/in the Postmodern*. New York and London: Routledge.

Lave, J. and E. Wenger (1991) *Situated Learning: Legitimate Peripheral Participation*. Cambridge, New York and Melbourne: Cambridge University Press.

Leadbetter, C. and Lownsborough, H. (2005) *Personalisation and Participation: The Future of Social Care in Scotland. Final Report*. London: Demos.

Levin, P. (1997) *Making Social Policy: The Mechanisms of Government and Politics, and How to Investigate Them*. Buckingham: Open University Press.

Lipsky, M. (1980) *Street-Level Bureaucracy: Dilemmas of the Individual in Public Services*. New York: Russell Sage Foundation.

Lupton, T. (1983) *Management and the Social Sciences*. Harmondsworth: Penguin.

Lyotard, J-F. (1984) *The Postmodern Condition*. Minneapolis: University of Minnesota Press.

Martin, J.P. (1984) *Hospitals in Trouble*. Oxford: Blackwell.

McLellan, D.E. (ed.) (1977) *Karl Marx: Selected Writings*. New York: Oxford University Press.

Meyer, J. (2009) 'Breakfast Debate: RCN International Research Conference, Cardiff, March 2009', *Journal of Research in Nursing*, 14: 371–81.

Mills, C.W. (1959) *The Sociological Imagination*. London and New York: Oxford University Press.

Nesbitt, S. (1995) *British Pensions Policy Making in the 1980s: The Rise and Fall of a Policy*. Aldershot: Avebury.

NIHR (2008) *NIHR Clinical Academic Training Pathway for Nurses, Midwives and Allied Health Professionals*. London: National Institute for Health Research

Parker, I. (2007) *Revolution in Psychology: Alienation to Emancipation*. London: Pluto Press.

Phillips, E.M. and Pugh, D.S. (2005) *How to Get a PhD: A Handbook for Students and their Supervisors*. Maidenhead: Open University Press.

Pithouse, A. (1998) *Social Work: The Social Organisation of an Invisible Trade*, 2nd edn. Aldershot: Ashgate.

Porter, L.W. and McKibbin, L.E. (1988) *Management Education and Development: Drift or Thrust into the 21st Century?* New York: McGraw-Hill.

Prime Minister's Strategy Unit (2005) *Improving the Life Chances of Disabled People: Final Report*. London: PMSU.

Reith, M. (1998) *Community Care Tragedies: A Practice Guide to Mental Health Inquiries*. Birmingham: Venture.

Richards, G. (1997) *'Race', Racism and Psychology*. London: Routledge.

Robinson, L. and Schulz, J. (2009) 'New avenues for sociological inquiry', *Sociology*, 43(4): 685–98.

Roethlisberger, F.J. and Dickson, W.J. (1939) *Management and the Worker*. Cambridge: Harvard University Press.

Rose, N. (1985) *The Psychological Complex*. London: Routledge and Kegan Paul.

Rose, N. (1990) *Inventing Ourselves*. London: Routledge.

Savage, M. and Burrows, R. (2007) 'The coming crisis of empirical sociology', *Sociology*, 41(5): 885–99.

Scott, J. (2007) (ed.) *Fifty Key Sociologists*. London: Routledge.

Scourfield, P. (2007) 'Social care and the modern citizen: Client, consumer, service user, manager and entrepreneur', *British Journal of Social Work*, 37(1): 107–22.

Stenhouse, L. (1975) *An Introduction to Curriculum Research and Development*. London: Heinemann.

Taylor, F.W. (1947) *Scientific Management*. London: Harper and Row.

Trinder, L. and Reynolds, S. (2000) *Evidence-Based Practice: A Critical Appraisal*. Oxford: Blackwell Science.

UKCRC (2007) *Developing the Best Research Professionals*. Report of the UKCRC Sub-Committee for Nurses in Clinical Research. London: UK Clinical Research Collaboration.

Wertsch, J.V. (1998) *Mind as Action*. New York and Oxford: Oxford University Press.

Woodward, J. (1970) *Management and Technology*. London: HMSO.

2

Working with Literatures

Barbara Kamler, School of Education, Deakin University, Australia

Pat Thomson, School of Education, Nottingham University, UK

Summary
- Mapping the field
- Identifying texts that are most pertinent to the research
- Creating the warrant for the research
- Key theorists and writers
  - Howard S. Becker
  - Christopher Hart
  - Barbara Kamler
  - Pat Thomson

Key concepts

Work with literatures is an integral part of scholarship. There are four key tasks accomplished through engagement with texts that others have produced. These are:

(1) To map the field or fields relevant to the inquiry. This is likely to involve both showing something of the historical development of the field(s), discussing its empirical and theoretical bases and biases, as well as identifying major debates, key figures and seminal texts.
(2) To establish which studies, ideas and/or methods are most pertinent to the specific research being undertaken. No project starts from scratch – new research both uses and builds on existing findings. These pre-made building blocks are acknowledged through scrupulous citation practices.
(3) To create the warrant for the research. This may involve identifying gaps, bringing together ideas

and approaches which have previously remained separate and/or speaking to a particular difficulty, puzzle or debate within the field.

Through these three processes, researchers are equipped to not only argue why their research is needed and important, but they also are able:

(4) To identify the particular contribution that their research will make. Work with literatures allows researchers to name the conversation(s) which they will enter into and to articulate the 'chunk' of knowledge they are offering to the scholarly community.

Scenario

It is for these reasons that when doctoral students begin their studies, they are told to read and read a lot. This is in part to help define their research question. But there is also an expectation that this reading will become the basis of 'the literature review'. Students rapidly become anxious about this open-ended and never-ending task. Where to start? What are the key texts? How can pivotal authors be identified? How many texts are sufficient? When does reading stop? Too often the focus on reading is so overwhelming that the significance of writing about and with the literatures is overlooked. And while students do have a sense that someone, somewhere, sometime – The Examiner – is going to read what they have written, the question of what it means to write for a reader is often not considered.

We want to explore the notion of the reader. Imagine an examiner sitting down with a completed manuscript. They open the big book, read the abstract and then check the table of contents. They skim the introduction, then move to the list of references, spending time scanning each page of bibliographic data. To the uninitiated this might seem odd; as if the reader is simply looking to see if their own work is cited. Even if this is the case, something else is going on here. In this brief engagement, the examiner has accomplished a series of tasks. They can see the argument that is to be made in the thesis – or not – and they can see if the work is logically structured – or not. They know the field in which the candidate is working and the kinds of scholars they have drawn on. They will form an opinion at this early point, and as they read the text from beginning to end, they will confirm whether this impression is justified – or not.

What is clear from this scenario is that the reader-examiner is not checking to see if the doctoral researcher has read everything. They are checking to see whether they have read sufficiently; too little reading is a sign that the research may be conceptually thin. They are checking to see if the references are technically correct; sloppy referencing may be a sign that the candidate has not grasped the required scholarly conventions. They are also getting a sense of the candidate's positioning within the field, with whom they appear to be in conversation and what the potential contribution of the research might be. The bibliographic references act, together with the list of contents and the abstract, as a kind of map for the reading ahead and they create a strong impression of the scholar who is to be encountered.

We've indulged in this scenario not because we want to add to the agitation that emerging academic researchers might feel about 'the literature,' but because we want to examine the complex work it accomplishes. Rather than literature work being a technical matter – simply reading a lot, summarizing and grouping books and articles and then writing a chapter as a series of thematized lists – we suggest it is more helpful to think that:

(1) The literature is not a monolith, it is plural. Many researchers find that, in order to position, legitimate and connect their work to that of others, they need to use a range of texts – policy documents, professional reading, articles from the popular press and web-based documents as well as books and journal articles that are 'scholarly'. In some instances, the range may even include novels, films and cartoons. And the texts may well straddle a number of different fields. We suggest, therefore, that it is appropriate to talk about the literatures, rather than imply that there is a single homogenous corpus.

(2) The literatures comprise a field or fields of knowledge production. The purpose of reading the literatures is to ascertain what is known about a particular topic. We read to see the categories that are used by others to sort, sift, foreground and background the field. We look to see what previous work has been mobilized and what has been ignored. We evaluate the methods used to generate the data and the argument; we might ask, for example, who are the research participants – how many, when, where and how were they involved? We also look to see what view of knowledge underpins each text. Taken together, these questions allow us to compare and contrast and to develop a view of the 'clumps' of literatures which share common characteristics or approaches.

(3) The task is not to review. While it is necessary to summarize texts and to make lists of findings and arguments, this is only a first step in constructing what is commonly called 'the literature review'. We think the notion of *review* is unhelpful because it implies that what is required is to produce a list of summarized texts. This summarizing often results in the 'he said, she said' laundry list formula, where each sentence begins with the name of the researcher, as in this example.

> *There are significant differences in opinion on how to define school improvement. Gray et al. (1999) point out that school improvement secures year-on-year improvement in the outcomes of successive cohorts of similar pupils. Improvement is measured in terms of raising attainment of all students over time (Chapman, 2002). In other words it increases the school's effectiveness over time. In contrast, Mortimore (1998) describes school improvement as the process of improving the way a school is organized, its aims, expectations, ways of learning, methods of teaching and organizational culture. For Gray et al. (1999) student outcomes are pre-eminent, whereas for Mortimore (1998) it is the process that is vital. Hopkins (2001) combines these two ideas, i.e. school improvement and school's capacity, by describing school improvement as a 'distinct approach to educational change that aims to enhance students' outcomes as well as strengthening the school's capacity for managing change (p. 23).*

What this writing clearly lacks is a point of view and an evaluative stance from the writer. The listing technique may be inclusive, but it can obscure the ideas being discussed because they remain so disconnected.

(4)   The task is to map the field. The job of engaging with the literatures is to locate the place for the research and decide which conversation the research is joining. The work is to clarify and make explicit the contribution that the research will make and its relationships with prior scholarship. This example of an introductory paragraph to a literature chapter effectively signposts the mapping that is to be undertaken.

> *I turn now to what is already known about teenage pregnancy and education. I look first at why, according to the literatures, pregnant and mothering teenagers are viewed as educationally vulnerable and I detail the policy guidance to local authorities and schools that has resulted. I note the minimal focus on education in the lives of teenage mothers relative to other research and also the limited work which foregrounds the views and experiences of young mothers themselves. It is this gap to which I aim to contribute.*

The writing clearly identifies the topic of the research and announces its intention to address patterns and types of knowledge and their sources. In doing so, a space is created to situate the research. Below we delete the content from this passage in order to make explicit the syntactic moves that have been made.

> I turn now to what is already known about _____ I look first at why, according to the literatures, _____ and I detail the _____ that has resulted. I note the minimal focus on _____ relative to other research and also the limited work which foregrounds the _____ It is this gap to which I aim to contribute.

This 'syntactic skeleton' is one of several strategies we've developed to help researchers attend more closely to language and to understand alternative ways of thinking/writing about literatures (see Kamler and Thomson, 2006; Thomson and Kamler, 2010 for further examples and strategies).

Alternative approaches to work with literatures

Situating and mandating the research through engagement with literatures is not simply a matter of learning new techniques and new tricks. Rather, the approach to literatures we've described is underpinned by three key concepts: (1) writing as discursive social practice; (2) writing as dialogic; and (3) writing as text work/identity work.

Writing as discursive social practice

Academic writing does not occur in a vacuum. It is productively understood as a discursive social practice, embedded in a tangle of cultural, historical practices that are both institutional and disciplinary. Using Fairclough's (1992) three-tiered model of discourse, we see writing as shaped 'not only by the local circumstances in which students are writing, but by the social, cultural and political climate within which the thesis is produced' (Clark and Ivanic, 1997: 11). Seeing research writing as discourse makes visible the complex ways in which it is regulated and constituted by discipline-specific conventions and protocols, by conversations with supervisors, mentors or colleagues who embody the discipline and institution, and by prevailing higher education policy regimes that constrain what can be researched and written about. Such discursive practices take time for academic writers to understand and put into practice.

Writing as dialogic

The Russian literary theorist Mikhail Bahktin (1981) suggested that texts could be either monologic or dialogic. A monologic text is one that attempts to define meaning tightly, defining and redefining what is intended until the opportunities for readers to create meaning are limited. Monologic prose can be leaden and plodding and/or full of alienating jargon. Ritualistic engagements with literature that read like laundry lists tend to the monologic. By contrast, Bahktin argued, dialogic text is not simply lively and pleasurable to read, but also invites the reader to find within it multiple resonances with other texts, and multiple possibilities for engagement. Dialogic text engages the reader in a conversation.

Writing as text work/identity work

Rather than a set of rules and default structures, doctoral writing is best understood as text work/

identity work. By this we mean that texts and identities are formed together, in and through writing. The practices of academic writing produce simultaneously a scholar and a text. In the academic world, texts and their authors are inseparable. Research as a public and documented inquiry is communicated through texts that are an extension of the scholar and her/his scholarship. Research students, in particular, fret about whether they are interesting or persuasive; they fear that they will not make a contribution to knowledge. Not surprisingly, these stresses often surface in the writing, but are frequently misunderstood as 'poor writing', when what is at stake is the difficulty of writing as an authority when one does not feel authoritative.

Stories from the field

We suggest that the three intertwined concepts of writing as social discursive practice, writing as dialogic and writing as text work/identity work are imbricated in all work with literatures, be it a dissertation literature chapter, a commissioned review or an elaboration of relevant literatures in a journal article. In the two stories we tell from the field we see emergent researchers grappling with literature work. We highlight how their struggles involve not only the technical tasks of sorting, selecting, categorizing and writing succinctly, but are intimately connected with their identities as scholars being formed in specific institutional and disciplinary contexts.

Mapping the field: Denise's story

Denise is a former school principal. When she began her doctorate she had already decided that she wanted to investigate the reasons why principals leave their posts preretirement. She was particularly interested in researching the situation in Anglican primary schools, the sector in which she had worked. She already knew the literatures emanating from the National College for School Leadership and those reported in the national press. As could be expected, her first task in beginning her doctorate was to read, and read widely about the issue.

Denise felt overwhelmed by the quantity of material and she began by simply dividing texts into two categories: (1) that which was the product of scholarly research; and (2) all other texts, including policy documents, media articles, and government reports.

Denise's reading and writing was scaffolded by an academic writing class at her university, where she followed a set of strategies offered by the tutor. The emphasis in the first part of the course was on making economical summaries. So, as she read she entered each text into Endnote together with brief notes about:

- the aspect of principal supply addressed;
- the research sample (who, how many, which sector, country of origin) and method;
- the argument made.

This was a process that the writing course helped Denise understand as reviewing. Denise was also encouraged to develop some initial comparisons of selected texts, in order to understand the basis on which individual texts could be discussed in relation to each other.

The next strategy that the tutor introduced was that of mapping the field – sorting literatures into identifiable groups, with each group addressing a similar aspect of the relevant topic. Denise was daunted by the sheer quantum of material she had collected about the process of principal departure from schools. However, she worked her way systematically through over 100 texts. This was not a rapid process.

Eventually, she identified six 'clumps' of texts; she checked out the groupings with her supervisor at this point to see if they made sense to someone with more expert knowledge of the field. She then did three things: (1) she allocated a different colour to each of the six 'clumps'; (2) she wrote a post-it note about each text in the colour of the group to which it belonged; and (3) she put the post-its onto large A3 sheets on her living room floor. She was then able to sort each A3 sheet of post-its to establish the major themes within each 'clump' and then summarize each in written form (see Figure 2.1 for an example of a 'clump').

The challenge for Denise was to then develop these 'clumps' into an argument. The writing tutor asked her to think visually by putting the clumps onto a map. She was then asked to talk to her peers in the writing class about the relationships between the groups and to argue for her research.

The textual result of this sorting, sifting and clarifying work was that Denise then produced an A3 sheet with post-its organized into six major clumps (Figure 2.2). Denise's conversation 'with the field' went roughly like this: Here are the facts and figures on principal departure (Figure 2.1; Figure 2.2, clump 1). The reasons that are given for retirement are boredom, wanting a new challenge and/or no longer

Facts and figures about supply and recruitment

What do we know?
- Large numbers of headteachers are leaving their posts (national surveys by Howson, 2002, 2005, 2007, 2008)
- There are predictions of a demographic 'time-bomb' (NCSL, 2008; see also comparison in Australia – D'Arbon, 2003; Duignan et al., 2001)
- There are difficulties in recruiting headteachers, particularly in Anglican schools (Howson surveys)

Figure 2.1   A 'clump' of literatures

feeling competent (Figure 2.2, clump 2) and the changing role of the headteacher (Figure 2.2, clump 3). The effects of boredom and/or the changing role are that principals must choose between sanity and self-sacrifice. Many choose to leave the profession early (Figure 2.2, clump 4). This leads to a haemorrhaging of expertise from the system – although this view is contested (Figure 2.2, clump 5) as well as potential applicants being dissuaded to apply for jobs (Figure 2.2, clump 6).

In addition, Denise identified from policy documents the 'solutions' that were being implemented (Figure 2.3). These paid attention to recruitment,

rather than premature leavers and the reasons for their departure, which might coincidentally also be the reasons that put off possible new principals.

There was thus a need to change policy to accommodate what was already known. This set of policy texts became a seventh clump of literatures. (We have not shown this diagrammatically, but it would become a seventh circle in Figure 2.2.) As a result of this literature work, a key question for Denise became: Is what is already known all that there is to be known?

Finally, Denise was able to identify the gaps in the literature that related to her particular research inter-

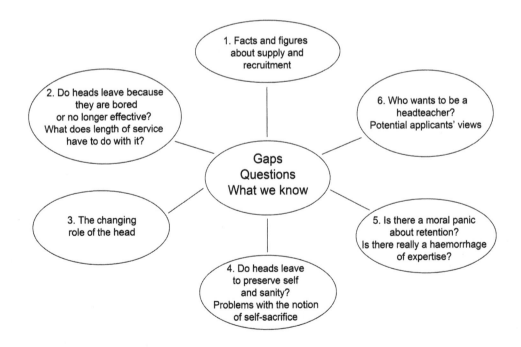

Figure 2.2   Six clumps of texts

Policy 'solutions' to the question of headteacher supply

- Succession planning – grow your own schemes, co-headship, phased retirements
- Structural-organizational responses – emergence and professionalization of business managers, federations, co-headship, executive headships

---

Figure 2.3   Policy solutions on offer

est. While there was information about shortages in principal supply, there was little disaggregation of data about premature departures. How old were the principals? Where did they go after they departed? How did these two issues relate to the particular Anglican sector of schooling she was interested in? There was no specific research into this sector. It was not clear, therefore, if the major reasons cited for the general departure of principals might also apply to this group, or whether there might be other reasons related to the faith-basis of the schools. On the basis of her mapping of the field, Denise could argue that if there was going to be a change in policy, which existing research recommended, then her research needed to be conducted in order to avoid creating wrong policy solutions for this specific sector.

The example shows how Denise, at an early stage of candidature, has been able to take her professional knowledge base into her doctoral research and use it to assist in building her scholarly project and persona. Importantly, she had substantial support and scaffolding in order to 'get on top' of the literatures. The mapping strategy created a space for her research project, constructed the mandate for it, and delineated the contribution to be made. Mapping allowed Denise to focus on the field of knowledge production rather than engage in a technical summarizing and reviewing process. Because she began the research process with a structured approach to the 'reading' task, she never produced a laundry list of 'he said, she said'. Rather, she learned to speak with authority about the various trends, assumptions, empirical bases and debates within the field.

While she has not yet written the literature section of her dissertation, she has produced an extended research proposal, which used this mapping in order to argue for her topic and for its focus. The mapping also became the basis for a powerpoint conference presentation where she argued the necessity for her research. Thus even at this early stage of candidature her relationship to the literatures is authoritative and confident – even if this is not what she feels about

her fieldwork and her findings, she knows that there is a firm basis and argument for her study.

Conversing with the field: Calvin's story

Calvin is a former middle years teacher with extensive expertise in digital and multimodal literacies. His doctoral research adopted a practitioner research paradigm to examine the digital literacy pedagogies he developed with his first- and second-generation Chinese American students. In his thesis he argued that students' engagement with web-based literacies allowed them to mobilize their out-of-school literacy expertise and also improve their in-school literacy achievement.

After graduation, Calvin gained a full-time position in a university, where he was under pressure to publish from his research and gain a profile in peer reviewed journals. We look at excerpts from an article he submitted to a high profile literacy journal to examine the text work/identity work struggles he continued to experience when working with literatures. Excerpt 1 comes from the introduction where Calvin attempts to situate his study in recent scholarship.

Excerpt 1

Changing social conditions brought about by globalization and shifts in communication technologies have elicited new, inventive pedagogical responses. They include multiliteracies (NLG, 1996; Cope & Kalantzis, 2000; Albright, Purohit & Walsh, 2006a; Walsh, 2006), multimodality (Jewitt, 2008; Kress, Jewitt, Ogborn, & Tsatsarelis, 2001; Kress & van Leeuwen, 2001) and design (NLG, 1996; Kress, 2000, 2003; Janks, 2000). These pedagogies build on a range of traditions from critical literacy studies (Lankshear & McLaren, 1993; Lankshear, 1998; A. Luke, 1996; C. Luke, 1992). The New London Group (1996) introduced the term multiliteracies and called for a literacy pedagogy that moved beyond the constraints of linguistic texts to provide students with improved social futures.

Multimodality, like multiliteracies has also emerged in response to the changing social and semiotic landscape (Jewitt, 2008). In terms of literacy education, multimodality is about making meaning through a variety of modes (linguistic, image, audio, gestural, gaze and spatial), where no one mode is necessarily privileged. The theory of multimodality (Kress & van Leeuwen, 2001) focuses on all modes of communication and what it is possible to express and represent in particular contexts. Teachers who enact multiliteracies pedagogies apply the theory of multimodality to explicitly instruct students to analyse all modes in any text (linguistic, audio, visual and so on) or communicative event (talk, gesture, movement and gaze) . . .

This text demonstrates many of the problems we have already noted in literature work. There is an extended listing of prominent researchers and a mini exposition on multiliteracies and multimodality theory and pedagogy. This piling up of scholarship is not selective, and continues for six pages where Calvin seems to stand aside and let the experts do the talking. He makes no evaluations and provides no signals about where his work fits. One way to understand this tedious way of writing is to say that Calvin is still 'stuck' in his doctoral student identity. He still seems to be writing for examiner-readers and parading his knowledge as a tactic for asserting his credentials as a scholar who knows the field.

Of course, journal reviewers and editors are very different readers than examiners. And Calvin has not yet fully grasped the new readers he is writing for. One of the journal reviewers captured the problem when he wrote:

The paper sets out to connect with the key theories in the first section of the paper. The author tries to use the literature to frame the case study but I don't think it adds very much to the empirical data and the theoretical ground it covers will be well trodden for the readers of X Journal. The writing suggests the author is much more at home with the study than the literature review aspect of the paper and I would suggest that much of this first section be deleted and/or substantially condensed . . .

This is useful commentary in pointing out the disconnection between previous literatures and Calvin's own research and the need to delete much of it. Calvin talked with a mentor about how to operationalize the advice and was given articles to analyse how other scholars created an evaluative stance in

text. The mentor emphasized the dialogic nature of the writing, the way writers create a conversation with the field: they argue, agree, qualify and select in order to situate their own contribution. And they talked about Calvin's contribution. What prior research had he used and why? What was he adding and where did his work fit in? What was not relevant to the research he was now reporting? Excerpt 2 comes from Calvin's revision, where he reduced six pages of literature work to one and a half pages and drastically changed his textual and identity stance.

Excerpt 2

This article describes practitioner-research where I enacted a multiliteracies curriculum (The New London Group, 1996; Walsh, 2006) that required students to engage in a discourse analysis of school and media texts (Albright, Purohit & Walsh, 2006a; Walsh, 2007, 2008). As a teacher practitioner working in the new media age (Kress, 2003), I integrated internet communication technologies with my literacy instruction (Albright, Purohit & Walsh, 2002, 2006b; Kamler & Comber, 2005; Lankshear, Snyder & Green, 2000; Marsh, 2005; Snyder & Beavis, 2004) and asked students to re-represent their literacy learning through multimodal digital design. The paper first outlines the multiliteracies curriculum that provided a new framework to help me cope with the access, production and distribution of digital texts. It then illustrates how digital technologies were incorporated into the curriculum, through a school–museum partnership. I argue that this partnership provided spaces where students could interact, socialize and learn in both the real and virtual world (Beavis & Charles, 2007; Lam, 2006; Marsh, 2003; Sefton-Green, 2006). Importantly, they were also able to develop a new set of multimodal literacy practices to talk back to and challenge racist and exclusionary discourses they find problematic.

Here Calvin uses the literature to make an argument for his contribution. A more confident scholarly identity is performed as an informed teacher-researcher trying to make a difference to his students. He *uses* multimodal theory (rather than parades it) to argue for the new multimodal practices he has designed through a museum partnership. The article was accepted and became a pivotal textual moment in his identity reconstruction, where he felt more able to take his place alongside scholar peers competing for academic journal publication.

Last words

Denise and Calvin are at different stages of their academic careers. One is entering the field and the other trying to emerge from it as an expert scholar. Our two stories suggest that both Denise and Calvin benefited from guidance and support to do literature work. Denise learns early in her candidature the importance of creating a relationship between previous research and her own. Calvin is still learning in a new context of journal writing. He came to see that he could not know which literatures to include or exclude until he was clear about his contribution.

The kinds of literature work researchers need to do changes at different stages of a research project. All researchers need to map the relevant field(s), locate their project within it and create the space and mandate for their work. They need to keep the literatures in tension with the research as it proceeds. And finally, they need to peel away the plethora of prior scholarship to foreground the particular contribution they make and highlight the conversation in which they are involved.

The ways in which researchers need to write about the literature also needs to change according to the purposes of the writing. While researchers may do the same wide reading for all research, different forms of publication will require different ways of writing. Reviewers of journal articles often despair when they have to wade through a comprehensive section called 'literature review', particularly when this comprises massive chunks of literature taken from the dissertation. Writers need to seriously consider their readers and genre (a book, an article, a research report for sponsors, a thesis) and write or rewrite accordingly. What is the best way to create a lively conversation with peers in a journal community and assert the significance of the work? What kind of literature conversation is possible when one has the luxury of a book length manuscript rather than the constraints of a 5,000 word article? And how much detail do sponsors really want about the field in which funded research is located?

The importance of engaging with literatures is not just a ritual or mechanistic process. It is, as we have suggested, always a process which involves understanding the discursive social practice of scholarly research/writing, the dialogic nature of the texts produced and the text work/identity work inextricably involved. Ultimately the readership will shape the kind of literatures text that is produced. And because there are different readers and different purposes for different kinds of research texts, there will never be ONE way of writing a literature 'review'.

Annotated bibliography

Becker, H.S. (1986) *Writing for Social Scientists: How to Start and Finish Your Thesis*. Chicago, IL: University of Chicago Press.
Becker's aptly named chapter 'Terrorized by the literature' suggests that students need to think of scholarship as a cumulative enterprise, using the work of others to help build their arguments. The domestic nature of his table metaphor helps take the fear out of engaging with expert scholars.

Boote, D.N. and Beile, P. (2005) 'Scholars before researchers: On the centrality of the dissertation literature review in research preparation', *Educational Researcher*, 34(6): 3–15.
Boote and Beile argue that a sophisticated literature review is the basis of a good research dissertation. We agree and recommend, in particular, their exploration of standards and criteria for judging a good literature review.

Dunleavy, P. (2003) *Authoring a PhD: How to Plan, Draft, Write and Finish a Doctoral Dissertation or Thesis*. London: Palgrave.
We like Dunleavy's use of the term authoring. His metaphor of the thesis as front loaded with literature or back loaded with reported results is helpful in pointing out the need to emphasize the 'core contribution' of the research. We like the way he argues for not giving too much space and deference to the work of others.

Golden-Biddle, K. and Locke, K. (1997) *Composing Qualitative Research*. Thousand Oaks, CA: Sage.
This is one of the few texts that offer ways of conceptualizing how to locate the distinctive contribution in the field.

Hart, C. (1998) *Doing a Literature Review*. London: Sage.
This is the most cited text on literature work. We have found Hart's mapping approaches useful.

Herr, K. and Anderson, G. (2005) *The Action Research Dissertation. A Guide for Students and Faculty*. Thousand Oaks, CA: Sage.
Herr and Anderson do not spend a lot of time discussing literature per se, but their argument that literatures are extended in line with cycles of action research is important. So too is their insistence that action research also adds to literatures.

Kamler, B. and Thomson, P. (2006) *Helping Doctoral Students Write: Pedagogies for Supervision.* London: Routledge.

Our book contains two chapters on work with literatures. These offer further strategies and examples of text work/identity work in various fields of knowledge production.

Lillis, T. (2001) *Student Writing: Access, Regulation, Desire.* London: Routledge.

Lillis offers an extended illustration of academic writing as a discursive social practice. She focuses on identity issues experienced by 10 undergraduate non-traditional students in higher education. She shows the complexities and ambiguities required to become an 'insider' in a research field.

Wallace, M. and Wray, A. (2006) *Critical Reading and Writing for Postgraduates.* London: Sage.

Wallace and Wray offer a range of strategies for doing the work required to map the field. Their exercises are the starting point for getting a grip on debates and looking for patterns in what might first appear to be a big mess of texts.

Further references

Bahtktin, M. (1981) *The Dialogic Imagination. Four Essays.* Trans. C. Emerson and M. Holquist. Austin, TX: University of Texas Press.

Clark, R. and Ivanic, R. (1997) *The Politics of Writing.* London: Routledge.

Fairclough, N. (1992) *Discourse and Social Change.* London: Polity.

Thomson, P. and Kamler, B. (2010) 'It's been said before and we'll say it again: Research *is* writing', in P. Thomson and M. Walker (eds), *The Routledge Doctoral Student's Companion: Getting to Grips with Research in Education and the Social Services Handbook.* London: Routledge. pp. 149–60.

Ethical Issues in Generating Public Knowledge

Heather Piper, Education and Social Research Institute,
Manchester Metropolitan University, UK
Helen Simons, School of Education, University of Southampton, UK

Summary

- Informed consent
- Confidentiality and anonymity
- Pre-publication access
- Situated ethics
- 'Doing good' as well as 'doing no harm'
- Key theorists and writers
  - Dianna L. Newman
  - Robert D. Brown
  - Pat Sikes
  - Heather Piper
  - Helen Simons

Key concepts

Helen Simons

Ethical principles are abstract and it is not always obvious how they should be applied in given situations . . . Some of the most intractable ethical problems arise from conflicts among principles and the necessity of trading one against the other. The balancing of such principles in concrete situations is the ultimate ethical act. (House, 1993: 168)

Introduction

Ethics in research is a situated practice as the quotation above implies. Ethical decisions are the result of a weighing up of a myriad of factors in the specific complex social and political situations in which we conduct research. Frequently sets of principles are drawn up to protect the rights of participants in research as well as guide the researcher's actions in the field. In some disciplines research proposals have to pass through ethical committees which judge not only whether the research is sensitive to human 'subjects' but in many cases also whether the methodology is sound and appropriate for the research in question. This chapter outlines different ways of conceiving how to act ethically in social research and highlights the moral dilemmas we may encounter. It first outlines the traditional key concepts associated with conducting ethical social science research, such as informed consent, confidentiality and anonymity and pre-publication access. Secondly it briefly examines the increasing trend in publishing of ethical principles and guidelines by professional organizations and the institutionalization of ethical committees. Thirdly the concept of situated ethics is elaborated. Finally the role of the researcher is examined as ethical guidelines more often than not pay more attention to the rights *of* participants than the ethical rights of and/or danger *for* the researcher. Ethical practice is often defined as 'doing no harm'. In this chapter we take the view that we should also aspire to 'do good'; in other words to conduct research that benefits participants in positive ways.

Common ethical concepts

Informed consent

With some exceptions – those who argue that certain participant observation studies could never be conducted if informed consent was the norm – most writers of social science ethics adhere to a concept of informed consent. This means that those interviewed or observed should give permission in full knowledge of the purpose of the research and the consequences for them of taking part. Frequently, a written informed consent form has to be signed by the intending participant. However, achieving informed consent is not a straightforward process. First, there is often a tension between 'fully' informing and gaining access; outlining all possible consequences could make potential participants wary or decline to take part. Secondly it may not always be possible to foresee consequences in advance. A more appropriate concept is 'rolling informed consent' or 'process consent', that is, renegotiating informed consent, throughout the research, attentive to risks in the field and how participants perceive these at every stage. Thirdly, informed consent is needed from each person interviewed and/or observed, not simply the major gatekeeper in an institution or project. Fourthly, there is the difficulty of gaining informed consent from groups where there may be peer pressure to participate, or from particular individuals, for example, those with learning difficulties or children, in contexts where an adult has authority and/or responsibility for their behaviour or assessment.

Confidentiality and anonymity

The second common assumption in ethical social science practice is confidentiality in the process of conducting the research and anonymization of individuals in reporting. These are often linked as though the second, that is to say using pseudonyms in reporting, justifies the reporting of information obtained in confidence. However, these two concepts require separate consideration. Confidentiality is a principle that allows people not only to talk in confidence, but also to refuse to allow publication of material that they think might harm them, frequently expressed as 'please keep this in confidence'. Anonymization is a procedure which offers some protection of privacy in its aspiration not to identify people, but it cannot guarantee that harm may not occur. How people will react to research reports cannot be foreseen. The context, unless massively disguised, often reveals clues to identity even when names and places are changed. Moreover, not all people in a research study can be anonymized and the number to whom this applies is often more than we envisage. In such situations, a sound ethical principle is to seek clearance from the individuals concerned for use of the data in a specific context or report.

Apart from the obvious situation where the law is breached, in which case no one can hide under a confidentiality agreement, there are some situations, where anonymization is not the right course to pursue. For instance, in bereavement counselling the argument has been made that in order to help individuals cope with the grieving process, it is important to keep the person who has died 'alive', so to speak, visibly and through discussion using their real names and faces. To anonymize in this context is tantamount to a double death. A second reason for not anonymizing is to encourage the development of ethical reflexivity between the participants and the researcher, through a process of honest, open deliberation of the issues and possible consequences so that the outcome is morally and ethically defensible to all. Finally, anonymization may be inappropriate in those forms of action and participatory research, where participants, individually or jointly, research their own practice or policy context. In such contexts naming is important to acknowledge an individual's contribution to generating knowledge.

Pre-publication access

This principle of giving participants the opportunity to read a research report before it goes public appears on first sight to adhere to the principle of respect for persons. However, much depends upon the intent. If it is merely to warn participants of critical elements, so they will not be shocked when a report goes public, this offers more protection to the researcher than to participants. If it offers an opportunity for the participants to comment upon and possibly add to the report, this demonstrates greater respect for potential difference of interpretation and the right to a fair voice.

Ethical guidelines

Many social researchers draw up ethical principles and procedures reflecting the above concerns, based upon traditional research ethics of duties and rights and analysis of harm and benefit. Others embody in such statements democratic values of justice, fairness and respect for privacy of persons and public knowledge. For example, see Simons (2006) and, in relation to children, Alderson and Morrow (2003).

Many professional associations have also published guidelines to facilitate ethical practice (see e.g. AERA, 1992; UKES, 2003). Some aspire to set standards to judge the quality of the research. Others are couched in terms of codes and rules. Yet others prefer statements of principle, which offer guidance for ethical decision-making and a basis from which possible codes and rules might be developed. Such guidelines traditionally embody a normative ethics – concerned with how people ought to behave (Newman and Brown, 1996).

Ethical guidelines vary on a number of other dimensions, such as the extent to which they do or do not make a distinction between ethical-moral issues and scientific-methodological issues and the quasi-legal language in which they are sometimes written. Often there is a lack of clarity between ethical and legal issues. For example, treating participants 'fairly and equally' is written into the Human Rights Act and is now a legal imperative. It still remains an ethical issue, however, how 'treating fairly' is interpreted.

Ethical committees

Ethical committees have long been established in the field of medicine and increasingly they are being set up in the social sciences and other professional fields. They exist to ensure that researchers have considered the ethical issues that are likely to arise and have developed protocols to protect participants from harm. In many cases such committees also act as the guardians of what is to count as research methodology. Some have claimed (see e.g., Lincoln and Tierney, 2004) that ethical committees are in practice acting as gatekeepers, defenders of reputations, and in the prevention of litigation. As a consequence they may inhibit freedom to research, especially topics that may be sensitive. Where this happens, their function has become part of the culture of managerialism and is not necessarily to do with ethics at all (Lincoln and Tierney, 2004; Sikes and Piper, 2008).

Situated ethics

Principles provide a shared frame of reference and are useful to guide ethical decision-making. However, they are abstract statements of intent and cannot be followed simply as rules. Ethical practice depends on how the principles are interpreted and enacted in the precise socio-political context of the research. For examples of such concrete ethical decisions in practice see Simons and Usher (2000), Lee-Treweek and Linkogle (2000) and Simons (2009: 96–111).

The application of general principles and codes of practice nearly always stems from a rational, reasoning approach to the consideration of individuals' rights, duties and obligations of different groups. With the growth of feminist research, postmodern thinking and participatory and democratic practices, a different concept of ethics is being invoked – the ethics of care or relational ethics (Noddings, 1984). This is more concerned with relationships, people's lives and context than universal laws and principles. This approach has much in common with the ethical discourse of social justice (House, 1993) and the redistribution of power in research and evaluation relationships (MacDonald, 1976). It also has affinities with forms of participatory research (Etherington, 2007) which encourage participants to develop their own ethical practice in the groups and contexts in which they work and an ethics which takes into account the specific cultural differences between people.

Situated ethics, in summary, acknowledges the uniqueness and complexity of each situation; any ethical decision needs to take cognizance of the precise way in which many of the above factors are played out in the specific socio-political context. To what should the researcher appeal?

Some have suggested the ultimate recourse is to one's own conscience. However, to be justifiable as an ethical practice, this would need to be accompanied by a disciplined self-reflexive approach to one's own behaviour. Others have recommended broadening the reference point. Soltis (1990) suggests that an issue/ situation be considered from three different perspectives: of the person (the researcher in this case), the profession, and the public, noting the different dilemmas that occur for each. Newman and Brown (1996) offer a framework for ethical decision-making that includes intuition, rules and codes, principles and theory, personal values and beliefs and action, listing a few questions to ask of oneself in regard to each. This may appear overly rationalistic. However, given the uncertainty, complexity and finely tuned professional judgement we have to make in the 'ethical moment' (Usher, 2000), it draws our attention to a range of issues we may need to integrate into our consciousness to inform ethical decision-making in research.

Ethics for the researcher

Ethical principles and guidelines tend to focus on protecting participants from harm or in some cases on empowering them. Rarely is so much ethical attention paid to the researcher. However, this is changing as awareness grows about the risks and ethical danger a researcher may face studying certain contexts. Lee-Treweek and Linkogle (2000) make a strong case for redressing the predominant focus on participants by considering the risks and ethical dangers that can confront a social researcher in field situations, drawing distinctions between emotional, physical, and ethical danger. It is only the ethics that concern us here, that is to say the risks associated with making moral judgements in the field, though there may be links with emotional – and even physical – danger in facing ethical dilemmas. Making wrong judgements about what to study or how to study social life has consequences for how one's research is seen by others. The first story in the next section illustrates another side of this coin, where others make judgements through their gatekeeping about whether or not researchers can or should take risks. Ethical danger is perhaps at its most critical, say Treweek and Linkogle (2000: 5–6), when studying unfamiliar cultures, where there is the risk of unconsciously breaching cultural norms through the lens of one's own, and when studying extremist groups. It is sometimes for this reason, or in order to study groups for which one might not gain research access, that covert participant observation is employed (Bulmer, 1982). In some forms of research, however, such as naturalistic or phenomenological inquiry, deceptive research practices are inherently unacceptable (Lincoln, 1990).

Implications for research design

While it is rarely possible to anticipate all the ethical dilemmas you may encounter, there are steps you can take in your research design to indicate that you are thinking ethically:

- Consider at the outset what ethical issues might arise (numerous questions and frameworks exist in the literature to facilitate such thinking), and think through, in one or two instances, how these would be addressed.
- Be conscious of what kind of ethics you personally aspire to and what values you hold in relation to the research topic.

- Think through the ethical implications of any methodology you choose – for example, does it respect participants' rights? Does it balance this with the responsibility for generating public knowledge? Does it provide scope for participants' ethical development if this is part of your purpose? Does it honour those who are less enfranchised? Does it respect cultural, gender and age differences?
- Draw up a brief set of ethical procedures to guide data collection and dissemination. This is especially important if you have to submit your research proposal to an ethics committee. It will not be possible to encapsulate all the ethical dilemmas that may arise, but it will demonstrate that you have thought about the issues and have some reference points for acting ethically in the field. Indicate that you are working within the ethical guidelines (where they exist) of your department, profession or university.
- Pilot any potential methodological tools (e.g. questionnaire or interview schedule) to ensure questions are unobtrusive (though do not equate this with non-challenging) as well as cultural, gender and age sensitive.
- In your ethical procedures indicate how you will maintain respect for persons while making research knowledge public. Include a consideration of issues such as non-coercion (do you require an opt-out clause?); potential benefit to participants (what might they gain from this research, what might they learn?); and potential harm (what might be the consequences and for whom?).
- Think through how and in what form you might report in-depth experiences of individuals and what rights you will give them in this process.
- Become familiar with any legislation that exists in relation to your topic and act within it.
- Decide what position you will adopt on informed consent, confidentiality and anonymity, control over data, access before publication. Decisions on these issues will to some extent be determined by the choice you make as to whether you prefer to be guided by an ethical tradition that favours universal laws and principles, one that is more relational and situation specific or one that is democratic in intent and/or participatory in process and outcome.

Stories from the field

Heather Piper

The purpose of these stories is to illuminate contextual pressures which can impact on particular research intentions and ethical judgements. Both relate to research areas which engage strongly held emotions and assumptions, issues around which the personal and professional tend to become hard to distinguish. Both illustrate how what *counts* as ethical considerations can, in the field, prove to be fluid and problematic.

For some years, with a colleague (Pat Sikes) I sought funding and ethics approval for research into the growing phenomenon of teachers being accused of sexual misconduct by pupils. Some allegations are true. However, it is a very small proportion that has enough substance to result in formal disciplinary action or a guilty verdict in court. Yet all such allegations cause lasting damage to careers and lives. Although an important research topic, we have been unsuccessful in gaining funding, and secured ethical clearance for our non-funded research only with great difficulty (Sikes and Piper, 2008). Acquiring research grants is challenging and competitive but it was clear from feedback that the negative responses we received were to a significant degree related to the topic, which was seen as 'sensitive' or 'risky'.

When the proposal was considered by a university ethics committee, such messages became louder and more explicit. It appeared that members were challenged not only by ethical considerations, but also by calculations of risk in terms of public concern and potential media interest in the proposed research topic, and what it could mean for the university. Further, it became clear that, for some, the very act of talking with teachers about 'false' allegations was objectionable (or worse) because it involved breaching the mantra that children never lie about abuse. It was argued that the research could be seen as perpetuating abuse by suggesting to (wholly notional) victims that they might not be believed. It also confronted deeply held beliefs and commitments to child protection. For one such person, approval was simply out of the question as it challenged their personal commitment and professional integrity. In spite of these difficulties, although the quest for funding remains unfulfilled, ethics approval was finally achieved following a lengthy and tortuous process. As a result, modest unfunded research was possible

(Sikes and Piper, 2010). This first story illustrates the problem in real situations of achieving a shared agreement about what counts as an ethical issue or ethical research. It also highlights the potential that ethical committees (or some members) have to curtail important research on sensitive issues.

The second story, of a project commissioned by the Royal Society for the Prevention of Cruelty to Animals (RSPCA), is chosen for the ethical issues it raised before, during and long after the research was completed (Piper et al., 2001). It illustrates how it is not always possible or necessarily desirable to have a pre-prepared blueprint for ethical research practice. It exemplifies situated ethics and ethical reflexivity – concepts raised in the previous section – where ethical issues are treated as a collaborative venture, resolved in a particular context at a particular time.

The project sought to identify why children harm animals, in response to fears that such violence was on the increase. The steering group comprised colleagues from within the university (including teacher and social work educators) and an RSPCA officer. During the planning stages many potential ethical problems were raised, particularly around the proper response to young people stating they had harmed an animal because they had been, or were being, abused. This expectation stemmed from a common assumption (in the RSPCA and elsewhere) of links between types of abuse – based largely on US research (Ressler et al., 1988). There was disagreement amongst the steering group on the correct response to any such admission. Most thought that children claiming abuse should be dealt with through child protection procedures, reporting the claim to the relevant professional, but one member differed and was adamant that all such information be treated as confidential. Lengthy discussions exposed previously hidden ethical differences (e.g. contrasting views on confidentiality if children divulged harming behaviour, safety issues, etc.) essentially based on the differing professional socialization of teachers, social workers and RSPCA officers.

The issue was not resolved in one meeting. I consulted members of the university ethics committee to learn from their experience, but this and the literature indicated that many were confused about this issue. However, it was resolved by a briefing paper, identifying literature that indicated the reporting of abuse as a legal imperative, not just a moral or ethical one. This allowed progress, though not everyone was happy. We agreed all interviews would begin with the statement 'I can promise confidentiality on anything you may tell me except on anything that leads me to be concerned for your own or another's safety, in which case I must do whatever is necessary to ensure that you or the person being harmed is protected'. This example serves to demonstrate the difficulty in getting people with opposing views to agree and also how, following a resolution, ethical issues generally become enshrined as law, no longer the subject of discussion (Masson, 2000).

As it transpired, during the research no child or young person claimed that they had been harmed themselves, so the lengthy preparation for this event-uality was unnecessary, although the issue clearly needed airing. Significantly the concerns of the RSPCA officer differed from those of other contribu-tors. The worry was that should the researcher become aware of animal abuse s/he should report it to *her*, because for her this was a legal *and* moral imperative. In a lengthy exchange, she was persuaded that it would be impossible to conduct research that asked children for examples of harming behaviour towards animals, and then report them for telling us. We would be acting in bad faith, would risk disrepute, and children, schools and families would accuse us of deceit and coercion. All information passed to the RSPCA, verbal or written, was anonymized to make it impossible to identify any individual or group or school by what was said. Again, progress ensued but not everyone was content. The resolution perhaps indicates that some of us privilege people over animals in unquestioning ways, contrary to the re-sponses from many young people: 'We need to learn how to look after animals . . . teach how they are just like people'.

It is significant that I had underestimated my own response to hearing stories of children harming animals. I had naively thought that I would be quite hardened, whereas I knew from previous experience that hearing children describe their own abuse is hard. In the event it was difficult not to be affected by young people describing how they fastened cats to railway lines to watch them die, or lit fireworks tied to cats' tails. I did not want to report the young people to the RSPCA, but in a few cases it became apparent that the young people were seriously disturb-ed. Fortunately these disclosures took place with other professionals present (often their teachers) who were in a longer-term position of care, otherwise I might have felt compelled to pass on my worries even if not the detail. On reading interview transcripts

some colleagues questioned whether the children were truthful or saying things for effect. It is of course impossible to know whether what one is told in such research is truthful, but there was little doubt in my mind or the minds of other adults present that we were hearing accounts of real events and actions. Yet the young people could be shocked by each other's accounts, and demonstrated an 'ethical' code of their own: 'I'd kill anyone who harmed my dog'!

Another issue was whether young people could give consent to their involvement in the research or whether their parents or carers should do so on their behalf. This is a matter on which there is considerable disagreement. While the United Nations Convention on the Rights of the Child agreed in 1995 that children should make their own such decisions, it was only in 2000 that the UK, through the Human Rights Act, ratified this principle. In this as in other projects we adopted the practice of the participating schools. Frequently schools ask for a letter which they distribute to various classes or particular young people and I would only see those who brought back a signed letter of parental consent. But in this case, schools distributed questionnaires for completion during Personal, Social and Health Education lessons, permitting follow-up in another PSHE lesson by a group interview, usually led by the teacher. This was recorded and passed to me for transcription and analysis. In other instances I or another researcher carried out the interviews, but with a teacher usually present. The teachers clearly thought it an interesting and appropriate topic for PSHE and many volun-teered to be involved in any future work. Of course, there was the possibility that the children and young people were less likely to give accurate accounts of violent behaviour in the presence of their teacher (or indeed the researcher), regardless of conditional promises of confidentiality – but most found their own way around this difficulty. The majority of harming stories were told in the third person: 'I saw someone throw a bag of gerbils from the top of the flats'. Either the majority of our sample had witnessed harming whilst not taking part themselves, or we were left with the possibility that they were describing their own behaviour. However, in terms of ethical respon-sibility, such information could only be treated as a third-person account.

Ethical dilemmas emerged throughout the research and its aftermath. From meetings with the RSPCA we became aware of a joint initiative with the National Society for the Prevention of Cruelty to Children

(NSPCC) which was likely to attract considerable publicity and funding. It was premised on the assumption that violence and abuse are linked and that if a child harms an animal they will either have been abused or will have witnessed severe violence within their home environment, but the findings of our research project were not compatible with this view. Rather, we concluded that *many* children (depending on the definition of harming) harmed animals, not just the few known to the RSPCA and other services, but the transmission of this message from the research was inhibited. For example, during the research process, groups of 'respectable' adults (trainee teachers, social workers and others) admitted to harming animals as children, and we had hoped to explore this significant outcome further. However, our intention to distribute a short questionnaire at a joint NSPCC/RSPCA conference on children harming animals was prevented at the last moment.

The research received a great deal of media coverage and many invitations to appear on radio or TV programmes, but the story journalists (and others) wanted to hear is not the research-based and measured one we wished to present, but rather the sensational one (favoured more by fundraisers and their PR teams) that damaged children become damaged adults and in some instances mass murderers. Academic papers based on the research, arguing against a simplistic (but mainstream) application of dubious causal explanations, were initially rejected by (mainly) American journals, but are now in print (e.g. Patterson-Kane and Piper, 2009; Piper, 2003).

These two stories indicate how ethical considerations can impinge on research activity at all stages of the research and how ethical concerns can be blurred with other types of arguments, more to do with personal beliefs and institutional protection than ethics. This does not diminish the significance of the issues raised in the first section of this chapter. Rather it reinforces the need for the researcher to have thought through the ethical issues likely to arise in their proposal or project and to draw up ethical procedures that will guide their decision-making in the field. From that position of security they can confront the other considerations and arguments which may come between them and the completion of their work.

Annotated bibliography

Alderson, P. and Morrow, V. (2003) *Ethics, Social Research and Consulting with Young People*. London: Barnados.
An extensive discussion of ethics in research with children and young people raising a series of questions and dilemmas for the researcher in relation to traditional ethics and recent legislation and ethical practice.

Burgess, R.G. (ed.) (1989) *The Ethics of Educational Research*. Lewes: The Falmer Press.
Explores ethical dimensions in different forms of educational research such as case study, action research and quantitative research, and in different contexts. Several chapters suggest specific principles and procedures to guide ethical decision-making in practice.

Lee-Treweek, G. and Linkogle, S. (eds) (2000) *Danger in the Field: Risks and Ethics in Social Research*. London and New York: Routledge.
Focuses through case examples on how researchers have faced danger in the field. Only one section refers to actual ethical danger (the others being physical, emotional and professional). Important for drawing our attention to the need to consider ethics for the researcher as well as for participants.

Mauthner, M., Birch, M., Jessop, J and Miller, T. (eds) (2002) *Ethics in Qualitative Research*. London: Sage.
Examines the theories and intentions of ethics in the 'lived experiences' of the research process by a group of feminist researchers conducting qualitative research largely in family and household studies.

Newman. D.L. and Brown, R.D. (1996) *Applied Ethics for Program Evaluation*. Thousand Oaks, CA: Sage.
A thorough exploration of ethics and morality, ethics and methodology, differences between standards, codes, rules, principles and theories, in evaluation of social programmes.

Oliver, P. (2003) *The Student's Guide to Research Ethics*. Maidenhead: Open University Press.
Explores ethical issues the research student may encounter at each stage of the research process from design to publication and dissemination.

Punch, M. (1986) *The Politics and Ethics of Fieldwork*. London: Sage.
Focuses on participant observational studies in sociology and anthropology, exploring the ethical dilemmas and hidden moral agendas the fieldworker encounters in close relationships in the field.

Simons, H. and Usher, R. (2000) *Situated Ethics in Educational Research*. London: Routledge/Falmer.

Makes the case for ethics as a situated practice in different research traditions and contexts – feminist, postmodern, evaluation, participatory, image-based. Each chapter is case-based exploring the particular ethical issues that arose in unique socio-political settings including those of race, post-colonial situations, and health care.

Many books on qualitative research also include chapters on ethics, which cover and extend many of the issues discussed in this chapter. Only books focusing entirely on ethics are included in this Annotated Bibliography.

Further references

American Educational Research Association (AERA) (1992) 'Ethical standards of the American Educational Research Association'. *Educational Researcher*, 21(7): 23–6.

British Educational Research Association (BERA) (2004) *Revised Ethical Guidelines for Educational Research*. (http://www.bera.ac.uk/publications/pdfs/ETHICAL).

Bulmer, M. (ed.) (1982) *Social Research Ethics*. London: Macmillan.

Etherington, K. (2007) 'Ethical research in reflexive relationships', *Qualitative Inquiry*, 13(5): 599–615

House, E.R. (1993) *Professional Evaluation: Social Impact and Political Consequences*. Newbury Park, CA: Sage.

Lincoln, Y.S. (1990) 'Toward a categorical imperative for qualitative research', in E.W. Eisner and A. Peshkin (eds) *Qualitative Inquiry in Education: The Continuing Debate*. New York: Teachers College, Columbia University. pp. 277–95.

Lincoln, Y.S. and Tierney, W.G. (2004) 'Qualitative research and institutional review boards', *Qualitative Inquiry*, 10(2): 219–34.

MacDonald, B. (1976) 'Evaluation and of the control of education', in D. Tawney (ed.) *Curriculum Evaluation Today: Trends and Implications*. London: Macmillan.

Masson, J. (2000) 'Researching children's perspectives: legal issues', in A. Lewis and G. Lindsay (eds) *Researching Children's Perspectives*. Buckingham and Philadelphia, PA: Open University Press. pp. 34–44.

Noddings, N. (1984) *Caring: A Feminine Approach to Ethics and Moral Education*. Berkeley, CA: University of California Press.

Patterson-Kane, E.G. and Piper, H. (2009) 'Animal abuse as a sentinel for human violence: a critique', *Journal of Social Issues*, 65(3): 589–614.

Piper, H. (2003) 'Children and young people harming animals: intervention through PSHE?', *Research Papers in Education*, 18(2): 197–213.

Piper, H., Johnson, M., Myers, S. and Pritchard, J. (2001) *Why do People Harm Animals? Attitudes of Children and Young People*. Manchester and Horsham, West Sussex: Manchester Metropolitan University and RSPCA.

Ressler, R.K., Burgess A.W. and Douglas J.E. (1988) *Sexual Homicide: Patterns and Motives*. Lanham, MD: Lexington Books.

Sikes, P. and Piper, H. (2008) 'Risky research or researching risk: The role of ethics review', in J. Satterthwaite, M. Watts and H. Piper (eds) *Talking Truth, Confronting Power*. Stoke-on-Trent: Trentham.

Sikes, P. and Piper, H. (2010) *Researching Sex and Lies in the Classroom: Allegations of Sexual Misconduct in Schools*. London: Routledge.

Simons, H. (2006) 'Ethics in evaluation', in I.F. Shaw., J.C. Greene and M.M. Mark (eds) *The International Handbook of Evaluation*. London: Sage. pp. 243–65.

Simons, H. (2009) *Case Study Research in Practice*. London: Sage.

Soltis, J.F. (1990) 'The Ethics of Qualitative Research', in E.W. Eisner and A. Peshkin (eds) *Qualitative Inquiry in Education: The Continuing Debate*. New York: Teachers College, Columbia University. pp. 247–57.

United Kingdom Evaluation Society (UKES) (2003) *Guidelines for Good Practice in Evaluation*. (www.evaluation.org.uk/resources/guidelines.aspx).

Usher, R. (2000) 'Deconstructive happening, ethical moment', in H. Simons and R. Usher (eds) *Situated Ethics in Educational Research*. London: Routledge/Falmer. pp. 162–85.

PART II

LISTENING, EXPLORING THE CASE AND THEORIZING

Introduction

This part of the book presents two methodological approaches – Ethnography and Case Study – which provide a basic foundation for qualitative research in the social sciences, along with two of the most common ways of collecting data within these approaches – Research Diaries (or field notes) and Interviewing.

Research is about the generation of public knowledge through systematic – and often private – processes. We have deliberately started the book by looking at methodologies and methods which focus on the personal, and on the person of the researcher as a 'research instrument' (Peshkin, 1988).

None of the chapters is, of course, discrete. The methodologies and methods presented in Part II have implications for others which follow in Parts III–VIII, and vice versa. For example, a core concept in both Ethnography and Case Study is culture, which is also dealt with in considerable depth in Part V on Identity, Community and Representation. The difference is perhaps that chapters here draw more heavily on anthropology and sociology whereas, in Part V, Chapters 19, 20 and 21 focus on sociocultural interaction and representation which have been strongly influenced by the sociocultural psychology of Vygotsky and the semiotics of Saussure.

Many issues are raised in the chapters in Part II which will be further explored and clarified later in the book. In particular, Torrance's focus on 'the social construction of meaning' (Chapter 6) and Altrichter's observations about 'the fuzzy borderline between description and interpretation' (Chapter 5) invite cross-references to the chapters on Observing, Querying and Interpreting in Part IV. The methodologies and methods introduced here also provide the starting point for the more politically oriented approaches presented in Part III on Addressing Issues of Power and Researching for Impact. Essentially Parts II, III and IV are all concerned with understanding the meaning for individuals of their lives and experiences and to varying extents with giving them a 'voice'.

Further references

Peshkin, A. (1988) 'In search of subjectivity – one's own', *Educational Researcher*, October: 17–21.

Ethnography

Jo Frankham, CERES, Liverpool John Moores University

Christina MacRae, Education and Social Research Institute,
Manchester Metropolitan University, UK

Summary

- Field work
- Participant observation
- Suspending taken-for-granted assumptions
- Receptive to multiple possibilities that present themselves
- Different modes: e.g. critical ethnography; performance ethnography
- Key theorists and writers
  - James Clifford
  - John Van Maanen
  - Clifford Geertz
  - Norman Denzin

Key concepts

Jo Frankham

Ethnography is a methodology which has its origins in anthropology. Anthropological study, historically, involved western academics studying other, usually distant, cultures (e.g. Margaret Mead studying sexual mores in Samoa, or Evans-Pritchard studying the Nuer religion in Southern Sudan). Their approach was, in essence, immersion. It involved living, sometimes for long periods, in the environment – or 'the field' – in which they were interested. Their 'fieldwork' involved extended observation, and recording, of naturally occurring events, supplemented by interviews and the gathering of other forms of data (e.g. artefacts) which helped them to piece together the

meanings of the culture they were studying. Over time, this non-interventionist approach to research was seen to be helpful in the study of local events and people. The same broad principles apply to ethnography as they do to anthropology; if we wish to understand the 'other', and how they behave, we need to suspend our taken-for-granted understandings and watch and wait for the meanings in what we see to become clear. Participant observation remains at the centre of the endeavour – getting involved and looking and listening intently – over time.

Ethnography is an approach characterized by uncertainty and contradictions. It is a field defined by ambitious claims (holism, immersion, depth, rapport) accompanied by discussion of the impossibility of ever reaching those goals. That should not mean – some texts imply – that we stop trying. And the open-endedness and the open mind that distinguish the practice of ethnography mean continually having to make choices, but in ways which do not close down their possibilities. All of this makes for an emotionally demanding experience.

But why such unsettlements? This relates to the aspirations I mention above – holism, depth, and so on. The suggestion is that we can only begin to understand why people behave as they do, and the stories they tell, if we see these actions and words as entangled with many other 'worlds' and words that we likely cannot see or hear, but that we need to gain insight into. The past and the future are seen as connected to the present as people re/present themselves to others (and to themselves) and, as conscious actors, these stories will change according to context. And none of this 'stands still' because of the dynamism of social situations, including the effects that the conduct of research will have on those involved (including the researcher). Human beings, in this construction, are regarded themselves as 'in process', not open to 'fixing' as this or that, as ultimately *unknowable*. Ethnographers, then, try to mimic this complexity in terms of both processes and outcomes.

Where might you begin, then, when every beginning will suggest other possible beginnings and connections? In such a context, in a sense, it doesn't matter; the most important thing is to begin. And in this 'beginning' to wait, watch and listen in ways which allow yourself to be provoked – to be drawn in particular directions and to be receptive to the multiple possibilities that will next present themselves. At this early stage it is important to try to record, as far as possible, all that you see and hear. This makes for an arduous experience, both in terms of what you do 'in the field', and afterwards when notes are written up. Try to do this writing as soon after fieldwork as possible as you will be able to add many further details from memory. It is important to differentiate between what you see and hear and what you *think* about what you see and hear; early interpretations, while inevitable, may well need to be reviewed and revised and this will be facilitated by keeping a close record of 'raw' data, as well as of thoughts and impressions. Although many studies will include interviews as well as observations these are, typically, semi-structured and/or informal conversations that take place during and after observations.

What constitutes data is problematized in ethnographic practice. Direct forms (observation and interviewing) are likely to be accompanied by more indirect forms of data. These are those fragments that accumulate without the researcher necessarily being aware of them at the time, in scraps of conversation, in silences, in emotional responses at the borders of notes, in the ways a story is repeated, in the importance a myth holds (Frankham and Edwards-Kerr, 2009). In other words, data exists in what cannot be told as well as what can. This is not because research participants don't want to tell or that they don't trust researchers (which may well also be the case), but because these stories are *untellable*, in a direct sense.

Analysis, thinking, writing, theorizing in ethnography are bound up with this conceptualization of data as something (often) intangible, elusive, circumstantial. This is not a standardizable process. Instead, analysis, interpretation and writing in ethnography is itself likened to 'telling stories', also 'making pictures, concocting symbolisms, and deploying tropes' (Geertz, 1988: 140). The idea is that the researcher tries (using analogy, metaphor, dialogue, description, allusion and so forth) to communicate how this place, these people, these practices 'work'. These stories are the researcher's constructions of others' constructions and the language foregrounds that ethnographers 'play' with versions of the real. This does not mean, however, that these stories are fictional. 'Fact is not "lost", if literalism is lost' (Geertz, 1988: 140). This is a process which combines very close attention to the details of what has been seen and heard, over time, and careful but ultimately highly flexible approaches to interpretation of that data and the communication of ideas. This is what Geertz (1973) called 'thick description'.

Reflexivity is central to the process both of doing and writing ethnography. Van Maanen's conceptualization is helpful, where reflexivity is regarded as encounters with 'hermeneutic and representational issues' (1988: 126); the researcher 'tacks' between theory and experience and the writing of those things in ways which open up new questions about the self, responses to the data and the theoretical resources brought to bear. It is not regarded that this focus on the self will (or can) result in final conclusions (Stronach et al., 2007). Rather, through problematizing our interpretive processes, there is the potential for new thoughts to emerge that we can bring to bear on the research.

It is best not to use, apply or develop theory prematurely, although 'thinking with' existing theories is inevitable in the sense-making process. The general point, however, is to try to avoid 'shoehorning' what you think you see into pre-existing ways of making sense of similar phenomena. After all, one of the central reasons for doing ethnography is to work in ways which open up new ways of thinking about things.

Estrangement or defamiliarization remains the distinctive trigger of ethnographic work, giving it the sense that there is something to be figured out or discovered by fieldwork. What provides this estrangement now is ... the determined effort to refuse the couching of one's work

... in naturalized, commonsense categories that is so easy to do otherwise. (Marcus, 1998: 16)

The nature of ethnography raises particular ethical issues because of its 'open-ended' character; drawing up agreements about confidentiality, the limits of the work, how it will be used and so on, are problematic. Marcus suggested that we are 'always on the verge of activism' (1998: 122) when doing ethnography. Participant observation – indeed – means precisely to try to become a (very) (semi) 'insider'. In turn, this means being asked questions, sometimes being asked for help, perhaps changing the course of the research according to others' interests and desires. This, in my experience, provokes difficult questions about what you think you are trying to achieve and the part research might play in the day-to-day realities of the people you are working with. This sort of reflexive consideration of values and intentions underlines the politics of ethnography. It foregrounds the human in the human act of trying to understand. This is in contrast to research that is characterized as a technology and where the preparation of researchers is reduced to the transmission of skills. Choosing to do ethnographic research in the twenty-first century, then, in this reading of it can help to 'restore social science to its classical position as a practical, intellectual activity aimed at clarifying the problems, risks, and possibilities we face as humans and societies, and at contributing to social and political practice' (Flyvbjerg, 2001: 4, cited in Ramaekers, 2006). In Ramaekers's terms, this contribution is best made by research which provokes researchers into confronting the real and on-going problems, risks and possibilities we face in the *conduct* of research.

Ethnography allows for changing forms of sociality and new ways of understanding to be incorporated in its practices. A range of different approaches are summarized below. Critical ethnography explicitly eschews the notion of neutrality and is an approach that is put to use by researcher/activists in support of the goals of the participants. Typically, topics for exploration would be identified with those one is working with and some advocates go so far as to describe themselves as being a 'pen for hire' (Foley and Valenzuela, 2005: 220). Performance ethnography takes ethnographically derived data and 'stages' that data (through poetry, drama, dance) in order to communicate and evoke ideas from that work. Practitioners emphasize that *doing* – in bodily performances – is an important component of what it means to

be human. Performance, then, is more than a 'translation' of the verbal/textual and is an important way to 'know' culture. Autoethnography overlaps with performance ethnography inasmuch as data about the self is often fashioned into a performance. This is a self-narrative which sets out to interrogate what it means to 'be' through reflexive consideration of stories about oneself. Outcomes are likely to be in the form of re-imaginings of aspects of the self as an on-going production. Performance may be an important opportunity for new beginnings and refractions of the 'self'. The development of online ethnography reflects the increasing role the internet plays in everyday life. The internet allows for new kinds of connection and communication and these are explored either online or in 'blended' fashion using both online and face-to-face methods (see Chapter 18, this volume). Visual ethnography draws attention to data which is best collected through film, photography and other visual means. It might also include the analysis of participants' visual artefacts, such as family photos.

Implications for research design

The greater the time that can be spent in the field before you start to (formally) study it, the better. This will help you begin to define the field, identify key individuals to work with, forms of data collection that are appropriate and some sense of the challenges you will face. If you can find 'insiders' who will help you identify the challenges you are likely to face this will help you make informed decisions in the early stages, when you could easily misjudge situations. At the same time, of course, the perspectives of these informants are *data* and need to be read, as such.

Given that ethnography is open-ended (at least to an extent) it is probably best to explain this to your research informants and, as fieldwork continues, return to the subject of the ethical issues that are being raised. At some point, you may have to develop a written agreement but this will be very much dependent on context.

Participant observation is hard work. One day in the field may take as long as two days to write up if you have comprehensive notes. Then you need to build in thinking and reading time to capitalize on what you have seen and heard and to work out what you need to do next. It may be important, however, to spend at least some uninterrupted periods in the field according to the 'rhythms' of the fieldwork site(s). For example, think about what you might learn if you spend an entire week in an institution compared with five days spread over a number of weeks. Each time fieldwork occurs, multiple opportunities and further avenues for exploration will become evident. For some time, it is best to pursue as many of these as you can (those that 'feel' as if they might be productive, yield relevant material, help cement important relationships); trust your judgements, while also keeping a close eye on those judgements and what they tell you about you.

Your observations should help you think about what you do next, who you might talk to, what would constitute data in the context, what stories you might begin to be able to tell and how all of these relate to, and disturb, one another. And as Josephides describes:

> . . . our ethnographic strategies are also shaped by the subjects' situations, their global as well as local perceptions, and their demands and expectations of us. There can be no blueprint for how to do fieldwork. It really depends on the local people, and for this reason we have to construct our theories of how to do fieldwork in the field. (1997: 32)

This is an important part of staying 'open' to reviewing and revising your priorities and, crucially, remaining open to how you interpret what you see. However, at some point, you will also have to put boundaries around what you do, who you speak to, and so on. You will almost inevitably, in the process, be acutely aware of what you have *failed* to understand; this is in the nature of ethnography, however, if you take seriously its intentions and values.

Stories from the field – making Matthew's train

Christina MacRae

This 'field' story revolves around three fragments of data collected during a year of fieldwork as part of doctoral research in an early years classroom: a photograph, a scribbled 'note from the field', and a typed transcription of a conversation. The original aim of my enquiry had been to look at how children appropriate images that circulate in early years classrooms as part of their identity construction in order to ask questions about notions of expression and authenticity in children's art-making. However, as I

reflected on my data I found that my attention was unexpectedly drawn away from my original interests, towards an interest in the encounter between the children and the material world. This shift occurred through the process of observation and documentation, yet the way my attention was turned by my looking is something that is difficult to elucidate. Somewhere at the heart of the process is the nature of the field itself, and the artefacts that I produced as ethnographic observer. As Renton has noted, as a term of reference 'field' is usefully ambiguous, as it indicates both a site and an active practice: 'field is both place and production, always expanding' (2004: 99). This is a reminder of how time is layered into the field; at first the experience of an encounter unfolds in the present, and then this encounter takes a new life in the artefacts that continue to exert an influence as we look back at them to make sense of the encounter. In this sense the field 'leaks', since the field note is 'enmeshed in writing and reading that extends before, after and outside the experience of empirical research' (Clifford, 1990: 65).

When I set out to collect data as part of my research I thought of them as evidence that would shed light on children's understanding and purposes as they engaged in art-making activities. However, they became things in which I started to see my *own* understandings and purposes reflected back at me, but these understandings simultaneously changing as the artefacts from the field, in turn, became something new. This intense relation of looking and transformation made it increasingly difficult to pin down a 'self' that looked at the field, or objects from the field that I could simply look at. As Elkins notes, seeing is metamorphosis, it 'alters the thing that is seen and transforms the seer' (1996: 12). As my notes, photos, and sketches from the field proliferated, I found the objects exerting irresistible forces, and matters of fact became impossible as I found that my interpretation was continually on the move.

The story behind the photograph (Figure 4.1), the field note (Figure 4.2) and the transcription unfolded when I noticed Matthew working in the junk-modelling area. He informed me excitedly that he was making a train, waving in his hand a short cardboard tube and saying, 'that's the funnel'. In front of him was a tightly rolled piece of corrugated card held in place by masking tape. It was covered by green tissue paper that had been glued on. Matthew started to attach the cardboard tube/funnel to the thick green cylinder, which I took to be the body of the train. I

Figure 4.1   Matthew's train

immediately picked up a scrap of paper to take notes. I recorded that Matthew worked alongside Oliver and that he assisted Oliver in attaching two short cardboard tubes together by suggesting using a long strip of masking tape glued over the two tubes. When he returned to the problem of fixing his own cardboard tube/funnel onto the body of his train, the tape was not strong enough to hold the tube and it fell off. I suggested that he could try to attach the tube by cutting a hole in the corrugated card, and Matthew asked me to cut a hole out. Once I'd cut out a hole, he pushed the short cardboard tube in and it was firmly attached. However, the train now kept rolling over because of the uneven weight of the newly attached tube, and he used objects lying on the table to prop it up on either side. I asked him if trains had wheels, to which he replied 'yes, six. I need to go to the drawing area to make them'. He went off to the drawing area, and somewhat to my surprise, returned

with only three strips of paper. Matthew said 'we'll roll them up [the strips of paper], but first I need to cut them in half'. As I scribed his words I was mentally impressed both by his idea of using rolled strips to make wheel shapes, and by his numeracy skills: he knew that three strips cut in half would make six.

Figure 4.2 is a fragment from my field notes and until this point my notes were similar to ones that I would have made in the past, as an early years teacher. Out of an ingrained habit I noted his use of language to plan and to explain his project, his numeracy skills, concentration, problem-solving and his social skills.

At this point my notes take a slightly different turn, as Bethany (in a pink fairy costume) sat down at the table. She watched Matthew, got a piece of paper and covered it with glue. She then initiated a conversation that I also recorded. When I later came to write this transcription up, I included a commentary that to some degree records the 'tugs and pulls' (Elkins, 1996:

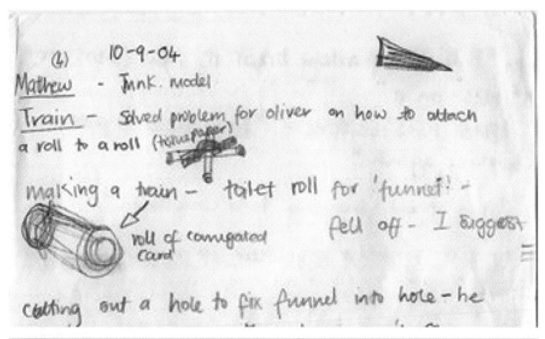

Figure 4.2 Field notes from ethnographic observation of Matthew creating his train

19) inside my head as I tried to make sense of their conversation. This was an attempt to make visible how my interpretation formed the basis for my own turns in the conversation. In the following transcript, my interpretations are in square brackets in italics:

Bethany: I'm going to do a picture of a train

Matthew: mine's a real train [*is this because his is a three-dimensional model as opposed to Bethany's two-dimensional version?*]

(Bethany gets a pink pair of scissors and starts to cut up pink bits of paper in circles for wheels for her collage train.)

Bethany: I've got a track at home [*she has a 'real' train at home, redressing the challenge made by Matthew to her 'less real' picture?*]. (She then studies her picture) I'm going to cut it out when I've finished [*to make it more three-dimensional, more real?*]

Me: you mean so you can put it on the tracks at home? [*make it more real?*]

Bethany: (laughing, as if I was stupid) no, it's not a real train

Matthew: mine's a real train [*is his more realistic because it corresponds more accurately as a replica? Or because of relative power as a boy, and hence someone more rooted in*

the world of real things; after all Bethany can't be serious with her pink wheels, dress, etc.? Anyway he has the final word . . . maybe Bethany doesn't care that much in the end . . . boys will be boys. She was just making conversation and she has a brother at home, hence the train track at home, and knows it is something that she can talk to Matthew about.*]

Here my interests are turning the children's conversation into an object from the field for collection. The observation that had initially been framed as a teacher evidencing Matthew's intellectual and social skills was interrupted as my ethnographic gaze attempted to grasp the children's representational intent. Now, as objects of my concern, the photograph of Matthew's work was eclipsed by the transcription of the children's conversation. This fragment was now transformed into evidence of the children's discursive construction of reality and of hierarchies of the real within this. As I wrote up the field note and included my thoughts as part of the transcription certain aspects came to the fore: Bethany was wearing a pink dress, used pink scissors and cut up pink paper for the wheels on her train. I began to think about Matthew's insistence on the realness of his train in relation to Bethany's, not simply as a question of different levels of real, but as a gendered hierarchy of different reality regimes. Matthew seemed to employ realism as a ploy to maintain a dominant position in relation to Bethany's collage. I also became acutely aware of my complicity in privileging Matthew's over Bethany's in my initial teacherly response to his model. It also became telling that I had only taken a photo of Matthew's model, whereas not one of Bethany's collage. This in turn led me to remember that other children stopped to admire Matthew's model, but no children commented on Bethany's collage.

Curiously, the effect of my shifting attention was to re-erase Matthew and Bethany from the encounter. Matthew's train became a sign of my collaboration with his masculine and rational desire for mastery of the real, and the way my gaze was averted from Bethany. However, my reading of Bethany as caught at the wrong end of an unequal opposition rendered her marginal. Again I appropriated the artefacts from the field, borrowing the phrase from Bakhtin: 'to overpopulate them with my own intentions' (Bakhtin, cited in Morris, 1994: 77).

However, once again, my initial encounter underwent yet another transformation at a much later stage in the research. When I was writing up the research, I fell upon the initial piece of paper where I had written down my observations. I now noticed the drawing I had made to indicate how Matthew had helped Oliver, which for some reason I had never paid attention to. Looking at this visual rather than written note, I was suddenly struck by two things: first that I was looking at a series of rolled pieces of card (the cardboard tubes of Oliver's, attached together by a strip of paper curving over them, and the rolled piece of corrugated card). Secondly, that I never knew if Matthew had made the rolled piece of corrugated card with the intention of making a train or if he found or rolled it up himself. Might the cylindrical form have suggested a train to him? My assumption had always been that he had intended to make a train from the start. That I sketched the tubes that Matthew attached for Oliver and the rolled piece of corrugated card indicates that in some sense words were lacking. But it was only now, at this later moment of reflection, that these visual sketches became significant. I recalled the surprise that I had noted at Matthew's use of rolled strips in order to make the wheels. Looking again at the sketch, I now see the traces of the *idea* of rolled paper both in the

strip used to attach Oliver's cardboard rolls and in the rolled corrugated card that made the cylinder. I was reminded how the model kept falling over. This in turn made me look back at the photograph to see how he had finally stabilized the model, and I saw that again he used cardboard rolls glued onto each side of the model in order to keep it upright. With this emerging theme of rolled card and paper, I now saw a somewhat different relationship between Matthew and his model. The *likeness* to a train as the principal force guiding Matthew as he imposed form onto the materials was displaced by the possibility of a relationship where the qualities and potential of the materials themselves were also an important factor in the form that the model took.

The potential of paper and card to be transformed into cylinders now could be seen to have given Matthew an idea that he subsequently started exploring. My reading of Matthew as having set out to represent a train as realistically as possible, assuming this figurative intention was what gave form to the materials that he assembled, was blind to the transformative process that was occurring at the level of the materials themselves. Perhaps it was the visual qualities of the sketched observation, rather than the written one, that allowed me to make these new connections.

This new reading of the process that unfolded as Matthew made his train led me to re-read his conversation with Bethany. I returned to the moment when Bethany laughed at me 'as if I was stupid', saying 'no, it's not a real train'. My first reading had cast Bethany as victimized by a dominant realist discourse. However, Bethany's laughing rebuke could be seen as her objection to my narrative. Perhaps Bethany wasn't taking the need for the models to be 'real' that seriously; she had simply entered a conversation with Matthew and then responded to his insistent claim that his model was more real than hers. There is nothing to indicate to me that Bethany accepted his claim; and her laughing put-down to me could be read as playfulness. Far from being oppressed, Bethany might have been putting language into play and using it to resist the classification of others. Once again I found that objects from the field were exerting a force beyond the initial encounter. Field notes continued to have an unruly effect, transforming the initial meanings I gave them, nudging me into thinking otherwise and reminding me about the complexity of the encounter.

Annotated bibliography

Atkinson, P., Coffey, A., Delamont, S., Lofland, J. and Lofland, L. (eds) (2001) *Handbook of Ethnography*. London: Sage. Comprehensive work on the many different approaches to ethnography and its conduct. Central issues (such as ethics) are also debated, and key figures describe their current thinking and practices.

Clifford, J. and Marcus, G. (1986) *Writing Culture: The Poetics and Politics of Ethnography*. Berkeley and Los Angeles: University of California Press.
After analysing some 'classic' examples of cultural description, the authors go on to consider more recent trends in ethnographic writing. Their premise is that everything we write is an invention (of others, of self, of culture) and this requires us to rethink our writing practices and our intentions for ethnographic work. This is a text for later in a study if writing/reflexivity becomes a particular interest or to dip into so that you are aware of the arguments.

Denzin, N. (1997) *Interpretive Ethnographic Practices for the Twenty-First Century*. Thousand Oaks, CA: Sage.
After summarizing key challenges for ethnography, Denzin describes recent developments in ethnography – with many useful examples – and urges researchers to find ways to use ethnography as a stimulus for action.

Fine, M. and Weis, L. (1998) 'Writing the "wrongs" of fieldwork: Confronting our own research/writing dilemmas in urban ethnographies', in G. Shacklock and J. Smyth (eds) *Being Reflexive in Critical Educational and Social Research*. London: Falmer.
An important piece in which the authors talk the reader through their methodological and ethical dilemmas during research which aims to contribute to social change. The book (Shacklock and Smyth) contains many other worthwhile pieces.

Geertz, C. (1973) *The Interpretation of Cultures*. London: Harper Collins.
An important classic text, which points to many 'fundamentals' in ethnography. The chapter on 'Thick Description' is really helpful.

Hammersley, M. and Atkinson, P. (2007) *Ethnography: Principles in Practice*, 3rd edn. London: Routledge.
This book will give you lots of practical advice and is a really good starting point if you want to begin ethnographic fieldwork.

Rosaldo, R. (1993) *Culture and Truth: The Remaking of Social Analysis*. London: Routledge.

A very accessible text which debates, in a very helpful style, key dilemmas in ethnography/anthropology.

Scheper-Hughes, N. (1992) *Death Without Weeping: The Violence of Everyday Life in Brazil*. Berkeley and Los Angeles: University of California Press.
A vivid account of life in shanty-town Brazil, focusing particularly on mother/child relations in a context of high fertility and high death rate. In documenting mothers' reactions to routine infant mortality the book provides fascinating insight into the cultural specificity of 'maternal love'. The author uses observations, interviews, documents and literature by others writing in the same field, to build the account. It also contains many 'personal' anecdotes by the author.

Sparkes, A. (2009) 'Novel ethnographic representations and the dilemmas of judgement' *Ethnography and Education*, 4(3): 301–19.
This article provides a useful introduction to the importance of writing in ethnography and goes on to provide possible ways of judging the quality of different approaches to ethnography.

Further references

Clifford, J. (1990) 'Notes on (Field) Notes', in R. Sanjek (ed.) *Fieldnotes. The Making of Anthropology*. London: Cornell University.

Elkins, J. (1996) *The Object Stares Back*. San Diego: Harvest.

Foley, D. and Valenzuela, A. (2005) 'Critical ethnography: The politics of collaboration', in N.K. Denzin and Y.S. Lincoln (eds), *The SAGE Handbook of Qualitative Research*. Thousand Oaks, CA: Sage.

Flyvbjerg, B. (2001) *Making Social Science Matter: Why Social Inquiry Fails and How It Can Succeed Again*. Cambridge: Cambridge University Press.

Frankham, J. and Edwards-Kerr, D. (2009) 'Long story: Beyond 'technologies' of knowing in case-study work with permanently excluded young people', *International Journal of Inclusive Education*, 13(4): 409–22.

Geertz, C. (1988) *Works and Lives: The Anthropologist as Author*. Cambridge: Polity.

Josephides, L. (1997) 'Representing the anthropologist's predicament', in W. James, J. Hockey and A. Dawson (eds) *After Writing Culture: Epistemology and Praxis in Contemporary Anthropology*. London: Routledge.

Marcus, G.E. (1998) *Ethnography Through Thick and Thin*. Princeton: Princeton University Press.

Morris, P. (1994) *The Bakhtin Reader*. London: Arnold.

Ramaekers, S. (2006) 'No harm done: The implications for educational research of the rejection of truth', *Journal of Philosophy of Education*, 40(2): 241–57.

Renton, A, (2004) 'Everything matters: Anthony Gormley's Ethics of Materiality', in A. Gormley, *Making Space*. Gateshead: Baltic.

Stronach, I., Garratt, D., Pearce, C. and Piper, H. (2007) 'Reflexivity, the picturing of selves, the forging of method', *Qualitative Inquiry*, 13(2): 179–203.

Van Maanen, J. (1988) *Tales of the Field: On Writing Ethnography*. Chicago: University of Chicago Press.

Research Diaries

Mary Louise Holly, Teaching, Learning, and Curriculum Studies, Kent State University, Kent, Ohio, USA

Herbert Altrichter, Department of Education and Psychology, Johannes Kepler University, Linz, Austria

Summary

- Writing to increase self-understanding
- Multiple modes of capture (including digital tools)
- Data and reflection, interpretation and analysis
- Ethical issues: e.g. other people's diaries are usually private
- Key theorists and writers
  - Herbert Altrichter
  - Michael Armstrong
  - Mary Louise Holly
  - Bronislaw Malinowsky

Key concepts

Herbert Altrichter and Mary Louise Holly

History

While research diaries have long been the site of rich description and conjecture, the tools to capture, record, analyse and portray the researcher's story have expanded greatly in recent years. With the advent of digital media, research diaries acquire multiple modes of capture and analytical strength, moving from black and white to Technicolor, from static to dynamic. Whether they are called diaries, log books, journals, blogs, field notes or lab books, 'external memory' has

been used by researchers in many disciplines for recording their daily observations in the field: for example, in ethnographical research (see Malinowski, 1967) or in zoological field research (see DeVore, 1970). Qualitative social researchers (see Whyte, 1955) make intensive use of research diaries as a means to record data from participant observation and from conversations with key informants, be these individuals or groups.

Inspired by sociological field research, qualitative educational research has developed using similar methods. An early example is Philip Jackson's (1968) *Life in Classrooms* where the author tried to 'move up close to the phenomena of the teacher's world' (1968: 159). Interestingly, he argued that 'in addition to participant observers it might be wise to foster the growth of observant participators in our schools' (1968: 175). A step in this direction is taken by another landmark book, *The Complexities of an Urban Classroom* (Smith and Geoffrey, 1968), written collaboratively by a participant observer and an observant teacher. In Britain, Armstrong (1980) worked with a diary as the basis for detailed description and analysis of a primary classroom in his book *Closely Observed Children* about intellectual growth and intellectual achievement; about understanding the understanding of children.

There is another source diary writing may tap into. 'From the very beginning of European culture, texts have been written with the aim of increasing self-understanding, becoming aware of self-delusions, and articulating and reducing pain' (Werder, 1986: 4). Diaries in which the self and its surrounding conditions were investigated have ranged from Saint Augustine's *Confessions* to scores of anonymous diaries by which everyday people reflect on their lives. At first sight, such diaries appear as introspective texts or as 'literature', but only rarely as research. Yet, introspective diaries can lead to important insights. As Elias Canetti (1981) points out, conversation with oneself in a diary can be a 'dialogue with a cruel partner'. In a digital age, in addition to one's self, there are often multiple partners and modes for conversing and capturing the action for later reflection.

Elements

Research diaries include a range of items:

- *data* obtained by observation, interviews and informal conversations, threaded discussions, and focus groups;
- additional '*found items*', such as photographs, letters, videos, websites, wikis, blogs;
- *contextual information* about the forms and ways these data were collected;
- *reflections* on research methods;
- *ideas, examples, and plans for subsequent research steps.*

Obviously, research diaries include items of different type and quality, including both 'data' and reflection, interpretation and analysis. This heterogeneity may make some researchers feel uneasy; however, this is also the source from which major and *specific qualities* may be developed:

- Diaries invite 'miscellaneous entries' which otherwise may get lost: short memos or occasional observations, interpretative ideas and reflections about research issues. With this *continuity*, a diary may become the researcher's companion, documenting the development of perceptions and insights across various stages of research.
- By including data and interpretation, commentaries and reflection, diaries enable *ongoing analysis* throughout data collection and can be used to push forward the research; preliminary results of analysis can indicate data needed to fill in the gaps in a theoretical framework and to evaluate intermediate results.

Recommendations for different kinds of diary entries

Memos are produced when recalling experiences over specific time periods (e.g. during a classroom lesson, a court session, etc.). Often providing the only possibility of collecting data on quickly flowing practical activities, memo recording requires sufficient detail and accuracy, Bogdan and Biklen (1982) suggest that the earlier a memo is recorded after an event, the better. Discussing the event before initially recording evidence can modify both memory and what is recorded. Even if little time is available at the time of the event, capturing words and phrases, photographs, or other artefacts can later prove useful as aides-memoire. Narration in the form of detailed or even 'gist' memos can be surprisingly useful when one returns to them for elaboration. Arranging records chronologically, at least initially, is recommended. Using software such as NVIVO, data can be manipulated and details added. Plan an hour for recording a memo on a one-hour activity. While *descriptions* and *interpretations* are often interspersed in memos, it is useful to distinguish between them.

Descriptive sequences within memos and other records contain accounts of activities; descriptions of events; reconstructions of dialogues, gestures, intonation and facial expressions; portraits of individuals – their appearance, their style of talking and acting; description of a place, facilities, etc. With electronic means, such as photography, audio and video taping, snippets of action can be captured and later described. When acting as a participant researcher, your behaviour is an important part of these descriptions. Detail is more important than the summary, the particular is more important than the general, and the account of an activity is more important than its evaluation. Whenever possible, provide exact quotations or paraphrase (marked as such).

Interpretative sequences (feelings, speculations, ideas, hunches, explanations of events, reflections on assumptions and prejudices, development of theories, etc.) are valuable entries in research diaries. Interpretations occur both when recording experiences and later when reflecting upon them.

In daily life, writing is often re-read, mistakes discovered, and clarity enhanced. Data analysis is a kind of re-reading of existing data with the intention of making connections, reorganizing, interpreting and evaluating them with respect to your research interest. On re-reading, it is often easier to judge which things are important than it is at the time of writing. You may discover new relationships between ideas, and insights to follow up. Questions emerge. It becomes easier to see what needs to be done and how thoughts expressed in the text can be usefully restructured. We distinguish three types of 'interpretative sequences':

(1) Research entails making connections between data and understanding them. In reflecting on data, various ideas come to mind. In *theoretical notes* you try to capture these ideas and save them from oblivion. Put forward explanations relevant to the research question being investigated. Relationships between events are noted for further research. Theoretical notes are useful for:

- clarifying a concept or an idea;
- making connections between various accounts and information;
- identifying surprising or puzzling situations worth following up;
- connecting your experience to existing theory;
- conjecturing and formulating new hypotheses;
- realizing hitherto unconscious assumptions and formulating their theoretical implications.

(2) *Methodological notes* contain observations and reflections on research strategy, methods and activities. Issues of methodological critique and ideas for alternative methods and procedures may help to develop the quality of the research project and the competence of the researcher. Theoretical notes can be an integral part of the diary entry or added in the preliminary analysis. They might address questions such as:

- Under what circumstances did I use particular research methods; what biases might be associated with them?
- What role did I play in the situation under investigation?
- What comments arise from my experience of specific research strategies?
- What decisions did I make about the future course of my research, and why?
- What conflicts and ethical dilemmas were encountered; how did I deal with them?

(3) In research strategies which combine research with practical action, such as action research, or organizational development, a third type of 'interpretative sequences' become important: *planning notes*. When writing or re-reading diary entries, new ideas emerge for the improvement of practical action, for example, about:

- alternative courses of practical action;
- forgotten ideas and how to address them;
- ideas to be thought through more carefully;
- additional information that seems essential.

Planning notes enable more systematic use of the stream of ideas. The diary becomes a 'memory bank' reminding us of plans to put into practice, and facilitating the plan by recording the context of the original aspirations enabling us to keep its purposes clear in the course of development.

Suggestions for keeping research diaries

Keeping a diary is a personal matter. In an electronic age it is often also a collaborative matter. Depending on the research, every diary writer or group develops a style and idiosyncrasies that make diary-keeping a valuable research tool. Some suggestions are offered below for your consideration (for further recommendations see Altrichter et al., 2008: 15).

(1) *Record regularly.* For example, entries might be recorded after each lesson in which a particular teaching strategy has been implemented, or after each meeting with a social group to be studied. Some people reserve times for recording to prevent it from being drowned in the whirlpool of daily necessities. Taking photographs, collecting artefacts, or jotting during an activity can be narrated as soon as time permits.

(2) People unaccustomed to diary-keeping often experience a *difficult period before diary keeping becomes personally satisfying*. We find diary-keeping easier when we collaborate with a research partner with whom we can read and discuss extracts and artefacts. Blogs and wikis enable individuals and groups to capture information in multiple formats as well as to garner other people's perspectives in a heuristic and timely manner. Critical colleagues and inquiry communities can lend support to on-going diary-keeping as a normal part of research, especially with action research and other formative methods of scholarship.

(3) Collaboration does not take away from the *private nature of a diary*. The decision to make excerpts

available to other people remains with the author. The privacy of the traditional diary makes it easier to disregard considerations of style and punctuation. Self-censorship disturbs the free flow of thoughts; editing can come later if the results are to be published. With blogs and electronic capture tools the richness and timeliness of data expands which can include public documents and evolving data, thus complicating public and private issues of ownership and display.

(4) *Structure and space* can make orientation and data analysis easier. Paragraphs, headings, numbers, underlining, various fonts, etc. may be used to *structure the text*. Programs such as NVIVO can enable one to capture and organize on multiple levels and dimensions, as well as to store and analyse data in new ways. Capturing rich data in one's diary provides the foundation for making connections across time and data sources – often in seconds or minutes.

(5) With the factual account, include information for understanding the situation and for reconstructing it later: 'Observations, feelings, reactions, interpretations, reflections, ideas, and explanations' (Kemmis and McTaggart, 1982: 40). When using electronic means, text can easily be added, copied, and moved without disturbing the original text, and artefacts scanned into the diary.

(6) *Include relevant items*: notes, photographs, video clips, websites, copies of documents, pupils' work, etc. If research activities and the data obtained by them (for example, an interview or lesson transcript) cannot be recorded, directly cross-reference them in the diary.

(7) Because research diaries contain various kinds of records, this wide-ranging approach brings with it challenges. One is coping with the fuzzy borderline between *description and interpretation*. The 'ladder of inference' described by Argyris et al. (1985: 56) may be helpful in this respect. *Coherence*, how the captured stories and vignettes (Holly, 1989) hold together as accounts, may be as important as is accuracy or truth.

(8) *Provisional analyses of the diary entries* (Altrichter et al., 2008: 157) enable the researcher to view the data from different altitudes, to see whether descriptions and interpretations are coherent and in useful balance, which of the initial research questions can be answered from existing data, and which additional data are necessary. This helps in planning next research steps. Last but not least, it

reduces the danger of being flooded by 'data overload'.

Implications for research design

In any type of research where a person or a group is trying to make sense of experience, and where the eye of the beholder is a variable in the research, research diaries are called for. Geertz (1983) refers to researchers as 'spectators'. The forms used to document the subjects of the researcher's gaze in these cases shape what can be seen and what is available for later scrutiny. While no one would dispute the challenges involved in understanding other's lives, it is usually more difficult for researchers to become spectators of their own observations and interpretations.

Like all data, a diary constitutes a record. Diaries are usually private and contain intimate accounts and reflections. Other persons' diaries cannot be made public (i.e. used in written or spoken accounts of the research) without clearance from their authors. With the advent of almost instant communication, blogging, wikis, facebook, youtube, and other public forums and outlets for what would have been private documents, the ground shifts as the boundaries between public and private domains continue to blur.

When diaries contain interview data or observation notes made by others, it is usually best to clear the data immediately with the person concerned. This can be done by providing the person with a photocopy of the relevant passage. Diaries are also frequently used in covert social research. For the ethical issues which arise thereby see Piper and Simons, Chapter 3, this volume.

Diaries are nearly always used in concert with other forms of documentation and data collection, most notably interviews, observations, and artefacts. When diaries are used as data, they too are subjected to procedures of qualitative analysis as part of a comprehensive process of data analysis. Diaries can be particularly useful for making detours, for taking side roads that offer possible insights into phenomena that were not obvious or predictable when the research journey began. What might have seemed a diversion may become an important discovery in the light of new information.

In projects where the primary methods of research are quantitative, diaries may be employed as log books where notations provide a sense of continuity to various activities. Multi-person projects may commission a person to keep a project diary in which decisions, the ways they were arrived at, the arguments used for them, and the alternatives that were discussed, are documented.

Stories from the field

Mary Louise Holly

If, as Foucault (1972) observed, everything is already interpretation, the research diary can make interpretation more visible, enabling the researcher to be a spectator of the 'facts' and of the reconstructive process which brings them into being, and, from that, to generate new understanding. To illustrate different uses of research diaries and issues related to their use, we draw from the diaries of recognized scholars, and from teachers and students trying to understand and improve their learning.

Whose eyes can see what?

Several important issues attend the researcher's points of view.

What are the assumptions and perspectives of the researcher?

What, by virtue of the researcher's tools and perspectives (philosophical assumptions, past experience, biography, motivation, biology), is the researcher able to see? Where are the blind spots, those derived from the research (explicit unknowns) and researcher (explicit and implicit), and how might these influence the inquiry and results? Sartre's 'intellectual' is relevant: 'the mind that watches itself' (Camus, 1965). What is the researcher's warrant for the 'story'? A look into Malinowski's diary (1967) says as much about what Malinowski was able to see as it does about those he observed.

> *Tuesday, 4.17:* Overall mood: strong nervous excitement and intellectual intensity on the surface combined with inability to concentrate, superirritability and supersensitivess of mental epidermis and feeling permanently being exposed in an uncomf. position to the eyes of a crowded thoroughfare: an incapacity to achieve inner privacy. I am on a war footing with my boys . . . and the Vakuta people irritate me with their insolence and cheekiness although they are fairly helpful to my work . . .

As researchers write freely they can begin to see biases and distortions in their own thinking; unconscious processes are made conscious through language. Many a writer, like Florida Scott-Maxwell (1968: 8), has discovered this.

> [My diary is] my dear companion, or my undoing. I put down my sweeping opinions, prejudices, limitations, and just here the book fails me for it makes no comment. It is even my wailing wall, and when I play that grim, comforting game of noting how wrong everyone else is, my book is silent, and I listen to the stillness, and I learn.

What do mental and biological factors like emotion, motivation, and memory contribute to documenting and reconstructing experience in the diary?

As is apparent in these examples, the researcher is subject to the same emotions and mental operations as are casual observers. 'Our hopes, fears, and desires influence how we think, perceive, and remember' (LeDoux, 2002: 24). The mind is both liability and asset. Learning involves emotion – whether it is Scott-Maxwell's wailing wall or Malinowski's irritation – that calls forth particular ways of observing and interpreting experience. Emotion indicates an area where unconscious interpretation is more obviously at work. The mind constantly shifts. Whatever happens 'now' is over-emphasized: 'The normal strategies of mind – simplification and exclusion of information – make us continuously overreact from the little information we have' (Ornstein and Dewan, 2008: 141).

Keeping a research diary is both an aid to memory and a process for critical reflection where emotional and cognitive processing enables different levels of analysis, synthesis, interpretation, and portrayal. Thus, Einstein's observation that one cannot solve a problem by thinking at the same level at which it was created provides a research tool. Holding data constant long enough to manipulate and consider it from alternative angles can also make conscious what one knows unconsciously.

Craig Carson, a kindergarten teacher, uses his research diary as a workspace to record and process classroom experience. As he describes a disturbing incident with a parent, he begins to identify and integrate salient pieces of a puzzle that the incident uncovers.

> I was ambushed . . . in a conference . . . Near the end of our time she asks 'do you think there is

something strange about Melody?' What a shot! There has been a feeling I could never grasp but always disturbing that, yes, something is strange about Melody . . . She does not seem to be a whole child but I could never lead myself past vague generalities . . . Now I'm committed to figuring this puzzle out . . . Melody is spotless jumpers, fancy blouses, patent leather shoes, socks with no holes, and freshly curled blond hair . . . Melody shares, cares for her friends, isn't bossy and never gets in trouble or causes anyone else to have difficulty. The children regret that she has only two sides since that limits the number of people who can sit by her . . . I failed to realize that here was a five-year-old who acted nine . . . (Holly, 1989: 64–5)

Interpretation and description: Inseparable?

What is interpretation and what would other observers see as factual accounting? What is my logic here? What is missing? Often the issue is less interpretation, than consciousness of interpretation.

Becoming conscious of interpretation *during* the process of describing phenomena is possible, but comes more easily *after* interpretation has been rendered: 'How do I know what I think until I see what I say?' Interpretation is part of observing, and 'all understanding is interpretation' (Gadamer, 1975: 350) but most observation, interpretation and understanding are unconscious. With meagre data of a conscious nature we replace absent stimuli with theorizing and imagination. The richer the data collected, including sense and context, the more the researcher has to work with – on both conscious and unconscious levels.

Take a scholar in the arts, naturalist poet Mary Oliver, for example, who, for over 30 years, has kept small 'notebooks' which inform her poetry.

What I write down is extremely exact in terms of phrasing and cadence . . . back to the felt experience . . . I can, then, think forward again to the idea – that is, the significance of the event – rather than back upon it. It is the instant I try to catch in the notebooks, not the comment, not the thought. (Oliver, 1995: 46)

Art may be closer to 'reality' as people know it than so-called objective (sans obvious interpretation) accounts. The research diary, as Leonardo da Vinci's 'sketchbook' illustrates, can be a space where ideas are generated and connected. The diary is also a place where one can zoom in on a phenomenon and then place it back into a larger context.

Commitment to becoming the storyteller?

Committed to clear vision and disciplined interpretation, the researcher is vulnerable to what Schacter (2001) describes as the 'seven sins of memory', including bias, distortion, and misattribution. Though not avoidable, these sins can be identified and taken into account by using the research diary to identify attachments that obviously distort vision. The research diary 'can help us see around our normal habits' (Ornstein and Dewan, 2008: 157), to see how our mind 'shifts and wheels', how we can become storytellers, able to see and interpret experiences beyond the actor's perspective. 'The light that illuminates processes of action . . . reveals itself fully only to the storyteller . . . to the backward glance of the historian, who indeed always knows better what it was all about than the participants . . .' (Arendt, 1958: 192). The scholar becomes the story teller: 'What the storyteller narrates must necessarily be hidden from the actor himself, at least as long as he is in the act or caught in its consequences' (1958: 192).

The mind's propensity to look for novelty, to over-emphasize 'now', and to look through rose- or dark-coloured glasses depending on circumstance and motivation, is captured in an excerpt from the research blog of a young high school science teacher who struggles with wanting to intervene as his learning community students make mistakes. Using a Netbook to narrate his observations in real time, he takes himself into account and leaves traces of a transformative process that ultimately alters his understanding of teaching and learning, curricula, and environments for learning.

I am very nervous – the students are being struck down again & again. I hear them misreading and not knowing toothed vs. lobed, etc. It's killing me to sit back and let them make these mistakes, knowing Forrest is about to tell them they're incorrect. Interestingly, I am more invested in each one of their successes than I am during school. If this had been a school assessment, I would never have even known they needed help because they'd be quietly and secretly sweating on a multiple choice test . . .

Update – students did just fine and even got the bonus! (John Moore's ISLS Blog, 15 June 2009)

The following example (see box), from another teacher's diary, illustrates how an elementary school teacher documents a conversation with a child on one side of his diary, struggles with conscious interpretation and attachment to his own point of view in the middle, and later responds to a colleague's questions.

We conclude this discussion of research diaries with examples from two researcher blogs. The first researcher, Keith Manring, is a journalist and a Woodrow Wilson Teaching Fellow, who studies his journey to becoming a science teacher. In this excerpt he summarizes four months of study – ending with an invitation to his 19 Fellow colleagues to contribute their recollections and ideas to his blog. Manring is clearly part of a learning community – and profession.

... One log every week (let's say roughly 12) showing what we have been up to.

A log of the key lessons we have observed.

Our own log of good teaching ideas.

At least three lessons we designed, videotaped, and evaluated.

A complete plan on how we will teach and implement safety procedures in our science labs, including lessons, rules and organizational details.

Essays on everything from how teachers spend their time to ways they incorporate different approaches to help different kids learn. At least 10 of those. Which means at least 30 research papers read, a minimum of three for each essay. . . .

Hang with your own class of students for at least two half days and one full day a week.

And if anyone notices something I left off, let me know! (Manring, Blog, 17 December 2009)

	Actual conversation	Interpretation	Researcher questions
Adam:	Mr Jensen, would you tell me how to spell igloo?	Perhaps I'm too structured – Rigid. I am concerned that Adam doesn't participate in a lot of the classroom activities as I feel he should. It comes down to responsibility.	How so?
Me:	Sure Adam. (I write it for him on the board.) What assignment are you working on?		
Adam:	Assignment?	I am responsible for what Adam does in his second year of schooling and so far he has been uncooperative. *I need a sense of direction with him and we haven't found a common ground so far.*	I am responsible?
Me:	Yes (looking toward the board). Spelling? Phonics? Language? Reading? Which assignment?		What would that look like? Direction? A common ground?
Adam:	Oh, I'm done with all those things.		
Me:	Are you writing a story then?		
Adam:	Well, yes, and no, well, yes I guess I am. Well, I'm going to.		
Me:	So you've finished up and you are going to write a story?		
Adam:	Well, no not exactly. I haven't finished my reading yet.		

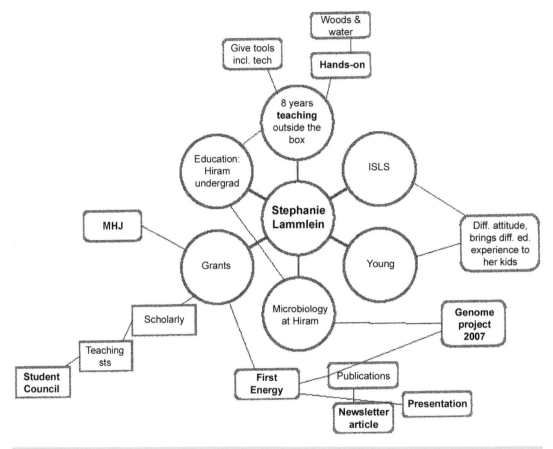

Figure 5.1   Using a mind map to create a visual representation of data

In our last example, the second researcher, Holly Wells (2009), captures the richness of a science teacher's experience in a mind map where she draws together various data sources and layers of data that can easily be accessed with hypertext. As with Manring, Wells steps back from chronological recording to bring together data and artefacts that have been collected over time. She creates a visual snapshot that enables her to move easily between data sources and layers of analysis (Figure 5.1). Each of the underlined links leads to the data – publications, photographs, video clips, the teacher's research blog, interview excerpts. From this map ideas are captured, conjectures and connections made, and plans generated for next steps in her research.

In each of these examples researchers zoom in on specific data and back out to a larger context; each records their experience and uses the research diary to sift and connect bits to tell the scholar's story. If the researcher's diary is a rich 'dialogue with a cruel partner' (Canetti, 1981) it is also the site of discovery and creativity, where the terrain can become a rich, evolving, heuristic map the researcher draws in conversation with other researchers and the 'facts'.

Annotated bibliography

Altrichter, H., Feldman, A., Posch, P. and Somekh, B. (2008) *Teachers Investigate their Work. An Introduction to Action Research across the Professions.*, 2nd edn. London and New York: Routledge.
For practitioners who want to research their own practice, this book contains practical exercises for developing research competence and a chapter on 'research diaries', which is considered to be one of the most important

research methods and as 'companion of the researcher's development', giving form and continuity to the research process.

Armstrong, M. (1980) *Closely Observed Children: The Diary of a Primary Classroom*. London: Writers and Readers in association with Chameleon.
This classic study takes you into the classroom of Stephen Rowland and 32 nine-year-old students, as meticulously described by Michael Armstrong who focused on children's 'moments of intellectual absorption'.

Burgess, R.G. (ed.) (1982) *Field Research: A Sourcebook and Field Manual*. London: George Allen & Unwin.
See the chapters 'Recording field data: "Keeping Field Notes"' by R. Burgess, 'The art of note-taking' by B. Webb, and 'The diary of an anthropologist' by B. Malinowski for valuable insights and suggestions from the researchers.

Burgess, R.G. (1984) *In the Field: An Introduction to Field Research*. London: George Allen & Unwin.
Of note here is 'Methods of field research 3: using personal documents' includes 'diaries and diary interviews', containing excerpts from diary entries and commentary, and diary interviews and commentary.

Denzin, N. and Lincoln, Y. (1998) *Collecting and Interpreting Qualitative Materials*. Thousand Oaks, CA: Sage.
Note chapters by: N. Denzin, 'The art and politics of interpretation'; L. Richardson, 'Writing: A method of inquiry'; and J. Clandinin and M. Connelly: 'Personal experience methods'.

Holly M.L., Arhar, J. and Kasten, W. (2009) *Action Research for Teachers: Travelling the Yellow Brick Road*, 3rd edn. Boston: Allyn & Bacon.
As the action research process unfolds in this book, so too can readers' research journals as they complete related exercises. Of interest are case studies, journal examples, and chapters on 'Writing as a research process', and 'Narrative writing'.

Holly, M.L. (1989) *Writing to Grow: Keeping a Personal Professional Journal*. Portsmouth, NH: Heinemann.
This book, based on a study of seven elementary school teachers who kept journals to document everyday experiences and life in their classrooms, introduces journal writing for reflective practice, case studies, and action research.

Malinowski, B. (1967) *A Diary in the Strict Sense of the Term*. London: Kegan Paul and Harcourt.
This book contains inside perspectives on details of daily life and motivations of the anthropologist during his research.

Stevens, D. and Cooper, J. (2009) *Journal Keeping: How to Use Reflective Writing for Learning, Teaching, Professional Insight, and Positive Change*. Sterling VA: Stylus.
Examples and methods for using journals to learn from practice with sections on blogs, concept mapping, and journal writing in the computer age.

Further references

Arendt, H. (1958) *The Human Condition*. Chicago: University of Chicago Press.
Argyris, C., Putnam, R. and McLain Smith, D. (1985) *Action Science. Concepts, Methods, and Skills for Research and Intervention*. San Francisco, CA: Jossey-Bass.
Bogdan, R. and Biklen, S. (1982) *Qualitative Research for Education: An Introduction to Theory and Methods*. Boston, NJ: Allyn and Bacon.
Camus, A. (1965) *Notebooks, 1935–1942*. New York: Modern Library, p. 28.
Canetti, E. (1981) *Das Gewissen der Worte*. Frankfurt/M: Fischer.
DeVore, I. (1970) *Selections from Field Notes. 1959 March–August*. Washington, DC: Curriculum Development Associates.
Foucault, M. (1972) *The Archaeology of Knowledge*. London: Tavistock.
Gadamer, H. (1975) *Truth and Method*. New York: Crossroad.
Geertz, C. (1983) *Local Knowledge: Further Essays in Interpretive Anthropology*. New York: Basic Books.
Jackson, P.W. (1968) *Life in Classrooms*. New York: Holt, Rinehart and Winston.
Kemmis, S. and McTaggart, R. (1982) *The Action Research Planner*, 2nd edn. Geelong, Victoria: Deakin University Press.
LeDux, J. (2002) *The Synaptic Self*. New York: Penguin.
Manring, K (2009) *Emerging Species: A Veteran Journalist's Path to Becoming a Teacher* (http://emspecies.word press.com).
Moore, J. (2009) John Moore's 'Igniting streams of learning in science' Blog, 15 June 2009 (http://islsOhio.org).
Oliver, M. (1995) *Blue Pastures*. New York: Harcourt Brace.
Ornstein, R. and Dewan, T. (2008) *Mindreal: How the Mind Creates its own Virtual Reality*. Cambridge, MA: Malor Books.
Schacter, D. (2001) *The Seven Sins of Memory: How the Mind Forgets and Remembers*. Boston, NJ: Houghton Mifflin.
Scott-Maxwell, F. (1968) *The Measure of My Days*. New York: Alfred A. Knopf.

Smith, L.M. and Geoffrey, W. (1968) *The Complexities of an Urban Classroom*. New York: Holt, Rinehart & Winston.

Wells, H. (2009) Holly Wells' 'Igniting streams of learning in science', Researcher Blog, 30 November 2009 (http://islsOhio.org).

Werder, L. von (1986) *. . . triffst Du nur das Zauberwort. Eine Einführung in die Schreib-und Poesietherapie*. Munich/ Weinheim: Psychologie Verlags Union.

Whyte, W.F. (1995) *Street Corner Society: The Social Structure of an Italian Slum*. Chicago: Chicago University Press.

Case Study

Charlotte Chadderton, Education and Social Research Institute,
Manchester Metropolitan University, UK

Harry Torrance, Education and Social Research Institute,
Manchester Metropolitan University, UK

Summary

- Where to draw the boundaries of the case
- The social construction of the case
- Naturalistic generalization
- Comparing and contrasting across multiple cases
- Two traditions: anthropological / sociological; and applied research and evaluation
- Key theorists and writers
  - Howard Becker
  - Bent Flyvbjerg
  - Helen Simons
  - Robert E. Stake

Key concepts

Case study is not easily summarized as a single, coherent form of educational or social research. Rather it is an 'approach' to research which has been fed by many different theoretical tributaries. Some derive from phenomenological social science, and place emphasis on social interaction and the social construction of meaning in situ; some derive from medical or even criminological models, giving far more emphasis to the 'objective' observer, studying the single 'case', i.e. the individual patient or offender. What is common to all approaches is the emphasis on study-in-depth; but what is not agreed is where to draw the boundaries of a case, and the extent to which the researcher can produce a definitive account of 'the case', from the outside, so to speak, rather than a series of possible readings of 'the case', from the inside. In this chapter we shall be discussing the claims and problems of case study from the point of view of a broadly sociological perspective, rather than a medical perspective. Thus while case study can involve studying the pathologies of individual patients, pupils, etc. we focus much more on the social construction of the case, the site of the social/educational encounter and the nature of the case as realized in social action. Thus our definition of case study combines a policy focus (a 'case' of curriculum development) with a physical location (i.e. teaching carried out in particular sites). Where we include reference to the study of individuals in our definition, we do so from the position of asking what does 'the case' look like for this pupil or this teacher, i.e. from this person's point of view?

Thus case study is an 'approach' to research which seeks to engage with and report the complexity of social and educational activity, in order to represent the meanings that individual social actors bring to those settings and manufacture in them. Case study assumes that 'social reality' is created through social interaction, albeit situated in particular contexts and histories, and seeks to identify and describe before trying to analyse and theorize – i.e. it places description before explanation. It asks the basic question 'what is going on here?' – before trying to account for it. It assumes that things may not be as they seem, and privileges in-depth enquiry over coverage: understanding 'the case' rather than generalizing to a population at large. When the case study researcher has to make a decision about depth versus coverage, the recommended choice is always depth. As such educational case study is aligned with and derives much of its rationale and methods from ethnography and its constituent theoretical discourses – symbolic interactionism, phenomenology, and ethnomethodology (cf. Torrance, 2010). It is very much within the 'social constructivist' perspective of social science, though even within this perspective there are variations, especially with respect to the balance to be struck between observation and interview – between the researcher's role and perspective, and that of the participants.

The strength of case study is that it can take an example of an activity – 'an instance in action' (Walker, 1974) – and use multiple methods and data sources to explore it and interrogate it. Thus it can achieve a 'thick description' (Geertz, 1973) of a phenomenon in order to represent it from the participants' perspective. Case studies can thus be produced of new institutions (e.g. Charter Schools in the USA, or Academies or Trust Schools in England), new programmes (e.g. changes in the National Curriculum) or new policies (e.g. using assessment to drive the reform of schooling), which aspire to tell-it-like-it-is from the participants' point of view, as well as hold policy to account in terms of the complex realities of implementation and the unintended consequences of policy in action. Case study is thus particular, descriptive, inductive and ultimately heuristic – it seeks to 'illuminate' the readers' understanding of an issue (Parlett and Hamilton, 1974).

A criticism often levelled at case study is that it is not possible to generalize from one or a small number of cases to the population under study as a whole. Nevertheless many case study reports imply that their findings are at least of general relevance and interest: we are asked to give them credence precisely because they are not idiosyncratic accounts, but because they claim to illuminate more general issues. Clearly this is a matter for judgement and the quality of the evidence presented. Some have argued that good case studies appeal to the capacity of the reader for 'naturalistic generalization' (Stake, 2005); that is, the reader recognizes aspects of their own experience in the case and intuitively generalizes from the case to their own situation, rather than the sample (of one) being statistically representative of the population as a whole.

The other major epistemological issue to be addressed by case study is where to draw the boundaries – what to include and what to exclude and, thus, what is the claim to knowledge that is being made – what is it a case of? Too often in the past the boundaries of a case have been assumed to be co-terminous with the physical location of the school or the factory or whatever was the focus of interest. But of course schooling involves local authorities (school districts), parents and, perhaps, local employers; manufacturing involves suppliers, customers, etc; drawing boundaries around a phenomenon under study is not so easy. Also, moving beyond the contemporaneous, institutions have histories and memories manifested through the understandings and actions of individuals. Likewise policies impinge on practice – teachers do not just 'choose' what to teach and how to teach it – they teach within a context determined by curriculum and assessment policies and procedures. Similarly our understandings of what is the purpose of schools, or other social institutions, are generated in particular social and historical circumstances, as are our understandings of definitions of professionalism and the proper role for teachers, nurses, pupils, etc. So case studies need to pay attention to the social and historical context of action, as well as the action itself (Ragin and Becker, 1992). This can be accommodated by the methods employed, as long as they are self-consciously looking beyond the immediate. Thus interviews offer an insight into respondents' memories and explanations of why things have come to be what they are, as well as descriptions of current problems and aspirations. Documents (e.g. children's schoolwork, school prospectuses, etc.) can be examined for immediate content, changing content over time and the values that such changing content manifests. Observations can offer an insight into the sedimented, enduring *verities* of schooling – rows of desks, percentage of teacher talk as against pupil talk, etc. – which are often at variance with new policies and/or the espoused preferences of participants. Sometimes of course data must be obtained from well beyond the physical location of the case, and the case becomes not just one example of a policy in situ, in action, but of the policy itself. Thus a vertical 'core' of data can be extracted from 'the system', by studying central policy-making, through local authority interpretation of policy, to local implementation and mediation, asking questions at each level of the system about where this policy has come from as well as where it is going ('antecedents, transactions and outcomes', Stake, 1967).

Having said this, it is also nevertheless the case that these aspirations have been developed in different ways in different disciplinary settings and are currently practised differently in different professional contexts. Essentially, the current practice of educational case study derives from an anthropological/sociological tradition on the one hand, and an applied research and programme evaluation tradition on the other.

The anthropological/sociological tradition emphasizes long-term participant observation of, usually, a single setting, and is exemplified in the 'Chicago School' of sociology, for example Becker et al.'s study of medical training (*Boys in White*, 1961). Education examples from the UK would include Lacey (1970), a case study of a grammar school, and Ball (1981), a case study of a comprehensive school. The emphasis in the fieldwork is very much on coming to know the 'insider' perspective by observing participants going about their 'ordinary' business in their 'natural' setting – i.e. by long-term immersion in 'the field'. Some interviewing and informal conversations will also be used to help interpret the observations. The underpinning idea is that of accessing the participants' perspective – the meaning that action has for them – but reporting is oriented towards theoretical explanations of the action and contributing to social theory 'to arrive at a comprehensive understanding of the groups under study [and] to develop general theoretical statements about regularities in social structure and process' (Becker, 1970).

The applied research and evaluation tradition arose later, in the late 1960s in the USA and the early 1970s in the UK, largely as a reaction to quasi-experimental curriculum evaluation designs which revealed too little useful information, especially about how innovations were implemented in action (Parlett and Hamilton, 1974). While the basic orientation and methods of ethnography were borrowed – i.e. interview and observation – the balance between them had to be radically altered because evaluative case studies had to be completed in weeks, rather than months (or years), and because the researchers had a substantive interest in the particular professional dilemmas and problems of participants. Thus interviewing became widely used to gather data, rather than observation, and the validity of the findings were based on comparing and contrasting across multiple cases and respondent validation of draft reports, rather than just the researcher's long-term observations and interpretations. Key features of such an approach are intensive, interview-based 'condensed fieldwork' (Walker, 1974)

and 'multi-site case study' (Stenhouse, 1982). Respondent validation, initially a methodological tool to check the veracity of draft accounts, also developed into a defining ethical and political aspiration of the approach, whereby representing the participant's perspective was elevated to reporting the participant's views in their own (interview-derived) words. Ultimately this returns us to crucial epistemological issues about who defines what 'the case' is a case of – the researcher or the researched? Key theoretical articulations of the applied research and evaluation tradition can be found in Stake (1967, 2005) and House and Howe (1999), while further engagement with the issue of whether or not researchers can ever really represent 'the other' can be found in Stronach and MacLure (1997) and Hopson (2009). Examples from the UK include MacDonald and Walker (1976), Norris (1990) and Kushner (2000). The underpinning idea is to identify and describe the impact of a programme or innovation-in-action, with the report being oriented towards improving decision-making and practice, not social theory. Thus the evaluative case study should respond: 'to audience requirements for information, and [to] ... different value perspectives ...' (Stake, 1983: 292).

Currently both of these approaches to case study can be found in practice and discussed in the literature, though often the divergence and genealogy of different approaches is either largely ignored or treated as irrelevant for present investigative purposes. Certainly there is no point in inventing typologies of case study just for the sake of them, yet how case studies are accomplished and, even more important for novice researchers, how they are judged, still largely depends on the 'tradition' in which they are conducted. Moving beyond origins, current practice can probably be said to include ethnographic case studies (as above); policy ethnographies (related to ethnographic case studies, as above, but treating policy as the case), evaluative case studies (as above), educational or professional case studies (as above but with more of an emphasis on professional improvement rather than evaluative decision-making) and action research case studies (related to evaluative case studies, as above, but with the emphasis on planned development in situ; cf. Noffke and Somekh, 2009).

Implications for research design

Case study analysis tends to be inductive, with the boundaries of the case and the key issues emerging from the data. However, decisions have to be taken about which case or cases to select for study, how much time can be spent in each fieldwork site and what methods of investigation to employ. A key issue concerns depth versus coverage, and within the logic of a case study approach, the recommended choice is always depth. Where resources allow it is helpful to compare and contrast across cases if possible and investigate the range of possible experience within a programme, for example studying an apparently 'good' and successful example of a new social programme, as compared with an apparently 'bad' and unsuccessful example. How have such intuitive judgements come to be made by key informants? Are there substantive differences between the cases? What might account for the differential implementation and perception of policy in action? If only one case study is being conducted an element of comparison can also be brought in by reference to other studies reported in the literature. Another way to address the breadth versus depth issue is to visit a range of potential fieldwork sites and conduct interviews with key personnel, then engage in 'progressive focusing' (Parlett and Hamilton, 1972) whereby the particular sites selected for detailed study emerge from an initial 'trawl' and analysis of key issues.

Most commonly employed research methods are interviews, documentary analysis and observation, with the balance between them being largely determined by the resources available and the disciplinary and professional tradition in which the case study is being conducted. It can be particularly helpful to ask respondents to identify and reflect on a 'critical incident' in their work or situation – a key example for them of what are the important issues in the case. An important criticism is that reliance on such methods, and especially on interviewing alone, can result in an overly empiricist analysis – locked into the 'here-and-now' of participants' perceptions. As noted above, this can be addressed by attention to relevant literature and by the methods employed, as long as they are used to look beyond the immediate and explore participants' memories and explanations of why things have come to be what they are, as well as descriptions of current problems and aspirations. Flyvbjerg (2001, 2006) argues that case study produces practical knowledge to inform practical action.

The story from the field explores these issues with respect to the issue of race taking description and analysis beyond the boundaries of 'the case'.

Stories from the field

Charlotte Chadderton

I now discuss the genesis and accomplishment of case study in the field – the focus of my PhD. The decisions taken about designing and undertaking the study were derived in principle from its location within the ethnographic tradition of long-term immersion in fieldwork, but combined with the topic's location within the educational field of 'curriculum innovation and evaluation'.

The study focused on the potential of the recently introduced Citizenship Education (CE) curriculum programme to address racism in UK secondary schools. Although some research had been conducted around CE policy, there had been very little work which explored how the policy was implemented in school classrooms. Therefore this study aimed to examine the ways in which CE is taught and how this is experienced by students with regards to race, racism and diversity (Chadderton, 2009).

Establishing the boundaries of the case study, I chose to combine observations of CE lessons and examination of teaching materials with interviews and discussion groups in two schools, in order to afford depth but also some comparative element to the study. I specifically wanted to conduct interviews and discussion groups, in order to try to access the frequently marginalized perspectives of minority ethnic pupils. Anonymity and confidentiality were agreed. I chose to conduct discussion groups with most pupils rather than one-to-one interviews, in the hopes of relaxing them and to enable me to observe the interaction. Due to the group situation, an individual may need to explain more fully or defend their views, possibly developing arguments in a way which would not have been produced in a one-to-one interview situation. These advantages were weighed against the disadvantage that certain points of view might be suppressed or encouraged in front of a group.

Access issues

As an outsider researcher, I was dependent on the cooperation of the relevant institution for data. I had great difficulty gaining access to schools, and individuals within the schools. Besides the barriers to access discussed below, there may have been other barriers, such as the busy nature of schools and the fact that research tends to be much more important to the researcher than to the researched, who are not necessarily prepared to make much time for it (Mirza, 1995). Government demands for the routine production of data for accountability purposes are now much more significant than even a few years ago and the lone PhD researcher can be perceived as little more than an irritant in an already pressurized institutional context.

Gatekeepers

I had planned to conduct my study in two comprehensive schools. However, access to schools was only achieved after multiple attempts to contact institutions. In the end, in order to gain the data I needed, I collected data in five schools, meaning that I spread myself thinner than I would have liked. Consequently, I was unable to acquire an in-depth knowledge of the individual schools in the way that I had originally intended. However, the result was a very diverse sample of schools and the contrasts were illuminating.

I wrote letters of introduction to about 30 secondary schools, and initially received answers from an ethnically mixed, selective boys' grammar school and a mainly white, mixed-sex comprehensive. I gained access to an ethnically mixed boys' comprehensive by working on a funded piece of research. In an effort to find more female participants, I wrote twice to a girls' school, but to no avail. At this point, I turned to my PhD supervisor for help and a letter signed by her was answered after many months' delay, and I was able to spend a short time there towards the end of my data collection period. About halfway through this period, I also gained access to a mixed comprehensive school through a personal acquaintance, which was exactly the type of school I had originally intended to study. This brought the total of schools at which I collected data to five in all.

At several points while trying unsuccessfully to arrange school visits, I became concerned that I would never have enough data to conduct a study. It turns out that this is a common concern for novice researchers (Mirza, 1995). Just having permission from the head teacher to conduct the research was not enough to carry it out in practice. I had to arrange interviews and observations with the individual teachers involved, which normally meant contacting them by phone, at school. Surprisingly, most teachers did not regularly use email, and many, though not all, were reluctant to give me a mobile phone number.

Gaining pupil participants was even more difficult, and achieved in a different way not only in each school, but also each time I conducted a discussion group. Consequently, although I had planned to conduct repeated interviews, I managed to speak to some groups only once, some twice, and two groups three times. I had intended that those pupils who took part should have some understanding beforehand of what the study was about and be willing volunteers. However, this was not possible as pupils were mostly simply chosen by members of staff. The students follow a strict timetable and no individual teacher felt that they had the authority to let students off the following lesson with another teacher, to be interviewed by me, resulting in a very opportunistic sample. Classroom teachers did sometimes allow me to take small groups out of their own lessons, but never liked the same group to go more than once, possibly twice, as they felt they would be missing too much schoolwork.

Racial issues as the focus of enquiry

At times I felt the topics of citizenship and race might have been the cause of the lack of willingness on the part of some staff to engage with my project. All the examples of sceptical reactions to the research below are from white staff. This does not mean that all white staff were unhelpful; on the contrary, I could never have conducted the research had it not been for the help of at least one person at each school, and at three schools this was a white staff member. However, most members of staff displayed a lack of understanding as to why I would want to research racial issues. Moreover, they tended to deny that racism existed at their school, or that race mattered at all. This was equally the case whether in schools where the population was ethnically mixed or overwhelmingly white British. Below are some examples of comments, characterized by avoidance strategies to silence or render invisible issues of race and difference – such comments were common.

- *'There is no multiculturalism here!'* (school mainly white). A refusal to see how issues of multiculturalism could be relevant for young people who grow up in a mainly white British area, despite the fact that it is located in the outskirts of a large, multi-ethnic city. Also, a disavowal of ethnic minority presence.
- *'Racism isn't really a problem here. We have far more urgent problems, such as bullying'* (ethnically mixed school). A refusal to see racism as an issue at all.

Also, a disavowal that bullying can have racist origins or implications.

- *'There are lots of vulnerable kids, black, white, green and pink, and they all need help'* (ethnically mixed school). A refusal to see how minority ethnic young people might be vulnerable in ways specific to that particular group. Also, a disavowal that a person's ethnic origins affects how they are treated by others.

- At a school with a mostly white pupil population, the research was delayed many times because the deputy head (a white woman) felt that there should be no discussion groups that did not include white pupils, as it was non-inclusive. Every time I tried to get an audience with her, she was unavailable and never rang back. The discussions did eventually take place, after the intervention of the only minority ethnic staff member, but we had far less time than initially planned.

The staff attitude should not necessarily be viewed as deliberate racism (Gaine, 2005; Jones, 1999), but rather as shaped by dominant, racializing discourses which mean that many teachers may have no understanding of racism.

Control and surveillance

A further barrier to the collection of data was the surveillance I and the student participants experienced from the schools during the research. Something I did not realize initially was that as a researcher I was also, inevitably, surveilling the school and its population, as 'all research is to some degree surveillance' (McCoy, 1998, cited in Lather, 2001: 482). Staff may therefore have resisted this surveillance.

However, I did feel that I was under particular surveillance. One example was the way some teachers policed which lessons I observed: only with one teacher was I able to set a timetable of regular visits to school, without having to arrange them in advance. Most stipulated an individual morning or lesson meaning that the teacher, not I, decided which lessons I observed.

Equally, I felt the discussions with students were under surveillance. For example, at one school I had conducted other research on the school's behalf some months previously, during which I was given a quiet room to conduct confidential interviews. The same was not provided for my own PhD study. Indeed, although in every school I explained the need for a quiet room, it appears that such a room was not readily available due to shortage of space. Even when we did have a room, I felt that little attention was paid to issues of confidentiality by the staff member who had organised the rooms. My discussion groups were disturbed in rooms which turned out to have been double booked, empty classrooms which teachers came in and out of, senior staff offices which were actually only available for a short time, after which we were expected to find somewhere else. This disturbance raises ethical questions for the young people as I had assured them of confidentiality. Although it is unlikely that much was overheard by staff, I did take care to anonymize the data when writing up the study. All these incidents highlight the need to try to agree with key gatekeepers in advance the 'rules of research engagement' so to speak: the proposed research schedule; sample of respondents; need for privacy. But this is hard to establish when one is simply grateful for gaining any access at all, and in any case such agreements can still break down in practice.

Representing the 'other'

Most student participants belonged to a minority ethnic group or minority religion or both, as I specifically aimed to speak to those who are positioned by discourses of citizenship which construct them as separate, essentialized groups. I therefore sometimes asked for groups who self-identified as Muslims, or as 'black'. This is ethically problematic because, in the event, the teachers chose the participants, and thus the young people were not given the chance to self-define, but were defined by their mostly white teachers and myself, a white researcher. This categorization is not neutral: indeed, it creates racial difference and others individuals (Noble, 2005: 133). It has been argued that categorizing people for research purposes is only ethically defensible if the focus of the study is not their ethnicity (or indeed, gender, disability), but rather their experiences of being positioned, in order to reveal structural inequalities (Humphries and Truman, 1994). However, importantly, despite my aim to conduct social justice research and challenge structures of racialization, I found myself (unwittingly) complicit in those very structures. This challenges the notion that research can be objective, and that participants' perspectives can be unproblematically accessed. A researcher should acknowledge her own participation in the construction of the subject position of others, and unless the power relations involved are deconstructed, she runs the risk of reinforcing inequalities rather than challenging them.

There remain many such acknowledged tensions in the work. A case study can be seen as providing an interpretation of a situation rather than a single representative truth. Nevertheless, this study provides important insights into the ways racism operates at a structural level in the education system which may have general relevance.

Annotated bibliography

Brown, T. and Jones, L. (2001) *Action Research and Postmodernism*. Buckingham: Open University Press.
A very well informed review, grounded in empirical data and a series of excellent examples of the extent to which case study researchers, especially those conducting action research, can or should impose their own meanings and interpretations on the actions of others.

House, E. and Howe, K. (1999) *Values in Evaluation and Social Research*. Thousand Oaks, CA: Sage.
A review and summary of case study approaches within the 'applied research and evaluation' tradition, particularly focusing on the design of qualitative evaluations of social programmes, the need to seek out and represent stakeholders' views, and the need to recognize the role of values and value judgements in social research.

Ragin, C. and Becker, H. (eds) (1992) *What Is a Case?* Cambridge: Cambridge University Press.
A collection of papers exploring and representing the 'anthropological/sociological' participant observation tradition in case study.

Schostak, J. (2002) *Understanding, Designing and Conducting Qualitative Research in Education*. Buckingham: Open University Press.
A theoretically very well informed guide to designing and conducting qualitative research, especially through case study approaches, including a great deal of experienced, practical advice and how to 'frame the project' guidance.

Simons, H. (2009) *Case Study Research in Practice*. London: Sage.
A review of the theory and practice of case study by an expert practitioner who has worked in the evaluative tradition for 30+ years.

Stake, R. (1995) *The Art of Case Study Research*. Thousand Oaks, CA: Sage.

Excellent treatment of different approaches to case study but particularly focusing on the role and sensitivity of the researcher in teasing out the nuances of a case.

Torrance, H. (ed.) (2010) *The SAGE Handbook of Qualitative Research Methods in Education*. London: Sage.
A four-volume handbook including key papers on case study from the 'Participant Observation' and 'Evaluation' traditions, along with more recent work discussing the implications of post-modernist and post-structuralist critiques of 'naturalistic' qualitative inquiry.

Further references

Ball, S.J. (1981) *Beachside Comprehensive*. Cambridge: Cambridge University Press.

Becker, H., Geer, B., Hughes, E. and Strauss, A. (1961) *Boys in White*. New Brunswick, NJ: Transaction Books.

Becker, H. (1970) *Sociological Work: Method and Substance*. Chicago: Aldine.

Chadderton, C. (2009) Discourses of Britishness, Race and Difference: minority ethnic students' shifting perceptions of the schooling experience. PhD Thesis, Manchester Metropolitan University.

Flyvbjerg, B. (2001) *Making Social Science Matter: Why Social Inquiry Fails and How It Can Succeed Again*. Cambridge: Cambridge University Press.

Flyvbjerg, B. (2006) 'Five Misunderstandings About Case Study. *Quantitive Inquiry*. 12, 2, pp. 219–45.

Gaine, C. (2005) *We're All White, Thanks: The Persisting Myth About 'White' Schools*. Stoke-on-Trent, UK and Sterling, USA: Trentham.

Geertz, C. (1973) *The Interpretation of Culture*. New York: Basic Books.

Hopson, R. (2009) 'Reclaiming knowledge at the margins: Culturally responsive evaluation', in K. Ryan and J.B. Cousins (eds), *The SAGE International Handbook of Educational Evaluation*. Thousand Oaks, CA: Sage. pp. 429–46.

Humphries, B. and Truman, C. (1994) *Re-Thinking Social Research*. Aldershot, Hants and Brookfield, VT: Avebury.

Jones, R. (1999) *Teaching Racism – or Tackling It? Multicultural Stories from White Beginning Teachers*. Stoke-on-Trent: Trentham Books.

Kushner, S. (2000) *Personalising Evaluation*. London: Sage.

Lacey, C. (1970) *Hightown Grammar*. Manchester: Manchester University Press.

Lather, P. (2001) 'Postmodernism, post-structuralism and post (critical) ethnography: Of ruins, aporias and angels', in P. Atkinson, A. Coffey, S. Delamont, J. Lofland and L.

Lofland (eds) *Handbook of Ethnography*. London: Sage. pp. 477–92.

MacDonald, B. and Walker, R. (1976) *Changing the Curriculum*. London: Open Books.

Mirza, M. (1995) 'Some ethical dilemmas in fieldwork: Feminist and anti-racist methodologies', in M. Griffiths and B. Troyna (eds), *Antiracism, Culture and Social Justice in Education*. Stoke-on-Trent: Trentham. pp. 163–81.

Noble, D. (2005) 'Remembering bodies, healing histories: The emotional politics of everyday freedom', in C. Alexander, and C. Knowles (eds) *Making Race Matter: Bodies, Space and Identity*. London and New York: Palgrave Macmillan. pp. 132–52.

Noffke, S. and Somekh, B. (eds) (2009) *The SAGE Handbook of Educational Action Research*. London: Sage.

Norris, N. (1990) *Understanding Educational Evaluation*. London: Kegan Page.

Parlett, M. and Hamilton, D. (1972) 'Evaluation and illumination', reprinted in H. Torrance (ed.) (2010) *The SAGE Handbook of Qualitative Research Methods in Education*. London: Sage.

Ragin, C. and Becker, H. (eds) (1992) *What Is a Case?* Cambridge: Cambridge University Press.

Stake, R. (1967) 'The Countenance of Educational Evaluation', *Teachers' College Record*, 68: 7.

Stake, R. (1983) 'Program evaluation, particularly responsive evaluation', in G. Madaus, M. Scriven and D.L. Stufflebeam (eds) *Evaluation Models: Viewpoints on Educational and Human Services Evaluation*. Boston: Kluwer.

Stake, R. (2005) 'Qualitative Case Studies', in N.K. Denzin and Y.S. Lincoln (eds) *The SAGE Handbook of Qualitative Research*, 3rd edn. Thousand Oaks, CA: Sage. pp. 443–66.

Stenhouse, L. (1982) 'The conduct, analysis and reporting of case study in educational research and evaluation', reprinted in H. Torrance (ed.) (2010), *The SAGE Handbook of Qualitative Research Methods in Education*. London: Sage.

Stronach, I. and MacLure, M. (1997) *Educational Research Undone: The Postmodern Embrace*. Buckingham: Open University Press.

Walker, R. (1974) 'The conduct of educational case study: Ethics, theory and procedures', reprinted in H. Torrance (ed.) (2010) *The SAGE Handbook of Qualitative Research Methods in Education*. London: Sage.

Interviewing and Focus Groups

Rosaline S. Barbour, School of Nursing & Midwifery, University of Dundee, UK

John Schostak, Education and Social Research Institute,
Manchester Metropolitan University, UK

Summary

- 'Performance' of those engaged in communication
- Vulnerability of those who 'leak' knowledge to others
- Trust
- Imposition, grounding and emergence
- Participants in focus groups co-produce an account of themselves and their ideas
- Key theorists and writers
  - Rosaline S. Barbour
  - Pierre Bourdieu
  - John Schostak

Key concepts

Everyone thinks they know something about interviewing – and quite rightly too! The media images are everywhere: the crime series showing the rough tough cop interrogating the suspect to find the 'truth'; the psychiatrist during a clinical interview delving into the mind of the client to uncover repressed realities; the job selection committee interviewing a candidate who puts on a performance to present the best image possible; the reporter interviewing a politician and trying to dig out a clear, unambiguous statement. And, as a final image, there is the street survey where 'random' passers by are interviewed for their views about some topic of the day, product or service.

Between one-to-one interviews and the groups of everyday life sits the focus group. What about focus groups? They've attained unprecedented popularity with researchers. Politicians and marketing consultants love them, and they have, consequently, become a household term. We all discuss and debate in a variety of groups and, to some extent, we all possess some of the skills required to moderate or participate in focus group discussions, whether we chair committee meetings, run or take part in workshops, or attend dinner parties. However, there can be a downside to the over-enthusiastic use of any method and it is crucial that focus groups are not employed in a formulaic and unthinking manner.

Implicit in our images of interviews and focus groups are a number of key concepts that fundamentally impact on their utility as methods to be employed by researchers:

- the 'messiness' of encounters with others;
- the 'performances' of those engaged in communication;
- the level of 'commitment' to being engaged in communication;
- 'truth';
- 'reality';
- 'suspicion';
- the hidden agendas at play;
- the tactics and strategies employed to 'unearth' information.

This list is not exhaustive. However, it is indicative of the problem: what status can we give to the words of the other?

Take the example of the investigative reporter interviewing an informant who is in fear of losing a job, or indeed, of being injured or killed if found out, but who feels it is right to tell others what it means to live and work within a given organization. Knowledge is power. But those who leak 'knowledge' that others wish to remain suppressed are in positions of great vulnerability. And when the statements are printed, they are taken out of the lived context and placed into another – the public domain, the domain where words are twisted, given alternative meanings, 'interpreted' in the light of other evidence. Investigations and pressure may be brought to bear to find the 'informant' – will the cloak of secrecy be lifted? Think too of the pressures that may bear upon a focus group member whose views are clearly out of step with the majority in the group – there is the temptation to conceal those views, or, for some, there may be the temptation to play the radical outsider and give wildly exaggerated opinions.

Taking such thoughts as these into account, the key concepts can be refined as:

(1) *Power* – the power structures that are the context to the exchange taking place between interviewer and interviewee, or within the focus group.

(2) *Social position* – the relative positions of the actors involved in the interview or focus group process in the context of the social arrangements that embed them (the legal, economic, religious, community, organizational, cultural, gender, ethnic, and so on, structures).

(3) *Value* – the value that the 'information' has as a commodity for sale (in the media, as blackmail, as 'leverage' in some dispute, as a 'juicy quote' to enliven a dissertation or publication); the value of the interview as evocative of 'truth', of 'reality', of the 'conditions of everyday life'; the value of the interviewees' words as 'testimony' of a way of life.

(4) *Trust* – given all the vulnerabilities, the desire to make a good impression, the desire to conceal shady dimensions, trust is a delicate gift, easily broken. To what extent is it the guarantor of accuracy, the underwriter of 'truth', 'honesty', 'reality', 'objectivity'?

(5) *Meaning* – the meaning heard by one individual may not be the same as that intended by the speaker. Interviews and focus groups provide an opportunity to check the meanings intended. However, it can be argued that there are unconscious or latent meanings that, although not

intended, may provide a 'truth', or reveal an alternative 'reality' that underpins apparent actions. The words employed to represent experiences, realities, points of view, expressions of self are all open to alternative meanings.

(6) *Interpretation* – if there are multiple meanings, then interpretation is critical. However, what rules, what approaches, what frameworks can be employed to underpin the process of making and selecting appropriate, 'correct', 'significant' interpretations?

(7) *Uncertainty* – with multiple meanings and multiple interpretations a stable resting place may be difficult, even impossible, to find.

These concepts – and others – *problematize* interviewing and focus group discussions as natural ways of 'getting the data' or the 'sense of the real'. There are three kinds of strategy for getting at the 'real'. These are: imposition, grounding and emergence.

Impositional strategies begin with a list of themes, issues, problems, questions to be covered. These may be drawn from a review of the literature, the imagination, or an 'expert group'. Once identified they are generally tested with small groups, to reduce ambiguity and identify questions that produce the most useful spread of information, as a way of standardizing the questions that can be applied across a large sample. The aim of this 'closed interview' format is to generate the conditions for generalization across populations. Some flexibility may be built in by including some 'open ended' questions, thus generating semi-structured interviews. These enable the interviewer to capture unexpected issues and information. However, this contrasts with open interviews that have no prior list or pre-set questions but are grounded in the views and agendas of the interviewee in order to adopt strategies appropriate to the specific nature of social contexts and processes (Schostak, 2002). Finally, in contrast to grounded strategies, impositional strategies reinforce the power of the interviewer over that of the interviewee and create the suspicion that the other is 'hiding something'. What does the interviewer really want, what is it that the interviewee is keeping secret? What is it that the interviewer is really going to do with the data collected? In whose interests will it be used? There is, as Bourdieu has pointed out, an implicit violence here, a symbolic violence.

Bourdieu and his team wanted to evoke French working-class experience (Bourdieu, 1993). How should the interviews be conducted? The aim was to provide a stage for the *emergence* of the *voices* of those who live in the slum suburbs to testify to the inequalities, the injustices, the tensions, the anxieties of everyday life in a country that is one of the richest in the world. Bourdieu (1993: 1389–447) provided a rationale for his approach where, through an ever-vigilant self-reflexivity during interviewing, the researcher guards against the multiple complex influences of all the social pressures and traps (1993: 1391). However, can this rationale escape the impositional nature of the research process? It can be argued that there is a symbolic violence in the presumed power, social status, and knowledge of the researcher that may be used to manipulate the interview. There is the agenda the interviewer may impose upon the interview which may prevent the interviewees raising the concerns of their own lives. Alternatively, it can be argued that the interviewer should adopt the pose of the listener in a way that parallels the language and manners of the interviewee, and does not impose or objectivize the person who is invited to speak. In this way, the possibility is increased that the views of the interviewee will *emerge* as their voices are freed from the impositional power of the research. This would mean that the data collected and the analyses that follow would be *grounded* in the experiences of the interviewee rather than grounded in the demands of the research.

Focus groups pose many of the same problems, but offer access to a wider range of voices in a similar timeframe. Yet focus groups are not simply cheap and dirty surveys (Barbour, 2007). Treating them as such ignores fundamental differences in sampling. Focus group studies generally employ either convenience or purposive sampling, neither of which produces a representative sample. Treating focus group data as if they can simply be aggregated and 'multiplied up' is to overlook the importance of group dynamics. Focus groups are not an effective way of measuring attitudes or, even, of eliciting people's 'real views'. This is because they are, fundamentally, a social process through which participants co-produce an account of themselves and their ideas (Brannen and Pattman, 2007), which is specific to that time and place.

Clearly, the interview or the focus group is much more than just a tool, like a drill to screw deeper into the discursive structures that frame the worlds of 'subjects'. It is as much a way of seeing, or rather, a condition for seeing anything at all. Kvale (1996) regards the 'InterView' as a way of bringing together the multiple views of people. Schostak (2006) sees it as the space between views, not the views themselves

but the negative condition under which people may express their views to each other and to themselves. It is the very condition for critical reflective dialogue in public space to *emerge* and be maintained and for a provisional consensus 'for all practical purposes' to be framed without it falling into sterile, totalitarian monologue (see Schostak, 2002). Focus groups allow participants to debate issues and to provide the researcher with insights into the lengths to which they are prepared to go to defend their views in a specific context. Participants may also individually or collaboratively formulate and revise their perspectives. This kind of dialogic approach to the interview and the focus group that is *grounded* in the voices of people in order to enable multiple views to *emerge* has implications for research design (see below).

Rather than convening groups of strangers as focus groups – advised by most marketing research texts – it is generally better to get as close as possible to the real-life situations where people discuss, formulate and modify their views and make sense of their experiences as in peer groups or professional teams. However, there are problems, such as obvious and hidden 'pecking orders', the histories group members have with each other, their possible animosities, and the considerable potential for confusion about the purpose of the meeting.

Once convened, focus groups can – and do – take on a life of their own. Although capitalizing on the privileged 'fly on the wall' status, the researcher cannot abdicate responsibility for the impact which taking part in a focus group discussion may have on continuing relationships within the group. Some of the banter observed during sessions is, of course, part and parcel of social interaction and the usual way in which group members act towards each other (and may or may not be inherently interesting to the researcher – depending on the topic of the research). However, in bringing even a pre-existing group together for research purposes, we may ask people to cross boundaries which they do not normally do in the contexts in which they usually meet. This raises the particular challenge of ensuring confidentiality which is crucially important to address 'up front' at the start and not assume this work has already been done.

Implicatons for research design

There is no recipe for research design. However, design must take into account such issues as access, representation, sampling, ethics, data elicitation, data processing and analysis in identifying a *key list of people* each of whom acts in relation to some other individual and/or group (cf. Schostak, 2002). As each person adds their view, challenges or denies the views of others there is a complex of interacting views, that is, a public space of views where meanings, validity, generalizability and so on can be contested (Schostak and Schostak, 2008, 2010).

Initially, it may involve snowball sampling when the researcher may not be aware, at the outset, of all the relevant players involved. However, gaining access in this way requires building trust. This is important when selecting focus group participants, and, especially, when utilizing existing social groups or networks. Groups and communities are fluid entities, making it difficult to secure agreement from everyone. Representation is also tricky, since participants may very well have their own agenda. Gatekeepers can play a key role in setting up focus groups, but time spent briefing such individuals on the purpose of our work is time well spent – otherwise they may inadvertently select people out as well as select them in (Kitzinger and Barbour, 1999).

Ethical frameworks are crucial and spell out the principles under which anonymity, confidentiality and rights of access are to be constructed. The danger is that such principles are developed routinely, or indeed quasi-bureaucratically, via a plethora of ethics committees. To reduce symbolic violence the principles should be individually negotiated with each interviewee before each interview (see Enquiry Learning Unit website). More recently online discussion groups have afforded the opportunity of engaging with groups who might otherwise be marginalized (see e.g. Fox et al., 2007).

For both one-to-one interviews and focus groups the researchers are the principal data generating tool, thinking on our feet, and inviting participants to explore the limitations they might place around their responses, and how to contextualize their views (Barbour, 2008). Semi-structured interview schedules and focus group topic guides tend to be much shorter than 'interviewer-administered questionnaire tools'. Open-ended interviews build conversationally, mapping the themes as they unfold, with researchers entering and learning how to behave in the worlds of others (Schostak, 2010).

In thinking about designing either interview or focus group studies, sampling holds the key to the comparisons that can be made – that is, the basis of

the 'constant comparative method', as advocated by Glaser and Strauss (1967). Most textbooks advise that focus groups should be convened in order to bring together individuals who share some important characteristic. Setting up a range of groups (e.g. with old and young, men and women, parents and non-parents – depending on the topic on hand) gives us a useful basis for making inter-group comparisons. If we also pay attention to variations in views expressed by individual group members (intra-group differences) and the nuances in the discussion, however, we can produce much more textured and theoretically informed accounts. It is also possible, in some studies, to convene additional groups in order to take advantage of distinctions we have uncovered and these can allow us to test out theoretical propositions and emergent explanations (Barbour, 2007).

Stories from the field – interviewing

John Schostak

Much has been written on the interview as a research method, but it is the experience of doing it that matters. I hope, then, to evoke this by starting with a story.

After a 26-hour flight without sleep to Sydney, we were whisked from the airport to meet the senior police officers who would be our initial contacts for the evaluation of police training that we were to undertake. I had hoped to go straight to the hotel and go to sleep. 'While you're here, you may as well interview me' said the senior police officer. I recall taking out the tape-recorder but nothing else of the interview. Apparently the interview took about an hour and a half. About a week later, I was in a police car being driven to interview officers at police stations when my driver said, 'I hear you're really good at interviewing'. The interview he was referring to was the one I still had no recollection of. 'Really?' I said, 'Why?' 'Well', he said, 'you never let go, you just keep circling around until you get the real answer.'

I have never been certain whether to take that as a compliment or not. However, there is a grain of truth in the response. I have always considered that it is not what is in my mind that is important but what is in the mind of the interviewee. The question is how to get at it. Being asleep may not be the answer! But maybe it is about being sufficiently relaxed in the company of another in order to create the conditions for them to speak. When I looked at the transcript of the interview, it was clear I had been on autopilot. I said little, all my questions were open ended, designed to get the other to talk. Of course this was not the first time I had interviewed. There had been several hundred before. Typically I start with a question that puts the other into 'home territory', such as: 'Can you tell me something about your role so that I can get a bit of context . . .?' or, 'Been a long time since I was at school (or since I was 10, 14, . . .), what's it like for you here?'

And whatever their response, particularly when the answer is something like 'it's OK', I tend to ask for examples: 'I can't quite get a picture of that, I like to be able to *see* what you're talking about, can you give me an example?' 'What made school OK/awful today?' For me it is about getting the interviewee to paint a picture in my mind of the world that is in his or her head. What are the features of this world? What words are used to describe it? What are the concrete instances of the general concepts that are employed to describe roles, relations, aims, values, intentions, motives, hopes, ambitions, fears . . . Who are the people that populate this world? Who are the friends, the allies, the enemies? What are the kinds of events that take place? What are the resources, the structures, the routines? The questions multiply as the interviewee talks, so that I continually prompt: 'That's interesting, can you tell me more, can you paint a picture for me of how you . . .?'

Preceding this, of course, I will have done my homework. I will have listed the key themes, issues, questions that are relevant to the project in hand. I will have outlined my opening statements about why I am doing the research and how the interview will be confidential, names will not be used, data will be anonymized. As a new researcher I would have my questions and key thematic areas listed in my notebook. However, I always felt the artificiality of just routinely going through the list. I also didn't like the sense of imposing questions. I soon realized that if my questions, themes and issues were relevant in their lives, the interviewees would generally raise them during the interview. That meant, I had to be alert to the flow of the conversation, asking for further information and concrete description when relevant to the key points on my list. At the end of an interview, if any of my key points had not been covered, I could simply raise them. And finally, often the most important part of all, I would end by saying, 'We've talked for quite a long time now, I'm conscious of your time, but is there anything that we

have not covered that you think is important for me to take into account?' Mostly the answer is 'No, I think we've covered everything'. But sometimes it is, 'Yes, I'm surprised you didn't ask about . . .'.

By the ways in which the interview evolves and is elaborated during my attempts to 'get the picture', analysis is already implicit in the questions and answers posed. What emerges is the sense of the public scenes of action and their borders with the private realms of feeling, hopes, ambitions, frustrations, fears and things that cannot be said in public. Briefly, the interview provides an insight into how the public spaces of everyday life are organized for this individual in terms of the 'dramatis personae' of people, how those people are categorized, how the views of those people are interpreted and engaged with, the kinds of resources (tools, knowledge, networks, structures) that are within reach or out of reach and the kinds of outcomes, events or products that are accomplished or not accomplished. Most importantly, it provides a basis for the next interview and the next observation. Using a kind of circling strategy I can identify from the dramatis personae of one interview the people who need to be added to my list of interviewees. I can compare and contrast, identify what features were given prominence by one and not by another, what was seen or heard or experienced by one and not by another, thus analysing, cross checking (or validating) and triangulating the views of interviewees. For me, then, the interview is a critical strategy in generating the intersubjective features of the public and private spaces of social life.

Stories from the field – focus groups

Rosaline S. Barbour

I am sitting in the maternity hospital clinic with the research midwife and the crèche worker, drinking yet another cup of coffee. We've been here for nearly an hour and, shamefully, the stock of biscuits is somewhat depleted. Despite a telephone reminder the previous evening, no one has turned up for our scheduled focus group discussion on experiences of taking folic acid (recommended by the Department of Health for women trying to conceive and pregnant women up to 12 weeks' gestation in order to help prevent neural tube defects). However, we can't leave, as we're still hoping that at least three women will show up for the group scheduled to follow this session.

I feel particularly bad about this as I've been waxing lyrical to the research midwife (an experienced quantitative researcher) about the merits of qualitative work. The research team (a nutritionist, obstetrician and social scientist) have selected focus groups as our method of choice, due to their capacity to elicit data on issues not of prime importance to respondents (Barbour, 2007). I'm not revising my views about the decision to avoid individual interviews, as it would be difficult to sustain a one-to-one conversation about something someone hasn't done. However, I am beginning to question our choice of the maternity hospital as the venue for groups. This is our second such experience, following a session which produced two women (and a hastily-made decision to conduct a joint interview). The team subsequently decided to hold sessions in peripheral clinics, hoping that these would be more accessible for the mothers we were trying to recruit. This amendment required us to re-contact the ethics committee for approval, as well as contacting staff at these peripheral clinics in order to seek permission to attend and to ascertain the times when these happened.

The study team breathed a collective sigh of relief when the change of venue was approved and set to re-convening groups based on the localities in which women live, hoping for fewer 'no shows'. This proved logistically quite challenging, as some of the women have, by this stage, returned to work and we also had to fit focus groups around nursery and school timetables for older children. Certainly first-time mothers might have been easier to accommodate, but we have elected to include women of varying parity (i.e. number of previous pregnancies) and so must be philosophical about the practical challenges of this choice.

Focus groups in peripheral clinics were marginally more successful, with five visits resulting in two focus group discussions (and due caution having been exercised on the biscuit front). We are, however, still a long way from our target and I find myself toying with the slightly surreal – and ethically indefensible – option of resorting to cruising around the area in a stretch limo snatching up women with pushchairs. One last option is still at our disposal in the form of telephone focus groups, which also afford the relative luxury of not having to take locality into account, but still allow the researcher to capitalize on interaction between participants, provided that these are moderated accordingly. Although these require the same amount of groundwork in terms of phoning around,

after a couple of aborted attempts (due, respectively to technological challenges and unavailability of participants) we eventually manage to carry out three focus groups and two joint interviews by telephone.

We have still been hoping to recruit the same spread of women of differing ages and socio-economic background (using postcode deprivation categories as an indicator). Although the research team is concerned with establishing the reasons for suboptimal uptake of folic acid, previous focus group work has convinced me of the value of also exploring the views of those who do follow advice, as we can learn much from the resulting comparisons (Clark et al., 2004). Therefore, we had decided to include those who have taken folic acid (pre-conception and/or during early pregnancy), those who have taken it but not entirely according to recommendations, and those who have not taken folic acid at all. In order to avoid putting those who had not taken folic acid 'on the spot' we elected not to mix those at opposite ends of the 'compliance continuum'.

However, our neat sampling grid has to be relaxed due to recruitment problems and categories also prove, in practice, to be somewhat more malleable. Some women who had ticked the box (on the screening questionnaire) to indicate that they had taken folic acid, reveal in discussions that they had taken it intermittently or had stopped taking it – either because they forgot or because they thought it caused morning sickness. In the event, women seem happy to give consideration to others' sometimes different views, but do not appear reticent about sharing their own experiences. For ethical reasons we had elected not to recruit pregnant women, since we were concerned about the potential of the research to raise anxiety. However, all such desk-generated plans can be more difficult to follow in the field and four of the women who turned up to focus group sessions were pregnant again. None of these women, in the event, appeared disconcerted by discussions about the role of folic acid in preventing neural tube defects – even where they had not taken folic acid with the current pregnancy. One was almost defiant. She told us: 'I've got a wee girl of four, a wee girl at three and a wee boy on the way. And I've not taken folic acid in my life, and it didn't make any difference because they're just like any other normal bairns [children]' (Focus Group D). This serves to remind us that participants may not be as susceptible to researchers' 'wisdom' as we anticipate.

One of our most interesting findings is that even

women who had taken folic acid might remain unconvinced about its efficacy, with good outcomes being seen as having occurred independently. Including women of varying parity provided the useful insight that receptiveness to health promotion advice appears to diminish with subsequent pregnancies, with women valuing their own experiential knowledge and giving more credence to a 'lay evidence base'. Thus, although the best laid plans of researchers may have to be modified in the light of the realities of the field, some research design decisions do pay off in the end.

Annotated bibliography

Barbour, R. (2007) *Doing Focus Groups*. London: Sage.
This book (part of the Sage Qualitative Research Kit) provides practical advice on planning and conducting focus group research projects. It pays particular attention to sampling and research design. Also covered are uses and abuses of focus groups, theoretical underpinnings and detailed advice on analysing focus group data. Chapter 1 ('Introducing focus groups') and Chapter 2 ('Uses and abuses of focus groups') are available via the companion website.

Bloor, M., Frankland, J., Thomas, M. and Robson, K. (2001) *Focus Groups in Social Research*. London: Sage.
This has a particularly useful chapter on virtual focus groups, which provides a thoughtful discussion of the potential and pitfalls of using online sources to carry out focus group research.

Bourdieu, P. (1993) *La Misère du Monde*. Paris: Éditions du Seuil.
It was published in English as *The Weight of the World: Social Suffering in Contemporary Society*, translated by Priscilla Parkhurst Ferguson et al. (1999) Oxford: Polity. This is a collection of interviews, powerfully representing the lives of the poor. The methodological Appendix by Bourdieu is especially worth reading.

Crabtree, B.F., Yanoshik, M.K., Miller, W.I. and O'Connor, P.J. (1993) 'Selecting individual or group interviews', in D.L. Morgan (ed.) *Successful Focus Groups: Advancing the State of the Art*. London: Sage. pp. 137–49.
This chapter is helpful with regard to deciding when it is appropriate to use interviews and when focus groups are more appropriate.

Enquiry Learning Unit: http://www.enquirylearning.net/ELU/SubFrame.html
This website contains a nine chapter introduction to qualitative research. The site also has a further 20 + articles on research issues.

Gubrium, J.F. and Holstein, J.A. (2003) *Postmodern Interviewing*. Thousand Oaks, CA: Sage.
The book provides insights into the ways in which postmodern researchers have employed the process of interviewing.

Rubin, H.J. and Rubin, I.S. (1995) *Qualitative Interviewing: The Art of Hearing Data*. Thousand Oaks, CA: Sage.
The task of hearing is not easy. Too often people hear only what they want to hear. Worth a read.

Schostak, J.F. (2006) *Interviewing and Representation in Qualitative Research Projects*. Maidenhead, England and New York: Open University Press.
This book extends the notion of interview from being a method to being a methodology fundamental to research design in social science research.

Further references

Barbour, R. (2008) *Introducing Qualitative Research: A Student Guide to the Craft of Doing Qualitative Research*. London: Sage.

Brannen, J. and Pattman, R. (2005) 'Work-family matters in the workplace: The use of focus groups in a study of a UK social services department', *Qualitative Research*, 5(4): 523–42.

Clark, A.M., Barbour, R.S. and McIntyre, P.D. (2004) 'Promoting participation in cardiac rehabilitation: Patient choices and experiences', *Journal of Advanced Nursing*, 47(1): 5–14.

Fox, F.E., Morris, M. and Rumsey, N. (2007) 'Doing synchronous online focus groups with young people: Methodological reflections', *Qualitative Health Research*, 17: 539–47.

Glaser, B.G. and Strauss, A.L. (1967) *The Discovery of Grounded Theory*. London: Weidenfeld & Nicholson.

Kitzinger, J. & Barbour, R.S. (1999) *Developing Focus Group Research: Politics, Theory and Practice*. London: Sage.

Kvale, S. (1996) *InterViews. An Introduction to Qualitative Research Interviewing*. Thousand Oaks, CA: Sage.

Schostak, J.F. (2002) *Understanding, Designing and Conducting Qualitative Research in Education: Framing the Project*. Buckingham: Open University Press.

Schostak, J.F. (2010) 'Participant observation', in P. Peterson, E. Baker and B. McGaw (eds) *International Encyclopedia of Education*, Vol. 6. Oxford: Elsevier. pp. 442–8.

Schostak, J.F. and Schostak J.R. (2008) *Radical Research. Designing, Developing and Writing Research to Make a Difference*. London: Routledge.

Schostak, J.F. and Schostak, J.R. (eds) (2010) *Researching Violence, Democracy and the Rights of People*. London: Routledge.

PART III

ADDRESSING ISSUES OF POWER AND RESEARCHING FOR IMPACT

Introduction

All the chapters in this section foreground issues of power. The three chapters on feminist methodologies, critical race theory and queer theory focus on difference and raise issues in relation to power and knowledge. The voices of marginalized groups (their standpoints) are celebrated and the authority of the traditional constructors of knowledge is questioned. These chapters share with the chapter on action research, which follows, a concern with resisting oppression and promoting social justice. Practitioners at the centre of action research often need to negotiate their role carefully in relation to others involved including those perceived to be in positions of greater power such as managers/administrators and 'expert researchers'. At the same time they need to be confident that the outcomes of such research, whilst contributing to improving practices in their own setting, will be of value to others and treated respectfully.

The final chapter in Part III, on the purpose, practice and politics of sponsored evaluations (often called program evaluation), engages with power issues at a different level. In sponsored evaluations, which by definition are undertaken on behalf of a sponsoring body such as a government department or an international body, power issues enter the terrain of the research itself, inherent in the relationship between the independent evaluator and the commissioning sponsor with a vested interest in the outcome. Evaluation research also places the evaluators in a position of power vis-à-vis the team responsible for implementing the program or initiative, so that evaluators need to take considerable care to set up procedures that enable them to operate ethically, while still remaining independent so that they can act effectively in the interests of the public whose taxes have funded the initiative.

The chapters in this section all deal with approaches to research that are designed to make an impact, whether on personal practice, national policy or society as a whole. In this sense none of them conforms to the traditional model of research as an objective, impartial set of procedures aimed at uncovering facts and 'the truth'. In reality, none of the chapters in this book supports an approach based on such a naive epistemology; nevertheless the chapters in Part III challenge these notions more directly and more fundamentally. Whereas some of the approaches put forward in the chapters in Part VIII are more radical in their epistemological and ontological assumptions, they tend to be less engaged with research participants and hence more detached from the field of study than the chapters in Part III. The exception is sponsored evaluation which often adopts a more traditional model of relationships with programme participants and sponsors; here, too, however, researchers often undertake evaluation work because it offers the opportunity of making an impact through influencing policy development.

8

Feminist Methodologies

Diane Burns, University of East Anglia, UK
Khatidja Chantler, University of Manchester, UK

Summary

- Gender as a social construct
- Research into the lived experience of women and unequal gender relations
- Research as an inherently political process
- Standpoint theory
- Challenges to the category 'woman'/strategic essentialism
- Key theorists and writers
  - Erica Burman
  - Judith Butler
  - Sandra Harding
  - bell hooks
  - Mary Maynard

Key concepts

Khatidja Chantler

Feminist research methodologies are closely linked to the histories of feminist struggles and are broadly categorized into first, second and third wave feminisms. Concerns that are important to feminists at different historical, social and political moments influence ideas about methodology and the types of research conducted. However, it should be noted that there is no singular feminist methodology.

First wave feminism began in the mid-nineteenth century and ended around 1945. Key campaigns included the right to vote for women, rights to property, and access to education. The quest for these basic rights means that the question of feminist

research methodology was not salient at the time. Second wave feminism (1945 onwards, but with concerted activity from the 1960s to the 1990s) built on the achievements of first wave feminism as well as on the civil rights movement in the US. Second wave feminism called for an opening up of the professions for women, equality in the workplace, payment for domestic labour and the right for women to control their own reproduction. The key pivot for an exploration of feminist research methodology therefore arose from the women's liberation movement. It was second wave feminism that began to challenge traditional forms of knowledge production by arguing that women's experiences had hitherto either been excluded from research or, where included, served to maintain existing unequal gender relations. Whereas feminist research in second wave feminism focused on women's lived experience as a way to recover what had been omitted (Fonow and Cook, 2005), third wave feminism (early 1990s onwards) can be broadly characterized as focusing on 'difference' alongside the shift to postmodernism. This shift is well explained by Fonow and Cook (2005) who argue that second wave feminism was primarily concerned with establishing gender as a social construct and challenging the biological determinism of sex. Third wave feminism took this analysis further and, influenced by the work of Judith Butler, argued for 'sex' to also be seen as a social construct (Butler, 1990). These ideas are taken up by feminist post-structuralism, discussed by Davies and Gannon in this volume. This chapter primarily focuses on the contribution to research methodologies made by second wave feminist scholarship and argues for the continuing relevance of research into the lived experiences of women and unequal gender relations, particularly where patriarchy is used in conjunction with a range of other social divisions, such as race, class, disability and sexual orientation. It therefore argues for ideas from both the second and third waves as integral to feminist knowledge production.

The transformation of social life, particularly the pursuit of social justice for women is central to feminist enquiry (Hesse Biber and Yaiser, 2004). Feminist enquiry starts from the premise that research is an inherently political project and so feminist research necessarily seeks to interrogate power relations in the production of knowledge. Arguments have therefore been made for feminist research to be located within critical, emancipatory frameworks (Humphries, 2008: 105). Critical approaches to social research are closely allied to oppositional social movements.

A key theoretical development in second wave feminist research is standpoint theory and Sandra Harding is one of its main proponents (1987). She argues that in a society marked out by different forms of oppression, marginalized peoples have different perspectives and accounts based on their experiences and struggles and are therefore best placed to challenge dominant accounts. The different perspectives here are envisaged as those that have traditionally been silenced and/or subjugated, and so Harding's idea is to privilege those voices in the production of knowledge. Therefore, it is argued that women as a subjugated group have specific experiences that have traditionally been overlooked in knowledge production. Moreover, much research that claims to be universal and objective is in fact partial knowledge. In relation to this, Harding reminds us that there is 'no news from nowhere'.

In second wave feminism, the central organizing feature of feminist scholarship rested on the notion that as women experienced very similar forms of oppression and discrimination, 'woman' was a powerful and unifying category in which women's experiences could be interrogated and analysed, and through which social relations could be made explicit. However, black feminists (e.g. Amos and Parmar, 1984; hooks, 1981), in particular, argued that this category worked to exclude women of colour, lesbian women, disabled women and working-class women and therefore 'women' served to privilege the accounts of white middle-class women. Hence the very category

that was created to counter inequalities and injustices was at the same time generating its own exclusions. This intervention poses some interesting questions as to whether the categories 'woman' or 'black' are viable ones given the levels of internal differentiation within them. Black feminist writing therefore paved the way for third wave feminism. Post-structuralism (Davies and Gannon, this volume) utilizes 'difference' and multiple voices as the key epistemological stance and forms a central feature of third wave feminisms. The use of the term 'feminisms' recognizes the importance of multiple locations and the need for previously silenced voices within feminism to be articulated.

However, the central conundrum remains as to whether it is possible to use labels such as 'woman' or whether they have been rendered redundant as they can lead to a refusal of difference. It is clear that if the category 'woman' is to be used, it must simultaneously recognize internal differentiation and multiple axes of oppression, resist the dangers of essentialism (the notion that identities are fixed in specific ways) and be cognizant of the social construction of the labels involved as well as their material realities. If on the other hand we were to do away with categories completely, this has the dangerous potential of fragmentation with implications for political action. Successful campaigns for social justice are more likely where there is unity rather than fragmentation. To circumvent fragmentation, the notion of strategic essentialism has gained ground. Strategic essentialism refers to the possibility of forming alliances to engage in collective action. It offers one way of contingently managing the vexed question of how to attend to the specificities of a group without the risk of total fragmentation (the logical conclusion of which takes us to an individual, rather than group level of analysis) and at the same time guarding against 'grand narratives' at the expense of specificity. However, some postmodernist feminists object to even a strategic use of the category 'woman' (see Hesse Biber and Yaiser, 2004).

The brief discussion above highlights the contested epistemological and ontological terrain of feminist inquiry. However, it is still possible to identify four key characteristics of feminist research. They are: (a) feminist research as critical enquiry; (b) 'voice' and grounding research in women's experiences; (c) reflexivity; and (d) an ethic of care. These four aspects are closely interrelated and each of these is discussed briefly below.

Proponents of critical approaches argue that a constructionist ontology which offers a range of different realities as equally valid (relativism) is problematic. Critical positions object to relativism, as the notion of different realities which are equally weighted does not engage sufficiently with issues of power relations. So whilst sympathetic to constructionist ontology in that it allows for multiple realities, critical approaches differs from this by locating these realities within a social and political context. Critical approaches may also adopt a realist ontology (but not necessarily in the positivist sense) to accept 'lived experience' as significant and to highlight inequalities and social divisions within society.

As a way of elucidating gender relations, 'voice' or experience has a central place in feminist methodology. However, from the perspective of 'difference', claims to 'voice' are problematic as they can lead to a warranting of a particular reality whilst simultaneously silencing others. For example, what are the research implications of interviewing women who might express racist or homophobic views? Should such views be challenged during the research process and how would such views be written up? Secondly, we should always ask which women's voices are being privileged and which are silenced. One way of working with such tensions is to locate 'voices' within a political and social context, which helps to ward off the individualizing tendencies associated with experience, and opens up the possibility for a multiplicity of voices – including marginalized voices within oppressed groups. Given that dominant discourses rely on and value individualism and self-responsibility, this can pose particular problems in researching 'private' lives, for example when dealing with issues of domestic violence. Private lives are likely to be spoken about by participants as individual experiences, but Maynard (1994) argues for the importance of analysis rather than a simple reiteration of women's words. This is helpful as it legitimizes the theorizing of participant (and researcher) accounts and moves away from a sense of voice or experience that is seen to reside purely in the participant. A fruitful approach is to consider the discursive practices which 'other' people, and to locate 'voices' within these.

The third key characteristic of feminist methodology is its emphasis on reflexivity. Reflexivity is difficult to define precisely, but there is general agreement that reflexivity is primarily about challenging the notion of objective, neutral and value-free research, focusing instead on accounting for subjectivity. Debates on reflexivity, influenced by feminist ideas on unequal power relations, and on multiple

axes of oppression and disadvantage, are crucial. Reflexivity should not be read as purely to do with an expression of the researcher's feelings and emotions through the research process. There are two dangers of a very personalized and individualistic take on reflexivity: firstly, the focus becomes the researcher, rather than research topic or the relationship between researcher and researched; secondly, a personalized reflexivity serves to strengthen the researcher's position, rather than attending to the power relations inherent within researcher-researched relationships and their respective institutional and social contexts. Hence, ideally, reflexivity focuses on positioning the researcher within relationships in a move towards more egalitarian research practices and towards creating knowledge that incorporates an understanding of the power relations that are constitutive of, and reproduced through, research.

This leads to consideration of the fourth characteristic of feminist research: an 'ethic of care'. Firstly, feminist approaches foster non-hierarchical relationships and aspire to research relationships that are based on valuing the contributions of research participants. This valuing is in part assumed to stem from the researcher and researched sharing the same gender or on the basis of similar experiences (e.g. of motherhood). This similarity is not only thought to deepen empathy, but also to facilitate an increased understanding of participant accounts and subsequent analysis, thus producing accountable knowledge. Despite the advantages of 'sameness', focusing on similarity assumes that it is relatively easy to identify a position from which to speak or that similarity automatically aids understanding (see Hurd and McIntyre, 1996). Identities are not only shifting, but the multiplicity of variables between any two people makes this a problematic proposition to implement. Secondly, an ethic of care involves forming appropriate supportive relationships with research participants, for example by linking them to local or national networks engaged in activist work, such as organizing campaigns or local support organizations, for example rape crisis. Thirdly, an ethic of care calls for accountable knowledge. This refers to knowledge production which engages with reflexivity and positionality, representing the accounts of research participants in ways that do not fuel existing stereotypes, and providing an analysis which can be easily traced to participant accounts.

Recent developments in feminist methodologies include interrogating the ways in which 'difference' is used. Burman (2003) argues that the focus on difference can work to erase power relations from feminist scholarship and practice. The current (re)focus on *intersectionality* rather than 'difference' is proposed as one way of locating difference within a complex web of power relations (Collins, 2000). Intersectionality interrogates categories such as 'women' or 'black', attends to intra-group differences (including trans-national feminisms), conceptualizes identities as multiple, shifting and dynamic and engages with structural and material realities. It also advocates coalitions using categories such as 'women' or 'black women' according to which category might best meet the political objects of a specific project, and recognizes that such alliances may well be transient. Intersectionality draws on standpoint and feminist post-structuralism to carve a space that seeks to avoid previous exclusions while still keeping true to the ideal of transforming social lives.

Implications for research design

In the early phases of second wave feminism, there was considerable debate about which research methodologies and methods were appropriate to feminist inquiry. Maynard (1994) outlines how quantitative approaches were perceived to be 'masculine' forms of inquiry, which frequently overlooked, rendered invisible or pathologized women's experiences. The emphasis in this early phase (which still persists) was to document women's experiences by an open-ended exploration via semi-structured or unstructured interviews. While this legacy continues to be enormously valuable, quantitative methods are also important. As Stanley (2004) points out, much feminist research was actually quantitative at the time, and Maynard comments on how some of this scholarship was also critical and important work. Thus, there is considerable agreement that there is no singular feminist method (Ramazanoglu with Holland, 2002; Stanley, 2004). Key examples of quantitative work that aligns with the principles of feminist research include studies on the prevalence of domestic violence, income levels for men compared with women, the proportion of time spent on housework by men and women, and so on. These studies have been important in highlighting and quantifying levels of discrimination. Further, given the privileging of quantitative information in the hierarchy of knowledge, this continues to be an important strand of feminist

inquiry. Equally important are qualitative studies which have illuminated experiences and meanings of women's lives by locating them firmly within the political and social arena.

Just as there are a plurality of approaches to feminist research, so there are a wide variety of research questions, covering any aspect of gendered lives. The research question needs to be in line with the characteristics of feminist research discussed above. Methods used can include semi-structured or unstructured interviews, focus groups, (video) diaries, journals, photographs, experimental methods, surveys, ethnography, etc. to produce a rich account of a particular topic. Thematic analysis, content analysis, conversational analysis, narrative and discourse are frequently used, as is statistical analysis. The sampling techniques used depend on the research question and methods to be used. For many feminist researchers, research is linked to social justice and thus knowledge produced is frequently used to highlight and campaign for a change in social relations.

Women as well as men can be participants in feminist research. The question of whether men can be feminist researchers is more contested, although men's studies (and qualitative methodologies, e.g. Denzin, 1997) often draw on feminist theory.

Story from the field

Diane Burns

My story from the field draws upon an ethnographic, action-based study of a self-help, lobbying organization that works toward improving the lives of lone parents in the UK. During the research the organization provided information, training, childcare, and campaigned on behalf of its membership. In 1995 I was elected to become a member of the National Co-ordinating Committee and, in 1996 the organization became the focus of my doctoral research. My voluntary work and research plans were a reflection of my interests in, and commitment to engage in, action aiming to achieve social change. In the research I explored issues of organizational culture and change, through an examination focusing on women's identities, experiences and collective action. I sought to develop a methodology where it would be possible to analyse organizational practices and as a means for us to reflect on this analysis as a way of informing our work. Furthermore, I sought to ground the research in women's experiences of single parenting while addressing power issues within the research process.

I was researching the organization from the 'inside'. This meant I was both privy to, and a participant in, the kinds of conversations and discussions someone researching from a position 'outside' the organization may not be. However, this closeness also meant that I was more subjected to the power dynamics that figure within organizations.

Ethical considerations, therefore, were not merely steered by research guidelines but also by practices concerning who gets to speak and what sort of things become spoken and written about in organizations. Nearing the end of the study it became necessary to create a distance between the organization and the research to prevent my analysis from being shaped by processes through which accounts of the organization were usually produced. For ethical reasons, I have not illustrated the specifics of these dilemmas much further – opting instead to frame the issues involved within wider debates around feminist methodologies.

Feminist methodologies

Chantler points out, earlier in this chapter, that feminism and feminist methodologies are not monolithic but numerous, a contested terrain and a source of continuing debate. However, there is a core of agreement. As DeVault (1996) says, feminist research tends to seek methodologies that:

- shift the focus of practice from men's concerns in order to reveal the locations and perspectives of women
- minimize harm and control in the research process
- support research of value to women, leading to social change or action beneficial to women.

In this study, I similarly sought a methodology to give voice to women and ground the research in women's experiences; attending to an ethic of care; and engaged with collective action to challenge welfarist assumptions and dominant accounts that tend to pathologize single mothers. This involved analyses of a range of data, including research diaries, collated documents and interviews with 15 people involved in the organization. For this chapter I outline two methodological dilemmas that arose – particularly when conducting interviews and analysing the transcribed audio recordings.

Issues of accountability in research relations

Each participant was interviewed separately, loosely following a set of open-ended questions about their involvement in the organization. The participants were aware of their rights, the purpose of the research, and that they would be given access to the transcribed interview and have the opportunity to make changes to their transcript. I was also committed to making the interviews as confidential as possible but was aware that, due to the close-knit relationships between members of the organization, there was a strong possibility that someone's identity might be recognized from even a snippet of transcript. Issues around confidentiality were complicated further by the conversations that took place between participants who chose to talk to each other about their experiences of taking part and the content of their interviews.

The interviewing took place over a three-year period and I was aware that we were engaging in more critical discussions as time went by. This was possibly due to our growing familiarity and developing relationships and our growing awareness of each other's shared and different positions and perspectives on the organization. Our discussions included negotiations about participants' rights, and the obligations that were directing my practice as a researcher, rather than as a volunteer manager. The shift in my positioning from manager to researcher perhaps figured in permitting a more critical dialogue about the organization during the interviews. Certainly some participants informed me that they had decided to participate because they wanted to voice their views on our organizing and felt it important that I heard, and ultimately the research chronicled these.

Many feminist scholars have written about the power differentials between researcher and the researched and many have worked to challenge and reshape research practices. I also was concerned about power differentials and prepared to name and discuss these with participants, developing the research process accordingly, in an attempt to remedy them. For example, alongside the backdrop of the researcher–participant relationships, we were also aware of reflecting on our differences and whom we were speaking 'as' and 'to' when we spoke (paid and unpaid workers, our experiences as white woman and black woman, and so on). This was important as our experiences, and the positions we occupied, influenced our dialogue and action. Participants could speak in a critical way about issues and events as 'a friend' that they might not choose to share with me as a manager, for example. Thus the interviews arguably created a new didactic space and provided the potential for occupying different discursive subject positions (Garvey, 1992) from those which figured within the dynamics of the organization. In creating these possibilities I necessarily became bound by the particular informal 'contract' negotiated with each participant – invoking questions about how to maintain participants' confidentiality and simultaneously privilege women's voices.

This ethical tension mirrors another as the privileging of women's voice and experiences in the research on the one hand produced a set of diverse accounts about the organization, but, paradoxically, giving voice created risks for our organizing. Accounts voiced by participants were not always consistent with the public representations we produced about who we were and what we sought to achieve and why. Considering all that I have outlined so far, I was then faced with the tough question of how I was going to analyse the interview transcripts.

Presenting and analysing women's 'voices'

I am sure participants had many different concerns when articulating accounts and were speaking to different audiences (potential and imagined). The aim of giving voice and privileging women's particular standpoints on single motherhood, without presenting any one voice or position as if it was more valid than another, raises problems of essentialism on the one hand and relativism on the other. In addition I felt a responsibility, sometimes placed on me by participants, to address the organizational issues they were voicing in interviews.

The way I approached addressing this dilemma was to develop a discursive analytical framework that combined:

- Narrative analysis, as it permits a focus on the stories women tell about organizing. I chose to draw attention to how such stories function, and to consider questions of why they are being told in that way, at that particular moment (Riessman, 1993).
- Discourse analysis which, following the work of Foucault, aimed to understand how power and ideology operate through systems of discourse. I

took the approach that discourses produce different speaking positions that we occupy, with impacts for how we understand our experiences of organizing and our identities. Hence it becomes possible to interpret the organization as being, in part, discursively produced.
- Poetic ethnography which is concerned with writing that breaks with the idea that there is a connection between lived experience and the written word – this is about showing not telling experience (Denzin, 1997).

Firstly I identified narratives within the interview transcripts which told a variety of stories about the history of the organization, and members' involvement in working together for social change and how such experiences were informed by, and impacted on, our everyday lives. At this level of analysis I identified what issues participants seemed to be associating with organizational change and development and considered why it was important to tell these stories. I then re-analysed the narratives, explicating the discourses that figured within these stories (e.g. 'family', 'motherhood' and 'organization'). I paid attention to the ways in which the discourses functioned within the texts, in shaping organizational identities and the power effects these produced. This allowed a critical reflection of the ways in which language is implicated in organizing and organizational change. I then shaped the broken transcripts (and the now fragmented voices) into poems. I did this by discarding my own utterances to leave only the participant's words and I then reshaped these words into poems. In effect the poems offered a way to *show women's experience* while also creating a way to reinsert the voices of women as uttered at the moment of speaking.

My commitment to incorporate women's voices into the research process and my attempt not to privilege one account over another raised wider concerns about who can speak about the organization and what it is legitimate to say (and to whom). The analytical approach allowed a range of voices and a variety of stories to be presented. In addition, within the institutional framework of the academy, conventions exist about accepted forms of authorial voice within a PhD thesis, and the multi-vocal (re)presentation went some way to disrupt and offer an alternative to constructing a singular, seamless account of the research.

Yet the multi-vocal (re)presentations were also problematic. Public accounts of organizations (their aims and purpose) tend to be consistent and coherent and in the case of campaigning groups may draw on notions that lone parents are subjected to similar forms of social discrimination and inequality. Participants have access to such accounts, and we actively contributed to their production, but there are also other voices that reflect different perspectives and identities – other storied experiences of organizing, of being a single mother and so on. In writing up the research I presented women's stories side by side, following my aim for a methodology that revealed the locations and perspectives of all participants. However, the multi-vocal accounts produced a rather messier picture than the official accounts of organizational reality. Furthermore, this approach leaves readers (whether internally or externally located to the organizations) open to judge, if they wish, which of the women's standpoints are more or less interesting or 'true', and so on, therefore, raising concerns about the validity of some voices. However, by locating the voices in the social and political milieu of the organization, it became possible to understand multi-vocal accounts of experience, as a practice of making sense of organizational change. The approach of taking seriously the different concerns and voices of women may be one that feminist scholars and other researchers appreciate – but in my research the process was problematic because it was also strategically important not to undermine our collective voice.

A final note

Engaging in action was an important part of my practice and I volunteered to be involved in the organization because I wanted to make a contribution to the organization's work and development. The research is one among other contributions I made, and the analysis of the thesis was both for the organization and in pursuit of my own ends in being awarded a doctoral degree. However, seeking a feminist methodology also raised problems. Firstly, placing women's narratives of organizing side by side gave a platform for their voices on the one hand, yet the differences between women's views and perspectives were made explicit and potential conflicts in interests exposed. Secondly, as I was positioned as a researcher, manager and friend my practice involved managing multiple relationships and competing accountabilities to the participants *and* the organization.

The analytical framework developed in response to these concerns is a product of my attempt to privilege women's voices, but not permanently fragment them when addressing differences and power relations between women.

Annotated bibliography

Butler, J. (1990) *Gender Trouble: Feminism and the Subversion of Identity*. London and New York: Routledge.
A revolutionary book which challenges the sex/gender divide and argues that gender is performative. It argues that sex, not just gender, operates within discursive fields and that they need to be considered simultaneously, rather than as a binary.

Collins, P.H. (2000) *Black Feminist Thought: Knowledge, Consciousness and the Politics of Empowerment*, 2nd edn. New York: Routledge.
An exploration of US-based black feminism, intersectionality and the call to make feminism relevant to ordinary black women.

Harding, S. and Norberg, K. (eds) (2005) *Signs*. Special edition on Feminist Methodology, Summer, 30(4).
A collection of useful and thought-provoking essays introducing and discussing new feminist approaches to social science methodologies. The essay by Fonow and Cook traces some of the historical developments in feminist epistemologies and methodologies since their 1991 publication *Beyond Methodology: Feminist Scholarship as Lived Research*.

Harding, S. (1987) *Feminism and Methodology*. Milton Keynes: Open University Press.
An essential and influential text of enduring significance discussing feminist epistemology, methodology and methods.

Hesse Biber, S.N. and Yaiser, M.L. (2004) *Feminist Perspectives on Social Research*. New York and Oxford: Oxford University Press.
Divided into three parts: (i) epistemology, methodology and methods; (ii) strategies on issues of race, class, gender and sexuality; and (iii) application and method, the book covers issues in feminist research across a range of disciplines in the humanities and social sciences.

hooks, b. (1981) *Ain't I a Woman?: Black Women and Feminism*. Boston, MA: South End Press.
An early challenge to the universalizing category 'woman' highlighting the specific positions of black women.

Hughes, C. (2002) *Key Concepts in Feminist Theory and Research*. London: Sage.
This book provides a clear introduction to the implications of postmodernism and post-structuralism for feminist theory and research. The text focuses on six key concepts: equality, difference, choice, care, time and experience, and usefully illustrates their application through case studies of feminist research.

Humphries, B. (2008) *Social Work Research for Social Justice*. Basingstoke: Palgrave Macmillan.
This book is about researching for social justice and thus fits well within feminist perspectives. It discusses a range of methods and highlights the possibilities for research to challenge injustices.

Maynard, M. and Purvis, J. (eds) (1994) *Researching Women's Lives from a Feminist Perspective*. London: Taylor & Francis.
A UK-based edited collection covering a range of important feminist research and thought.

Ramazanoglu, C. with Holland, J. (2002) *Feminist Methodology: Challenges and Choices*. London: Sage.
This book is particularly helpful for those embarking on a feminist research project as well as offering sound theoretical perspectives on feminist methodologies and the challenges posed to them.

Further references

Amos, V. and Parmar P. (1984) 'Challenging imperial feminism', *Feminist Review* 17: 3–20.

Burman, E. (2003) 'From difference to intersectionality', *European Journal of Psychotherapy, Counselling and Health*, 6(4): 293–308.

DeVault, M.L. (1996) 'Talking back to sociology: Distinctive contributions of feminist methodology', *Annual Review of Sociology*, 22: 29–50.

Denzin, N.K. (1997) *Interpretive Ethnography: Ethnographic Practices for the 21st Century*. Thousand Oaks, CA: Sage.

Fonow, M. and Cook, J. (2005) 'Feminist methodology: New applications in the academy and public policy', *Signs*, 30(4): 2211–36.

Garvey, N. (1992) 'Technologies and effects of heterosexual coercion', *Feminism and Psychology*, 2: 325–51

Hurd, T.L. and McIntyre, A. (1996) 'The seduction of sameness: Similarity and representing the other', in S. Wilkinson and C. Kitzinger (eds) *Representing the Other: A Feminism and Psychology Reader*. London: Sage. pp. 78–82.

Maynard, M. (1994) 'Methods, practice and epistemology: The debate about feminism and research', in M. Maynard and J. Purvis (eds) *Researching Women's Lives from a Feminist Perspective*. London: Taylor & Francis. pp. 10–26.

Riessman, C. (1993) *Narrative Analysis*. Thousand Oaks, CA: Sage.

Stanley, L. (2004) 'A methodological toolkit for feminist research: Analytical reflexivity, accountable knowledge, moral epistemology and being "a child of our time"' in H. Piper and I. Stronach (eds) *Educational Research: Difference and Diversity (Cardiff Papers in Qualitative Research)*. Aldershot: Ashgate. pp. 3–29.

Critical Race Theory and Its Use in Social Science Research

Laurence Parker, Department of Educational Policy Studies,
University of Illinois at Urbana-Champaign, USA

Lorna Roberts, Education and Social Research Institute,
Manchester Metropolitan University, UK

Summary

- Deconstructing the rationalized meanings of policies, practices and laws
- A social justice agenda
- Centrality of experiential knowledge
- The sociological myth of racial categories
- Key theorists and writers
  - Derrick Bell
  - Richard Delgado
  - Gloria Ladson-Billings
  - Daniel Solorzano
  - Tarra Yosso
  - William Smith

Key concepts[1]

Critical Race Theory (CRT) emerged in the last quarter of the twentieth century as a legal theoretical framework exploring the ways in which alleged race-neutral policies, practices, and laws perpetuate racial/ethnic subordination. It emphasizes the importance of viewing policies, practices, and laws within a proper historical and cultural context in order to deconstruct their racialized meanings (Bell, 1995; Crenshaw et al., 1995; Ladson-Billings and Tate, 1995). This framework challenges dominant liberal concepts such as colour-blindness and meritocracy

and shows how these ideas operate to disadvantage people of colour while further advantaging whites (Delgado and Stefancic, 2000a). Originally developed by legal scholars of colour, CRT is grounded in a 'social reality' that is defined by our experiences and the collective historical experience of our communities of origin. CRT theorists have typically utilized dialogues, stories, chronicles, and personal testimonies as a method in their scholarship because some members of marginalized groups, by virtue of their marginal status, are able to tell different stories from the ones white scholars usually hear and tell (Delgado, 1989). There are some key principles that form the basic assumptions, perspectives, research methods, and pedagogies of CRT (Parker and Lynn, 2002; Tate, 1997; Yosso et al., 2004).

The centrality of race and racism

CRT acknowledges as its most basic premise that race and racism are defining characteristics of American society. Race and racism are central constructs that intersect with other dimensions of one's identity, such as language, generation status, gender, sexuality and class (Crenshaw, 1990). For people of colour, each of these dimensions of one's identity can potentially elicit multiple forms of subordination (Montoya, 1994), yet each dimension can also be subjected to different forms of oppression.

The challenge to dominant ideology

CRT in education challenges the traditional claims of universities to objectivity, meritocracy, colour-blindness, race neutrality and equal opportunity (Bell, 2000). This theoretical framework reveals how the dominant ideology of colour-blindness and race neutrality act as a camouflage for the self-interest, power, and privilege of dominant groups in American society (Lopez, 2003).

A commitment to social justice and praxis

CRT has a fundamental commitment to a social justice agenda that struggles to eliminate all forms of subordination (Matsuda, 1996). In education, this struggle is conceived as a social justice project that attempts to link theory with practice, scholarship with teaching, and the academy with the community (Parker and Stovall, 2005).

A centrality of experiential knowledge

CRT recognizes that the experiential knowledge of people of colour is legitimate and critical to understanding racial subordination. The application of a CRT framework in an analysis of research and practice in the field of education requires that the experiential knowledge of people of colour be centred and viewed as a resource stemming directly from their lived experiences (Bell, 1987; Delgado, 1989). The experiential knowledge can come from storytelling, family history, biographies, scenarios, parables, *cuentos*, chronicles, and narratives (Yosso, 2006).

An historical context and interdisciplinary perspective

CRT challenges ahistoricism and the unidisciplinary focus of the dominant interpretation of current constitutional law (Bell, 2004; Delgado and Stefancic, 2000b; Tsosie, 2000). We can currently see this trend in legal thought rooted in a colour-blind perspective that either ignores the legacy of historical discrimination and remedy, or stands history on its head to say that to end racism, we have to simply stop making legal decisions in education based on race. Critical Race Theory has ties to other race-based social science and philosophical critiques related to the ontology and epistemology of racism (Goldberg, 1993).

The genealogy of CRT in education can be found in the traditions of other disciplines such as ethnic studies, women's studies, multicultural education and critical pedagogy (Yosso, 2005). CRT also pushes for an analysis that centres the origins of race and racism and its connection to modernity, history, philosophy and the origins of the nation-state both in the U.S. and Europe (Goldberg, 1993; Smedley, 1999; Winant, 2001).

We can see part of this in the UK, for example through the work of Sewell (2000) and his description of how the popularization of black youth culture creates conflict in British schools when black males 'act out' black youth culture and white teachers are overtly threatened by what they view as black male predatory behaviour that has to be disciplined.

Comparisons can be drawn between the US and the UK regarding how race and racism play out in social relations and education policy. Gillborn's (2008) research, using CRT, on educational policy and its impact on students of colour in the UK maintains that racism is pervasive and endemic and that persons of colour are subject to subtle discrimination despite the passage of national civil rights laws and general heightened concern about racism. Moschel (2007) argues that there is an avoidance of using CRT in the European context because most nations in the EU only view overt or structural racism as 'American' problems that are invalid to apply to the European context. This is despite the fact that immigration from their former colonies has had an adverse impact on the racial and religious tolerance of many EU democracies, especially since the onset of the global recession.

Additions to CRT: second generation movements

The basic tenets of CRT spawned new additions to the critical study of race, racism and the law by examining how these areas worked within and against feminism or the black–white binary. From this new frameworks emerged such as critical race feminism; in which both feminist and racial analysis were placed at the centre of the counter-narrative expeience and counter-story telling of women of colour as well as using it to examine the deleterious impact of public policy effects on women of colour (Wing, 1997). LatCrit (Latina and Latino Critical Legal Theory), Asian American CRT and some Tribal Nation scholars in the US have also used CRT to centralize the racial discrimination experiences of Latinos/Latinas, Asian/Pacific Island

Americans, and American Indians, as well as a critique of whiteness and its continued superiority as a global construct (Haney López, 2003; Leonardo, 2009; Tsosie, 2000). Critical Race Theory has also been pushed by outside scholars (Darder and Torres, 2003) and some of the original founders (Delgado, 2003) to make more explicit links between race and the material conditions of daily socio-economic existence, in terms of seeing that racism and class discrimination are interconnected. Both need to be fought on multiple levels as global capitalism creates greater inequalities between poor persons of colour and the rich in the global economy. This has also been viewed as a call for active and intensive social justice work in education and the larger political economy (Parker and Stovall, 2005).

Critical Race Theory's latest trends include a focus on the law and economics of race. One trend is to look at ways in which racialized choices by employers and employees shape the context of discrimination (Carbado and Gulati, 2003). Another new area is critical race realism; this off-shoot of CRT seeks to use more quantitatively based research methods to: '(1) expose racism where it may be found; (2) identify its effects on individuals and institutions, and (3) put forth a concerted attack against it, in part, via public policy arguments' (Parks, 2007: 5). This new area of CRT seeks to combine qualitative narrative with quantitative data to point out to the general public and to public policy-makers that we are not in a post-racial era with the election of President Obama, and that various aspects of institutional and structural racism still exist in terms of inequality of resources among groups of colour. Neoliberalism's impact on K-12 and higher education has created an increased emphasis on individual self-interest in a global economy that is in a recession. This socio-economic context has had political implications for racism in terms of a greater overall tolerance of race, but also increasing hostility to racial groups when it comes to competition for scarce jobs, housing, and admissions to universities, and reactions to those racial 'others' seeking these resources for 'their kids too'. To be sure, the political discourse shifted swiftly after the election of the 44th President of the US, Barack Obama, in November 2008, as race and racism were reframed towards a discussion of colour-blindness. Indeed, the historic election of the nation's first African-American president has prompted increased calls to 'move past race'. As the nation's electorate have been praised by some for 'not seeing colour' in

their support of the first President of colour, discussions of systemic and institutionalized racism and subsequent inequities have been displaced by claims of a new 'post-racial' society. Although proclamations of an end to race and racism are prevalent today, from a Critical Race Theory perspective, the educational experience for a majority of students of colour continues to be mired in inequality and a lack of educational opportunity.

Implications for research design

Studies that adopt a Critical Race Theory approach require a theoretical sensitivity to race as a personal quality of the researcher. They acknowledge an awareness of the various meanings of the data, or situations, where race and ethnicity are central to the study of the issue. The research process involves reviewing the existing research on race and ethnicity; looking at one's own professional experience with race, and one's own personal experience with race. Solórzano and Yosso (2002) developed critical race methodology in terms of its utility as an analytical framework to ask research questions, review literature, analyse data and form conclusions and recommendations. They discussed five tenets of a CRT methodology: (1) placing race and its intersectionality with other forms of subordination (e.g. gender, social class, etc.), at the centre of research; (2) using race in research to challenge the dominant scientific norms of objectivity and neutrality; (3) connecting the research with social justice concerns and potential praxis with on-going efforts in communities; (4) making experiential knowledge central to the study, and linking this knowledge to other critical research and interpretive perspectives on race and racism; and (5) acknowledging the importance of transdisciplinary perspectives that are based in other fields (e.g. ethnic studies, women's studies, African-American studies, Chicano/a-Latino/a studies, history, sociology) to enhance understanding of the effects of racism and other forms of discrimination on persons of colour.

Critical Race Theory places race at the centre of the research analysis. Placing race in the centre is important, not only to frame the research issues to study, but also to interpret the evidence and provide a lens of focus for racial equity implications. A critical race methodology, for example, would seek to ask research questions focused on gaining an understanding of how students of colour experience school, and whether specific opportunities are provided or denied during the school day in order to pinpoint actions by all in schools that contribute to the success or failure of these students (Pollock, 2008: 15–16). A critical race theory perspective also involves being extremely sensitive to community issues and supportive of the community. For instance, researchers who are committed to a community of colour over a long period of time, and gain trust with that community, develop a unique degree of sensitivity to racial equity issues. Combined with their knowledge of the relevant research literature, encompassing theoretical understandings of the history of race and racism in the particular context, this allows the researcher to use race and cultural intuition to give meaning to the data (Bernal Delgado, 2002).

Research questions in the social sciences in race-centred nation states need to pose issues such as: (a) how does race (in conjunction with gender and social class in some cases) shape the educational conditions and outcomes of students of colour?; (b) what are the specific effects of policies and actions by government agencies on students of colour in terms of creating opportunities for learning?; (c) how do schools and teachers reinforce racial, class and gender inequality?; and (d) how do students of colour and their parents/community respond to this racism in the UK and USA?

Reporting of CRT studies is usually by means of narrative and stories to make the continuing situation of racism real to others, especially whites. It draws on interview and observational data gathered from the research process itself, as well as existing literature on race and racism, and the researcher's own personal and professional experience with race and racism (Solórzano, 1998). These kinds of studies have become a powerful and persuasive means for CRT research to inform education policy.

Stories from the field

Lorna Roberts

A small girl and her mother passed a statue depicting a European man who had barehandedly subdued a ferocious lion. The little girl stopped, looked puzzled and asked, 'Mama, something's wrong with that statue. Everybody knows that a man can't whip a lion.' 'But darling,' her mother replied, 'you must remember that the man made the statue.' (Cannon, cited in Collins, 1990: 201)

It is widely accepted that our perceptions of the world are framed by our positioning in the world. When one particular worldview becomes accepted as the norm, other ways of seeing become effaced. Earlier in this chapter, my co-author Laurence Parker indicated the significant role the social construct 'race' has played in shaping the world and our understanding of it. The story of the little girl and the statue reinforces this point. This has implications for the nature of the research topic, the way in which the research question is framed, the way in which research subjects are constituted and the ways in which data are interpreted. Consequently, undertaking research in race/ethnicity issues as a black researcher within a predominantly white institution can be fraught with difficulties. My story from the field concerns my experiences as one of two minority ethnic team members working on a project exploring issues related to the retention of minority ethnic trainee teachers. The account is very much from an 'insider' perspective, as someone who was actively involved in a piece of research and who is an African Caribbean woman; it is a personal report of the dilemmas I faced in the field, therefore the views expressed are mine alone. The story is offered as a contribution to the debate, as an invitation to confront the unease and silences engendered by 'race' and racism and to think through/disrupt the ways in which 'race' constructs, positions and shapes actions.

This is a story about power dynamics, emotional turmoil, intrigue and discovery – too much to cram into this limited space. What follows are the 'highlights' to illustrate the dilemmas faced by a novice researcher emotionally attached to a particular area of research.

About 18 months into my PhD I was invited to participate in a small-scale project exploring issues related to the retention of minority ethnic trainee teachers. Within the institution where I was based tutors had noted a worrying drop-out trend among particular groups of students. It was my understanding that the research sought to determine factors that might have contributed to trainees' failure/drop-out or intercalation with a view to reforming the initial teacher training course, providing support to 'at risk' students, and arriving at recommendations to feed into a nationally funded project examining retention more globally.

Of course I was initially delighted to be considered as part of the project team. However, doubts began to creep in. I started wondering if I had been asked to do the research because of the possible greater access afforded by virtue of my ethnicity rather than my ability as an interviewer. I discussed the issue with a friend who felt that the reasons for being asked were minor, of far greater significance was the positive role I could play in impacting positively on the situation. I therefore laid my concerns aside and decided to proceed with the project.

I was not involved in the initial discussions to shape the scope of the project or identify the trainee sample. The areas to be investigated were informed by the findings from previous research and tutors' own perceptions of likely difficulties. There was a desire to gain an understanding of the religious and cultural barriers. From my perception of the discussions there seemed to be an impression that the minority ethnic trainees at risk of failing, repeating or intercalating tended to be mature students with alternative entry qualifications to the traditional 'A' levels (formal assessments undertaken in the UK, post-16) and those who had to negotiate family and course commitments.

Previous research in the area had identified a number of barriers to retention of minority ethnic trainees, including feelings of isolation in a predominantly white environment, lack of awareness of cultural and religious issues and racial discrimination. I did not want to make assumptions about the possible barriers but felt that racism might be at the heart of the problem. I felt that focusing on cultural and religious barriers somehow placed the emphasis on the trainees and ignored the issue of racism. I was very mindful of the fact of my own background and how this could impinge upon my framing of the situation. Although racism was foregrounded in my mind, I was aware that minority ethnic trainees are not a homogenous group and that a number of other factors could be at play, hence I did not want to limit the field of vision. I wanted to encourage trainees to tell their own story rather than what I thought their story would be. I also needed to bear in mind concerns tutors had raised. I therefore designed the interview schedule to be as open as possible to encourage trainees' own narratives. I asked interviewees to tell me about experiences at university and in placement schools, and I also asked students to tell me how they would define their own identity.

I drafted a letter of introduction to invite trainees to participate in the research. I briefly outlined my background and explained the aims of the project. It was suggested that my picture be included on the letter to provide a personal touch. I remember feeling some embarrassment, but finally agreed. Would this 'personal' touch have been suggested if the project had not been focused on 'race' and ethnicity? The letters were sent to 22 individuals: some were active students including a certain number who were repeating a year; some had successfully completed the course and some had withdrawn. I experienced some difficulties contacting a small number of students. Nineteen agreed to participate; some were quite exasperated at the prospect of yet another study into minority ethnic issues. A few expressed anger that it had taken so long before their experiences had been investigated. In one case the student had agreed to participate because of my ethnicity; had I been white she would have refused.

I found interviewing in some cases distressing and would on occasions leave interviews feeling angry. I could not be a dispassionate observer as I sympathized with the struggles some of the participants were experiencing, having had similar experiences myself. On two occasions trainees were reduced to tears as they recalled experiences during their school placement block. Some trainees reported incidences of covert or overt racism. One student spoke about instances which displayed the perceived 'ignorance' and 'prejudice' of her white peers. She raised her concerns and had been referred to a tutor within the department who was seen as 'the expert' on such matters. The tutor was 'a professor ... white ... middle class' and had 'written loads of books'. They had 'this high brow conversation, picking up and dissecting everything' the trainee had said. The trainee was told 'basically ... without evidence you can't say whether that's racism or not'. The trainee tried to explain that 'unless you have got this badge on and you have got to walk with it everyday you won't know. Half the time these subtle things you won't be aware of.' The trainee was left feeling 'paranoid, like [she] was the one with the problem because [she] had highlighted it'. In some instances trainees spoke about ways in which they were made invisible: for instance there were examples of teachers in placement schools who avoided making eye contact with minority ethnic trainees, instead focusing attention on their white peers, thereby excluding the minority ethnic trainee from the discussion. At other times some trainees were made to feel very visible as a result of their perceived difference. One trainee told of an overtly racist incident which had occurred beyond the school gates in an area known for its racism. The school itself had been very supportive, 'the teachers were brilliant,' 'the staff was absolutely excellent ... really facilitating,' but there were perceived tensions with parents and the local community: 'the parents ... just stare in such a demeaning way, they've just got those stereotypical views ...'. Not all the experiences had been negative; a number of trainees spoke very positively about the training, declaring that they had not encountered any racism. In many ways experiences were very similar to the majority ethnic group. The research dispelled a number of myths about the type of student who might fail or drop out, but raised a number of questions in my mind about the nature of racism, and the implications for minority ethnic researchers engaging in 'race' based research in predominantly white institutions.

Personal dilemmas faced during the research process

I was fully committed to this piece of research, not as an academic exercise but for its potential to make a real difference to the trainees' lives. My earlier conviction that I could feed into a process of change soon waned, and I began to feel uncomfortable with my role as researcher. Despite my feelings of powerlessness as I listened to the more disturbing accounts, some trainees actually looked to me as someone who could impact directly on their situation. Because I could empathize, I think I was trusted and many trainees opened up, releasing a lot of the tensions and frustrations they had had to keep bottled up. This raised all sorts of ethical issues related to how respondents are co-opted into the research, what is done with the data – particularly very sensitive information – and the relationship between the researcher and respondents.

I was far more emotionally attached to the participants in the research and had a strong investment in my particular understanding of the research aims. This possibly narrowed my vision to some extent. I could not escape the feeling of being 'the outsider' when discussing certain issues with fellow researchers. Certainly I felt that maybe I read the data differently. My perception was that the trainees' voices had been silenced – revealing their stories to me was one way of being heard and I wanted them to have that voice. Some of the data generated by the research made for uncomfortable reading. I was uncomfortable with writing protocols for reporting findings which had the effect of 'neutralizing' the language. In my mind this

was another way of silencing the trainees' voice. I would have presented the data differently, had I had sole control.

I have found this research problematic in many ways. Research into minority ethnic experiences of education – be it pupils' educational attainment or issues to do with trainee teachers – has been punctuated by silences and inertia.

The way forward

Interrogating 'race' based issues and questions of ethnicity is an extremely sensitive enterprise. It is very easy to attack or be defensive, but the way forward is not about attack or defence, rather it is about engaging in a critical dialogue; the issues need to be confronted head on and dealt with rather than sidelined or cushioned in more palatable language. For me this entails acknowledging myself as a black researcher as opposed to a researcher. It means allowing minority ethnic communities to tell their narratives in their own voices, and for those accounts to be heard and acknowledged. It means looking critically at how 'race' and racism shape possibilities and daily practices. The processes are hidden, difficult to detect, yet are clearly felt.

Note

1. This section draws on an editorial: 'A race(cialized) perspective on education leadership: Critical Race Theory in educational administration', by Laurence Parker and Octavio Villalpando. The final, definitive version of this paper has been published in *Educational Administration Quarterly*, 43(5), 2007, pp. 519–24 by Sage.

Annotated bibliography

Bell, D.A. Jr. (1980) 'Brown v. Board of Education and the interest-convergence dilemma', *Harvard Law Review*, 93: 518–33.
This work by Bell is a landmark article to understand the notion of interest convergence and how it works under CRT (i.e. incremental civil rights gains for persons of colour only come when their interests 'converge' with those of white European Americans who still are in a superior political and socio-economic position.

Harris, C.I. (1993) 'Whiteness as property', *Harvard Law Review*, 106(8): 1709–91.
This article links the concept of whiteness to property rights in US law and cites examples of how African Americans were considered 'property' and American Indians had 'property' and how each was exploited through US Constitutional Law and court rulings.

Lawrence, C.R. III (1995) 'The id, the ego, and equal protection: Reckoning with unconscious racism', *Stanford Law Review*, 47(5): 819–48.
Lawrence documents the concept of unconscious racism and this is the precursor to subsequent work on this topic and the role that cognitive psychology and racial schema theory play in shaping racist actions and institutional racism.

Lopez, I.F. (1997) 'Race, ethnicity, erasure: The salience of race to LatCrit theory', *California Law Review*, 85(5): 57–125.
Lopez's article serves as an excellent introduction to the critique of the black–white binary and why LatCrit is important in looking at how Latinos are racialized in the US context.

Tate, W.F. IV (1997) 'Critical race theory and education: History, theory, and implications', in M. Apple (ed.) *Review of Research in Education*, 22: 195–247; and
Ladson-Billings, G. (1998) 'Just what is critical race theory and what's it doing in a nice field like education?', *International Journal of Qualitative Studies in Education*, 11(1): 7–24.
Both of these works build off the landmark 1995 article that appeared in *Teachers College Record* written by Ladson-Billings and Tate. The Tate chapter links CRT's roots to the legal realist movement and critical legal studies movements in law and then connects it to education research and policy, while the Ladson-Billings article presents readers with the principals of CRT and how they can be applied to important aspects of schooling (e.g. curriculum, resources).

Wing, A. and Weselmann, L. (1999) 'Transcending traditional notions of mothering: The need for critical race feminist praxis', *Journal of Gender, Race, & Justice*, 3(1): 257–82.
Adrien Wing's legal scholarship is important in understanding how the law works for and against women of colour and why critical race feminism is a legitimate framework to analyse law and policy related to women of colour.

Chapman, T.K. (2007) 'Interrogating classroom relationships and events: Using portraiture and critical race theory in education research', *Educational Researcher*, 36: 156–62.
DeCuir, J.T. and Dixon, A.D. (2004) '"So when it comes out, they aren't that surprised that it is there": Using critical race theory as a tool of analysis of race and racism in education', *Educational Researcher*, 33: 26–31.
Solórzano, D.G. and Yosso, T.J. (2002) 'Critical race methodology: Counter-storytelling as an analytical framework for education research', *Qualitative Inquiry*, 8(1): 23–44.
These three texts provide key information regarding how Critical Race Theory has been defined and used in education research and in qualitative research studies. The last reference in particular by Solórzano and Yosso presents important information and specific examples of what a critical race methodology looks like and how it can be used in a research study.

Race, Ethnicity & Education: Special issue on Critical Race Praxis, 12(2).
All of these works in this special issue of *Race, Ethnicity & Education* (July 2009) represent a sample of new articles that take CRT in a more applied methodological perspective in order to seek its utility as a viable interpretive research framework of research questions, data collection, mode of inquiry and informing findings and conclusions.

Further references

Bell, D. (1987) 'Neither separate schools nor mixed schools: The chronicle of the sacrificed black schoolchildren', in D. Bell (ed.) *And We Are Not Saved: The Elusive Quest for Racial Justice*. New York: Basic Books. pp. 102–22.

Bell, D. (1995) 'Who's afraid of Critical Race Theory?', *University of Illinois Law Review*, 893–910.

Bell, D. (2000) *Race, Racism, and American Law*. Chicago: Aspen Publishers.

Bell, D. (2004) *Silent Covenants: Brown v. Board of Education and the Unfulfilled Hopes for Racial Reform*. Oxford: Oxford University Press.

Bernal Delgado, D. (2002) 'Critical race theory, Latino critical theory, and critical raced-gendered epistemologies: Recognizing students of color as holders and creators of knowledge', *Qualitative Inquiry*, 8(1): 105–26.

Carbado, D.W. and Gulati, M. (2003) 'The law and economics of critical race theory', *Yale Law Journal*, 112: 1757–828.

Collins, P. (1990) *Black Feminist Thought: Knowledge, Consciousness, and the Politics of Empowerment*. Boston, MA and London: Unwin Hyman.

Crenshaw, K. (1990) 'Demarginalizing the intersections of race and sex: A black feminist critique of antidiscrimination doctrine, feminist theory and anti-racist politics', in D. Kariys (ed.), *The Politics of Law: A Progressive Critique*. New York: Pantheon. pp. 195–217.

Crenshaw, K., Gotanda, N., Peller, G. and Thomas, K. (eds.) (1995) *Critical Race Theory: Key Writings that Formed the Movement*. New York: The New Press.

Darder, A. and Torres, R.D. (2003) 'Shattering the "race" lens: Toward a critical theory of racism', in A. Darder, M. Baltodano and R. Torres (eds) *The Critical Pedagogy Reader*. New York: Routledge. pp. 245–63.

Delgado, R. (1989) 'Storytelling for oppositionists and others: A plea for narrative', *Michigan Law Review*, 87: 2411–41.

Delgado, R. (2003) 'White interests and civil rights realism: Rodrigo's bittersweet epiphany', *Michigan Law Review*, 10(5): 1201–24.

Delgado, R. and Stefancic, J. (2000a) 'California's racial history and constitutional rationales for race-conscious decision making in higher education', *UCLA Law Review*, 47: 1521–614.

Delgado, R. and Stefancic, J. (2000b) *Critical Race Theory: The Cutting Edge*, 2nd edn. Philadelphia, PA: Temple University Press.

Gillborn, D. (2008) *Racism and Education: Coincidence or Conspiracy?* London: Routledge.

Goldberg, D.T. (1993). *Racist Culture: Philosophy and the Politics of Meaning*. Oxford: Oxford University Press.

Haney López, I.F. (2003) *Racism on Trial: The Chicano Fight for Justice*. Cambridge, MA: Harvard University Press.

Ladson-Billings, G. and Tate, W.F., IV (1995) 'Toward a critical race theory of education', *Teachers College Record*, 97: 47–68.

Leonado, Z. (2009) *Race, Whiteness and Education*. London and New York: Routledge.

Lopez, G.R. (2003) 'The (racially neutral) politics of education: A critical race theory perspective', *Educational Administration Quarterly*, 39: 68–94.

Matsuda, M. (1996) *Where is Your Body?: And Other Essays on Race, Gender and the Law*. Boston: Beacon.

Montoya, M. (1994) 'Mascaras, trenzas, y grenas: un/masking the self while un/braiding Latina stories and legal discourse', *Chicano-Latino Law Review*, 15: 1–37.

Moschel, M. (2007) 'Color blindness or total blindness? The absence of critical race theory in Europe', *Rutgers Race & Law Review*, 9: 57–128.

Parker, L. and Lynn, M. (2002) 'What's race got to do with it? Critical race theory's conflicts and connections to qualitative research methodology and epistemology', *Qualitative Inquiry*, 8(1): 7–22.

Parker, L. and Stovall, D.O. (2005) 'Actions following words: Critical race theory connects to critical pedagogy', in Z. Leonardo (ed.) *Critical Pedagogy and Race*. Oxford, UK: Blackwell. pp. 159–74.

Parks, G.S. (2007) *Critical Race Realism: Towards an Integrative Model of Critical Race Theory, Empirical Social Science and Social Policy*. Cornell Faculty Law Papers.

Pollock, M. (2008) *Because of Race: How Americans Debate Harm and Opportunity in Our Schools*. Princeton, NJ: Princeton University Press.

Smedley, A. (1999). *Race in North America: Origin and Evolution of a World View* (2nd ed.). Boulder, CO: Westview Press.

Sewell, T. (2000) *Black Masculinities and Schooling: How Black Boys Survive Modern Schooling*. Staffordshire, UK: Trentham Books.

Smedley, A. (1999) *Race in North America: Origin and Evolution of a World View*, 2nd edn. Boulder, CO: Westview Press.

Solórzano, D. (1998) 'Critical Race Theory, racial and gender microaggressions, and the experiences of Chicana and Chicano scholars', *International Journal of Qualitative Studies*, 11: 121–36.

Tsosie, R. (2000) 'Sacred obligations: Intercultural justice and the discourse of treaty rights', *UCLA Law Review*, 47.

Winant, H. (2001) *The World is a Ghetto: Race and Democracy Since World War II*. New York: Basic Books.

Wing, A. (1997) *Critical Race Feminism: A Reader*. New York: New York University Press.

Yosso, T.J. (2005). 'Whose culture has capital? A critical race theory discussion of community cultural wealth,' *Race Ethnicity & Education*, 8: 69–91.

Yosso, T. (2006) *Critical Race Counterstories Along the Chicana/o Pipeline*. New York: Routledge.

Yosso, T.J, Parker, L. Solórzano, D.G. and Lynn, M. (2004) 'From Jim Crow to affirmative action and back again: A critical race discussion of racialized rationales and access to higher education', in R. Flodden (ed.) *Review of Research in Education*. Washington, DC: American Educational Research Association. pp. 1–27.

Queer Theory/Lesbian and Gay Approaches

Gloria Filax, Equality and Social Justice, Athabasca University, Athabasca, Canada

Dennis Sumara, Faculty of Education, University of Calgary, Canada

Brent Davis, Faculty of Education, University of Calgary, Canada

Debra Shogan, University of Alberta, Canada

Summary

- Challenges categorization/normalization
- Post-structuralist critique of subjectivity and discourse
- Theoretical and political affiliations with feminism
- Foucauldian discourse analysis, deconstruction and psychoanalysis
- Key theorists and writers
  - Judith Butler
  - Michel Foucault
  - Eve K. Sedgwick

Key concepts

Gloria Filax and Debra Shogan

Queer theory addresses the problem of a two-sex, two-gender, one-sexuality ordering, which systematically categorizes and then divides humans into what counts as normal and deviant. The idea of *normalization* is integral to understanding the significance of queer theory. Research processes that draw on queer theory pay close attention to processes of normalization including those that construct categories of race, class, able-bodiness and age along with the context of place, culture and time in researching experiences, discourses and identities related to this normalizing sexual order. Queer theory problematizes and historicizes the foundational assumptions of all categories which human science research mostly takes for granted. Queer theory borrows from and has close theoretical and political affiliations with feminist, gay and lesbian theories and studies.

Introducing the word 'queer' into academic discourses suggests both a rupture as well as continuity with the older categories of lesbian and gay. 'Queer', as reclaimed identification, was given intellectual capital at a conference theorizing lesbian and gay sexualities held at the University of California, Santa Cruz in February 1990. The conference was based on the speculative premise that homosexuality is no longer defined either by opposition or homology to a dominant, stable form of sexuality (heterosexuality) or as merely transgressive or deviant in relation to a proper or natural sexuality. Participants were invited to reconceptualize male and female homosexualities as social and cultural forms in their own right, even if under-coded and discursively dependent on more established forms of sexuality. In the words of Teresa de Lauretis:

> [R]ather than marking the limits of the social space by designating a place at the edge of culture, gay

sexuality in its specific female and male cultural (or subcultural) forms acts as an agency of social process whose mode of functioning is both inter-active and yet resistant, both participatory and yet distinct, claiming at once equality and differ-ence, demanding political representation while in-sisting on its material and historical specificity. (1991: iii)

While 'queer' has come to stand in for a range of subjectivities that defy 'the normal', including lesbian, gay, bisexual, transsexual and transgender, specifically queer theory works to problematize, transgress or transcend the ideological baggage of distinctions produced by the terms lesbian, homosexual and gay. 'Queer' is contentious and many refuse to be con-tained by 'queer' because it is perceived to be Euro-western, white, male and therefore exclusionary.

Queer theory brings a perspective to social science research, which has been influenced by how *post-structuralism* conceptualizes *subjectivity* and *discourse*. Post-structural theory provides a critique of the human subject or individual and calls into question the stability or fixedness of categories that are normally assumed. Subjectivity represents the post-structuralist notion that a human being is formed or produced through discourse. Post-structuralist the-ories of subjectivity insist there is no fixed, unified, biological, essential or pre-discursive self. Instead human subjects are born into language, culture and discourse. How we talk, act, think, what is said, what can be said, who is authorized to speak, when and where, and the ways in which our lives are organized, constitute unified ways of thinking about things, people, culture and events. An example of a discourse is gender. Gender is a systematic way of organizing and thinking about humans, which has the effect of producing male and female subjects. How bodies are produced as male and female through discursive practices of gender include: ways of dressing, family arrangements, laws regarding who can marry and inherit, appropriate leisure and work activities, and emotional responses and responsibilities. Discourses are multiple, overlapping, and contradictory. Queer theory is interested in how gender, sex, desire and sexuality organize all human behaviour including religion, education, family and kinship, politics, work and so on. By destabilizing categories, queer theoreti-cal reworkings of post-structuralist theories of subjec-tivity reveal that human identity is a constellation of multiple and unstable positions.

Four overlapping principles operate in relation to queer theory.

(1) Queer theory works to problematize identity categories by showing how the assumptions on which they are based are falsely normalizing, reifying, hom-ogenizing, naturalizing and totalizing. Queering the norm or standard (Shogan, 1999) reveals the arbitrari-ness of all social categories. Further, queer theory shows how fixed categories like lesbian or gay, even when these are used as a corrective to heteronor-mativity, leave heteronormative discourse unaltered and that 'gay' and 'lesbian' specify sexual identities that reproduce the ideology of heterosexual society. The effect of these categories is to fix a normal human identity in a two-sex, two-gender, one-sexual orientation system in what Warner calls the 'sexual order' (1993: x–xi). Because the sexual order per-meates all social institutions (family, religion, work, leisure, law, education), challenging this order has the effect of challenging common-sense ideology about what it means to be a human being. To theorize sexualities outside of the heterosexuality/homosexual-ity binary is to proliferate sexual categories. Bisexual-ity, transgender, transexuality, third sex and queer-straight are just some terms to capture sexuality and gender category proliferations. These, in turn, are proliferated by problematizing racial categories.

> Finally, it is because sexuality is so inevitably personal, because it so inextricably entwines the self with others, fantasy with representation, the subjective with the social, that racial as well as gender differences are a crucial area of concern for queer theory, and one where critical dialogue alone can provide a better understanding of the specific-ity and partiality of our respective histories, as well as the stakes of some common struggles. (de Lauretis, 1991: xi)

To sexuality, race and gender we add class, physicality, religion, age, colonial, post-colonial and culture cat-egories. Each of these is unstable and further destabil-izes fixed sexual identities by proliferating categories. Differences are interlocking, producing hyphenated identities. Different perspectives, histories, experien-ces and different terms make crucial the reformulation of questions posed by queer theory. For example, *tombois* and *leshi* in West Sumatra (Blackwood, 1999) and *two-spirited* for some indigenous peoples in North America (Wilson, 1996) are contemporary categories informed by sexuality, culture, gender, colonialism, racism, ethnocentrism and post-colonialism.

Two theorists are of particular importance in understanding the disruption of identity categories. Eve Sedgwick's *Epistemology of the Closet* (1990) troubles the assumed connection between gender and sexuality as well as troubling the open secret of the closet, an awareness of the existence of homosexuality alongside exclusion, denial and silence about homosexuality. Judith Butler's *Gender Trouble* (1990) problematizes the assumption that sex is a biological given which prefigures a cultural gender.

(2) Queer theory works to problematize *heteronormativity* as the dominating form of sexuality. This problematization challenges and destabilizes how normalization works by exposing incoherencies between gender, chromosomal sex, sexuality and sexual desire (Jagose, 1996: 3). Rather than see heterosexuality as the original or that from which homosexuality deviates, both are seen as mutually productive of each other. They are both effects of each other's exclusions. Processes of normalization produce all other sexuality categories as outside the norm, that is as abnormal or deviant. To understand the myriad ways in which heteronormativity organizes and structures everyday life, queer theory explores how education, law, religion, psychiatry, family, and any other area of human activity all embed assumptions of what counts as normal and are normalizing mechanisms in human relations. As Warner writes: 'Realization that themes of *homophobia* and *heterosexism* may be read in almost any document of our culture means that we are only beginning to have an idea of how widespread those institutions and accounts are' (1993: xiii, our emphasis). For example, accounts of proper age-stage models of maturation embedded in educational, legal and family discourses assume a standard family form as well as normal sexual development in youth towards heterosexuality.

(3) Queer theory opens up possibilities for human relations by producing and/or noticing other ways of living and thinking differences. The least known and represented forms of desire may produce new and different forms of identity, community and social relations (de Lauretis, 1991). Living differently will be productive of different sorts of hierarchies whose effects cannot be predicted in advance. For some, queer theory shuts down potential as it reproduces another generic identity: white, colonial, male, well-resourced, Euro-western, gay, adult, United States. For others, queer is a word that cannot be reclaimed and symbolizes horrific forms of homophobia. Taking up queer theory obligates a researcher to work within what Hutcheon calls complicitous critique (1989) and Flax calls recognition of one's own non-innocent forms of knowledge (1992). This requires researchers to be vigilant about how their own assumptions are an ongoing site of conflict, ambivalence and power/knowledge.

(4) Queer theory mostly draws on three specific forms of analysis. These are *Foucauldian discourse analysis, deconstruction* and *psychoanalysis.*

Foucault offers a method which traces *conditions of possibility* (1970) or what he has termed as a history of the present (1979) which reveals the myriad ways in which discourses overlap and reinforce one another to produce particular kinds of human subjects. In *The History of Sexuality, Volume I*, Foucault (1980) described ways in which human sciences of sexuality create an imperative for people to know the Truth about themselves and others through 'knowing' and confessing sexual practices. Indeed, knowing one's self and others through sexual practices, 'in modern Western culture [is] the most meaning intensive of human activities' (Sedgwick, 1990: 5). Through confessional technologies and their supporting discourses, sexual identities are created and regulated which, in turn, are central to the constitution of the subject as both subject to and subject of sexual (and other) discourses (Foucault, 1980). Both identity and consciousness of identity take place in contexts that constrain available identity categories. To problematize identity, then, is to interrogate ways in which individuals take up identity categories, as well as ways in which categories are socially produced.

In order for heterosexuality to function as the normal, natural and given, it must have its abnormal, unnatural, absent other: the homosexual. Both deconstruction and psychoanalytic theory make it possible to expose the ways in which heteronormativity is constructed through *exclusion* of the queer '*other*'. Deconstruction interrogates a category's 'construction as a pregiven or foundationalist premise' (Butler, 1992: 9) and demonstrates 'how the very establishment of the system as a system implies a beyond to it, precisely by virtue of what it excludes' (Cornell, 1992: 1). Deconstruction calls into question, problematizes and 'opens up' a category for 'a reusage or redeployment that previously has not been authorized' (Butler, 1992: 15). Homosexuality is not a stable or autonomous term but a supplement to the definition of the heterosexual. 'The homosexual' functions as a means of stabilizing heterosexual identity and, as such, is the *limit* or the beyond of 'the heterosexual'.

Psychoanalytic theory makes it possible to see 'the homosexual' as an *imaginary other* whose flamboyant difference deflects attention from the contradictions inherent in the construction of heterosexuality. Often this deflection is through a demonization process in which the actions of queer people are always already perverse in the negative sense by virtue of being queer. Perverse actions then become the defining features of what is queer. Heterosexuality is able to thrive precisely by preserving and consolidating its internal contradictions at the same time as it preserves and consolidates ignorance of them.

Implications for research design

Dennis Sumara, Brent Davis and Debra Shogan

Research informed by queer theory can utilize many established social science research methods, although most research is multi-methodological.

Because queer theory is primarily interested in how particular orderings of sexuality and gendering have been given primacy over others, the questions, related research instruments, methods and analyses that shape research focus on both the constructions and the experiences of personal and collective identities. These questions, methods, and analyses might be sociological, investigating, as examples, how gay, lesbian, transgendered and heterosexual identities are socially structured and policed or how capitalism and globalization have influenced the development of a two-sex, two-gender, one-sexuality ordering. They might be anthropological, exploring, for example, what meanings those who identify in different sexuality categories bring to their daily, lived experiences. The questions, methods, and analyses might be historical, detailing, for example, what social and cultural circumstances have led to particular views of sexuality and gender. Or they might be psychoanalytic, examining how trauma and repression contribute to the organizing of sexualized and gendered identities. While all these methods and related analyses are used, most research informed by queer theory is primarily interested in expressing historical and cultural perspectives, while exploring how human beings experience the way sexuality and sexual identities are shaped by discourses of race, class, gender, and other axes of difference and how these experiences of identity are influential to the organization of societies and cultures, including research collectives. Participants are often self-selected, since naming in advance what counts as membership in an identity category precludes an investigation into how these categories are established in the first place and how individuals come to identify with them. As we elaborate in the Stories from the Field section below, queer theory pays attention to how research methodologies affect relationships between researchers and others involved in research, including how a research collective may contribute to the reproduction of insider and outsider identities.

Research informed by queer theory generally views the posing of research questions, the development of data-gathering activities and the processes of analysis and interpretation as iterative and recursive. That is, all aspects of research informed by queer theory continue to shift as the research develops. For example, in Stories from the Field, the research began with questions about how gay and lesbian teachers develop their pedagogical practices but, over time, evolved to include more fine-grained analyses of how minority sexuality categories can develop hierarchies of what is considered normal and deviant.

Outcomes from research developed with queer theory can be as varied as the different methodologies employed. However, what all research shares is a commitment to revealing the usually-not-perceived relationships between experiences of human sociality and culture, and expressions and experiences of sexuality. All outcomes of research informed by queer theory must in some way illuminate the ways in which sex, sexualities and sexual identities are both influenced by and influence individual and/or collective experiences.

The outcomes of research informed by queer theory can be presented in what are now considered to be traditional qualitative research forms (e.g. anthropological or sociological reports, case studies, reports of action research). However, in keeping with the queer theoretical imperative to interrupt status quo discourses and practices, the use of alternative representational forms such as literary, narrative, new journalism and other creative non-fiction forms that are able to more fully represent the complexity of human identities is encouraged.

Stories from the field – troubling identities with literary forms: action research informed by queer theory

Dennis Sumara and Brent Davis

From 1995 to 1997 we conducted an action research project with eight teachers who identified as gay, lesbian and transsexual. The purpose of our research was to try to gain some insight into what it meant to occupy a minority sexuality identity category and be a public school teacher. All eight participants in the research were experienced teachers in a large Canadian urban centre. Four were men, three were women and one was transsexual in the process of transitioning from male to female.

Our reading of the theoretical literature in queer theory had suggested to us that we needed to create a research methodology that was collaborative and, at the same time, that remained critically aware of how collaboration, in itself, functioned to reproduce structures we were trying to interrogate. For us, this meant developing methods that not only allowed for a representation of the identities that participated in research processes, but, as well, of the ways in which the forming of a research collective functions to reproduce particular sorts of identities and not others. As well, we needed to create research processes that highlighted the complex ways in which identities continually shift and proliferate through processes of identification and representation. Therefore, although telephone and face-to-face interviews were initially used to gather demographic and autobiographical information about participants in the research, these were not considered to be central to our 'data gathering'. Instead, we aimed to create research structures that we hoped might help all participants in this collaborative research (including ourselves as the university-based researchers) to continually call into question the ways in which we presented and represented our identities as human beings and as human beings who were also teachers. Our reading of post-structural theories had helped us to understand the ways our identities were structured by various discursive practices (including, e.g., the discourse of gender, class, race, age, ability, schooling, teaching). Our reading of queer theory had elaborated these insights by reminding us that the normal/deviant binary has been supported by a two-sex, two-gender,

one-sexuality ordering, which assumes the 'naturalness' of a narrow view of heterosexuality and the 'unnaturalness' of any other presentation of identity that departs from this normalized version of human identity.

Following methods developed by Sumara (2002) we used shared readings of literary texts as sites for critical inquiry in order to interrupt the usual ways in which identities are both experienced and re-presented during processes of interpretive inquiry. These reading activities required readers to form literary identifications with characters and situations that challenged and expanded remembered and currently lived experiences. By working with our co-researchers to interpret these literary identifications, moments of insight occurred that often interrupted the transparent structures of our perceptions and our thinking. For us, these shared responses to literary texts create possibilities for what Iser (1993) has called 'literary anthropology' – an interpretive activity where the relationships among memory, history and experiences of subjectivity were made available for analysis. Because we all read the same texts, and identified in 'minority' identity categories, we predicted that our responses would be similar. Of course, this proved not to be the case.

In reading and responding to Audre Lorde's (1982) *Zami: A New Spelling of My Name*, for example, we discovered that no two members of our group identified similarly. Not only were the responses noticeably structured by learned gender differences, they were also clearly influenced by the members' racial and ethnic backgrounds. Some of the responses, particularly from several male participants of the group, were puzzling in that they seemed unable to acknowledge that anger and frustration were very much part of the experience of women depicted in the novel. As Jim explained:

I just don't understand why the main character is always so angry. Surely, things were not as bad for women as is suggested. Even if they were, I think that maybe some of what she is experiencing she is bringing on herself.

Here it became clear that, although some male members of the group expressed the need to unite under the banner of same-sex identification, many of their responses were structured by a profound and largely unnoticed (by them) misogyny. The women in the group, however, did notice and, for them, these responses confirmed past experiences with gay men. As Jan explained:

I guess I shouldn't be surprised by some of the things I hear from the men in the group. I mean, that's one of the reasons that lesbians must have their own communities. Gay men can be just as sexist as straight men.

These curious experiences of identification and non-identification continued in our group's reading and discussion of Califia's (1995) short story, 'The surprise party', where we learned that personally familiar erotic identifications can become restructured by literary identifications: As Sandy explained:

After reading this story, I had some vivid dreams that include sex of the kind the characters had in the story ... I didn't think that I could be interested in that kind of sex.

These responses to literary fiction informed our understanding about the relationships between and among expressed and experienced identities, regulated and disciplined forms of sociality, and experiences of pleasure, desire and imagination. Although it is obvious that human beings experience events of identification and pleasure that are not necessarily understood as 'normally' heterosexual, the various technologies of regulation around gender and sexuality force open secrets about what constitutes both identification and pleasure. And, although 'the closet' is usually understood as the place where queer identities simultaneously hide and make themselves comprehensible to themselves, we suggest that the closet's boundaries must be understood to include the polymorphous ways in which identification and pleasure are produced. It is important to note that we used queer theory to analyse any identity that defines itself as counter to normative constructions of heterosexuality, including those who sexually identify with members of the opposite sex and/or gender, but not in ways that are heteronormative. If sexuality is understood as a category of experience that emerges from various and overlapping technologies of self-creation and re-creation, then the cultural mythologies of what constitutes the categories that are understood as 'normal' – particularly the category heterosexual – must be critically interrogated.

At first, calling into question the construction of heterosexuality seemed easy for those of us in the research group who identified with minority sexuality positions. As we discussed our responses to literary characters who identified as both heterosexual and 'not-heterosexual' we were able to deconstruct the ways in which what is considered a 'normal hetero-sexual' identity is represented in almost every struc-ture that we could identify, including everyday uses of language. What we eventually came to learn, however, was that 'normalization' occurs at every level of culture, including the gay, lesbian and cultural groups with which we identified.

Most surprising in this research were insights that emerged from the presence of Terry, our transsexual research group member. In her mid-fifties, Terry joined our group in the middle of her three-year programme of transitioning from a male to female identity. Terry suggested to us that her 25-year history as a husband and a father meant that she had had no history of involvement with the gay and lesbian communities and therefore felt like an outsider in our group. During most meetings, Terry continually at-tempted to represent the ways in which she did and did not identify with male/female gender systems or with straight/gay identity categories. During one of our meetings, Terry suggested that if our group was to be called the 'queer teachers study group' then she was the 'queerest' of us all.

The primary challenge for those of us who initiated this research and who were most familiar with the theoretical structures that guided the methodologies we were using, was to continually publicly surface and analyse the ways in which our research was reproduc-ing the very normative structures that we were trying to both understand and undermine. As our group continued to meet, it became clear that the 'normal/ not-normal' binary was being created in our group – those who presented unambiguous gay or lesbian identities and Terry, who presented a much more fluid and ambivalent identity – one whose features (both physiological and psychological) continued to shift as Terry moved through her sex-reassignment transition. Some members of our group confided privately to us that they were not comfortable having Terry in our group:

She continues to insist that she is a woman and I'm trying to see her that way. But she continues to respond to the women in the group like a man, and she insists that she was a heterosexual man. Well, I just can't accept that! To me, Terry is just not a woman and never will be, no matter what sorts of surgical and hormonal interventions are made.

Terry had her own responses to the group:

You all seem to be so sure about your identities and you seem to have friends and activities that support who you are. I have none of that. When I was married and raising children I did not feel like I was a 'proper' heterosexual man and now that I'm doing what feels right to me, I don't feel like I'm a 'proper' member of this queer research group.

Terry's presence in our research group helped us to understand how strong the impulse to create fixed identity categories can be, and how easy it is for individuals and groups to make decisions about what counts as a 'normal' identity and what will be designated 'deviant'. While all members of our research group identified as activists for the civil rights of all members of society, we continued to make judgements about how the normal/not-normal binary was to be structured within our study/research group.

These issues were never fully resolved. Most members continued to feel dissonance with the different ways identities and experiences were presented within the context of group meetings. However, in final interviews with Sumara, it was clear that everyone had a much more well developed consciousness of how processes of normalization are reproduced at all levels of cultural involvement, even when there is an awareness of how these structures are created and enacted. As persons who identified as 'queer' and who were also teachers, we realized that we needed to abandon the idea that we could draw a neat line between different ways people identify and how others experience those identities. In fact, what this research showed us was that not only could we not make a correlation between features of our experienced and expressed identities, but we couldn't even be certain that we knew exactly what we meant when we used signifiers like 'gay', 'lesbian', 'transsexual' or 'heterosexual' to represent our and other identities. While these identity markers did help to connect us with historical and contemporary cultures and communities, at the same time, close identification with any of them seemed to require a reproduction of processes of normalization that we, as persons working within a queer theoretical framework, aimed to avoid. However, we did learn that participating in literary identifications helped us to render more visible the usually transparent ways in which we both identified others and created identities for ourselves. In order to conduct research that is informed by queer theory, we learned that we as researchers must consciously and conscientiously continue to queer the ways in which we are involved in language forms that explicitly aim to produce heteronormativity. For us, this did not mean merely bringing a critical eye and ear to the ways in which language and cultural practices function to produce normalized identities. It also meant creating research structures that deliberately aimed to interrupt familiar ways of presenting, representing, and interpreting knowledge and knowing identities.

Annotated bibliography

Gloria Filax

Barnard, I. (2004) *Queer Race: Cultural Interventions in the Racial Politics of Queer Theory (Gender, Sexuality, and Culture)*. New York: Peter Lang Publishing.
One of the strongest critiques of queer theory is the absence of race as a point of analysis and a parallel point is the whiteness of much queer theory and research. This book is worth reading because it racializes queer theory thereby countering the lacuna in much existing queer theory/research.

Butler, J. (1990) *Gender Trouble*. New York: Routledge; (1993) *Bodies That Matter*. New York: Routledge; (2004) *Undoing Gender*. New York: Routledge.
The work of Judith Butler is a primary source for scholars taking up gender, sexuality, and queer theory. Taking up deconstruction, psychoanalytic theory and Foucauldian discourse analysis, Butler shows how gender and sex are productive of one another, effectively disrupting the notion that sex is a prior and more biological moment in identity formation.

Foucault, M. (1980) *The History of Sexuality, Volume 1: An Introduction*. New York: Vintage.
A key reading in which Foucault traces the conditions of possibility that have given rise to modernism's sexualized identities and subjectivities. Prior to the mid-nineteenth century diverse sexual practices existed but no corresponding identities. With the rise of the human sciences (*scientia sexualis*), both an accumulation of knowledge and a continuous refining of detail about identity categories were linked to behaviours which were labelled normal or deviant, and became fixed, hardened and productive of forms of human identities.

Hawley, J.C. (ed.) (2001) *Postcolonial Queer: Theoretical Intersections*. New York: SUNY Press.

This edited collection counters the colonizing tendencies of North America (Canada and USA) by looking beyond to other contexts and cultures.

McRuer, R. and Wilkerson, A.L. (2003) 'Cripping the (queer) nation', *GLQ: A Journal of Lesbian and Gay Studies*, 9(1/2): 1–23.

All of this GLQ volume is devoted to the articulation of queer theory and critical disability studies and worthy of reading because of the important questions and insights it contains. Disability, like race, is a lacuna in much queer theory and research.

Sedgwick, E.K. (1990) *Epistemology of the Closet*. Berkeley, CA: University of California Press.

The introduction is absolutely essential reading, setting out Sedgwick's six axioms that have become central to much queer research.

Sullivan, N. (2003) *A Critical Introduction to Queer Theory*. Edinburgh: Edinburgh University Press.

Sullivan brings ideas about the self, sexuality and society together in this introduction to central debates and questions of queer theory including identity politics, fetishism, transsexualism, performativity, community and race. The text provides historical context to how and why queer theory emerged in the west in the late twentieth century.

Wilson, A. (1996) 'How we find ourselves: Identity development and Two-Spirit people', *Harvard Educational Review*, 66: 303–17.

This article points to the intersection of sexuality studies, aboriginal cultural practices and colonial legacies, showing how these cannot be understood separate from one another. This article continues to be important because of the disruption to dominant white narratives and research in sexuality studies.

Further references

Blackwood, E. (1999) '*Tombois* in West Sumatra: Constructing masculinity and erotic desire', in E. Blackwood and S. Wieringa (eds) *Same-Sex Relations and Female Desires*. New York: Columbia University Press. pp. 181–205.

Butler, J. (1992) 'Contingent foundations', in J. Butler and J. Scott (eds) *Feminists Theorize the Political*. New York: Routledge. pp. 3–21.

Califia, P. (1995) 'The surprise party', in P. Califia and J. Fuller (eds) *Forbidden Passages: Writings Banned in Canada*. San Francisco, CA: Cleis Press. pp. 110–24.

Cornell, D. (1992) *The Philosophy of the Limit*. New York: Routledge.

De Lauretis, T. (1991) 'Queer theory: Lesbian and gay sexualities. An introduction', *differences*, 3(2): iii–xviii.

Flax, J. (1992) 'The end of innocence', in J. Butler and J. Scott (eds) *Feminists Theorize the Political*. New York: Routledge. pp. 445–63.

Foucault, M. (1970) *The Order of Things*. Trans. A. Sheridan. New York: Pantheon.

Foucault, M. (1979) *Discipline and Punish*. Trans. A. Sheridan. New York: Vintage.

Hutcheon, L. (1989) *The Politics of Postmodernism*. New York: Routledge.

Iser, W. (1993) *The Fictive and the Imaginary: Charting Literary Anthropology*. Baltimore, MD: Johns Hopkins University Press.

Jagose, A. (1996) *Queer Theory: An Introduction*. New York: New York University Press.

Lorde, A. (1982) *Zami: A New Spelling of My Name*. Freedom, CA: Crossing Press.

Shogan, D. (1999) *The Making of High-Performance Athletes*. Toronto: University of Toronto Press.

Sumara, D. (2002) 'Creating commonplaces for interpretation: Literary anthropology and literacy education research', *Journal of Literacy Research*, 34(2): 237–60.

Warner, M. (1993) 'Introduction', in M. Warner (ed.) *Fear of a Queer Planet*. Minneapolis, MN: University of Minnesota Press.

11

Action Research

Susan Noffke, Department of Curriculum and Instruction, College of Education,
University of Illinois at Urbana-Champaign

Bridget Somekh, Education and Social Research Institute,
Manchester Metropolitan University, UK, and the University of Canterbury, New Zealand

Summary

- Inter-relationship between practice and theory
- Research from inside a social setting
- Dimensions of action research: professional, personal, political
- Critical/emancipatory action research
- Methodology that adapts and develops in relation to participants' values
- Key theorists and writers
  - Mary Brydon-Miller
  - Wilf Carr
  - John Elliot
  - Stephen Kemmis
  - Susan Noffke
  - Bridget Somekh

Key concepts

Action research is a broad family of practices. As with most families, there are differences and conflicts. There are varied assumptions about the purposes and processes of research, but also a set of shared assumptions (Editors, 2009). Action research directly addresses the problem of the division between theory and practice, and assumes that the two are inter-twined, with neither at a more valued position. Rather than research being a linear process of knowledge production that is later applied to practice settings, action research integrates the development of practice with the construction of research knowledge in a cyclical process. Practice generates knowledge, including theory, and theory can be tested in practice, not just applied.

Instead of being research *on* a social setting and the people within it, it is research *from inside* that setting and is carried out either by the participants themselves or researchers working in collaboration with them. In most cases it involves a collaborative process that transcends distinctions between researcher(s) and subject(s). One goal is to have an immediate impact on practice, through its integral connection to day-to-day work. Many forms of action research also emphasize the potential for knowledge generation, and incorporate new processes for establishing ethics and quality standards. In addition, there has been an increase in saliency of forms of action research that emphasize a strong connection to the larger social context in which practices are embedded, highlighting issues of social and economic justice.

Multiple forms from multiple sources

The search for a form of research that connects careful study with impact not only on the development of practice but also on large social issues stretches back to the development of the social sciences at the beginning of the twentieth century and has both feminist and anti-racist origins. While most of the historical literature focuses on the US, the emergence of this form of research has global roots in social struggles (Brydon-Miller et al., in press) including many projects in post-colonial settings. These forms of action research emphasize its role in social struggle and highlight the importance of local knowledge and knowledge production towards those ends. While these roots are integrally connected to the development of participatory action research (PAR) in organizational settings and the work of non-governmental organizations (Whyte, 1991) they are particularly connected to post-colonial settings. Emanating from South America, a tradition of PAR has been influenced by the work of Paulo Freire and others who worked to theorize and practise a form of research which aimed at emancipatory ends. Starting out as a grassroots movement carried out in small-scale work in local 'popular education' settings, PAR has become a movement 'search[ing] for a new type of scientific plus activist/emancipatory work' (see Borda, 2001). The most recent work along these lines highlights the voices of young people in understanding the social context and creating means for social change (Cammorota and Fine, 2008).

The most frequently noted source for action research is in the work of Kurt Lewin during the years surrounding World War II. As a psychologist and refugee from Nazi Germany, he worked within the USA to address wartime concerns, such as the changing of family diet to use new food sources, but also worked to address questions around democratic processes and issues such as prejudice. Trist, influenced by Lewin, worked in a similar way at the Tavistock Institute in London, focusing during the 1950s on experimental work in organizations to help them address their practical problems. Lewin's theory of action research divides the work into distinct stages within a series of cycles, starting with 'reconnaissance' and moving on to the collection of data, analysis, and the development of 'hypotheses' to inform action. This then leads into the second cycle in which the hypotheses are tested in practice and the changes evaluated. The cyclical process of action research does not come to a natural conclusion, although at some point it is necessary to bring it to a close and disseminate the outcomes in some form. This emphasis on the cyclical construction of the research process has become an integral part of many forms of action research.

In the USA, action research in education flowered briefly during the 1950s, but then drew criticism from established researchers and declined. In the UK, it first became important in education as a result of Stenhouse's Humanities Project and Elliott's Ford Teaching Project during the 1970s (Elliott, 2007; Stenhouse, 1975). Stenhouse saw research as a necessary component of the work of every teacher and his definition of curriculum as a set of processes, principles and interactions, rather than a specification of subject matter content, led to his belief that curriculum development was an impossibility without the involvement of teachers-as-researchers. In Australia, Stephen Kemmis, Robin McTaggart and colleagues built from a significant base of teacher researchers to develop action research at Deakin University (Carr and Kemmis, 1986) and were later influenced by the PAR work, especially that of Fals Borda. In Europe, for example in Austria, through the work of Peter Posch and colleagues at the University of Klagenfurt, action research has made a significant impact on government policy for education.

Since the mid-1980s there has been a resurgence of interest in action research in the USA and more recently in many other countries. One area has been the development of a sustained tradition of teacher research focused on improving learning and teaching (Cochran-Smith and Lytle, 2009), and more recently a tradition of self-study by teacher educators (Loughran et al., 2004). There has also been substantial growth in the use of action research within local school districts and national ministries of education as part of their professional development agendas.

Some see action research as being carried out by practitioners – whether in a professional group or university – to understand and improve their own practice. This tradition often places importance on an outside facilitator who has expertise in supporting the practitioner-researchers. The relationship between the facilitator and 'insiders', such as nurses, social workers or teachers, is crucially important but it raises ethical issues related to their differential power. Sometimes the whole research process (identification of the problem, data collection and analysis, writing up and presentation at conferences and in publications) is carried out by insiders. The facilitators' research focus is 'second order', concerned with improving their own practice as facilitators rather than the 'first order' issues of practice. Another approach is for the action research to be led by a participant who comes into the practice situation from outside and negotiates the boundaries and parameters of the study with the participants, involving them as co-researchers without expecting them to undertake substantial amounts of additional work. The 'outsider' may be a professional who has become a graduate-student or a university-based researcher working on a funded project. Again, there will be imbalances of power and control so that the working relationship will need to be carefully negotiated. In all cases the ethical issues raised are acknowledged to be integrally connected to issues of power and voice. A resolution to this problem often involves developing an agreed code of practice to ensure that such power/ethics issues are discussed and addressed in advance. Recent works (Campbell and Groundwater-Smith, 2007; Editors, 2006) take ethical issues further, highlighting the ways in which research ethics intersect with the ethics of practice.

There is a wide range of different approaches to action research. The *SAGE Handbook of Educational Action Research* (Noffke and Somekh, 2009) groups these within three dimensions: the professional, the personal and the political. The first focuses on improving and contributing to the professional knowledge base for practice while the second is concerned with issues such as developing self-knowledge and understanding of the individual's own practice. While all are considered political, the third approach directly addresses research aimed at social action to combat oppression. The *Handbook* presents these categories as being of equal and interconnected status, whereas Grundy's (1982) earlier categorization suggests a hierarchy of status: the 'technical', the 'practical'; and the 'critical'. Based on three kinds of knowledge, in Aristotle's *Ethics*, the technical focuses upon making a better product (for example more efficient and effective practice), the practical focuses upon developing the 'practical judgement' of the participant-researcher grounded in experience and self-reflection, and the critical leads to 'emancipatory' action research. The latter, for which Grundy drew on Habermas' critical theory, involves group reflection and action to emancipate participants from the coercive power of traditions and their own prior conceptions.

Including the works already cited, a considerable body of writing has supported the development of action research, theorizing its similarities to, and differences from, other forms of research, and exploring the special value of generating theories as an integral part of development work in social settings. Much of this has focused upon the nature of practitioner knowledge and the special contribution it makes to research (e.g. Cochran-Smith and Lytle, 2009). Action research is closely linked by many writers with the concept of 'reflective practice' which has its roots in the work of Dewey (1933) and of Schön (1983). The latter has been influential in developing concepts of reflection-in-action and reflection-on-action as core attributes of expert professional practice. While it is true that action researchers necessarily engage in reflective practice, it is not true conversely that all reflective practitioners are action researchers. Crucially, action research involves a process of the collection and analysis of data that provides the practitioner with some objectivity and distance, looking at his/her own practice from another point of view, sometimes through bringing to bear more than one kind of data in a process of triangulation. Compared with action learning where the emphasis is on groups supporting reflection based on the perceptions and memories of individuals, action research is also based on consideration of data collected during practice.

Action research is always rooted in the values of the participants. Somekh (2006) points out that its close links with the values of practice tend to mean that action research methodology adapts and develops in rather different ways within different social groups. Action research among nurses, for example, is strongly influenced by the need to establish credibility alongside the research of the medical profession so it tends to conform rather more to standards of traditional research rigour (Hardy et al., 2009). In the UK, much action research in education has focused on the professional development of teachers and teacher educators. In the USA, an important strand of participatory action research, originating in the civil rights movement of the 1960s, has emanated from the work of the Highlander Center, which contributed significantly to social action to promote social justice through focusing on the role of information gathering as an important part of the construction of social action. Martin Luther King encouraged researchers to make a close link between social research and social problems, which invokes earlier work by activist researchers such as W.E.B. DuBois and Myles Horton, who worked to build a tradition of close connection between the methods (data collection) of social research and the practice of social activisim. Similarly, action research in South Africa, with its roots in the struggle against oppression in the time of apartheid, was often overtly political with a strong emphasis on issues of social justice (Robinson and Soudien, 2009). For writers working from a feminist stance (Maguire and Berge, 2009) action research has emerged as a means to examine women's issues through research.

Implications for research design

Action research does not always start with a research question. The driving force rather is an impetus for change/innovation. Through the process of designing 'actions' (interventions in the social situation) there is a deepening of the participants' understanding of social processes as well as a development of new strategies to bring about improvement. There will be a focus on some aspect of the social setting in which the work takes place, but the starting point may be something rather vague, such as a feeling of dissatisfaction without being sure of the reason, or a desire to understand some aspect of activity more deeply.

At the start it will be necessary to make some broad decisions. First, who will be involved? This will depend on whether the action research will be a study of one individual's practice in a clearly-defined setting, such as a hospital ward, or a study of organizational change, for example in a school or hospital. In either case, a lot will depend on who is prepared to volunteer to participate. A partner prepared to act as an observer will be invaluable in providing a different point of view and enabling triangulation of data. Participatory action research often intends to draw more and more people into the process as the work progresses. In practice, this approach intentionally leads to the outsider becoming unnecessary to the project. While perhaps stressful to the external researcher, it is essential to the development of self-sustaining research-change efforts.

Collaboration is never easy, as such ethical issues need to be clearly identified and working principles agreed upon in advance to safeguard the interests of all. Alongside this, analysis of the data is the most difficult as well as the most interesting aspect of the work. It is not only a collaborative process, it is an on-going process, integral with reflection during data collection. The development of action strategies and their implementation, based on the findings of the initial stage of the research, need to be followed by further data collection to evaluate these. The validation of action research outcomes involves multiple means, but emphasizes the testing out of conclusions through new actions, to see if the expected improvement results. While action research frequently involves qualitative data sources and means of analysis, it often involves quantitative methods.

In action research design, it is important to remember that the action aspect is central to the process and influences the methods. When the goal of the research is to influence policy, there is a stronger component of quantitative data to support the knowledge claims; when the goal is sharing in-depth understandings of the particularities of practice, there might be a stronger qualitative component to the data collection and analysis process. The data collection procedures may be a way to record, preserve, and use the knowledge of a specific community, to influence larger scale policy change, or to provide a rich body of information that a community might use to understand and move forward the social agendas of their group in new ways. Theoretical resources relevant to equity issues are often employed when planning the action research, for example feminism, activity theory, critical race theory. These influence the process of data analysis, as does the intended outcome of research: the dual aim of improved practice, alongside the development of new knowledge about that practice. For many action researchers, there is an added component to the research design: the improvement of the overall social situation in which practices occur, including local aspects, but also global intentions.

Stories from the field

Action research can begin in multiple settings, with many kinds of participants. These 'stories from the field' are representations of how one action research issue, parent involvement in the education of school children, can emerge from differing perspectives which, in turn, affect the process as well as the outcomes of the research. In each story, the process of research is cyclical and focused both on producing new knowledge and on creating actions which will affect directly the social situation in which the issue emerges. It is temporal, as well as cumulative.

This series of small 'stories' is built from actual experiences. Theory plays a role, both academic and generated from the hopes and dreams of those most closely connected to practice. Change and thereby improvement in the immediate social situation is a goal, alongside the generation of better understanding of the social context – hence, action and research.

The teachers' story

Many conceptions of action research focus initially on an individual teacher's concerns, but then move on to collaborative projects:

I wonder about some of my students who are not doing as well as they could. If parents could be more 'partners' in the educational process, these children could do so much better in school.

After dialogue between colleagues and administration, and a search of some of the relevant literature, the group devises a survey to gather information on both parent and teacher views on the issue of participation. While the survey results reveal much in terms of teacher attitudes, the parent response rate is small, involving primarily parents who are already involved in school activities. For some teachers, this response 'proves' their belief that 'these parents just don't care'. For others, who know parents and community members outside the school setting, that is clearly not the case. It makes no sense for parents not to want their children to do well in school.

In the next cycle they design a focus group protocol, make use of their personal contacts, and invite parents to discussions at local community sites, at times when parents would be likely to be able to attend. Child care is provided, as well as refreshments. This time there is wide participation. The field notes taken were analysed and the patterns that emerged provided a basis for staff development, but the results were also shared with other schools in the area.

An administrator's story

A school administrator has a parallel concern:

The school staff is highly qualified, and very successful with many of the students, especially those who come from backgrounds similar to their own. Yet they constantly talk about parents and children in ways that I feel are a reflection of their lack of understanding of the local community culture. They seek to explain gaps and weaknesses and not find strengths on which to build.

Together with the school advisory committee, which includes teachers, paraprofessionals, parents, other local community members, as well as participants from a local university teacher education programme, they brainstorm ways to bring the various segments of the staff and community closer together. They decide to make 'community' a theme for project work for the year. Each grade level team designs inquiry activities that will provide opportunities for families and community members to share stories and local

history. As the work emerges, the school staff begins to see parents and children in a new and positive light, especially through collecting information over time (interviews, student work, parent comments, attendance and achievement records) and using it as a focal point for team discussions of learning plans.

A parent and community story

A similar goal looks somewhat different from a parent and community perspective:

I know that our son could be doing better at school, but I have a hard time finding out how to help. The regular progress reports and parent–teacher conferences are helpful, but I often feel that as long as my child isn't causing problems in class, there is little offered in terms of really tapping into what he could do. A 'C', or average grade, seems to the teachers to mean that everything is fine. But isn't more than that needed if he wants to go to college?

The parent talks with friends, other community members, and starts a focus group, meeting in a local church. She learns that her concerns were widely shared. Together, they work out a network of parents, sharing concerns, and develop a plan for bringing their initial concerns closer to a deeper understanding of the nature of the problem, as well as closer to concrete actions for change. Teachers known to be very successful, with high expectations for students, are invited to participate. Over the next year, they meet regularly, collecting data through interviews, meeting notes, and field notes, hold focus group discussions with parents and teachers, and examine school documents. As they sort and analyse their data, their understanding of 'meaningful parental involvement' emerges over time. Both teachers and parents take on leadership roles, and all gain research skills. They share their findings by producing a booklet that other groups can use in assessing their school's family–school relationships, including suggested actions for each of the seven points of their findings (Tellin' Stories Project, 2000).

A community organizing story

A community activist and research group has long been interested in addressing the widely acknowledged gaps in achievement between various racial/ethnic and socio-economic groups. Building on longstanding traditions of community organizing, with direct links to the ideas of people like Myles Horton and Saul Alinsky (two well-known USA community organizers), they work at developing a broad sense of parent involvement, that includes not only attention at the school level to curriculum and teaching, but participation in the policy making, and also budget making processes.

One such group working in Chicago, IL (US) noted:

> Many educators say that they cannot do the work of educating children alone, particularly low- and moderate-income children and children of color. Unfortunately, there are few mechanisms that allow parents and community members in low-income neighborhoods to play a meaningful role in the education of their children ... The common viewpoint is that parents are seen as the people who drop their kids off at school, conduct fundraisers, and occasionally volunteer time in a classroom. Community organizing seeks to change that dynamic. (Gold et al., 2002: 4)

Groups such as this 'Strong Neighborhoods, Strong Schools' project work with the assumption that public schools are neither equitable nor effective for all students. Unlike other contemporary efforts, which focus on 'standards' and high-stakes testing of students, these efforts begin with building a large base of members with solid relationships, and shared responsibilities. Through such efforts, leadership emerges not from the professional community alone, but from community residents, taking charge of the education of their own children through democratic processes. In this way, the organizing efforts are also educative efforts, which build a power base for the communities through knowledge and action linkages.

Information gathering plays a major role, as parents share concerns and ask questions such as 'Why do our children have to drink out of lead fountains, and play in dirt? Why do some communities have better facilities and more programs than ours does?' Instead of ending with the listing of grievances, the process reveals a need to research the questions, to document the disparities, to analyse budgets, to make plans to present findings to governing bodies, etc. Such data are used to further understand the issues, but also to plan strategic actions for improvement.

A student story

Some educational action research projects look at issues from the standpoint of the students. A student voice might start an action research project as well:

> It's so boring. But it's also confusing. I think that I know what I'm supposed to be doing and learning, but then the tests don't seem to match. I want to do well, but every time I study, it seems like it just doesn't work. When I learn things at home, from my family, it's so clear. They tell stories, show me how to do things, let me practice, and enjoy the products when we're finished. It's a group effort, not just me under the spotlight.

Working with an after-school group and its leader – a local graduate student – the children share similar stories and note a common theme of how their families help them learn in different ways than the school does. They want to know more about how their parents see learning at home and learning at school. The group generates a list of possible avenues to pursue, and agrees to begin with a 'family stories of school' project.

The students learn to develop interview protocols, and use audio recording and digital cameras to gather parents' views on learning and schools. As the interviews are being completed, students learn how to analyse the material for recurrent themes and patterns. These are in turn used to organize excerpts for public sharing. Vignettes of family 'learning times' – covering a wide range of skills and contexts (e.g. housework, child care, construction, automotive work, the arts; in churches, libraries, businesses) – are included.

The data showed a tendency to work collaboratively on a concrete task which had mutual benefits, with the students learning as they worked. They also showed the many ways in which families support their children's schooling. But another theme emerged as parents moved from concrete conversations about family learning to remembrances of their own experiences with schooling. Many parents, most often parents of colour or those from low-income families, shared stories that spoke of alienation – times when as children they felt and even today feel disrespect or a lack of cultural awareness by school staff. Their anger and hurt came through as powerful indicators of their commitment to their children's education; they worked with and encouraged the children despite these experiences.

When the research was shared with school personnel, the impact was mixed. Some were angry and 'tired of being called a racist'. Others, though, wanted to find out more about how they could learn how to teach in new ways, how to interact with the communities differently. A small group said, 'Finally. Now perhaps we can move forward.'

Each of these stories highlights different communities of researchers, and embodies differing values, which are, in turn, related to different ideological orientations. All of the projects share a concern with a particular political agenda, although one group identifies this as a professional concern while another articulates the concern in terms of its sense of community. Likewise, all of the 'stories' involve a personal dimension in the sense that they all require rethinking of one's actions in the world and revaluating their worth and effectiveness. The projects do not emerge in a linear fashion from research questions derived solely from academic definitions of researchable topics. Rather they revolve around questions that are integrally tied to practice; they are formed from a need for change which is driven by and, in the process, is generative of, new knowledge. They are research from 'inside', but at the same time show how the participants in the research, through the cycles of research, define and often redefine who counts as an insider and outsider. All of the stories too work toward a new form of theory-practice relationship, in some cases through including 'popular' as well as 'academic' knowledge forms.

Annotated bibliography

Brydon-Miller, M., Kral, M., Maguire, P., Noffke, S. and Sabhlok, A. (in press) 'Jazz and the banyan tree: Participatory action research', in N. Denzin, *The SAGE Handbook of Qualitative Research*, 4th edn. Thousand Oaks, CA: Sage.
Addresses the history and practices of Participatory Action Research.

Cammorota, J. and Fine, M. (eds) (2008) *Revolutionizing Education: Youth Participatory Action Research in Motion*. New York: Routledge.
Includes case studies of PAR with youth and community work with a Freirean orientation.

Campbell, A. and Groundwater-Smith, S. (eds) (2007) *An Ethical Approach to Action Research*. New York: Routledge.

Addresses ethical concerns within higher education and practice contexts.

Carr, W. and Kemmis, S. (1986) *Becoming Critical: Knowing through Action Research*. London: Falmer Press.
A detailed rationale for action research as a way of putting into practice ideas from critical theory.

Cochran-Smith, M. and Lytle, S. (2009) *Inquiry as Stance: Practitioner Research for the Next Generation*. New York: Teachers College Press.
Contextualizes practitioner research in education within a socio-political context. It includes examples by practitioners.

Editors (2009) 'Multiples perspectives on action research', *Educational Action Research*, 17(1).
Offers insights into various contexts and purposes for action research.

Elliott, J. (2007) *Reflecting Where the Action is: The Selected Works of John Elliott*. New York: Routledge.
This text brings together the key contributions to the field by John Elliott, who contributed to the development of action research in education in the UK.

Loughran, J., Hamilton, M., LaBoskey, V. and Russell, T. (2004) *International Handbook of Self-Study of Teaching and Teacher Education Practices*. Dordrecht, The Netherlands: Kluwer Academic.
Contains basic works related to self-study as a form of action research.

Noffke, S.E. and Somekh, B. (2009) *The SAGE Handbook of Educational Action Research*. London: Sage.
Contains perspectives across many countries and approaches to action research.

Phillips, D. and Carr, K. (2010) *Becoming a Teacher Through Action Research*, 2nd edn. New York: Routledge.
Introductory text for preservice teachers, but suitable for many practitioners. Offers critical perspective.

Reason, P. and Bradbury, H. (eds) (2008) *The SAGE Handbook of Action Research: Participative Inquiry and Practice*, 2nd edn. London: Sage Publications.
New material complementary to the first edition. A wide range of contexts and processes are explored.

Further references

Borda, O.F. (2001) 'Participatory (action) research in social theory: Origins and challenges', in P. Reason and H. Bradbury (eds) *The SAGE Handbook of Action Research: Participative Inquiry and Practice*. London: Sage. pp. 27–37.

Dewey, J. (1933) *How We Think*. New York: Heath.

Editors (2006) Special Issue: Ethics and Action Research, *Action Research*, 4(1).

Gold, E., Simon, E. and Brown, C. (2002) *Strong Neighborhoods, Strong Schools: The Indicators Project on Education Organizing*. Chicago: Cross City Campaign for Urban School Reform.

Grundy, S. (1982) 'Three Modes of Action Research', *Curriculum Perspectives*, 2(3): 23–34.

Hardy, S., Tichen, A., McCormack, B. and Manley, K. (2009) *Revealing Nursing Expertise through Practitioner Inquiry*. Chichester: Wiley-Blackwell.

Maguire, P. and Berge, B. (2009) 'Elbows out, arms linked', in S. Noffke and B. Somekh (eds) *The SAGE Handbook of Educational Action Research*. London: Sage. pp. 398–408.

Robinson, M. and Soudien, C. (2009) 'Teacher development and political transformation', in S. Noffke and B. Somekh (eds) *The SAGE Handbook of Educational Action Research*. London: Sage. pp. 467–80.

Schön, D. (1983) *The Reflective Practitioner*. New York: Basic Books.

Somekh, B. (2006) *Action Research: A Methodology for Change and Development*. Maidenhead, UK: Open University Press.

Stenhouse, L. (1975) *An Introduction to Curriculum Research and Development*. London: Heinemann Educational Books.

The Tellin' Stories Project Action Research Group (2000) *Between Families and Schools: Creating Meaningful Relationships*. Washington, DC: Network of Educators on the Americas.

Whyte, W.F. (ed.) (1991) *Participatory Action Research*. Newbury Park, CA: Sage.

The Purpose, Practice, and Politics of Sponsored Evaluations

Tineke Abma, Department of Medical Humanities, VU University Medical Center, Amsterdam, The Netherlands

Thomas A. Schwandt, Department of Educational Psychology, College of Education, University of Illinois at Urbana-Champaign, USA

Summary

- Determining value (merit, worth, significance)
- The social practice of evaluation and its role in society
- Differing purposes (improving performance, knowledge building, social critique)
- Making value judgements – subjectivist and objectivist stances
- The relationship between evaluation and politics
- Key theorists and writers
  - Egon B. Guba
  - Ernest R. House
  - Yvonna Lincoln
  - Michael Quinn Patton
  - Robert E. Stake

Key concepts

Thomas A. Schwandt

Evaluation is a professional social practice concerned with determining the value (merit, worth, significance) of a programme, policy, or project. Much evaluation work is for hire, with contracts issued by national and international agencies, private foundations, and public agencies. Evaluation is undertaken in a variety of fields including education, health care and nutrition, technology, economic development, social welfare (e.g. poverty, family assistance, youth development), transportation, energy, the environment, and agriculture. It is practised by academics whose first affiliation is as a university-based researcher and by privately employed professional evaluators. Generally – as with any form of disciplined, systematic investigation of human affairs – evaluation requires expertise in methodologies for generating and analysing both qualitative and quantitative data as well as knowledge of substantive issues implicated in the policy or programme that is being evaluated. Audiences for evaluation reports vary but include the client commissioning the study and different groups with a vested interest in the success or failure of a programme or policy (i.e. stakeholders) including programme developers and managers, programme participants, government officials, politicians, legislators, and the public at large.

Although there is nominal agreement among evaluators that the purpose of their practice is to determine value, there is considerable disagreement on just what that means and how it should be accomplished; hence, there are a variety of views on the purposes, perspectives and methods of the undertaking (Chelmisky and Shadish, 1997; Shaw et al., 2006). This is far more than a simple debate over the choice of methods for doing evaluation: it concerns the very definition of the social practice of evaluation and its role in society.

Several of the more prominent, though not necessarily mutually exclusive, persuasions on the purpose and role of the practice include: *Evaluation to improve performance and accountability*. Influenced by neoliberalism and the programme and ideology of new public management, this view holds that evaluation is about the assessment and measurement of performance. The rationale here is that performance in public (and non-profit) organizations requires improvement (e.g. services should be more effective, efficient, and transparently accountable to users, clients or customers) and the best way to achieve that is by adopting a results-oriented or outcomes-based approach. *Evaluation for knowledge building* defines evaluation as a scientific undertaking that generates explanations of how and why a programme or policy works and under what circumstances. Various methodologies and perspectives are employed here under the rubrics of theory-driven evaluation, scientific realist evaluation, and social experimentation. In *evaluation for development* the evaluator partners or consults with an organization engaged in programme or organizational development. Evaluation is focused on organizational learning and capacity building, on facilitating engagement of members in the task of development, enhancing their sense of ownership for the process and its results, and so on. Utilization-focused, participatory and collaborative, and empowerment evaluation are among the types of practices focused on development. *Evaluation for understanding* envisions evaluation as primarily a pedagogical rather than a technical undertaking. It is oriented to the practices of teachers, health care workers, social workers, and the like. It aims at enhancing these practitioners' grasp of issues and concerns surrounding the judgement of the quality of their practice and their understandings of the meanings they attach to their practice and it often employs both dialogic and narrative strategies to accomplish these goals. It may be primarily descriptive and illuminative in intent and/or transformative. Fourth-generation evaluation, responsive evaluation, evaluation informed by hermeneutics and practical philosophy, as well as some forms of case study evaluation are of this kind. *Evaluation for social critique and transformation* is a close cousin to the foregoing view

and differs primarily in its avowed focus on power and the reduction or elimination of exploitation, inequality, and oppression in social relations. Evaluation approaches of this kind are informed by the tradition of critical hermeneutics, feminist theories, and social action perspectives.

Several significant debates within the field swirl around the very meaning of the words 'evaluate', 'value' and 'politics'. One important discussion deals with the proposition that evaluation *ought* to be concerned with making value judgements, and just what making a value judgement means. Some evaluators argue that their responsibility is primarily scientific description and explanation. Thus, if the object in question is a drug-treatment programme (X), they would describe its features – what is done, by whom, how often, to whom, when, and so on. They would also determine the relationship between X and its desired outcomes (Y, Z), taking into account factors (e.g. B and C) that might mitigate or confound that relationship. They might also consider whether X achieves its desired outcomes efficiently (i.e. consider costs). Having done this they would render a judgement to the effect that 'X (under conditions B and C) leads to Y and Z'. Judging value here is synonymous with scientific appraisal or explanation of what happened and why. A generous interpretation of this way of thinking is that evaluation involves judgement of the *instrumental* value of X, namely, whether X is effective and efficient in achieving its desired purpose(s). Other evaluators argue that scientific appraisal is not equivalent to evaluation. They claim that judging the value of a programme or policy means taking into account a variety of value considerations beyond utility (or beyond whether the programme is effective). For example, the evaluator must judge the value of the desired purpose(s) of the programme, the conduct of the staff in view of legal and ethical considerations, and determine the basis for saying that the programme has utility or instrumental value (e.g. is the criterion one of the greatest good for the greatest number?), and so on. In sum, these evaluators argue that the judgement of value extends well beyond the matter of scientific appraisal of whether and how a programme works.

This dispute relates to concerns over whether value judgements are an objective or subjective matter. The *subjectivist* holds that value judgements are in the eye of the beholder, so to speak. They are nothing more than expressions of personal or political preferences, tastes, emotions, or attitudes on the part of individuals or groups. They are to be distinguished from statements based on facts that describe and explain some state of affairs. The facts of the matter are capable of being rationally debated and resolved, and hence descriptions and explanations can be judged as either true or false. Thus, determining the utility (effectiveness, outcomes) of a programme – whether it is instrumental in achieving its intended objectives – is really the only 'judgement' that can be 'objective' because that assessment rests solely on the facts of the matter. Judgements of value, because they are subjective, can never be resolved by rational means; they will be endlessly argued. This subjectivist position is typically held by evaluators who claim it is the primary *responsibility of stakeholders*, not the evaluator, to make the judgement of value. The evaluator's responsibility is limited to, at best, describing and reporting the various value positions at stake in what is being evaluated and making descriptive statements to the effect that 'if you value A, then B is the case'. Evaluators who assume that their task is primarily one of scientific appraisal and explanation often take this position.

The *objectivist* disagrees and holds that value judgements (e.g. 'X is a good, poor, corrupt, programme') are rationally defensible and that disputes over whether such statements are true and objective are resolvable. Thus, there is such a thing as moral disagreement, moral deliberation and moral decision. Objectivists disagree on the procedure for objectively determining value questions. Some claim that it is primarily the *evaluator's responsibility* to render a judgement of value by taking into account all relevant values bearing on the merit, worth, or significance of what is being evaluated. These evaluators identify and synthesize various pertinent sources of value – for example, needs assessments, professional standards for a practice, legal and regulatory considerations, programme objectives, and relevant comparisons – in each particular evaluation. There is disagreement on just how this synthesis and judgement is to be made. Different procedures are defended including clinical inference, an all-things-considered synthesis that provides the most coherent and defensible account of value, a heuristic qualitative weight and sum procedure, and non-deductive reasoning to develop an argument scheme. Other objectivists argue that determining the value of a programme or policy should not be undertaken exclusively by the evaluation expert but via some kind of democratic procedure or forum in which *stakeholders and the evaluator jointly discuss and*

deliberate the matter of value and reach agreement or consensus. At issue here is the role that evaluator expertise is accorded in the determination of value.

The relationship between evaluation and politics is also contested, in large part, because the 'political' is defined in different ways. A common assumption is that politics is about power, or more precisely the wrong kind of power – power in the form of guile, imposition, partisanship, threat, authority and command. Evaluation practice and its results are surely implicated in this political arena of bargaining, negotiating, and deal-making. The inevitability of this state of affairs is owed to the facts that: (1) programmes are created and maintained by political forces; (2) higher echelons of government, which make decisions about programmes, are embedded in politics; and (3) the very act of evaluation has political connotations (Weiss, 1991). Yet, despite the fact that evaluation practice inescapably brushes against this world of politics, steps must be taken so that politics of this kind do not taint or influence evaluation practice. Thus, in the politics of negotiating evaluation contracts, including access to and control of data, as well as the politics involved in the myriad types of interactions between evaluator, sponsor, client, and stakeholders, every effort must be made to avoid polluting the evaluation process with the wrong kind of power politics. In other words, an evaluation must be planned and conducted in such a way that the cooperation of stakeholders is obtained, while any efforts by these groups to curtail or otherwise influence the conduct or conclusions of the evaluation are averted or counteracted.

In this way of thinking, the milieu and discourse of politics – conceived in terms of norms, values, ideology, power, influence, authority, and so forth – is contrasted with the world of science – pictured in terms of facts, objectivity, and empirically warranted descriptions and explanations. The world of politics and values lies outside of the scientific practice of evaluation and presents a threat to its legitimate exercise of authority and persuasion grounded in information and scientific analysis. The findings of evaluation might well enter the arena of politics and become part of political rationality, but evaluators ought to take steps to minimize the contamination of scientific rationality by political influences. In a nutshell, this is the doctrine of value-free science as applied to evaluation (Proctor, 1991). This relationship between politics and evaluation neatly fits the representative liberal model of democratic theory

(Ferree et al., 2002) in which disinterested, apolitical experts inform public decision-making in a detached (i.e. emotion- and value-free) manner thereby enhancing both the rationality as well as the civility of the debate about a suitable course of action in the free marketplace of ideas.

A different view holds that politics is primarily a matter of practical problem solving. In this technocratic view of politics, the 'political' is paradoxically transformed into an outwardly apolitical phenomenon – a style of formalized accountability that becomes the new ethical and political principle of governance (Power, 1997). In this way of thinking, social service practices (education, health care, etc.) are treated as devices or technologies for engineering desired levels of output. Targets are set for practices to achieve. Evaluation becomes a means for quality assurance – it measures the *performativity* (efficiency) of practices against *indicators* of success in achieving the targets – and it takes on the characteristics of an engineering practice, aiming to exert direct influence on action in social and educational policy and practice by generating evidence of what works (Elliott, 2001).

A third view holds that politics is critical reflection on value-rational questions – Where are we going? Is this desirable? What should be done? Who gains and who loses, by which mechanisms of power? (Flyvbjerg, 2001). Here, evaluation practice is not envisioned as engineering or applied science concerned with establishing the rigour and reliability of its assessments of programme and policy performance. Rather, it is recast as a process of deliberation about values embodied in social action and human experiences (Schwandt, 2002). Evaluators are not neutral brokers of scientific information that informs public decision-making: rather, they are more like deliberative practitioners connecting the worlds of is and ought, politics and ethics, in order to help clients and stakeholders 'learn not only about technique but about value; how we can change our minds about what is important, change our understanding and appreciation of what matters, and more, change our practical sense about what we can do together' (Forester, 1999: 62).

Implications for research design

Evaluation 'problems' do not come ready made, such that one can neatly select a design and set of tools to solve the problem. What comprises an acceptable study design and appropriate means of investigation depends greatly on how the 'object' of evaluation is framed and what one thinks the activity of evaluation should be. For example, when evaluations are viewed primarily as the scientific study of cause and effect, then designs follow standard principles of experimental and quasi-experimental studies; case study designs are often (but not exclusively) used by evaluators committed to evaluation as a form of understanding; evaluation as performance assessment employs a logic that entails precise specification of goals as tangible and measurable outcomes or targets, objective means with which to measure actual performance and standards against which the quality of the performance can be judged. Choices among various means of generating data (e.g. unstructured interviews or open-ended questions on surveys; questionnaires; structured or unstructured observations; archival data; document and record analysis; focus groups) and analysing/interpreting those data (e.g. constant-comparative method; cluster analysis; narrative portrayal; factor analysis) are determined in light of the kind of evaluation undertaken as well as practically in view of available resources and logistics. It is difficult to spell out a definitive list of design principles applicable to all evaluations beyond a list of epistemological virtues whose meaning is only determinable in context. This list includes (but is not necessarily limited to) responsiveness to client/stakeholders' needs and interests; open-mindedness; responsible use of means for generating and analysing data; honesty; objectivity (understood as the willingness and ability to provide reasons and evidence for one's claims); fallibility (accepting that one's claims are always corrigible and subject to reinterpretation); a commitment to making one's study useful and its findings comprehensible to clients and stakeholders.

Stories from the field – the politics of responsive evaluation

Tineke Abma

This is a story about the politics of evaluation and subtle mechanisms of exclusion. A few years ago, an executive manager at Welterhof, a psychiatric hospital in the south of the Netherlands, approached me to conduct a responsive evaluation of a vocational rehabilitation project. The project was meant to assist and train (ex-)psychiatric patients in their search for a meaningful day activity or job. Project participants wanted to start on a small experimental scale in the garden and greenhouse. 'Learning-by doing' was their motto, and they also reasoned that this 'development along the way' might profit from an evaluation. The purpose of the evaluation was not to assess the project on the basis of its effectiveness, but to motivate participants to reflect on their actions and to improve their practice. I considered the evaluation a wonderful opportunity to gather material for my PhD on responsive evaluation. A responsive approach to evaluation focuses on stakeholder issues and a dialogue between stakeholders (Greene and Abma, 2001; Guba and Lincoln, 1989). The approach requires a certain power balance to give all stakeholders equal opportunities as participants in the process. The challenge was how to conduct a responsive evaluation in a situation characterized by asymmetrical relationships and marginalized groups (Mertens, 2009).

Managers and staff

A creative therapist, who worked on a part-time basis for the project, assisted me in the evaluation. The first question we confronted was *with whom* to start. The assistant suggested that the people who were most directly involved in the development of the project should be interviewed first, in this case the members of a specially formed task force. She had the feeling that some members were afraid that their work was not acknowledged, while the manager was taking the credit for it. I took this observation seriously, because I did not want to ignore the *invisible work* of those who actually do the work. Being blind to these activities would be to succumb to the perils of managerialism.

The task force consisted of a heterogeneous group of practitioners with differing disciplinary backgrounds. Including them in a task force was uncommon in the hospital. Usually, projects were developed by a relatively homogeneous group of professional people. They would present their plans to the decision-makers and having decided what to do, the plans would be carried out by practitioners. The manager, who was relatively new in the hospital, considered this a very traditional leadership style. Her motto was participation: 'Involve people and share responsibility!' She liked to emphasize that 'involvement' was part of her participatory management philosophy, and that this also corresponded with the rehabilitation philosophy. In her own words: 'Not an expert-role towards the practitioner or an expert-role towards the patient, but jointly seeking the way'.

The vision of the manager differed remarkably from the experience of some of the members in the task force. We interviewed the staff and their stories suggested that they were not very happy with this new, participatory style of management. They liked being involved, but there were also signs that they did not like it. Some said, for example, that they wanted to be told what to do. Others interpreted the involvement as a delegation of work that needed to be carried out by them but that was not acknowledged. These paradoxical responses did not surprise us, because the message of the manager was also very paradoxical. On the one hand, people were invited to share responsibility; on the other hand several things were already pre-determined. The manager for example preordained the planning: 'The first year to experiment, the second year to improve, and third year to make a 'go-no go' decision'. The members accepted these time constraints as hard and fast deadlines that could not be changed. This caused a feeling of panic, especially among those who actually had to carry out the project: 'We haven't enough time to do the things that are needed to realize the quality we want'.

The imposition of the timeframe formed a *hidden conflict* between the manager and staff, because the available time for the 'experiment' would have serious implications for their work. Compared with the hidden emotional response there was only slight overt resistance and this was only aired in private to a colleague of mine. The fact is that the staff did not encounter an overt conflict related to their self-definition. They did not consider themselves active 'subjects' who could influence the planning; rather, they behaved as if they were merely passive 'objects' that had to adapt to the situations that confronted them.

As evaluators we decided to support the staff by suggesting to them that they should draw attention to their problem. Since my colleague was also a member of the task force she could join the little coalition. Furthermore, we brought the subject up in one of the occasional meetings with the manager. We told the manager about the pressures of time that task force members felt under and asked her to adjust her deadlines to the rhythms of the people who were actually doing the project. Although this idea was at first contested, eventually the manager loosened her grip on the original plans. The negotiations over the planning and particularly the allocation of time to different phases were re-opened.

Therapists and patients

The members of the task force were very eager to know what the patients thought of the project. 'Are they satisfied with what we are doing?' they asked. As evaluators we also found it important to take the patients' perspective into account and wondered how we could make their silenced voices audible (Mertens, 2009). We were very aware of the fact that madness was excluded from society the very moment that modern reason was born (Foucault, 1961/1984). How could we, as evaluators, let madness speak for itself? How could we talk with the silenced in their (silenced) language? I was not satisfied with the procedural rules offered by Guba and Lincoln (1989). These excluded all those actors – young children, mentally handicapped, psychotics – who lack communicational skills, but who in fact only lack the skills that are required in a specific context created by evaluators to succeed with their chosen method. I thought that if one sticks to an 'academic marketplace of ideas', then metaphorical, playful and embodied aspects of everyday speech would be excluded. Furthermore, I was afraid that a rational debate would only reproduce the process of 'othering' instead of emancipating them.

In line with an 'ethics of care' that requires attention to particular others in actual contexts we began to participate in the activities of the group of patients who were participating in the project. Initially we felt like voyeurs looking at people, but soon we began to forget about our role as an 'observer'. Both of us liked gardening and got caught up in the work. We developed a relationship with the patients and their facilitator, and learned about their activities, their lives and their concerns. 'Patients', the facilitator (gardener) said, 'are much more spontaneous in their reactions when they actually do something.' We recognized this ourselves; sitting or kneeling near someone's body on the ground with your hands in the mud is less threatening than a face-to-face situation where one is interviewing the other. One could say that the question-answer method – even if the tone is nice – is always feeding dualism.

The facilitator was not the only one who was sensitive to the connection between knowledge and power. The managers, for example, remarked that 'screening' was not an appropriate word in the context of rehabilitation, because it maintained the *distance* between professional and patient. Ironically, the manager was also the one who promoted the development and standardization of new methods

and techniques to test and screen people. Most of the therapists embraced this proposal under the cloak that it would enhance the quality of their work. We showed them that observational methods also (or primarily) served another purpose: they established and maintained the professional power of therapists who are literally disciplining the bodies of those who are the subjects of these experts. A therapist tried to explain what this meant: 'You create a different sort of relation. I mean, the relation therapist-patient is still there . . . and the patient does not need to be dependent . . . though . . . I have some expertise and that I find important too.' There was still another even more subtle way by which therapists tried to hold power. We discovered this mechanism only later when we confronted them with our ideas about approaching patients.

After having developed a trusting relationship we decided to do a group interview with the patients. This was not encouraged; members of the task force reminded us that we had to take all the precautions required by the law that protected the rights of patients. We felt in two minds about this. We could not bypass the ethical commission, but it was somewhat patronizing that the patients could not decide for themselves whether to participate in the evaluation. While discussing the form of the group interview we suddenly came up with the idea of a picnic. This was less threatening than an individual interview. Moreover, we found it important to meet the patients in a surrounding where they felt comfortable; in this case, nature. Again the task group warned us with the sentence 'They might become psychotic!' We interpreted this caution as a resistance to share power, because asking patients what they think is indirectly an attack on the power-expertise of the professional. No longer would they (the professionals) be the ones who knew what was best for the patients. Therefore, we remained convinced about our idea, and had a picnic. To everyone's surprise the outcome surpassed all expectations. Patients were capable of expressing their wishes and their dissatisfaction once we adjusted to their world and language. The task force members acknowledged they had underestimated the patients. The picnic as a different interaction with patients stimulated reflection and re-opened fixated social relations between staff and patients.

In this story I have discussed the politics among project participants and how we as evaluators dealt with subtle mechanisms of exclusion as well as conflicts. Responsive evaluators have to be extra sensitive to power relations given the deliberate attempt to acknowledge plurality of interests and values and the genuine dialogue they want to facilitate (Abma, 2005; Koch, 2000). In the case under consideration we as evaluators deliberately attempted to give voice to people and groups that are less powerful. Nowadays we even work with those groups in our research and evaluation teams (Abma et al., 2009). Here we conducted in-depth interviews that acknowledge the personal identity of people and created a safe environment where people felt comfortable to speak up. These stories and voices were amplified in the process. The discrepancy between what was said and actually done stimulated reflection on the side of both managers and therapists.

Annotated bibliography

Guba, E.G. and Lincoln, Y.S. (1989) *Fourth-Generation Evaluation*. Newbury Park, CA: Sage.
Although dated, this book has had remarkable influence in shaping conceptions of the issues and practices of a social constructivist approach to evaluation.

House, E.R. and Howe, K.R. (1999) *Values in Evaluation and Social Research*. Thousand Oaks, CA: Sage.
Explores the meaning and use of the concept of value in evaluation theory and practice. Advances a view of evaluation as wedded to deliberative democratic theory.

Mertens, D.M. (2009) *Transformative Research and Evaluation*. New York and London: The Guilford Press.
This book examines the contribution of transformative theory to becoming more inclusive to marginalized groups within evaluation practice. It starts from the idea that knowledge reflects power and social relationships within society, and that an important purpose of evaluation is to help people improve society.

Patton, M.Q. (1997) *Utilization-Focused Evaluation*. Thousand Oaks, CA: Sage.
Extensive explication of the theoretical and practical view that evaluations should be judged by their utility and actual use, where use includes both the application of evaluation findings and the value of participating in the process of evaluation. Also covers other forms of development evaluation.

Pawson, R. and Tilley, N. (1997) *Realistic Evaluation*. London: Sage.

A strong critique of current evaluation practice and an equally strong defence and explanation of evaluation methodology grounded in scientific realism.

Ryan, K.E. and J.B. Cousins (eds) (2009) *The SAGE International Handbook of Educational Evaluation*. Thousand Oaks, CA: Sage.
Coverage of context, key concepts, methods, and areas of application in diverse national contexts. One part is devoted to 'Educational evaluation in a political world'.

Russon, C. and Russon, K. (eds) (2000) *The Annotated Bibliography of International Program Evaluation*. Dordrecht, the Netherlands: Kluwer.
Annotated bibliographies on evaluation theory and practice for Africa, Asia, Australasia, Europe, Latin America, the Middle East, and North America written by authors with extensive work experience in the respective regions. Approximately 700 references are discussed.

Schwandt, T.A. (2002) *Evaluation Practice Reconsidered*. New York: Peter Lang.
A series of essays criticizing a narrow conception of evaluation as scientific methodology and arguing that evaluation practice ought to be redefined as a form of practical philosophy informed by the tradition of philosophical hermeneutics.

Shaw, I.F., Greene, J.C. and Mark, M.M. (eds) (2006) *The SAGE Handbook of Evaluation*. London: Sage.
Some leading theorists' views of evaluation as (social) practice, its role and purpose in society and its application in various domains.

Stake, R.E. (2004) *Standards-Based and Responsive Evaluation*. Thousand Oaks, CA: Sage.
This book offers a balanced treatment of the choices evaluators face in framing programme evaluation in terms of standards and performance or in terms of the activities, aspirations, and accomplishments of programme participants.

Further references

Abma, T.A. (2005) 'The practice and politics of responsive evaluation', *The American Journal of Evaluation*, 27(1): 31–43.
Abma, T.A., Nierse, C. and Widdershoven, G.A.M. (2009) 'Patients as research partners in responsive research: Methodological notions for collaborations in research agenda setting', *Qualitative Health Research*, 19(3): 401–15.

Chelmisky, E. and Shadish, W.R. (1997) *Evaluation for the 21st Century*. Thousand Oaks, CA: Sage.

Elliott, J. (2001) 'Making evidence-based practice educational', *British Educational Research Journal*, 27(5): 555–74.

Ferree, M.M., Gamson, W.A., Gerhards, J. and Rucht, D. (2002) 'Four models of the public sphere in modern democracies', *Theory and Society*, 31: 289–324.

Flyvbjerg, B. (2001) *Making Social Science Matter*. Cambridge, UK: Cambridge University Press.

Forester, J. (1999) *The Deliberative Practitioner*. Cambridge, MA: MIT Press.

Foucault, M. (1961/1984) *De geschiedenis van de waanzin* (translation of *Folie et déraison: histoire de la folie à l'age classique*) [published in English translation as *Madness and Civilization: A History of Insanity in the Age of Reason*]. Amsterdam: Boom.

Greene, J.C and Abma, T.A. (eds) (2001) *Responsive Evaluation*. New Directions for Evaluation no. 92. San Francisco, CA: Jossey-Bass.

Guba, E.G. and Lincoln, Y.S. (1989) *Fourth Generation Evaluation*. Beverly Hills, CA: Sage.

Koch, T. (2000) '"Having a say": Negotiation in fourth generation evaluation', *Journal of Advanced Nursing*, 31(1): 117–25.

Power, M. (1997) *The Audit Society: Rituals of Verification*. Oxford: Oxford University Press.

Proctor, R.N. (1991) *Value-Free Science? Purity and Power in Modern Knowledge*. Cambridge, MA: Harvard University Press.

Weiss, C.H. (1991) 'Evaluation research in the political context: Sixteen years and four administrations later', in M.W. McLaughlin and D.C. Phillips (eds) *Evaluation and Education: At Quarter Century*. Chicago: University of Chicago Press. pp. 211–31.

PART IV

OBSERVING, QUERYING, INTERPRETING

Introduction

This part of the book presents two methodological approaches – grounded theory and phenomenology – which have strongly influenced the development of qualitative research practices. Together with the chapters which follow, on observation and discourse analysis, these chapters build on the approaches and ideas presented in Part II. They focus more deeply on making meaning from human experience and social interactions in relation to different ways of understanding the nature of being (ontology) and knowledge (epistemology).

All five chapters are primarily concerned with observing people, interactions, discourses and activities in naturalistic settings. These data are then interpreted to present rich stories about people and the world they live in from their perspective rather than that of the researcher.

The first chapter provides an exposition and re-appraisal of grounded theory, probably the most influential methodological approach developed in the twentieth century to the analysis of qualitative data. The chapter that follows provides a contemporary re-appraisal of phenomenology. During the first half of the twentieth century, phenomenology led the way in providing a philosophical basis for the use of subjective data and methods of analysis in qualitative research. Both of these methodological approaches place emphasis on interpreting phenomena as experienced by research participants (or informants) in natural world settings.

The chapter on observation provides an insight into how different ontological and epistemological starting points result in the collection of very different kinds of data, ranging from numerical records of instances of particular behaviours to reflexive accounts that involve the researcher in an interpretive dialogue with data recorded holistically. This is followed by a chapter on discourse analysis, an analytical tool used to make sense of human communication through written and oral texts – interpreting and constructing meaning – going beyond apparent surface meanings to uncover the connotations of power and emotion that lie beneath. The chapter clarifies how discourse analysis is not merely a method for data collection and analysis, but a research approach in its own right.

The fifth chapter, 'Researching Online Practices', explores the emerging patterns of social interaction in the use of the internet and online environments in general. Its focus is on how social practices are co-constructed by virtual environments, and on the interrelationships between the virtual and the physical in online practices.

Observation is a valuable tool used in many research approaches, whether quantitative or qualitative. But in Part IV the focus is mainly on immersion in the field, gathering data intensively from a variety of sources in naturalistic – as opposed to experimental – contexts, drawing on the researcher's direct experience and often attempting to view participants' experience from the inside (whether directly or indirectly). Interwoven with observation is querying or questioning, but not only questioning the participants or people upon whom the research is focused.

A crucial aspect of the researcher as data gatherer is the capacity to question him/herself through a reflexive approach that takes account of the role of the self as a research instrument. In order to interpret meaning, researchers need to take careful account of the context in which the data were collected or recorded, and the effects of interactions.

Once again, these chapters cross-refer to chapters in other parts of the book. Variants of grounded theory are often used in case study research (Chapter 6 in Part II) and in the approaches presented in Part III. Likewise observation is the key method in ethnography (Chapter 4 in Part II) and is widely used in case study and the approaches in Part III. Variants of discourse analysis are commonly used by researchers using all of these approaches, and critical discourse analysis is a method for many of the approaches presented in Part VIII.

There are also obvious cross-links to Parts VI and VII where observation reappears as an important method of recording quantitative data and some of the Stories from the Field focus on the collection of observation data within naturalistic settings.

13

Grounded Theory

Juliet Corbin, International Institute for Qualitative Methodology, University of Alberta, Canada

Nicholas L. Holt, Faculty of Physical Education and Recreation, University of Alberta, Canada

Summary

- A theory-generating research methodology
- Symbolic interactionism
- Theories are constructions
- Naturalistic data
- Key terms include: coding; concept identification; categories
- Key theorists and writers
  - Kathy Charmaz
  - Juliet Corbin
  - Barry Glaser
  - Anselm Strauss

Key concepts

Juliet Corbin

Introduction

Grounded theory is a theory generating research methodology. The end product of the research is not a set of findings or a few themes. It is a set of grounded concepts integrated around a central category/theme to form a theoretical framework that explains how and why persons, organizations, communities, or nations experience and respond to events, challenges, or problematic situations. Since the purpose of the research is to generate theory there is no need to begin the study with a predefined theoretical framework or set of concepts. However, a researcher may have an underlying general perspective or belief system such as feminism or symbolic interactionism that influences the questions that are asked and the approach taken towards analysis, making it important for the researchers to clarify their underlying philosophy and assumptions when presenting their final theory.

Theories are constructions (Schwandt, 1998). They are constructed from data provided by participants that is interpreted, framed, and retold by researchers (Charmaz, 2006; Corbin and Strauss, 2008). In fact data is itself a construction and not a direct reflection of reality. External events do occur. But what is important from a researcher's standpoint is how persons experience and give meaning to those events. According to symbolic interactionism (the general framework underlying grounded theory (Clarke, 2005; Corbin and Strauss, 2008)) persons act/interact/generate emotion based on their experience and the meaning that they give to significant events that occur in their lives (Blumer, 1969; Clarke, 2005). In a postmodern world, where nothing is 'real' and everything is subject to multiple viewpoints, methodologies leading to theory development are often subjected to criticism (Denzin, 1998) leading to the question: are theory constructing methods still relevant? The answer is yes. It is difficult to imagine a profession such as education without theories that explain how and why knowledge is acquired, processed and used. Despite its many imperfections, theory remains the cornerstone upon which professions are built and from which knowledge flows. The powerful thing about a grounded theory is that it is directly rooted in the problems and issues faced by a discipline.

Background

Glaser and Strauss developed grounded theory methodology during the course of a research study of persons dying in hospitals (see *Awareness of Dying*, 1965). They then went on to write *The Discovery of Grounded Theory* (1967). Their book was an argument against the 'armchair' theorizing and the 'positivistic' approaches to theory development and research popular at the time and urged researchers to 'get out into the field' and develop theory grounded in naturalistic data, providing researchers with a method for doing so. Later Denzin and Lincoln (1994) criticized grounded theory as a post-positivistic method. Perhaps their viewpoint was accurate at the time they wrote it. However, the grounded theory of today does not merit that label. It has evolved as the 'methodological' mantle has been passed on to the second generation of students of the original founders (Morse et al., 2009), not only in response to such criticism but because methodological knowledge, like any knowledge, advances with time. Today grounded theory is a methodology used around the world. And there seem to be as many versions of the method as there are persons using it – most likely because researchers adapt the method according to their understanding (not always accurate) and in response to the methodological problems they encounter 'in the field'. Despite philosophical differences between the original grounded theorists and their disciples there are certain key elements that transcend the differences, techniques and procedures that, if used as designed, enable researchers to construct valid and quality grounded theory for evaluative criteria see Charmaz, 2006; Clarke, 2005; Corbin and Strauss, 2008). The key elements are explained below.

Key terms

Description is a recounting or depiction of events or happenings organized around central themes often using the words of participants to tell the research story. Description can be grounded and it can be rich and dense **but** description is not theory.

Theory is a set of concepts that are integrated around a central theme to form a theoretical framework that can by used to explain the why, what and how of phenomena. There are elements of description in theory; however, theory takes description to a higher level of abstraction by integrating themes/categories around a central theme through statements of proposed relationships.

A grounded theory is a theory grounded in qualitative data. It provides **one** possible explanation for how and why persons, groups, organizations, communities, or nations experience and act/interact emotionally to the events/happenings/situations/problems they encounter in life.

Coding is the name given to process of doing analysis. The products of analysis are concepts and are referred to either as concepts or codes.

Analysis is the act of examining, interpreting, conceptualizing, reducing, and integrating data. Analysis may be of a large section of data or paragraph or it may be more focused on a word or phrase, a process called micro-analysis.

Micro-analysis is sometimes referred to as line-by-line analysis. It is analysis that is focused on a specific line, sentence or phrase in the data. This form of analysis is not used throughout a study because it is too intense and time consuming. However, it is useful at different points in the research process such as at the beginning of a study or when a researcher becomes stuck in a 'conceptual rut' (can't seem to move beyond standard ways of thinking about a section of data).

Concepts are abstract interpretations of a piece of data. They are words that stand for and represent events, happenings, situations, and problems described in data as viewed through the eyes of the researcher. Concepts are more useful than paraphrasing because concepts allow researchers to group data that have a common element or purpose under the same heading. This reduces the amount of data researchers have to work with and allows them to place similar events under the same heading. For example, a researcher interested in child development is observing children on a playground. There he or she might see some children 'swinging', other children 'building' sandcastles, and still other children 'yelling and chasing' a ball. These are concepts that denote or stand for what the children are doing. It doesn't tell you anything about how or why but does describe their actions/interactions. These concepts can then be placed under a broader heading as will be explained below.

Categories often referred to as themes, are higher-level more abstract concepts that group together lower-level concepts. Many concepts are derived in the course of a research study, but only a few will reach the status of a category or theme. To continue with the example above, a researcher might have a list of concepts such as 'swinging', 'yelling' and 'chasing' and 'building'. At this point a researcher can say: What do I think these activities are indicative of? One possible response is: 'play'. 'Playing' is a higher-level concept because it explains what the children are doing when they 'swing', 'build', and 'chase'. Furthermore, many different activities done for the same purpose can be subsumed under it. Once a researcher has a category, the lower-level concepts such as 'swinging' and 'chasing a ball' and 'having tea' are not discarded. Instead they become grouped even further under another heading, which in this case, we can call 'forms of play', the concept of forms now becoming a property of the category 'playing'. Considerable condensing and shuffling of concepts occurs over the course of the research. It is not until the research progresses that a researcher can sort out which concepts are the categories and which concepts and sub-concepts are properties and dimensions of those categories.

Properties and dimensions are the conceptual descriptors or qualifiers of each category. Properties and dimensions define and differentiate each category. They give it specificity, provide variation and detail, and keep a theory grounded in data. Properties and dimensions also help researchers to identify patterns and establish relationships between categories.

Core category is the highest and most abstract concept of the research. It is the theoretical thread that unites the other categories into an explanatory whole. A researcher might have 10 major categories. However, until those categories are integrated under a larger umbrella concept that integrates them all through statements of relationship there is no theory. The core category is derived from the data and is often one of the concepts that were identified earlier in the research. To continue with the example of the observations of children on a playground, once a researcher has many different categories (all being well developed of course) he or she might ask, what are all of these categories pointing to or aiming at? After mulling it over and reading all the many memos written over the course of the research a researcher might conclude that play helps children develop the physical, interpersonal, psychological and moral skills that they need to function in an adult world. The researcher decides that this interpretation can be

conceptualized as 'Play: Socializing for Adulthood'. Once a researcher has chosen a core category, then he or she will have to integrate all of the other categories and sub-categories (lower-level concepts) around it. If the researcher is not able to integrate the categories around it, then he or she has to return to the data and come up with a different core category that will work to unify the other categories.

Making comparisons is the analytic procedure of examining different pieces of data in order to identify conceptual similarities and differences. Concepts that share a similar feature or purpose can be grouped under the same conceptual heading.

Asking questions of the data is another procedure for probing data during analysis. When asking questions analysts make comparisons such as: 'is this data the same or different from that piece of data?', or, 'what larger idea is this concept indicative of?' Questions, such as who, what, when, why, where and how also help analysts identify properties and dimensions of categories and will suggest ideas for theoretical sampling.

Context represents the set of structural conditions in which action/interaction/emotion are located. Action doesn't just occur, it occurs in response to something. Grounded theorists are different from other qualitative researchers. They are interested not only in how persons or groups experience events but also in how persons or groups respond in terms of action/interaction/emotion based on the meanings that they give to the goals, events or situations or problems. Conditions can facilitate or constrain response to situations and events through action/interaction/emotion.

Process represents changes in the flow of action/interaction/emotion over time occurring in response to changes in contextual conditions. Context and process are intertwined in that action/interaction/emotion as explained above occur in response to context and can be located within it. As conditions change, adjustments in activities, interaction and emotional responses are called for. For example, to return to the earlier example, if 'Play: Socializing for Adulthood' was determined to be the core category of a study, a researcher would want to explain how the actions/interactions/emotions leading to socialization change or take different forms as a child matures.

Memos and diagrams are the written records of analysis and are depictions of how concepts relate. Memos and diagrams lie at the heart of qualitative analysis because there is no other way of keeping a record of what the researcher is thinking or doing as he or she works with data. Memo writing begins with the first analytic sessions and continues through the writing phase. Memos evolve in complexity, length and content over time.

Theoretical sampling denotes data gathering based on concepts generated from data. In grounded theory it is not persons that are being sampled but concepts. To theoretical sample the researcher follows the lead of the data, asking questions about important concepts, then going out to the field to find answers.

Theoretical sensitivity is the ability on the part of an analyst to respond to nuances or implied meaning in the data. Theoretical sensitivity grows over time as analysts 'work' with data.

Saturation represents the point in the research process when the researcher determines that categories are fully developed in terms of their properties and dimensions. This means that categories show variation and density and that relationships between concepts have been established. Saturation is more than 'no new categories'. Categories must also be well developed. Nor should there be some categories more fully developed than others. Naturally data collection can't go on forever and much of what a researcher learns after a while becomes redundant. So a researcher has to make a judgement based on time and money about when to stop collecting data.

Since concepts form the foundation of theory, the first step in developing a grounded theory is 'concept identification'. In grounded theory, the discovery of concepts begins with the first interviews or observations. The importance of alternating data collection with analysis cannot be overemphasized because it is what enables researchers to do the theoretical sampling necessary to build categories in terms of their properties and dimensions. Analysis leads to identification of concepts and it is those concepts that determine what a researcher will look for (in addition to anything new) or the kinds of questions that will be asked in subsequent interviews.

It is important to point out that researchers conceptualize differently and that they might put different emphasis on data depending upon their professional backgrounds and underlying philosophical perspectives. The important thing is not what conceptual names are applied to data but that other

researchers and critics are able to follow the analytic logic that led to a particular choice of concepts and subsequent theory.

Some researchers continue data collection until they discover a 'negative case'. If a researcher thinks in terms of concepts and identification of properties and dimensional ranges rather than cases, the negative case represents one point along the range of possibilities regarding concept. A negative case does not necessarily contradict a researcher's theoretical formulation but adds to the theory's breadth by expanding its possibilities.

Pros and cons of grounded theory

Developing a grounded theory is a lengthy and time-consuming process. A researcher must be willing to work hard and live with considerable ambiguity because at first nothing in the data makes much sense. However, the methodological process outlined in grounded theory methodology does work and eventually a researcher is able to see the analytic story unfold. One of the method's strengths is its ability to explain not only how persons experience things and the meaning that they give to events but also why and how people act/interact/emote in response to their experiences and given meanings. Perhaps the most valuable aspect of grounded theory methodology is its ability to generate concepts grounded in data, thereby providing the stepping stones upon which to build knowledge and frameworks to guide practice.

Implications for research design

Developing a grounded theory is not for everyone. From the onset one has to be very clear that the purpose of the research is to develop theory and not just do description. That said, here is some practical advice for those who wish to develop theory. Begin by finding colleagues or academic advisers who are knowledgeable about and sympathetic to the approach. (Students who do not have a mentor familiar with the method on their committees will have difficulty convincing committee members of the validity of what they are doing.) Next, determine the question. The question driving a grounded theory is purposefully open and broad allowing the researcher to discover relevant variables in the data. An example of such a question is, 'How Does Having a Chronic Illness Affect the Experience of Pregnancy?'. Notice that this question does not specify any variables, leaving them to evolve in the research process. Meeting the requirements of Human Subjects and Research Committees necessitates providing specific information about data collection procedures. This sometimes presents a problem for grounded theorists but not an insurmountable one. It is advisable to write a proposal that is honest and that adheres to the designated guidelines providing an estimate of the number of participants that are needed (it is best to overestimate, leaving room for theoretical sampling). The researcher can also provide a list of topics for possible observations and/or questions, making the lists conceptual and broad, leaving room for flexing the design and updating questions as the research progresses. Though data collection sessions should always be followed by analytic sessions it is not always possible to complete the analysis before going back to the field. A researcher has to take participants when and where they can be obtained and work with what he or she has. It is easier to collect data on a concept while the researcher is 'in the field' but not impossible to go back if it is later discovered that there are gaping holes in the evolving theory. There is another benefit to keeping up with analysis. It allows the researcher to bring interpretations back to participants in order to obtain their reactions. Participants' feedback not only contributes to the co-construction of the theory but also enables the researcher to make changes or modifications to theory as needed (Charmaz, 2006).

It is important for a researcher to keep a journal of his or her experiences, feelings, and difficulties while doing the research. It helps to put final interpretations into context and explain why this particular researcher arrived at one theoretical explanation and not another. Writing a grounded theory is more difficult than writing up a quantitative research study because there are fewer guidelines; however, there are plenty of models available, published in academic journals.

Stories from the field

Nicholas L. Holt

This section focuses on some challenges that may arise when conducting grounded theory and the evolution of my understanding of the methodology. First, challenges related to theoretical sampling and falling into an analytic rut are discussed. Next, a strategy for refining an initial grounded theory is provided.

Overview of PhD work

The two challenges discussed here primarily arose from my PhD work (see Holt and Dunn, 2004). The purpose of this study was to create a grounded theory of talent development in the sport of soccer. Four major psychosocial competencies were identified: *Discipline, Commitment, Resilience,* and *Social Support.* By placing these competencies in a wider framework a grounded theory of the psychosocial competencies and environmental conditions associated with becoming a professional soccer player was created.

Challenge #1: Theoretical sampling

One of the more predictable challenges I faced was recruiting an appropriate sample. Although sampling traditionally tends to become more focused as research advances (Corbin and Strauss, 2008), I identified a specific group of elite participants at the start of the project. Initially I recruited a total of 20 players during fieldwork trips to training camps of the Canadian under-20 and under-17 male international soccer teams. To increase the potential of developing a useful theory, I took a third fieldwork trip to England, where I sampled 14 young players employed by professional soccer clubs in England and six professional youth-level coaches. Overall then, data collection involved three fieldwork trips to Montreal, Toronto and England.

In grounded theory the researcher engages in data analysis as soon as the first data are collected, which helps direct on-going sampling. However, for my PhD study each fieldwork trip involved intensive data collection with two or three interviews per day, so it was difficult to fully analyse data immediately. I engaged in more extensive data analysis between fieldwork trips, but the interplay between data analysis and data collection was limited at times. In fact, once all the fieldwork had been completed I discovered that new questions arose as I became more involved in the complexities of data analysis. I realized that I needed to go *back into the field* but I could not afford another set of fieldwork trips. To solve this problem during the final stages of data analysis and theory development, six informal confirmatory interviews were conducted with older players who possessed professional playing experience in both England and Canada. These players were able to provide alternative examples by reflecting on their own experiences as youth soccer players, and they commented on my evolving theoretical interpretations. Maintaining a flexible approach to sampling was crucial to the success of the study.

In my subsequent research my understanding of the flexibility needed in order to maximize theoretical sampling has been invaluable. In a recent study (Holt et al., 2008) we collected data from families using interviews and audio diaries to examine parenting behaviours at youth sport events. There was interaction between data collection and analysis as we worked with each family, and new families were sampled in order to obtain a range of experiences. Initially we anticipated that the interviews and audio diaries would provide enough data to reach adequate saturation. However, we failed to anticipate that when asked about poor or negative behaviours, the parents we interviewed would almost always refer to *other parents'* poor behaviour – it was never them! Following the principle of theoretical sampling, we realized the need to observe parents' behaviours *during* sport events. This required a new application to our institutional research ethics board, a new round of data collection and analysis, and ultimately resulted in a two-phase paper being published. This example reinforced the need for a flexible and responsive approach to research design.

Challenge #2: Falling into an analytic rut

During the PhD study described earlier, I faced a problem that I described as 'falling into an analytic rut'. In other words, I had trouble theorizing, especially while I was in the iterative process of moving between fieldwork and data analysis. This may not be unusual for students engaging in grounded theory for the first time. Theorizing is based on developing explanations between the data whereby concepts are connected (using statements of relationship) to form an explanatory theoretical framework. But during my PhD I found I was initially working at a descriptive rather than theoretical level. It seemed that I had focused too much on following the order of moving in a linear manner from description to conceptualization to theory building, rather than approaching every step of the process with the intention of developing theory. This extract from my memos revealed the problem:

Although I've got a range of concepts, sub-categories, and categories they don't seem to be coming together. I might be concentrating too much on describing what I think is going on, but

the more I 'interpret' the further away from the data I get. I thought that by going through all the steps in the process, the theory would come together. Maybe I got some of the description wrong (maybe I missed a step?). Go back and check.

Following the recording of this memo I engaged in a circular process of going back to the raw data and juggling certain concepts and sub-categories, hoping that the connections between the data would be revealed. And thus the analytic rut deepened because I was still thinking descriptively. I somehow expected the theory to come together as long as I got the description right. In fact, I realized that I was thinking too descriptively, rather than looking at the bigger picture and attempting to make theoretical connections. Fortunately, my supervisor (Juliet Corbin) encouraged me to use a range of analytic tools to move beyond this rut.

Inherent within the grounded theory coding procedures are certain techniques that enable the analyst to make theoretical interpretations and form statements of relationship between concepts. I fully embraced these techniques in an attempt to break out of my analytic rut. The data were ordered to form a storyline that explained what was apparently going on. Diagrams were used to visually examine relationships between categories. I reviewed and assessed my memos and notes intermittently and compared them with the emerging theory. The emerging theory was also compared with previous talent development research to illuminate plausible connections. Finally, using the comparative techniques of 'flip-flop' and 'systematic comparison of two or more phenomena' (Corbin and Strauss, 2008: 79–80), I compared adolescent soccer players' careers to the career of a lawyer I knew. The techniques helped change my mode of thinking, which subsequently enabled me to move out of my analytic rut, and helped me to develop a better understanding of factors that underpinned the pursuit of a soccer career. The key lessons I learned were to think theoretically from the moment the idea for the study begins, and to use the analytic techniques described above with the goal of developing theory as soon as data collection and analysis begins.

Refining the grounded theory

As Strauss and Corbin (1998) explained, a misconception is 'that qualitative research never "validates" theory. Some qualitative studies do and some do not ... it is a process of comparing concepts and their relationships against data during the research act to determine how well they stand up to such scrutiny' (1998: 24). Therefore, to build on the initial grounded theory (Holt and Dunn, 2004), in a second study (Holt and Mitchell, 2006) we used negative cases to examine alternative conditions that may not have been included in the original grounded theory. The analysis of negative cases may produce exceptions that prove the rule, but they may also broaden, change, or raise doubts about the rule.

Participants in the second study were nine adolescent soccer players who played for the youth team of a club in the lowest professional league in England. The 'level' these players competed at was vastly different to the international and top professional youth players recruited in the first study. In fact, two months after the second study ended, eight players were released by the club. One player was offered a 12-month contract, but he has also since been released. Therefore, these athletes were negative cases in that they were talented enough to be selected to the professional adolescent level of performance, but they were unable to make the transition to professional adult soccer. We also interviewed three coaches to ascertain the reasons why the players were not going to 'make it'. The findings suggested that players lacked volitional behaviour, delaying gratification, determination to succeed, strategic career planning, coping strategies and tangible support. We interpreted these findings against previous research and presented a revised grounded theory of soccer success during adolescence. This study showed a way in which an initial grounded theory could be tested and refined by sampling negative cases.

Conclusions

These 'stories from the field' present what I learnt from my experiences of using grounded theory. Ultimately, I have realized that while some problems can be anticipated and planned for, others can only come to light in the process of doing research. It seems that the lesson is to anticipate as many problems as possible while remaining flexible, reflexive, and responsive to difficult decisions as they arise.

Annotated bibliography

Charmaz, K. (1990) 'Discovering chronic illness: Using grounded theory', *Social Science Medicine*, 30: 1161–72.
This article demonstrates the range of insights and understandings that a researcher can gain on a subject – here chronic illness, using the grounded theory approach. It is also an excellent example of how to write up one's grounded theory findings using a blend of theoretical formulations and the words of participants.

Charmaz, K. (2006) *Constructing Grounded Theory*. Thousand Oaks, CA: Sage.
This book presents a constructivist view of grounded theory.

Clarke, A. (2005) *Situational Analysis*. Thousand Oaks, CA: Sage.
This book takes grounded theory methodology beyond constructivism. It addresses differences and complexities of social life articulated from a postmodern perspective. The article provides another option for thinking about grounded theory and brings it into the postmodern era, while retaining the theory-building foundation.

Corbin, J. and Strauss, A. (2008) *Basics of Qualitative Research*. 3rd edn. Thousand Oaks, CA: Sage.
The third edition is a much needed updating of the previous two editions (Strauss and Corbin, 1990, 1998). It takes a more updated approach to grounded theory while still remaining true to the basic ideas of Anselm Strauss.

Creswell, J.W. and Brown, N.L. (1992), 'How chairpersons enhance faculty research: A grounded theory study', *The Review of Higher Education*, 16(1): 41–62.
This is an example of a theory generated using grounded theory methodology. Again it is useful to study the article in terms of how findings are presented in an article format.

Glaser, B. (1992) *Basics of Grounded Theory Analysis*. Mill Valley, CA: Sociology Press.
An alternative approach to grounded theory written in response to Strauss and Corbin's (1990) book.

Holt, N.L. and Dunn, J.G.H. (2004) 'Toward a grounded theory of the psychosocial competencies and environmental conditions associated with becoming a professional soccer player', *Journal of Applied Sport Psychology*, 16: 199–219.
This article summarizes the PhD dissertation referred to in the Stories from the Field section. It gives a detailed description of the theory that emerged and an account of how certain techniques associated with grounded theory were used to produce it.

Morse, J., Noerager Stern, P., Corbin, J., Bowers, B., Charmaz, K. and Clarke, A. (2009) *Developing Grounded Theory: The Second Generation*. Walnut Creek, CA: Left Coast Press.
The value of this book is that it lays the various versions of grounded theory side by side.

Patton, M.Q. (2002) *Qualitative Research and Evaluation Method*, 3rd edn. Thousand Oaks, CA: Sage.
This is a favourite book about qualitative research. It is well written, complete and charming. It doesn't detail how to do analysis but it does take the reader through the entire research process.

Further references

Blumer, H (1969). *Symbolic Interactionism*. Englewood Cliffs, NJ: Prentice Hall.

Denzin, N.K. (1998) 'The art and politics of interpretation', in N.K. Denzin and Y.S. Lincoln (eds) *Collecting and Interpreting Qualitative Materials*. Thousand Oaks, CA: Sage. pp. 275–81.

Denzin, N.K. and Lincoln, Y.S. (1994) 'Introduction', in N.K. Denzin and Y.S. Lincoln (eds) *The SAGE Handbook of Qualitative Research*. Thousand Oaks, CA: Sage. pp. 1–17.

Glaser, B. and Strauss, A. (1965) *Awareness of Dying*. Chicago: Aldine.

Glaser, B. and Strauss, A. (1967) *The Discovery of Grounded Theory*. Chicago: Aldine.

Holt, N.L. and Mitchell, T. (2006) 'Talent development in English professional soccer', *International Journal of Sport Psychology*, 37: 77–98.

Holt, N.L., Tamminen, K.A., Black, D.E., Sehn, Z.L. and Wall, M.P. (2008) 'Parental involvement in competitive youth sport settings', *Psychology of Sport and Exercise*, 9: 663–85.

Schwandt, T.A. (1998) 'Constructivist, interpretivist approaches to human inquiry', in N.K. Denzin and Y.S. Lincoln (eds) *The Landscape of Qualitative Research Theories and Issues*. Thousand Oaks, CA: Sage. pp. 221–59.

Strauss, A and Corbin, J. (1998) *Basics of Qualitative Research*, 2nd edn. Thousand Oaks, CA: Sage.

14

Understanding Phenomenology through Reverse Perspectives

Angie Titchen, Knowledge Centre for Evidence-Based Practice,
Fontys University of Applied Sciences, The Netherlands; University of Ulster,
Northern Ireland; Charles Sturt University, Australia; and University of Warwick, UK
Dawn Hobson, School of Community and Health Services, City University, London, UK

Summary

- Lived, human phenomena
- Pre-cognitive knowing
- An interpretive science – two approaches:
  - A conscious actor in a world of objects
  - Actors immersed in the world and not separate from it
- Key theorists and writers
  - Alfred Schutz
  - Martin Heidegger
  - Edmund Husserl

Key concepts

Angie Titchen

Angie: We need to understand phenomenology through reverse perspectives.

Dawn: Angie, that sounds like a riddle!

Angie: What I mean is that there are two very different approaches in phenomenological research to look at the same phenomenon. The first approach is direct – looking at the phenomenon, as it presents itself in the consciousness of the people who live it. The researcher is on the outside, looking in. The second approach is to get inside the

social context of the phenomenon, to live it oneself, as it were, and look at the phenomenon more indirectly. Like the way we sometimes understand things by reading between the lines. So the key message I want to get across in this section is that researchers have to be very clear about the distinctive philosophical roots of each approach to enable them to choose between the two (or even to choose both for one study). Clarity is essential because these roots determine the nature of the research questions, the kind of research products and the whole research methodology and design. It's that different!

Dawn: I agree. In my study everything hung on the philosophical stance I used, for example, the observer role I developed. The philosophical stance is like the acorn from which the oak tree grows in all its diversity.

Angie: Exactly. I want to use two reverse perspectives, as a device, to show these differences. The first perspective is holistic, using metaphor and imagery. The second separates out the key concepts through a comparative analysis.

Dawn: OK. Will you start?

Phenomenology is the study of lived, human phenomena within the every day social contexts in which the phenomena occur, from the perspective of those

121

who experience them. Phenomena comprise anything that human beings live/experience. Increasingly, the value of examining the phenomena of professional practice has been emphasized. For example, Dawn and I have both studied nursing phenomena, that is, nurses' ethical decision-making when their patients were dying (Hobson, 2003) and patient-centred nursing and its development (Titchen, 2000).

Phenomena can be *directly* researched by exploring human *knowing*, through accessing consciousness or cognitive knowing, that is, our owned and conscious journey into knowing and meaning-making. Conversely, phenomena can be studied *indirectly*, by investigating human *being*, through accessing pre-cognitive knowing (perceptual awareness, bodily sense or the wisdom of the body). Pre-cognitive knowing that is embodied and embedded in practices is ineffable, tacit, without mental representation or verbal communication. It includes shared background meanings and practices (Figure 14.1). This is where the idea of different perspectives comes in, the perspectives being the foreground and the background of the phenomenon. It is as if the researcher shines a light **on** the foreground (white circle in Figure 14.1 (direct approach)) or **within** the background (white ring in Figure 14.1 (indirect approach)).

People can usually talk easily about the foreground because they have personal knowledge of it in their heads. So the uninvolved, detached researcher using a *direct approach* shines a light on the foreground of the phenomenon to engage in a systematic study of participants' mental representations of the phenomenon as they experience it. For example, the researcher asks participants questions about their rational actions when designing a building, nursing patients, teaching students or whatever, exploring their underpinning logic, intentions, rationale, choices, decisions and so on. The researcher's detached observation and contemplation, throughout data gathering, analysis and interpretation, can be understood by remembering that to shine a light *on* some 'thing', we have to be outside of the 'thing'. Researchers, in this approach, may know about the pre-cognitive background; so much a part of us that it goes unnoticed and untalked about because it is transparent to us, just like the air we breathe. But they are not interested in it, so it remains dark, in the shadows (black ring in Figure 14.1).

In contrast, researchers using the *indirect approach* reverse perspectives and light up the background (white ring, Figure 14.1). This light is shone from

within the life and social worlds of the participants, rather than at a distance. Researchers adopt an involved, connected observer stance and immerse themselves, literally, in the concrete, everyday world they are studying, so that they can better understand participants' wisdom of the body, intuitions, shared looks of unarticulated understanding and undisclosed, shared meanings between the words and in the practices. They engage in dialogue with the data emerging from the background.

Dawn: This observer stance is exactly the one I adopted and it wasn't easy at all! But I must wait until I tell my story.

Another way of looking at this reversal of perspectives is to think of studying the light around you that enables you to see this book (symbol of a phenomenon), rather than investigating the book (phenomenon) itself. Without the light, you would be unable to read this chapter at all and so it is here.

> It is only the pre-cognitive, transparent background that enables us to experience the foreground and know it cognitively. The background is, therefore, a prerequisite for human knowing by the mind.

Before reversing perspectives to undertake a comparative analysis of the two approaches, I outline their origins.

Origins

During the 1800s and reacting to ways of construing the world only through empiricism, German philosophers began the search for a new interpretive science. Their ideas were based on the investigation of the life and social worlds through the study of context and individuals' own constructions and meanings within that context. This work led to the development of two philosophical frameworks that influence interpretive research methodologies today. Edmund Husserl (1859–1938) founded phenomenology, premised on epistemological concerns, so the starting point of his framework is the separation of a conscious actor in a world of objects (Husserl, 1964). This is the root of the *direct approach* in which researchers investigate the foreground of the phenomenon, and so develop research questions that lead to the systematic study of the mental content of

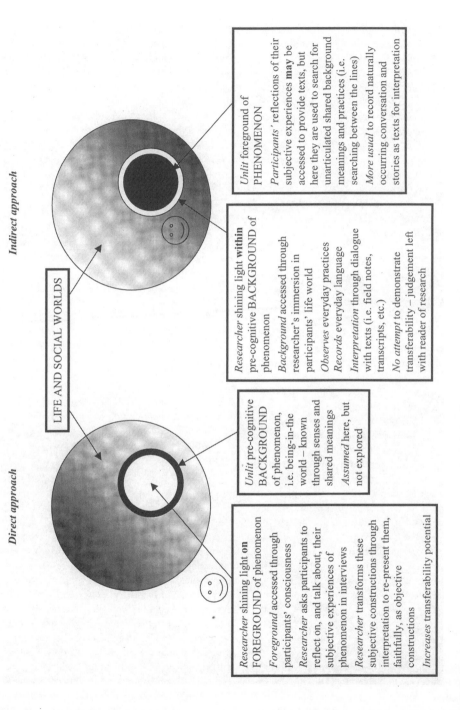

Figure 14.1   Reverse perspectives: direct and indirect approaches to researching phenomena

individuals' inner worlds, for example, Carol Edwards's (Edwards and Titchen, 2003) question, 'How do patients reflect on their healthcare experiences?'

Whilst accepting this epistemological premise, Husserl's student, Martin Heidegger, did not see it as the starting point (Heidegger, 1962). Rather, he saw that we are first and foremost, rooted, immersed in the world and not separate from it. So, the ultimate goal for Heidegger's phenomenology is to deepen our understanding of what it is to be. His concern is, therefore, ontological. The *indirect approach*, used to study the background of the phenomenon, grows from this root. Research questions here ask how participants interpret and make sense/seek meaning of their worlds. For example, 'What is the meaning of autonomy in a relationship between a nurse and an older patient?' (McCormack, 2001).

The writings of Husserl and/or Heidegger are seminal to all phenomenological approaches. They are rather obscure and difficult to understand, but we are fortunate that rigorous commentaries by philosophers (e.g. Dreyfus and Magee, 1987), psychologists (e.g. Giorgi, 2005) and literary critics (e.g. Steiner, 1978), amongst others, have made their work more accessible to us. Neither Husserl nor Heidegger, nor the philosophical giants who followed them, for example, Hans-George Gadamer, Jean-Paul Sartre and Maurice Merleau-Ponty, developed methodological frameworks and procedures for research. This work fell to others, for example, in sociology (e.g. Alfred Schutz, 1970), education (e.g. van Manen, 1990) and nursing (Benner, 1994). Their works link philosophical underpinnings to methodology and can, therefore, help us to understand how we can create our own theoretical and methodological frameworks. Doing phenomenological research well is challenging and a few scholars recently, in nursing, are questioning whether it is worth the effort (e.g. Muncey, 2006; Porter, 2008). Judging by the subsequent utility of good quality phenomenological research (e.g. Dewing, 2007) in terms of illuminating, developing and improving practice, Dawn and I say, 'Yes, it is!'

Reverse perspectives: A comparative analysis

In this section, I offer an analytical perspective on the direct and indirect approaches that builds on the philosophical and methodological ideas above. In a sense, this is another reverse of perspectives, that is, from the holistic (i.e. metaphorical and visual) perspective in Figure 14.1, to an analytic perspective that separates out key concepts. To give focus, I have used an analysis of Schutz's phenomenological sociology and Heideggerian/Gadamerian existential phenomenology. However, the material in Tables 14.1 and 14.2 is also likely to be of use in other phenomenological research approaches (see companion website for further information).

Table 14.1 shows the baseline, empirical and methodological differences between the two illustrative approaches. Note that the decontextualized product (i.e. theory) in Schutz's phenomenological sociology *can* be contextualized through grounding typifications in rich description (see Titchen, 2000).

Resting place

Distinctions between *direct* and *indirect* phenomenological approaches have been shown, using holistic and analytical perspectives. Whilst researchers tend to adopt one or other approach due to the philosophical and methodological oppositions, the methodological distinctions are not as sharp as they have been made out to be. Being fully aware of the distinctions and their implications, I reconciled their differences and used them in complementary ways in my research to give a fuller picture of the phenomenon (Titchen, 2000). Reflexivity, in particular the ability to reflect upon one's own epistemological and ontological authenticity, is key in enabling the adoption of different stances, roles and using different observing, questioning and interpreting methods within them.

Implications for research design

Weaving throughout both holistic and analytic perspectives above, significant clues have been laid to illuminate the design of research using direct and indirect approaches. The nature of research questions and product are summarized in the empirical differences in Table 14.1 and the examples given both there and at the beginning of the chapter. In phenomenological research, having clear research questions at the outset is of utmost importance because the nature of questions (i.e. whether they are epistemological or ontological or a combination) will determine the research design and methods chosen (as shown in Table 14.2). Phenomenological researchers select people who experience the phenomenon in question for their studies and tend to use the term 'participant'

Table 14.1 Baseline, empirical and methodological differences

	DIRECT APPROACH Phenomenological Sociology	INDIRECT APPROACH Existential Phenomenology
CENTRAL CONCERNS	Looking for shared intersubjective meanings among participants Generation of general types of subjective experience	Analysis of everyday, masterful, practical know-how Interpretation of human beings as essentially self-interpreting
CONCEPTS	Consciousness, acting in the outer world, experience, rational action, subjective meanings, meaningful intersubjectivity	Dasein, i.e. being-in-the-world, being with, shared background meanings, involved coping in world
UNDERSTANDING	Rational understanding Verstehen – finding out what participant means in his/her action, in contrast to the meaning this action may have for someone else (including a neutral observer)	Ontological understanding – suspension of conventions of common logic/hermeneutics Background pre-reflective understanding in pragmatic, involved activity Understanding of being is embedded in language, social practices, cultural conventions and historical understandings
LIFE WORLD	Natural attitude (cognitive setting of the life world) which is embodied in the processes of subjective human experiences of the phenomenon Acting in the life world	Shared background practices Involved coping with the world
SOCIAL WORLD	Intersubjectivity 'We-relationship' (shared stream of consciousness) 'They-relationship' (adopted by the researcher because of need for objectivity)	Being with Shared, social, situated way of being
EMPIRICAL DIFFERENCES	Description and interpretation of social action through typification Empirical questions about knowledge and meaning attached to 'inner worlds', e.g. what is the nature of the professional craft knowledge of person-centred nursing? Development of abstract practical knowledge, decontextualized universals or theory, e.g. a conceptual framework for person-centred nursing	Description and interpretation of human being Empirical questions about shared meanings, e.g. what does it mean to be a person-centred nurse? Development of contextualized, practical knowledge and situated, relational and temporal meanings, e.g. interpretations that illuminate the meaning of being a person-centred nurse
METHODOLOGICAL DIFFERENCES	Separation: – subjective and objective – truth discovered through detached contemplation Everyday language as a key to getting at subjective meaning context of individual Researcher concerned with rational thinking of the actor Analysis of data to develop decontextualized 'ideal-types'	Holism: – notions of subjectivity and objectivity abandoned – truth discovered through involved contemplation Everyday language as a key to getting at background meanings, practices, social context Researcher concerned with intuitive thinking; embodied, non-verbal knowing Synthesis according to hermeneutic principles to uncover pre-cognitive evidence

Adapted from Titchen (2000: 47, 51).

for those who agree to take part. This is especially so in the indirect approach because of the stance the observer adopts (see Table 14.2). However, researchers working in a critical hermeneutic approach also invite those people to investigate the phenomenon with them collaboratively. In this case, participants are likely to be called 'co-researchers/co-inquirers'.

The nature of observing, questioning and interpreting from a methodological standpoint has also been illuminated above. Table 14.2 gives a summary of their implications for gathering data through, for example, participant observation, unstructured interviews, storytelling, written reflections, clinical supervision notes, photographs, video-recordings, poems, paintings and music. Data analysis, synthesis and interpretation through an approach (Titchen and McIntyre, 1993) shaped by Schutz's (1970) ideas and a hermeneutic approach, inspired by Gadamer's (1981) 'fusion of horizons' are also summarized.

Stories from the field

Dawn Hobson

This is a story about the collection and subsequent analysis of 18 months' worth of observational and interview data using the 'indirect approach' in phenomenology. The story highlights the great benefits of such an involved research focus for environments where many of the working challenges are not explicit. It also explores the difficulties of such a close integration. The challenges of allowing phenomenological principles to drive the management of a large and complex data set are also explored.

The study formed the basis of my PhD thesis (Hobson, 2003), and aimed to explore individual nurses' engagement with perceived moral problems as they occurred on an acute cancer unit. The backdrop to the study was an inadequate empirical base in ethical decision-making. Existing evidence demonstrated a lack of focus on clinical practice, with a subsequent lack of insight into the encounter between the nurse and a moral question. I felt that this indicated a participative research approach where nurses' intuitive ethical judgements were the focus of the study. It was apparent from the literature that such judgements were difficult for nurses to put into words, and were likely to be hidden within day-to-day clinical practice.

I therefore needed an approach that would preserve the 'voices' of individual participants, by a

process of rich description both of their perceived and embodied values. I found the philosophical approach of Heidegger especially useful in this regard. Studying the involved practical viewpoint of people in situations in order to examine meaning and significance was exactly what I wanted to do. I chose an existential phenomenological approach for this reason.

Data collection was undertaken over a period of 18 months, based on one acute cancer treatment ward at a London teaching hospital between 1999 and 2001. During this time, observation participation was employed to gain access to the everyday experience of nurses on the ward. Informal interviews later explored nurses' perception of ethical issues occurring on the ward.

Access to the 'everyday'

As Angie describes in Figure 14.1, the indirect approach in phenomenology examines the pre-cognitive background of participants, in order to illuminate aspects of their life and social worlds. I participated in the work of the ward to gain familiarity with the everyday experiences of nurses, and also to develop trusting relationships. My own training as a registered nurse gave me initial understanding of the language and types of activities undertaken. I also enjoyed easier access to the nurses' shared background practices and involved coping with the world (Table 14.1). These aspects of integration into the ward facilitated access to nurses' expressed and enacted values, and particularly to the ways in which they attached ethical significance to certain aspects of patient care.

I was interested both in accessing nurses' consciousness of their ethical values and their embodied values. Nurses' expressed values were known cognitively and I accessed them by questioning (see Table 14.2 – questioning). Their enacted values were accessed by observing through 'being with' in a shared, social situated way of being (Table 14.1). In practice this meant hearing nurses' everyday language with patients, their stories told to colleagues, and what they emphasized at key times of information exchange in order to understand what was ethically significant for them.

Gaining their trust

An initial hurdle to becoming accepted on the ward was the difficulty in negotiating access to the real world of nurses and the care they provided. I came to

Table 14.2   Differences in research methods

	DIRECT APPROACH *Phenomenological Sociology*	INDIRECT APPROACH *Existential Phenomenology*
OBSERVING	Detached, uninvolved observer Observation not key method because cannot reliably access participant's subjective meaning contexts Sometimes used to provide: – common, shared experience for discussion in in-depth interview – opportunity, through focused conversations during observation, to get inside participants' heads Naturally occurring/focused conversations audio-taped for stimulated recall in interview	Connected, involved observer Essential method because of required 'being with' participants/sharing ontological meanings and background practices and immersion in participants' life world Field notes capture unreflective activity of others and self, i.e. body skills and ways of being-in-the-world (physically, energetically, emotionally, intuitively, imaginatively, soulfully)
QUESTIONING	Researcher asks open questions to encourage reflection upon everyday experience and common-sense theorizing Seeks participants' understanding of their conscious ways of construing social contexts, situations and logic by which they conduct their activities Prises open the taken-for-granted (doubting) Asks how they judge own situations, decision-making and action-taking Takes open approach to ensure participants dependent on own ways of construing actions/social context Asks participants specific rather than general questions to give closer access to practice and taken-for-granted knowledge (general questions get general answers about theory or what they typically do)	Questioning during interviews and spontaneous conversations helps participants to tell stories in everyday language rather than reflection-on-action or theorizing Questions not aimed at encouraging reflection upon experience, rather at helping participant to focus on stories that matter, have value (thus accessing what is significant for participant) Inviting participants to express and question meaning of meanings in everyday practice through paintings, clay-modelling, movement, drama, music
INTERPRETING (see Titchen and McIntyre (1993) for an approach based on Schutz's (1970) ideas and Titchen (2000) for a hermeneutic approach inspired by Gadamer's (1981) 'fusion of horizons')	Purpose is to re-present participants' own understandings, subjective meaning context or 'first-order' constructs with researcher's objective meaning context or 'second-order' constructs to create a typification or abstract 'ideal-type' Typification describes and interprets way participants made sense of a situation which was either common to all participants or to all instances within one case Seeks to understand participants' constructs by leaping from objective to subjective meaning context – achieved through bracketing/ suspending prejudices and prior theoretical understandings	Researcher uses own knowledge, senses, emotions, intuitions, imagination to understand nuances, subtleties and meanings embedded in texts Interprets meaning of meanings within texts Brings own interpretations, prejudices, 'horizons' to dialogue, dialectically, with text within hermeneutic circle Hermeneutic circle – reiterative process of looking at parts in relation to whole and whole in relation to parts Interpretation is synthesis or 'fusion of horizons', i.e. 'horizons'/prejudices of participants and researcher Artistic expression, e.g. metaphor, imagery, poetry for synthesis of data and dissemination

Source: Titchen, 2000.

the ward with the explicit aim of becoming a participant, and entering a dialogue with the nurses on the ward about their practice. I was not prepared for the difficulty in negotiating a kind of 'being with' research relationship with the nurses. I found that in order to achieve this I had to be willing to do the things nurses had to do, and to share in background practices and the 'everyday' – with commodes, beds, and trips to pharmacy. Only then could I share in the situation in which they were operating (Table 14.1 – shared, social and situated ways of being with). Nurses then began to actively seek me out to tell me of things they thought I should know, or events I should attend. It was interesting to see what they thought was significant for me to hear. As a result I could access what was significant for them (Table 14.2 – listening and questioning). Nurses also began to share their private feelings about particular episodes of care management – often in whispers. In this way, access to the everyday world of nurses facilitated further access to their 'ethical stories,' revealing what they felt to be morally significant.

I took extensive field notes during this period of working alongside the nurses. These involved an account of events, records of conversations, and impressions of how nurses had responded to particular events. These were collated in a qualitative analysis software package, called Nud.Ist (Non numerical unstructured data: Indexing, searching and theorizing). I chose this because it allowed the coding and storage of data, line by line, around central analytical concepts called nodes. In practice this meant that I could first group data around individual nurses, and from this develop further shared categories to build the analysis.

My thesis was jointly supervised by the departments of philosophy and nursing. My philosophy supervisor was a phenomenologist for whom interacting with clinical situations in interviews and field notes was startling, but also energizing, as he came to apply existential concepts to observable realities. He gave guidance during both data collection and analysis, to ensure that the 'face' of individuals was not lost in the pressure for overriding analytical concepts.

Interviews took place with the same 18 nurses I had been working alongside, who already felt familiar with me and able to discuss their feelings freely. I returned to working with them after the interview, so that contextual data would provide a commentary on what had been shared. The interviews provided an opportunity for nurses to talk further and explore areas of concern in their field of practice.

During the interviews, questions and responses were developed and shaped by dialogue between us. I don't mean that I was sharing *my* experiences but that by listening to the answers to questions, it was possible to see their interpretation of the question, and to let this shade the meaning constructed. Questions became part of a circular process in this way. In other words, both through observing and questioning, the participants and I entered a hermeneutic circle and were interpreting meanings through a synthesis or 'fusion of horizons' (Table 14.2 – interpreting); a process that I continued throughout data interpretation. Recording details such as pauses and emphasis in the subsequent transcription enabled this process and the developing meaning to become clearer. As described above, after the interview I would return to working alongside the nurses. In this way a broader understanding could be gained (see Table 14.2 interpreting: first point).

Dealing with the data

Observational and interview data were interlinked in order to achieve a contextual account of individual nurses' ways of being. This enabled the analysis to draw on an integrated understanding of nurses' experiences, where different types of data were interlinked rather than used to critically review the other. The interview transcripts and field notes were used to create a text for each nurse, whereby key experiences connected with ethical concerns were identified. The fact that I had shared in the events in question provided insight into the nuanced meanings attributed by nurses in such situations. The synthesis of nurses' texts led to the identification of shared experiences between nurses.

The length of time spent in coming alongside individual nurses, and the level of access it allowed, meant that the study was able to examine the many barriers to ethical decision-making. Perceived ethical issues were avoided, both by individual nurses and by the medical team as a whole. Nurses often did not feel able to ask questions about the care in which they were involved, and their coping strategy of emotional distancing appeared to contribute to a lack of moral engagement with patients. This finding was a product of having been involved with the life world of the participants (Table 14.1).

The lack of a credible ethical language in practice and the effects of hierarchical decision-making also hindered open discussion of ethical issues. These discoveries were first made at the individual level, and then as the study progressed it was impossible not to notice that they were shared across the nurses, and even more widely to the systematic treatment of dying patients.

At the same time, the pattern of my involvement in the ward began to affect my ability to remain a researcher, as well as a participant. There were costs associated with being an involved, connected researcher (Table 14.2).

Costs of emotional involvement

I had realized that ethical issues were not discussed, and that decisions about them did not appear to get made. However, I was not asking critical questions about this, because having shared so much with the nurses I identified with them very strongly. I was therefore not following crucial lines of enquiry. Instead, there was some temptation to abandon all pretence at research in order to be totally involved and just help out. Writing and reviewing journal entries and field notes during this time proved to be a crucial means by which I realized what was happening. I saw that I was becoming too immersed in the surroundings to be able to function effectively as a researcher.

I had heard and read about the benefits of clinical supervision, and as a result sought to find an appropriate mentor. Fortunately there was a senior researcher within my university who had significant clinical experience in oncology, and was not involved with either the research or the site. This meant that she could remain impartial whilst understanding the nature of patient care on the unit. She listened to my accounts of events on the ward, and reflected with me on my responses to them. This strategy proved to be very effective in regaining a participant stance as opposed to one of unquestioning involvement. It enabled me to plan the focus of data collection more clearly.

Doing existential phenomenological research requires emotionally mature, reflexive researchers who can maintain a critical stance whilst living the daily experience of those they are alongside. Good emotional and intellectual support is crucial. A good research supervisor will provide this to some extent, but further emotional support is of great value in keeping the researcher on the right path.

However, the benefits of an involved research stance, with a focus on the individual's construction

of what is significant, were to lay bare what many nurses felt to be 'under the carpet'. Events taking place in the everyday were articulated for the first time, offering the potential for health care staff to openly confront ethical issues.

Resting place

My research methodology was tailor-made for the questions at hand. I was interested both in accessing nurses' consciousness of their values and their embodied values. However, I decided to locate the study firmly in existential phenomenology because of the need for an involved, connected observer stance in order to access practical ethical concerns. I also wanted to interpret data arising from expressed values, described in Figure 14.1 as 'searching between the lines'. As Angie points out, methodological distinctions can be reconciled given a transparent epistemological and ontological position. Of great assistance in achieving this was my philosophy supervisor, who showed that, by a firm grasp of phenomenological commitments, the approach can be less restrictive and more creative than when assumptions are not explicit. Rather than requiring researchers to read philosophical tomes, phenomenology can prompt them to a stronger handling of the available methodologies for this reason. Using expert help can be a vital inspiration to the process.

The method I used had great benefits for eliciting unarticulated concerns hidden in the everyday. It also had pitfalls for reflexivity during periods of intense exposure to participants' social and life worlds.

Annotated bibliography

Benner, P. (ed.) (1994) *Interpretive Phenomenology: Embodiment, Caring, and Ethics in Health and Illness.* London: Sage.
Provides theoretical and practical support for all stages of Heideggerian hermeneutic inquiry, for example how to dialogue with texts through the development of paradigm cases, exemplars and thematic analyses.

Dewing, J. (2007) 'An exploration of wandering in older persons with a dementia through radical reflecion and participation'. PhD thesis, University of Manchester.
This creative thesis contributes to our understanding of: involving older people with a dementia in research; application of van Manen's principles of human science; and the

use of Merleau-Ponty's ideas in research methodology and findings.

Dey, I. (1993) *Qualitative Data Analysis*. London and New York: Routledge.
I (DH) used this book to help me employ qualitative data analysis software without prejudicing the phenomenological approach.

Draper, P. (1994) 'Nursing research and the philosophy of hermeneutics', *Nursing Inquiry*, 3(1): 45–52.
Gives a useful 'worked' account of one phenomenological approach in nursing.

Dreyfus, H. and Magee, B. (1987) 'Husserl, Heidegger and modern existentialism', in B. Magee (ed.) *The Great Philosophers: An Introduction to Western Philosophy*. London: BBC Books. pp. 254–77.
Hubert Dreyfus, in critical conversation with Brian Magee, lucidly explains the key ideas of, and differences between, Husserl's and Heidegger's phenomenologies.

Higgs, J., Titchen, A., Horsfall, D. and Armstrong, H. (2007) *Being Critical and Creative in Qualitative Research*. Sydney: Hampden Press.
Immersing self in the hermeneutic circle requires us to create open spaces, let go of clutter, suspend conventions of common logic and engage in processes more akin to artistic appreciation and expression. This book could provide a trigger for researchers to find their own ways. Inspiration also for creative research methods.

Krishnasamy, M. (1999) 'Nursing, morality and emotions: Phase 1 and phase 2 clinical trials and patients with cancer', *Cancer Nursing*, 22(4): 251–9.
An example of the sensitive use of a phenomenological approach in palliative care.

Riessman, C.K. (1993) *Narrative Analysis*. Qualitative Research Methods Series 30. Newbury Park, CA: Sage.
An excellent insight into the hermeneutic analysis of interview transcripts.

Schutz, A. (1970) *On Phenomenology and Social Relations*. Ed. H.R. Wagner. London: The University of Chicago Press.
Sets out a system of sociological thought and procedure in accessible language with concepts that can be used by researchers to develop systematic data gathering and analysis strategies.

van Manen, M. (1990) *Researching Lived Experience: Human Science for an Action Sensitive Pedagogy*. New York: State University of New York.
A must read for researchers exploring contemporary understandings of phenomenology.

Further references

Edwards, C. and Titchen, A. (2003) 'Research into patients' perspectives: Relevance and usefulness of phenomenological sociology', *Journal of Advanced Nursing*, 44(5): 450–60.

Gadamer, H-G. (1981) *Reason in the Age of Science*. London: The MIT Press.

Giorgi, A. (2005) 'The phenomenological movement and research in the human sciences', *Nursing Science Quarterly*, 18: 75–82.

Heidegger, M. (1962) *Being and Time*. New York: Harper & Row (1st edn, 1927).

Hobson, D. (2003) 'Moral silence? Nurses' experiences of ethical decision-making at the end of life.' Unpublished PhD thesis. London: City University.

Husserl, E. (1964) *The Idea of Phenomenology*. Trans. W. Aston and G. Nakhikan. The Hague: Nijhoff.

McCormack, B. (2001) *Negotiating Partnerships with Older People: A Person-Centred Approach*. Aldershot: Ashgate.

Muncey, T. (2006) 'Mixing art and science: A bridge over troubled waters or a bridge too far?', *Journal of Research in Nursing*, 11: 223–33.

Porter, S. (2008) 'Nursing research and the cults of phenomenology', *Journal of Research in Nursing*, 13: 267–8.

Steiner, G. (1978) *Heidegger*. London: Fontana.

Titchen, A. (2000) *Professional Craft Knowledge in Patient-Centred Nursing and the Facilitation of its Development*. University of Oxford DPhil thesis. Kidlington, Oxon: Ashdale Press.

Titchen, A. and McIntyre, D. (1993) 'A phenomenological approach to qualitative data analysis in nursing research', in A. Titchen (ed.) *Changing Nursing Practice through Action Research*, Report No. 6. Oxford: National Institute for Nursing, pp. 29–48.

15

Observation

Liz Jones, Education and Social Research Institute, Manchester Metropolitan University, UK

Bridget Somekh, Education and Social Research Institute, Manchester Metropolitan University, UK and the University of Canterbury, New Zealand

Summary

- Ways of conceptualizing the world (positivist; social interactionist; ethnographic; deconstructive)
- The subjectivity of the researcher
- The impact of the observer on the observed
- Using technology to record
- Key theorists and writers
  - Michael V. Angrosino
  - Maurice Galton
  - Clifford Geertz
  - Erving Goffman
  - Phillip Jackson

Key concepts

Bridget Somekh

Through the habit of observation, social science researchers become sensitized to the fascinations of observing people going about their daily lives. An interesting phenomenon in recent years is the behaviour of people using cell phones: as soon as they make a connection their discourse and their non-verbal behaviour become appropriate to the person they are talking to 'virtually', and in varying degrees inappropriate to their physical environment and the people around them. Patterns are easily observable – they nearly always start by saying where they are ('I'm on the train . . .'), and they reveal personal details of their lives and work in a way which often seems extraordinary to those nearby. We notice this because it is new. Other kinds of patterned behaviour are equally easy to observe if we set out to do so systematically.

Observation is one of the most important methods of data collection. It entails being present in a situation and making a record of one's impressions of what takes place. In observation the primary research instrument is the self, consciously gathering sensory data through sight, hearing, taste, smell and touch. By various means of record-keeping, traces of those impressions are stored for careful scrutiny and analysis after the event. An obvious problem is the enormous complexity of human behaviour, whether as individuals or in groups, and the impossibility of making a complete record of all the researcher's impressions. Add to this the subjectivity of the researcher who, at the same time as collecting sensory data, is actively engaged in reflecting on impressions and interpreting the meaning of observed behaviour and events. The record of the observation becomes, necessarily, a product of choices about what to observe and what to record, made either at the time of the observation in response to impressions, or in advance of the observation in an attempt prospectively to impose some order on the data.

Ways of seeing the world

What is observed is ontologically determined, that is it depends to a very great extent on how the observer conceptualizes the world and his or her place within

131

it. For example, if the starting point is a positivist belief that the world is external to the observer, and that facts about people, locations and events can be recorded unproblematically (see Jones, Chapter 23, this volume), the main methodological issues will relate to how to make accurate observations and reduce observer bias. Observation will need to be a systematic, structured process, so that data can later be categorized for quantitative and statistical analysis. A good example of observation data collected and analysed in this way would be the many studies carried out on the length of time that teachers in classrooms pause after asking a question before either re-phrasing the question or answering it themselves. It is now recognized that the pause is almost universally too short to give students a real opportunity of replying if the answer requires thought. This important finding resulted from classroom observations that measured the amount of time taken up by teachers' and students' utterances and the exact length of pauses between utterances.

If, on the other hand, the starting point is the symbolic interactionist assumption that behaviour is constructed through interaction between individuals and groups, and that much of it is strongly patterned, or 'routinized', in a kind of symbolic action-response performance (Garfinkel, 1984; Goffman, 1959) the observer will be looking for – and thus is likely to see – 'patterns' of behaviour. The interpretation of teacher–student interaction given above would then incorporate recognition of the mutual performance that they are engaged in, with both parties expecting students' answers to be short (between three and five words) and given rapidly (without any need for prior thought) and expecting teachers who receive no response to quickly re-direct their question to another student or answer it themselves. This would imply that observation should focus on collecting as full a record as possible of words and behaviours by means of tape- or video-recording and scrutinizing these in a search for patterns. These might be obvious because of their novelty (as in the case of mobile-phone users) or unnoticed until they emerge through analysis because they are embedded in the observer's prior experience (as in the case of teacher and student).

Yet again, if the research is underpinned by an ethnographic approach (see Frankham and MacRae, Chapter 4, this volume), the process of observation will be highly participatory and the researcher will seek to observe in an open-ended way, screening nothing out and noting as many details as possible,

guided by some overarching categories (e.g. the concepts of culture, gender and social class). The aim here is that, through immersion, the researcher will become able to interpret the cultural meanings inherent in verbal and non-verbal behaviour. Analysis of the observation data will then adopt what Geertz (1973: 24) calls the 'semiotic approach' to 'the interpretation of cultures', through making meaning from complexity. Geertz says of this kind of observation that 'the aim is to draw large conclusions from small, but very densely textured facts' (1973: 28).

If, however, the starting point is deconstruction (see Burman and MacLure, Chapter 33, this volume) the observer will be expecting to challenge any 'obvious' interpretation of what is observed, and seek ways of revealing underlying layers of meaning. This approach is exemplified in Liz Jones's story from the field in the second part of this chapter.

Ways of observing

As we have seen, the methodological framework for the research will largely determine what is 'seen' and is, therefore, the key factor in the choice of observation method from the options set out below.

Structured observation

One approach is to structure the observation around a schedule prepared in advance. Schedules predetermine the categories of behaviour/talk that will be observed, and are inevitably influenced by the researcher's expectations, so it is usually best to develop a schedule specifically for a particular research study. Flanders Interaction Analysis Categories, FIAC, is an example of an observation schedule developed as a replicable method of observing teacher and student talk in classrooms with inter-observer reliability (i.e. minimal differences due to researcher bias) (Flanders, 1970: 34). The observation schedule offers:

- 7 categories of 'teacher talk' – three 'response' categories (accepts/clarifies; praises or encourages; accepts or uses ideas of pupils) and four 'initiation' categories (asks questions; lecturing; giving directions; criticizing or justifying authority);
- 2 categories of 'pupil talk' – response and initiation;
- 1 category for 'silence or confusion'.

The observer's job is to 'code' the observed talk by jotting one of the category numbers on an observation schedule at regular intervals (e.g. every five seconds). FIAC is an excellent tool for the purpose it was designed for, but it leads to highly selective observation. For example, there is no distinction made between 'closed' questions which expect a yes/no answer or recall of a fact, and 'open' questions which ask for an opinion. There is bias built into the FIAC categories since seven categories apply to teacher talk and only two to pupil talk and in fact it works best in situations where the teacher is working with the whole class (and teacher talk is more likely to be dominant). In classrooms organized around group work with the teacher moving around the room, researchers have either to make a decision to observe and record only one group, or make very frequent use of category 10 ('silence or confusion').

Unstructured observation

Another approach is to sit at the side or back of the room and make detailed notes. In this holistic approach, the researcher is guided by prior knowledge and experience and 'sees' through the unique lens of her own socioculturally constructed values dependent upon life history and factors such as gender, ethnicity, social class, and disciplinary and professional background. Broad decisions are usually made in advance about the kinds of things to be recorded, either on the basis of analysis of other data already collected (e.g. interview or questionnaire data) or derived from the focus of the research. It is best to record key utterances verbatim, as this reduces the extent to which intended meanings are obscured, and is usually quicker. It is useful to draw a 'map' to show the position of furniture, numbering participants, and recording movements with dotted lines, arrows and secondary numbers (2a, 2b); the time can be noted in the left-hand margin to record the speed of the sequence of events.

Shadow studies

Here the researcher tracks one of the participants, with or without prior agreement (there are ethical considerations in the latter case). The purpose is either to study the person shadowed, or to share that person's experiences. For example, in the latter case a shadow study might be carried out in a prison in an attempt to understand the nature of the experience of being a prisoner. If researchers go into role and

imitate the general behaviour of the group they often attract surprisingly little attention and have relatively little impact on group behaviour.

Participant observation

Participant observers gain unique insights into the behaviour and activities of those they observe because they participate in their activities and, to some extent are absorbed into the culture of the group. Disadvantages include that they may be distracted from their research purpose by tasks given to them by the group, and note-making becomes much more difficult and may have to be done after the event, ideally the same evening. It is also necessary to guard against becoming too immersed in the group's culture and losing sight of alternative perspectives.

The impact of the observer on those observed

Observers always have some kind of impact on those they are observing, who, at worst, may become tense and have a strong sense of performing, even of being inspected. Negative effects are reduced if the purposes of the observation, how the data will be used, and who will be given access to them, are made clear in advance. It helps if the clothing worn by the observer merges into the context and signals equality of status with those who are being observed.

Using technology to record observations

Neither audio- nor video-recording replaces the need to make field notes, since technology only keeps a partial record and cannot replace the sensitivity of the researcher's 'self', open to nuances of meaning and interpretation.

Tape-recording and transcribing

The sound quality of the recording is of paramount importance, especially when recording in a noisy environment. Digital 'voice recorders', such as the Olympus range, are small and light and produce high quality recordings. Those which come apart to reveal a USB memory stick are particularly useful, as files can be accessed directly from a computer. Voice recorders with a noise reduction feature that focuses on the main speaker are good. Choose where to place the voice recorder, since this will determine what is recorded most clearly. It can be kept in a pocket (not necessarily the researcher's) at the most appropriate height (e.g. waist height when working with small children). In order to analyse the data, the voice-recording has to be transcribed: either a full transcription of every utterance, or a partial transcription of selected passages. In the latter case, listen first to the whole tape and make brief running notes of its contents before making the selection. Transcribing is very time-consuming but yields excellent data.

Video-recording

Digital video is very much more useful than traditional video-recording because editing is quicker and easier, and individual frames can be easily selected for display or printing. Remember that the video-camera is pointed in one direction which screens out a considerable amount of activity. It can be placed on a tripod and set up to record continuously, which is a good way of reducing the impact on participants as well as preventing further 'screening out' through discontinuities in the recording. There is a balance to be achieved here, however, as the researcher has more control over what is observed if the camera is manually operated. As with audio-recording, considerable work needs to be done to prepare video data for analysis. The first step is to watch the complete recording and select extracts for detailed study. Video data can be analysed by an inductive open coding process. This requires transcription of talk and some means of recording additional notes of the visual images. There is also a variety of software packages that enable on-screen analysis of video-data. These provide the means for very detailed scrutiny, but the process is extremely time consuming so that often only a small amount of the data can be analysed. It may be more important to work with a wide range of data and opt for a more holistic method of analysis. Focused discussions of video clips (without transcription in the first instance) are almost always extremely productive in helping everyone involved to 'see' more.

Digital still images

A small digital camera, with automatic focus and zoom facilities, is ideal for recording still images. One approach is to use it to systematically record a sequence of events over a period of time (e.g. by taking one picture every minute). There is a big difference between taking pictures socially and taking them for research, so it may be useful to plan carefully in advance what kinds of images will be most useful as research data. It is important that images containing people are not 'posed' but are, as far as possible, a record of normal behaviour. Provided that participants have given permission to be photographed in advance, they are likely to forget about the camera very quickly.

Implications for research design

The approach taken to collecting, recording and analysing observation data depends on the methodological framework for the research. How the researcher understands 'being in the world' (ontology) and the nature of knowledge (epistemology) will fundamentally shape both the observation process and analysis of the data collected. Regardless of the approach to observation, it is crucially important to prepare well in advance. In the case of structured observations, schedules need to be prepared to ensure that exactly the right data will be collected to explore specified research questions. In the case of unstructured observations, considerable thought should be given to the kind of relationship that needs to be established with participants – and how to present the researcher in order to achieve this. This will also involve a number of practical decisions such as what to wear and how much information about the purpose of the research to give in advance. Fundamentally, all kinds of observation involve invading other people's space and constructing meanings from the experience of participating in their activities, rather than through the filter of their accounts about their activities. The key issue here is the well-known mismatch between intentions and effects (e.g. interviewees usually make claims of behaving in ways that are not fully corroborated by observation). This means that the researcher's construction of meaning from observation data is unlikely to match the participants' own constructions of meaning from their experience of taking part in what has been observed. Observation is, therefore, much more threatening than interviewing and gives rise to a number of ethical issues. Hence, it is of the utmost importance to seek 'informed consent' and negotiate a 'code of practice' governing ownership and use of the data in advance of carrying out the observation (see Piper and Simons, Chapter 3, this volume).

Stories from the field – undertaking observations within a practitioner researcher enquiry

Liz Jones

And because the stories were held in fluid form, they retained the ability to change, to become yet new stories, to join up with other stories and so become yet other stories. (Salman Rushdie, Haroun and the Sea of Stories, 1990: 73)

My aim is to illustrate how written observations, undertaken as part of a practitioner enquiry for doctoral studies, became a means for self-scrutiny. In general, teachers who work with very young children, as I did, spend considerable amounts of time observing them closely. Careful observations are the bedrock of good teaching, where current strengths and weaknesses of the children are identified so that subsequent learning can be mapped. Observations in this instance aim to be objective and can be seen as reflections of reality. But what are the reverberations if an alternative position is adopted regarding language and meaning? What are some of the consequences if a sceptical attitude is taken in relation to language and its capacity to tell us how it – including the nursery classroom – really is?

What follows tries to illustrate the dynamic interplay between observing events, writing about them and then subjecting these texts to practices of deconstruction. The consequences of such an engagement can be fruitful, where observations can become 'enabling stories' (Bernstein, 1983) that can be used to: 'understand ourselves reflexively as persons writing from particular situations at specific times' (Richardson, 1993: 516).

A reflexive reading has, I think, the capacity to foreground how certain personal blind spots (Lather, 1993: 91) work at blocking the vision necessary for creative thinking. In brief, I want to enact how one story changed and became a new story . . .

Observing the mercurial world of the nursery classroom

Research for the doctorate took place in a nursery that is part of an inner-city primary school situated in Manchester, England. A central aim of the research was to provide an account of how children's identifications, as evidenced in their use of language, contributed to their own evolving identity, with particular reference to gender. Specifically, this entailed collecting examples of interactions between the children and their teacher, as well as the children with one another. Choosing which interactions to focus on was clearly an issue. Within the nursery classroom the children experienced a relatively large degree of physical autonomy. They were encouraged to take some control over their own learning and as a consequence the children often made their own decisions about where they wanted to be located in the room and the type of activity that they wanted to be engaged with. The mercurial nature of this particular context had implications for the way in which observations could be undertaken. Undertaking Masters work – which was also a piece of practitioner research – had helped to evolve my observational techniques. It was here, for example, I learned never to be without my research journal. In this, rough notes about aspects of classroom life were quickly noted, including descriptions of children's play and snatches of their conversations. Having worked for some time with young children I had also become quite skilled in being able to work alongside one group of children whilst simultaneously being able to 'eavesdrop' on others. At other times the children involved me in their play. As a consequence, there were opportunities to observe both as a participant and a non-participant and, because the research journal had become such a familiar feature – part of my teacher persona – its presence was readily accepted by the children. Thus, I made on-the-spot observations and, at more leisurely points in the school day, added reflections to enrich and categorize the initial notes.

Clearly decisions were made about what should and should not be recorded. To imagine that such recordings could comprehensively capture everything was a nonsense. As Martin and Bateson note: 'The choice of which particular aspects to measure, and the way in which this is done, should reflect explicit questions' (1986: 12–3).

My own criteria for selecting particular phenomena did not, however, rest on 'explicit questions'. Rather, instances were selected where it seemed that the children, through their imaginary worlds, were exploring a range of 'social positionings' (Davies, 1989). Role-play was a rich data source. I also noted extracts of children's conversations where they demonstrated a capacity to move between everyday, matter-of-fact talk to more wishful, imaginative musings. I was particularly attracted to moments that worked at destabilizing my own understandings and assumptions that I inevitably brought to notions such as 'the child' and 'identity'. Moreover, I recorded examples that had, for a number of reasons, touched the ideological and theoretical baggage that accompanied me into the nursery.

The written observations functioned on two levels. First, they fleetingly captured features of classroom life and, secondly, they revealed aspects of myself including particular attachments to specific value systems. Deconstructing the observations helped me to tease apart these attachments and in so doing created a necessary conceptual space where more creative ways could be considered. What follows illustrates this process.

An observation from the field

(Journal entry)

> Lisa and Michael are in the area where the dressing-up clothes are kept. Lisa ties a narrow band of cloth around Michael's head. He then does the same for her. Both children have now become karate fighters. There is no actual fighting between them. Just a lot of posturing, with arms, legs, hands and faces indicating that they are executing some form of martial arts. Michael declares that he's 'Leonardo'.[1] Lisa states, 'I'll be Leonardo's friend'. Michael responds 'Girls can't be your mates'. At this point I intervene in order to reason with Michael. I try to point out to him that as he and Lisa had been 'playing so well together' then 'weren't they friends, so why couldn't Lisa be the mate?' Michael makes no verbal responses. He looks uncomfortable as if he is being told off. He shifts around, avoids my eyes and looks down at his feet. Lisa looks bewildered. I make one more appeal to Michael: 'Couldn't Lisa be the mate?' I move away from the children hoping that by so doing the situation will be resolved.

Ground-clearing activities

Clearly, given the position that has been articulated concerning language and meaning the notion that the above is an unbiased account is untenable. Better perhaps to see the above story/observation more as an invention than a description (St Pierre, 1997: 368). So, what fuelled the above account? What libidinal investment helped in its enframing (Lather, 1991: 83)?

Why did I intervene? I think my intervention was prompted because I perceived Lisa as being treated unjustly. That is, Michael was refusing Lisa an opportunity to be a mate and it was a refusal that was premised on her gender – '*Girls can't be your mates*'. His refusal confounded me because it seemed to me to be irrational and illogical. On the one hand it appeared that Michael could befriend a girl in that they could play together. They could share their collective knowledge of a television programme with Lisa introducing headbands into their play so that both she and Michael could undertake transformations into karate fighters. Michael therefore appears to be accepting of Lisa when she is in the guise of a karate fighter, but nevertheless he is disbarring her from being a 'mate'. My intervention was I think guided by a sense of wanting to right a wrong. However, retrospectively I now perceive my action not as an intervention but as an intrusion. In part, I think my interference was fuelled by disappointment. My reading of the children's play was filtered through a number of adult perspectives, including a feminist one and as a consequence I found it wanting. Michael's particular reading of friendship precludes not just Lisa but all girls. There is of course a certain irony in his declaration because in the interest of reproduction girls have to be your mate. But for Michael, and indeed for a great number of men, mate is the favoured term for a same-sex friend. So what within the context of the play does 'mate' signify for Michael? My infringement into their play prevented opportunities occurring whereby this question might have been addressed. As it was, by truncating their narrative I managed to close a gap that had briefly been opened and which had allowed some insight into a young child's perception of the social order.

The observation illustrates, I think, how both Michael and I are caught up in undertaking what Connell (1983) refers to as category maintenance work. Categories are used in order to impose order on the world but it is a practice that can have negative implications. They can, for example, work at narrowing conceptions of what is and is not acceptable. In this instance, Michael has established which groups can and cannot be your mate. Meanwhile my own investment in feminism prompts me to act in ways that are unproductive, where an over-readiness to intercede in the children's play curtailed opportunities to fathom or appreciate why girls can be a playmate but not a mate.

Tentative conclusions

In general terms, researchers who undertake observations are involved in first looking at 'the field'. Their task is then to analyse: to establish the 'essential meaning in the raw data' and to begin to tame the chaos by using 'the lenses we have at our disposal at any given time' (Ely, 1991: 140–54), These lenses are those tried and tested modes of qualitative analysis that are 'perfectly learnable by any competent social researcher' (Strauss, 1987: xiii) and are, in effect, filing mechanisms that work at organizing and categorizing the data (Goetz and LeCompte, 1984; Strauss, 1987) so that the researcher is better placed to stake a claim for certainty and impose absolute frames of references.

In contrast, what is being suggested here is a shift from observation of the classroom events to enquiry into the observation itself. As such, a 'generative' as opposed to a reductive methodology is proposed (Lather, 1993: 673). Texts within a generative methodology do not purport to be transparent, where explicit findings are available. Nor are they attempts to capture the real. Rather, they are 'reflexive explorations of our practices of representation' (Woolgar, 1988: 98). Moreover, they are attempts at struggling with those boundaries and categories that work at stipulating what it is to know and do. In all, they are textual undertakings that endeavour to dislocate mastery.

Notes

1. Leonardo is a cartoon character drawn from a children's television series *Teenage Mutant Turtle Heroes*. The characters are highly trained in karate skills that are used to ensure that good triumphs over evil.
2. Thanks to Dr Julia Gillen of the University of Lancaster, UK for assistance in developing this Annotated Bibliography.

Annotated bibliography[2]

Angrosino, M.V. (2005) 'Recontextualizing observation: Ethnography, pedagogy, and the prospects for a progressive political agenda', in N.K. Denzin and Y.S. Lincoln (eds) *The SAGE Handbook of Qualitative Research*, 3rd edn. Thousand Oaks, CA: Sage. pp. 729–45.

A comprehensive and scholarly overview of approaches to observation. Particularly helpful in setting out the complexities between observing and the subjectivity of the observer, as well as drawing attention to the ethical dimensions of undertaking observations.

Brown, T. and Jones, L. (2001) *Action Research and Postmodernism: Congruence and Critique*. Buckingham: Open University Press.

Draws upon extensive examples of classroom-based observations. These are deconstructed in order to create a necessary conceptual space in which to think differently about – amongst other things – teaching, and young children and their social worlds.

Galton, M.J., Hargreaves, L., Comber, C. and Wall, D. (1999) *Inside the Primary Classroom: 20 Years On*. London: Routledge.

Donna started school in 1965 and her daughter Hayley in 1996. This book charts the difference in their likely experiences based on detailed research into teaching in UK primary-school classrooms, using an observation schedule. An excellent example of the strengths of this approach.

Geertz, C. (1973) *The Interpretation of Cultures*. London: Fontana. (First published 1973, Basic Books: New York.)

A classic text which is essential reading for those taking a sociocultural approach to observation. The final chapter on Balinese cock-fighting is a treat.

Harper, H. (2005) 'What's new visually?', in N.K. Denzin and Y.S. Lincoln (eds) *The SAGE Handbook of Qualitative Research*, 3rd edn. Thousand Oaks, CA: Sage. pp. 747–62.

Discusses new themes, technologies and practices in the field of visual methodologies – in particular, the status of 'visual thinking' in the sociological community, the impact of new technologies on visual methods, and problematical ethics within the visual research world. Case studies illustrate the scope of visual methodologies.

Jackson, P.W. (1968) *Life in Classrooms*. New York: Holt, Rinehart and Winston.

Provides a good example of how participant observation can transform our understanding of social practices – in this case elementary school classrooms in the USA in the 1960s. A fascinating read.

Rolfe, S.A. (2001) 'Direct observation', in G. MacNaughton, S.A.Rolfe and I. Siraj-Blatchford (eds) *Doing Early Childhood Research: International perspectives on Theory and Practice*. Buckingham: Open University Press. pp. 224–39.

A comprehensive guide to undertaking observations in general but within early years specifically. This chapter would be of particular benefit to the novice researcher as it clarifies a number of fundamental issues including, for example, the establishment of research questions.

Sanger, J. (1996) *The Compleat Observer? A Field Guide to Observation*. London: Falmer Press.

Izaac Walton (1593–1683) in *The Compleat Angler* wrote 'I undertake to acquaint the Reader with many things that are not usually known to every angler'. Sanger's book sets out to do the same for Observation and is full of unexpected delights.

Sparkes, A. (1995) 'Writing people: Reflections on the dual crises of representation and legitimation in qualitative inquiry', *QUEST*, 47: 158–95.

A fascinating paper on the issues that lie behind the writing up of observations. Sparkes demonstrates how the 'objective, author-evacuated' stance of third-person scientific writing up of observations is a rhetorical device designed to persuade, and, as such, as deeply subjective a stand as any more ostensibly personalized style of writing-up.

Webb, E.J., Campbell, D.T., Schwartz, R.D. and Sechrest, L. (1966) *Unobtrusive Measures: Nonreactive Research in the Social Sciences*. Chicago: Rand McNally.

A classic work. The authors organize their discussion of simple observation around five topics: (i) exterior physical signs; (ii) expressive movement; (iii) physical location; (iv) spontaneous conversations, randomly selected; and (v) behaviour associated with time.

Further references

Bernstein, R. (1983) *Beyond Objectivism and Relativism: Science, Hermeneutics and Praxis*. Philadelphia: University of Pennsylvania Press.

Connell, R.W. (1983) *Which Way is Up? Essays on Class, Sex and Culture*. Sydney: Allen and Unwin.

Davies, B. (1989) *Frogs and Snails and Feminist Tales: Preschool Children and Gender*. Sydney: Allen & Unwin.

Deluze, G. and Guattari, E. (1987) *A Thousand Plateaus: Capitalism and Schizophrenia*. Trans. B. Massumi. Minneapolis: University of Minnesota Press (original work published in 1980).

Ely, M. (1991) *Doing Qualitative Research*. Basingstoke: Falmer.

Flanders, N.A. (1970) *Analyzing Teaching Behavior*. Reading, MA and London: Addison-Wesley.

Garfinkel, H. (1984) *Studies in Ethnomethodology*. Cambridge and Oxford: Polity Press.

Goetz, J.P. and LeCompte, M.D. (1984) *Ethnography and Qualitative Design in Education Research*. Orlando, FL: Academic Press.

Goffman, E. (1959) *The Presentation of Self in Everyday Life*. London: Penguin.

Lather, P. (1991) *Getting Smart*. London: Routledge.

Lather, P. (1993) 'Fertile obsession: Validity after poststructuralism', *The Sociological Quarterly*, 34(4): 673–93.

Martin, P. and Bateson, P. (1986) *Measuring Behaviour: An Introductory Guide*. Cambridge University Press: Cambridge.

Richardson, L. (1993) 'Narrative and sociology', in J. van Maanen (ed.) *Representation in Ethnography*. Thousand Oaks, CA: Sage. pp. 509–41.

Rushdie, S. (1990) *Haroun and the Sea of Stories*. Harmondsworth: Granta Books.

St Pierre, E. (1997) 'Nomadic inquiry in the smooth spaces of the field: A preface', *Qualitative Studies in Education*, 10(3): 365–83.

Strauss, A. (1987) *Qualitative Analysis for Social Scientists*. Cambridge: Cambridge University Press.

Woolgar, S. (1988) 'The next step: An introduction to the reflexive project', in S. Woolgar (ed.) *Knowledge and Reflexivity*. London: Sage.

Discourse Analysis

Alison Lee, Faculty of Arts and Social Sciences, University of Technology, Sydney, Australia

Alan Petersen, Sociology, Faculty of Arts, Monash University, Australia

Summary

- An epistemological shift, loss of certainty, radical questioning about the nature of knowledge
- Textualization of the contemporary world
- Critical theory tradition – fields of meaning and power that categorize and regulate
- Linguistic tradition – specific forms of meaning-making (language but also other modes)
- Critical discourse analysis (CDA) combines linguistic and critical theory traditions
- Key theorists and writers
  - Norman Fairclough
  - Michel Foucault
  - Gunther Kress

Key concepts

Alison Lee

Discourse is an umbrella term, with a range of different meanings within different theoretical traditions, implying different methods of analysis that serve different purposes and produce different kinds of knowledge. As Gee (1999: 5) notes: 'any method always goes with a theory. Method and theory cannot be separated, despite the fact that methods are often taught as if they could stand alone.' This issue is crucial to newcomers seeking to work with discourse analysis.

This chapter briefly outlines a range of traditions that produce different approaches to discourse and its

analysis. In what follows, some concepts that are elaborated in the chapters in Parts V and VIII of this book will be referred to, since theories of discourse and its analysis cross over from linguistic and broadly structuralist frameworks into postmodern theoretical spaces of power-knowledge, desire and subjectivity.

Why discourse analysis?

The investigation of discourse has become increasingly central to the task of understanding society and human behaviour. Some form of discourse analysis has become an essential element of many academic disciplines, including linguistics, literary theory, philosophy, anthropology, sociology, psychology, cultural studies, media studies, geography, economics, political science, education, and organization studies. This interest has been spurred by two particular features characterizing postmodernity. First, there has been an epistemological shift, a loss of certainty and a radical questioning about the nature of knowledge. This has led to an increased focus on how knowledge is produced and represented, rather than simply whether or not something is 'true'. Second, there has been an increasing 'textualization' of the contemporary world. As societies and economies become increasingly geared to the global production and consumption of information, knowledge, and human services, so language and other media of representation and communication become primary sites, tools and instruments of social meaning and the exercise of power. Social analysis is increasingly focused on discourse, broadly defined. What is clear, however, is that there are no simple answers to the questions 'what is discourse analysis?' and 'what do I do?'

Traditions of discourse analysis

The growing interdisciplinary field of discourse analysis is informed by three major theoretical traditions or clusters which, in some versions, overlap and mutually inform one another. First, within a broadly critical theory tradition, discourse refers to fields of meaning and power that categorize and regulate social practices and kinds of people. Examples include neoliberal discourse or environmental discourse. Second, within the discipline of linguistics, discourse is used to refer to specific forms of meaning-making (semiosis) that can occur relatively autonomously, pre-eminently language (speech and writing) but also visual, aural and gestural modalities. Meaning-making occurs also in simultaneous modes (e.g. linguistic, visual or aural modalities; see Mavers and Kress, Chapter 19, this volume). Third, there is a cluster of socially oriented frameworks for analysis of language, action and interaction that broadly sit under this umbrella of discourse analysis. These include conversation analysis from within ethnomethodology, rhetorical analysis and discursive psychology. These do not belong to one theoretical tradition and are certainly not primarily critical or linguistic, nor are they simply sites of application of discourse analysis. Rather, they have emerged from within sociology, psychology and English studies as modes of analytic engagement with discourse.

Discourse and critical theory

A critical theory approach to discourse is concerned with how social phenomena are named and organized. Of central interest are questions of the analysis of power in society, how societies are governed, and how access to resources, both symbolic and material, is distributed. For critical theorists, discourses are about much more than language: they encompass all the practices through which meanings are produced and circulated, subjects (categories of people) are formed and social conduct regulated, within particular institutions or social formations and at particular historical periods. The history of discourse within European philosophy and social theory is wide-ranging and encompasses the shifts into structuralism and post-structuralism (see Williams, 1999). The work of Foucault has been particularly influential.

Discourses, in Foucault's (1972: 149) sense, are 'practices that systematically form the objects of which they speak'. Foucault's work on discourse was concerned with the ways in which contemporary practices governing individuals became possible and powerful. Hence he traced 'genealogies' of discourses and the practices they govern in terms of the historical conditions of their production. Though Foucault himself never specified a method for his historical analyses, others have (e.g. Dean, 1994; Kendall and Wickham, 1999).

Feminist and other minoritarian critical theorists have also developed particular kinds of critique and methods of discourse analysis focusing on the primacy of gender in social meanings and relations (e.g. Smith, 1999; Threadgold, 2003). Issues of power in relation to other vectors of social difference, are taken up by critical discourse theorists, for example: race (van Dijk, 1991), national identity (Wodak et al., 1999) and sexuality (Cameron and Kulick, 2003). Central to all of them is the analysis of relations of power, the governing of people and the production of subjects, or forms of personhood.

Linguistically informed approaches to discourse analysis

Within linguistics, the development of tools for investigating what people do with language emerged strongly in the 1970s. Of particular interest was the role of language in the establishment and maintenance of identity as members of groups (including nation, class and gender) and in negotiating social relations. This work in sociolinguistics, pragmatics and discourse analysis used linguistic concepts and categories in conjunction with others drawn from philosophy (particularly speech act theory), sociology (e.g. class/status and ethnomethodological approaches) and feminist theory. Linguistic forms of discourse analysis encompass both written and spoken language, as well as multiple representational modalities (see Mavers and Kress, Chapter 19, this volume). Two significant kinds of linguistically-informed discourse analysis are distinguished below.

Analyses of spoken language are the most technical, requiring formal training. Work in these traditions investigates spoken interactive language, including media interviews, everyday spoken interaction and classroom talk. Schiffrin (1994) outlines six approaches (including speech act theory, ethnography of communication and pragmatics). In practice, much discourse-analytic research works across these boundaries rather than simply within them. In particular, conversation analysis (CA), developed in the framework of ethnomethodology (see below), has been influential in a range of different approaches (see Cameron, 2001).

Critical discourse analysis (CDA) works with both spoken and written language and combines linguistic and critical theory approaches. Many CDA practitioners (e.g. Fairclough, 2005) have a particular interest in 'public' texts such as print media, policy and bureaucratic documents. The approach can also be used for more privately circulating texts such as email. CDA is often described as 'critical and hermeneutic'; its detailed analytic methods, however, emerged from linguistics, in particular the critical linguistic and social semiotic work of Halliday (1985; Halliday and Hasan, 1985) and those working from his framework (e.g. Kress, Hodge, Fairclough, van Leeuwen) and from European sociolinguistics, notably van Dijk and Wodak. CDA focuses on ideological, institutional and social perspectives in discourse and its theoretical frames are a synthesis of the critical theory of the Frankfurt School, neomarxism and post-structuralism. What is 'critical' in this work is the political and social commitment brought to the analysis of unequal power relations and possibilities for social transformation (see Blommaert, 2005; Luke, 2002; Phillips and Jorgensen, 2002).

Sociological, psychological and rhetorical traditions

A third cluster of theoretical traditions growing up alongside, but somewhat independently of, critical theory and linguistics, have in common a focus on the psycho-social-interactive dimensions of discourse. From within the sociology of scientific knowledge, a distinctive set of approaches to discourse analysis has grown that has taken hold in fields such as discursive psychology and interactionist sociology. This work has also been influenced by ethnomethodology, based on the seminal work of Garfinkel and Sacks. Analytic approaches of particular note here are conversation analysis (CA) and membership categorization analysis (MCA) (see Wooffitt (2005) for an overview of both). Some of the most accessible and influential texts on discourse analysis and conversation draw on these traditions (see Davies and Harré, 1990; Wetherell et al., 2001). The analytic tradition known as rhetorical analysis, based largely in North America, focuses on discourse as social action and attends to the pragmatic force of genres and interactions (see Bazerman and Prior, 2004). This cluster, taken together, is often known as 'psycho-socio-linguistics' (Davies and Harré, 1990). It merits attention here because these traditions have produced some of the most widely read introductory textbooks on discourse analysis (see e.g. Phillips and Jorgensen, 2002).

Navigating the terrain

While each of these traditions has a disciplinary 'home', with a set of theoretical assumptions about the nature of knowledge and research, in practice, contemporary discourse-analytic research is interdisciplinary. A challenge for researchers is to become able to 'read' the methods and procedures of particular traditions or interdisciplinary mixes of traditions in terms of the kind of knowledge they will produce. Furthermore, if a researcher understands what they want to achieve through their research, and is aware of the possibilities and limitations of particular approaches, then their choice of method will produce a useful result. Discourse analysis can usefully complement and supplement other methods in social research, provided there is a coherent theoretical framing for the study.

A common problem for researchers new to discourse analysis is to find themselves bewildered by the amount and diversity of literature dedicated to introducing discourse-analytic methods. It is difficult to manage the differences as well as the relationships among critical theory, linguistic, ethnomethodological, psychological or rhetorical conceptions of discourse in the literature. Different theoretical traditions encompass different conceptions of discourse, and so both the *object* and the *unit* of analysis will be different.

The *object* of analysis refers to how a research problem within that topic is defined and focused. Different traditions of discourse analysis define problems differently and produce different objects for analysis. Within a broad research topic, for example literacy testing, objects for analysis will be constituted differently. The research problem within a Foucault-influenced critical theory framework would typically be how power operates through a particular literacy discourse to produce objects (e.g. tests, school league tables) that have certain effects in the distribution of material resources and the constitution of categories of people such as high scorers or successful schools. Within linguistic frameworks, the problem will be defined in terms of how language operates in discourse to produce meanings and social relations. The objects will be texts, written or transcribed spoken discourse, here the actual literacy tests, or instructions, or transcribed testing processes, and so on. Within ethnomethodological frameworks the problem is to understand how testing is accomplished interactively, and so the objects will typically be audio- or video-recorded instances of interactions around the actions of testing.

The *unit* of analysis refers to how data are generated and analysed in terms of scale, timeframe, degree of technicality and so on. Critical theory traditions are typically more theory-driven, so not highly technical in terms of the units and methods of analysis, and explicitly concerned with social and historical specificity. For example, a focus of analysis in literacy testing might be to identify 'subjects' – kinds of people with high or low literacy scores – and actions – streaming, remediation, career advice – that are the effects of literacy testing within particular historical and social circumstances.

A linguistically-based analysis would typically take as its units of analysis the lexical and grammatical features of relevant material such as tests, theoretical and policy documents, and the interactions between testers and the tested. Critical discourse analysis (CDA) would focus on the ways power operates within and among texts to reproduce or transform social inequalities. Units of analysis typically remain smaller-scale, with different degrees of technicality, as specified in different versions, including modality and inter-textuality (e.g. Fairclough, 2005; see Lee and Otsuji, 2009 for a critical review). Ethnomethodological analysis will focus on how literacy testing is accomplished *in situ* in the actions and interactions among participants; units of analysis include turn-taking and the negotiation of categories. Rhetorical analysis is interested in the activities and activity systems in which the tests operate and how they form part of larger systems of meaning and action. Units of analysis range from classical rhetorical functions such as how participants address each other, to the analysis of specific genres of speech, writing and action.

Implications for research design

As demonstrated above, discourse-analytic research is strongly framed by theory and by purpose. Theory shapes the definition of the problem and the constitution of the object of inquiry, and it influences, though does not determine, the units of analysis.

Within critical theory traditions, for example, it is common to find close attention to linguistic features of texts or interactions, drawing on linguistic units such as grammar. CDA draws on critical theory as well as having specific sets of methods and units of analysis for examining particular texts, as described above. As anything in principle can be subjected to discursive analysis, it is the particular purpose to which the analysis is to be put that will shape a research question (and hence the object of analysis) and determine the focus of data collection and the units and methods of analysis. However, while the research question is central for achieving focus, the nature of the analysis may change through the course of the research, through reflexive and iterative processes of review.

Discourse analysis is often textually focused and can involve the analysis of existing documents without the engagement of active participants. Often discourse-analytic social research involves a range of documentary and interactive forms of data collection. It is often deployed as a method of data analysis within broader social research methodologies, such as case studies and ethnographies. Sampling and selection of participants in that case would follow the principles of those research traditions. Similarly, these methodologies will shape the kinds of relationships with participants, including co-researching and co-analysing data.

A potential trap for novice researchers in blending discourse-analytic methods with other qualitative research approaches, however, lies in the assumption that these methods are merely technical and can be applied within broader interpretive frames. Too often the selection of methods for data analysis is left until too late in the design process and studies can become tangled in an unsatisfactory blend of interpretive and descriptive methods. Elements named as 'discourses' can often look uncannily like 'themes' or 'topics' in an interpretive study, unless the researcher is working with a conception of discourse clearly located within a coherent theoretical framework.

The methods used for discourse-analytic research are numerous and varied, ranging from quite abstract ideas of discourses as historically produced systems of meaning and power (in critical theory approaches) down to the close lexical or grammatical analysis of written or transcribed texts (within linguistics) or the fine-grained analysis of technically nuanced transcriptions of interactive data (within ethnomethodological conversation analysis) and so on. This is where textbooks offer a useful guide to the development of a range of possible methods but always guided by a theoretical frame and a focused research question. Knowledge outcomes are similarly varied, though what all discourse-analytic traditions have in common is a focus on how meanings are made and enacted in social contexts and situations, rather than looking through texts and language to meanings that reside elsewhere, in people's minds or intentions or in social structures. In this way discourse-analytic research is always reflexive, more or less, as it draws attention to the systems and resources for representation and for human meaning and action.

Stories from the field

Alan Petersen

My work is motivated by theoretical and political concerns, rather than by the desire to use a particular method or methods. I use whatever methods I believe are appropriate for the problem or issue at hand. My discourse analysis (DA) work has focused on news media portrayals of genetics and medicine, on assumptions about sex or gender differences in documents produced for a specific readership, and on discourses pertaining to medicine and public health. I have explored how assumptions are manifest in texts and how a particular use of language may serve to make these assumptions seem natural. My empirical materials have included a range of texts, including newspaper articles, anatomical texts, psychological journal articles, and various expert documents: for example government reports, health promotion literature. Depending on the particular question(s) explored, I may focus on the use of rhetorical devices, the narrative structure, the inclusion of quotations or citations and of drama (in the case of news), the positioning of text relative to other items, and the use of accompanying illustrative material.

Although I have undertaken a great deal of DA-related work, I have never found DA to be straightforward. Although some scholars see DA as an easy research methods option, there is rarely a clearly defined path for the researcher. This is a contested area and there are no blueprints as to how 'best' to proceed. Subjective evaluations impinge on every stage of the research process. In my experience, every new project requires one to rethink the issue of methods: how they relate to the aims and research questions, what empirical resources are likely to be

most useful or illuminating, and how to 'operationalize' concepts (i.e. put them in a form that can be measured). DA has proved particularly valuable in my recent work on news media portrayals of genetics and medicine, which I will focus on here.

In recent years, versions of DA have been used by a number of scholars in analysing the portrayal of medical genetics issues in news media and other popular cultural texts. The rise of public interest in genetics in the 1990s corresponded with media interest in the Human Genome Project and, later, its 'race' with the rival Celera to map the human genome. I was following some of the debates in newspapers about discoveries of 'genes for' X, Y, and Z, and, in light of what seemed to be a kind of genetic determinism in these reports, I believed it would be interesting and useful to examine news reports in detail. Coming from a background in the sociology of health and illness, my concerns were informed by sociological questions about the formation of public discourse. That is, I was interested in how a particular 'framing' of issues may shape public responses to the issues being reported and thus potentially shape public policies. When I commenced study in this field, I had only a few writers as guides to the kinds of questions worth pursuing and how DA might 'work' in practice in relation to news media. However, I had developed some relevant expertise and insights through earlier research into the portrayal of research into genetic-based differences of sex and sexual orientation in 'popular' science journals (see Petersen, 1999).

My research materials included a national broadsheet newspaper (*The Australian*) and two state-based tabloid newspapers (*The Sydney Morning Herald* and *The West Australian*). Because these newspapers are owned by different proprietors, I felt that they were less likely to share news stories than newspapers that are owned by the same proprietors. They also have different format styles, being oriented to different audiences and, as I discovered, had somewhat different ways of presenting medical genetics issues. I located news articles for these newspapers via a news monitoring service. One can now do this more easily online, via Newsbank and Lexus-Nexus (though these sources don't include accompanying illustrative material and sometimes don't include page numbers), and these I find useful when making assessments about the prominence and framing of issues. As a first step, I made note of the location of articles in the newspapers: on what page they appeared, where they were positioned relative to other articles, and whether they appeared in special sections (e.g. 'Health and Medicine'). I found that for all three newspapers, a large proportion of articles on genetics and medicine appeared in the first three pages, and the majority in the first ten pages, which suggested that these stories were seen by editors as highly 'newsworthy'.

 Besides positioning, I also made a note of the type of news items (article, editorial, opinion pieces, letters to the editor), and of the amount and kind of detail presented. I also recorded details of the authorship of articles – whether they were written by journalists, scientists, bio-ethicists, or other writers – and of any evidence of authors' efforts to verify information and to present alternative or disconfirming information. Finally, I made a note of the news source(s), if this was stated. Again, such information was useful in assessing how stories were 'framed'. As I discovered, news stories did not always include details on the professional identity of writers. Consequently I was unable to draw firm conclusions about the impact of the author type on the content and style of stories. In *The Australian* and *SMH*, regular contributors of articles were sometimes described as either 'medical writer', 'science writer', or 'science correspondent'; however, in all three newspapers, such descriptions often did not appear in articles. In some articles, most notably in *The Australian*, only the news agency (e.g. Reuters, AFP, AP, or AAP) or another newspaper (e.g. *The Sunday Times, The Times*) that was the source for the news was cited. In others, most evidently in *The West*, neither the writer's name nor a news agency source appeared in the article.

 I read and then re-read each news item, taking note of use of titles, sub-titles, and of accompanying illustrative material that helped attract readers' attention and shape the portrayal of stories, and of words, phrases, metaphors that imported particular images and associations. I made note of themes and sub-themes, and recorded who was cited or quoted in stories. I discovered that in many articles the scientists themselves were often cited or quoted, which allowed them to place a particular interpretation on research and its implications. Quotations or citations from experts lent credibility to stories by conveying the impression that information was straight from the expert's mouth, and hence irrefutable.

 Many articles relied heavily on the scientist's own descriptions and generally positive evaluations of research and its significance. Since no other alternative information was presented, there was little reason

for the reader to doubt the veracity of the scientist's claims. The use of quotes from experts is an important element in the framing of news stories on medical genetics. I discovered that scientists frequently use terms such as the 'killer cells' and analogies such as 'prospecting' in describing research which provided insight into how scientists may seek to 'popularize' scientific information for lay readers and emphasize the significance of their work. The research literature on science news production suggests that there are 'two cultures' of science and journalism and that this may lead to misunderstanding between scientists and journalists about the role of news reporting. One influential perspective on the production of science news, the so-called 'popularization' model, suggests that scientists generate objective knowledge which is then popularized for lay readers or audiences by the use of simple language, particular metaphors and rhetorical devices. It is argued that this may lead to the distortion or misrepresentation of science fact. However, along with other recent research, my own work suggests that this model, although useful, is too simplistic and does not take account of the more subtle ways in which scientists may seek to influence the media portrayal of science through, for example, the use of popular metaphors and the promotion of positive images of science and its applications.

 I found that good news stories and stories about discovery figure prominently in medical genetics news and that stories tend to neglect non-genetic and 'multifactorial' explanations of disease, thereby tending to convey an over optimistic impression of the potential of genetics. The frequent use of particular metaphors such as those of the book, map, and code help to convey the nature and significance of research. For example, in one article a scientist is cited as saying that 'the new screening technique complemented black and white strips of DNA resembling bar codes used on shopping centre goods'. He is also quoted as saying, '*Without the maps you do not know where to go . . .* They have immediate applications in clinical work where *the colour bar codes* can identify changes or rearrangements in the chromosomes' (*The West*, 25 July 1997: 10, my italics). Military metaphors were also common and reinforce an image of scientists as heroes who are pitted against an evil enemy (a 'killer disease') which is seen to threaten the public's health. For example, an article, 'Resistance to drugs cracks' announced that '*Genetic scientists are on the verge of defeating life-threatening organisms* that have developed strong resistance to conventional antibiotics . . .' (*The Weekend Australian*, 18–19 July 1998: 40, my italics). It was not always easy, however, to determine who originally introduced a particular metaphor – whether it was the scientist who was originally cited or quoted, or the journalist who wrote the story. This is something that would need to be explored through further research, by talking to quoted/cited scientists and journalists, and perhaps editors.

I found that news reports of medical genetics are not always unequivocally positive. The nature of portrayals depends on the nature of the issue. In my study of medical genetics news, and also in a related project on news media portrayals of cloning in the wake of Dolly the sheep, I have discovered a recurring tension between utopian and dystopian themes and images of genetics, particularly in relation to reproductive issues (see Petersen, 2001, 2002). Public reaction to Dolly, which reflected concerns about the applications of cloning technology to humans, led many scientists to make extensive use of the media to defend and explain their work. The torrent of news articles on cloning in the months after the announcement of Dolly made considerable reference to the views and predictions of scientists, who extolled the medical virtues of cloning research, and emphasized the distinction between 'therapeutic cloning' and 'reproductive cloning'. As this research revealed, following the unfolding news stories of genetics and medicine over an extended period of time allows one to identify themes and patterns in styles of reporting that are unlikely to be evident within a short timeframe.

While DA is very useful in revealing how news issues are portrayed, it doesn't tell us much about the social processes of news production, or about how readers engage with stories. One needs to 'get behind the news' and talk to journalists, editors, and sources to understand why certain issues get reported and how they are portrayed. And one needs to develop methods for studying how readers interact with, interpret and use information gleaned from news media in order to assess the impacts of stories. DA, however, can provide a useful starting point for exploring processes of news production and news reception. For me, the application of DA methods in the analysis of news media has proved extremely fruitful. It has generated new questions, and opened up new avenues for exploration, which is what all research should be about.

Annotated bibliography

Bazerman, C., and Prior, P.A. (eds) (2004) *What Writing Does and How It Does It: An Introduction to Analyzing Texts and Textual Practices*. Mahwah, NJ: Lawrence Erlbaum.
An overview and practical guide to working within rhetorical, narrative and linguistic analysis traditions.

Cameron, D. (2001) *Working with Spoken Discourse*. London: Sage.
A wide-ranging account of methods of analysing spoken language from one who identifies as a linguist but is familiar with work in the critical tradition.

Fairclough, N. (2005) 'Critical Discourse Analysis', *Marges Linguistiques*, 9: 76–94.
A succinct overview of Fairclough's methodology, which entails three stages of analysis: description, interpretation and explanation. These stages exist within a three-dimensional conception for analysis: analysis of discursive practices (processes of text production, distribution and consumption); text (grammar, vocabulary, cohesion and text structure); and social practices (ideological effect and hegemonic process of discourse).

Kendall, G. and Wickham, G. (1999) *Using Foucault's Methods*. London: Sage.
A practical guide to begin the process of working within Foucault's theoretical frameworks.

Luke, A. (2002) 'Beyond science and ideology critique: developments in critical discourse analysis', *Annual Review of Applied Linguistics*, 22: 96–110.
A scholarly and wide-ranging critical account of the theoretical underpinnings of CDA, including a discussion of theoretical limitations and challenges.

Phillips, L. and Jorgensen, M. (2002) *Discourse Analysis as Theory and Method*. London: Sage.
Useful account of three traditions: discourse theory in the European tradition, CDA, and discursive psychology, discussing how they are theoretically distinct yet inter-related. This book attempts to integrate these into a methodological framework for a critical practice of discourse analysis.

Wetherell, M., Taylor, S. and Yates, S.J. (eds) (2001) *Discourse as Data: A Guide for Analysis*. London: Sage.
Practical discussion of six different approaches to discourse analysis with a focus on the kinds of data produced within different traditions. See Carabine's chapter for a practical example of genealogical analysis.

Williams, G. (1999) *French Discourse Analysis: The Method of Post-structuralism*. London and New York: Routledge.

A complex but comprehensive discussion of a broad range of theoretical issues involved in undertaking discourse-analytic research in post-structuralist traditions.

Wooffitt, R. (2005) *Conversation Analysis and Discourse Analysis: A Comparative and Critical Introduction*. London: Sage.

A useful two-part account of conversation analysis within ethnomethodology and discourse analysis within sociolinguistics. Wooffitt categorizes discourse analysis narrowly within linguistics, draws a distinction with ethnomethodological traditions of CA and compares the two. This distinction differs from the broader conception of discourse analysis outlined in this chapter.

Further references

Blommaert, J. (2005) *Discourse: A Critical Introduction*. Cambridge: Cambridge University Press.

Cameron, D. and Kulick, D. (2003. *Language and Sexuality*. Cambridge: Cambridge University Press.

Davies, B. and Harré, R. (1990) 'Positioning: The discursive production of selves', *Journal for the Theory of Social Behaviour*, 20(1): 43–63.

Dean, M. (1994) *Critical and Effective Histories: Foucault's Methods and Historical Sociology*. London: Routledge.

Foucault, M. (1972) *The Archaeology of Knowledge*. Trans. Alan Sheridan. London: Tavistock Publications.

Gee, J.P. (1999) *An Introduction to Discourse Analysis: Theory and Method*. London: Routledge.

Halliday, M.A.K. (1985) *Spoken and Written Language*. Geelong, Australia: Deakin University Press.

Halliday, M.A.K. and Hasan, R. (1985) *Language, Context and Text: Aspects of Language in a Social-Semiotic Perspective*. Geelong, Australia: Deakin University Press.

Lee, A. and Otsuji, E. (2009) 'CDA and the problem of methodology', in T. Lê, Q. Lê and M. Short (eds) *Critical Discourse Analysis: An Interdisciplinary Perspective*. New York: Nova Science Publishing.

Petersen, A. (1999) 'The portrayal of research into genetic-based differences of sex and sexual orientation: a study of "popular" science journals, 1980 to 1997', *Journal of Communication Inquiry*, 23(2): 163–82.

Petersen, A. (2001) 'Biofantasies: genetics and medicine in the print news media', *Social Science and Medicine*, 52(8): 1255–68.

Petersen, A. (2002) 'Replicating our bodies, losing our selves: News media portrayals of human cloning in the wake of Dolly', *Body and Society*, 8(4): 71–90.

Schiffrin, D. (1994) *Approaches to Discourse*. Oxford: Basil Blackwell.

Smith, D (1999) *Writing the Social: Critique, Theory and Investigations*. Toronto: University of Toronto Press.

Threadgold, T. (2003) 'Cultural studies, critical theory and critical discourse analysis: histories, remembering and futures', *Linguistik Online*, 14(2). http://www.linguistik-online.de/14_03/index.html

van Dijk, T.A. (1991) *Racism and the Press*. London: Routledge.

Wodak, R., de Cillia, R., Reisigl, M. and Liebhart, K. (1999) *The Discursive Construction of National Identity*. Edinburgh: Edinburgh University Press.

Researching Online Practices

Colin Lankshear, School of Education, James Cook University, Australia

Kevin Leander, Department of Teaching and Learning, Vanderbilt University, USA

Michele Knobel, Department of Early Childhood, Elementary and Literacy Education, Montclair State University, USA

Summary

- Online social practices
- Connective inquiry that resists a sharp online/offline distinction
- Affinity spaces
- Practice theory
- Key theorists and writers
  - James Gee
  - Michele Knobel
  - Colin Lankshear
  - Kevin Leander

Key concepts

Practice (social practices)

This chapter considers what is entailed in researching activities involving use of the internet from the standpoint of people engaging in social practices like blogging, online shopping, participating in online social networks, and being a fanfiction writer or music video creator. It outlines what we mean by 'practices' as a technical concept, and identifies some key implications for research design and methodology of taking a practice approach to researching social phenomena. We pay particular attention to a concept of 'connective inquiry' that disrupts the online/offline distinction and to the idea of 'affinity spaces' as a

useful construct for understanding how people become proficient in certain kinds of internet-related practices. The chapter privileges attempts to gain 'insider' understandings of internet-related practices, as experienced from the perspective of the actors themselves (emic), rather than imposing observer meanings upon these practices (etic) from the outside or on the basis of generalizations presumed to hold across a range of cultural contexts. We live in a period of massive technological and institutional change, where new things to be done and new ways of doing things – increasingly on a global scale – are emerging apace, mediated to a large extent by the internet. Internet-related practices are the 'nuts and bolts' of a great deal of the culture and history being made in this conjuncture. Understanding these nuts and bolts, then, is crucial to understanding our times – locally and globally.

Practice theory is a form of *cultural* theory of social phenomena, based on the idea that humans share ways of making sense, or ascribing meaning, to the world as the means for 'doing life together' (or 'being social'). As a particular cultural theory of the social, *practice theory* locates this shared knowledge in everyday social practices, with practices comprising the smallest units of social theory. In a formulation consistent with Silvia Scribner and Michael Cole's (1981) classic statement of 'practice' developed from an activity theory perspective, Andreas Reckwitz (2002) describes a practice as a routinized type of behaviour that consists of several interconnected elements:

namely, 'forms of bodily activities, forms of mental activities, "things" and their use, a background knowledge in the form of understanding, know how, states of emotion and motivational knowledge' (Reckwitz, 2002: 254). Wherever a practice exists we necessarily find all of these elements present, and connected to one another in specific and distinctive ways. A practice cannot be reduced to one or two of these elements, and differences in the ways they are interconnected constitute variations in the practice or, even, different practices. In short, practices are routinized ways of moving our bodies, handling objects and using things, understanding and describing the world, desiring and conceiving of tasks and purposes, of treating subjects, and so on (Reckwitz, 2002).

Humans are bearers or carriers of practices, through which they do and are and understand. As carriers of practices, through participation in practices, individuals 'perform' their bodies and their minds, their desires and ends, their emotions and values, in particular ways. They thereby achieve identity and membership, roles and relationships, understandings and accountabilities.

It is important to recognize that while practices are *routines* and, to that extent (relatively) stable and recognizable as particular ways of doing things, they are nonetheless dynamic, mutable and not completely monolithic. There are different versions of particular practices, more and less expert versions, and there is room for a degree of innovation and variation. Bloggers, for example, may blog quite differently from one another – thematically, in terms of additional media and applications used, regularity of posting, etc. – while nonetheless being recognizable as bloggers. Their mental, bodily and dispositional performances, use of tools, and so on, may vary significantly while remaining versions of blogging. The sense they respectively make of blogging may differ, as may their understandings of the blogosphere. Yet they are bloggers and engaged in blogging. The details of the 'elements' of blogging and the interconnections between these elements can vary from case to case – within recognizable limits – and it is these nuances that good social research will identify and document and explain, thereby contributing to our knowledge of the social world: of action and order. Furthermore, to contribute to knowledge of social practices it is not necessary to deal with the 'whole' of a practice. It may be sufficient and useful to focus primarily on particular interconnections

between elements or, even, particular elements of a practice.

'Connective' inquiry and the online/offline distinction

During the early years of internet research there was a strong tendency to bracket the online world or practice being studied and to distinguish quite sharply between on- and offline social lives, and between real world and online 'communities'. Much discussion about research methods centred on the extent to which conventional research tools and techniques 'might be transferred and adapted for the unique characteristics of online social spaces' (Leander, 2008: 36). In an early collection of essays the editor, Steve Jones (1999: 9), argued that there was a risk of restricting and confining online experience if researchers used old methodological tools for new internet experiences, since '[t]he range of experience is somehow changed online, both qualitatively and quantitatively, and our explanatory abilities must change with it'.

Work in the 'adaptation paradigm' continues, exploring the appropriate range of uses of familiar methods and developing new ones. However, researchers of internet-related practices have increasingly resisted a sharp online/offline distinction and sought to develop 'connective' methodological approaches (Hine, 2000) based on the assumption that 'people routinely build connections to internet-related practices and sites and myriad offline practices and sites' (Leander, 2008: 36). Practices exist in time and space and move, or 'travel' through time and space. What we do online now is usually intimately connected to things we do offline, from the past extending into the future (e.g. what we blog about or bring to our Facebook profiles). Hence, practices like blogging or being a blogger travel seamlessly across and between connected aspects of our lives in physical and virtual spaces. Since practice travels, so must social research approaches, like ethnography and qualitative case study. 'Connective' social research of internet-related practices regards (social) relations and connections as normative social practices and sees online social spaces as complexly related to other social spaces. The distinction between 'online' and 'offline' might indeed best be seen as a 'holding place' or as an 'analytic heuristic' that may serve provisionally until researchers can formulate more grounded means of understanding and discussing human experiences that are mediated by internet technologies.

We would argue that the binaries between online/offline, virtual world/real world, and cyberspace/physical space must be disrupted. In part, they are imperfect, fuzzy distinctions. In addition, however, they provide *a priori* answers to some of the most intriguing questions about internet practices. As Miller and Slater (2000: 5) observe, the extent to which some people seem actually to treat various internet relations as a 'world apart' from the rest of their lives should not be taken as the assumed point of departure for investigation but, rather, be seen as something that needs to be socially explained as *a practical accomplishment* (Leander, 2008: 37).

Internet-related practices

For precisely the kinds of reasons just mentioned, some researchers prefer to speak of 'internet-related practices' rather than 'online practices'. We might think of a continuum along which everyday social practices are mediated to a greater or lesser extent by the internet. Nearer one pole we might find practices like online multi-player gaming, weblogging, and participating in social networking sites where the immediate engagement and activity are conducted almost wholly online, albeit by material bodies and minds situated in the material world, surrounded by and often drawing upon accoutrements of that material context and interacting with anyone else who may be in that space. Of course, gamers, bloggers, and online social networkers draw upon relationships and experiences from their offline worlds and integrate them into their online activities. Nearer the other pole we might find particular instances of practices like music video remixing where much of the activity can occur offline, and participants might go online mainly to collect source video, to post their creations and check out feedback on their work within spaces like YouTube.com.

Allowing for such considerations and variations across on- and offline spaces, some typical examples of widely subscribed online/internet-related practices include:

- Digitally-mediated social networking: Facebooking, for example, can maintain a range of relationships through wall posts, news feeds, status updates, collaborative game playing, and the like. It can be used to network professionally through

group memberships, 'friending' known figures in the field, and posting website links and resources. Facebooking can focus on interests, too, through posting interest-focused photos and news, joining Facebook causes, linking to online bookmarking services, and so on.

- Fan fiction practices can involve drafting stories collaboratively using instant messaging, using discussion boards to role-play character development, posting polished stories to Fanfiction.net for review and reviewing others' stories. It can include creating fan art, movie trailers, manga/comics, podcasts and more to accompany these narratives.

- Machinima are short movies made using video games. Machinima practices include video game playing, developing storylines using game characters and sets, storyboarding, video editing, watching machinima for enjoyment and ideas, participating in discussion forums, posting videos to machinima archives for comment and review, attending festivals in person or online, and so on.

As in the case of blogging, we assume from the outset that each of these internet-related practices involves or possibly 'recruits' a broad range of offline practices, relationships, purposes, and materials, and that individual users will locate themselves at particular points along online/offline continua in each case, shaping unique social-digital webs. Other everyday internet-related practices include online shopping, participating in user-generated social news or recommendation sites, instant messaging and real time chatting, contributing to user-generated media sites, collaborative online writing, and so on.

Affinity spaces

James Gee (2004) introduced the idea of 'affinity' spaces as an alternative construct to 'communities of practice' for thinking about how people learn to become proficient in a practice. Affinity spaces may exist online as virtual space, or in the physical world as material and face-to-face space. They are *designed* spaces that have been built in order to resource people who share a particular interest or endeavour (an affinity). They are social spaces where members of an affinity can 'affiliate' to share and gain knowledge, interact, locate resources, and so on. They are not *locations* so much as dispersed 'environments' serving their respective affinities. With respect to websites like

Fanfiction.net, which serves authors and readers of fan fiction, Rebecca Black (2008: 36) explains how thinking in terms of a *space* for this affinity 'is a way of focusing attention on the interplay among engagement, active participation, a sense of belonging, and the production of a social space'.

Gee provides an ostensive definition by reference to the popular video game, 'Rise of Nations':

> The many websites and publications devoted to ['Rise of Nations'] create a social space in which people can, to any degree they wish, small or large, affiliate with others to share knowledge and gain knowledge that is distributed and dispersed across many different people, places, Internet sites and modalities (magazines, chat rooms, guides, recordings). (2004: 73)

Affinity spaces, then, are defined in part by content – what people interact around, what the space is about. Any resource that provides access to the content of the affinity and to ways and means of interacting with that content can be seen as a 'portal' (Gee, 2004: 81). Gee refers to the sources of the content that galvanise affinities as 'generators' (2004: 81). These include people, institutions, artefacts, signs, conceptual frameworks, signifying systems, and so on (Black, 2008: 36). Anyone at whatever level of proficiency can participate in the space and, to this extent, can interact with and otherwise contribute to furthering the participation of others, whoever and wherever they may be and regardless of their level of expertise.

As such, affinity spaces constitute crucial 'sites' of online or internet-related practices. They will typically be radically dispersed and will traverse online and offline spaces.

Implications for research design and methods

A *practice* approach to internet-related activities means that *from the outset* research design must be focused on getting at participant experiences and understandings of elements of practice – bodily and mental performances, things and how they are used, purposes, motivations, knowhow, etc. – and how these are connected when participants enact (their particular versions of) the practice. This is compatible with questions and design and methods choices evolving during the early phases of a study, in accordance with

researcher experiences *in situ* and latest knowledge developments. For example, researcher experiences with participants may dictate using fewer or more participants than originally planned, or doing more observation and less interviewing, or shifting from a focus on participant information and paying greater attention to observing how tools are used or on the features and qualities of artefacts – but always on the basis of generating better quality knowledge and understanding of elements of practice and how they are connected in this instance. Whether research objectives are framed as specific questions, and the extent to which these questions are 'in place' from the outset, is less important than the requirement that the data collected and the ways in which it is analysed and discussed be constantly accountable to illuminating elements of practice and their connectedness.

In some cases (e.g. Black, 2008), aspects of practice can be studied in depth without having offline access to participants. Finding appropriate participants will involve getting to know them as well as possible online to establish trust, identify possible points of vulnerability, and to be satisfied that they can provide sufficient good quality data to meet research purposes (see Stories from the Field). This takes time, but is crucial work, sometimes assisted by public markers (e.g. number of reviews, comments or views), peer networks, and through access to affinity spaces, where finding one participant may lead to another. Negotiating participation requires researchers and participants working through ethical issues concerning privacy, consent (and what constitutes data when 'informants' may not be participants), and forms of vulnerability (risk, security) that are exacerbated by online environments and electronic 'searchability' and tracking facilities (Leander, 2008).

In other cases it will be necessary also to have offline access to participants, to see how they use tools, work through processes integral to the practice, or do things in their daily lives that are carried over into their online lives and interests (Jones, 2008; Leander and Lovvorn, 2006). To make informed judgements about the particular version or versions of a practice they are witnessing, in relation to one another and to other versions of the practice – e.g. more/less expert, more/less 'mature', more/less typical or peripheral – researchers will benefit from participatory experience of that practice (or relevant similar practices), and from having access to other people's 'insider' perspectives (see the third story from the field below). This might incline a researcher towards adopting participant observation techniques, or immersing themselves in the practice as they move into the research.

Participant observation (comprehensive fieldnotes), in-depth interviewing, artefact collection, screen capture, *in situ* conversations with a purpose, think alouds, walk-throughs and talk-throughs, written transcript production, textual documentation of technical resources, network mapping, audio and video recording of interactions, use of eliciting devices, and the like are among the staple means of data collection (Lam, 2005; Lewis and Fabos, 2005; Miller and Slater, 2000).

A focus on practice(s) directs researchers' attention towards the constitutive elements of practice and their connections, but does not narrowly circumscribe theoretical perspectives to be adopted for informing data analysis and it does not prescribe analytic codes and categories. Grounded theory approaches to data analysis have often been used to good effect (Lewis and Fabos, 2005) but are not obligatory. Open coding and category development using constant comparative techniques will have wide applicability. At the same time, analytic approaches informed theoretically by narrative theory, activity theory, discourse analysis (Steinkuehler, 2006), rhizomatic analysis (Hagood, 2004), or other frames will often be productive. Some researchers (e.g. Leander and Lovvorn, 2006) find actor network theory useful because it helps map relationships between the material – 'things' – and the semiotic – 'concepts' – for example, between people (e.g. fanfiction writers), their ideas and purposes, and their technologies and other resources; all of which collectively constitute a 'network', and practices themselves involve precisely such networks (Latour, 2005). Finally, qualitative archiving and analytic tools, like Atlas or NVivo, can help with organising, analyzing and searching through data.

Stories from the field

1. Email interviews and depth of data (Michele Knobel and Colin Lankshear)

Email-mediated interviews are a popular data collection method for researching online practices. Since they are asynchronous, interviewees can respond in their own time – which is ideal when researchers and participants are in different time zones and otherwise remote. Respondents needn't complete interviews in

one sitting and can spend time reflecting on and crafting responses. The text-based nature of email-mediated interviews obviates transcription, which is often tedious and time-consuming.

In our experience, unfortunately, email-mediated interviews haven't delivered the depth we seek for obtaining 'insider' perspectives and know-how with respect to a practice – especially email interviews with young people. In a recent study we were interested in how a successful young anime music video (AMV) remixer learned to create AMVs (song-length videos created using anime as the visual resource). We had access to his AMVs in online affinity spaces (e.g. AnimeMusicVideos.org) and to commentaries and feedback conversations between the remixer and viewers, and access to other spaces documenting his everyday life as an anime fan. But what we really wanted to know was more process-oriented, for example: how he became involved in creating AMVs and posting them for feedback; what kept him remixing when each polished video required hundreds of hours to complete; what kept him engaged as an active participant in the AMV universe online and offline. Email-mediated interviews seemed most appropriate, given we had never met the remixer in person and considered a telephone or voice-over-internet call too intrusive during the early stages of the study.

Our informant was enthusiastic about participating, and interviewing began, with questions like: 'How did you learn to make AMVs? What resources do you draw on to help you? (e.g. software manuals, Google, discussion boards, friends?)' This question set, for example, yielded two sentences:

I learned how to make AMVs like I learn everything else, I jump into it head first and have fun with it. After a while I looked up a guide on DVD ripping which would be the only resource I've probably ever used besides feedback from friends.

The problem may lie with how we framed our questions, yet in previous case study interviews conducted face-to-face we have had little difficulty getting interviewees to elaborate at length about some process or how they complete some task. The opportunity to prompt for more information at a specific point in an exchange with a research participant is lost in email-mediated interviews. They are not like in-person interviews, where interesting comments can be followed up immediately, and requests to 'tell me more' are easily made on the spot. Subsequent emails with the remixer invited elaboration (e.g. what jumping in and having fun with creating AMVs actually looked like). Responses, however, remained stripped back, leaving us feeling we were only skimming surfaces in terms of coming to understand the practice of AMV creation and sharing.

We've found that researching online practices with 'unknown' participants-at-a-distance creates particular challenges for researchers. Writing about processes and insider know-how in email-mediated interviews is to expect a lot from respondents, especially when they are relatively young and perhaps not well-practised in reflecting on how one participates in or creates something. Using specific examples of our inform-ant's work and having him discuss editing decisions concretely helped obtain more detailed email re-sponses, but these remained less satisfying than conducting voice-to-voice interviews.

2. Privacy hazards (Rebecca Black)

Networked, online spaces simultaneously open excit-ing new research vistas and pose heightened method-ological challenges for qualitative researchers. My ethnographic study of adolescent English language learners (ELLs) who were writing online fan fiction was particularly concerned with two aspects of their writing: (1) how they used their online texts to elicit feedback from readers as a means of improving their English skills; and (2) how they used their texts to represent aspects of their identities and work through issues that they were dealing with from their everyday lives, such as sexuality, peer pressure, and school violence. Many of these teens were using screen names to publish their stories, so parents and even friends were often unaware that they were writing these stories, posting them online, or even that they were dealing with these issues.

During recruitment I found a potential research participant who was writing powerful anime-based fan fictions about male characters who were struggling with their sexuality. I contacted him about possibly participating. He was enthusiastic and willing to have a parent/guardian sign the consent forms, which would entail letting them know that he was writing fan fiction. However, as I read more of his public interactions with other fans on the site, it became clear to me that he was struggling with his own sexuality and had not yet discussed any of this with his offline friends or family members. This posed an

ethical dilemma. He was enthusiastic about participa-ting, and having his parent/guardian sign consent forms did not necessarily entail revealing his screen name or the content of his texts. On the other hand, as a researcher, I felt I had an ethical obligation to weigh the benefits of his participation in the study against the risks.

Another complicating factor involved the public nature of online texts. At the time, search engines like Google were not indexing pages from this particular site. Hence, you could enter text from a fan fiction story and it would not yield an accurate result in a search. However, I was worried that this might change at some point. Because participants' online stories are linked to their author profiles, which in turn could contain links to the participants' LiveJour-nal accounts, their personal web pages, and other potentially identifiable information, there was risk of breach of confidentiality. Ultimately, I decided that there was too much at stake for this young man for me to feel comfortable including him in the study. Moreover, this experience led me to carefully re-examine the sort of information that my other participants were revealing in their texts, their author profiles, and on any linked websites.

This example underscores the difficulty of doing any sort of textual analysis of web documents that are linked to participants' personal or interview data. The 'search-engineable' nature of online text poses a unique challenge for online researchers. It also under-scores the need to carefully consider potential ramifi-cations of our research for members of vulnerable populations, like adolescents, who are so accustomed to living life online with their peers that they do not realize or think about the possibility that 'offline' institutions like parents, schools, employers, etc., also may have relatively easy access to their online lives.

3. A participatory research approach (Rodney Jones)

There are two important challenges to studying online literacies: being able to access the lived experiences of people participating in these literacies, and being able to capture the complexity of this participation as it moves across multiple physical and virtual spaces. Our project (Jones, 2008) sought to explore and compare school-based and non-school-based com-puter-related literacy practices of young people in Hong Kong. We attempted to address these chal-lenges through: (1) a participatory framework in which participants collaborated with researchers in posing the research questions, collecting data, and reporting results; and (2) a multimodal approach to data gathering in which as much attention was paid to how online practices affected what happened 'off-screen' in the physical environments in which computers were used as to what happened on-screen.

The participatory model was extremely effective in helping us obtain an insider's perspective on young people's literacy practices and the social strategies they had built around them. Since participant researchers felt a sense of ownership of the project, they worked hard at soliciting cooperation from their friends and recruiting them into researcher roles. The project began with 15 participant researchers and ended with the active collaboration of more than 100 young people participating in overlapping online social networks and actively reflecting on this participation. Through this process, the questions the research sought to answer were negotiated and refined. While participants were interested in many of the questions that the researchers had posed – about, for example, the ways new literacies were learned and the effects of new literacy practices on old literacy practices – they were also interested in other issues such as the effect of online interaction on their friendships, how they could use online tools more effectively in their social and academic lives, and how they could expand their social networks online. They were also keenly aware of the questions their parents and teachers were concerned about (such as the effect of online language on their English and Chinese proficiency) and included them as well, but not just to ventriloquate them, but to engage with them critically. One of the most interesting aspects of the project was observing the participant researchers report their findings to different audiences through written reports to researchers, a webpage for their peers, and a formal presentation to their parents and teachers. In each of these exercises they highlighted different aspects of their findings and framed them in different ways. This helped to bring home to us the fact that an important aspect of literacy is being able to appropriately represent one's literacy practices to different kinds of people.

Participant researchers collected a wide variety of data in different modes. They kept diaries in which they reflected on their online and offline practices; they saved samples of chats; they took screen movies of their computer use using a program called Spector; they installed webcams to monitor the physical activity occurring around them when they were using their computers, and they video-taped themselves and their friends using computers at home, at school, and in other venues like internet cafes and gaming halls. This combination of data allowed for an understanding not just of the products of new literacies, but the complex online and off-line *processes* and interactions that go into producing these products. One of the major findings of the study, in fact, had to do with the ways computers affect the organization of social situations and the ways attention is managed within those situations.

Researching online literacies poses a host of complex ethical problems, such as obtaining informed consent from participants in virtual networks whose participation is often uncertain, contingent and peripheral. Another challenge it poses is in negotiating the ambiguous boundaries between etic and emic perspectives. More participatory models of research, while not resolving these issues (and, in many ways, complicating them), at least open up avenues of access and create opportunities to re-conceptualise research as an ongoing conversation among interested parties in which all of these parties might be somehow empowered.

Annotated bibliography

Black, R. (2008) *Adolescents and Online Fan Fiction*. New York: Peter Lang.
An ethnographic and discourse analytic study of English language learners participating in the popular online fan fiction writing space, fanfiction.net

Coiro, J., Knobel, M., Lankshear, C. and Leu, D. (eds) (2008) *Handbook of Research on New Literacies*. Mahwah, NJ: Erlbaum.
State-of-the-art accounts of research covering diverse online practices, with a section on qualitative, quantitative and mixed methods designs and methodologies.

Hine, C. (2000) *Virtual Ethnography*. London: Sage.
Argues that researching the internet, as both a site for cultural formations and a cultural artefact shaped by our understandings, requires a new kind of ethnography.

Jones, R. (2008) 'Technology, democracy and participation in space', in V. Koller and R. Wodak (eds) *Handbook of Applied Linguistics Vol. 4, Language and Communication in the Public Sphere*. New York: Mouton de Gruyter. pp. 429–46.

Provides an account of an innovative approach to participatory research of internet-related practices.

Jones, S. (ed.) (1999) *Doing Internet Research: Critical Issues and Methods for Examining the Net*. Thousand Oaks, CA: Sage.
This collection identifies key issues of internet research from a wide-ranging academic standpoint.

Lam, W.S.E. (2005) 'Second language socialization in a bilingual chat room', *Language Learning and Technology*, 8: 44–65.
Case study of two young Chinese immigrants participating in a bilingual Chinese/English chat room, using participant observation, in-depth interviews, textual documentation, and data about the technical set-up, demographics and social dynamics of the chat room.

Leander, K. (2008) 'Toward a connective ethnography of online/offline literacy networks', in J. Coiro, M. Knobel, C. Lankshear and D. Leu (eds) *Handbook of Research on New Literacies*. Mahwah, NJ: Erlbaum. pp. 33–65.
Surveys works by researchers developing 'connective' ethnography using diverse complementary qualitative methods for collecting and analysing data.

Leander, K. and Lovvorn, J. (2006) 'Literacy networks: Following the circulation of texts, bodies, and objects in the schooling and online gaming of one youth', *Cognition & Instruction*, 24(3): 291–340.
Draws on actor network theory to reconceive literacy and its relations to space–time through the construct of the literacy network.

Lewis, C. and Fabos, B. (2005) 'Instant messaging, literacies, and social identities', *Reading Research Quarterly*, 40(4): 470–501.
Uses interviews and videotaped IM sessions to explore what functions instant messaging served in participants' lives and its relationship to identity. Data analysis used qualitative coding procedures informed by grounded theory.

Miller, D. and Slater, D. (2000) *The Internet: An Ethnographic Approach*. New York: Berg.
Classic study of the uses of the internet and meanings of internet culture in the context of Trinidad and the Trinidad Diaspora, using a house-to-house survey, in-depth individual interviews in households and cybercafés, online conversations and observations in cybercafés.

Further references

Gee, J. (2004) *Situated Language and Learning: A Critique of Traditional Schooling*. London: Routledge.

Hagood, M. (2004) 'A rhizomatic cartography of adolescents, popular culture, and constructions of self', in K.M. Leander and M. Sheehy (eds) *Spatializing Literacy Research and Practice*. New York: Lang. pp. 143–60.

Latour, B. (2005) *Reassembling the Social: An Introduction to Actor Network Theory*. Oxford: Oxford University Press.

Reckwitz, A. (2002) 'Toward a theory of social practices: A development in social theorizing', *European Journal of Social Theory*, 5(2): 245–65.

Scribner, S. and Cole, M. (1981) *The Psychology of Literacy*. Cambridge, MA: Harvard University Press.

Steinkuehler, C.A. (2006) 'Massively multiplayer online videogaming as participation in a discourse', *Mind, Culture & Activity*, 13(1): 38–52.

PART V

IDENTITY, COMMUNITY AND REPRESENTATION

Introduction

Part V brings the concept of 'culture' to the centre of research activity and meaning-making. It begins with life history and narrative approaches, in a chapter which presents these approaches as socially constructed, and argues that human actions and agency are contingent upon sociocultural, historical and political influences. This is followed by a chapter dealing with social semiotic approaches to interpretation, illustrating processes of multimodality. The next two chapters focus on the overlapping theoretical frameworks of 'communities of practice' and activity theory, both of which see human interaction, co-construction of meaning, and mutual cooperation as central to human agency and empowerment. The final chapter is on researching policy. Its focus is on the analysis and evaluation of policies and initiatives of governments, which frame social practices and issue directives, and which are increasingly influenced by processes of globalization and by the copycat phenomenon that Blackmore calls 'travelling policies' (Chapter 22).

An important common denominator for these chapters is that they are all concerned with the process of 'reading' sociocultural data and making meaning. Three of them (Chapters 19, 20 and 21) draw explicitly on the sociocultural psychology of Vygotsky and are concerned with learning as a process of transformation through engaging in human activity. Experience and meaning-making are encultured and co-constructed, whether in daily life or through engaging in research. The emphasis on the visual – video-recordings and drawings as research data – and multimodality as a norm of representation

opens up new opportunities for qualitative research. The tyranny of the written text is particularly challenged in the chapter on social semiotics and multimodality. The chapter on researching policy adopts an overtly political stance and analyses how a focus on power and control is a factor in the poor articulation between policies and their enactment in practice.

These chapters also privilege the practical and focus on the integration of theoretical insights with practical action – in some cases through a focus on community engagement and change processes, in others through in-depth interpretation of representations as both expressions of human identity and encultured artefacts. The Stories from the Field portray learners of all ages from small children, through adolescents, to employees in industry, and teachers coming to terms with technology. In all cases they are portrayed as unique individuals whose identity is mediated and sustained by the socio-historical and cultural contexts in which their life experience is embedded.

Again, there are many cross-links between this part of the book and chapters in other parts. The chapter on Life History and Narrative should be read in relation to Interviewing in Part II; the chapter on semiotic engagements links forward to the chapter on deconstruction in Part VIII; the Story from the field in the Communities of Practice chapter illustrates the integration of qualitative and quantitative data described in several of the chapters in Part VII; and all of the chapters need to be read in the light of the chapter in Part I on Ethical Issues.

The sociocultural-historical theories that underpin Chapters 19, 20 and 21 provide a useful alternative to some of the mainstays of qualitative research portrayed in Parts II–IV, such as hermeneutic interpretation on the one hand or critical engagement with political processes on the other. If these sociocultural theories have a limitation it tends to be in their neglect of the political, but this is specifically addressed by the chapters on activity theory and researching policy.

Life History and Narrative Methods

Scherto Gill, Centre for Research in Human Development, Brighton, UK

Ivor Goodson, University of Brighton, UK

Summary

- Narrative: temporality, meaning and social encounters
- Meanings are socially constructed
- Human actions and agency are contingent
- Life becomes human in and through narratives
- Narrative identity
- Key theorists and writers
  - Anthony Giddens
  - Ivor Goodson
  - Paul Ricoeur
  - Pat Sikes

Key concepts

In social research, both life history and narrative approaches share a common root in the concept of narrative or stories. Hinchman and Hinchman (1997: xvi) define 'narrative (stories) as discourses with a clear sequential order that connect events in a meaningful way for a definite audience and thus offer insights about the world and/or people's experiences of it'. This definition highlights three characteristics of narrative: temporality, meaning and social encounters. Clearly, these authors underline the significance of social interaction in the construction of narratives and transforming human experience into meaning. Other authors tend to focus their attention on the structure of the narrative, the organization of plots and how they are determined by the inherent value or meaning the narrator assumes (Bakhtin, 1981; Mishler, 1999).

Originating in the Chicago School of Sociology in the 1930s, the life history tradition has long been employed in anthropology and sociology. Closely linked to the notion of narrative, life history is a collection of individuals' or groups' lived experience in the past and present which is analysed by researchers who then place the narrative accounts within the social, political, economic and historical contexts where these experiences took place. The focus of life history is to understand the interplay between social change, individual (and group) lives and agency. Goodson and Sikes (2001: 18) add that 'by providing contextual data, the life stories can be seen in the light of changing patterns of time and space in testimony and action'. Accordingly, life history forms a 'linkage in a chain of social transmission, a strand of complicated collective life in social and historical continuity' (2001: 18).

Both narrative and life history approaches recognize that meanings are socially constructed, and human actions and agency are contingent upon sociocultural, historical and political influences. At times we use the terms narrative research and life history study interchangeably. This is for good reason. The most sociologically sophisticated and pedagogically rich traditions in both narrative and life history work often converge. There is, however, an important and potentially challenging distinction between the two genres. Narrative research focuses on the stories recounted by the teller. It can, and often does, see this as the starting point but also the finishing point of the process. The role of the narrative researcher is to facilitate and promote the voice of the participant, and often to present that voice unchanged, for fear of 'academic colonization'. Indeed colonization has been a real issue in social research. However, forgoing all collaboration is, we would argue, a form of abdication. It can leave the teller or the participant with their story 'uncontaminated' but also unchanged. In other words, no further understanding is pursued.

Not all research using narratives follows this route of abdication and some explore more complex contexts and agencies, making it akin to a fully-fledged life history study. The crucial point is that the life story is the starting point of our exploration of and search for a story of actions set within historical, social and cultural transitions, as well as personal landscapes.

Hitchcock and Hughes suggest the life history approach is 'superior' to other narrative methods because:

> it enables the researcher to build up a mosaic-like picture of the individuals and the events and people surrounding them so that relations, influences and patterns can be observed ... The retrospective quality ... enables one to explore social processes over time and adds historical depth to subsequent analysis. (1995: 187)

In some narrative research, life stories can be used by individuals for self-inquiry and self-reflection. This kind of narrative approach is not limited to the researcher's interpretation and analysis, and involves the participants' self-interpretation and collaborative interpretation with others in a group, such as in research using life writing and biographical research (Dominicé, 2000).

Why narrative and life history?

Some thinkers have argued that life and narratives are inextricably related and that human life is interpreted in and through narratives. In other words, from a hermeneutic point of view, human life is perceived as a process of narrative interpretation (Ricoeur, 1992). Life is meaningful, but the meaning is implicit, and it only becomes explicit in our narratives or stories.

Social researchers are often drawn to life narratives for two inter-related reasons.

First, narrative has been perceived to be an inherently human concept (Barthes, 1975). Similarly, according to Ricoeur (1983), life and even time becomes human in and through our narratives. Narratives are considered as central to being human because our sense of purpose and meaning, our selfhood, values and aspirations are based on our narratives; and narratives are essential for humans to construct coherence and continuity in their lives (Taylor, 1989). Furthermore, narratives permit us to adapt, modify and shift our stories towards transformation. Continuity is refined (Brooks, 1984).

Second, human life is chaotic, whereas narratives, through their plots, temporality and meaning, allow the chaotic nature of life to assume a certain structure and configuration as well as coherence, direction and unity (MacIntyre, 1984). Narratives can thus be a helpful mode to explain human actions, and by recounting our lives, we place our actions in the context of intentions, 'with reference to their role in the history of the setting or settings in which they belong' (1984: 208). In this way, we 'write a further part' of our histories, and human actions are unified in their narrative construct; life becomes 'enacted narratives' (1984: 208). The latter consolidates a mutually constituted relationship between life and narrative – life forms the fundamental basis of narratives or stories, and narratives and stories provide order, structure and direction in life, so helping develop the meaning in life in richer and more integrated ways.

At the core of the above relationship is the recognition of humans as social actors with agency. Narrative and life history work provides an opportunity to re-examine social research by acknowledging the complexity of human encounters and by integrating human subjectivity into the research process.

Narrative identity and human action

The relationship between life and narratives has a profound implication for another concept – self-identity. Here, identity in itself is not simply a psychological concept of ego identity. Rather, it is simultaneously cultural, historical, social and personal. Identity and narrative are intrinsically connected and Paul Ricoeur has put forward a notion of narrative identity which has been used widely in the studies of human narratives. Ricoeur (1992) suggests that the self holds two notions of identity at the same time: *idem* identity and *ipse* identity. Idem-identity – the persisting self – is what Ricoeur describes as 'keeping one's promise', which includes genetic identification and the self as physical and metaphysical continuity;

whereas ipse-identity is selfhood, the answer to the question 'who am I', and can initiate without being dependent on something permanent for its existence. Ricoeur maintains that narratives play an important mediating role between a number of dialectics, including harmony and dissonance in human experience; narratives as lived and narratives as told, innovation and sedimentation, fact and fiction; what is and what ought to be; exalted cogito and shattered cogito; the person as the interpreter and the interpreted; and as the reader and the writer of one's own life; and finally, the lived world and the told world.

Ricoeur (1988: 246) argues that to answer the question 'Who?' is to tell the story of a life, and thus, narrative identity, 'constitutive of self-consistency, can include change, mutuality, within the cohesion of one life time'. Similarly, McAdams (1996: 307) sees it as 'an internalized and evolving narrative of the self that incorporates the reconstructed past, perceived present and anticipated future'. Narrative identity thus allows the individual to live life in a continuum.

Writing from the point of view of late modernity, Giddens (1991: 55) points out that a person's self-identity is fundamental to their ontological security, which is 'robust' and 'fragile' at the same time. He argues that the sense of self-identity is robust because it 'is often securely enough held to' during major tensions or transitions in a person's social environments; and that it is fragile because 'the biography the individual reflexively holds in mind is only one "story" among many other potential stories that could be told about her development as a self'. Giddens stresses the significance of maintaining the continuity of self-identity in the everyday world. He sees a person's self-identity in their capacity to 'keep a particular narrative going' (1991: 54). Giddens concurs with Taylor (1989) on this point: 'In order to have a sense of who we are, we have to have a notion of how we have become, and of where we are going' (1991: 54.).

In this sense, the reflexive project is not merely a narcissistic obsession of the ego, but also involves an understanding of what it means to be a 'person', which applies to both the self and others, and the concept of the person will facilitate individuals with the capacity to 'use "I" in shifting contexts' (Giddens, 1991: 53). Personal meaning is at the centre of the search. What Giddens terms 'existential isolation' raises moral issues and calls for 'life politics' which are 'concerned with human self-actualization, both on the level of the individual and collectively'.

At this juncture, let us return to our earlier discussion of human action. This is where narrative identity can provide an entry point for the discussion of the 'value-generating capacities' of narrative's function (Gergen, 1992). Hitchcock and Hughes (1995: 186) maintain that research using life narratives 'facilitates a deeper appreciation of an individual's experience of the past, living with the present, and a means of facing and challenging the future'.

Other authors argue for the connection between life narratives and the development of the moral or ethical self. Ricoeur states 'the self of self-knowledge is the fruit of an examined life' (1988: 247). The ethical self or moral identity is further placed by Ricoeur in the light of culture and community. Similarly, Charles Taylor argues that identity is defined by 'the commitments and identifications' which provide the 'frame or horizon' within which the individual can try to 'determine from case to case what is good, or valuable, or what ought to be done', or what one endorses or opposes. In other words, to define one's identity is to determine the horizons within which one is capable of 'taking a stand' (Taylor, 1989: 27). MacIntyre summarizes:

> the key question for men [sic] is not about their own authorship; I can only answer the question 'What am I to do' if I can answer the prior question 'Of what story or stories do I find myself a part?' (1984: 211)

Hence, narrative identity shows that what is good for me has to be good for those communities of which I am a part. Ricoeur further concludes that both individuals and their communities are 'constituted in their identity by taking up narratives that become for them their actual history' (1988: 247).

Implications for research design

Narrative and life history are both reciprocal processes of developing understanding. Part of the research aspiration is co-constructing meaning. The research can resemble a process of people coming together to know about their lives and why they are so lived. Inevitably, research questions are reflexively engaged by the researcher, whose personal life and stories are intertwined with those of the participants. This relationship ultimately determines narrative learning (Goodson and Gill, forthcoming) about oneself, the social world, and how the different factors interact, resulting in our lives as such.

Data collection

Narrative and life history research often takes a qualitative approach to data collection using in-depth interviews (although some researchers also take a mixed-method approach). The process is collaborative and requires establishing trust and close relationships. In the first instance, the researcher often encourages a 'flow' in the interview with minimal interrogation to let the participants control the ordering and sequencing of their stories and reduce the issue of researcher power (however, we realize that this can never be completely obliterated).

Building on the initial interview(s), further dialogues or follow-up interchange(s) can be developed. When the researcher and the participant move the 'inter-view' towards a 'grounded conversation' and away from the somewhat singular narrative of the initial life story, it can signal the move from life story to life history. This means approaching the question of why stories are told in particular ways at particular historical moments. The life history, together with other sources of data, 'triangulates' the life story to locate its wider meaning (see Figure 18.1).

Narrative analysis

The purpose of narrative analysis is to unfold the ways individuals make sense of their lived experience and how its telling enables them to interpret the social world and their agency within it. More often the focus is not on revealing the 'truth' of the stories. The approach to analysis is determined by the research questions, the researcher's epistemological position and his/her lived experience in connection with the research topic(s).

Sociological models of analysis draw attention to the ways that sociocultural, historical and political contexts influence how stories are told and how the structure of the narrative relates to the contexts of the telling (Cortazzi, 1993). Some researchers choose to focus their narrative analysis on the inherent structure of the stories (Labov, 1973; Ricoeur, 1983) and others on the discourse in order to unfold the ideologically invested, and power-allied nature of meaning and knowledge (Gergen, 1994).

The social construction of subjectivity in relation to dominant discourses, and its potential for reflexive openness, makes narrative analysis a specific discourse methodology capable of critically contributing to the interplay between personal and social change (Riessman, 1993).

What is seldom mentioned by the research literature, but often used by researchers, is their own intuition in analysing and interpreting the narrative data. Hence for some time, narrative researchers and life historians have tended to 'write themselves' into the research in order to acknowledge that research insights are the result of a fusion of voices, interactions and collaboration between those involved.

Stories from the field

Working with narrative and life history approaches as research methodology has presented us both with many challenges throughout our research experiences. The first and foremost challenge lies in the deeper epistemological and methodological domain. Indeed, we feel that our own positionality has been really crucial in guiding our research questions, the way we collect, analyse and interpret narratives, and the writing of final texts. Our positionality also affects the way we perceive the nature of the research relationship. For us, empathy, collaboration, dialogue and intersubjectivity are important ingredients in the relationship. In all our research work, we aim to

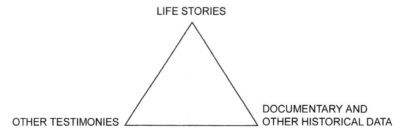

Figure 18.1   Data sources of life history

engage actively with the participants, and connect closely with them on both a personal level and within the research. We respect the participants as persons, not merely as the means to research insights, so we often find ourselves in a situation of 'self-disclosure', sharing our own life stories with the participants.

Our struggle with such challenges makes us believe that it is necessary to embrace the contradictions and possibilities narrative and life history methods pose, and use 'ethics-in-context' to negotiate the 'give and take' of research relationships (Riessman, 2005).

In Scherto's research into Chinese postgraduate students studying in the UK, she chose in-depth interviews to gain insights into the participants' life stories of living in another country and experience of intercultural encounters. During her very first interview with Yang (participant's pseudonym), she began by explaining what her research was about and shared personal details, that she had also been an overseas student herself a few years before the research and that it had motivated her to find out more about other students' experiences. Scherto also explained to him about her research design, the number of interviews expected, confidentiality, recording and transcribing, and how she planned to arrive at the research texts.

Yang appeared to be listening intently, whilst Scherto felt rather embarrassed about her long monologue. She asked if he had any questions about the research and hoped that this would break the ice. Yang took her by surprise and asked directly: 'Tell me what it was like for you to be an overseas student?' Scherto paused at this invitation for stories. During that short pause, many methodological keywords such as 'leading' the participants, 'researcher power', 'vow of silence' and more jumped into her head. Then she decided: 'Do you mind if I make it brief? I have already talked too much?' 'Of course.' Yang smiled kindly.

In fact, what followed was a long conversational exchange about their mutual experiences of studying abroad. The same dialogical approach thus characterized her research fieldwork and the writing of the final research text. Sharing the researcher's own stories was the beginning of a trusting and close relationship throughout the research, and later friendship with a few of her research participants. Over a one-year period, Scherto met regularly with her participants/collaborators both on an individual and group basis to have conversations about their experience over time and the change in their sense of self. They collaborated in constructing meaning and developing

understanding about intercultural learning in the context of Chinese economic growth and shifting social, cultural and political landscapes. These frequent research encounters provided fertile ground for a 'fusion of horizons' (Gadamer, 1975) and collaborative interpretation. In her final research report, Scherto was able to include narrative sketches for all the participants. She describes the process as follows:

(1) transcribing the recorded interview/conversations;
(2) re-reading the text using her understanding of the participants' intercultural adaptation over time and in view of their current narrated experience;
(3) re-writing the transcripts into a draft narrative sketch – a shorter and more accessible text depicting the main threads of the participants' experiences, bringing in other documentation and social, cultural, historical and political data, highlighting issues relevant to the research questions;
(4) co-interpreting and editing (with the participants) the draft sketches;
(5) finalizing the texts and getting the participants' approval (Gill, 2005).

Inevitably, research ethics were the most challenging aspect of all the research fieldwork. It was comforting to know that there are no strict rules or prescriptions for ethical conduct in narrative and life history work (Clandinin and Connelly, 2000). What we are most concerned with is that there is no clear boundary between what is ethical and what is not in 'informed consent'. We often ask ourselves whether our participants are aware that they have given us the consent to come into their lives and take a closer look at them from within. It is never possible to predict the impact of our research on the participants, nor could they understand or anticipate the risks and benefits of a process-based and contextualized commitment. Furthermore, because of the centrality of life narrative to self-identity and the temporal orientation of narrative encounters, in particular, in enabling the person to identify the direction of their future actions, Scherto's research provided opportunities for change in these individuals which would otherwise not have happened. Thus narrative and life history research is potentially an intervention and interruption to participants' lives.

In Scherto's initial interviews with Lin, Lin explained that she came to study in the UK mainly to 'experience the world outside of China'. This participant had chosen the MA in international education because she believed that this might lead to a well paid and respectable university job after returning to China. As the MA progressed and the research reflection deepened, Lin said that she was prompted to think about many questions she would otherwise not have had the chance to consider, such as what she was learning about herself, what she valued in life and work, and what she wanted to do with her learning afterwards. The narrative construction of herself led to Lin's decision to do something more 'meaningful and worthwhile' for herself and for other people. Lin realized that her true interest was to work in education development in the poorer regions in China. This was totally at odds with her initial plan and against the current graduate employment trend in China, where materialistic pursuits take priority over concern for others. The research enabled Lin to change her course of action. As Mishler points out, through their narratives, participants 'may be moved beyond the text to the possibilities of action ... to apply the understanding arrived at to action in accordance with one's own interests' (1986: 119).

Over time, Scherto's research process resembled the three-stage approach described by Goodson (2006), as in Figure 18.2:

(1) Narration – Interview(s) and recalling individual lives. The sharing of stories in her research also included the participants' use of photos, objects, journals, etc. to support their narration.
(2) Collaboration – After narration, the participant(s) and the researcher had follow-up conversations/ interviews when they examined the transcripts to identify gaps in the narrative. This was where questions were posed about meanings in order to gain a better understanding of the told experiences.

(3) Location – Following the dialogic exchange and drafting the first narrative sketch, the participant and the researcher would locate individual stories in their wider historical context and social and cultural practices. This was also where links between individual stories were made to form a picture of a collective experience.

As Scherto continued to explore this collaborative process, she came to realize that as the result of analysis, interpretation and critical self-reflection, some participants (like Lin) were willing to delineate one or two further steps in the location process – 'explicit meaning-making' and 'direction'. Explicit meaning-making seemed to allow individuals to intentionally perceive their experiences within the contexts that had contributed to who they are and how they have lived their lives; direction followed whereby the participants were able to use reflection during the research to determine a course of action adhering to their own values and personal interests. In Goodson and Gill (forthcoming), we spell out the ingredients of the location process as a pursuit of holistic understanding, an integration of one's purpose in life and elaboration of commitment in order to write one's own history.

Emotions played a big part during the narrative exchange. For instance, in Yang's stories, home was a significant concept and the need to find a 'home' and search for belonging and acceptance was a theme to which he frequently returned. These were emotional stories for Yang and unfolded many problems he had with his parents, teachers at school and authority in general. They were also poignant to Scherto as they reminded her of her grandfather's experiences during his youth. Like Yang, her grandfather became a stranger in his home country and an outsider in his own house. When he went to study abroad, her

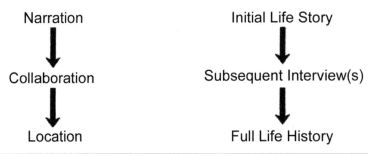

Figure 18.2   Interview collaboration (after Goodson, 2006)

grandfather found a home in a foreign land. Scherto was thus drawn to this aspect of Yang's experience. However, the conversation and interpretation enabled both Scherto and Yang to see beyond Yang's childhood trauma – in twenty-first century China, inequality and the demand for academic attainment as a means to social mobility are amongst factors that oppress many children and young people like Yang.

This was a different cultural and historical context from where Scherto's grandfather had his 'outcast' experience. Yet, it was an emotional response to such stories that brought their attention to Yang's experience. After the research, Yang wrote to Scherto from his new home in Finland and thanked her for involving him in the research. He said 'my life has become more interesting simply by talking about it with someone'. 'Above all', he wrote, 'I know now that home is where I am. In this sense, I am always at home.'

This research story raised two interesting questions.

The first is about engaging with our emotions during the research, echoing Riessman's (2005: 476) view that both the researcher and the participant bring with them 'subjectivities and emotional lives' in the research encounter. Emotions add to the complexity of the constantly negotiated and interrogated power dynamics in the research field.

The second is the distinction between research and therapy. In our research story above, Yang went through an unravelling process and was able to derive meaning from his own narratives and the story-telling, and began to re-author his stories. Of course, there is a therapeutic dimension to the narrative engagement. However, there are fundamental differences between Scherto's interview with Yang and a therapeutic intervention. Her research aimed to foster understanding of individual experience and how it is placed within social historical contexts. In this way, narrative and life history research wrestles with the tensions between the individual and the social, as well as questions of structure and agency. These essential tensions are explored in a dialogic process. This exploration should provide the culminating phase of life history work and thereby provide a story of action within contexts for both the participants and the researcher. It demonstrates the powers and forces that have shaped our experience, and how our narrative further allows us to identify ways to change our lives and the social world.

In short, narrative and life history research has, at its core, the purpose of understanding and learning, in particular, reciprocal learning between researcher and participant. This joint experience is at the root of narrative pedagogy (Goodson and Gill, forthcoming).

Annotated bibliography

Atkinson, R. (1998) *The Life Story Interview*. London: Sage Publications.
Atkinson gives a detailed explanation of the art and science of life story interviewing. The book makes useful suggestions in terms of the collection, transcription, analysis and interpretation of life stories with practical examples.

Bertaux, D. (ed.) (1981) *Biography and Society: The Life History Approach in the Social Sciences*. London: Sage Publications.
This collection is a comprehensive survey which maps out the contemporary uses of the life history approach in sociology. The authors focus their exploration on the relationship between the individual and collective within social and historical shifts. The texts point out that macro questions concerning class, gender and agency can be explored through micro analysis of human lives.

Fraser, H. (2004) 'Doing narrative research: Analysing personal stories line by line', *Qualitative Social Work*, 3(2): 179–201.
This article takes a comprehensive approach to discussing how narrative analysis might be undertaken. The author begins with a broad overview of general approaches to doing narrative research before offering a specific method to analyse personal stories.

Gadamer, H. (1975) *Truth and Method*. New York: The Seabury Press.
This book provides an idea of 'philosophical hermeneutics' to those who are interested in exploring the conceptual framework for life history and narrative research. Gadamer puts forward a robust argument for a 'fusion of horizons' which is the basis for human understanding.

Giddens, A. (1991) *Modernity and Self-identity: Self and Society in the Late Modern Age*. Cambridge: Polity Press.
Giddens argues that in the late modern age, self-identity has become a reflexive project. Self-identity is considered to be embedded in a person's capacity to 'keep a particular narrative going'. Through narratives, individuals create and revise the story of who we are, where we have come from and how we ought to act in the world.

Goodson, I. and Sikes, P. (2001) *Life History Research in Educational Settings – Learning from Lives*. Buckingham: Open University Press.

This useful book provides the context and rationale for using the life history approach in education and social research in general. The authors make a clear distinction between life stories and life history and offer a step-by-step guide in terms of how to move from life stories to life history. The book also addresses ethical dilemmas, research relationships and the issue of representation.

Hatch, J. and Wisniewski, R. (eds) (1995) *Life History and Narrative*. London: Falmer Press.

This is one of the earlier books to expose novice life historians to an understanding of the 'many exceptionally difficult decisions that need to be made' in carrying out social research of this genre. The book also offers an insight into the critical debates within the field.

Plummer, K. (2001) *Documents of Life 2: An Invitation to Critical Humanism*. London: Sage.

This book offers a coherent argument for a humanist approach to the methodologies in social sciences, and another opportunity to understand the history and development of life history as a research method. It argues against the notion of life stories as 'telling it like it is', rather the writing of a life is an exercise of agency and change.

Ricoeur, P. (1992) *Oneself as Another.* Trans. Kathleen Blamey. Chicago: The University of Chicago Press.

In this book, Ricoeur develops a hermeneutics of the self that allows for both its spatio-temporal sameness and its unique ability to initiate something new, which together constitute narrative identity. The author goes on to link one's narrative identity to an ethical exploration of the self which requires a person to be accountable for his/her acts in the world.

Riessman, C.K. (1993) *Narrative Analysis*, Qualitative Research Methods, Series 30. London: Sage.

This is a helpful book for those who have just started collecting life stories and persona narratives as research data. It provides a systematic approach to understanding individuals' lived experience by analysing their stories and tales.

Tierney, W. (1998) 'Life history's history: subject foretold', *Qualitative Inquiry*, 4(1): 49–70.

This article is useful for narrative researchers who are struggling with how we might present the narrative (qualitative) data, especially when we are torn between the risks of 'essentializing' individuals and relationships and that no understanding is possible in the postmodern sense.

Wengraf, T., Chamberlayne, P. and Bornat, J. (2002) 'A biographical turn in the social sciences? A British–European view', *Journal of Cultural Studies, Critical Methodologies*, 2(2): 245–69.

This article contains an insightful account of the contexts and developments in biographical and life history research methods. Most of the major works in the field have been reviewed and located as part of a broader picture of shifting configurations of concerns, concepts, and methodologies in the history of the social sciences.

Further references

Bakhtin, M. (1981) *The Dialogic Imagination*. Austin, TX: University of Texas Press.

Barthes, R. (1975) 'An introduction to the structural analysis of narrative', *New Literary History*, 6: 237–62.

Brooks, P. (1984) *Reading for the Plot: Design and Intention in Narrative*. Cambridge, MA and London: Harvard University Press.

Clandinin, D. and Connelly, F. (2000) *Narrative Inquiry: Experience and Story in Qualitative Research*. San Francisco: Jossey-Bass.

Cortazzi, M. (1993) *Narrative Analysis*. Washington DC: Falmer Press.

Dominicé, P. (2000) *Learning From our Lives: Using Educational Biographies with Adults*. San Francisco: Jossey-Bass.

Gergen, K. (1992) 'Beyond narrative in the negotiation of therapeutic meaning', in S. McNamee and K.J. Gergen (eds) *Therapy as Social Construction*. London: Sage. pp. 166–85.

Gergen, K. (1994) *Realities and Relationships: Surroundings in Social Construction*. Cambridge, MA: Harvard University Press.

Gill, S. (2005) 'Learning across cultures', unpublished DPhil thesis, University of Sussex, Falmer, Brighton, UK.

Goodson, I. (2006) 'The rise of the life narrative', *Teacher Education Quarterly*, Fall: 7–21.

Goodson, I. and Gill, S. (forthcoming, 2010) *Narrative Pedagogy*. New York: Peter Lang Publishing.

Hinchman, L.P. and Hinchman, S.K. (1997) *Memory, Identity, Community: Idea of Narrative in the Human Sciences*. Albany, NY: SUNY Press.

Hitchcock, G. and Hughes, D. (1995) *Research and the Teacher: A Qualitative Introduction to School-Based Research*. New York: Routledge.

Labov, W. (1973) *Sociolinguistic Patterns*. Philadelphia: University of Pennsylvania Press.

MacIntyre, A. (1984) *After Virtue: A Study in Moral Theory*. Notre Dame: University of Notre Dame Press.

McAdams, P. (1996) 'Personality, modernity and the storied self: A contemporary framework for studying persons', *Psychological Inquiry*, 7: 295–321.

Mishler, E. (1986) *Research Interviewing: Context and Narrative*. Cambridge, MA: Harvard University Press.

Mishler, E. (1999) *Storylines: Craftartists' Narratives of Identity*. Cambridge, MA: Harvard University Press.

Ricoeur, P. (1983) *Hermeneutics and the Human Sciences*. Cambridge, England: Cambridge University Press.

Ricoeur, P. (1988) *Time and Narrative, Vol. 1*. Trans. Kathleen McLaughlin. Chicago: University of Chicago Press.

Riessman, C. (1993) *Narrative Analysis.* Thousand Oaks, CA: Sage Publications.

Riessman, C. (2005) 'Exporting ethics: A narrative about narrative research in South India', *Health*, 9(4): 473–90.

Taylor, C. (1989) *Sources of the Self: The Making of the Modern Identity*. Cambridge, MA: Harvard University Press.

Social Semiotics and Multimodal Texts

Diane Mavers, Institute of Education, University of London, UK

Gunther Kress, Institute of Education, University of London, UK

Summary

- Multimodality of texts
- Sign-making – signs constantly newly made
- The relation of form to meaning is iconic
- Transformations
- Representation
- Key theorists and writers
  - Carey Jewitt
  - Gunther Kress
  - Theo van Leeuwen

Key concepts

A need for new thinking

Language alone can no longer give us full access to the meanings of most contemporary messages, which are now constituted in several **modes**: on pages in the mode of *writing*, of *image* and of *layout*; on screens, through CD-ROMs and on the web, in *speech, music, image* – moving or still, in *gesture, colour* and *soundtrack*. In such **texts** each mode, the linguistic modes included, is a partial bearer of meaning only. The co-presence of modes in a text other than speech or writing raises the question of their function: are they merely replicating – echoing perhaps – what the linguistic already does? Are they ancillary, marginal, or do they play a full role in **representation**? If they do,

is it the same role as that of writing, or is it different? And if they play a different role, is that because their different materiality (say *sound* compared with *graphic matter*) and their differing cultural histories provide different potentials for making meaning? The **materiality** of mode does provide different **affordances**, which may be taken up, worked on and used differently in different cultures.

That being the case, we would need to look again at *speech* and *writing* and ask: if all modes have specific potentials, then what are those of *speech* and of *writing*? What are their potentials, their limitations, their particular affordances? That is a new question to ask of all modes used in representation and communication. It is a question of near Copernican import, with its implication that speech and writing do not occupy the central and privileged place in the firmament of communication.

We deal with that issue from the perspective of a general theory of meaning (-making), that of *Social Semiotics*; and the perspective of *multimodality* with its assumption that all modes have a specific part to play in the making of meaning. The shift of discipline from linguistics to *semiotics* is a move with two profound effects: (1) it is a move from a *concern with form alone*, to a *concern with form-and-meaning*, and (2) it is a move from a *concern with one mode* to a *concern with many modes*. It is a move from a theory in which form (as grammar and syntax) is dealt with separately from meaning (as semantics and pragmatics). It challenges the assumption – implicitly or explicitly held – that linguistic theory can provide a satisfactory and generally applicable account of all meaning in representation and communication, and posits that we need a theory which can account equally for *gesture, speech, image, writing, three-dimensional objects, colour, music.*

Semiotics, sign-making and signs

For one of the founders of semiotics, Ferdinand de Saussure (1857–1915), **semiotics** was 'the science of the life of signs in society'. To get a grasp on that 'science' we need to understand the characteristics of the formation of signs of whatever kind, at all levels. (Social) semiotics provides categories which, at one level apply to all modes equally, to *speech* as much as to *image*, to *gesture* as much as to *music*, to *writing* as much as to *three-dimensional objects*, and so on: categories such as **sign, text, genre, discourse**, or those of **metaphor** and **analogy**. At the same time we need descriptions which focus on the characteristics of specific modes; categories such as **verbs** or **vectors** (to deal with dynamism, action, movement), **subjects** and **objects**, or **salient entities** (to deal with grammar-like functions), **nouns** or **depictions** (to deal with the representation of object-like things and phenomena in the world).

Throughout much of the twentieth century, mainstream linguistics had, by and large, dealt with language in highly abstracted ways. Seen from a semiotic perspective, it had focused on form, on the **signifier**, while meaning was exported to peripheral enterprises – semantics, pragmatics, socio-linguistics, stylistics. Linguistics has been the science of the signifier, focused on form; semiotics has been the science of the sign, focused on a fusion of form and meaning, of **signified** and **signifier**. In the multimodal social semiotic approach taken here, the language-modes of *speech* and *writing* are also described semiotically, as a part of the landscape of modes available for representation; even though they remain special still in having highly valued social status; and while speech certainly carries the major load of communication in very many environments.

In social semiotics, the idea of sign-*use* is replaced by sign-*making*, a move away from the conventionally accepted view of stable signs **used** in representation and communication. Instead of an assumption of stability, signs now are seen as constantly newly made, out of the **interest** of the (socially and culturally formed and positioned) individual **sign-maker**. Their interest gives shape to the signs made.

The relation of form to meaning in social semiotics is *iconic*, that is, the signifier aptly 'resembles' the 'shape' of the signified (i.e. the shape of an oblong is a signifier that aptly indicates the look of what is signified – a bar magnet). If we think in terms of principles of connection, the relation of form and meaning is **motivated**, never **arbitrary** as it is assumed to be in the still dominant common-sense in mainstream semiotics. 'Motivation' assumes that the form of the signifier aptly expresses the content of the signified: 'what is being meant' is indicated by the shape of 'that which means it': wavy lines 'meaning' the movement of magnetic force (see Figure 19.2c in the Stories from the Field section).

If we look at the signs made in the drawing in Figure 19.2, we can see these principles at work in a number of ways: in the *selections* made by the children (e.g. the teacher's hands, seen on the whiteboard screen, were excluded from the scientific prediction) and in the *different ways* in which signs are realized (e.g. the drawings of the magnets-as-objects). Each of these signs is a (double) metaphor, for example 'togetherness means attraction and attraction means magnetic force'. These are motivated signs, where form and meaning are intrinsically connected, always in an iconic relation, always as metaphor; in fact they are always both. The interest of the sign-maker at the moment of making the sign leads to the selection of the criteria for representing that which is to be represented – 'attraction' say – and for selecting the signifier/form which most aptly, most plausibly represents it, namely conjoining. Signs are also made in the relationship between image and writing, in how meanings are *distributed* across modes (e.g. prior experimental conditions and hypothetical outcome in drawing and writing, as in Figure 19.2b).

Representation is never neutral: that which is represented in the sign, or in sign-complexes, realizes the interests, the perspectives, the positions and values of those who make signs. The outwardly-made sign functions in **communication**, and so it must necessarily fit into the structures of power which characterize environments of communication. In its form, the sign must factor that in as well – it must be fit for its role in the social field of communication.

We can now ask about the relation of *the sign that is made* to *signs (like it) that were made before*: is the relation one of copying, of imitation, or of imperfectly understood use? The shapes of the bar magnets in Figure 19.2 have strong similarities to shapes that might conventionally represent bar magnets; and yet each differs in specific ways, actually indicating quite precisely the functions that the child sign-maker wished to indicate. In other words, the signs are neither copies nor imitations: they are well-understood uses of existing signifier material. They are, in each case, specific *transformations* of culturally available material. As transformations they are always new, specific, and creative in a non-trivial sense: something that had not been there before is made from culturally available material. Such a view of sign-making has profound consequences for theories of meaning and therefore for theories of learning: the latter is not ever seen as mere and limited acquisition, as imperfect copying, as deficient imitation, but as the best possible new making from existing cultural material transformed in line with the sign-maker's interest.

The process of outward meaning-making has a transformative effect: the sign made outwardly is a new sign, a material instantiation of the sign-maker's changed resources. The inner transformations produce what we call 'learning'; which in turn can be seen as the (re-)shaping of the subjectivity of the maker of signs. The outward transformations produce syntactic, textual forms which are – however minutely – different from what they had been before; and these play their role, however slightly, in the change of the resources which the sign-maker used in making meaning. This accounts for semiotic and cultural change – whether in changes to writing, to speech, to gesture. It shows semiotic change, whether as the change in the modal resources or change in resources for making 'arrangements' such as syntax, as reflecting and tracking the values, structures, meanings of the social and cultural world of the meaning-maker. Engagement in these processes constantly transforms the subjectivity of the maker of signs.

The new technologies of information and communication facilitate the ready use of many modes together on the screens of the contemporary period; through that the now possible choice of modes has become a crucial issue. *Mode* has material form and bears everywhere the stamp of past social-cultural work, among other things the stamp of regularities of social institutions and practices. This regularity has traditionally been referred to as *grammar* and *syntax*.

One fundamental distinction in the potentials of modes – that of *space* and of *time* – is due to their materiality. *Time-based modes* – *speech, music* – have potentials for representation which differ from *space-based modes* – *image, layout, sculpture* and other *three-dimensional forms* such as *architectural arrangements,*

streetscapes; both differ from modes which combine *time* and *space*, such as *dance, gesture, action*. The fundamental logics of these types of mode differ: the *logic of time* affords the possibilities for making meaning through the temporal succession of elements, their place in a sequence constitutes a resource for meaning. The *logic of space* affords the possibilities for making meaning through the spatial distribution of simultaneously present elements; relations of elements in space are a resource for meaning. These lead, in all modes, to preferred textual/generic forms: *narrative* in speech and in writing; *display* in visual modes (and perhaps *displayed narrative* in the case of modes resting on both logics).

When choice of mode has become easy, the question about the characteristics of mode arises in ways it could not do before: what can this specific mode do, in relation to that which I wish to do? What are its limitations and potentials? What are the *affordances* of this or that mode? Such questions bring up the central question of *design*. Multimodally constituted texts rest on *design*, with its question: what resource is best to achieve that which I wish to communicate now, for this audience? To answer that question we need to understand fully the potentials, the affordances, of the different modes – what can *writing* do best? What can *image* do best? But also address the questions: is my intended audience more likely to respond to *image* or to *writing*, to *moving image*, sound of various kinds (*speech, music, soundtrack*, etc.) on a screen rather than writing alone in a book?

Implications for research design

The relevance of a multimodal social semiotic approach depends on what it is that is being investigated. From a multimodal perspective, people make and interpret signs made bodily (e.g. speech, gesture, gaze, movement) and graphically (e.g. writing and drawing), extending to moving image and sound in digital texts, as well as in objects (e.g. clothing, buildings, toys). Recognizing and studying the multimodality of face-to-face interaction and graphic texts is not new. It is well acknowledged in the disciplines of anthropology, interactional sociology, cultural studies, media studies, visual studies and design, to take just some examples. This approach is well suited to the study of a range of activities, such as working, playing, moving through and socializing in a variety of sites, including the street, the workplace, the museum and the home (e.g. Goodwin, 2000; Macken-Horarik, 2004; Scollon and Scollon, 2003). Social semiotics provides a particular theoretical lens. With its focus on representation and communication, it provides certain key concepts as it seeks to understand the social action of sign making. The Stories from the Field section that follows illustrates the use of a multimodal social semiotic perspective to research learning in a primary classroom. Together, this theoretical perspective and methodological approach frame what is studied, which materials are gathered, how they are analysed and the claims that are made.

In studying how people make meaning, video recording – which is increasingly common in social research – provides a means of capturing and observing closely the detail of what goes on: complex interrelationships in face-to-face communicational exchange; processes of producing a text on the page or the screen; and the relationships between them. When a researcher makes choices about what will be video recorded, this already constitutes a selection. Particular activities and participants are selected, and they are recorded from a particular angle, with a particular length of shot and over a particular period of time. Multimodal transcription is a further selection. Certain sections of footage are extracted for close attention in preference to others. Not everything is re-presented. Due to the complexity of interaction, the transciber may choose to include certain modes and exclude others. For example, speech and action may be incorporated, whilst facial expression and gaze may be omitted. Transcription is also varied with regard to which modes of reproduction are chosen. The original interaction might be remade as writing or as image (be that video stills, tracing of freeze frames or freehand drawing), or a combination of the two. Decisions are also made regarding how these are presented and arranged, whether as a table, a series of stills overlaid with writing, or a single drawing (see e.g. Bezemer, 2008; Flewitt et al., 2009; Goodwin, 2000; Norris, 2004). Transcribing video, which entails repeated viewings of extracts in real time, at speed and frame-by-frame, with and without sound, is immensely time consuming, and this should be factored into the research design.

Attending to the full repertoire of resources in representation and communication, a social semiotic approach to multimodal texts seeks to understand the meanings made with each mode, how those meanings are distributed, and the relationships between them. Examining texts entails study of each mode discretely and as an ensemble. The graphic texts people make consist of writing and image, presented and set out in different ways. Which resources of writing did the text maker select, and how did s/he put together not only words and wording, but also orthographic or typographic features such as font, style, colour, size and emphasis, and how is the text arranged? In drawing, how are the lines, shapes, positioning, directionality, colour and so on combined? What relationship is constructed between writing and image? In seeking to understand texts, the ideological shaping of meaning demands that the analysis is contextualized in the purpose, relations of power and environment in and for which it was made. Typically, questions that drive multimodal social semiotic analysis include: Which resources has the text maker selected to make which meanings? How have they been combined? How was the making of the text a response to the social environment?

Stories from the field

Investigating text-making in the classroom from a multimodal social semiotic perspective

To illustrate how social semiotic theory and a multimodal methodology can be used in a research study, we have chosen an episode in one science lesson.[1] A teacher frames a task, the class (7- and 8-year-olds) produces texts in response and there is subsequent whole-class interaction around these texts. The aim of the study was to investigate how teachers use whole-class digital technologies and what children do in response. Studying multimodal texts through a social semiotic lens provided a means of tracing relationships between pedagogy and children's engagement with curricular subject matter in the context of everyday classroom practices.[2]

Video recording was one means of gathering data: what the teacher said and did, how the children went about producing their texts (e.g. the order in which they drew and wrote, hesitation and flow, exchange with others) and whole-class interactions that subsequently went on around them. A hand-held camcorder enabled flexibility with regard to what was recorded. A second fixed camcorder provided sustained recording of a single child throughout the lesson. The children made their hypotheses on individual dry-wipe whiteboards. In the everyday busyness of the classroom, these are here and gone, made and erased soon afterwards. Photography was a means of capturing these fleeting texts. Notwithstanding their fixity in the paper, it is important to bear in mind their ephemerality in the course of the lesson. Interviews held separately with teachers and groups of children (with access to their whiteboard texts) provided information not available in observations, including prior experience and knowledge of the curricular subject entity, reflections on and explanations of what had been represented and why, and issues around assessment.

The 5 minutes 16 seconds of activity subject to particular analytical examination was located in a lesson of over one hour in length. Over the opening 13 minutes, the teacher introduced the topic of magnetic force. He asked questions, displayed and read pre-prepared writing, explained, showed objects, enacted processes, introduced new vocabulary, made a mind map and gave instructions. The children responded to questions, engaged in paired debate, read and copied from the screen, and observed different kinds of magnets. Enacting the 'push', 'pull', 'direction' and 'move' of magnetic force with ready-to-hand objects and those specified in the copied mind map framed the task of prediction.

After this introduction, the teacher asked the class to hypothesize what would happen if two magnets are moved closer together. He simulated the experimental procedures for the forthcoming hands-on investigation by displaying and acting on two bar magnets using a 'visualiser' (a digital display technology consisting of a high quality video camera connected to a data projector). Meanings were distributed multimodally, simultaneously and complexly between objects, actions, gestures and speech in intricately interwoven and constantly shifting configurations of communicational ensembles. What was displayed visually on the class screen and what the teacher said were transcribed, because these were the modes available on the video recording and because this is what the children were expected to attend to (Figure 19.1). Due to the unsatisfactory quality of the video stills, images and arrows were used to represent gesture, along with a description written in bold, selected for its typographical differentiation at a glance from the italics of speech. A tabular structure for the transcript enabled the visual (displayed on the screen) and the oral/aural (spoken by the teacher) to be separated. Not every shift in movement could be shown, and not every inflection of speech is included. Positioning gesture to the left of the transcript – an

indication that it should be seen as a critical feature of the teacher's framing of the task and not a mere appendage – it is shifts in movement that framed construction of the transcript rather than the pauses of speech. Repeated images (adjustment of the bar magnets and occasions when the hands are removed) and an instance of simulating inward movement pick out criterial moments.

One aim of the research was to investigate how children respond to digitally mediated pedagogy graphically. Analysing the multimodality of their texts made on dry-wipe whiteboards entailed cataloguing the signifiers of drawing (e.g. shape, dividing lines, colouring, position, orientation, plane, wavy lines, arrows) and writing (e.g. verbs, pronouns, adverbs, tense). This provided a means of examining how children had distributed meaning across modes and how they had created relationships between them. The texts were next examined in relation to the transcript in order to trace constancies and shifts in form and meaning. Brief, some of the hypotheses consisted of 'just' a quick drawing, and some also included a few words. This was not laziness. Constrained by the width of the marker and the size of the board, what the children did was shaped towards the familiar classroom practice of holding up their boards for whole-class display. Their representational economy presupposed opportunities for face-to-face interaction where additional bodily communicated information could be supplied.

The children's dry-wipe whiteboard hypotheses were not replications of what they had seen and heard in the teacher's framing of the task, but redesigns. The children remade what they saw with the resources of drawing. In a precise response to their teacher's instruction to 'show me', everyone in the class drew the bar magnets as two divided rectangles, some with shading to indicate the two ends. These features were not mentioned in speech. Without exception, drawing the bar magnets in a horizontal alignment and on the same plane showed methodological procedure. This was shown to the class, but not mentioned by the teacher. It was assumed that what was presented as a projected image on the screen would be recognized. This demonstrates the role of the visual in pedagogy, and the entirely ordinary process of transduction between modes in text production.

Of the 59 per cent of children in the class who chose to write as well as draw, two kinds of relationship were constructed between these modes. Meaning congruence was created where representa-

Gesture		Speech
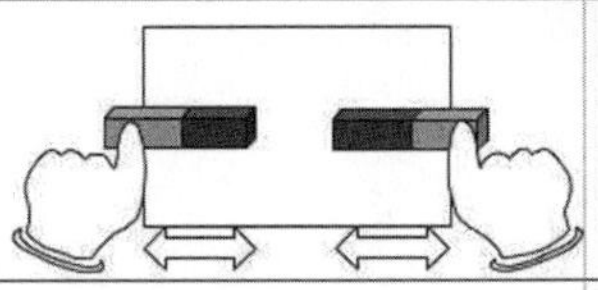	touches each bar magnet and adjusts them slightly	_so_ there are our two magnets _okay_ (..)
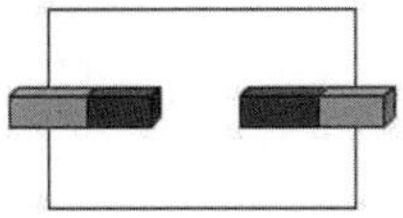		_what_ do you think (.) think about this (.) don't put your hands up for now (.)
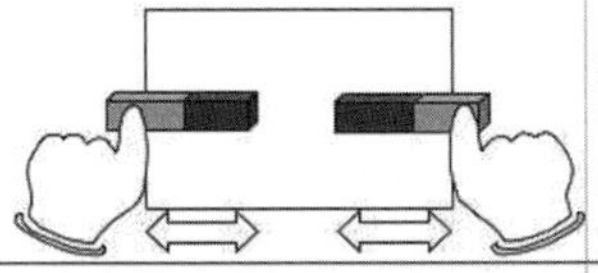	touches each bar magnet and adjusts them slightly	_if_ I (..) move them
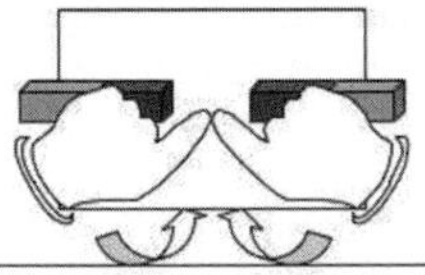	brings fingers together above the magnets	_closer_ together (..)
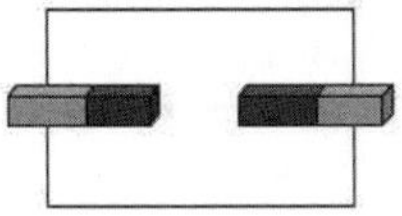		then let go (..) what do you think would happen to the magnets?

Figure 19.1   Extract from a transcript of the teacher's framing of the task

tion of the anticipated experimental outcome was shared by these two modes, for example when two magnets were drawn in a conjoined state and the writing stated 'Stick Together' (Figure 19.2a). Even so, this is not replication. Writing 'Stick Together' states in a concise combination of verb and adverb the prediction of attraction as dynamic conjoining. Drawing shows the attributes of objects in their matched shape and equal size, with division, labelling and lines of shading specifying the differently coloured ends of the bar magnets. It also shows the hypothetical post-experimental outcome as spatial relationships in joined positioning and sustained horizontal orientation, unlike the magnets that remained displayed in the screen. (One child later explained, 'I like drawed like three or four little lines in the bar magnet to make it look like two of them are stuck together.')

Elsewhere, method and prediction were distributed between drawing and writing. In a complementary semiotic relationship, pre-experimental conditions are shown in drawing as divided oblongs positioned apart

(e.g. Figure 19.2b). Writing 'they will go toghter (together)' – note the use of the future tense – anticipates the post-experimental outcome. Drawing and writing were made to perform particular and different functions. A connection was made between these two modes in the assumption that 'they' refers to the divided rectangles. Removed from the specificity of the lesson, this text might be difficult to decipher. In the context of the investigation, the children's meanings were readily understood.

Five children added wavy lines or arrows to indicate movement and to theorize the scientific phenomenon of magnetic force (e.g. Figure 19.2c). They show present conditions (the magnets positioned apart), specified methodology ('move lit (little) bit forward'), theorized scientific processes (lines described in the interview as 'magnetic waves') and predicted outcome (conjoined magnets and the writing '– then they are together'). Framed by the stipulation of the science curriculum in England, these texts meet the requirement to record method, hypothesis and explanation (DfEE and QCA, 1999: 83–4).

(a) Congruence

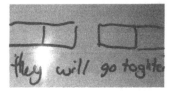

(b) Complementarity

(c) Recording scientifically

Figure 19.2 Dry-wipe whiteboard texts

Tracing the curricular entity of magnetic force provided opportunities to investigate constancies and changes between forms and meanings as one text became another. Even if entirely ordinary, this was not a case of mere 'translation', but rather demanded the semiotic work of interpretation and remaking. Shifts from the embodied communication of gesturing and talking around objects to the graphic representation of drawing and writing are transductions between modes. Something made in one way was redesigned with different resources, and for a very particular purpose. What could be done was dependent on the affordances – the possibilities and constraints – of the chosen modes in the very specific context of the science lesson. The children's sign making was not at all random, but was shaped by their own interests and motivated by the representational practices of the curricular subject and the practices of the classroom. So entirely ordinary that this passes by largely unnoticed, these shifts between modes are what, in part, constitute learning. A social semiotic perspective on multimodal communication and representation provided a means for re-seeing the complexities of the rhetorics of teaching and children's demonstration of their learning.

Notes

1. The research project Shapes of Representation, Shapes of Knowledge: From Object to Visualiser to Page (January to December 2007), directed by Diane Mavers, was funded by the Centre for Excellence in Work-Based Learning for Education Professionals (WLE) at the Institute of Education, University of London.
2. For an earlier version of this work, please see Mavers, D. (2009) 'Student text-making as semiotic work', *Journal of Early Childhood Literacy*, 9(2): 141–55.

Annotated bibliography

Hodge, R. and Kress, G. (1988) *Social Semiotics*. Cambridge: Polity Press.
In exploring how systems of meaning are socially contextualized, this book addresses issues of power and ideology, space and time, and gender and class.

Jewitt, C. (ed.) (2009) *The Routledge Handbook of Multimodal Analysis*. Abingdon: Routledge.
With contributions from leading authorities in multimodal research, this book is divided into four sections: theoretical and methodological tools, key factors, different theoretical perspectives and case studies.

Kress, G. (2010) *Multimodality: A Social Semiotic Approach to Contemporary Communication*. London: RoutledgeFalmer.
Looking beyond language, this book examines the multiple communicational modes of everyday life from a social semiotic perspective.

Kress, G. and van Leeuwen, T. (2006) *Reading Images: The Grammar of Visual Design*. London: Routledge.
Significant for its contribution to the field, this book provides analytical tools for examining image and 'visual' design (e.g. salience, framing and information value) across a range of examples including advertisements, fine art and diagrams.

Mavers, D. (2011) *Children's Drawing and Writing: The Remarkable in the Unremarkable*. New York: Routledge.
Examining features of text-making that pass by largely unnoticed, this book investigates the multiple ways in which children make meaning in the 'semiotic work' of their drawing and writing.

Norris, S. (2004) *Analyzing Multimodal Interaction: A Methodological Framework*. London: Routledge.
This book offers a methodology for examining multimodal communication in ordinary, everyday settings, and provides a practical guide for analysing the multiple modes of interaction.

Pahl, K. (1999) *Transformations: Meaning Making in Nursery Education*. Stoke-on-Trent: Trentham Books.
This book explores the multiple ways in which nursery-aged children make meaning as they draw, write, cut out, stick together and model, with implications for developing literacy.

Scollon, R. and Scollon, S.W. (2003) *Discourses in Place: Language in the Material World*. London: Routledge.
With a focus on the materiality of sign making, this book provides a methodology for analysing the language of interaction, such as road signs and notices, in a range of settings across the world.

Stein, P. (2008) *Multimodal Pedagogies in Diverse Classrooms: Representation, Rights and Resources*. London: Routledge.
This book explores how multimodality in the classroom can be a means of addressing democracy, politics and social justice in the diverse classroom contexts of post-apartheid Africa.

van Leeuwen, T. (2005) *Introducing Social Semiotics*. London: Routledge.
This book is an introduction to how semiotic resources carry cultural value in contemporary society, exemplified from a range of domains, including journalism, advertising and rap.

Further references

Bezemer, J. (2008) 'Displaying Orientation in the Classroom: Students' Multimodal Responses to Teacher Instructions', *Linguistics and Education*, 19: 166–78.

DfEE and QCA (1999) *The National Curriculum: Handbook for Primary Teachers in England Key Stages 1 and 2*. London: Department for Education and Employment and Qualifications and Curriculum Authority.

Flewitt, R., Nind, M. and Payler, J. (2009) '"If she's left with books she'll just eat them": Considering inclusive multimodal literacy practices', *Journal of Early Childhood Literacy*, 9(2): 211–33.

Goodwin, C. (2000) 'Action and embodiment within situated human interaction', *Journal of Pragmatics*, 32: 1489–522.

Macken-Horarik, M. (2004) 'Interacting with the multimodal text: Reflections on image and verbiage in ArtExpress', *Visual Communication*, 3(1): 5–26.

Communities of Practice

David Benzie, University College of St Mark and St John, Plymouth, UK

Bridget Somekh, Education and Social Research Institute, Manchester Metropolitan University, UK and University of Canterbury, New Zealand

Summary

- A theory of social practice
- Relational interdependence within a community
- Situated learning
- Legitimate peripheral participation
- Boundary objects and brokers
- Key theorists and writers
  - John Seely Brown
  - Paul Duguid
  - Jean Lave
  - Etienne Wenger

Key concepts

David Benzie and Bridget Somekh

The power of the conceptual model of a Community of Practice (CoP) depends on a proper understanding of what is meant by the terms 'practice' and 'community' within the literature of sociocultural psychology. The huge uptake of the term CoP, since it was used in the title of Part 4 of Lave and Wenger's book, *Situated Learning: Legitimate Peripheral Participation* (1991), has been extraordinary. However, it may have been more to do with associating the sense of mutual support suggested by 'community' with the everyday notion of 'practice' (and its links to efficiency in phrases such as 'best practice') – as they are used in common parlance – than with the actual meanings

that Lave and Wenger, and later Wenger (1998), intended. This is how Lave and Wenger define social practice:

> Briefly, a theory of social practice emphasizes the relational interdependency of agent and world, activity, meaning, cognition, learning, and knowing. It emphasizes the inherently socially negotiated character of meaning and the interested, concerned character of the thought and action of persons-in-activity. This view also claims that learning, thinking, and knowing are relations among people in activity in, with, and arising from the socially and culturally structured world. (1991: 50–1)

The last sentence of this quotation indicates the importance of community to developing and sustaining a social practice. In the CoP model, 'community' is made up of 'relations between people in activity'; and practice emerges from this 'relational interdependence' within a community.

The CoP model was derived by Lave and Wenger (1991) from ethnographic studies of apprenticeship among diverse groups – Yucatec midwives, Vai and Gola tailors, naval quartermasters, meat cutters, non-drinking alcoholics. Thus, narrative has always been seen as a core means of learning in, and from, Communities of Practice. The starting point of the book was an exploration of the process of 'legitimate peripheral participation' whereby learning came about through participation in a 'situated' community of practitioners. This was a deliberate move away from theories of learning as individual cognition, towards a new theory of learning as shaped by context and relationships. It was in line with important developments in theories of learning at the time. Brown et al. (1989) had argued that the environment in which the learner engages in learning is an integral part of the learning experience and shapes what is learned. For example, when students learn mathematics in a maths laboratory, working alongside mathematicians, the 'authentic' experience enables them to co-construct – with mathematicians – a particular view of the world through socially shared 'webs of belief' (1989: 33).

From the beginning, therefore, the CoP model has been centrally concerned with theories of 'situated' learning. These provide a challenge to previous theories, such as behaviourism and cognition, which are strongly embedded in the practices of schools. In a meta-analysis of case studies of learning, in a book she edited with Chaiklin, Lave (1996) shows that the case studies conducted in *authentic communities of practice* demonstrate that 'learning is an integral aspect of activity in and with the world at all times' (1996: 8), whereas the case studies of activity in settings dedicated to education show learning to be highly problematic. She suggests that these latter cases:

> provide evidence of the sociocultural production of failure to learn. . . . They are about how people learn identities and identify the situated meaning of what is to be learned, and the specific shaping of people's identities as learners. . . . Students who fail (and perhaps the most successful as well) are the sacrificial lambs whose fates give material form to legitimate knowledge. (1996: 10–1)

It is useful to compare the presentation of CoP in Lave and Wenger's *Situated Learning: Legitimate Peripheral Participation* (1991) with its elaboration into the full CoP model in Wenger's *Communities of Practice: Learning, Meaning and Identity* (1998). In the later book, Wenger only mentions legitimate peripheral participation (LPP) in passing (1998: 100–1). Nevertheless, it is important to note that some of the more recent critiques of CoP reveal a partial understanding of its original conceptualization as LPP. For example, critiques of CoP's failure to take account of the identity and agency of individuals ignore Lave and Wenger's specific focus on 'the person', and the transformative nature of learning for participating individuals: 'Learning thus implies becoming a different person with respect to the possibilities enabled by these systems

of relations. To ignore this aspect of learning is to overlook the fact that learning involves the construction of identities' (1991: 53).

Similarly, critiques of CoP's failure to engage with issues of power tend to overlook the emphasis that Lave and Wenger place on the contradictions and displacements that result from LPP of newcomers: 'The different ways in which old-timers and newcomers establish and maintain identities conflict and generate competing viewpoints on the practice and its development' (Lave and Wenger, 1991: 115). LPP is not concerned with the 'internalization' of knowledge, whether discovered or transmitted, but with 'sociocultural transformations' resulting from newcomers and old-timers participating in the context of 'a changing shared practice' (1991: 47–9); and this process is characterized by 'the contradictions and struggles inherent in social practice and the formation of identities' (1991: 57).

In his 1998 book, Wenger develops CoP into a fully described theoretical framework. His starting point is that 'a social theory of learning must . . . integrate the components necessary to characterize social participation as a process of learning and of knowing' (Wenger, 1998: 4–5). He lists these components as 'meaning', 'practice', 'community' and 'identity'. He then defines communities of practice as all those overlapping social groupings which are an integral part of our daily lives.

The next step in Wenger's thesis is the presentation of two vignettes and a coda about the community of practice of workers processing health claims at Alinsu. These then become points of reference for elaborating the theory in each of the main sections of the book – on practice, identity and design. Meaning for health claims processors – and, it is argued, for us all – is constructed within communities of practice through the dual process of 'participation' and 'reification'. It is important to note that whereas many writers use the word reification to describe loss of subjective meaning in a negative sense, for Wenger this process of de-personalizing and naming concepts and procedures plays a key part in strengthening and developing the power of ideas. He argues that through participation we mutually construct our identities and through reification we identify and accord meanings to abstract concepts so that we can own them and manipulate them.

Community is constructed and made coherent by practice. There are three dimensions of this process: 'mutual engagement', 'a joint enterprise' and 'a shared repertoire' (1998: 73). After detailed analysis of how these operate in practice, Wenger points out that they are not always in place in a community of practice. However, he goes on:

> Still, most of us have experienced the kind of social energy that the combination of these three dimensions of shared practice can generate. Conversely, we may also have experienced how this social energy can prevent us from responding to new situations or from moving on. (1998: 85)

In Part II of the book the emphasis is on the impact on individual identity of membership in a community of practice, and the power implications and politics of membership. The focus is upon the individual's membership of multiple communities of practice and the way that the boundaries between these communities need to be negotiated. Members of one CoP need to engage in external relations with other CoPs whose work impinges on their own. The continuities and discontinuities of these boundary relations are critical factors in the continuous co-construction and transformation of practices. In this context 'boundary objects' such as artefacts, procedures and concepts that reify practices are useful in helping CoPs to 'organize their interconnections' (Wenger, 1998: 105) and there is an important role for brokers who have the legitimacy to lead the process of interconnection by engaging in 'translation, coordination and alignment between perspectives' (1998: 109).

In the final section of *Communities of Practice*, entitled 'Epilogue: Design' Wenger extends the CoP analytical model discussed in Parts I and II, and illustrated in the Alinsu vignettes, and re-casts it as a 'design framework, laying out basic questions that must be addressed and basic components that must be provided by a design for learning' (Wenger, 1998: 229). This broadening of the CoP model to encompass both an analytical framework and a framework for designing and implementing change is one reason why the CoP literature over the last decade has become so rich and diverse.

The research literature provides examples of the CoP model being used for a wide variety of purposes. Perhaps its primary use is as a theoretical framework for the analysis of qualitative data about social processes: for example, Oliver and Carr's (2009) study of learning in the online role-playing game, World of Warcraft. Others use CoP as a framework for research design as well as analysis: for example

Denscombe (2008) suggests that CoP might be an ideal 'research paradigm' for mixed methods research, because of its ability to accommodate cross-cultural variations and inconsistencies. Wenger himself has led the way in using the model for consultancy work with organizations and writing texts for managers (Wenger et al., 2002). DePalma argues that Wenger's vignettes of health claims workers have focused CoP too much on 'closed and reproductive systems' and illustrates its use in developing 'learning and practice communities that are more transformative and less reproductive' (DePalma, 2009: 353–4). Cobb and McClain (2006) suggest that Communities of Practice that share similar values and practices, through adhering to the CoP model of situated learning, can be linked to form 'networks of practice' and that these provide a powerful tool for upscaling reforms in teachers' instructional practices from one CoP to the whole network.

Many writers, like DePalma, engage critically with the CoP model, analysing its strengths and weaknesses and suggesting ways of extending it. Johnson (2007) uses it as an analytical framework in international development projects and suggests it needs a stronger focus on the history of social relations, sensitivity to contestation and difference, and to multiple agendas of participants. Busher and colleagues use it in a study of middle leadership in schools and colleges and find its usefulness limited by 'its inadequate theorizing of power and micro-politics' (2007: 418). Fuller and colleagues, in a study of workplace learning, show that CoP undervalues the role that teaching plays, is too dismissive of formal education, pays too little attention to the diversity of students (gender, ethnicity, social class) and 'acknowledge[s] but never fully explore[s] the significance of conflict and unequal power relations' (Fuller et al., 2005: 66). The edited collection by Barton and Tusting (2005) provides a critique of CoP in terms of its under-theorizing of the relationship between language and power in communities, followed by case studies that reveal weaknesses, for example in relation to theorizing responses to 'risk' (Myers, 2005: 198– 213). In the final chapter, Gee (2005: 214–32) argues that CoP should be seen as one model among alternatives, and suggests that participation in online 'affinity spaces' requires an analytical framework that is not predicated on 'membership'. The edited collection by Hughes and colleagues (2007) provides a scholarly critique of a number of specific aspects of the CoP model, with case studies that assess its strengths and weaknesses when used in various settings. Together, these two edited collections have made a substantial contribution to the CoP literature.

Implications for research design

A key feature of CoP is its focus on learning and transformation, through continuous co-construction of identities within a social practice. Thus CoP is a theory well suited to research that has a developmental focus, and by implication poorly suited to research that is looking for outcomes that are narrowly defined. It can focus on the experiences of individuals, but always sees them as 'situated' within the social practices of the groups to which they belong.

An important first step will be to decide if CoP theory is to be used for the analysis of data in situations where the researcher is also a participant. If the aim is to use CoP theory for participant research, a number of ethical issues will need to be addressed, regarding the power relations between the researchers and participants, and ownership of the change process.

In CoP research, a community will be selected and the research will focus on the inter-relationship between the community as a whole and the individuals that make it up. The research is likely to begin by focusing on the nature of individuals' engagement with the CoP as a whole. CoP research can also focus on a selected sample that has commonality within a larger community, for example, children who fail in numeracy or literacy at school.

The CoP model provides a number of very useful analytical tools which can be used to develop a constellation of interrelated research questions. What is 'the joint enterprise'? Who is participating – or not participating – in the 'mutual engagement'? What jokes, stories and memories make up the 'shared repertoire'? What concepts, artefacts, procedures have been reified? Where are the boundaries with other CoPs? How does membership of other CoPs impact on the CoP in question? Who are the 'brokers' for external relations? What 'boundary objects' are being used, and by whom?

Research methods are likely to include participatory observation, the collection of artefacts including documents, interviewing of participants, perhaps the use of key informants to provide access to specialist knowledge.

There is usually a strong element of narrative in the reports of CoP research, in order to portray the situated nature of the community's practice. A useful approach is to present vignettes with accompanying analytic commentary.

Don't forget that if you decide to use CoP theory, the quality of your research will depend on using it as a model to be explored and developed, rather than as a rigid framework that is applied mechanically. The best research reported in the literature has made a contribution to CoP theory by approaching it critically and looking for ways of customizing it to the needs of particular contexts. The core feature of CoP research must always be to reach the best possible understanding of CoP practices, and/or the practices of individuals within and between CoPs, and this may entail additional theoretical work.

Stories from the field

David Benzie

Some of my students are really good with IT while others just don't get it. Why? And what can I do about it?

I teach students in higher education to use computers. In broad terms, the aim is to develop their Information Technology (IT) capability to the point where they are able to make effective personal and professional use of technology. Some of my students are aspiring schoolteachers and their courses take place in a context where there is considerable pressure to make effective use of computers in the classroom.

It was against this background that I decided to conduct a three-year longitudinal study of a cohort of undergraduate students with the initially stated aim of illuminating the way in which undergraduate students perceive, acquire and deploy IT skills during the course of their study (Benzie, 2000). As with much practitioner research, it was not driven by the desire to explore the issue from a particular theoretical perspective. Rather, the driving force was a desire to provide an interpretation of the student experience that would be helpful to those who are responsible for teaching and supporting students in contexts where there is an IT dimension. What I failed to notice at the start, and for some considerable time, was the extent to which the implicit assumption that IT capability is an individual attribute and that the acquisition and deployment of IT skills are separate, albeit related, activities was framing my thinking. These assumptions were first exposed, and then rejected, as Lave and Wenger's (1991) and Wenger's (1998) theories slowly moved from off-stage to centre-stage during the main analytical phase of the research. The story of the research illustrates how and why this happened.

The starting assumption was that a number of research tools would be needed in order to track changes in IT skills and in IT-related attitudes over time. (Literature suggested that the latter might be significant.) Additionally, it was assumed that instruments would be needed to illuminate the actual use of IT by students and to identify the contexts in which their learning occurred. Against this background an IT skills self-assessment questionnaire and three IT-related attitude scales were developed. These instruments also collected routine nominal data. In addition, an 'IT Diary' was created which individual students used to record IT-related activities over a week. These diaries were themselves linked to a series of interviews. After two and a half years, 225 students had completed the questionnaires on three occasions. About 20 students kept IT diaries covering 182 distinct weeks. Eighty-three interviews were conducted, the majority being linked to a recently completed IT Diary.

Early assumptions were also made about the relationship between the data from the different instruments. Foremost amongst the assumptions was the expectation that the large IT skills questionnaire and attitude data sets, together with basic coded data from the IT Diaries, would be the main source of insight. The interviews were merely seen as having a role to play in assessing the reliability and validity of the IT Diaries. But it did not turn out that way!

As the research progressed, the stories from the interviews became ever more fascinating. An early change of perspective came when it became clear that the real power of the IT Diary came from its ability to trigger interview dialogue. Attributing a code to the diary entry 'spent 2 hours word-processing an essay' and subsequently analysing many hundreds of similar entries is all very well, but it simply fails to catch the social reality that often lies behind such bald statements. It was not untypical, for example, for a diary entry like this to be the product of a complex social negotiation between family members who each wished to use the single available computer. In this situation, power relationships and value systems within the family lead to one claim becoming privileged. Experiences like this had two important consequences. Firstly, the perceived relationship between

diary and interview switched, with the diary ultimately seen as an interview discussion starter. Secondly, the stories generated by the interviews began to highlight the profound significance of social context in shaping the way in which students interact with computers.

The full data set was available shortly after the self-assessment questionnaire and the attitude surveys were completed for the third time. By then it was clear that the interview data was going to be as least as significant as the quantitative data but it was not clear how the various data sets would finally relate to one another, or even how a single theoretical framework could be used to create a coherent account of all the available data. Against this background, an extensive exploration of the quantitative data set was undertaken and a number of statistically significant patterns did emerge. There was, however, one pivotal pattern that shifted the theoretical focus of the research. The quantitative data showed, with exceptional clarity, that patterns in the development of self-assessed IT skills varied tremendously from student to student. Some students who started their degree course with very low skills made huge progress whilst others made almost none. This pattern of differential progress was repeated for students at every level of initial skill.

The nominal variables of age, gender and degree course provided no accessible explanation for this pattern, though the nominal variables associated with attendance on an IT course and with computer ownership did point to other intriguing patterns. IT-focused courses, unsurprisingly, made a significant difference to self-assessed IT skills but it was also clear that some students who did not attend a course also managed to make gains. Where and how was that learning taking place? What was more, attending an IT course did not appear to affect the future development of self-assessed IT skills. In other words, students did not appear to have learnt how to continue learning about IT.

It was at this stage, over three years into the research, that the full analytical focus switched to the qualitative data generated by the interviews. Could it explain the patterns evidenced in the quantitative data? The interview data had already been explored to some extent using Strauss and Corbin's (1990) approach to grounded theory and this acted as a powerful sensitizing agent. In particular, that exploration highlighted the significance, and complexity, of context related features in shaping each individual's 'IT story' over a period of time. This experience, together with a preliminary reading of Lave and Wenger (1991), led to an 'informed guess'. The hunch was that Lave and Wenger's framework, with its focus on the situated nature of learning, might illuminate the data from a perspective that would lead to a coherent account of the patterns that had been observed.

The next stage in the research involved a close reading of Lave and Wenger (1991) with two main aims. The first being to immerse myself in their perspective and the second being to highlight key questions, given what I already knew from the interview data. Those key questions included fundamental ones concerning the concept of a community of practice – how does it translate from the well-bounded contexts described by Lave and Wenger (1991) to the rather different settings that are found in higher education? Other key questions were less fundamental but equally intriguing. Lave and Wenger (1991: 57, 93), for example, draw passing attention to the role that near-peers play in learning, yet the first reading of my data suggested this role was highly significant.

Following this, the full data sets (quantitative data, IT diaries and interviews) for two students, Adam and Hazel, were used as the basis for detailed case studies. These were designed to explore the questions that arose from the reading of Lave and Wenger (1991). Wenger's (1998) later book was published around this time, and from that point on it too had an impact on the analysis. The exploration of the experiences of these two students now moved to centre-stage in the research. The quantitative data, originally seen as having the leading role, now moved to become part of the supporting cast.

Both stories provided challenges to theory whilst also affirming many key tenets. Communities of Practice were clearly visible as discernible and useful analytic units in the stories of both students, though the demarcation of boundaries was more problematic than even Wenger (1998: 103) suggests. The experiences of Adam and Hazel, for example, suggest that the demarcation of a community is itself a situated act (Benzie, 2000: 163). Where a boundary is drawn depends on who is drawing the boundary and for what reason. This is particularly important to recognize when seeking to use this theory in settings where the unit labelled as a community is either transient or of secondary significance (or both) to those involved.

As the analysis proceeded it also became clear that Adam and Hazel's experiences could only be understood by recognizing that they were both members of multiple communities of practice and that they were both members of contemporary and historic communities. It also became clear that both students needed to be seen as active agents in multiple communities with their membership in each community having an impact on their membership in others. This in turn led to a theory of participation that suggests that the pattern of an individual's participation in a Community of Practice is shaped by the resulting force from three web-like structures. The first web concerns legitimacy: what are the values and rationales that a community uses to legitimate and promote certain activities? For a given individual these legitimating rationales have to be set against the legitimizing rationales that are available to them through their membership in other communities. Inevitably, the individual actively traverses this web of available rationales as they choose to engage, or otherwise, in community activity. The other webs concern power and motivation.

Hazel's story powerfully illustrates this theory of participation. She knew that playing and 'fiddling around' are leading legitimate activities in many IT-related communities, yet deep in her value system was the notion that learning and playing are illegitimate bedfellows. She always struggled when her courses involved work with a computer. The explanation for the difficulties that she experienced is grounded in Lave and Wenger's (1991) and Wenger's (1998) theories. It illustrates how they can be used as a foundation for accounts of learning that respect social complexity.

There were two other significant outcomes from the research that could be directly attributed to the decision to use a theory concerning Communities of Practice. Firstly, a theory of IT capability was created that recognizes the mutually constitutive nature of a community and its members (Benzie, 2000: 190). A distinctive feature of the theory is its inclusion of IT capability descriptors for the community, as well as for the individual. This symmetry is a consequence of working in a theoretical framework that relentlessly drives issues of context and relationship to the fore.

The second significant outcome was an explanatory model for the failure of some individuals to make effective use of IT. The distinctive feature of the model is that it explains failure without giving primacy to matters of individual cognitive inadequacy (Benzie, 2000: 217). Again, this arose because the underlying theory shifts the focus in discussion of learning from matters of cognition to ones of enculturation.

The strength of working with an analytical framework that has the concept of a Community of Practice at the centre is that it emphasizes the situated nature of knowledge and brings matters of context to the fore. It highlights relationships both between individuals and between individual and community. In this way, it is well suited to supporting accounts that capture social complexity.

Working with Community of Practice theory does, however, bring particular challenges. Any given community has a complex set of relationships with other communities and so consideration of its affairs inevitably requires matters in other contexts to be scrutinized. Wenger (1998) provides a comprehensive taxonomy of entities and concepts that assist analysis. The complexity of the terminology may be seen as a barrier but it does provide a vocabulary that enables social complexity to be probed.

There is a mutually constitutive relationship between a Community of Practice and the individuals who belong to it. In research terms, this is particularly powerful because it forces individual-centric studies to take account of social structures and provides the means to do so. Conversely, it forces studies that focus on social institutions and groupings to account for active individuals whose behaviours are shaped by their experiences in multiple contexts.

Annotated bibliography

Barton, D. and Tusting, K. (2005) *Beyond Communities of Practice: Language, Power and Social Context*. Cambridge and New York, Cambridge University Press.
An edited collection of ten chapters, each exploring the concept of CoP from a different point of view. The Introduction provides an excellent overview.

Busher, H., Hammersley-Fletcher, L. and Turner, C. (2007) 'Making sense of middle leadership: Community, power and practice', *School Leadership and Management*, 27(5): 405–22.
By showing how the authors attempted to use theories of power in conjunction with the CoP framework, this article both points to a shortcoming in the CoP model, and explores ways of overcoming it.

Cobb, P. and McClain, K. (2006) 'The collective mediation of a high-stakes accountability program: Communities and networks of practice', *Mind, Culture and Activity*, 13(2): 80–100.

The concepts of 'boundary encounters', 'brokers' and 'boundary objects' are used to explore how innovative practices can be upscaled. Communities that have a shared ethos can be said to form 'networks of practice'.

Denscombe, M. (2008) 'A research paradigm for the mixed methods approach', *Journal of Mixed Methods Research*, 2(1): 270–83.
This article suggests that CoP provides a theoretical framework that has particular advantages for mixed methods research, because it focuses on issues of practice rather than methodological concerns.

DePalma, R. (2009) 'Leaving Alinsu: Towards a transformative community of practice', *Mind, Culture and Activity*, 16: 353–70.
This describes use of CoP theory to support the process of transformation in a participatory action research project.

Hughes, J., Jewson, N. and Unwin, L. (2007) *Communities of Practice: Critical Perspectives*. Abingdon, Oxon and New York, Routledge.
An edited collection of 14 chapters that provide an analysis and critique of the concept of CoP. The Introduction provides an excellent overview.

Johnson, H. (2007) 'Communities of practice and international development', *Progress in Development Studies*, 7(4): 277–90.
The CoP model is used to explore the dynamics of social learning in the field of international development. It provides a situated model of learning that is responsive to diversity.

Lave, J. and Wenger, E. (1991) *Situated Learning: Legitimate Peripheral Participation*. Cambridge and New York: Cambridge University Press.
This is the seminal text in which the term 'communities of practice' was first used. It draws on ethnographic data to describe the learning process of apprentices in various fields of practice.

Oliver, M. and Carr, D. (2009) 'Learning in virtual worlds: Using communities of practice to explain how people learn from play', *British Journal of Educational Technology*, 40(3): 444–57.
An example of research that uses CoP as a framework for analysing interactions in virtual environments. It provides case studies of how two couples learn when they play a massively multiplayer online role-playing game (MMORPS), 'World of Warcraft'. CoP was chosen because the chronology of games playing 'revealed a striking resemblance' to Wenger's 1998 model.

Wenger, E. (1998) *Communities of Practice: Learning, Meaning and Identity*. Cambridge and New York: Cambridge University Press.

Wenger elaborates the concept of a CoP into a theoretical framework for describing and analysing group practices. The book includes two illustrative vignettes.

Further references

Benzie, D.H. (2000) 'A longitudinal study of the development of information technology capability by students in an institute of higher education'. PhD dissertation, University of Exeter. Available from: dbenzie@marjon.ac.uk

Brown, J.S., Collins, A. and Duguid, P. (1989) 'Situated cognition and the culture of learning', *Educational Researcher*, 32 (Jan–Feb): 32–42.

Fuller, A., Hodkinson, H., Hodkinson, P. and Unwin, L. (2005) 'Learning as peripheral participation in communities of practice: A reassessment of key concepts in workplace learning', *British Educational Research Journal*, 31(1): 49–68.

Gee, J.P. (2005) 'Semiotic social spaces and affinity spaces: From *The Age of Mythology* to today's schools', in D. Barton and K. Tusting (eds) *Beyond Communities of Practice: Language, Power, and Social Context*. Cambridge and New York: Cambridge University Press. pp. 214–32.

Lave, J. (1996) 'The practice of learning', in S. Chaiklin and J. Lave (eds) *Understanding Practice: Perspectives on Activity and Context*. Cambridge and New York: Cambridge University Press.

Myers, G. (2005) 'Communities of practice, risk and Sellafield', in D. Barton and K. Tusting (eds) *Beyond Communities of Practice: Language, Power, and Social Context*. Cambridge and New York: Cambridge University Press. pp. 198–213.

Strauss, A. and Corbin, J. (1990) *Basics of Qualitative Research*. London: Sage.

Wenger, E., McDermott, R. and Snyder, W. (2002) *Cultivating Communities of Practice: A Guide to Managing Knowledge*. Cambridge, MA: Harvard Business School Press.

21

Activity Theory

Ines Langemeyer, Institute of Work and Social Sciences,
Brandenburg University of Technology, Germany
Morten Nissen, Department of Psychology, University of Copenhagen, Denmark

Summary

- Language is a cultural tool that organizes human psychic phenomena
- Thoughts and actions are creations, appropriations and uses of cultural forms
- We gain understanding through intervention
- We co-create the objects we study
- Basic theoretical work is integrated with empirical-practical engagement
- Key theorists and writers
  - Lev Vygotsky
  - Aleksei N. Leont'ev
  - Alexandre Luria
  - Klaus Holzkamp
  - Yrjö Engeström
  - Michael Cole

Key concepts

Morten Nissen

CHAT – Cultural-Historical Activity Theory – was born when Lev Vygotsky, in the 1920s and 1930s, inspired by the Russian revolution, began to reformulate his research in linguistic and developmental psychology into an outline of principles for a psychology drawing on Marxist insights. Psychic phenomena, in particular the higher functions specific to humans, must be viewed primarily as social activities mediated by tools. Tools are cultural objects, social forms that develop historically, and language is the overall most important structure of social forms which organize thinking, perception, emotion, action, and so on, conceptually.

In psychology, these are highly controversial ideas, since psychology has typically attempted to establish itself by demarcating a field which is precisely not sociocultural and historical. And if we try to spell out their implications in terms of research methods, we run into yet another provocation: while much psychology is strictly 'going through the movements' of what is perceived as a 'scientific' methodology, regardless of its object of study, CHAT is carried out in a wide variety of activities, many of which would normally not be recognizable as scientific methods at all. Nevertheless, this is what we will do – asking the reader to be prepared to question everything, even the concept of method itself.

The first implication is that of an inherently interdisciplinary approach to any phenomenon studied. This has been most outspoken at psychology's borders with philosophy and sociocultural studies. In the latter case, various concepts have been adapted that serve to mediate phenomena which appear to be features of individuals and their functions. Prominent among these have been broadly anthropological and sociolinguistic ideas such as Bakhtin's notion of dialogism or, more recently, Latour's idea of actor-networks (Middleton and Brown, 2005). With the help of such mediators, thoughts and actions can be viewed as creations, appropriations and uses of cultural forms rather than merely 'natural' entities, and as forming part of wider social practices.

In relation to philosophy, Jensen (2003) has referred to CHAT as a 'science of categories', since it not only begins by reworking the theoretical categories that frame research, but also, in general, takes categories, as human-made cultural forms, to be part of its subject matter. For reworking categories, a genuinely theoretical methodology is derived from the dialectical tradition of Hegel, Marx and their followers (Ilyenkov, 1977). According to this, the point is not to stipulate terms that 'match' things that exist. Rather, it is to create models which, in their conceptual hierarchies, reconstruct contradictory moments (or aspects) of development. Thus the theoretical questions are the likes of: 'How did this quality (this function, dimension, aspect of life, this feature) come to be? What does it presuppose? How does it transform, and how does it differentiate into opposing forms?'

This way of questioning leads us to the second implication for methodology: Vygotsky stressed the historical approach as the most fundamental principle:

> To study some thing historically means to study it in the process of change; that is the dialectical method's basic demand. To encompass in research the process of a given thing's development in all its phases and changes – from birth to death – fundamentally means to discover its nature, its essence, for 'It is only in movement that a body shows what it is'. (Vygotsky, 1978: 64–5)

In CHAT, we can distinguish at least three important historical dimensions. First, there is the all-encompassing history in which all forms of existence – such as the psyche, meaning, learning or play – were developed, even long before humanity. To gain a theoretical framework, we must reconstruct the emergence and transformations of such most basic qualities, using data from biology, paleontology, philosophical anthropology and so on, and the most decisive issue is how life changed with the advent of humanity. For instance, 'learning' is no longer, as in apes, just building from experience or socialization into given norms but, as 'human learning', it is the appropriation of culture and the enhancement of participation in a proactive control of life circumstances. Secondly, there is the cultural history of any issue at hand; thus, for instance, studying the way the ideas and the forms of 'learning' changed when schools, and later school disciplines (subjects), were invented helps us understand how the issue itself has been framed, how learning is bound up with 'knowledge' and 'teaching', and how the 'scholastic' prejudices that arise from this may be overcome. Finally, investigating the specific histories of the living communities, individuals and activities being studied, forms the overall approach to live empirical data: in CHAT, all psychology is 'developmental psychology'.

The way this developmental approach is realized is itself another methodological implication of the basic ideas. If thinking is basically a social activity mediated by tools, and research is no exception, the implication is that we always gain understanding through intervention. This is true of natural processes and conditions, the general laws of which we conjecture from manipulating their particular instances. And it is even more obvious if we consider cultural forms: if the objects we study are sociocultural creations, we do not stand outside them and watch; neither do we just manipulate them: we co-create them. In psychology, the understanding of research as basically interventionist leads to an experimental approach, and the understanding that intervention is basically productive leads to the idea of what Vygotsky called an 'experimental-genetic' method: studying 'higher mental functions' by creating them. Accordingly, the particular people and activities studied are not viewed as a sample but as a *prototype* (cf. Nissen, 2009). A prototype is different from a sample in that it is something new. And, as in the case of industrial design, the questions of generality and validity are important, of course, but they are subsumed to the idea of relevance, and thus allow and demand – and include in methodological reflection – all the adjustments and mediations on the way from the abstract idea (drawn from the prototype) to its various concrete realizations.

A striking early example was the expedition to Uzbekistan in the 1920s (Luria, 1976). Vygotsky was critical of developmental psychology, notably that of Piaget, for regarding cognitive functions as merely maturing or developing in the course of the individual's own activities. The developmental level of formal logical thinking was seen by Vygotsky to evolve through the social practice of schooling. So, his colleagues Luria and Leont'ev accompanied the literacy campaign in Central Asia to contribute to, and record, the historical development of this highest form of conceptual thinking, demonstrating qualitative differences between peasants' conceptual reasoning before and after learning to read, write and calculate.

The researchers not only documented events, but themselves suggested practical interventions. Sometimes, special arrangements were constructed for the sake of research itself – such as the cognitive tests the peasants were asked to perform – but in general, the prototype was the 'real-life' practice of teaching and learning. The core of the methodology was the ongoing reflections that connected the emerging practical prototype with general theorizing, leading to renewed practical changes and/or new tests, and so on.

The implication of this process is that research methods develop as part of the social practices studied. This has been called a tool-and-result dialectics of method, referring to a famous quote from Vygotsky:

> The search for method becomes one of the most important problems of the entire enterprise of understanding the uniquely human forms of psychological activity. In this case, the method is simultaneously prerequisite and product, the tool and the result of the study. (Vygotsky, 1978: 65)

In other words, rather than a fixed set of rules or recipes to be followed, method is the ongoing theoretically informed reflection of the social practices in which research participates; yet method is also, still, a tool for research, a specific cultural object produced to form and transform that activity.

Objections have since been raised to the underlying colonial evolutionism of the Uzbekistan expedition which rendered the Russian cultural form as the 'highest'. But the expedition exemplifies the social engineering which lies at the heart of early CHAT. The project of understanding generic properties of the human psyche was closely connected with the project of creating the 'new man' of the 'new society' in the Soviet Union (cf. Stetsenko and Arievitch, 2004); the assumed general features of 'Humanity' were at once the overall determination, the germ cell from which later forms evolved and the ideal to be realized. This is, admittedly, a tricky idea, although essential to dialectics since Hegel. It has been much criticized as teleological and self-confirming dogmatism; it is often felt that understanding 'laws' and 'necessities' should be not only distinguished but kept apart from espousing 'values' or 'preferences'. Today, a CHAT scholar would reply that, while it is true that evolutionist ideas about a necessary development of our societies – such as the current belief that welfare

states must succumb to a globalized neoliberalism – are ideologies that obscure powerful interests, we would deceive ourselves if we were to think that laws can be studied with no values in mind, or that preferences are not subject to necessities. 'Teleology' is inescapable, but it should be regarded as the projects of people rather than of God, Spirit or History.

In other words, CHAT, methodologically, is a form of action research that stresses the integration of basic theoretical work with empirical-practical engagement. This integration is always a challenge, since it is a critical and inventive process – which implies some distance from the everyday. The idea of 'social engineering' suggests an inherent pitfall that sometimes has removed CHAT from the democratic standards of action research. Especially during Stalinism and the Cold War, political climates have nurtured elitist and technocratic conceptions of experimental-genetic methodology: dressed in the white cloaks of a 'science' aloof from controversial everyday life, researchers, in the East as in the West, could gain some protection from political censorships and still be funded to make a better world.

A strong counter-current emerged in the 1970s with the reception of CHAT into the context of the students' movement, the New Left and academic Marxism in the Western (European) countries. This was most outspoken in the 'critical psychology' which developed in West Germany and the Nordic countries. Here, the agenda was one of democratic emancipation and, above all, critique of ideology: subjectivity as directly immersed in contentious social practice was the focus and the starting point for a process that would seek to reconstitute subjects as they reconstructed and transformed the cultural categories and conditions that shaped their lives (see Haug, 1999). In this context, building on CHAT as a Marxist foundation of psychology was an alternative to either abandoning psychology altogether as a form of 'bourgeois ideology' or developing it from critical psychoanalysis. The CHAT legacy implied a notion of subjectivity as a productive and reflective agency, but the irrevocable implication of ideology critique was an anchoring of research in participants' experience. This was elaborated in the seminal 'Foundation of Psychology' (Holzkamp, 1983), where the phenomenologically inspired consequence was drawn that people should never be made the objects of research, only its agent-subjects. Viewed in the larger framework of CHAT, this epitomizes a discernible general tendency toward employing hermeneutic methodologies – above all, the qualitative interview – to elicit participants' subjective perspectives. Sometimes this amounts to a pitfall opposite to that of technocratic experiments, responding in a different way to the challenge inherent in critical research: seeking to carve out a space of free inter-subjective communication and disavowing the objectification inherent to research as to any social practice. But on the whole, contemporary CHAT embraces the democratic lessons that date back to Aristotle's notion of phronesis, where each participant has something to contribute to the truth, while also maintaining that achieving this 'truth' is the practical production of a real-life prototype.

Implications for research design

Your first step – although these points should not be read as occurring in a linear sequence – is to develop your research question in an historical reconstruction of its main categories. Although its dimensions vary from preliminary readings to full blown research projects, this goes beyond the traditional state-of-the-art review in three ways: (1) it seeks out theoretical core problems and thus inevitably becomes interdisciplinary; (2) it transcends science to reconstruct the history of your category as a cultural element (not unlike a Foucauldian 'genealogy'); and (3) it construes your topic as an instance of fundamental aspects of human life, reconstructing relevant concepts into this overall historical framework, and recasting the present issue critically in the light of these assumptions about what is human. For instance, if you want to understand 'humour', you might retrace the (historically recent) emergence of our current preparedness to consider humour legitimate in almost all spheres of life, read studies of anthropoid play behaviour or review theories of humour in philosophical anthropology in the light of basic CHAT ideas.

Your second step is to design or engage in a prototypical practice, a practice which embodies the relevance of your research question. Typically, of course, things work the opposite way around: various practical 'development projects' first exist and may or may not call for research. Either way, you should consider the relations of relevance between research questions and development problems: humour in learning may be an interesting topic, but it may not be the most promising approach to the problems faced in an urban secondary school. This is not simply a question of match; it is a ceaseless negotiation and developing of relevancies that run parallel to your ongoing analysis of social conditions and is intimately connected with a 'political' dynamics of power balances, alliances and so on. In this process, your subjects are recruited as participants – not sampled or selected – and, given existing differentials of power, resources, capacities, etc. This is likely to be far from a smooth and trivial process.

The third step is to objectify and inscribe the processes into data. Here, some relatively rigid discipline is required so that the structure of the transformations made can be retraced and critically reflected – whether your data are observation field notes, video or audio tapes, or samples of field materials (e.g. school homework, official documents, websites, etc.). Specialized 'data production' activities may be useful as a deliberate part of both research and development of the prototype – such as interviews, diaries or documented reflection meetings, and so on.

The fourth step is that of analysis, of objectifying activities into theoretically organized models which are constructed to challenge experience and theory (seek out contradictions), and to suggest ways to meet those challenges (mediate and resolve contradictions). Analysis involves oscillating between using the model to organize data, and using data to revise the model – and doing this, above all, without bending data to confirm theory, or watering down theoretical ideas to match intuitive experience: analysis is precisely about creating new ways of seeing things, ways which are as unexpected as they are convincing.

As far as possible, data and analyses should be produced and treated as the property of all participants, mediating a critical dialogue which transforms relevant cultural elements in participants' lives. Yet, while analytical models are half-made artefacts used by all participants, academic writing achieves a closure that embodies the distances and tensions between the communities of your prototypical practice and of academia. Since this is likely to be both problematic and productive, itself conducive to generalization, there are no stylistic conventions to cover that gap, but the gap, and the movements and transformations across it, is an important source of methodological reflection.

Finally, your target outcome is itself cultural-historical: not a universal truth or a value-free piece of knowledge to be added to the edifice of pure science; but neither is it just a unique narrative of a local practice. If it matters, it suggests forms of knowing and doing that are prototypical, that is, contingently, contentiously, and in innovative ways, relevant to its readers.

Stories from the field

Ines Langemeyer

My story reports on a vocational course that provides a qualification in programming software tools, applications and databases. This state-subsidized training programme was kept at low cost through adopting relatively self-dependent learning practices, among others 'e-learning' and workplace learning, in a 14-month apprenticeship (which was partially financed by private companies). Several changes characterized the research field: the shift in the technological mode of production; the 'modernization' of the relations of production that include a political change towards a 'lean state' (analogous to 'lean production'); and the current 'reforms' of the German public education system. By interviewing seven trainees four times (during 2002–3), I tried to reconstruct how each participant coped with the responsibility of learning under these conditions. My other focus was the notion of learning itself. To compare the trainees' with the teachers' perspectives I arranged a group discussion with the latter.

The first contact with the trainees was at the beginning of their apprenticeship after eight months on the course; two further interviews followed, and the last contact was after 15 months, one and a half months after they had finished the course. Their ages ranged from 27 to 52 and the ratio of five men to two women constituted an approximately representative sample of all the students on the course. My research aimed at a comparison of cases to analyse the particular developmental processes in relation to general societal transitions. It was motivated by specific theoretical results from former studies; nonetheless, the implications of the methods and the theoretical concepts that I referred to needed further reflection at every step of intervention and analysis.

My view of socio-technological change induced by information technologies was inspired by the Berlin research project on automation work (1972–87, directed by Haug – see PAQ, 1987) which can be summarized as follows: inventing, planning, and managing were previously carried out on a higher

hierarchical level than executing tasks. Given the division of intellectual and manual labour, human involvement in the actual production process required above all physical power and manual skills. However, as a result of automation and computer technologies, manual labour tends be eliminated and the remaining work activities have become mainly intellectual: regulative, investigative, experimental and generally increasingly scientific. Today, the creative work of inventing, planning, and managing is no longer separated from executing, so that not only is the division between physical and mental labour largely removed but, partly as a result, hierarchies have lost their legitimation. Due to a radical revision of the competences of, and demands on, the individual employee, industrial work has been partially 'humanized', but it also entails new contradictions and conflicts. The new, less hierarchical, organization of work gives relative autonomy to the workers, but it is also experienced as an indirect form of coercion.

This contradiction became the starting point for a previous case study of programmers in 2000, in which I investigated subjective conflicts associated with this kind of autonomy. To analyse interview data, I reconstructed how the new type of work and its mode of regulation conferred various responsibilities and uncertainties onto the employees. These made them think and act like entrepreneurs although they were not formally employed as such. The crucial question turned out to be whether, on the one hand, responsibilities had been 'individualized' or whether, on the other hand, cooperative and mutual support structures existed among the programmers. This clarified that the organization of responsibilities brings up power structures which foster an extension and an intensification of work over which employees often have little control.

In this study I challenged Holzkamp's (1983) view of competitive wage labour, in which he attributed constraints, such as the subordination of the self or self-adaptation to requirements (e.g. to work harder and faster than others), as indications of a 'restricted agency', whereas the expansion of possible actions and increased solidarity signified a tendency towards a 'generalized agency'. His conceptualization suggested a dichotomy between a restricted and an extended range of action possibilities. But in my project where the programmers' conflict resulted from contradictions arising from this new 'autonomy', analysis in terms of such a dichotomy would have been misleading.

Likewise, in this new research I challenged Holzkamp's analytical categories of learning. His foundation of a 'subject science of learning' (1993) focused on the articulation of premises and motivations for learning. He assumed that contradictory educational practices resulted from whether someone learns 'defensively' or 'expansively'. He assumed a polarization between learners' efforts to adopt appropriate behaviours to avert negative effects (like bad grades) and positive endeavour that arises from learners' intentions to increase their power to learn. He argued that learning is not merely a mechanical internalization of ready-made facts, nor simply a performance of behaviour evoked by teaching. Rather, an individual always needs to be aware of a subjective problematic in order to start learning intentionally. Any institutionalized form of learning should take into account that the individual learners (subjects) need to recognize their own concerns within educational practice.

Although these reflections were quite useful, my interviews document that the conflicts did not stem from the power relations of a repressive institution that imposed its rules on the learners, but rather crystallized around the issue of responsibility. The trainees wanted to expand their agency and obtain qualifications in information technology (IT), but faced a discrepancy between their desired and their actual performance, and between planned achievements and any shortfall. Therefore, I decided to focus on the learning activities, their trajectories and boundaries, rather than conscious learning intentions. With regard to the scientific logic of IT, the interviewees reported how they organized their learning activities on their own. For them, it became paramount to identify strategies to orientate their efforts, to collect the information that was relevant for solving a certain problem and to distinguish between irrelevant nuisance and prototypical problems that help to broaden their comprehension of the scientific logic of IT-work.

Most of the trainees discovered the convenience of addressing their questions to websites, chatrooms, newsgroups and also personally to their colleagues, yet during face-to-face meetings they were dissatisfied with their relationship with their teachers. The latter were organizing the programme as a team and in the group discussion they complained that poor communications among themselves had adversely affected the coordination of the programme, but that they did not see a way out. They said this was due to lack of time and blamed the trainees for deficiencies in 'social

skills'. In interview, the trainees admitted being part of a 'difficult group'. On the other hand, they complained that the teachers neither kept their promises to support them individually nor managed to respond effectively to the wide disparity of aspiration levels during classes. In a few cases, the ineffectiveness of teaching did not affect the learners so badly, since their employers were able to support learning at work. In 1999, at the beginning of this programme, successful employment after the apprenticeship assured the success of this shortened job training (22 months instead of three years), but the conditions did not remain the same. Because of a precarious economic situation, not many of the trainees in my study had prospects for employment. Since they needed to qualify for a tight labour market, they felt highly responsible for their own learning, but in view of the lack of job opportunities and the shortcomings of the programme they also felt discouraged. The impact of this situation on their commitment nurtured permanent conflicts between trainees and teachers on the one hand and hassles among the classmates on the other. Repeatedly, conflicts arose about the methods and the organization of the course. These debates were symptomatic of a number of organizational inconsistencies and a rather 'mechanical' application of 'new' forms of learning which largely ignored the scientification of work and the uncertainties deriving from it. In spite of the potential for the trainees' critique to be instructive for the teachers, those debates did not cure the problematic situation, they rather impeded any improvement. A 40-year-old trainee starkly pointed out that it was 'so stressful' for her to put up with 'stupid people' at the course and at work that she pretended to be sick in order to skip classes. She described experiencing a sense of 'being abandoned' on the one hand and 'not finding the right place in life' on the other. This not only indicates her suffering but also the resulting stalemate that made any development impossible – due to lack of support and her own loss of motivation.

During the research process, the generation of empirical methods or strategies and of explanatory theoretical assumptions were intertwined. I constructed several theoretical perspectives that made the cases comparable as well as distinguishable: the mode of participation, the forms of cooperation, and the aspects of situatedness (cf. Langemeyer, 2006). While elaborating these perspectives as components of a theoretical explanation of the respective problems in practice, I also figured out what kinds of question were important for the next series of interviews and the next step of evaluation.

Through the analysis of conditions and relationships between specific educational practices, possibilities for development could be generated. Similarly to Clot et al. (2001), I came to understand how generative structures of a learning culture not only depend on the material resources that are at someone's disposal but also on a certain kind of experience. As Clot et al. (2001: 23) explain, with reference to Vygotsky and Bakhtin, it is a new way of perceiving things and conditions that enables individuals to adopt new possibilities for action. This means that the personal activity process is generalized and its comprehension becomes richer by recontextualizing it.

Thus, the individual (subject) gains the capability to reorganize his or her own activity. Of course, such a development is not achieved in isolation. Only in cooperation with others can subjects develop, on the basis of their spontaneous reactions, new cultural resources and a space for collective as well as individual reflexivity. This always takes place within the diversity of possible (realized and unrealized) activities, when someone focuses on an activity's distance from its potential advanced form, when individuals measure the distinction between an intended activity and its realization, when they understand the difference between isolated and cooperative engagement in an activity or learn about less and more adequate forms of cooperation, and so on. Although I 'discovered' these generative structures by analysing and comparing the interview data, I did not initiate a process of joint reflection between interviewees on these available resources nor make any attempt to generate them in practice as Clot et al. did, for example, with their methodology of a 'crossed self-confrontation' – although this could have been a good way of extending this research project. Nevertheless, during the enquiry, I tried to support each interviewee to become aware of generative structures and common resources. For this purpose, the interviews were characterized by three major types of questions: first, questions to find out how the trainees relate themselves to the learning demands and to the different learning practices; second, questions to let them report how they perceive and judge the activities and attitudes of their classmates, their teachers and their colleagues; and third, questions to generate reflection on their own way of doing things and on alternative possibilities for changing practice.

The problems that emerged between the teachers and the course participants in relation to learning showed how important it is to develop those activities as an 'organic' whole in which its components (instrument, object, community, division of labour, and rules) are integrated, so that it forms a coherent complex (cf. Engeström, 1987: ch. 3.3) and thereby a cooperative power of action. Otherwise, it is likely that the subjects (those involved) internalize the respective contradictions, deal with them as internal conflicts and try – inevitably unsuccessfully – to solve them as individuals only.

Annotated bibliography

Chaiklin, S., Hedegaard, M. and Jensen, U.J. (eds) (2003) *Activity Theory and Social Practice: Cultural-Historical Approaches*. Aarhus: Aarhus University Press.
Papers by renowned authors centring mostly on philosophical and theoretical contributions. Useful in showing how CHAT is situated in contemporary off-mainstream psychology and cultural studies.

Daniels, H. (ed.) (2005) *An Introduction to Vygotsky*. London: Taylor & Francis.
Accessible overview of Vygotsky's work combining reprints of key journal and text articles with editorial commentary and suggested further reading.

Engeström, Y. (1987) *Learning by Expanding: An Activity-Theoretical Approach to Developmental Research*. Helsinki: Orienta-Konsulit.
Provides an overview of CHAT approaches to learning and founds the approach to experimental-genetic studies of activity systems widely employed, especially at the Helsinki centre.

Ilyenkov, E.V. (1977) *Dialectical Logic: Essays on its History and Theory*. Moscow: Progress Publishers (http://www.marxists.org/archive/ilyenkov/works/essays/index.htm)
Reconstructs history of philosophy to achieve a dialectical understanding of the ideal as based on activity. Ilyenkov is one of the very few of the more recent Soviet philosophers who is still respected in today's philosophy.

Langemeyer, I. and Roth, W-M. (2006) 'Is cultural-historical activity theory threatened to fall short of its own principles and possibilities as a dialectal social science?', *Outlines. Critical Social Studies*, 2: 20–42. Available online at: http://ojs.statsbiblioteket.dk/index.php/outlines/article/viewFile/2090/1854

Investigates the role of dialectics in Vygotsky's thought and methodology and discusses critically Engeström's model of activity systems in relation to his method of 'developmental work research'.

Leont'ev A.N. (1981) *Problems of the Development of the Mind*. Moscow: Progress Publishers.
Systematic collection of papers from the 1930s and 1950s demonstrating general and specific research methodologies. This is the classic that introduces the overall historical approach to the psyche.

Tolman, C. and Maiers, W. (eds) (1991) *Critical Psychology. Contributions to an Historical Science of the Subject*. Cambridge: Cambridge University Press.
Central classical papers in the critical psychology branch of CHAT collected, introduced and contextualized for the English-speaking audience.

Vygotsky, L.S. (1962) *Thought and Language*. Boston: MIT Press.
The ultimate CHAT classic. Most of the text available as 'Thinking and Speaking' at: http://www.marxists.org/archive/vygotsky/works/words/index.htm

Vygotsky, L.S. (1978) *Mind and Society*. Cambridge, MA: Harvard University Press.
Central text stating overall approach illustrated by experimental data. Most of the text available at: http://www.marxists.org/archive/vygotsky/index.htm

Websites

The official website of the International Society for Cultural and Activity Research: http://www.iscar.org

Oldest and biggest international journal: *Mind, Culture & Activity*: http://www.education.bham.ac.uk/research/sat/publications/mca/ default.htm

Open access international journal based in Denmark: *Outlines – Critical Practice Studies*: http://www.outlines.dk

The Laboratory of Comparative Human Cognition (LCHC) at the University of California, San Diego, United States: http://lchc.ucsd.edu/

Centre for Sociocultural and Activity Theory Research (CSAT): http://www.bath.ac.uk/csat/

Center for Research on Activity, Development and Learning (CRADLE): http://www.helsinki.fi/cradle/index.htm

Further references

Clot, Y., Prot, B. and Werthe, Chr. (2001) 'Special Issue: Clinique de l'activité et pouvoir d'agir', *Education permanente*, 146(1).

Haug, F. (1999) *Female Sexualisation. A Collective Work of Memory*. London: Verso.

Holzkamp, K. (1983) *Grundlegung der Psychologie*. Frankfurt am Main: Campus Verlag.

Holzkamp, K. (1993) *Lernen. Subjektwissenschaftliche Grundlegung*. Frankfurt am Main: Campus.

Jensen, U.J. (2003) 'Categories in activity theory: Marx' philosophy just-in-time', in S. Chaiklin, M. Hedegaard and U.J. Jensen (eds) *Activity Theory and Social Practice: Cultural-Historical Approaches*. Aarhus: Aarhus University Press. pp. 79–99.

Langemeyer, I. (2006) 'Contradictions in expansive learning – towards a critical analysis of self-dependent forms of learning in relation to the contemporary socio-technological change', *Forum: Qualitative Social Research*, 7(1). Available online at: www.qualitative-research.net/fqs-texte/1-06/06-1-12-e.htm

Luria, A.R. (1976) *Cognitive Development: Its Cultural and Social Foundations*. Boston: Harvard University Press.

Middleton, D.M. and Brown, S.D. (2005) *The Social Psychology of Experience: Studies in Remembering and Forgetting*. London: Sage.

Nissen, M. (2009) 'Objectification and Prototype', *Qualitative Research in Psychology*, 6(1): 67–87.

PAQ (Projekt Automation Qualifikation) (1987) *Widersprüche der Automationsarbeit*. Berlin/W: Argument Verlag.

Stetsenko, A. and Arievitch, I.M. (2004) 'Vygotskian collaborative project of social transformation', *International Journal of Critical Psychology*, 14: 58–80.

Researching Policy

Jill Blackmore, School of Education, University of Deakin, Australia

Hugh Lauder, Department of Education, University of Bath, UK

Summary

- The rational model of policy analysis
- The critical tradition of policy analysis
- Globalization
- Discursive shifts in policy
- Disjunctures between policy and practice
- Key theorists and writers
  - Stephen Ball
  - Jill Blackmore
  - Hugh Lauder
  - Jenny Ozga
  - Fazal Rizvi

Key concepts

Jill Blackmore

What is policy?

Policy studies is a highly contested field in terms of how policy should be understood, the role of policy researchers and who does policy research (Ozga et al., 2006). Policy is more than 'official' texts produced by and on the authority of governmental or executive power. Policy has multiple dimensions within any field of activity, whether education, health or welfare education. Policy could be considered to be a text, a process, a discourse, a political decision, a programme, even an outcome. Policy is also a form of intended and actual social action, and is therefore inevitably incomplete in terms of how it maps into

practice (Ball, 1993). Policy is also normative. Policy-makers seek to change behaviours through the distribution of scarce resources and in so doing change values (Le Grand, 1997). Whether it is at the state or institutional level, policy is 'the authoritative allocation of values' (Prunty quoted in Taylor et al., 1997: 1).

The issues for policy researchers are about how and why certain policies come to be developed in particular contexts, by who, for whom, based on what assumptions and with what effect. On whose authority is policy produced and disseminated, what are the principles of allocation, whose values are being promoted, who wins and who loses?

Understanding the 'field' of policy research

In the twentieth century policy studies emerged as a discipline that sought legitimacy by claiming to be a 'science'. This *'rational' model of policy analysis*, which dominated until the 1970s, was premised upon statistical techniques, large population samples, and linear hierarchical processes. In this model, research was done by experts, policy was developed by government and then disseminated/implemented by practitioners. Any failures were blamed on technical problems rather than the assumptions underlying the policy. Poor dissemination/communication, failed implementation, and flaws in statistical procedures and sampling were also possible 'culprits'. Government has historically favoured such 'rational or technocratic models' based on quantitative research because it claims to be generalizable, objective and offers simple ways of understanding a problem. This rational model was often associated with an incrementalist position in which policy is perceived as a pluralist, consensual process mediated by the state in relatively benign ways. If policy is seen as proceeding by consensus through a benign state then underlying assumptions about inequalities in power and who will win and lose as a result of a policy(s) need not be interrogated (Bacchi, 1999).

However, these rational models were coming under increasing criticism as the period of post-war reconstruction and 'consensus' was challenged by questions of social class, gender and ethnicity. By 1986, Dale (1986: 68) named three main orientations to policy analysis, particularly in education, arising from three fields of activity: those of social administration (prescriptive and ameliorative), of policy analysis (pragmatic and problem-solving) and of social science (theoretical and relatively distant from the action).

The new sociology of knowledge and the rise of a critical social science and feminism during the 1970s, informed by the work of cultural studies, critical theorists and Gramsci's notions of hegemony, questioned the value neutrality of the research methods underpinning the rational model and its claims to generalizability. This critical tradition perceived policy sceptically: rather than being about social justice it was about social control because the state was seen as complicit with the power of entrenched interests. In essence, policy was a product of political contestation and negotiation between stakeholders with unequal political power.

However, during the 1980s and 1990s, globalization on the one hand, and democratic demands of diverse populations on the other, challenged the conception of the state as a unitary, monolithic source of power (Dale, 1986). But social theorists increasingly conceptualized the state as a contested site of political action, in which a set of, often contradictory, processes and relationships mediated policy production, simultaneously producing new opportunities and closing down others for particular groups (Blackmore, 1999). This approach has highlighted the importance of theorizing policy in terms of local/global relations. It has also led to re-conceptualizing the nature of policy, as 'new forms of public administration' which have given rise to a new managerial class of multi-skilled generic managers who 'wrote policy' but whose loyalty was to Ministers rather than an 'imagined public'(Yeatman, 1998).

At the heart of the reconstruction of the post welfare state has been the notion of *performativity*: the idea that each institution would have targets against which performance could be measured. Behind such targets was a new social technology of control involving accountability systems, strategic planning, quality assurance and performance management. This social technology raised a new set of policy questions ranging from the obvious: do systems of performativity, such as external standards regimes imposed on the professions, improve performance, to examining the related questions concerning the way performativity reconstructs professional identities, motivations and effectiveness (Ball, 2003). For example, in health a new cadre of managers was introduced to make resource and organizational decisions which were taken out of the hands of clinicians, in order to gain financial efficiencies. But this strategy changed the professional identities of clinicians because priorities were determined by 'targets' rather than by their experience and judgement.

The above 'critical' analysis draws upon what has been termed the 'new policy sociology'. The new policy sociology, itself a product of the critical tradition, emerged in the context of the rise of the dominance of New Right policies in many Anglophone nation-states during the 1980s on the one hand, and post-structuralist theory in the academy on the other. The focus here widened policy concerns from the production, reception and effects of policy to how discourse, language and text set the context for how policy questions are framed.

To better analyse these discursive shifts in policy in the field of education, Ball (1993) distinguishes between the notion of *policy-as-text* and *policy-as-discourse*. *Policy-as-text* distinguishes between more open-ended 'readerly' texts that allow for interpretation by policy actors, and more closed 'writerly' policy texts that are more prescriptive and constraining of re-interpretation by teachers. In both cases policy texts are seen as inherently ambiguous and open to degrees of interpretation. *Policy-as-discourse* sees policy as part of a wider system of social relations, framing what is said and thought. Policy texts simultaneously emerge out of, but also produce, particular policy discourses. Groups and individuals position themselves, and are positioned by, these texts and discourses, and their acceptance, rejection or modification is shaped, in part, by them. Discourse analysis, therefore requires policy researchers to uncover the normative nature of decisions that appear to be obvious, inevitable or natural, to test judgements about truth claims, and to consider alternative more socially just ways of developing policies and practice (Luke, 2002).

However, a theme running through policy studies concerns the nature of the links between policy as intended by policy-makers and its relationship to what actually happens in practice. Do the recipients of policy initiatives faithfully do as they are bid? A more radical interpretation of the disjuncture between the community of policy makers and practitioners is provided by Ladwig (1994). He utilizes Bourdieu's notions of field and habitus to argue that educational policy has little to do with what goes on in education systems and schools because education *policy* as a social field is marked out by players outside education – universities, journals, researchers (public and private), commercial providers, ministerial departments – which only partially overlaps with education as a field in which teachers, parents and students are the actors. Policy research, Lingard et al. (2005) argue, is a relatively autonomous field with its own rules, hierarchies and players with their own predispositions seeking to position themselves optimally. Policy actors in this perspective both protect and advance the field but its relationship to practitioners may be only tenuous. This approach would explain why practitioners are often alienated by policy initiatives since policy-makers may have little understanding of the day-to-day realities of practitioners and understand less about their senses of professional identity.

These approaches also highlight how policy also has a *wider representational* or *symbolic power*. Recent policy research has focused on the role of the media in mediating policy, exemplified in how the New Right were able to mobilize popular opinion by producing 'de facto' policies (more standardized literacy testing, increased reporting of the unemployed) in response to 'de facto' problems (e.g. literacy crisis, welfare cheating) through the media. Governments, through the media, test public opinion about policies and provide policy solutions (often under-researched, under-resourced and poorly timed).

The problem of the lack of articulation between policy and practice has been extended by globalization. Globalization has also led to a focus on the *articulation of policy trans-nationally* with the phenomenon of 'travelling policies' between nation-states during the 1990s, for example, new public administration, devolution and privatization (Phillips and Ochs, 2004). Here the questions are: why have some policies been taken up in different nation-states; how appropriate is policy importation and in whose interests is it undertaken; and what have been the differential effects of such importation? Here again, Bourdieu's

notion of policy 'fields' has been useful in conceptualizing the emergence of overlapping 'global policy communities', for example OECD, UNESCO, international financial organizations such as the IMF and World Bank and non-governmental organizations (Henry et al., 2001). But while there may be overlapping views held by these multilateral agencies, their policy prescriptions, hatched high up in the glass towers of New York and Washington may have little relevance to solving social problems on the ground.

Feminist critical theorists similarly view policy research as contested, socially constructed, 'situated', and value laden. *Critical feminist policy* studies focus on how gender permeates the categories of analysis in policy and the organizational contexts in which policies are produced, the need for interdisciplinary and multiple theoretical and methodological approaches, and the power relationships between researchers and researched. They identify the gendered silences and gaps in policy texts and discourses, unpack the categories and assumptions underpinning policy, and consider the effects of policies on marginalized groups (e.g. Blackmore, 1999). For example, health, welfare and education policies often ignore the reality of women being the primary carers of the aged, sick and young, thus positioning women to take up the slack of the post welfare state's withdrawal from responsibility. Critical feminist policy analysis has been particularly effective in criticizing the dominant New Right policies because they assume a human capital theory premised upon the self-maximizing, freely-choosing, autonomous individual who is a man, *homo economicus*. Yet individual choices are framed by material conditions and relationships of interdependency with different cultural and social capital – there is no race, gender and class neutral individual. Feminist policy researchers, particularly in Australia, New Zealand and Scandinavia, have contested the *state centric view* of policy that focused on male policy elites. Feminist bureaucrats (femocrats) *working through the state* conceptualize policy as a 'dialogue' between the policy actors in the state and grassroots social movements, in particular policy communities (Yeatman, 1998).

Post-structuralist theories of policy, therefore, have addressed the fundamental question of whether the recipients and readers of policies have a sense of agency. On this basis we can construct more powerful explanatory theories of how social change occurs. The notion of discourse draws attention to the idea that power works through institutionalized discursive hierarchies in which some policy discourses are treated as 'truths', while more radical perspectives are marginalized. Questions for policy researchers are:

- How do some discourses become hegemonic or commonsensical, and under what conditions and with what effects?
- How are policies mediated through the state and articulated globally/nationally/locally, and with what unexpected outcomes?
- How are discourses appropriated and reworked?

This review of approaches to policy research has highlighted the importance of discourses and the theories they produce and the critical analysis and testing of the theoretical assumptions underlying policy initiatives (Lauder et al., 2004). It has also emphasized the different ways in which there may be a disjuncture between what policy-makers intend and what occurs in practice, which may give rise to unintended consequences. This concern is also fuelled by discourses of evidence-based policy and practice, and the relevance of research for policy production (Young et al., 2002).

Implications for research design

Doing policy research requires a notion of the intentions for undertaking policy research, a capacity to frame the policy 'problem'; and some clarity about the boundaries. One way of locating oneself in the field of policy research is to make the distinction as to whether you are doing 'research for policy' and/or 'research about policy'. A second question is whether you are an 'outsider' or 'insider', the latter is more likely to be the case if you are a practitioner-researcher undertaking a workplace-based professional doctorate, and how that shapes your approach. Third, is your investigation about all or any of the processes of policy production, dissemination and implementation or policy effects? Finally, is your focus at the global, macro (e.g. governmental), meso (regional) or micro level (e.g. hospital, employment agency, school) level or the articulation between levels?

Research for policy

The question for policy researchers is whether they are doing 'policy critique' or 'policy service'. While these are not necessarily mutually exclusive, each approach creates different ethical issues about definitions of the problem, ownership, outcomes and intended use. Researchers can warn policy-makers about problems, inform them of possible policy options, assist them in reframing policy problems or provide policy-makers post hoc with rationalizations of politically desired policy options. Your relation with key policy-makers may determine what you can research and what can be published in the public domain. The rise of contract research means that policy researchers may be restricted from publishing material as controversial reports are 'shelved'.

Research about policy

Ozga (2000: 1) states that the 'orientation of a policy researcher towards a policy problem is likely to have consequences for the kinds of investigations he or she carries out'. Action research is often appropriate for practitioner-researchers who wish to develop policy within their own workplace. Here policy critique and policy service can provide a useful tension but require high levels of reflexivity on the part of researchers. Feminist policy researchers overtly seek to be interventionist, visionary and provide alternative ways of conceptualizing a problem or doing policy, what Yeatman (1998) refers to as 'policy activism'.

What is the policy problem here?

Policies define a problem in a particular way and then set up categories and certain logics that typically go unquestioned. Policy is often less about 'problem solving' and as much about 'problem setting' in terms of setting up an agenda for social action (Yeatman, 1998). Bacchi's (1999) 'What is the problem?' approach explores 'strategic representations' of the policy problem and argues that 'policy solution' approaches of rational models close down debate. It is important, therefore, not to take official definitions of a problem at face value but ask how that definition was generated and how it fits into the state's agenda for social programmes.

Multiple methods

The primary issue is what constitutes a policy question – is it defined by government, by research, or by stakeholders? In turn, the policy question impacts on how one does the research. Policy studies does not have a distinctive set of methodologies, but calls upon a range of methodological positions and methods in order to achieve the most powerful explanations for policy questions. The strong tradition of large-scale statistical models continues to have greater influence amongst policy-makers because of its perceived generalizability and a belief that 'hard quantifiable data' has greater validity than what is perceived as 'anecdotal' case study or qualitative research. This falls into the trap that sees quantitative research as providing 'real data' and qualitative research 'the colour' (Ozga, 2000: 91–2). Increasingly, the complexity of social problems has led to recognition that quantitative analysis often provides inadequate responses to many policy questions. Large-scale quantitative data sets tend to view individuals as 'averages' or as exhibiting ideal type behaviours and cannot always be contextualized in terms of particular locations or communities (Lauder et al., 2004). Equally, such studies can identify a problem, make associations between particular factors, but often cannot explain the phenomena. The complexity of the 'problem' is often best addressed by in-depth qualitative analysis. Quantitative and qualitative methods can augment one another to flesh out this complexity, issues which arise when undertaking comparative policy analysis (e.g. Mazur, 1999). Ideological positions that equate particular methods with particular policy ideologies or perspectives should be rejected.

The following case study explores and explicates some of these traditional aims of policy research and the often 'mysterious' processes by which research moves from a phase of creation to one of presentation.

Stories from the field – a story of serendipity in the field of policy research

Hugh Lauder

This case study indicates the gap between official policy discourses about the knowledge economy that are being used (often post hoc) to justify workplace restructuring and new technology, and the actuality of what happens on the ground. My work in the policy field has always sought to link the quantitative and qualitative to investigate such gaps. This story is based on an interview with my banking relations manager. Fitting the interview into the broader statistical picture about the changing demand for skills helped to challenge the dominant policy discourse about the relationship of education to the economy. It also

helped to provide an alternative explanation of the links between the two and, more controversially, raise the question of whether the middle class is safe in its investments in higher education or whether, as the novelist J.G. Ballard has suggested, they will become *the new proletariat.*

In 2003 I (Lauder) worked with Phil Brown on the links between globalization, the knowledge economy and higher education. The general hypothesis we investigated was that the knowledge economy would not deliver on the rhetoric of policy-makers by providing increasing numbers of highly skilled jobs. Indeed, we took the view that all the indications were that there would be a decline in opportunities for the middle class. Our aim, therefore, was to test the truth claims underlying the rhetoric that was taken as common sense or a natural part of the post-industrial landscape. Broadly speaking most of the evidence marshalled in the resulting paper (Brown and Lauder, 2003) is quantitative. However, the chance to engage in some-small scale qualitative research enhanced the explanatory power of the paper.

One aspect of the study involved an idea first developed by Brint (2001) that the view taken by policy-makers of the knowledge economy is a-contextual and a-historical. Brint had noted that knowledge-based jobs in the previous century had, over time with the development and transfer of 'best practice', become routinized. The consequence was that many jobs that originally required a high degree of knowledge and skill no longer required that level of skill.

Could such an analysis be applied to some of the knowledge economy sectors to-day? Around the time that I was pondering this question I took time off to phone my personal relations banking manager. I wanted a loan to buy a second-hand car. In the past he, let us call him Henry, had the discretion to loan up to £30,000. In this case I was only after a fraction of that sum and was expecting him to agree to it over the phone but he did not.

> 'It's a bit more difficult these days', Henry explained. 'I don't have that kind of discretion any more to agree the loan on the nod. You're going to have to fill in some paperwork and we'll have to send it up the line to get the loan agreed.'

I was surprised and asked him what was going on. Henry was close to 40, had worked in the same bank for a long time, was perceived as successful and with strong knowledge of his local customer base.

'It's all changed' he said, 'since we've been taken over.'

There was a pause on the line and then he said he'd send the paperwork out to me. I replaced the receiver and went back to the research but something had triggered a connection between Henry and my present preoccupation. The forms duly arrived and I filled them in, although most of the information should already have been with the bank. As I went to post the forms back to him, the hunch or intuition that had been working away at the back of my mind clearly presented itself. I should say, that walking, as I had to the Post Office, is one way in which ideas present themselves; it's precisely when I am away from writing and doing something totally different that they seem to emerge.

Returning home I read back through some of the literature on national skills profiles in the UK. Sure enough the quantitative research showed that the banking industry was one where employees reported that their discretion in making judgements on the job was being reduced. One of the reasons why an economy would want better educated workers and especially more graduates is precisely that they are able to make independent judgements. After all, in order to study for a degree a high level of autonomy is required. However, the process of management de-layering that started in the 1980s enabled many middle management jobs to be stripped out with closer communications between senior managers and workers. What facilitated this process was the new technology related to the introduction of the PC. In turn this has meant that many in intermediate positions and indeed those in lower positions now have to cope with greater complexity. However, greater complexity does not entail greater discretion and judgement over the tasks undertaken.

The assumption that policy-makers have made is that the introduction of new electronic technologies will create an increased demand for skills. But it 'ain't necessarily so'. Technology and skill can be used in a complementary way in order to raise productivity, but electronic technology can also be used for purposes of surveillance and control. Initially it was thought that because banks had invested in new technology they would become a paradigm of the new knowledge economy. But what I had read, fired by Henry's comments, suggested otherwise. I needed to know what lay behind the figures on skill in the banking industry.

Within a week I was in Henry's office with a tape recorder, our usual positions reversed because I was now interviewing him. Henry was frustrated by what had happened to his job and he was happy to spend some time, in fact two hours, talking about it.

He took me through my personal file and showed me the paperwork involved in my loan application. What had come back from the 'credit controller' was effectively a computer print-out that contained a series of criteria by which my application was judged. Interestingly, these included my postcode area and the percentage of those in the postcode that had de-faulted on loans. Somehow my credit worthiness was to be judged against where I lived and the 'honesty' of my neighbours.

However, it emerged that this 'credit controller' is, in the first instance, a computer programme that automatically assesses a loan application according to pre-specified criteria. Only in appealing against the credit controller's judgement, as represented by the computer program, does Henry have a role. But even here there is no indication that his judgement will carry weight. Effectively, the role of the personal relations manager is no more than one of 'front of office' sociability. As Henry put it to me, 'a junior with a ready smile could do my job now'. And, in this particular case juniors on far lower salaries are being introduced to do the job. Indeed, salespeople were being hired from the next door clothes chain which was closing down.

But this was not the limit to the control and surveillance that had reduced Henry's ability to make independent judgements. His job now was one of mainly selling the bank's products to customers. Here he was a given a script that he was meant to follow based presumably on what was supposed to work and including various ways of manipulating potential customers' emotions. It was a script that Henry ignored. But there were many aspects of his job where that was impossible. His PC was brim full of manuals that governed the processes that had to be adopted for every conceivable problem or question that might arise. Failure to follow the manual would be subject to disciplinary procedures or a slap on the wrist depending on the gravity of the 'offence'.

But this was not all. The bank worked a five-day week which started on Fridays not Mondays. Every Friday his area manager, with data on Henry's performance on his PC screen, would phone him to review his performance for the week and whether he was on target to meet his annual financial goals.

Starting a week on a Friday is psychologically telling because it could leave Henry with the weekend to worry about how his performance could be improved if he was not meeting his targets. Henry was actually very successful in what he did and the bank used him to convey best practice to his colleagues but the changes in his job left him with a dilemma. He enjoyed that part of the job where he could meet people and, where possible, help them with their financial problems. But the devaluing of his knowledge and experience, by the systems of control and surveillance that had been installed, was another matter and he was considering leaving the bank.

Henry had given me rich insights into how the introduction of new technology had changed his job and to some extent his life. But when linked to the quantitative data patterns thrown up by the national surveys on skill, his interview filled out important aspects of the wider picture by providing an explanation of why corporations had restructured his job and many like it.

Corporations were using the new technology to create as consistent and predictable outcomes as possible. It ensured that the variables leading to under or over performance could more easily be measured and therefore identified. No one could escape from this computer-driven micro management. By this process, the bank was able to calculate the practices that could minimize risk while maximizing profits. It reduced workers' discretion and left decision-making to those at the top who processed the information coming up to them and then through manuals developed codes of best practice.

This piece of the jigsaw also fitted in with another odd 'fact' about the knowledge-based economic revolution: it is not generating the productivity gains that might be expected given that this economic revolution, supposedly, is meant to be as significant as the industrial revolution.

The interview with Henry linked to the statistical data patterns we had analysed showed that our picture of the knowledge-based economy is not the one that policy-makers like to paint. It also raises further questions about who benefits from the official picture.

Annotated bibliography

Bacchi, C. (1999) *Women, Policy and Politics. The Construction of Policy Problems.* London: Sage.

Overviews traditional and current approaches to policy studies. Uses feminist and post-positivist theories to develop a conceptual framework for policy analysis that starts with the question 'what is the problem here'?

Ball, S.J. (1993) 'What is policy? Texts, trajectories and toolboxes', *Discourse*, 13(2): 10–17.
An early explication of the new policy sociology drawn from post-structuralist theory.

Blackmore, J. (1999) 'Localisation/globalisation and the midwife state: Strategic dilemmas for state feminism in education?', *Journal of Education Policy*, 14(1): 33–54.
Explores effects of changing relations between state, social movements and education and their implications for equity.

Henry, M., Lingard, B., Rizvi, F. and Taylor, S. (2001) *OECD, Globalisation and Internationalisation.* Sydney: Allen and Unwin.
Maps the changing role of the OECD as part of an emerging global policy field in education.

Lauder, H., Brown, P. and Halsey, A.H. (2004) 'Sociology and political arithmetic: some principles of a new policy science', *British Journal of Sociology*, 55(1): 3–22.
Argues that we can learn from the tradition of political arithmetic about rules by which we can best view theories and judge between them.

Le Grand, J. (1997) 'Knights, knaves or pawns? Human behaviour and social policy', *Journal of Social Policy*, 26(2): 149–69.
Argues that policies assume that people are knights, who have a sense of duty, knaves who operate out of self-interest, or passive pawns who are simply passive and shape how to act accordingly.

Luke, A. (2002) 'Beyond science and ideology critique: Developments in critical discourse analysis', *Annual Review of Applied Linguistics*, 22: 96–110.
Indicates how critical discourse analysis can be a useful tool in policy analysis.

Ozga, J., Seddon, T. and Popkewitz, T. (2006) *World Yearbook of Education 2006: Education Research and Policy: Steering the Knowledge Economy.* New York: Routledge.
A comparative cross-national study of research that considers how research informs educational policy and specific global–local national politics of education research.

Rizvi, F. and Lingard, B. (2009) *Globalising Education Policy.* London: Routledge.
Explores key drivers of policy change in education and how they articulate differently within nation-states through critical issues such as centralized/decentralized governance,

public/private funding, access and equity, curriculum, and international education.

Yeatman, A. (ed.) (1998) *Activism and the Policy Process.* Sydney: Allen and Unwin.
Case studies in fields of health, welfare and education illustrating how activists work to change policy. Informed by conceptual work on policy discourses, educational change, gender equity.

Further references

Ball, S.J. (2003) 'The teacher's soul and the terrors of performativity', *Journal of Education Policy*, 18(2): 215–28.

Brint, S. (2001) 'Professionals and the "Knowledge Economy": Rethinking the theory of Post Industrial Society', *Current Sociology*, 49(4): 101–32.

Brown, P. and Lauder, H. (2003) 'Globalisation and the Knowledge Economy: Some Observations on Recent Trends in Employment, Education and the Labour Market'. Keynote Address to the BAICE/BERA Conference on Globalisation, Bristol University, June.

Dale, R. (1986) *Introducing Education Policy: Principles and Perspectives.* Milton Keynes: Open University Press.

Ladwig, J. (1994) 'For whom this reform? Outlining educational policy as a social field', *British Journal of Sociology of Education*, 15(3): 341–63.

Lingard, B., Rawolle, S. and Taylor, S (2005) 'Globalizing policy sociology in education: Working with Bourdieu', *Journal of Education Policy*, 20(6): 759–77.

Mazur, A. (1999) 'Feminist comparative policy: A new field of study?', *European Journal of Political Research*, 35(4): 483–503.

Ozga, J. (2000) *Policy Research in Educational Settings: Contested Terrain.* Buckingham: Open University Press.

Phillips, D. and Ochs, K. (2004) 'Researching policy borrowing: Some methodological challenges in comparative education', *British Educational Research Journal*, 30(6): 773–84.

Taylor, S., Rizvi, F., Lingard, B. and Henry, M. (1997) *Educational Policy and the Politics of Change.* London: Routledge.

Young, K., Ashby, D., Boaz, A. and Grayson, L. (2002) 'Social science and the evidence based policy movement', *Social Policy and Society*, 1(3): 215–24.

PART VI

QUANTITATIVE METHODS: THEORIES AND PERSPECTIVES

Introduction

Part VI presents the theoretical origins of quantitative methods and an overview of the wide range of tools and techniques that can now be applied in social science research. 'Quantitative methods' is a broad umbrella term for a huge range of specialized topics and approaches. Our focus in this book is on arguing the case for why these methods are important, and illustrating the variety in how they are used in practice. There are many textbooks that focus entirely on one specific statistical technique and it is not our aim here to replicate that work. What we seek to do, as we do elsewhere in this book, is to provide a focused introduction to the relationship between theories, methods and practices, and advice on further reading for those who decide to specialize in these approaches.

The first chapter discusses what quantitative methods do, how to use them well and how this all relates to different philosophical positions. It argues for the importance of quantitative methods because of the fallibility of human reasoning and confronts the unthinking hostility of some students. It provides an appraisal of critical realism as a strong philosophical basis for quantitative research in the social sciences. This is followed by a chapter that begins with a historical analysis and critique of positivism and moves on to a presentation of how quantitative methods can be adapted for use by psychologists, within a sociocultural theoretical framework. These first two chapters (23 and 24) provide the theoretical

base for the chapters on methods which follow (25, 26 and 27).

The third chapter provides an overview of many elements associated with quantitative methods, from defining terminology and underlying principles, to explaining sampling strategies, approaches to questionnaire design, and statistical methods of organizing descriptive data. In the fourth chapter, techniques for identifying differences between groups (usually of people in the social sciences) and relationships between characteristics of a single group are presented. The fifth and final chapter discusses a range of approaches for modelling relationships between characteristics. In particular, multilevel modelling is introduced as an important, sophisticated yet flexible technique that has the potential to serve the needs of social scientists very well. It is based on the premise that analysis should take account of the similarities of members of a group (students in a class, nurses in a hospital, and so on) because the contextual factors and influences are shared. Of course there will still be individual variation but this is also accounted for.

These three chapters (25, 26 and 27) provide the reader with the language required to understand quantitative approaches and an overview of what can be achieved with the diverse tools and techniques available, either in isolation or in combination with other methods. The accompanying Stories from the Field, providing exemplification of some of the techniques in practice, including multilevel modelling, and drawing on elements from all three chapters, are presented in Part VII.

There is a multiplicity of links between Part VI and others in the book. Part VI and Part VII are of course inextricably linked, the latter providing four Stories from the Field, and a chapter on mixed methodologies. Questionnaires are not exclusively quantitative and have a place in many qualitative and mixed method approaches. Sampling strategies are required in many spheres of research – how do you select which members of society should be interviewed? For example, Holt (Corbin and Holt, Chapter 13, this volume) refers to sampling issues that he faced and describes his samples in terms of their average ages. Observation can be applied within both quantitative and qualitative research. Some techniques applied in discourse analysis involve counting occurrences of words in texts. In fact numbers occur in almost all research, whether it be statistical analysis in a large-scale survey or reporting the number of people involved in an ethnographic study.

23

The Practice of Quantitative Methods

Kelvyn Jones, School of Geographical Sciences, University of Bristol, UK

Summary

- Quantitative methods in social science (QSS)
- Positivism
- Critical realism
- Closed and open systems
- Key theorists
  - Roy Bhaskar
  - John Tukey
  - Ann Oakley
  - Wendy Olsen
  - Ray Pawson

Key concepts

Introduction

This chapter is concerned with why we use quantitative methods in social science (QSS), what they do and how to use them well, and how this all relates to different philosophical positions. In teaching quantitative courses I am often confronted by barely concealed hostility. The approach is seen as hard, trivial, bloodless, reductionist, reactionary and even dead. I want to begin by confronting these views.

- *Hard*: Quantification is undoubtedly demanding. A pervasive problem is that this type of knowledge is highly cumulative and you cannot fully appreciate the more sophisticated approaches without knowing the simpler ones. This is exacerbated by focusing on technique and failing to get

over what Abelson (1995) has called 'statistics as principled argument'.

- *Trivial*: There is undoubtedly mindless empiricism where techniques are just used because they can be. But questions of real importance can only be tackled with good quality extensive data and tools that can reveal pattern and guard against over-interpretation. To take poverty; how otherwise would you answer such questions as 'has inequality increased in the last 50 years?', or 'is there a permanent underclass?', or the causal question 'does poverty produce failure or does failure cause poverty'? While ethnography provides rich knowledge about those in poverty, such work cannot inform on how extensive such findings are.

- *Bloodless*: Quantitative work stresses objectivity because experience has shown that we find pattern where none exists. I give my students a set of maps with cot deaths marked by a dot and they find clusters of birth defects in pure noise. A great deal of care is needed in making inferences; but that does not mean our work should not be impassioned. Indeed, removal of ignorance and false views is, I contend, genuinely emancipatory.

- *Reductionist*: Much quantitative work has indeed been over-generalizing – seeking the same results for all people for all time – and too atomistic in focusing on individuals and ignoring the context in which individuals find themselves. But this is changing as quantitative work is being developed that takes context seriously (Jones, Chapters 27 and 29, this volume).

- *Reactionary*: In part this related to the last point that much work has been atomistic and ignores context. But I believe that there is no necessary connection between political ideology and method. Thus, the *Bell Curve*'s[1] argument that life outcomes are based on intelligence which can in part be genetically and racially inherited was based on quantitative analysis, but quantification was also used by the protagonists in the *Bell Curve Debate* (Russell and Glauberman, 1995) to argue that this was scientific racialism. Undoubtedly, you need a good understanding of quantitative social science to engage effectively in such debate and critique.

- *Dead*: Nothing could be farther from the truth. Subjects and approaches do wax and wane and currently Quantitative Social Science is seen by the UK government as a 'strategically important and vulnerable subject'. But if you look more widely thousands of postgraduates are being trained in quantitative-orientated summer schools every year (e.g. at Essex, Ljubljana, Michigan), prestigious universities are setting up QSS institutions and the mainstream social science journals routinely publish a large range of quantitative studies. Indeed in *Freakonomics* (Levitt and Dubner, 2005) the approach has a best seller which is being made into a film!

Quantification and philosophies of science

The philosophy of science is concerned with the underlying logic of the scientific method. It tries to make sense of what researchers do, as well as how to do things better. It consists of two parts: ontology – what exists – and epistemology – what can be known, and how can we know it? The answers are highly contested, with a number of competing 'isms'. Much of the claim that QSS is defunct rests on the elision that science = positivism = quantification. As positivism is discredited, so is quantification. Here, I want to argue two things. First, that some of the tenets of positivism debar what is current state-of-the-art procedures in QSS. Second, a contemporary philosophy of science, Critical Realism (CR), does see a role for quantification alongside other practices, and does so for more than simple counting or enumeration.

Positivism

The many variants of positivism have two distinguishing features:

- Explanation can only be based on observable and measurable events. This empiricist ontology aims to guard against metaphysical mysticism where explanation is based on authority – accepting what someone said without looking and measuring. Science as positivism focuses on data as value-free facts, where observation is performed through a one-way mirror; what is being measured is not changed by being observed. Observations are independent of any theoretical statements that might be subsequently constructed around them. At the extreme, beliefs, emotions and values are outside science, the purpose of which is to stick to what we can observe.

- Explanation as a regularity: One event causes another if it is regularly followed by it. Generalized knowledge is obtained by identifying such constant conjunctions or event regularities, hence the quantitative search for order and pattern as associations between variables. In this successionist epistemology, causation is replaced by universal regularity. This dispenses with any mysterious causal necessity or unobservable processes, like explanations based on God's will. Scientists should seek 'covering' laws where events are seen as specific instances of a general law which is applicable universally for all time and all places. Thus, this shopper goes to this store because of the rational law of distance minimization.

In practice, this approach has often degenerated (of necessity?) into instrumentalism whereby the world is treated as a black box without need to understand processes. The truth/falsity of theoretical statements is not the issue, for they are just regarded as computational devices; knowledge is judged true, because it is useful. Being able to predict is to be able to explain; and being able to predict allows control. To be able to 'drive' the system does not require understanding how the 'engine' works; and we have an instrumentalist rationality, whereby scientific thinking itself has become an ideology; the ends justify the means.

Critical realism

Unlike positivism with its early nineteenth-century origins, critical realism has been initiated more recently by Roy Bhaskar (1975, 1979) and Rom Harré (Harré and Madden, 1975).[2] It offers a radical alternative to positivism (the goal is not generalizable laws); to interpretivism (the goal is not solely to appreciate the lived experience of social actors); and to postmodernism (there are truths, and knowledge is more than just some undetermined socially-constructed linguistic system). A critical realist believes that there is an independent reality that science can study – each of us is not making it all up! It aims to develop deeper levels of explanation as causal necessity, not just regularity. It provides a logic of enquiry based on the fundamental formula:

$$Mechanism + Context = Outcomes$$

Mechanisms are not regularities but are potentially causal generative processes that operate in particular historical, local, or institutional contexts to produce particular patterns of outcomes. For me, CR provides a much more congenial home for the practice of quantitative research. Congenial because it makes sense of my practice and I do not have to pretend that I am doing something else. It provides a strong bastion against the radical unreason and relativism of the strong constructionist viewpoint where what is true depends entirely on where you stand; it explains why scientific practices work; it also puts sensible limits on what can be achieved.

Critical realism has a multi-layered and stratified ontology. The world and our knowledge of it can be seen as three overlapping domains which of necessity must exist to permit the intelligibility and success of scientific practice. These domains have specific propensities:

- the empirical: aspects of reality that can be experienced and observed directly or indirectly; these experiences constitute parts of the 'events', which we can identify as the domain of
- the actual: aspects of reality that occur, but may not necessarily be experienced; these are in turn the outcomes of the domain of
- the real: 'deep' structures and mechanisms or tendencies that generate phenomena.[3]

The last are the key objects of knowledge in both natural and social science. In the social sciences, mechanisms are social practices which are outcomes of structures of social relations. Disputed entities such as class relations exist independently of us and are not simply human constructs; but unlike in positivism they may also be not directly observable, but still real

with observable outcomes. These structures are intransitive in operating independently of our knowledge of them (except when we intervene), but our knowledge of them is transitive and capable of being changed. Moreover, this transitive knowledge is not only a product of our fallible cognitive capacities, but also of the ideological pressures of the culture of any given scientific community. Mechanisms have the tendency to behave in such a way because of the structure of the underlying object. Thus a landlord–tenant structure necessitates the mechanism of the payment of rent. Such mechanisms are contingent and there may be countervailing tendencies in certain contexts which may prevent them from operating. Consequently, what causes something has nothing to do with the number of times it has happened; necessity implies neither regularity nor universality. Moreover, we can have emergent powers, new ways of operating due to the complex interplay of mechanisms. Water has the power to extinguish fire, a property which is not contained in the constituent parts of hydrogen and oxygen. Simply breaking down objects into their parts, reductionism, is therefore a fallible strategy.

Closed systems and the role of experiments

The aim of CR science is to uncover these causal powers and structures. Natural science is greatly helped by having access to closed systems either through their natural occurrence (as in the near clockwork universe of planetary astronomy) or by creative intervention (in a machine or experiment). With closure it is much easier to see mechanisms as regularities because everything else is kept constant. Thus, both the regularity conception and instrumentalism are effective in such a system so that laws not only explain but predict such things as solar eclipses. To achieve this, two aspects of closure are required. First, the intrinsic condition requires that there is no change in the object possessing the causal powers. Second, the extrinsic condition requires that the relationship between the causal mechanism and external conditions remains constant. To achieve clockwork regularity and predict the hour requires that the spring must not suffer metal fatigue and the mechanism must be isolated from any tampering. CR clarifies that the purpose of a well designed experiment is to intervene to isolate a mechanism and trigger its outcome in a regular sequence: experimental production as well as experimental control. In a closed world we create the conditions for the formula

Regularity = triggered Mechanism
+ stable Context

and thereby considerably aid the elucidation of explanatory mechanisms and structures.

Open systems and the need for methodological pluralism

Some natural sciences – climatology and geology – have difficulty in securing closed systems, but still make great progress in understanding the world. They do so by inferring that mechanisms are operative in open environments, but may be hidden or counter-acted by other powers. Thus geology uses knowledge of mechanisms to appreciate where oil may have been formed but needs to drill – empirical enquiry – to substantiate this; it is not knowledge of the causal mechanism that is incomplete, but lack of knowledge of accidental contingent conditions that are the hallmark of open systems. All science does this to some extent and transfers knowledge gained under artificial constructed environments to open systems. The social world is undoubtedly open for we are capable of conscious reflection and change (akin to cogs of a clock deciding to change the gearing ratio) and we have the capacity to re-configure the system (the fall of communism is akin to an acid-bath for the clock). While not expecting to find universal regularities within the social world, underlying causal structures may well give rise to differences or contrasts that are relatively enduring over space or time. Such patterns or 'demi-regs' (Lawson, 1989) may prove a good starting point for a CR investigation to uncover the mechanisms or constraints generating them.

The multi-layered depth ontology and open systems that characterize social science require different types of practice to obtain knowledge (Sayer, 1992). Methodological pluralism is a necessity, but this cannot be adopted unthinkingly. The concrete multi-faceted objects of our observable world require rational theoretical abstraction to distinguish contingent from necessary relations, to identify structures and counter-factuals. Intensive work, including quali-tative research, is required to see how mechanisms work out in particular cases; extensive work means looking at the demi-regs to see the evidence for processes in action and how widespread are phenom-ena. Finally, a synthesis is required to put it all together as explanation building; not just whether this causal process produces an effect but why, when, and how, and for whom. We need to be realistic about

this: the heterogeneity and complexity of what we are studying limits what can be achieved, and this is not just lack of skill or maturity of social science, but is constrained by the open nature of the social world.

Returning now to the practice of QSS, I want to look at what we do in light of these 'isms'.

Putting thoughts into quantitative practice

The positivist blueprint of confining explanation to observables is not the way that quantification works. Usually we want to use measurements to infer beyond the immediate. After interviewing 5,000 households about their income we want to infer robustly about the people we have not measured to answer such questions as what proportion of the UK population are in poverty. Theory and a representative sample guarantee that we can make the inference to the unknown proportion with a known degree of confi-dence (Barnes and Lewin, Chapter 26, this volume). This inference to the directly unobservable is becom-ing a prominent part of quantitative work. Chapters 27 and 29 discuss multilevel models in which there are random effects. We posit that schools have a differ-ential effect on student progress, and while we can only measure pupils, we can estimate the school differential effects. Such latent modelling is focused on the quantitative analysis of what cannot be directly measured.

Another important area is causal inference. To know the causal effect of going to university on subsequent earnings, we need the outcome for the same individual who has and has not gone to university. Without both counterfactuals we cannot be sure that nothing else has affected the outcome, or operated as a confounder between earnings and learning. It is obviously impossible to observe both potential outcomes, one is always missing. Conse-quently, the effect of higher education cannot be measured but can only be estimated. The develop-ment of the potential-outcomes approach to causal inference (Morgan and Winship, 2007) does not concern itself with correlational associations and the prediction of future events from past events (as in the positivist recipe), but with a logical framework for thinking about causality and under what conditions valid inference can be made (Pearl, 2009), and how to find evidence that the 'switching on' of a process and the 'holding off' of others lead to a difference in outcome. Positivist tenets, this time the irrelevance of causality, are at odds with current practice. Such quantitative work (contra most CR accounts) thus appears to be useful in intensive work in determining how things are caused.

I contend that the best quantitative work involves, often unknowingly, the practical realities that CR explains, and by understanding why, it enables us to do better. What follows is my list of rules of engagement for a post-positivist, CR-inspired QSS.

Pay attention to abstraction and classification: Abstraction and classification is a key process and we must try to distinguish the necessary from the contingent. Thus, the landlord/tenant relation is a necessary one, but whether the actors in these roles are male or female, young or old is contingent and arbitrary (Allen, 1983). In this context, theory is not grandiose speculation but rather mundane questions about what exists and what do social actors do, and to whom or with whom do they do it? This requires a more sophisticated social theory than either methodological individualism or totalizing structuralism and needs us to recognize that both agents and structures have causal powers. In Bhaskar's (1979) transformational model of society, people as agents create and reproduce structures which in turn enable or constrain the actions of agents. Unfortunately, a lot of quantitative research, especially that based on official statistics and aggregate analysis, uses poorly abstracted taxonomic collectives which classify according to formal similarities and not functional connections, thereby conflating very heterogeneous groups. Just think of the 'service industry': hairdressers and bankers may be placed in that group but they have very different powers to act. No methodology, however sophisticated, can rescue a poor abstraction and classification.

Practise retroduction but accept it is always fallible: This is the key epistemological method of CR in open systems; it involves guessing what are the underlying causal mechanisms that are operating. It is the form of reasoning used by detectives: here is the partial evidence – who could have caused the crime? Given a fallible hunch, what evidence do we need to corroborate it? In data analysis, we have to move from some observed phenomenon (or its absence) to posit some underlying mechanisms via a trial explanation which we call a model. Our job is to identify and to make sense of demi-regs as evidence that relatively enduring, and potentially identifiable mechanisms have been operating. Consequently, the technique of regression modelling (Jones, Chapter 27, this volume) can be seen as an attempt to identify spontaneously

occurring closures which may give us clues to processes (Ron, 2002). Demi-regs must be seen as the beginnings of causal explanation not as the end point. There is a need to open up the black box, to understand outcome patterns rather than seek outcome regularities, and to be sensitive to the context in which the patterns have been found. Regularities, even enduring ones, do not explain themselves.

Go back and forth between theory and the empirical patterns suggested by the data: The more extreme positivist would regard this as cheating – you are supposed to come up with a theory (without looking at data) which is then confronted and either confirmed or falsified. It is simply impossible to implement in open systems, which require an iterative process of understanding the data and developing constructs, and not a one-off calibration. In data analysis you need to try out models on the basis of a vague idea and discard them when they yield no explanatory return. This rarely succeeds on the first try and various models are needed to establish a good demonstration. Any account of what happens in reality must be able to account for this active role of the scientist in the process. The running of many models should not be regarded as 'sinning in the basement' (Kennedy, 2002) which must be hidden away; indeed it is both licensed and required by retroduction. At the same time there can be no pretence that the resultant estimates are the only ones that have been fitted and represent universal regularities across time and space that perfectly conform to theoretical expectation.

Choose appropriate techniques for the task in hand: In the context of all this philosophically-inspired advice, it is easy to forget that we do need technique. One of the great all-time statisticians, John Tukey (1962), distinguished between exploration and confirmation: the former brings data into sharper focus to see patterns and anomalies; the latter is the use of significance testing to confirm well-developed hypotheses and avoid unreliable results. The specific technique matters too. If we take the arithmetic mean (Lewin, Chapter 25, this volume), Canadians earn $2,000 dollars less than Americans, which may suggest a policy of lower taxes and cutbacks is needed. But if you calculate what the average Canadian earns, the median is $2,000 higher than in America, because the US is a much more unequal society with the arithmetic mean being pulled upwards by relatively few, big earners – different techniques, different answers, different implications.

Play with your data and use the tools of exploratory data analysis. EDA is close in spirit to retroduction; indeed Tukey saw it as numerical detective work in contrast to the judgemental confirmatory approach where the hypothesis is on trial. EDA is an attitude which encourages and licenses an iterative approach. It is based on the notion that 'better a good answer to a vague question than a precise answer to the wrong one' and 'by assuming less you learn more' (Jones and Almond, 1992). It has encouraged the development of procedures that reveal patterns in the data, and diagnostic, often graphical tools for exposing where assumptions are not met. In particular, residual analysis, the information that has not been accounted for by a model, has been likened to the magnifying glass of the story-book detective for bringing into sharper focus where the explanation is not working. However, we are not being data driven because we are exploring in the light of theoretically and substantively interesting questions as we investigate multiple working hypotheses.

Be alert for outliers and think what may be causing them. Outliers, cases which are 'far away' from the rest, are often thrown up by data analysis. If they are not just mistakes, they offer an opportunity to learn that the current model is not working and they may give clues to new mechanisms. These potentially explainable anomalies are known as contrastive demi-regularities. We may learn about the normal by considering the abnormal, and treating the outlier as a critical case. In data analysis, residual, post modelling, graphical analysis can be a powerful tool for their identification (Cox and Jones, 1981).

Appreciate the limited role of statistical hypothesis testing. The purpose of confirmatory approaches (Barnes and Lewin, Chapter 26, this volume) is to guard against chance results being interpreted as genuine pattern. Naive falsification – the testing of a null hypothesis – is unsupportable in open systems as the absence of an effect may be due to some other process preventing it. A significant p value really tells you that your sample size was large enough to detect an effect. Moreover, statistical significance says nothing about the magnitude and importance of the effect, and cannot be viewed as a substitute for judgemental assessments of the theoretical and practical significance of a particular model.

Do not indulge in data dredging. This activity tries to find 'rules' that link variables by maximizing the goodness-of-fit between the model and the observed data. This is usually achieved by machine-based algorithms using automated significance testing procedures. There is no contradiction between encouraging playing with data and denouncing dredging, for the former is retroduction and the latter is induction, seeking regularity as a black box without concern for illuminating causal mechanisms. Goodness-of-fit is a poor criterion for choosing one model over another; you can get perfect agreement by putting in the same number of variables as observations but you would have explained nothing. Such an approach can be likened to the Texan sharpshooter who fires at the barn door and then draws circles around where the bullets have clustered, and announces success. The explanations are being found solely in the results. Such unbridled empiricism is likely to capitalize on chance, finding pattern where none exists. Blind number crunching can be dangerous: you may have identified a black-box rule for profitable sub-prime lending but the market could change (breaking extrinsic closure) rendering the rule useless, with dire consequences.

Be very wary of predictions. Quantitative forecasts are based on equations capturing enduring relations of the past that continue into the future. In open systems this will not be the case, and no predictive system is able to deal with abrupt breaks of regime. Sherden's (1998) provocatively titled book examined the success of 16 types of forecasts. Only one-day-ahead weather forecasts and the aging of the population were more reliable than chance. A real danger is when fallible predictions are treated normatively, that is as goals that have to be achieved. This can degenerate into unthinking engineering to preserve the status quo; any systemic inequalities embedded in the equations are thereby reproduced into the future.

Use deduction but know its limitations. Deduction in QSS means using mathematics to represent the world to come up with potentially unexpected results. Thus, in the birthday problem, we can deduce from theory that we only need 23 people in a room to have a greater than evens chance that two people share the same birthday; a smaller number than most expect. Exploiting the power of mathematics requires making ruthless abstraction where the world is stripped back to just a few key terms. This can potentially bring new knowledge. For example, the spread of an epidemic can be reduced to the reproduction ratio of how many people a single person can infect and this allows the effective and realistic assessment of alternative futures, even on a global scale (Colizza et al., 2007). Recent years have seen the development of complexity social science (Byrne, 1998) with its feedback and non-linear dynamic systems, but the realism of the assumptions in relation to human social action remains a key issue for any deductive reasoning.

Use experimentation in all its forms: At the outset of a study, undertake a thought experiment as if you had unlimited resources and there were no ethical constraints. This ideal experiment will often allow you to formulate precise causal questions, appreciate what you need to control to get isolation, and will help identify a strategy for doing this in practice. If a randomized trial is possible, we can intervene and randomly allocate some individuals to receive the potentially causal exposure. This ensures that on average the exposed and non-exposed will be 'balanced' on all possible other influences. This state of equipoise holds off any other causal mechanism even if we do not know what they are! The desirability of the randomized experiment comes from this ability to deal with unmeasured confounders (the 'unknown unknowns') that could really be behind the apparent regularity between a causal exposure and an outcome. In recent years there has been an upsurge of interest in experimental social science. To take a single example, Oakley (1990) in her randomized study of social support for young mothers revealed that the standard practice of midwives involved discriminatory stereotyping based on race and class. You may be objecting that you cannot manipulate social dispositional variables like gender and race but researchers have designed ingenious experiments to examine sexism and racism where there is a consistent script but actors of different sex and race are used (Feldman et al., 1997).

If randomization is not possible, then look for quasi- or natural experiments: This when the causal mechanism has naturally been turned off and on, or there is a random-like process determining who gets exposed to the potentially causal process. An outstanding guide to identification strategies using naturally occurring randomization is Angrist and Pischke (2009). For this to work you need a variable known as an instrument which strongly influences exposure to the causal process but does not affect the outcome directly. One of their examples is trying to estimate the effect of family size on workplace participation and earning. It is not good enough to simply relate these outcomes to family size because reverse causality may be occurring (workplace outcomes affecting family size)

and there may be powerful preferences affecting having children and working that have not been measured (the unknowns). The study finds two-children families with same sex children are very much more likely to have another child than if the children are of different sex. The sex of the first two children forms a natural experiment: it is as if an experimenter has randomly assigned some families to have two children and others to have three or more, once we take account of the sex mix (the instrument). The authors are then able to estimate the causal effect of having a third child, finding that the labour-market consequences are more likely to be severe for poor and less educated women, while husbands experience little change. As always we have to be careful in transferring results from the rather artificial world of the 'closed' system. Here, the effect of going from two to three children does not necessarily apply to going from zero to one child, and from one to two.

Use the appropriate observational design for the problem in hand: If an experimental design is not possible, choose the most efficient design that requires the least resources to get evidential data (Jones and Subramanian, 2000). Thus, if there is a rare outcome, choose a design that samples on the basis of the outcome, a case-control design. A classic example is concern about sudden upsurge in birth defects in Germany. The researchers studied 46 cases of limb-defect babies and 300 normal birth comparisons. It was found that 41 of the cases had been exposed to the drug Thalidomide, compared with none of the controls: very strong evidence that this drug was the cause. In contrast, if there is a rare causal process operating, choose a multi-sample cohort design based on those who are and who are not exposed to the process. This design was used to follow those who did and did not work at the Sellafield reprocessing plant, finding that the father's pre-conceptional exposure to irradiation increased the child's risk of leukaemia. All observational designs, however, face the problem of not being able to control for unknown confounders as they are not measured. A chastening case being when the best observational studies found that HRT led to a relative reduction of 50 per cent in coronary heart disease, but subsequent randomized trials found an increased risk of 30 per cent. Despite the best efforts of the observational researchers, those receiving the treatment were systematically different from those not, and considerable efforts at statistical analysis had not been sufficient to achieve equipoise.

Recognize that the need for parsimony depends on what you are doing: Parsimony is often interpreted as the simplest explanation being the correct one. In data analysis this is frequently taken to imply that the model should be kept as simple as possible and have few terms. For me, the usefulness of the criteria differs by practice. In induction, this can be useful for black-box model building as, in the need to capture signal not noise, parsimony becomes our guard against over-fitting and capturing contingent fluctuations. In deduction, simplicity is often necessary to make the mathematics tractable, but if there is poor abstraction and key processes are missing, then the model is not complex enough. In retroduction, while we might start with simple models in terms of practicality, I see no reason why models should necessarily be limited to simple ones. In panel studies of people's changing behaviour over time, it is recommended that a separate term is put in the model for each and every person (Allison, 2009) so that each individual becomes their own 'control', just as if all stable unobserved variables had been measured, achieving the same function as random assignment in designed experiments. Such a model may well have thousands of terms. When the problem is complex, a complex model may well be needed. Parsimony should not be used to assert a naive view of causality, or to ignore demanding technical requirements.

Don't be afraid to explore for interactions: The CR account suggests that causal mechanisms may come together either to negate an effect or to act synergistically with emergent power to create an enhanced effect. Such interplay of causal mechanisms should show up in data analysis in what is known as interactions. Their exploration is an important part of opening up the black box to see the causal pathways behind the demi-regs. Thus, there may be a main effect of smoking on bronchitis so those that do smoke have a higher risk, there may also be elevated levels of the disease in those that live in higher air pollution, but the highest risk is for those who smoke and who live in high pollution. Including interactions in the model is also a way to have different models for different subsets of people. Indeed, these moderating interactions may be the most interesting part of a study. To take one example, the Head Start programme has been applied to millions of children. It is informed by a 1962 randomized experiment involving 123 black preschoolers, 58 of whom were treated to intensive education and home visits with 65 in the control group. They were followed until they were aged 27. A recent re-analysis (Anderson, 2008) found that the positive effects were driven by the results for girls; the intervention did little for boys. This example also shows that even randomized experiments do not analyse themselves.

Recognize that data in open systems are 'ficts': Data are seen in positivism as facts, the arbiters of theory. In CR, data obtained in open systems are seen as 'ficts' (Olsen and Morgan, 2005) which may not be true mirror-like representations of reality, but are still useful for warranted arguments in terms of speculation and as sources for explanation. Our understanding and analysis of data are of necessity theory-laden, but that does not mean our concepts fully determine the measurement. Theories suggest where to look and what to measure but do not determine what we find. Our best hope for approaching objectivity is not only by the actions of individual researchers (through randomization and blinding to outcome and exposure), but also through the social processes of scrutiny and criticism of the broader scientific community.

Do not expect textbooks to provide a cookbook recipe for your study: There are several aspects to this. First the majority of texts follow the positivist line – for exceptions, see the bibliography. Second, what we are researching should inform the choice of appropriate analysis. Sir Ronald Fisher was horrified that his statistical tests were used outside of the setting – agricultural trials – for which he had developed them. Thus, the use of the F test for judging difference in the means of interventions is based on independence of observations (Barnes and Lewin, Chapter 26, this volume). This assumption is guaranteed by randomization in trials, but is unlikely to be the case for observational studies. This dependency requires a more sophisticated modelling approach (Jones, Chapter 27, this volume). Third, there is a great deal of tacit knowledge that is required in any specific application. Magnus and Morgan (1999) conducted an experiment in which an apprentice had to replicate the analysis that might have been carried out by three different experts following their published guidance. In all cases, the results were different from one another, and different from that subsequently produced by the expert! This undermines claims to researcher-independent objectivity and suggests that experience is required not only in the subtleties of the method but also of the characteristics of what is being studied.

Be sensitive to context: Causal processes can produce different results in different settings. Pawson and Tilley (1997) have developed a realism-inspired form of evaluation which involves identifying CMO configurations where C is context, M is mechanism and O is outcomes. They argue that researchers should aim to identify the features of contexts that allow different mechanisms to be activated so as to generate particular outcomes. The theory is therefore used to derive the context that creates the ideal conditions for triggering the mechanism in question. The method seeks not generalization, but specification: what works for whom in a set of given circumstances and what is preventing change? As Deaton (2009) argues, success depends crucially not on evaluation of specific interventions but on the evaluation of theoretical mechanisms. Quantitative meta-analysis which pools information across contexts and averages the size of effect from different studies needs to be treated with considerable caution, as Pawson (2006) cogently argues.

Apply criteria of judgement in evaluating a theory: CR recognizes that, in the social world at least, there is unlikely to be a definite make-or-break study. Instead it encourages judgemental rationalism: there is fallibility (we can never prove a theory to be true for all time) but also the possibility of objective knowledge (not all theories are equally valid). This objectivity is possible because in the intransitive dimension, reality exists independently of us, and knowledge can be more or less like this reality. The process of obtaining objectivity in the transitive dimension is through competitive between-theory cross validation, a process of focused disputation between researchers. Explanation is itself therefore a social process whereby organized distrust produces trustworthy results (Campbell, 1984). Rational grounds for preferring one theory over another are their explanatory power, comprehensiveness, degree of supporting evidence, and coherence with other bodies of knowledge. Such criteria of judgement have a long history in observational research (Jones and Moon, 1987) and were responsible for regarding cigarette smoking as a cause of cancer even without the possibility of experimenting to produce a closed system. It is definitely not a matter of goodness-of-fit between the observed and predicted data.

Conclusions

I have argued that for science to be obviously successful there is an independent external world and we can gain reliable, if not provable, knowledge of it. There is a need for science to reveal deeper structures and mechanisms to counter irrationality, prejudice, superstition and 'bad science' (Goldacre, 2008); taken-for-granted commonsense may be false knowledge. Quantitative analysis can play a part in this by aiding the collection of reliable evidence, dealing with uncertainty, using analytical techniques to identify patterns and anomalies, and setting out a logical framework to make causal inferences. The aim of emancipatory social science is not to identify and reproduce universal regularities, but to recognize and change them. I have concentrated here on causality because of its centrality to science, but in reality much quantitative work is 'social mapping' and this counting and estimation of prevalence and change is important too for knowing what is happening in the world. At its best quantitative work is a rich, knowledgeable and reflective practice far removed from its positivist caricature.

Notes

1. A book by Richard J. Herrnstein and Charles Murray published in 1994: *The Bell Curve: Intelligence and Class Structure in American Life*. Regarded as controversial.
2. Pawson (2006, 19–20) provides a brief history.
3. The epistemic fallacy reduces the three domains to the one of the observable events of empiricism (Bhaskar, 1978: 36).

Annotated bibliography

Angrist, J.D. and Pischke, J-F. (2009) *Mostly Harmless Econometrics: An Empiricist's Companion*. Princeton: Princeton University Press.
A lucid account of what QSS is really about (that is, not just a bag of techniques). A state-of the-art account of how to do causal empirical research.

Brady, H.E. and Collier, D. (eds) (2004) *Rethinking Social Inquiry: Diverse Tools and Shared Standards*. Lanham: Rowman and Littlefield.
Something of a riposte to King, Keohane and Verba (see below) in arguing that distinctive standards must be set from exemplary qualitative work that do more than replicate those of quantitative studies.

Johnston, R.J. (1986) *On Human Geography*. Oxford: Basil Blackwell.

Integrates realism social theory and quantification in the study of places.

King, G., Keohane, R.O. and Verba, S. (1994) *Designing Social Inquiry*. Princeton: Princeton University Press.
Another lucid account of what QSS is really about, it caused quite a stir by laying out guidelines for conducting qualitative research from a quantitative viewpoint.

Lopez, J. and Potter, P. (2001) *After Postmodernism: An Introduction to Critical Realism*. London: Athlone Press.
Provocatively titled, this is a wide-ranging collection on the attractions of CR.

Marshall, G. (1997) *Repositioning Class: Social Inequality in Industrial Societies*. London: Sage.
A feisty account of why we are not a postmodern society requiring postmodern methods.

Oakley, A. (2000) *Experiments in Knowing: Gender and Method in the Social Sciences*. Cambridge: Polity Press.
A highly personal reflection on the need for experiments in social science by a noted feminist author.

Olsen, W. (2010) *Realist Methodology*, 4 volumes. London: Sage.
This compendium book covers the methodological implications of CR.

Pawson, R. and Tilley, N. (1997) *Realistic Evaluation*. London: Sage; Pawson R. (2006) *Evidence-Based Policy: a Realist Perspective*. London: Sage.
To see how critical realism can be put into practice in policy research.

Yu, C.H. (2006) *Philosophical Foundations of Quantitative Research Methodology*. Lanham: University Press of America.
An extended critique of how quantification does not equate to positivism.

Further references

Abelson, R.P. (1995) *Statistics as Principled Argument*. Mahwah, NJ: Lawrence Erlbaum.

Allen, J. (1983) 'Property relations and landlordism – a realist approach', *Environment and Planning D*, 1: 191–203.

Allison, P.D. (2009) *Fixed Effects Regression Models*. Thousand Oaks, CA: Sage.

Anderson, M. (2008) 'Multiple inference and gender differences in the effects of early intervention', *Journal of the American Statistical Association*, 103: 1481–95.

Bhaskar, R. (1975) *A Realist Theory of Science*. Hassocks: Harvester Press. (2nd edn, 1978.)

Bhaskar, R. (1978) *A Realist Theory of Science*, 2nd edn. Brighton: Harvester Press.

Bhaskar, R. (1979) *The Possibilities of Naturalism*. Brighton: Harvester Press.

Byrne, D. (1998) *Complexity Theory and the Social Sciences*. London: Routledge.

Campbell, D.T. (1984) 'Can we be scientific in applied social science?', in R.F Conner, D.G. Altman and C. Jackson (eds) *Evaluation Studies Review Annual*. Thousand Oaks, CA: Sage. pp. 26–48.

Colizza, V., Barrat, A., Barthelemy, M., Valleron, A-J. and Vespignani, A. (2007) 'Modeling the worldwide spread of pandemic influenza', *PLoS Medicine*, 4(1): e13.

Deaton, A.S. (2009) 'Instruments of development: Randomization in the tropics, and the search for the elusive keys to economic development', *Proceedings of the British Academy*, 162: 123–60.

Cox N.J. and Jones K. (1981) 'Exploratory data analysis', in N. Wrigley and R.J. Bennett (eds) *Quantitative Geography*. London: Routledge, pp. 135–43.

Feldman, H.A., McKinlay, J.B., Potter, D.A., Freund, K.M., Burns, R.B., Moskowitz, M.A. and Kasten, L.E. (1997) 'Non-medical influences on medical decision making: An experimental technique using videotapes, factorial design, and survey sampling', *Health Services Research*, 32: 343–66.

Goldacre, B. (2008) *Bad Science*. London: Fourth Estate.

Harré, R. and Madden, E.H. (1975) *Causal Powers*. Oxford: Blackwell.

Jones, K. and Almond, S. (1992) 'Moving out of the linear rut: The possibilities of generalised additive models', *Transactions of the Institute of British Geographers*, 17: 434–47 .

Jones, K. and Moon, G. (1987) *Health, Disease, and Society*. London: Routledge.

Jones, K. and Subramanian, S.V. (2000) 'Observational studies and design choices', in G.M. Moon, M. Gould and colleagues (eds) *Epidemiology*. Buckingham: Open University Press. pp. 70–85.

Kennedy, P.E. (2002) 'Sinning in the basement: What are the rules?', *Journal of Economic Surveys*, 16: 569–89.

Lawson, T. (1989) 'On abstraction, tendencies and stylised facts: A realist approach to economic analysis', *Cambridge Journal of Economics*, 13: 59–78.

Levitt, S.D. and Dubner, S.J (2005) *Freakonomics: A Rogue Economist Explores the Hidden Side of Everything*. London: Penguin Books.

Magnus, J.R. and Morgan, M.S. (1999) *Methodology and Tacit Knowledge*. New York: John Wiley.

Morgan, S.L. and Winship, C. (2007) *Counterfactuals and Causal Inference*. Cambridge: Cambridge University Press.

Oakley, A. (1990) 'Who's afraid of the randomised controlled trial?', *Women and Health*, 15: 25–59.

Olsen, W.K. and Morgan, J. (2005) 'A critical epistemology of analytical statistics: Addressing the sceptical realist', *Journal for the Theory of Social Behaviour*, 35: 255–84.

Pearl, J. (2009) *Causality*, 2nd edn. Cambridge: Cambridge University Press.

Ron, A. (2002) 'Regression analysis and the philosophy of social sciences – a critical realist view', *Journal of Critical Realism*, 1: 115–36.

Russell, J. and Glauberman, N. (1995) *The Bell Curve Debate: History Documents, Opinions*. New York: Random House.

Sayer, A. (1992) *Method in Social Science*. London: Routledge.

Sherden, W. (1998) *The Fortune Sellers*. New York: Wiley.

Tukey, J.W. (1962) 'The future of data analysis', *Annals of Mathematical Statistics*, 33: 1–67.

The Positivist Paradigm in Contemporary Social Research: The Interface of Psychology, Method and Sociocultural Theory

Charles Crook, Learning Sciences Research Institute, University of Nottingham, UK

Dean Garratt, Faculty of Education and Children's Services, University of Chester, UK

Summary

- Paradigms
- Falsifiability thesis
- Systemic nature of human activity
- Reflection, relationships and sociocultural contexts
- Learning as cultural practice
- Key theorists and writers
  - Michael Cole
  - Nathaniel L. Gage
  - Karl Popper
  - Gavriel Salomon
  - John K. Smith

In this chapter we begin, in the Key Concepts section, by tracing the origins and history of the positivist paradigm in social research, first from the point of view of educational philosophy and sociology (Dean Garratt) and second from the point of view of educational psychology (Charles Crook). The Stories from the Field (Charles Crook) focus on research carried out using an empirical toolkit from psychology with a sociocultural theoretical orientation.

Key concepts

Dean Garratt

The idea of a positivist *paradigm* in contemporary social research is a rather curious one and in many ways remarkably misleading. As Rowbottom and Aiston argue, 'educational research has been plagued by dubious bifurcations, the most significant of which is between "positivism", according to which social sciences ought to be modelled on the natural sciences, and "interpretivism", which rejects this view' (2006: 137–8). The modelling of educational research on the 'myth' of scientific method has strong antecedents in the work of Comte, dating back to the late nineteenth century. Comtean positivism argued for the unification of the sciences and thus gave historical sanction to the idea of a common *paradigm*, employing a single method in order to achieve certified knowledge.

Yet apart from the fact this has the tendency to caricature what science *is*, rather than accurately specifying what science *does* (Rowbotham and Aiston, 2006), it also rules out any notion of difference and roundly dispenses with the idea of simultaneously competing sociological or psychological perspectives.

This narrow view of science, seen through the positivist lens, takes social reality for granted, but at the same time dismisses the meaning of human activity, in particular the role of the subjective self in the discovery of new knowledge and/or in the process of making predictions about the world. Needless to say, this idealized methodological perspective appears out of step with the non-foundationalist belief system elaborated by many contemporary 'positivists' (see e.g. Phillips and Burbules, 2000). So, why is this so?

At the core of most on-going disputes concerning the idea of a positivist paradigm in contemporary social research is an ambiguity in meaning of the term 'paradigm', which can be traced back to the work of Kuhn (1970). For Kuhn, 'paradigm' is connected with the set of beliefs, procedures and working practices that inform the dominant world-view and which shape the context of modern science. Paradigms are nothing more or less than conceptual frameworks, providing 'models from which spring particular coherent traditions of scientific research' (Kuhn, 1970: 10), such as Newtonian physics or wave optics. Yet the essential point is that while Kuhn would acknowledge the presence of difference and inconsistency in the frameworks of modern science, he would also emphasize that any 'normal period' of science is governed by the regulative ideals that both shape and constitute the dominant view. There will, of course, over time be issues that are difficult to solve and recurring problems for which the dominant scheme can offer no straightforward solution. A crisis then ensues and a new paradigm is born. In this, the new framework is at odds with the old one, since its standards and practices are incommensurable with the new, emerging rationality (Kuhn, 1970; Lakatos, 1984). What this 'crisis' or 'revolutionary period' suggests is that one paradigm is completely dominant until displaced by a new scheme, as there can never be any mutual tolerance of differing ideologies.

Over time this view has received a great deal of critical attention. For example, Guba (1990), reflecting on Masterman (1970), has argued that Kuhn himself used 'paradigm' in no fewer than 21 different ways, suggesting that the term has no fixed meaning, universality or conceptual permanency. This being the case, it is not surprising that contemporary definitions within social and educational inquiry have tended to exploit more nuanced and fluid understandings of the term. Patton, for example, employs a definition in which 'paradigm' represents a basic belief system or:

world view, a general perspective, a way of breaking down the complexity of the real world . . . paradigms are deeply embedded in the socialization of adherents and practitioners telling them what is important, what is legitimate, what is reasonable . . . (Patton, 1975: 9)

Some years later, Sparkes (1992) used the term to suggest the possibility of different frameworks or perspectives containing contrasting sets of values, beliefs and assumptions. These factors are said to articulate with epistemological, ontological and methodological considerations in social inquiry, shaping and influencing the nature and conduct of research. They also assume the co-existence of different schemes that are often in conflict and where no single perspective is able to achieve total dominance over another.

Of all the criticisms lodged against the positivist philosophy of science perhaps the two most enduring issues are associated with: (i) the burden of 'proof' or the verification of knowledge; and (ii) the problem of sustaining a distinction between the researcher and that which is researched.

In terms of the burden of proof, it is Popper's work that provides the ultimate undoing of the verificationist theory of knowledge. In *The Logic of Scientific Discovery*, Popper [1959] (1990) outlines his falsifiability thesis, in which he challenges and effectively undermines the theory of induction: the logical basis on which science was affirmed and for which empiricism, as a foundational theory of knowledge, notably relied. Smith expresses this point well:

Popper convincingly pointed out that, no matter how many confirming or verifying instances have been accumulated for a theory, it is always possible that the next test of prediction will go astray. The problem is that induction does not allow one, with complete certitude, to predict the as yet unknown based on the known, or to predict the future based on what has happened in the past. Popper reversed the situation on traditional empiricism, so to speak, with his argument that one can never verify, but rather can only attempt to falsify, a hypothesis from a theory. A claim to knowledge must always stand as provisional in the sense that one can accept the claim only insofar as no one has been able to refute it or demonstrate it is false. (Smith, 1993: 71)

In terms of sustaining the distinction between the researcher and that which is researched, the problem is that the empiricist theory of knowledge rests, in part, on the possibility of realizing the Cartesian separation (dualism) and rationalist division of mind and matter. From this perspective, it is crucial to ensure that the researcher does not allow values and interests to interfere with the disinterested observation of events. Only if this is achieved can the researcher be sure of theory-free observation and hence be confident that knowledge is immunized and protected from the unwarranted intrusion of subjective ideas. Many writers, for example Popper [1959] (1990), Kuhn (1970), and Phillips and Burbules (2000), have pointed to the fact that in practice this type of dualism is impossible to achieve. There is simply no 'God's Eye' perspective and hence possibility of 'brute data', nor any 'theory-free observation' or transcendental view standing above the influence of the knowing subject (i.e. researcher). In essence this means that knowledge is no longer foundational, but only *conjectural* (Popper, 1972).

As a result of this on-going debate, in education, philosophy and the social sciences, positivism is now commonly referred to as 'postpositivism' (Phillips and Burbules, 2000), 'post-empiricism' (Norris, 2007), 'neorealism' (Smith and Hodkinson, 2009) or neo-positivism (Hammersley, 2008), to indicate a shift away from the old scheme towards something more sophisticated and arguably less naive. Some contemporary approaches have embraced the need for more subtle approximations of 'truth', where they have acknowledged that in the absence of the possibility of absolute truth, modern science may still adopt a non-foundational, fallibilistic approach to knowledge, (e.g. Hammersley, 2002). Others like Huberman and Miles (2002) have resisted the pressure to reject conventional criteria as a means of guiding the practice of post-positivistic research. For them, the conventional criteria and holy trinity of validity, reliability and generalizability, procured from the old positivist paradigm, provide an important working model for the production of defensible research findings. Moreover, in this spirit Gage has appealed to the reinterpretation of positivistic research, arguing that:

> Being positive can mean being certain or being affirmative. Behavioural scientists should indeed reject trying to be positive in the sense of seeking a certainty that tolerates no exceptions to generalizations ... [However], behavioural scientists should not reject trying to be positive in the sense of affirmativism, an attitude that affirms the value of the generalizations and theory thus far achieved and the value of the search for more. (Gage, 1996: 14–15)

A theory of knowledge affirmed on the idea of falsification does not entirely abandon the legacy of the old empiricist tradition. On the contrary, it transcends positivism in ways that are logically defensible, practically feasible and, by necessity, epistemologically non-foundational.

Charles Crook

My background in psychology makes me sensitive to a suspicion that educational researchers feel towards the discipline. It is the research of psychologists that is expected to do most violence to the subtle nature of educational phenomena. It is psychologists that promote attitudes of objectivity, analysis by reduction, and the methodology of control – to be positivists. Yet, ironically, this critique of psychological research itself illustrates one of the problematic issues: namely, a readiness to circumscribe or decontextualize what people are doing. Perhaps some critics of psychological methods seize too willingly on the rhetoric of 'definitive experiment'. When judged as part of a bigger investigative picture, much psychological research in education can be seen to be making a distinctive and valuable contribution to the field (e.g. Newman et al., 1989; Roth, 1998).

The empirical toolkit of psychology has most often resourced my own practical work. Yet, the theoretical orientation of that work has been very much sociocultural (Cole, 1996; Salomon, 1993). This might suggest a difficult tension to manage. For the supposed reductionist and impartial methods of psychology appear to sit uneasily with the supposed holistic and interpretative traditions of a cultural perspective. To be sure, if critics choose to detach studies arising from this methodology from the bigger picture of which they are often a part – then this tension may be real enough. However, from my own perspective, any method/theory tension I have encountered as a researcher has been more empowering than debilitating.

There are three features of a research agenda that are important to cultivate at this interface of psychology method and sociocultural theory. First, it is important to protect the *systemic* nature of complex human activity. So, the most useful research often succeeds by creating *perturbations* of an existing activity system – structured, perceptible but minimal forms of disturbance. Second, individual research projects are rarely 'definitive'; rather they are merely points on a trajectory of inquiry. For researchers (and their audience) they are pointers as to where to probe more tellingly next. They assist us in unfolding a problem. Finally, what is observed and reported by research can itself become a resource in our further engagements within the community of concern. That is to say, our research observations can serve as the focus of discourse and, thus, further enquiry within the community.

Implications for research design

Few social scientists these days would sign up wholesale to positivism – even from the mainstream of empirical psychology. Yet positivism's confidence and objectivity usefully persist as categories for reflecting on social science methodology. This is particularly so within a psychology influenced by sociocultural themes. Researchers who adopt this approach engage actively with the underlying categories of analysis that are contested within this epistemological debate. Hence, the (let us say) 'neo-positivist' perspective takes seriously a responsibility to be accountable in relation to the categories of reliability, validity, generalizability and quantification. This means giving close consideration to the descriptive tools and frameworks whereby we systematize what is observed. It means critical reflection on how any such systematization resonates with the phenomena we wish to understand through research. It means reflecting on the context in which a research project is located, in order to judge how far and in what way the observations that arise may predict events in other places at other times. Finally, it means finding ways to represent human action and experience that draw upon representational possibilities arising from the use of number. Note that these efforts to ensure accountability need not imply epistemological commitment to the belief that some absolute success or truth can be achieved in relation to reliability, validity, or generalization. There is certainly no assumption that numerically-grounded representations of social or psychological phenomena have some privileged status.

The positivist legacy places a pressure on researchers to be reflective (rather than prescriptive) about their methods, their relationships with participants in their research, and their conceptualization of the context in which that research is located. In practice, this entails striving for transparency around research tools and the management of data arising from their use. It invites triangulation across different methodological options. It encourages the formation of a relationship between researcher and research participant that permits negotiation of meaning and interpretation. It demands that the contexts of research should be approached as if confronting a social ecology rather than a structure of causal relations that is more rigidly mechanical. In general, it creates a healthy perspective on method that is both reflective and critical.

Some of these themes are taken up in the Stories from the Field that follows. For example, psychological methods, operationalized as a 'toolkit', are blended with sociocultural theory, so that two apparently disparate and diametrically opposed research orientations are imaginatively fused to present an intervention, 'perturbation' or disturbance of existing study practices, with undergraduates engaged in full-time, higher education.

Ultimately, as long as researchers within education and the social sciences more generally continue to attempt to measure social phenomena in ways that articulate with the conventional criteria of validity, reliability and generalizability, the tradition of positivism, modified and re-appropriated, will continue to influence research design in contemporary social inquiry.

Stories from the field

Charles Crook

My approach is to draw on a toolkit of research methods from psychology with a sociocultural theoretical orientation. I will illustrate this with an empirical example: one of interest to educational practitioners. The contemporary ambition is to 'virtualize' areas of higher educational practice. Sometimes this is motivated by interests of inclusion or economy, but sometimes by beliefs about learning: say, the belief that virtual educational methods can liberate the student into greater autonomy of study. Now, the sociocultural tradition of educational theorizing should find these ambitions provocative. Not just because that theoretical tradition has focused on the *interpersonal* dimension of learning (and virtualization seems set to dilute that) but because the sociocultural tradition theorizes learning (or, more tellingly, 'study') as cultural practice. And as a form of practice, study is likely to be resiliently grounded in a set of cultural resources: namely, those associated with particular institutions, places, routines, artefacts, and ways-with-words. If we shift learners away from this paraphernalia of cultural practice – shift them towards more virtual methods – then there may be trouble.

Of course, the visible success of some distance programmes might suggest that there are no serious obstacles to a virtualized university. Yet the equally visible rejection by school leavers of such routes into higher education surely presents a contrasting picture. What if we penetrate the established educational culture of these traditional undergraduates to explore this? What if we, as researchers, create a virtualizing perturbation in their system of activity? One good target for such meddling might be the lecture. We want to understand something about the status of this practice within the undergraduate's experience because, as virtualizing engineers, we want to redesign things. If so, then we must understand how the lecture integrates with the larger system of cultural practice in which undergraduates participate – as actors in a fulltime, campus-oriented higher education. What we, as researchers, do *not* aim to do is conduct a self-contained little study that legislates on the general viability of substituting traditional lectures with something more virtual. So, what then counts as a disturbance of this system that is both credible and genuinely informative?

My own answer was pretty simple, at least at one level. It was straightforward in terms of what was to be done, what was to be observed, what was to be compared. Yet credibility depended on more subtle features of the overall design, such as protecting continuity between the experience of my interventions and the existing ecology of this community. The formal structure of this intervention involved no more than audio recording weekly lectures and making them immediately accessible as MP3 files on web pages – along with associated visual aids. What was then at stake as 'outcome' was the students' continued engagement with the live lectures – when compared with parallel classes they take. Yet our view about any outcome of all this depends on how we judge our meddling in relation to the larger context in which the activity is set.

In the present case, getting it right was a matter of the intervention (a virtualization of the lectures) being realized in a manner that was *legitimate* for the participants. That demanded that this new form of resourcing be seamlessly woven into existing practices. So it mattered that these students were in an institution where networked communication was strongly emphasized: where campus-based students (half the total number) enjoyed broadband access to that network in their study-bedrooms. Where every university module had a local website to which students naturally turned for routine course materials. It was also relevant that this intervention was perceived as an innocently-conceived form of alternative resource – not an 'experiment' about which everyone might become rather self-conscious. In fact, it was originally designed merely to meet the legitimate need of one blind student requesting an audio record.

Against this background, the web-based lecture became an interesting disturbance of existing study practice: an interesting invitation for students to encounter a modest version of the autonomy promised by virtualization. However, attractive though this invitation might seem in the abstract, in practice it held little appeal. Compared with parallel and conventionally-resourced lecture courses, attendance was neither more nor less. This was reinforced by network system logs from the website. For although the course pages were visited frequently and most students accessed the recorded lectures, they typically only did so once and for lengths of time that suggested casual curiosity rather than engagement.

The example illustrates the three ambitions of empirical work noted above: first, structured observations making a useful 'perturbation' of a complex system; second, the construction of an outcome that becomes a point on a trajectory of enquiry (for it prompted further research – to be described below); but, finally, the work also furnishes a grounding for understanding changes in study practice by recruiting the sense-making interpretation of the participants themselves. In short, our intervention gives us something to talk with them about. The observations that make up the *results* of the intervention can themselves be recruited into discussion – to more effectively ground it. So we can talk about the documented stability of lecture attendance patterns and we can talk about the neglect of the audio web resource.

When we do this, we find students saying two kinds of thing. First, they make observations about lectures that concern the value added from simply attending. The corporate nature of the event seems reassuring, it affords casual (perhaps benchmarking) conversations with study peers, and it imposes a form of habitual or disciplined engagement with the curriculum. Second, they talk about the audio record being an 'uncomfortable' resource for studying. There is something unnatural about sitting down in one's room and listening to a recording of a lecture – even more so if the student endeavours to then take notes. This part of such conversations offered a helpful lever on understanding the resilience of existing study practices, the matter we set out to probe. But it was still just a point on a trajectory of enquiry, highlighting other forms of teaching practice that disturb the lecture format, and we picked this up for further research.

A parallel course which provided on its website full *written* notes of the lectures did manifest a more noticeable attendance decline. This resource was much praised by these students and, interestingly, it did seem more contiguous with students' preferred modes of private study. This tempts us to ask whether the experience of a course as a set of web-based lecture notes supports a different mode of study to the experience of a course as a sequence of live lectures. This is not an easy issue to address and, once again, there is no question here of invoking a 'definitive study' form of encounter with it. Yet structured observations are possible, again to discreetly disturb existing systems of practice.

The heart of the matter now shifts. It still concerns migration of lectures to the web, albeit in the form of text resources, rather than spoken ones; however, the issue now is whether this new form of mediation makes any difference to how learners study the material.

My approach invoked 'study practice' through the empirical device of orchestrating collaborative work sessions among peers. An advantage for the 'independently observing' researcher is that the resulting collaborative conversation makes more accessible the way in which students relate to certain study materials. The research was realized in something much more like a traditional experiment. What was at issue was the character of collaborative conversation under different circumstances of study resource. So some students revised together making use of a hypertextual set of web-based and lecturer-authored notes. Others talked around a linear (no hypertext links) version of those web documents. And still others talked around their *own* notes of the same set of lectures that were documented by the web material. In brief, the students collaboratively studying around their own notes were much more animated, on-task, and creative in their conversation. The packaged, authorized character of the web notes seemed to inhibit exploration around the lecture course ideas. Instead, topics discussed were strongly shaped by formal headings in the web texts, movements between topics were faster, and conversation dwelt more on what the lecturer wanted than on what the ideas themselves might amount to. Again, nothing is getting sewn up by this research, but the trajectory of enquiry does invite new forms of concern. It asks us to consider more carefully the mode of intellectual arousal that is supported by this kind of web resource – compared with personal records of live expositions.

This seems a rather classic form of psychological investigation. Participants are recruited into made-up associations; they are stage managed into 'sessions' – where they are closely monitored by 'independent observers'. Can this really advance understanding of issues arising out of new technology and higher educational practice? Again, our judgement about this requires that we look carefully at the larger ecology of this particular perturbation.

A critical onlooker might ask: Are such participant pairings not the typical 'nonsense groups' of experimental social psychology? Not quite: students chose their own partner and, indeed, chose whether to volunteer or not. Most said they understood it to be an innocent evaluation of resources and wanted the opportunity to be forced into a bit of study anyway. Was what they were asked to do relevant to them in their role (as students)? Yes: they were just weeks away from a finals examination and all their time was currently given to one form of such revision or another. Were the circumstances of their activities in the research project alien to them? Hopefully not: a large, comfortable, and familiar teaching room was used, with several pairings meeting at the same time in the same space. Coffee and snacks were always available and participants could stop, relax, and start just as they might in more private settings. The computer materials were similar to documents encountered for other courses. However, will there always remain a reflexivity problem inherent in observation? Well, not that the tapes themselves would suggest: some conversation was alarmingly frank and none suggested that the participants were inhibited by being recorded – or even consciously aware of it.

These observations converge on a general point that I hope is illustrated by these two interrelated examples. As researchers we will often position and equip ourselves to become well-resourced and well-positioned observers of events. Sometimes those events are flowing past us independently of our own design. Sometimes, our non-invasive role is complemented by us structuring our observations to afford relevant comparisons – say, between usefully contrasting flows of different events. But sometimes we do intervene and then we may configure such comparisons through our own engineering of events. I believe such interventions are a crucial ingredient of educational research and I have argued here that the issue for vigilance is the extent to which we manage them as 'perturbations to established activity systems' – rather than controlled manipulations of variables. Finally, the status of 'observer' in these scenarios will often be judged inadequate, for we may seem to deny ourselves access to the experience of those we observe by our insistence on protecting a sense of distance. But this is not an inevitable requirement of research inspired by the psychological tradition. Here I have argued that the human *relationship* inherent within research remains an important concern. What we do when we exercise this concern is cultivate intersubjectivity: a mutual understanding with the participants in our research. Moreover, the achievement of intersubjectivity is often discursively resourced by making reference to other research observations we have made – albeit observations that may have engaged us with these participants from positions of greater interpersonal distance. In this way our 'impartial' observations of events often dovetail creatively with our need to resonate more closely with experiences in the community we are concerned to understand.

Annotated bibliography

Cole, M. (1996) *Cultural Psychology*. Cambridge, MA: Harvard University Press.
A distinguished introduction to the cultural approach to psychology – with special attention to issues of cognitive development and educational practice.

Gage, N.L. (1996) 'Confronting counsels of despair for the behavioural sciences', *Educational Researcher*, 25(3): 5–15, 22.
This paper focuses on tensions that have arisen in the behavioural sciences as a result of their failure to produce long-lasting generalizations, and hence theories, from research. In 'Popperian' fashion, the paper concludes by suggesting that while the object of certainty is logically unattainable, researchers in the behavioural sciences may still display an attitude that affirms the value of generalizations and theory.

Hammersley, M. (2008) *Questioning Qualitative Inquiry – Critical Essays*. London: Sage.
Raises critical questions about the nature, purpose and future direction of qualitative research. Against a backdrop of recent changes in the field, which have seen social researchers attempting to incorporate and adapt a variety of different styles and approaches to the process of qualitative inquiry, Hammersley draws attention to the importance of preserving key principles and ideas. In the face of a perceived 'crisis', of the contribution that qualitative inquiry can make to the social world, he argues for a more pragmatic approach. This is one that acknowledges a greater need for transparency and bolder recognition that all analysis involves both theoretical abstraction and data reduction.

Kuhn, T. (1970) *The Structure of Scientific Revolutions*, 2nd edn. Chicago: University of Chicago Press.
A seminal text on the relativity of scientific knowledge. In rejecting the idea that science grows by accumulation of truths, Kuhn presents his thesis of scientific paradigms.

Leigh Star, S. (ed.) (1995) *Ecologies of Knowledge*. Albany: State University of New York Press.
Various papers that explore the consequences of approaching knowledge as embedded in local ecologies. Ranges widely and not exclusively on matters educational.

Newman, D., Griffin, P., et al. (1989) *The Construction Zone: Working for Cognitive Change in School*. Cambridge: Cambridge University Press.
The authors describe empirical work conceived to examine the problem of recognizing schooled cognition in out-of-school contexts. Their discussion of fieldwork thereby illustrates the challenges of adopting a cultural approach to cognition and educational practice.

Popper, K.R. (1992) 'Realism and the aim of science' (reprinted edition), in W.W. Bartley III, (ed.) *Postscript to the Logic of Scientific Discovery*. London: Routledge. II, III, IV, pp.159–216.
Popper elaborates his non-justificationist theory of knowledge, presenting the argument that while empirical science aims at true explanatory theories, it can never prove or finally establish any of its theories as true.

Roth, W-M. (1998) *Designing Communities*. Dordrecht, The Netherlands: Kluwer Academic Publishers.

The book explores an agenda of putting pupils at the heart of the educational enterprise by constructing a sense of learning community. The enterprise is discussed in terms of its rationale and the surrounding research is well illustrated.

Salomon, G. (ed.) (1993) *Distributed Cognitions: Psychological and Educational Considerations*. Cambridge: Cambridge University Press.

A collection of papers exploring the consequences of regarding human cognition in situated or distributed terms. While none is explicitly a report of empirical work, there is much discussion of such research and together these papers should give a strong sense of why human cognitive activity is best regarded as 'stretched' over social and material space and what implications this has for a research agenda.

Smith, J.K. (1993) *After the Demise of Empiricism – The Problem of Judging Social and Educational Inquiry*. New Jersey: Ablex.

This text explores the implications for contemporary social inquiry following the demise of traditional empiricism. Smith considers the problems and possibilities that are inherent in the process of judging social and educational inquiry.

Ward Schofield, J. (1995) *Computers and Classroom Culture*. Cambridge: Cambridge University Press.

An unusual book for its distinctive insistence on approaching educational computer use in a school from a cultural point of view – seeking to understand how patterns of using technology are related to the fabric of established traditions for institutional interactions. The book represents a full report of a substantial field study and gives insight into method and theory.

Further references

Guba, E. (ed.) (1990) *The Paradigm Dialog*. Newbury Park, CA: Sage.

Hammersley, M. (2002) 'Ethnography and Realism', in A.M. Huberman and M.B. Miles (eds) *The Qualitative Researcher's Companion*. Thousand Oaks, CA: Sage. pp. 65–80.

Huberman, A.M. and Miles, M.B. (eds) (2002) *The Qualitative Researcher's Companion*. Thousand Oaks, CA: Sage.

Lakatos, I. (1984) *The Methodology of Scientific Research Programmes*. Cambridge: Cambridge University Press.

Masterman, M. (1970) 'The nature of the paradigm', in I. Lakatos and A. Musgrave (eds) *Criticism and Growth of Knowledge*. Cambridge: Cambridge University Press.

Norris, C. (2007) *On Truth and Meaning: Language, Logic and the Grounds of Belief*. London: Continuum.

Patton, M. (1975) *Alternative Evaluation of Research Paradigms*. Grand Forks, ND: University of North Dakota Press.

Phillips, D.C. and Burbules, N.C. (2000) *Postpositivism and Educational Research*. Lanham, MD: Rowman and Littlefield.

Popper, K.R. (1972) *Conjectures and Refutations: The Growth of Scientific Knowledge*. London: Routledge.

Popper, K.R. (1990) *The Logic of Scientific Discovery* (14th impression). London, Unwin Hynam (I, II, pp. 27–56, IV, pp. 78–92).

Rowbottom, D.P. and Aiston, S.J. (2006) 'The myth of "scientific method" in contemporary educational research', *Journal of Philosophy of Education*, 40 (2): 137–56.

Smith, J.K. and Hodkinson, P. (2009) 'Challenging neorealism – A response to Hammersley', *Qualitative Inquiry*, 15(1): 30–9.

Sparkes, A.C. (1992) 'The paradigms debate: An extended review and celebration of difference', in A.C. Sparkes (ed.), *Research and Physical Education and Sport*. London: Falmer. pp. 9–60.

Understanding and Describing Quantitative Data

Cathy Lewin, Education and Social Research Institute, Manchester Metropolitan University, UK

Summary

- Statistical tools and techniques
- Sampling strategies
- Questionnaire design
- Experimental design
- Describing and exploring data using statistics

Key concepts

A wide range of statistical tools and techniques can be used to describe and interpret data that are quantitative or can be measured numerically. Numerical data can make a valuable contribution in both quantitative and qualitative research, whether it be simple percentages or the results of complicated techniques. The use of mixed methods (see Greene et al., in this volume) has become increasingly popular as a means to harness the strengths of both approaches, triangulate data and illuminate statistical findings with, for example, case studies and/or vignettes.

Quantitative researchers require knowledge of a range of very precise methods and procedures, all of which are associated with specific terminology and a range of principles arising from probability theory. This chapter seeks to provide the foundations required to understand quantitative research. The first section of this chapter provides the reader with an introduction to statistics – what can be measured and how – and introduces the concepts of reliability and validity. The second section covers sampling stra-

tegies: how to choose what will be included in quantitative studies in the social sciences. The third section provides an introduction to questionnaire design, a data collection instrument commonly used within quantitative paradigms to survey a large number of respondents. Finally, the last section explains how statistics can be used to describe and explore numerical data.

Introduction to statistics

What can be measured?

Statistics are applied to *variables* or measurements of attributes or characteristics of whatever is being studied, whether a person or an object, each of whom or which is often referred to as a *case*. Attributes can be real measurements or something that can be counted or quantified (e.g. height, income, test scores). Numbers can also be used to 'measure' opinions and attitudes through ranked responses to data collection methods such as survey questions or structured observations (e.g. educational level, socio-economic status, rating of services such as banking). Variables can also be assigned specific values (0, 1, 2 and so forth) to represent categorical attributes or characteristics that cannot be measured numerically or ranked in any way, such as eye colour or gender.

How can statistics be used?

Statistics are particularly useful when asking questions of large numerical data sets, enabling researchers to summarize and make comparisons. *Descriptive statistics* are used to describe and summarize data and include measures of central tendency (average) and dispersion (the spread of data or how close each case is to the measure of central tendency). Descriptive statistics have an important role to play, enabling data to be explored before any further analysis is undertaken but also as a primary means of describing how things are, rather than seeking to explain why phenomena occur. *Inferential statistics* are used to identify differences between groups, look for relationships between attributes and create models in order to be able to make predictions. Inferential statistics are introduced and discussed in Barnes and Lewin (Chapter 26, this volume) and Jones (Chapter 27, this volume). Statistics can be applied to a single variable (univariate analysis), two variables (bivariate analysis) or more than two variables (multivariate analysis). The kind of statistical tool that can be used also depends on the type of data involved and whether specific conditions have been met. The *significance level* of a statistical test is also established; that is the probability of achieving the test result assuming that there actually is no difference or relationship in the population. If the probability is very small it means it is less likely that the result (a difference in scores, or a relationship between two variables) has occurred by chance and so the researcher can be more confident about the findings.

What do we mean by reliability and validity?

Reliability refers to the stability or consistency of measurements; that is whether or not the same results would be achieved if the test or measure was applied repeatedly. For example, a question may be worded ambiguously and answered differently on subsequent occasions. *Validity* refers to whether or not the measurement collects the data required to answer the research question. A measure can be reliable (always generate the same result) but not valid (not measure the intended concept). However, if it is not reliable then it cannot be valid. There are various aspects of validity that should be considered when designing any measurement (see e.g. de Vaus, 1995, for more on this) and threats to validity can differ according to the statistical approach undertaken (see Jones, Chapter 27, this volume, for a discussion of threats to validity in relation to modelling).

Causality can be inferred if it can be demonstrated that changing the value of one variable, the *independent*

variable, has an effect on the value of another, the *dependent variable*. It is a means of explaining a phenomenon through its likely causes. *Internal validity* refers to the confidence that can be placed in causal inferences. There may be other (unaccounted for) variables at play. Some variables will have a direct effect on others whilst others may have an indirect effect. There are many threats to validity in quantitative research including history (circumstances changing over time), testing (test practice effects), mortality (attrition or being unable to collect data from all original participants) and maturation (developmental changes in participants). *Generalizability* or *external validity* refers to the possibility of expanding any claims of causality from the group or sample being studied to the population that the group represents – that is, that the same effect will be found in another group and/or in other contexts.

Quantitative designs

Quantitative research can employ a number of different designs, one of which is usually selected at the outset depending on the kind of research question being investigated. *Experimental design* involves the manipulation of at least one independent variable to see whether or not it has any impact on the dependent variable. Tests can be conducted before the experiment begins – *pre-test* – and after it has been completed – *post-test* – or just at post-test. These data are used to identify differences between two or more groups on measurements of the dependent variable. *Laboratory experiments* take place in contrived settings but allow researchers to have more control, whereas *field experiments* are conducted in naturalistic environments where it is often easier to recruit participants. Many argue that results achieved in laboratory settings are not generalizable to naturalistic settings, casting doubt on the external validity of such experiments. Often in social science research, *quasi-experimental designs* are adopted when it is not possible to allocate individuals randomly to groups (see 'Principles of sampling' below). For example, in educational research whole schools or whole classes are often assigned to groups (rather than individuals being randomly assigned to groups) because of practical and logistical issues.

Randomized controlled trials or RCTs are one form of experimental design in which participants are allocated truly randomly to an experimental group (e.g. those exposed to the independent variable such as a new drug) and a control group (those not), enabling unmeasured or unknown variables to be taken into account and strengthening claims for internal validity. These approaches are expensive due to the large numbers of participants required. Furthermore, random allocation can be hard to achieve in social science research and there are ethical considerations that necessitate constraints. Nevertheless, there are often opportunities to set up randomized experiments when an experimental and control group occur naturally, for example when there is a limited number of places on a course and participants are selected randomly. RCTs are often referred to as the 'gold standard' for quantitative research although the value of such an approach is not universally accepted by social scientists.

A *cross-sectional design* is often used in survey research and involves the collection of quantitative data on at least two variables, at one point in time and from a number of cases. These data are then used to look for patterns of association or relationships, either in the group as a whole (all cases) or in sub-groups sharing characteristics or attributes (females or males for example). It is problematic to establish causality in simple statistical tests of relationships (see Barnes and Lewin, Chapter 26, this volume) but causal inferences can be made using more sophisticated techniques such as regression analyses (see Jones, Chapter 27, this volume).

A *longitudinal design*, often an extension of a cross-sectional design when a survey is administered repeatedly at regular time intervals over a number of years, can be used to more easily establish causality but is expensive to conduct.

Principles of sampling

Social science research can focus on a specific *population* or complete set of units being studied (e.g. all state secondary schools in one country or all nurses working in a region) when time, costs and accessibility often prohibit the collection of data from every member or about every item. In these situations it is necessary to select a *representative sample* of the population, one in which the same range of characteristics or attributes can be found in similar proportions. It is only with a truly representative sample that you can *generalize* the research findings to the whole population. So judgements have to be made to ensure that the sample is as representative as possible, adopting one of a number of different *sampling strategies* to go

some way towards overcoming these limitations. A *census* involves collecting data from all members of the population and is a true representation. Sampling, however, results in an estimate of population characteristics because the sample selected may not be truly representative. Researchers should explain the sampling strategies used in their research so that readers can make judgements about potential bias that might be introduced or other limitations. In *probability sampling* each member or item of the population has an equal or known chance of being selected. It is usually possible to generalize findings from analysis of data collected from such a sample to the population overall. *Non-probability sampling* covers all other approaches.

There are many ethical considerations that need to be addressed, such as participant consent (see Piper and Simons, Chapter 3, this volume). Some samples will be easier to access than others by the nature of the population characteristics. For example, access to employees in companies will be easier than to self-employed people working from home.

Probability or random sampling strategies

Simple random sampling is the most straightforward strategy in which each population member has an equal chance of selection through 'pulling names from a hat', or assigning each member a unique number and using random number generators (tables of random numbers or a computer program that generates random numbers within a specified range). However, a complete list of the population is required and this is not always available. *Systematic sampling* is similar but uses the *sampling frame* (a complete unordered list of all members of the population) rather than random numbers in the selection process. A member of the population is selected at regular intervals from the sampling frame. The sampling frame should not be ordered (names listed alphabetically, for example) or there may be a bias in the selected sample.

Stratified sampling involves ordering the sampling frame by one or more characteristics and then selecting the same percentage of people or items from each sub-group either using simple random or systematic sampling. This will ensure that characteristics of the population are represented proportionately (e.g. males and females). The more characteristics that are used, the more complex this procedure will be. Only characteristics that are considered to affect the data analysis should be used.

When the population is large and widely dispersed it may be more appropriate to initially select sub-groups such as geographical areas rather than randomly select from the whole population, known as *cluster sampling*. For example, a number of hospitals could be randomly selected from the list of all hospitals in a country and then the sample identified through a random sampling strategy (simple, systematic or stratified) applied to lists of nursing staff at those hospitals selected initially. This can be extended when more than one level of grouping is used to generate the sample, such as selecting a region, then a school, and then a class, before selecting students within that class.

Sampling error

Probability or random samples have less risk of bias (selecting sub-groups disproportionately, for example twice as many men as women) but will still be subject to a degree of *sampling error* or the difference between attributes or characteristics of the sample and the population it is intended to represent. Consider a population of 15 female nurses and 15 male nurses, from which you wish to select a representative sample of 10. Each randomly selected sample (choosing names from a hat) is likely to be different. Common selections will include five females and five males, six females and four males, and four females and six males. However, there is a small chance that you might select 10 females and no males or vice versa, clearly not representative of the group being sampled.

It is easy to calculate the sampling error when the characteristic being measured is truly numerical and an average or *mean* value can be calculated (e.g. the average height of Chinese women). This is estimated using a statistic called the *standard error of the mean* which is a measure of the spread or distribution of all possible means of samples of a given size drawn randomly from a population. The smaller the standard error, the more closely grouped the possible means of all samples are, and therefore the more likely it is that a single sample drawn from a population is representative. So the standard error is an estimate of how much the sample mean differs from the population mean. The *confidence interval* can be calculated from the standard error and represents the range of values between which the population mean is most likely to lie, enabling the researcher to estimate the population characteristics from the sample characteristics. This should be used in conjunction with the *confidence level*,

which indicates the likelihood that the population mean lies within the specified interval. Common confidence levels that are used are 95 per cent and 99 per cent. The 95 per cent confidence level means that, 95 times out of 100, the population mean is likely to be in the range specified by the confidence interval. The confidence interval will vary according to the confidence level used – the higher the confidence level, the wider the confidence interval. See Fowler (2008: Chapter 3) for a more detailed and mathematically grounded explanation of sampling error.

Sample size

The absolute size of the sample is the crucial factor rather than the relative size or the proportion of the population sampled. The larger the sample size the smaller the error will be in estimating the characteristic(s) of the population but the more it will cost to administer a survey and analyse the data. The sample size will be dependent on the accuracy required and the likely variation of the population characteristics being investigated, as well as the kind of analysis to be conducted on the data. The larger a sample size becomes the smaller the impact on accuracy so there is cut-off point beyond which the increased costs are not justified by the (small) improvement in accuracy; a sample size of 1,000 is often referred to as a cut-off point beyond which rate of improvement in accuracy slows. Populations may be *homogenous* when the characteristics under investigation are largely similar or *heterogeneous* when the range of the characteristic is very diverse. It is good practice to overestimate rather than underestimate sample size to allow for attrition or non-response (participants withdrawing from research or failing to return a questionnaire, for example).

The size of the sample is an issue for any researcher. Suggested minimum sizes for different approaches are as follows:

- In surveys, the sample should be sufficiently large so that any major sub-groups contain at least 100 cases and minor sub-groups contain between 20 and 50 (Fowler, 2008; Oppenheim, 2000).
- In correlational studies (looking at relationships between particular characteristics of a population, for example smoking and health), there should be at least 30 participants.
- In experimental designs, in which one or more variables are controlled and comparisons are made between two or more groups over a period

of time, there should be at least 30 participants in each group.

Non-sampling error

A non-sampling error is one that relates to the sampling design or way in which data are collected. Such errors can occur in a variety of ways. For example, using a telephone directory as a sampling frame omits all members of the population who are ex-directory or do not own a landline. A poorly worded question may be interpreted in different ways by different respondents. The response from a question may be recorded incorrectly when preparing data for analysis.

Non-probability sampling

This approach is adopted when researchers target a particular group and are not always seeking to generalize findings to the population overall. This kind of approach is commonplace in small-scale research (particularly when costs need to be minimized) or qualitative approaches such as ethnography, case studies or action research. In fact, in the real world of social science research, non-probability sampling is widespread when time constraints and costs force the researcher to make compromises. The sample is often a group (a class, employees in a local company) that the researcher has easy access to or has selected for a particular reason. It is important to acknowledge the undoubted biases that will occur from this approach.

In *convenience sampling* or *opportunity sampling* easy access drives the selection process. For example, a local hospital or school is used, or a group with whom the researcher has an established relationship, or those who responded to a request for volunteers to participate in the research. *Quota sampling* is similar to stratified sampling but individuals are selected to fill quotas to represent relative proportions of specific characteristics. In *purposive sampling* cases are hand-picked for a specific reason such as use of a new product. In *snowball sampling* a small number of individuals are identified to represent a population with particular characteristics and they are subsequently used as informants to recommend similar individuals.

Questionnaire design

Questionnaires provide a way of gathering structured and unstructured data from respondents in a standar-

dized way, either as part of a *structured interview* or through *self-completion*. Often, the data collected are numerical (a measurement) or can be represented numerically (ranked in order of preference for example) and can thus be analysed using statistical techniques. Self-completion questionnaires are also a cost-effective way of collecting data from a large number of widely dispersed participants, particularly if postage costs can be avoided by, for example, asking individuals, such as teachers or employers, to supervise completion of questionnaires by groups. However, in questionnaire design there are many issues that need to be considered in order to (a) maximize the responses and (b) be confident that it is an instrument that is reliable and valid.

Thought needs to be given to whether the questionnaire should be completed anonymously or not, depending on the sensitivity of the questions being asked. Questionnaires may or may not be truly anonymized depending on the sampling strategy employed. Quota sampling can guarantee true anonymity for respondents whereas if a sampling frame has been used the researcher may know who the respondents are. Respondents can be asked to optionally give names and contact details if they agree to participate in the research further, for example through follow-up telephone interviews. It may be necessary to keep a record of who has and has not responded (in order to send reminders, for example) in which case questionnaires can be part-anonymized by giving respondents a unique identifier. In such cases, respondents should be assured that the information identifying them will be destroyed at the data processing stage or not taken into account during analysis.

A questionnaire should have clear aims and objectives, and be structured logically into sections and sub-sections (if necessary) with *filter questions* to ensure that respondents only answer relevant questions (for example, 'if yes, go to question 10'). The researcher should ensure that the data will be relevant and sufficient to answer the research questions as it is difficult to collect additional data after the questionnaires have been returned. It is often useful to include demographic data (those used to describe the population and its subgroups) such as gender, age and occupation. Often these questions appear at the beginning of the questionnaire because they can be answered easily and quickly, although some (e.g. Oppenheim, 2000) caution against this practice on the grounds that it can be seen as a personal intrusion by respondents and hence deter them from continuing. Either way, the first group of questions should be easy to answer. Be aware that if a limited amount of time is allocated to the completion of the questionnaire the respondent (e.g. young children) may not get to the end.

Highly structured *closed questions* are more suitable for large-scale surveys, as they are quick for respondents to answer and are easy to analyse using statistical techniques, enabling comparisons to be made across groups. Question types include: dichotomous questions (yes/no), multiple choice, and Likert (level of agreement with a statement) or ratings scales (e.g. indicating the frequency of an activity). In scales, odd scales (3, 5, 7 points) allow respondents to remain neutral. Some respondents may avoid extreme responses (either end of the scales) in which case a 7-point scale may need to be avoided. Even scales (4, 6 points) force respondents to indicate which aspect they favour (for example, to agree or disagree with a statement). However, scales may force a particular response, may not include all possible options and do not always allow for additional comments. *Open-ended questions* are more suited to qualitative approaches, allowing the respondent to give a free response in continuous text. Open-ended questions rather than closed questions can be more appropriate to elicit sensitive information. However, they are more difficult to code (categorize) and classify. In self-completion questionnaires, there should not be too many open-ended questions as they are more time-consuming to complete and respondents need adequate space to give their answers.

Questionnaires often have a combination of question types and collect data on facts, attitudes and beliefs. Questions can be direct or indirect. Attention must be given to the wording of the questions themselves in order to maximize reliability.

Questions should:

- be clear and unambiguous and not use technical language or language that is inappropriate for the respondents;
- not lead the respondents to particular answers;
- be simple rather than complex;
- avoid questions that are double-barrelled (ask more than one question simultaneously, e.g. 'do you own a mobile or a landline?' – if respondents say yes how do you know whether they own a mobile only, a landline only or both);
- avoid the use of negatives and double negatives;

- ensure that in multiple choice questions and ratings scales that all categories are mutually exclusive (if a single response is required);
- avoid questions that may antagonize or irritate respondents or could be perceived to be threatening.

Instructions on how to complete the questionnaire should be explicit, clear and polite. It is good practice to repeat instructions for each section as often as necessary. Researchers should be aware that respondents will interpret imprecise words such as 'sometimes', 'often', and 'very little' differently, so whenever possible more precise terms should be used – for example, 'at least once a week'. Researchers should be aware that respondents may not always answer accurately or may give the answer that they feel is expected – this can occur with children and adults alike. This will introduce an element of bias. Questions that introduce an element of cross-checking can be useful.

Questionnaires do not always have to rely on words to elicit information. With children and adults with poor literacy skills for example, pictures can be used to represent possible responses. Vignettes can be used to provide a context for a question and make it more meaningful and are often helpful for eliciting opinions and data relating to more sensitive issues. Use of graphics and colour can make questionnaires visually more interesting and stimulate responses, making completion more fun, especially for children. Layout should be uncluttered and inviting with plenty of space for open-ended answers but also be consistent (all responses indicated by ticking a box or by circling the appropriate answer).

For self-completion questionnaires, length and ease of completion should be considered. It is helpful to indicate at the beginning or in a covering letter how long completion might take. It is beneficial to include a brief note at the end of the questionnaire to ask respondents to check that they have answered all questions, remind them of the date by which the questionnaire should be returned and thank them for their time.

Piloting a questionnaire (testing it with a limited number of individuals who are similar to the sample) is crucial and can highlight ambiguities and other potential pitfalls.

Questionnaire administration

Questionnaires can be administered face-to-face, via telephone, via post or online. Ethical issues need to be considered such as anonymity and confidentiality depending on the sensitive nature of questions being asked (see Piper and Simons, Chapter 3, this volume, for a discussion of ethical considerations). A covering letter often improves initial response rates to self-completion postal questionnaires and should outline the aims of the research, highlight the importance of an individual's contribution, assure respondents of confidentiality and encourage their replies. It should also state how the questionnaire can be returned (a stamped addressed envelope – known as an SAE – eliminates costs for the respondent and avoids addressing errors on the return envelope) and what to do if any uncertainties arise (contact name and number for queries, for example). Questionnaires that are going to be administered by someone other than the researcher will require a clear and comprehensive set of administering instructions.

Questionnaires can be returned electronically or completed online, in which case data entry can be automated but may exclude some members of the sample (e.g. those without access to the internet), introducing a bias. Costs can be lower (no postage, printing, or data entry costs) but this will depend on the technical expertise required (costs of creating an online questionnaire). Many online survey services are available to enable rapid generation of questionnaires and simple analysis. Data can also easily be exported for more complex analysis using statistical analysis software.

A response rate of 40 per cent is typical to the original letter and questionnaire. Reminder letters can increase response rates and can be sent with a second copy of the questionnaire in case the respondent has mislaid the original. Three reminders can increase the response rate by up to 30 per cent. Offering incentives can also increase response rates (e.g. entering respondents into a draw for a highly sought after prize!). Response rates are likely to be lower in postal questionnaires than in face-to-face situations. Timing may need to be considered. A postal questionnaire in mid-December, for example, may not attract a high level of response in historically Christian countries. Non-responders should be considered and any resulting likely bias should be commented upon in reporting the research (e.g. poor literacy skills of respondents). There is disagreement over what an acceptable minimal overall response rate might be (e.g. from 50 per cent to 75 per cent). There is evidence that response rates are falling but that a low response rate does not necessarily lead to poor quality

data or indeed guarantee bias. However, it is still good practice to aim for the highest possible response rate.

If the questionnaire is being administered through a structured interview, either face-to-face, or over the telephone, care needs to be taken to ensure that the process is standardized for all respondents, particularly if more than one interviewer is involved. Interviewers should be briefed and trained prior to the data collection. There should be clear instructions to the interviewers on how to administer the questionnaire. For example, guidance should be provided on follow-up questions (probing or prompting) to ensure that the administration is consistent. It is also useful to hold a debriefing session for interviewers after the interviews have been completed to identify any matters which should be taken into consideration during analysis – questions that were unclear for example.

Data from questionnaires can be pre-coded for closed questions. It is helpful to code all responses numerically (for example no = 0, yes = 1). Where open-ended questions are to be coded, clear instructions need to be given to individuals undertaking this process, particularly if there is more than one person involved. A coding frame will be devised identifying how individual responses should be coded. There may initially be a number of queries relating to this process as new codes may emerge over time. Inter-rater reliability should be ascertained (the extent to which individuals make the same judgements about how to code a particular response). There should also be guidance on how to code variables when questions have been spoilt (more than one box ticked for example).

Describing and exploring data using statistics

As well as a wide range of statistical tests that can be applied to data, tables and graphical representations are often used as analytical tools. Tables can be used to present data in an easy to understand format. Graphs and charts can present data visually and often highlight patterns and issues that may be drawn out in interpretations of the data.

Many textbooks give detailed (mathematical) explanations of how each statistical test or tool is calculated. In reality, all calculations can be easily performed using computer-based statistical analysis tools (for example, SPSS/PASW). It is important to understand what tests are appropriate for the data that you have and why you might use them. It is not strictly necessary to understand the underlying mathematical principles but some researchers find this helpful. (Textbooks on statistical techniques in the social sciences vary; some pay lip service to the mathematics behind the tests whilst others provide detailed mathematical justifications.) You also need to be aware of any limitations that need to be acknowledged when interpreting results in relation to the kinds of data, the sample size and the sampling strategy that was followed. It is also helpful to have the same understanding of basic principles in order to be able to read the (quantitative) work of others and make judgements about whether or not their interpretations and conclusions are sound.

Data types

There are three main types of data that can be analysed statistically. *Nominal* data, such as dichotomies (responses that have two options only such as yes/no, male/female) or categorical data (year group or ethnicity), have no numerical meaning. *Ordinal* data have a rank order and are represented numerically, but differences between values may not be equal hence there is no true numerical meaning. For example, the responses to a question on how often online banking is used could be represented by the number zero (never use online banking) to the number four (use online banking at least once a week). *Continuous* data have true numerical values and can be of two types. *Interval* data have no true zero, for example temperature measurements. *Ratio* data do have a true zero, for example distances travelled to work.

Descriptive statistics

Frequency distributions are used to describe data indicating the frequency of all categories or ranks, either in a tabular form or in a graphical form as in a *bar chart*. The frequency distribution of two such variables can be compared with a *crosstabulation* as long as each variable does not have too many categories and each category is mutually exclusive. This would generate a two-dimensional table with rows (the categories for the first chosen variable) and columns (the categories for the second chosen variable). So for example a crosstabulation of gender with job category in health care would provide frequency counts for males and females according to their job (nurse, doctor, and so on). Percentages are often used to represent the number of responses to a categorical question. Frequency distributions for interval data can be represented graphically with a *histogram*.

The *central tendency* is a measure of the most typical value or central value in a frequency distribution and can be measured in three ways: mode, median and mean. The *mode* is the most common value in a set of data (the value or category that occurs most frequently). It is not often used but it is the only measure of central tendency that is appropriate for nominal data. The *median* is the middle value if all responses are put in order from the highest to the lowest value such that 50 per cent of the distribution is below the median and 50 per cent is above. The *mean* is the average value, which is calculated by adding up all the values in the distribution and dividing the total by the number of values. The mean can be influenced by extreme values.

Measures of dispersion, generating a number, are used to describe the 'spread' of the data or the distribution of values. It is possible for two frequency distributions to have the same central tendency (that is the same mean, median or mode value) but to be very different in the distribution of individual items. A measure of dispersion that is small indicates that the data are clustered closely around the measure of central tendency (i.e. the data are very similar). A measure of dispersion that is large indicates a wide and diverse set of responses or measurements. The *range* is the difference between the highest and lowest value. The *quartiles* are the values found at quarterly intervals if the data are ordered from the lowest to the highest and the *interquartile range* is the difference between the upper quartile (the value that is three-quarters of the way through the ordered list) and the lower quartile (the value that is one-quarter of the way through). The *standard deviation* is a measure of the spread based on all values, measuring the 'average' amount by which all values differ from the mean. This is explained further below.

The two most commonly used measures for continuous variables are the mean and standard deviation.

Normal distributions

The *normal distribution* is represented by a bell-shaped curve or *normal curve* (Figure 25.1) and represents a set of values that are commonly clustered around the mean value (the point where the curve turns) with a smaller number of values at each end of the range.

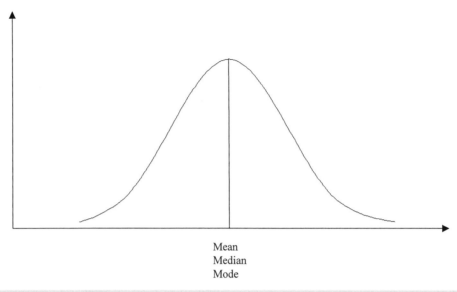

Mean
Median
Mode

Figure 25.1   The normal curve

For example, female adult shoe sizes are normally distributed. In the UK, common sizes are between four and six with a mean of say five, some of the population have shoe sizes of three and seven, a small minority of the population have sizes less than three or greater than seven. Many variables that are studied are assumed to come from populations with a normal distribution. Many statistical tools assume a normal distribution. In a normal distribution the values of the mean and the median will be about the same. It is worth noting that the 'norm' varies in different populations.

Standard deviation

As mentioned above, the *standard deviation* is a way of measuring the difference between each individual value of a variable and the mean value of the variable. It represents the spread of the data or the variability. In a picture of the normal distribution, the horizontal axis is usually measured in standard deviations. A normally distributed population with high variability (greater spread of differences from the mean) will be represented by a flatter bell-shaped curve (that is, with a lower central point) and a normally distributed population with a low variability will be represented by a thinner, higher curve, indicating a tighter clustering of individual values around the mean value.

Mean values should always be considered alongside a measure of variability. The *variance* is the mean of the squared deviation of all scores or values for a variable from the mean value. The deviations are squared to eliminate any negative deviations (those that are less than the mean value) that would otherwise result in the total deviations adding up to zero, preventing the calculation of the mean deviation. The standard deviation is the square root of the variance (which is measured in squared units), providing a measure of variability in relation to the original unit of measurement (e.g. average deviation from the mean salary in terms of salary rather than salary squared).

In a normal distribution two-thirds of all individual values of a variable will be within one standard deviation of the mean. Ninety-five per cent of all cases will lie within about two standard deviations either side of the mean (from $+1.96$ to -1.96 standard deviations). Ninety-nine per cent of all cases will lie within about two and a half standard deviations either side of the mean (from $+2.58$ to -2.58 standard deviations).

Hypotheses and statistical significance

A hypothesis in quantitative research has a particular meaning; it is the re-formalization of a research question (grounded in theory and/or literature) to form a precise declarative statement including a prediction of the outcome such that it can be operationalized and tested statistically. That is, the requirements for data collection and measurement become explicit and it is clear which statistical technique should be applied. Two hypotheses are required: the *null hypothesis* and the *alternative hypothesis*.

The *null hypothesis* assumes that there is no real difference or relationship between two variables. So for example if the research question was 'Does smoking cigarettes negatively affect health?' the null hypothesis would be:

H_0 = The scores achieved on a questionnaire assessing general health by a group of non-smokers will *not differ* from the scores achieved on the same questionnaire by a group of people who smoke at least 20 cigarettes a day.

The *alternative hypothesis* assumes that there is a difference or relationship. It can be non-directional if it is not possible to say which group will outperform the other. In this example, the research question suggests that the difference will be directional. That is, that the group of smokers will be less healthy than the non-smokers. So the alternative hypothesis would be:

H_1 = The scores achieved on a questionnaire assessing general health by a group of non-smokers will *be greater* than the scores achieved on the same questionnaire by a group of people who smoke at least 20 cigarettes a day.

It is the null hypothesis that is tested rather than the alternative hypothesis. Statistical tests enable researchers to reject the null hypothesis based on specific probabilities of achieving test results, assuming that there is no difference or relationship between two variables. When there is insufficient evidence to suggest the null hypothesis is false it is accepted, but not 'proved', and the alternative hypothesis is rejected. When the probability of achieving a test result assuming the null hypothesis to be true is small, then we can be confident in rejecting the null hypothesis and accept the alternative hypothesis. *Statistical significance* is used to indicate the probability of achieving the test result assuming that there actually is no difference or relationship in the population, that is, by chance. Thus if the probability is small we can be reasonably confident (but never certain) that the result

is a 'real' one. Significance testing is described in more detail in the chapter that follows (Barnes and Lewin, Chapter 26, this volume).

Implications for research design

Whilst the approach to designing quantitative research is generally planned in advance and top-down, as Doig (Chapter 32, this volume) comments, it is wise to consider the intended outcomes from the outset. The research question(s) will drive the design of the study but the researcher does need to ensure that the right approach is undertaken and the relevant data are collected to provide the answers. Does the study simply need to describe a population, as surveys such as the UK General Household Survey do? Or does it need to test a hypothesis regarding a potential difference or relationship? Or is the aim to develop a model enabling predictions to be made about a population? Which of these is the right approach to deal with the problem and be in a position to provide reliable answers? Other considerations are whether or not the chosen approach is feasible in relation to the constraints of the research project (e.g. available funds and time) and accessing the required population. Ethical and/or political issues may also need to be considered in quantitative approaches in social sciences research. It is arguably not ethical, for example, to study the impact of smoking by randomly assigning people to two groups, where those in the 'experimental' group smoke 20 cigarettes a day and the 'control' group do not. It would be more appropriate to identify a group of smokers and non-smokers and conduct a survey.

A sampling strategy needs to be considered and will be constrained by resource limitations (time and costs). Does the research need to be generalizable (as discussed under 'What do we mean by reliability and validity?' above), and if so will a truly random design be feasible? And what about sample size? Here considerations include the combination of research methods that might be included in the research design, the variation in the characteristics under investigation, and the required accuracy. What compromises will have to be made?

The next aspect to consider is how to collect the data. This chapter has provided an overview of questionnaire design as this research instrument is frequently employed in quantitative research, being a cost-effective way of collecting standardized data from large samples. Alternative approaches, however, may be more suitable, such as observation, structured interviews or the use of secondary data sources. A questionnaire needs to be reliable and valid (see discussion of reliability and validity above). Threats to validity must be considered. The questions asked need to be appropriate and suitable to test the research hypothesis. Anticipating likely bias can be helpful. Steps could be taken, for example, to ensure that ethnic minorities are not under-represented in a survey by providing the questionnaires in different languages. Non-response can be estimated in advance and sample sizes increased accordingly.

Descriptive statistics are helpful for providing a picture of the sample, whatever the design or approach. A measure of central tendency (appropriate for the kind of data collected) together with a measure of spread of the data can provide a useful summary. In addition, graphical tools and tables provide alternative means of summarizing the data. Descriptive methods can also be used to explore the data and identify outliers (extreme values) and to confirm that it is worth continuing with further data analysis.

Annotated bibliography

Connolly, P. (2007) *Quantitative Data Analysis in Education: A Critical Introduction Using SPSS.* London and New York: Routledge.
This book assumes no knowledge of quantitative methods or statistics. Although designed for those in education it will be of help to any beginner in a social science discipline. There are lots of examples to help novices get to grips with complex concepts with an emphasis on using a popular statistical analysis package, providing good examples of how to describe data in practice.

De Vaus, D.A. (2002) *Surveys in Social Research*, 5th edn. London: Routledge.
Chapter 6 provides a readable introduction to sampling. Chapters 7 and 8 provide details on questionnaire construction and design. Chapters 12 to 17 describe statistical analysis tools and techniques that are particularly relevant to survey research methods. The book usefully provides 'web pointers' – URLs to additional resources available on the internet. Each chapter finishes with a summary of the key concepts and recommendations for further reading.

Diamond, I. and Jefferies, J. (2001) *Beginning Statistics: An Introduction for Social Scientists.* London: Sage.
This textbook assumes no mathematical or statistical background and places little emphasis on statistical formulae. Full of examples to explain concepts, it focuses on description and graphical displays of data, providing an excellent starting point. There are lots of practice questions with answers and explanations given in the back of the book. It also contains some very helpful appendices explaining commonly used mathematical notation and some basic mathematical principles. A very readable book that is easy to follow. Chapters 8 and 9 are very helpful introductions to sampling, the standard error, confidence intervals and confidence limits.

Fowler, F.J. (2008) *Survey Research Methods*, 4th edn. London: Sage.
Chapter 3 covers the principles of sampling. Chapter 4 presents a detailed discussion of non-response and bias. Also includes aspects of internet and email based surveys and particular issues arising from these approaches.

Oppenheim, A.N. (2000) *Questionnaire Design, Interviewing and Attitude Measurement*, new edn. London: Continuum.
A comprehensive and practical guide covering design and implementation of questionnaires in the context of survey research. Each chapter has a list of follow-up readings for those who wish greater detail on a particular aspect.

Rowntree, D. (2000) *Statistics Without Tears: A Primer for Non-Mathematicians*, new edn. London: Penguin.
A classic introduction to statistics, assuming no mathematical knowledge and explaining the ideas behind their use rather than getting heavily into calculations.

Salkind, N. (2007) *Statistics for People Who (Think They) Hate Statistics*, 3rd edn. London: Sage.
Another helpful text for those who have limited experience of statistics or find the concepts difficult.

Sapsford, R. (2006) *Survey Research*, 2nd edn. London: Sage.
Chapters 3 and 4 cover sampling. Again a very readable guide, full of helpful examples to illustrate the points being made. Key points and useful mathematical explanations are presented in boxes within each chapter. Chapters 5 to 7 discuss aspects of questionnaire design together with interviews and systematic observation techniques.

Differences and Relationships in Quantitative Data

Sally Barnes, Graduate School of Education, University of Bristol, UK

Cathy Lewin, Education and Social Research Institute, Manchester Metropolitan University, UK

Summary

- Selecting appropriate statistical techniques
- Evaluating statistical results
  - Testing for significance
  - Probability theory
- Looking for difference
- Looking for correlations

Key concepts

Introduction to inferential statistics

Describing sets of data is often only the first step in data analysis. Frequently what we are most interested in doing is asking questions of the data, exploring relationships between different things we have measured. *Inferential statistics* cover all the techniques which allow us to explore in-depth relationships between variables. They provide a very powerful way of asking questions of numerical data. There are three main approaches: to explore differences; to explore the nature and extent of relationships; and to classify and make predictions (see Jones, Chapter 27, this volume). The focus of this chapter is to introduce some of the key concepts and some of the most commonly used procedures in exploring differences and relationships. The use of a statistics package can take the strain of calculating the mathematics required for each tech-

nique. However, no statistical package can make the decision about which technique to use in a particular situation nor how to interpret what the results mean.

Inferential statistical procedures are divided into two main types: *parametric* and *non-parametric*. Parametric statistics are based on the principles of the normal curve (see Lewin, Chapter 25, this volume) Therefore, in order to be able to use parametric statistics the data must be normally distributed and interval level data (some form of counting rather than categorical or a ranked response). Suggested sample sizes vary according to the kind of statistical test; a general rule of thumb is to have a minimum sample of about 30. When you have samples of less than 30 it is often better to use non-parametric statistics – or statistics which are distribution-free (i.e. not based on the principles of the normal curve). Category variables, either nominal or ordinal (see Lewin, Chapter 25, this volume), are analysed using non-parametric techniques because the mean and standard deviation should not normally be calculated.

One of the most difficult tasks in analysing data is to select the most appropriate statistical technique that both addresses the research question and fits the data you have collected. Howell (2002: 11) provides a useful diagram for selecting an appropriate technique according to:

- the type of data (categorical, ordinal, interval);
- whether testing for differences or relationships;

- the number of groups of participants (two or more);
- whether the groups are *dependent* or *related* (a single group exposed to different conditions or tested at different points in time) or *independent* (two or more unrelated groups of participants);
- whether the test should be parametric or non-parametric.

Several texts also provide guidance on how to select the appropriate technique. See, for example, Pallant (2007; Chapter 10), Salkind (2007; Chapter 9) and Field (2009).

Evaluating statistical results

Carrying out a statistical procedure is a three-stage process. First, we carry out a range of descriptive techniques to ensure the data are reliable, valid and meet the criteria required for statistical analysis (see Field, 2009; Salkind, 2007). Second, we select and compute the appropriate statistical test; and third, we carry out the appropriate test of significance to see what the probability is of achieving the test result assuming that there is no difference or relationship. The test of statistical significance enables us to say how confident we are that the result achieved from the analysis of the data from the sample is a 'real' result or if it is as a result of 'chance' (instead due to sampling error).

Probability theory allows us to ask what are the chances of achieving a similar result from another sample drawn from the same population. The better the chances the more confident we tend to be in thinking our result is valid. However, it is crucial to remember that significance testing is based on probability and that we are testing the null hypothesis (see Field, 2009: Chapter 2; Salkind, 2007: Chapter 9). It is possible to assume the null hypothesis is true, when in fact it is not, called a Type 2 error. Conversely, you may reject the null hypothesis when in fact it is true, called a Type 1 error. The implications behind significance testing (Freedman et al., 2007: Chapter 26) include two important assumptions. The first is that random selection needs to be used to select the original sample from a well-defined population. The second is that measurements need to be both valid and reliable – something often difficult to achieve in the social sciences (Freedman et al., 2007).

Significance testing uses 'degrees of freedom', or 'df' as it is commonly written. See Howell (2002: 56)

or Field (2009: 37) for clear mathematical explanations. Degrees of freedom refers to the number of items in a set (values of a variable for example) which can vary, and the calculation of this differs according to the statistical technique selected. In a classroom with 30 desks, the first student to arrive can choose where to sit, as can each of the following 28 students although from a decreasing number of possibilities each time. But the last student to arrive will have no choice because there will only be one empty desk left. So the degrees of freedom in this case will be the number of desks minus one: 29. In simplistic terms the degrees of freedom figure approximates to the sample size and so provides helpful information when reading quantitative research reports.

Parametric statistical procedures have a formula for calculating the degrees of freedom. Often it is:

$$n - 1 \text{ (if there is only 1 group of people, } n = \text{number in group)}$$

or:

$$n_1 + n_2 - 2 \text{ (if there are 2 groups, } n_1 = \text{number in group 1, } n_2 = \text{number in group 2)}$$

The results of statistical tests are written in conventional notation which typically includes four pieces of information: the statistical test used, the actual result, the degrees of freedom and the probability of achieving that result assuming the null hypothesis is true (see Coolidge, 2006; Freedman et al., 2007).

To evaluate the significance of results researchers present their findings in terms of different probability levels. The level of 0.05 ($p < 0.05$ – 'p' stands for probability value) for example means that the probability of achieving a result when the null hypothesis is true, is less than 5 times in 100. The probability values which we tend to use in the social sciences ($p < 0.05, p < 0.01, p < 0.001$) are based on the normal distribution curve.

There are a number of cautions about the interpretation of statistical results and their associated probabilities (Freedman et al., 2007).

- The .05 and .01 levels of significance used are arbitrary. Their use is common convention and that is the only reason they continue to be used. It actually makes more sense to state the actual probability value (p-value) rather than $p < .05$ – statistical packages report the actual probability value.

- The *p*-value is related to the size of the sample. The larger the sample the smaller the difference, or weaker the relationship, needed to reach statistical significance.
- Researchers should always summarize their data using descriptive statistics (see Lewin, this volume) so that readers can draw their own conclusions about the importance of any statistically significant *p*-values.
- *p*-values are only relevant for samples as they are based on probability, or chance models. When you have data from a whole population it is irrelevant to do a significance test as you would only be comparing the population with itself.
- Tests of significance do not check for design errors. If a researcher has chosen the sample incorrectly or used invalid or unreliable measures, or used an inappropriate test, there is no way to identify this statistically.

One aspect of significance testing that is often difficult for new researchers is the idea of one- or two-tail tests of significance. In the normal curve there are two 'tails', one in either direction, that stretch to infinity. If you have a research question that is very specific about the direction of the result (i.e. you expect a greater mean value of a variable in one group in comparison to a second group) then you can use a one-tailed test of significance. For example, the question 'Do boys complete more sit-ups in 5 minutes than girls?' is quite specific and directional; we can check the test statistic generated to see if boys do complete more sit-ups than girls. However, if we phrase this question as 'Is there a difference in the number of sit-ups boys and girls complete in 5 minutes?', this suggests that either group could complete more sit-ups. In this case, we cannot predict the direction of change so we consider both possibilities and use a two-tailed test (boys may do more sit-ups than girls or girls may do more than boys).

Grounding analysis in inferential statistics: looking for differences

How different do two things have to be before we get all excited about the results? In other words is a difference between several groups real or did it occur by chance? To test this out we carry out statistical tests that look at differences and then using methods of calculating statistical significance we evaluate the

probability of arriving at a particular result assuming that the null hypothesis is true.

Parametric techniques for identifying differences

For interval or ratio numbers the main parametric techniques are the t-test (when we have only two groups) and the Analysis of Variance or ANOVA when we have more than two groups.

We use the t-test when we wish to test and see if there is a significant difference between two sample means. In other words we are using this test to see if two samples can be thought of as coming from the same, or two different, population(s). Our null hypothesis is that there is no difference between two sample means. Our alternative hypothesis is that there is a statistically significant difference between the means.

There are two t-test formulas to consider when you have independent samples, that is two groups of people which are totally unrelated (for example, males/females; doctors/patients; 10 year-olds/12 year-olds). The *separate model t-test* is used when each group has the same number of participants. The t-test formula to use when you have unequal sample sizes is called the *pooled variance model t-test*. The difference in the two formulas comes in the way that the variance (distribution of data around the mean) of each sample is calculated.

One assumption of the t-test is that the variances of the two groups are the same. The Levene's test examines the equality of variances of two groups. The null hypothesis is that the two variances are equal. If the result of Levene's test is significant at $p < 0.05$ then the null hypothesis is rejected and the alternative hypothesis is accepted; the variances are not equal. If the results of Levene's test are not significant then the null hypothesis is accepted; the variances are assumed to be equal. It is then up to the researcher to decide which t-test is appropriate, based on the results of the Levene's test.

The result of the t-test is referred to as the t value. The larger the resulting value of t the greater the difference between the two means. To interpret the t value we check the probability value associated with that t for our sample, taking into account the sample size. Then we are able to interpret the finding and state whether or not there is likely to be a real difference between the two groups, and if so how confident we are that such a difference exists.

To report the results of t-tests it is important to specify which t-test formula was used; then state the outcomes including the degrees of freedom for this technique (df), for example:

$$t = 4.52, \text{ df} = 40, p < 0.01$$

This tells us that there were 42 people altogether in the two groups, as for this statistical technique the degrees of freedom is calculated by adding the number of people in each of the groups and deducting two. It also tells us the actual t value is 4.52 and the probability of accepting that there is a difference, assuming the null hypothesis is true, is less than 1 in 100. Therefore we can conclude that the means of our two groups are different and that this difference is statistically significant.

There is a third t-test formula used when there is only one group of people when data are collected about the same participants under two different conditions (known as a *dependent* or *related* design). This is called the paired sample t-test and is most commonly used in pre-test/post-test designs. Teachers often give a class a test at the beginning of term to assess pupils' knowledge of a subject. At the end of the term the pupils are tested again. Obviously teachers hope that pupils will have performed better in the end of term test than the initial test. A paired sample t-test would assess whether or not there was a statistically significant difference between the test score means, suggesting improvement.

When testing for differences between three or more groups, analysis of variance (ANOVA) is used instead of a t-test (see Field, 2009; Salkind, 2007). An ANOVA will identify whether or not there is a significant difference in the means across a number of different groups. The null hypothesis for this test is that there is no difference in the means for the different groups. For example, an ANOVA would be required to test for any variation among three exam markers, each marking 100 exam scripts. Here the variable being tested would be the exam mark given to each student and the grouping variable would be the exam marker. In this case, we would hope that there is no difference (i.e. that the test result is non-significant) demonstrating that the exam markers are consistent with one another.

In the ANOVA we are looking to see if the difference between the groups is greater than the difference within the groups. The result of the ANOVA test is called the F ratio. This ratio compares the variability (variance or sum of squares) between groups (the differences you might expect because of

Table 26.1   Example of ANOVA results

	df	Sum of squares	Mean squares	F	p
Between Groups	2	198.38	99.19	12.45	<0.01
Within Groups	72	95.62	7.97		
Total	74				

the grouping factor) to the variability within the groups (the differences that arise due to chance factors, irrespective of the group they are in). The larger the variability between groups and the smaller the variability within groups, the larger the F ratio will be and the more confident we can be of accepting that there is a difference between the groups.

For this technique two different degrees of freedom (df) calculations are required. The degrees of freedom for the between groups measure is the number of groups minus one. The degrees of freedom for the within groups measure is the total number in the sample minus the degrees of freedom for the between groups measure. The results of the ANOVA are often presented in a table – see Table 26.1.

The ANOVA result tells us whether or not there is a significant difference in the means of the groups overall. But it does not tell us if the significance is between all of the groups or just between some of the groups. To find out which pairs of groups are significantly different we carry out a post-hoc analysis (an analysis after the initial analysis). Commonly used post-hoc tests include the Bonferroni correction, Tukey HSD test and the Scheffé test (see Field, 2009: Chapter 10).

Non-parametric techniques for identifying differences

For nominal or ordinal data it is not appropriate to use t-tests, ANOVA, and other parametric techniques. Rather we use techniques that are distribution-free, that is not based on the principles of the normal curve. There are many non-parametric tests of difference (see Field, 2009; Salkind, 2007; Siegel and Castellon, 1988). Each technique has a specific purpose and each has specific requirements about the level of measurement (that is nominal or ordinal data), number of categories, number of groups, and type of difference explored. It is crucial to know what kinds of differences are being explored using what types of data in order to select the most appropriate technique. These techniques should also be used with interval data when you have very small samples or when there are violations of the assumptions which underlie parametric tests (e.g. when data cannot be described as having a normal distribution, see Lewin, Chapter 25, this volume). Non-parametric tests typically use ranking of data to compare groups and are based on fewer assumptions. The Mann-Whitney U Test is the non-parametric equivalent of the independent sample t-test. The Wilcoxon signed-rank test is the non-parametric equivalent of the paired sample t-test. The Kruskal-Wallis test compares differences between several different groups and is similar to the ANOVA.

Grounding analysis in inferential statistics: looking for relationships

To explore the relationships between variables we use a process called correlation. In social science research correlation procedures are very popular. We can use them to compare groups of individuals by different attributes. For example, we may correlate two different groups of 10-year-olds' performance on a maths exam, or we might compare one group of children's literacy scores with their numeracy scores, or explore the relationship between height and weight. In all cases what we are exploring is how the shape of the distributions of two variables is related.

In the parametric condition, the Pearson correlation coefficient (r) tells us the degree of linear association between the two variables, in other words the strength of the relationship. By linear we mean how straight a line they form when plotted on a graph showing their relationship. One of the implications of exploring linear relationships is that the things being measured must be able to form a straight line. Only interval and ratio numbers where means and standard deviations can be calculated can be used to explore linearity.

The correlation coefficient (r) will be between −1.0 and +1.0. When r = 1 or −1 it tells us the data fall in a perfect straight line. When r is positive then the correlation is positive meaning that scores on both variables increase together. When r is negative then the correlation is negative, meaning that as the value of one variable increases the value of the other variable decreases. When r = 0 it tells us that there is no association between the two variables. Values of r between 0 and +/−1 show the different strength of the relationship between the two variables. There is

no definitive rule about how to interpret the strength of a correlation. However, generally speaking, if r is between 0 and +/−0.33 it is considered to be a weak relationship; if r is between 0.34 and 0.66 it indicates a medium strength relationship; and if r is between 0.67 and 0.99 it indicates a strong relationship.

Scatterplot techniques

One way to understand what we mean by linear relationships is to draw a scatterplot of the two variables. The more 'line' or cigar shaped a scatterplot looks the greater the linear relationship. If the scatterplot is a straight line then it suggests a perfect correlation. For example, the scatterplot in Figure 26.1 shows a non-significant relationship between hours of sleep and year of birth among 90 people attending a statistics class.

When the scatterplot results in a mass of dots all over the paper there is unlikely to be a correlation and we would expect the resulting correlation coefficient to be very close to 0.

The next example, in Figure 26.2, shows a linear relationship between a mark given for coursework and a final module mark for 193 students. One would anticipate this scatterplot would be close to a straight line as quite obviously a grade on coursework would be included in a final grade.

Calculation requirements

To calculate the correlation coefficient requires two samples of scores, often called the X and Y variables.

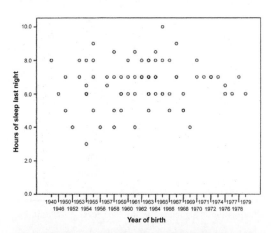

Figure 26.1 Example of scatterplot indicating no relationship between hours of sleep and age

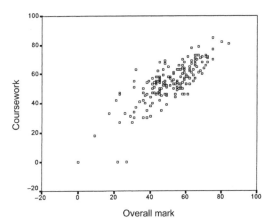

Figure 26.2 Example of scatterplot suggesting there may be a linear relationship between the mark given for coursework and the overall module mark

$$r = .908, \; n = 193, \; p < .01$$

In this case the size of the sample (*n*) is normally quoted instead of the degrees of freedom. (Sometimes the degrees of freedom figure is given instead which is calculated as the number of pairs – 2; in this case the df = 191.) It is important to give the sample size as it strongly effects the statistical significance of the correlation (see Figure 26.3).

There are a number of correlational methods. Which method to use depends on the scale of measurement of the two variables. The most common method is the Pearson product-moment correlation coefficient, used when both variables are interval or ratio. The correlational method appropriate when one or both variables are ordinal (ranked) is the Spearman rank order correlation coefficient, called Spearman's rho or if the data set is small with many observations equally ranked, Kendall's tau (see Field, 2009: 179–81). These techniques can also be used when assumptions for parametric tests are violated (i.e. the data is not normally distributed). There are also correlational methods to use with nominal data (chi-square, see below).

Interpreting correlations

To interpret a correlation we use three pieces of information: r (the correlation coefficient indicating strength of the relationship, described above); the statistical significance of r (the probability of accepting that there is a relationship, assuming that the null hypothesis is true); and the size of the sample. To interpret correlations all these factors can be taken

The scores are paired in some way. In most cases in social science research this pairing is by individual. Commonly, we have scores for a group of people on two measures. For example we might correlate a particular class of students' performance on the first term exam and the second term exam. This would tell us the degree of association between the two exam results. In this case each individual would have two scores. Or if we gave the same exam two years in a row we could calculate the correlation between last year's students and this year's.

The relationship between coursework mark and overall mark for 193 students from Figure 26.2 is confirmed as being very strong and the Pearson result shows that:

Correlations

		Coursework	Overall Mark
Coursework	Pearson Correlation	1	.908**
	Sig. (2-tailed)		.000
	N	193	193
Overall Mark	Pearson Correlation	.908**	1
	Sig. (2-tailed)	.000	
	N	193	193

**Correlation is significant at the 0.01 level (2-tailed).

Figure 26.3 Example of SPSS output from correlation test

into account. Clearly, statistical significance is relevant but so is the strength of the relationship. Correlation is greatly affected by sample size. With very large samples weak correlation coefficients may be statistically significant; with small samples only very strong correlations will reach statistical significance.

As with other tests, we first decide if we are hypothesizing a result in a particular direction or not – so do we use a one- or two-tailed level of significance? We then decide what is the minimum level of significance we are prepared to accept – .05, .01, .001, or whatever. The choice about what level of significance to use as the standard for a particular study depends on the reliability and validity of the data being analysed as well as the original research question being addressed. Always, your reasons for the decisions taken will need to be explained when reporting the outcomes.

Chi-square

Chi-square is one of the most commonly used techniques to explore relationships using nominal and/or ordinal data. It is a very unusual statistic because it does two things in one test. It is a test of independence and also a test of association. In chi-square we are formally testing the null hypothesis that two variables are independent. If we reject the null hypothesis because we have a significant result (i.e. we are confident that there is a relationship between the two variables) we can then do further tests to explore the kind of relationship that exists between two variables and the strength of that relationship.

Chi-square, whilst being a non-parametric test, does depend on assumptions that need to be met. Firstly, each case or person must contribute to only one cell in the contingency table (i.e. the characteristics for each variable must be mutually exclusive). Often this can be tested logically. If we collect information about gender and eye colour from 100 students you would expect the responses to each question to elicit only one answer (each student will be classified as being of one type of gender and having eyes of one particular colour). Secondly, the chi-square test works by comparing the distribution of observations in the cells of the contingency table with the distribution that might have been expected if there was no association, generating an *expected count* in each cell. If any of the expected counts are less than 5 then the chi-square test will be invalid, although with large contingency tables accepting no

GENDER* Use a computer outside school crosstabulation
Count

		Use a computer outside school		Total
		No	Yes	
GENDER	Male	322	2963	3285
	Female	288	2566	2854
Total		610	5529	6139

Figure 26.4   Example of a simple cross-tabulation

more than 20 per cent of cells with expected counts less than 5 is acceptable.

The first step in interpreting a significant chi-square is to look carefully at the values and/or percentages in a two-way frequency table as a way of understanding the association between different variables. The crosstabulation (or contingency table as it is also called) indicates how many cases (people for example) exhibit each of the possible combinations of the two nominal variables being tested. The example shown in Figure 26.4 shows how many boys and how many girls use computers outside school and how many do not.

However, the percentages in each column and row may make it easier to interpret the relationship between gender and out-of-school use of computers in the sample shown in Figure 26.5.

The percentages help us to take into account that there are many more pupils reporting use of computers out of school than not, and only slightly more boys than girls in this sample. The most commonly used chi-square statistic is the Pearson chi-square (χ^2). In the example presented here (see Figure 26.5) it is:

$$\chi^2 = 0.142, \text{df} = 1, p = 0.706$$

The df for chi-square is (number of rows – 1) multiplied by (number of columns – 1). For a table with two rows and two columns (a 2×2 table) the df = 1. It also tells us that for this distribution the probability of accepting that there is an association, assuming that the null hypothesis is true, is very high because $p > 0.05$ ($p = 0.706$). Therefore, we can be confident that the two variables are independent and that there is no association between gender and reported use of computers outside of school.

GENDER* Use a computer outside school crosstabulation

			Use a computer outside school		Total
			No	Yes	
GENDER	Male	Count % within GENDER % within Use a computer outside school	322 9.8% 52.8%	2963 90.2% 53.6%	3285 100.0% 53.5%
GENDER	Female	Count % within GENDER % within Use a computer outside school	288 10.1% 47.2%	2566 89.9% 46.4%	2854 100.0% 46.5%
Total		Count % within GENDER % within Use a computer outside school	610 9.9% 100.0%	5529 90.1% 100.0%	6139 100.0% 100.0%

Figure 26.5   Example of a cross-tabulation with row and column percentages

The chi-square statistic is the most used and most abused statistic in social science research. The abuse comes from researchers making interpretations about the association between variables beyond what the result indicates. In and of itself chi-square only tells us if there is an association between two things or if there is independence. To explore the strength of relationship requires using one of the post-hoc analyses in measures of association such as Phi or Cramer's V, Goodman and Kruskall Lambda (see Field, 2009: 695). Similar to correlation coefficients, these tests produce results which give a measure of strength between 0.0 and 1.0. The closer to 1.0, the stronger the association.

Implications for research design

One of the main issues to consider either when testing for differences or for relationships is whether or not to choose a parametric test or a non-parametric test. These decisions will be based on the size of the sample, the data collection techniques used, the way data is measured and any coding system used.

For example, the age of respondents can be asked in different ways which will result in different types of numbers. If the question is phrased as an open-ended question then 'How many hours of sleep did you have last night?' could produce responses of specific hours, so potentially an interval number where parametric techniques could be used. However,

the question could be asked to produce an ordinal scale and therefore require non-parametric statistics. For example:

How many hours of sleep did you have last night?
0–2 _____
3–4 _____
5–6 _____
7–8 _____
9–10 _____
11+ _____

Parametric tests are more sophisticated and many argue are more sensitive than non-parametric tests (and so are more likely to detect differences between groups, even if they are relatively small). However, parametric tests can only be used with interval level data and only if certain assumptions are met. The data should be normally distributed (see Lewin, Chapter 25, this volume). This can be determined by using statistical procedures such as the Kolmogorov-Smirnov test (see Field, 2009: 144–8). And, the variability of values in each group should be approximately the same – known as *homogeneity of variance*. This is tested in different ways for different procedures.

Non-parametric tests are more robust but less sensitive. They are sometimes referred to as assumption-free tests. The techniques are based on ranking rather than exact differences; that is whether scores or variable values are higher or lower than others. Non-parametric tests are appropriate for ordinal and nominal data. They can also be used when the necessary parameters for parametric tests are not in place (e.g. the distribution of the sample is not a normal distribution). See Salkind (2007: Chapter 16) for an overview of nonparametric techniques.

Prediction and causation – a caution

One of the most common mistakes researchers make when using correlations is to talk about cause and effect. If there is an association between two variables that does not necessarily mean that one causes the other. There are three conditions which must be satisfied in order to prove cause and effect relationships:

- There must be a significant correlation between the 'cause' and 'effect' variables.
- The correlation must be 'real', not do to with some other factor (we call this spurious).
- The cause variable must precede the effect variable in real time.

A significant correlation, on its own, does not provide any evidence for causality. For example, there is a positive association between height and weight – taller people tend to weigh more than shorter people or people who weigh less tend to be shorter than people who weigh more. We cannot say that tall people weigh more because they eat more because it is equally possible that they weigh more because they grow taller and need to eat more. Association does not mean causation.

Also, the significant correlation between the variables must be seen to be 'real'. Freedman and colleagues (2007) use the example of searching for the cause of polio back in the 1950s when there was a worldwide epidemic. Researchers gathered massive amounts of information from polio victims and their families and discovered two very significant correlations:

- an increase in the incidence of polio and an increase of drinking soft drinks;
- an increase in the incidence of polio and an increase in temperature.

Only one of these is a 'real' relationship. The other is 'spurious'. The polio virus spreads as the temperature rises and so that is a real relationship. However, as the temperature rises we tend to drink more liquids and so the connection between polio and soft drinks is spurious because it is connected to temperature and does not exist on its own.

The final condition which must be met to examine prediction and causality is that the cause variables must precede the effect variable. For example, an intervention to improve the teaching of reading must take place before the test measuring reading ability is undertaken. However, sometimes in the social sciences the cause and effect is harder to unravel. Think about the relationship between job satisfaction and productivity. Which comes first?

Annotated bibliography

Coolidge, F.L. (2006) *Statistics: A Gentle Introduction*, 2nd edn. London: Sage.
The book offers a good introduction to statistics and their underlying principles. Coolidge's examples and writing make some of these difficult concepts more easily approachable. His description of the ins and outs of t-test and ANOVA are very useful. His step-by-step calculations may help to understand what these tests actually do. He uses a style of notation which many people find accessible.

Field, A. (2009) *Discovering Statistics using SPSS*, 3rd edn. London: Sage.
The third edition is as friendly and even more accessible than the earlier editions. There are chapters geared to the novice researcher taking a first statistics course. There are also many chapters which are aimed at more experienced researchers carrying out sophisticated designs. The book has many helpful tips for using the SPSS/PASW package. Highly recommended.

Freedman, D., Pisani, R. and Purves, R. (2007) *Statistics*, 4th edn. New York: Norton.
This remains an excellent book which focuses on probability and significance testing and the use of root mean square (RMS) in developing statistical sophistication.

Howell, D.C. (2002) *Statistical Methods for Psychology*, 5th edn. Belmont, CA: Duxbury Press.
This is a very comprehensive text with careful conceptual and mathematical explanations together with helpful examples. It takes the reader through the underlying principles of statistical techniques to advanced methods such as multiple regression.

Mendenhall, W. (1987) *Introduction to Probability and Statistics*. Boston: Duxbury Press. Chapter 1 'What is statistics?'.

Mendenhall uses a case study to present his key concepts. He develops the idea and use of inferential statistics in sections 1.2, 1.3 and 1.4 and then applies them to his case study in 1.5. An interesting and useful technique.

Pallant, J. (2007) *SPSS Survival Manual*, 3rd edn. Buckingham: Open University Press.
Written in a friendly, detailed style with a good explanation of how to interpret and present the output from the statistical tests. Covers almost everything. One of the best features of this book is the table summarizing statistical tests, indicating when they can be used and how (116–17).

Salkind, N.J. (2007) *Statistics for People Who (Think They) Hate Statistics*, 3rd edn. London: Sage.
For beginners this book is the place to start. It is friendly, easy to understand and full of useful information. Chapters are in good, clear English with easy step-by-step procedures. Starts with the assumption that people don't know and may not want to know what they need to know about! The three chapters on t-test and ANOVA are a good progression. Highly recommended.

Siegel, S. and Castellon, J. (1988) *Non-Parametric Statistics for the Social Sciences*, 2nd edn. New York: McGraw Hill.
Siegel wrote the definitive guide to non-parametric statistics in the 1950s. It is a classic. The current text is an update on the original and though it is written in a statistical way most tests you will ever use are described and explained.

An Introduction to Statistical Modelling

Kelvyn Jones, School of Geographical Sciences, University of Bristol, UK

Summary

- Regression modelling
  - Researching 'cause and effect' relations that are neither necessary nor sufficient
- Multilevel modelling
  - Researching a specific problem – and how it relates to different forms of multilevel structures
- Key theorists and writers
  - Paul D. Allison
  - Harvey Goldstein
  - Stephen Raudenbush

Statistical modelling is a huge subject. In the space we have available I will concentrate on why you do modelling and what can be achieved. I consider what sort of questions it can answer, what sort of data looks like a 'regression' problem and what steps we can take to ensure we get valid results. I have written this introduction from the advanced perspective of the generalized linear model (McCullagh and Nelder, 1989) and have included a substantial discussion on the developing approach of multilevel modelling because of its major potential in the analysis of social research questions.

Key concepts: regression modelling

In the social sciences we research 'cause and effect' relations that are neither necessary (the outcome occurs only if the causal factor has operated) nor sufficient (the action of a factor always produces the outcome). Moreover, inherent variation or 'noise' may swamp the 'signal' and we need quantitative techniques to uncover the underlying patterns to produce credible evidence of a relation (see Jones, Chapter 23, this volume). A good exemplar comes from epidemiology. There are lung cancer victims who have never smoked, and people who have smoked for a lifetime without a day's illness. The link was once doubted but we now have unequivocal evidence. Men who smoke increase their risk of death from lung cancer by more than 22 times (a staggering 2,200 per cent higher). The estimate is that one cigarette reduces your life on average by 11 minutes.

To illustrate the arguments I will use a research problem of assessing the evidence for discrimination in legal firms. In that context, statistical modelling provides the following:

- a quantitative assessment of the size of the effect, for example the difference in salary between blacks and whites is £5,000 per annum;
- a quantitative assessment after taking account of other variables; for example a black worker earns £6,500 less after taking account of years of experience; this *conditioning* on other variables distinguishes modelling from 'testing for differences' (see Barnes and Lewin, Chapter 26, this volume);
- a measure of uncertainty for the size of effect; for example we can be 95 per cent confident that the

black–white difference in salary to be found generally in the population from which our sample is drawn is likely to lie between £4,400 and £5,500 (see Lewin, Chapter 25, this volume, for an explanation of confidence intervals).

We can use regression modelling in a number of modes: as description (what is the average salary for different ethnic groups?); as part of causal inferences (does being black result in a lower salary?) and in predictive mode ('what happens if' questions). The last can be very difficult to achieve, because change may be so systemic that the underlying relations themselves are altered, and past empirical regularities captured by the modelling no longer hold in a period of regime change (Lucas, 1976).

Data for modelling

Modelling requires a quantifiable outcome measure to assess the effects of discrimination. Table 27.1 provides several, differentiated by the nature of the measurement. There is a continuous measure of salary; the binary categorical outcome of promoted or not; the three-category outcome (promoted, not promoted, not even considered); a count of the number of times rejected for promotion; and a time-to-event measure, the length of time that it has taken to promotion, where a '+' indicates that the event has not yet taken place. All of these outcomes can be analysed in a generalized linear model, but different techniques are required for different scales of measurement. Suitable models going from left to right across the table are normal-theory, logit, multinomial, Poisson, and Cox regression but they all share fundamental characteristics of the general family (Retherford and Choe, 1993). Also shown in the table are a number of 'explanatory' or predictor variables, again with different scales of measurement. Gender is measured as two categories, ethnicity as four, education as a set of ordered categories, and years of employment on a continuous scale. All of these scales can be analysed in the general framework.

Relations

Figure 27.1 displays a range of relations between a response, salary, on the vertical axis and predictor variables on the horizontal. In (a) there is a sizeable difference between the male and female average income. In (b) to (d) we see a number of straight-line relations between salary and years of service. The first

is a positive one; the longer you have worked for the firm, the more money you get. The second is the flat one of no relation; there is no effect of length of employment on pay (think fast-food outlets!). The third shows a negative relation, the longer you have been there, the less you get paid (this can happen in physically demanding jobs).

A non-linear relation between salary and length of employment is shown in (e): an initial steep rise tails off indicating that the full salary is reached rapidly. In (f) salary increments get steeper and steeper with experience, and in (g) there is a curvilinear relation such that salary increases for the first six years then tails away. An interaction between gender and length-of-employment is shown in (h). At appointment there is no gender gap but this opens up the longer you are employed. The distinctive feature of (i) is that in addition to the solid lines displaying averages for the four categories of ethnicity, there are dashed lines representing the confidence interval (see Lewin, this volume). We can be 95 per cent confident that the true population value will fall within this interval given our sample data. Here, the average white salary is estimated with the greatest reliability and has the narrowest band. The Asian band is the widest; we are unsure what the average for this group is. While the black salary is unequivocally lower than the white as the confidence intervals do not overlap, the evidence is not sufficient to decide on white–Asian differences, nor on Asian-black differences. The unknown group looks indistinguishable from the white group, with a slightly wider confidence interval. The final graph (j) is a *three-way interaction* between gender, ethnicity, and length of employment. At the outset, there are substantial differences between the groups, and as time proceeds, black women would appear to be doubly discriminated against.

Conditioning

We may be interested in the effect of just one variable (gender) on another (salary) but we need to take account of other variables as they may compromise the results. We can recognize three distinct cases:

- Inflation of a relation when not taking into account extraneous variables: a substantial gender effect could be reduced after taking account of ethnicity; this is because the female labour force is predominantly non-white and it is this group that is characterized by poor pay.

Table 27.1 A dataframe for regression modelling for the discrimination study

Respondent number	Responses					Predictors			
	Salary (£k)	Promotion (2 category)	Promotion (3 category)	Number of rejections	Time to promotion (yrs)	Gender	Ethnicity	Years of education	Years of service
1	32.4	No	No	1	6.2+	Female	White	<11	9.1
2	40.1	Yes	Yes	0	3.2	Male	White	11-13	6.2
3	65.2	Yes	Yes	0	2.9	Male	Asian	14-16	4.9
4	32.1	No	No	2	8.2+	Female	Black	>16	8.2
5	21.6	No	No	4	6.7+	Female	Unknown	11-13	6.7
6	25.4	No	No	3	4.2+	Male	Black	<11	4.2
7	32.7	No	No	1	5.1+	Female	White	14-16	5.1
8	51.7	Yes	Yes	0	3.9	Male	White	<11	4.8
9	44.0	Yes	Yes	0	4.2	Female	Asian	14-16	7.2
10	32.6	No	No	1	3.9+	Female	Black	14-16	3.9
11	41.7	Yes	Yes	0	4.9	Male	White	11-13	9.7
.	.	.	.	.	.	.	.	.	.
.	.	.	.	.	.	.	.	.	.
500	39.7	No	No	2	5.2	Male	Unknown	14-16	8.1

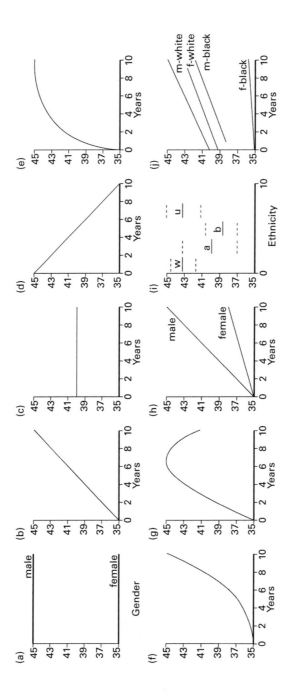

Figure 27.1   Relations between variables

- Suppression of a relation: an apparent small gender gap could increase when account is taken of years of employment; women having longer service and poorer pay.
- No confounding: the original relation remains substantially unaltered when account is taken of other variables.

While modelling can usually assess the partial relationship between two variables taking account of others, this cannot be achieved when predictor variables are so highly correlated that we have no effective way of telling them apart. In the pathological case of exact collinearity (complete dependence between a pair or more variables) a separate effect cannot be estimated. For example, if all Asians in the survey are women, we cannot determine the gender gap for Asians. More generally, collinearity is a matter of degree and as the correlation between predictor variables increases, so do the confidence intervals as there is insufficient distinctive information for reliable estimation.

Form of the model

All statistical models have a common form:

Response = Systematic part + Random part

The systematic part is the average relation between the response and the predictors, while the random part is the variation in the response after taking account of all the included predictors. Figure 27.2 displays the values representing the data for 16 respondents, and a straight line we have threaded through the points to represent the systematic relation between salary and length of employment. The line represents fitted values; if you have 10 years service you are predicted to have a salary of about £45,000.

All equations of the straight line involving two variables have the same form:

Fitted value = Intercept + (Slope*Predictor)

which here is:

Predicted salary = Intercept +
(Slope*Years of service)

which (say) we estimate to be:

Predicted salary = 30.3 + (1.7*Length of service)

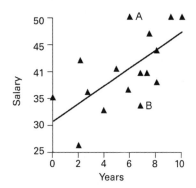

Figure 27.2 Simple linear regression

The intercept gives the predicted value of the response when the predictor takes on the value of zero, so we are predicting that the average salary on appointment (when years of service is 0) is £30,000. The slope gives the marginal change in the response variable for a unit change in the predictor variable. For every extra year with the firm, salary increases by £1,700. Importantly, the increase in salary consequent from staying 0 to 1 years in service is the same as from 5 to 6 years of service. This is a direct consequence of assuming that the underlying functional form of the model is linear and fitting a linear equation.

The term random means 'allowed to vary' and, in relation to Figure 27.2, the random part is the variation in salary that is not accounted for by the underlying average relationship with years. Some people are paid more and some less given the time they have been with the firm. We see that person A has an income above the line while B is below. The difference between the actual and predicted salary is known as the residual. In fitting the line we have minimized these residuals so that the line goes through the middle of the data points. Here we have used a technique called Ordinary Least Squares in which the sum of the squared residuals is minimized. Responses with other scales of measurement require other techniques, but all of them are based on the same underlying principle of minimizing the 'poorness of fit' between the actual data points and the fitted line.

In some cases there will be a close fit between the actual and fitted values but in other cases there may be a lot of 'noise', so that for any given length of employment there is a wide range of salaries. It is helpful to characterize this residual variability. To do so requires us to make some assumptions. We need to conceive the residuals as coming from a particular distribution. Given that salary is a continuous variable, we can assume that the residuals come from a Normal distribution (other scales would suggest other distributions). If we further assume that there is the same variability for short and long length of service (that is homoscedasticity) we can summarize the variability in a single statistic, the standard deviation of the residuals. For Figure 27.2 this value is 6, and we can anticipate (given the known properties of a Normal distribution) that the income for 95 per cent of employees on appointment will lay roughly 2 standard deviations around the mean value of £30,000. Most people will have an initial income between £18,000 and £42,000. This rather wide spread of values is due to inherent uncertainty in the system and the small number (16) of observations we have used. Another key summary statistic is the R-squared value which gives the correspondence between actual and fitted values, on a scale between zero (no correspondence) and 100 (complete correspondence). Chapter 23 warns about the over-reliance on such goodness of fit statistics, and you are encouraged to undertake a residual analysis to diagnose problems with the fitted model; a good account can be found at: http://www.ats.ucla.edu/stat/stata/webbooks/reg/chapter2/statareg2.htm

The model we have so far discussed is a 'simple' one with only one predictor. In a multiple regression model there is more than one predictor (there can be any combination of continuous and categorical variables) with the following differences:

- *Intercept*: this is now the average value for the response when all the predictors take the value zero;
- *Slope*: there is one for each predictor and this summarizes the conditional or partial relationship as the change in the response for a unit change in a particular predictor, holding all the other predictors constant;
- *Residual*: the difference between the actual and fitted values based on all the predictors;
- *R-squared*: the percentage of the total variation of the response variable that is accounted for by all predictors taken simultaneously.

Figure 27.1 (h) to (j) are all examples of multiple regression models, the key to their specification being the coding of predictor variables. A comprehensive discussion of how to do this can be found at: http://www.ats.ucla.edu/stat/stata/webbooks/reg/chapter5/

Implications for research design: regression modelling

We can recognize two broad classes of design that will produce suitable data for regression modelling; experiments where we intervene and observational studies. Experiments are artificial settings in which we change the predictor variable and see what happens to the response, while keeping other variables 'controlled'. We can also randomly allocate each case to an 'intervention' or not, thereby guaranteeing that any detectable change in the response is due to the intervention. Because of this closure and control of unknown factors, experiments are a very strong procedure for causal inference. It is often thought that experiments are more or less impossible in most social sciences due to ethics and relations being disposition-response, not stimulus-response. You cannot easily change a person's gender and keep everything else the same! But with some ingenuity we could get something like the data we need. If we are interested in how ethnicity affects whether a person is promoted or not, we could write scripts for an interview, varying some elements such as length of employment, but keeping all the rest the same. Actors of different ethnicity could record these, and the videos would be played to managers to see what decision they would come to. Modelling would then identify the size of the effect of ethnicity in relation to years of employment. This is a very strong design for causal inference but the external validity may be weak due to the artificiality of the process, so that everyone gets promoted!

Observational designs are less strong for causal inference, but if attention is paid to scientific sampling so that each member of the population has a known chance of inclusion, they can be highly representative. We can recognize four broad groups of design, each with their own strengths and weaknesses: administrative data, cross-sectional surveys, case-comparison study and panel design (see Jones and Moon, 1987). All of these designs can yield data that can be modelled by regression analysis, the choice of design being determined by the type of question being asked and the resources available. There is one golden rule that must be followed, however: 'the specifics of the design must be taken account of in the modelling'. For example, a panel survey (where people are tracked periodically) will generate data for respondents that will be patterned across time (salary now will be similar to what it was last year and the year before), and this 'non-independence' must be explicitly modelled.

Our aim in designing how we are going to collect the data and how we are going to analyse them is to get valid results. We can recognize two broad areas of validity that particularly apply to the analysis and the design of a model-based study, and we will discuss these issues using regression in causal mode.[1]

Conclusion validity

This is concerned with analysis, and asks if the conclusions we have reached about relationships in our data are credible. We can be wrong in two ways: missing a real relation; finding a relation where there is none.

The key threats to this sort of validity (and what to do about them) are.

- The assumptions of the systematic part (e.g. in terms of linearity) and the random part (in terms of the nature of the distribution and such properties as homoscedasticity, that is equal variance and independence)[2] must be met. This amounts to the systematic part of the model fully capturing the generalities of the world; equivalently the random part is just 'trendless' fluctuations. We can use 'diagnostics' to assess assumptions and robust procedures with less demanding assumptions. A useful guide to both these approaches is to be found in Cook and Weisberg (1999).
- Data dredging: This is analysing the data repeatedly under slightly differing conditions or assumptions, dropping these cases, transforming this variable, trying out a very large number of different predictor variables, or including every possible interaction to maximize the R-squared. If we do this, we are more or less bound to find something. But the status of what we have found is problematic; we cannot tell whether what we have found is idiosyncratic noise or generalizable signal. The best advice is to focus on a single topic. We should ask not the vague 'what determines salary?', but 'is there discrimination by ethnicity in annual salary when account is taken of gender and length of employment?' If you do

undertake such model searching, keep it limited, be honest in your write-up, adjust your level of significance to take account of multiple hypothesis testing, and use a hold-out sample as an independent test of the model.

- Lack of statistical power so that the sample is too small a sample to detect a real relationship: The required number of observations is determined by three factors: noisy systems need more observations, so do predictor variables lacking variability, and collinear predictors. As a very rough rule of thumb, you would not usually have more than 10 predictor variables in a single model, and you might plan on collecting at least 25 observations for each. Software is available (e.g. http://www.insp.mx/dinf/stat ... list.html) which indicates required sample size for a given power. A common rule of thumb is a power of 0.8; at least 80 per cent chance of finding a relationship when there is one.
- Measurement error: We can have imprecise measurements and we can have systematically biased measurements. In general, biased measurements will produce biased estimates of effects, unless all variables are off target by the same amount. Non-systematic errors in the dependent variable will require additional observations for the same power; while such errors in the key predictor variable usually biases estimates by attenuating them to zero. We can do a sensitivity analysis to appreciate the effects of measurement error, while during collection we can use a pilot survey to assess reliability and bias. Developing a consistent protocol, training the interviewers and careful wording of questions can all help.

Internal validity

This second type of validity addresses the question of whether the relationship we have found is a causal one. The key threats to validity (and what to do about them) are:

- *Omitted variables bias* refers to alternative explanation of results: to be problematic, such variables must be related to *both* the response and the included predictor variable. Specification error tests are available (Hendry, 2000), but while these may indicate a problem, they cannot suggest what variable is missing. This is the Achilles heel of regression modelling with observational data; with an experiment employing randomization this should not be a problem. The best possible advice is to think hard about a research problem and include all relevant variables. At the same time you do not want to include irrelevant variables, as this will reduce the power of the design to detect real effects. It can help a great deal to classify possible predictors into direct causes, indirect causes, moderating variables and mediating variables (Miles and Shevlin, 2001).

- *Endogeneity* is a fancy term for having a predictor variable that is directly influenced by the response, such that income is determined by health and health by income. In an experiment, this problem is ruled out by design as you can manipulate the predictors and see the subsequent effects. With observational designs there are specialist techniques such as instrumental variables for improved estimation of causal effects (Angrist and Pischke, 2009). Panel designs can also be vital here. In some situations it is possible to rule out this problem a priori; it is unlikely for example that gender or ethnicity are determined by salary!

- *Selection bias* is when we have selected our respondents so as to in some way systematically distort the relation between the predictor and the outcome. The problem is such that any selection rule correlated with the response variable will attenuate estimates of an effect towards zero. For example, if we had only been able to collect data on those above an income threshold, we would have attenuated the relation between salary and years of experience. People who do not return your questionnaire may be different, in some important way, to the people who did. Strict adherence to sampling protocols, well trained interviewers, and intensive follow-up to a pilot can help minimize this problem. There are also analytical techniques that can adjust the estimates to take account of this bias.

It is worth stressing in concluding this section what regression modelling is trying to do. It aims at generality and generalizable results. We are not primarily interested in why this specific person did or did not get a salary rise, but what is happening to females as a group. We can only collect sample data but we wish to infer quite generally what is going on across the country. Once identified, this generality throws into stronger relief any unusual cases. We are continually searching for evidence that supports/ challenges alternative explanations and we are always looking for the empirical implications of our theory to subject it to rigorous evaluation.

Key concepts: multilevel modelling

Multilevel modelling is a recently developed procedure that is now seeing widespread use. It is given a separate section here because of its potential for handling a wide variety of research designs. Although it grows out of regression, the approach represents a considerable increase in sophistication. We begin with a specific problem, and then show how this relates to different forms of multilevel structures and associated research designs.

A multilevel problem

My university (in the UK) like others has been keen to widen its participation. It may be that if an able student goes to a poorly performing school, their A level score at entry is an underestimate of their potential.[3] Alternatively, if they go to a fee-paying, highly-resourced school, their score has been temporarily boosted, and this does not carry over to their degree performance. If we can identify such situations we may justifiably recruit students with a lower point score on the basis of greater potential. But what is the evidence for such a policy? We can set this up as a regression-type problem in which the response of the degree result of the student is related to three predictors: A level score, the school average performance and an indicator of school type.

But there is a difficulty because we are dealing with a problem with a multilevel structure. Student and school are not at the same level in that (many) students are nested in (fewer) schools. Moreover, students belonging to the same school are more likely to be alike than students from different schools. If this 'non-independence' is not taken into account, we have fewer observations than we think we have and we run the risk of finding significant relationships where none exist. Technically the effective degrees of freedom (see Barnes and Lewin, this volume) are lower than we think they are. But this is more than a technical problem, for there are several sources of variation that need to be taken into account for a proper analysis. Thus, there is the between-student variation, between-school variation and, extending the analysis, between-university, and between-discipline variation. In relation to the last there may be disciplines where the A level score is a very poor guide to degree performance, and should not be used as the main entry requirement. Thus the effect of an A level score on performance is not fixed but varies from context to context, where context is provided by the different levels in the structure. In comparison with standard regression models, multilevel models have a more complex random part.

Research designs and multilevel structures

It turns out that a very large array of research questions can be seen as combinations of just three types of multilevel structure that can now be routinely handled by computer-intensive procedures. The simplest structure is the hierarchy in which a lower-level unit nests in only one higher-level unit (Figure 27.3). The classic example (a) is the two-level model in which pupils are nested in schools. This can readily be extended so that pupils at level 1 can be nested within classes (level 2) within schools (level 3) within local education authorities (level 4). This strict hierarchy includes a number of research designs that you might

not initially conceive as multilevel problems. A panel design is shown in 27.3(b) where repeated measures (at level 1) are elicited for voting behaviour for individuals (level 2) who are nested in constituencies (level 3). In 27.3(c), there is a multivariate design in which three responses measuring health-related behaviour (at level 1) are nested within individuals (level 2) within places (level 3); the responses are seen as repeated measurements of individuals, and individuals are repeated measures of places. Other examples with such a hierarchical structure include: an experimental design in which the intervention is not made for individuals (at level 1) but for communities (level 2); and an observational design in which there is a two-stage sampling process, first areas (which then become level 2), and then respondents within them (at level 1).

The other types of multilevel structure are two different non-hierarchical structures. The classic example (Figure 27.4(a)) of a cross-classification is students (level 1) being nested within neighbourhoods and also schools (both at level 2). Not all the students in a neighbourhood go to a particular school and a school draws its pupils from more

(a) Pupils nested within schools

(b) Repeated measures of voting behaviour at the UK general election

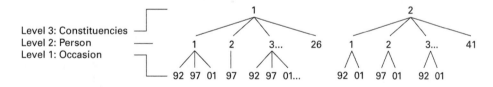

(c) Multivariate design for health-related behaviours

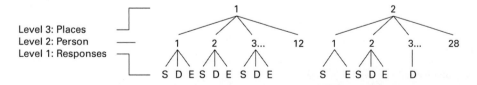

Where S is smoking. D is diet and E is exercise

Figure 27.3 Hierarchical structures as unit diagrams

than one neighbourhood. Thus schools and neighbourhoods are not nested but crossed. The final structure is the multiple membership in which a lower level unit 'belongs' to more than one higher level unit (Figure 27.4(b)). Thus a student (at level 1) may be nested within teachers (level 2) but each student may be taught by more than one teacher. We might include in the analysis a 'weight' to reflect the proportion of time each pupil spends with a teacher, so that student 2 spends 50 per cent of their time with teacher 1 and 50 per cent with teacher 2. Again a large number of problems can be cast within this framework, for example a dynamic household study in which individuals 'belong' to more than one household over time. A less obvious example is a spatial model in which individuals are affected by the neighbourhood in which they live and also by surrounding neighbourhoods – the weight in the multiple-membership structure being some function of distance from the home neighbourhood to the surrounding neighbourhoods. These models can be extended to look at pupil achievement in situations where there is 'competition' between the higher level units, such as schools with overlapping catchments, perhaps differentiated by school types.

An alternative way of conceiving and visualizing structures is as classifications. A 'classification diagram' is particularly helpful for complex problems. Figure 27.5 shows some examples of hierarchical and non-hierarchical structures using this type of diagram: (a) is a 3-level hierarchical problem; (b) is a cross-classified design; (c) is a multiple membership structure; and (d) shows a spatial structure. Boxes represent each classification with arrows representing nesting, single arrows for single membership and double arrows for multiple membership. Returning to the student performance example, we can see it as a combination of these three types of structure (Figure 27.5(e)). Students are nested within schools, and students are nested within disciplines within universities. Schools and universities are crossed because not all the students from a school go to one university. While the student/school relation might be conceived as a strict hierarchy (the last school attended) the university/discipline structure can be seen as a multiple membership one, in that students move between subjects and universities after starting courses.

Importance of structures

Is all this realism and complexity necessary? It is important to realize that a simple model tells you little about a more complex model, but a more complex model provides information about the simpler models embedded within it. Such complexity is not being sought for its own sake, but if the real world operates like this, then a simpler under-specified model can lead to inferential error.

There are in fact two key aspects of statistical complexity. We have so far concentrated on *dependencies arising from structures*. Once groupings are established, even if their establishment is random, they will

(a) Cross-classified structure

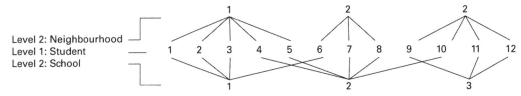

(b) Multiple membership with weights

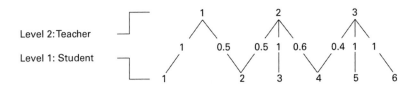

Figure 27.4 Non-hierarchical structures as unit diagrams

(a) 3-level hierarchical structure

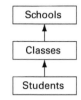

(b) Cross-classified structure

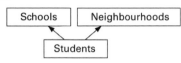

(c) Multiple membership structure

(d) Spatial structure

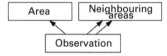

(e) Widening participation research problem as a classification diagram

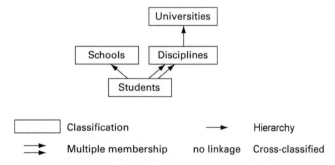

Figure 27.5   Structures as classification diagrams

tend to become differentiated as people are influenced by the group membership. To ignore this relationship risks overlooking the importance of group effects, and may also render invalid many of the traditional statistical analysis techniques used for studying relationships. An example is Aitkin et al.'s (1981) re-analysis of the 'teaching styles' study. The original analysis had suggested that children's academic achievement was higher if a 'formal' teacher using all-class activities taught them. When the structure of children into classes was taken into account, the significant differences disappeared and 'formally' taught children could not be shown to differ from the others. Some data, such as repeated measures and individuals within households, can be expected to be highly dependent, and it is essential this dependency is taken fully into account.

The second aspect is *complexity arising from the*

measurement process such as having 'missing' data or having multiple measuring instruments. In an observational study we can expect that there will be a different number of pupils measured at each school as shown in the unit diagram of Figure 27.3(a). In a panel study, each person may not respond every year, while in the multivariate design not all people respond to all questions that form the outcome variables. A defining case of the latter is the matrix sample design where all students are asked a core set of questions on, say, mathematics but different random subsets of pupils are asked detailed questions on either trigonometry, algebra, or set theory. Treating this design as a hierarchical structure allows the analysis of the full set of data in an overall model.

Prior to the development of the multilevel ap-

proach, the analyst was faced with mis-applying single-level models, either aggregating to the single level of the school and risking the ecological fallacy of transferring aggregate results to individuals, or working only at the pupil level and committing the atomistic fallacy of ignoring context. The standard model is mainly concerned with averages, and the general effect, where reality is often heterogeneous and complex. Thus females may not only perform better than males in terms of degree results, but they may also be more consistent (more homogenous) in their performance. It is this analysis of structures, contextual effects, and heterogeneity that is tackled by multilevel models.

Figure 27.6 portrays graphically some elements of the widening participation problem in terms of this

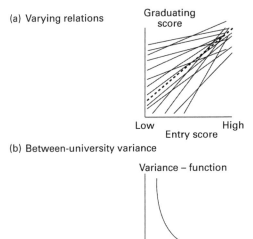

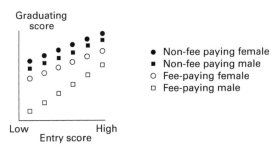

Figure 27.6   Achievement varying over context

heterogeneity and contextuality. In (a), the vertical axis is the final year points score of graduating university students, while the horizontal axis is the points score on entry. The lines shown are the different sampled universities. There is a noticeable 'fanning-in' so that highly qualified students on entry achieve the same excellence irrespective of where they study. But for those with a low-score at initial entry, it makes a great deal of difference where they study. This varying relation between pre-score and post-score is shown in an alternative form as a variance function in Figure 27.6(b) with the same horizontal axis, but the vertical axis is now between-university variance. As the pre-entry score increases, the between-university variation decreases. Finally Figure 27.6(c) shows what is known as a cross-level interaction; the axes are the same as (a), but the four lines represent fee-paying and non-fee paying schools for male and female students. The cross-level interaction is between a school-level variable (fee-paying or not) and two individual-level variables (gender and pre-entry score). The noticeable result in terms of our research question is that students who have attended fee-paying schools do less well across the entry range, but this is most marked for males, especially those with relatively low entry scores. If these results were confirmed, a university may be justified in taking students with lower entry grades from non-fee paying schools, particularly for males if it wished to pursue a policy of equal opportunity.

Implications for research design: multilevel modelling

A major difference between the design of multilevel and single-level studies is the requirements for sufficient power to detect effects. It is not the overall number of observations but the number at each level that is important. Advice depends on the amount of underlying variation in the 'system' being modelled, and what are the main aims of the analysis. Thus, in planning a school-effects study an absolute minimum would be 25 pupils in each of 25 schools, preferably 100 schools. Any less of the higher units will give poor estimates of the between-school differences, particularly if school effects are being examined on several dimensions, for example in relation to high and low ability pupils. At level 1 the number of pupils within a school is an important determinant of what can be reliably inferred about a particular school.

Little can be said about a particular school if only few students have been sampled. In contrast, if the higher-level unit is a household, there would be very few containing 25 individuals! But this is not a problem for we are unlikely to want to infer to a named household. Instead, we want to know about between-household variability in general, and that is determined by the number of households, and not by the number of people in a household. Finally if we only sample one person in each household we would be totally unable to separate household effects from individual effects. Hox (2002) provides an accessible discussion of statistical power in multilevel models.

Conclusion

Social reality is complex and structured. Recent developments in multilevel models provide a formal framework of analysis whose complexity of structure matches that of the system being studied. Modern software allows the estimation of very complex problems with multiple levels of nesting, and many units such as hundreds of thousands of students. Some examples of this approach are given in Jones (Chapter 29, this volume); the usefulness of multilevel models in reality in addressing the widening participation issue can be seen from a study entitled 'Schooling effects on Higher Education Achievement' available at http://www.hefce.ac.uk/pubs/hefce/, while Raudenbush and Bryk (2001) provide extensive discussion of modelling school effects.

Notes

1. Space precludes a discussion of construct validity (the extent to which variables faithfully measure concepts) and external validity (the extent to which we are able to generalize from our study).
2. To estimate correctly the confidence intervals for an effect requires that the residuals are independent: that is, knowing the value of one should tell you nothing about the value of another.
3. A levels are public examinations taken in the final year of secondary education, usually at 18 years; good scores are normally required to secure a university place.

Annotated bibliography

Regression modelling

Allison, P. D. (1999) *Multiple Regression: A Primer*. Thousand Oaks, CA: Pine Forge Press.
An excellent primer which introduces the underlying concepts with a minimum of algebra while covering a wide range of models and their motivation.

Angrist, J.D. and Pischke, J-F. (2009) *Mostly Harmless Econometrics: An Empiricist's Companion*. Princeton: Princeton University Press.
This spells out under what conditions quantitative results can have a causal interpretation.

Cook, R.D. and Weisberg, S. (1999) *Applied Regression Including Computing and Graphics*. New York: Wiley Interscience.
This stresses regression as conditional modelling and diagnostics, which are implemented in their freely available ARC software: http://www.stat.umn.edu/arc/

Gelman, A. and Hill, J. (2007) *Data Analysis Using Regression and Multilevel/Hierarchical Models*. Cambridge: Cambridge University Press.
Provides a comprehensive applied introduction that will take you a long way in appreciating the current practice and excitement of statistical modelling; highly recommended.

Retherford, R.D. and Choe, M.K. (1993) *Statistical Models for Causal Analysis*. New York: Wiley.
A very approachable account of generalized linear models in which the response can be categorical or timed to an event. The title is misleading, however, as there is little discussion of causality.

Tacq, J. (1997) *Multivariate Analysis Techniques in Social Science Research: From Problem to Analysis*. London: Sage.
Discusses quantitative analysis in the context of specific research problems.

Trochim, W. (2000) *The Research Methods Knowledge Base*. Cincinnati: Atomic Dog Publishing. Available at: http://www.socialresearchmethods.net/kb/
Available in printed form or as a website, this 'knowledgebase' provides lots of useful advice on minimizing threats to validity in observational and experimental studies.

Venables, W. and Ripley, B. (2002) *Modern Applied Statistics*. New York: SpringerVerlag.
One of the most comprehensive and up-to-date accounts of all sorts of developments in regression-like modelling with substantial online resources: http://www.stats.ox.ac.uk/pub/MASS4/. It can be used in the 'free' Open-source R software environment: http://www.r-project.org/

Wright, D.B. and London, K. (2009) *Modern Regression Techniques Using R*. London: Sage.
A very broad-ranging account achieved with brevity, and provides computer code.

Multilevel modelling

Hox, J. (2002) *Multilevel Analysis: Techniques and Applications*. New Jersey: Lawrence Erlbaum Associates.
Provides a well-written and approachable introduction to multilevel modelling.

Goldstein, H. (2003) *Multilevel Statistical Models*, 3rd edn. London: Arnold.
This is the definitive (but rather demanding) text. The author's team maintains a comprehensive website at: http://www.cmm.bristol.ac.uk/ including the Lemma online course which is a thorough and well-paced introduction.

Raudenbush, S.W. and Bryk, A.S. (2001) *Hierarchical Linear Models*, 2nd edn. Newbury Park: Sage.
Written by two American pioneers of multilevel modelling, this provides a detailed treatment that is linked to their HLM software.

Singer, Judith D. and Willets, J.B. (2003) *Applied Longitudinal Data Analysis: Modelling Change and Event Occurrence*. Oxford: Oxford University Press.
A very gradual account that shows in detail how the multilevel model can be used in the analysis of repeated measures; their worked examples in a number of different software packages (and much else) are provided at: http://www.ats.ucla.edu/stat/examples/

Further references

Aitkin, M., Anderson, D. and Hinde, J. (1981) 'Statistical modelling of data on teaching styles (with discussion)', *Journal of the Royal Statistical Society, Series A*, 144: 148–61.

Hendry, D.F. (2000) *Econometrics: Alchemy or Science*. Milton Keynes: Open University Press.

Jones, K. and Moon, G. (1987) *Health, Disease and Society*. London: Routledge.

Lucas, R.E. (1976) 'Econometric policy evaluation: A critique', in K. Brunner and A. H. Meltzer (eds) *The Phillips Curve and Labor Markets*. Carnegie-Rochester Conference Series on Public Policy, 1: 19–46.

McCullagh, P. and Nelder, J.A. (1989) *Generalized Linear Models*, 2nd edn. London: Chapman & Hall.

Miles, J. and Shevlin, M. (2001) *Applied Regression and Correlation Analysis in Psychology: A Student's Guide*. London: Sage.

QUANTITATIVE METHODS IN ACTION

Introduction

Part VII consists of a chapter on Mixed Methodologies and four Stories from the Field, providing examples of some of the quantitative tools and techniques presented in Part VI. The application of quantitative methods across the social sciences highlights a number of issues, demonstrating that the shift from theory to practice is not a smooth path.

To emphasize that quantitative and qualitative methods in the social sciences represent a continuum rather than binary opposites, Part VII begins with Greene et al.'s chapter on mixed methods in social research. The integration of contextual understanding forms one of the multiple perspectives adopted and serves to aid triangulation. The chapter argues for the importance of 'mixing' (linking) theoretical understandings through discussion, reflexion and critique, rather than merely using quantitative and qualitative methods alongside one another without any underpinning rationale.

Some authors in Part VII raise issues in relation to sampling, which is a central concern for any quantitative researcher. Pelgrum describes the difficulties inherent in international comparisons in defining what is meant by the population to be studied. In addition, he discusses the impact of sampling strategy and non-response in relation to sample size and representativeness. Ainley notes the difficulties of sampling in a school context when attrition (students moving to another school for example or being absent during data collection) can be high. Greene et al. stress that sampling strategies in mixed methods (which can be separate or integrated) need to take account of the study design.

Addressing the issue of validity, several authors discuss the need to be clear about what is being measured. Pelgrum looks at problems of comparability in the design of questionnaires to be used internationally when language translation effects, curriculum differences, and cultural interpretations all have potential to introduce bias. Doig describes how he used a model which 'preserved and reported all responses', in order to measure increasing levels of sophistication in students' understanding of science concepts when analysing data in which there was 'no single, correct response'.

One common theme throughout these chapters is the need to take account of context. Jones challenges the need for quantitative researchers to seek universal truths and instead uses multilevel modelling to tease out contextual differences in an analysis of voting behaviour in the UK. He argues that acknowledging context within modelling allows the quantitative researcher to build bridges with the qualitative researcher. Pelgrum, as has been noted earlier, shows how contextual issues such as national and regional differences in curriculum specification and delivery must be taken into account when designing international comparative assessments. Ainley describes how multilevel modelling was again used to take account of contextual factors, this time in educational research in Australia. This story, whilst focusing on quantitative methods, refers to the mixed method approach he adopted in order to be able to describe classroom practice and interpret the quantitative findings in relation to context.

The contributions in Part VII illustrate that boundaries between quantitative and qualitative approaches are blurring in contemporary social science research. The four Stories from the Field, commissioned as examples of quantitative research in practice, illustrate this, signalled by words such as: 'rich description', 'context', 'case study' and 'interpret'. The opening chapter on mixed methodologies highlights the benefits of drawing together multiple perspectives, not only the underlying theories informing research designs, but also multiple approaches to both data collection and analysis. This enables the social scientist to develop a more comprehensive understanding of human phenomena in our world, through multiple lenses.

Combining Qualitative and Quantitative Methods in Social Inquiry

Jennifer C. Greene, Department of Educational Psychology,
University of Illinois at Urbana-Champaign, IL, USA

Holly Kreider, Ed.D., Raising A Reader, Mountain View, USA

Ellen Mayer, Independent Consultant, Cambridge, MA, USA

Summary

- Representing human phenomena with numbers and words
- Mixed data gathering
- Mixing at the philosophical level – e.g. different stances to context
- Linking/connecting the different methods, data sets and results
- Key theorists and writers
  - John Creswell
  - Jennifer Greene
  - Abbas Tashakkori
  - Charles Teddlie

Key concepts

Jennifer C. Greene

Mixed methods approaches to social inquiry[1] involve the planned use of two or more different kinds of data gathering and analysis techniques – and more rarely different kinds of inquiry designs and different philosophical assumptions – within the same study or project. Using *methods* that gather and represent human phenomena with numbers (such as standardized questionnaires and structured observation protocols), along with methods that gather and represent human phenomena with words (such as open-ended interviews and unstructured observations) are classic instances of mixing data gathering techniques. Examples of mixing overall inquiry *designs* include the combined use of an experiment and an ethnography, or a survey and a case study. Examples of mixes at the *philosophical level* include the adoption of stances that honour both the generality and the particularity of social phenomena. Across these different levels of mixing, there is general agreement that what is importantly mixed in mixed methods inquiry extends beyond the numerical/quantitative or narrative/qualitative character of the different data sets gathered to comprise other dimensions of method. These dimensions include the degree of instrument standardization and structure (deciding in advance what specific questions to ask of all respondents or allowing different questions to emerge during interviews with different people), and the viewing of context as a source of unwanted variation or as partly constitutive of the phenomena being studied.

Also across multiple design variations, a defining characteristic of mixed methods inquiry is the intentional effort on the part of the inquirer to link or connect the different methods, data sets, and results. This connection can be instrumental, analytic or inferential. But a study without a connection is not a mixed methods study, agree most experts.

Why mix methods?

Mixed methods approaches to social inquiry are uniquely able to generate *better understanding* in many contexts than studies bounded by a single methodological tradition (Weisner, 2005). Various forms of better understanding are represented by five distinct methodological purposes for mixing: (a) *triangulation* seeks convergence, corroboration, or correspondence of results from different methods, thereby enhancing validity and credibility of inferences; (b) *complementarity* uses the different lenses of different methods to generate elaborated and comprehensive understandings of complex social phenomena; (c) for *development*, the results of one method are used to inform the instrumentation, sampling, or implementation of another method; (d) *initiation* invokes paradox through divergent results from different methods, and the consequent generation of fresh insights from analytic engagement with this dissonance; and (e) *expansion* extends the conceptual scope and reach of the study by extending methods choices to more than one methodological tradition, thus enabling selection of the most appropriate method for each construct within an expanded set of study foci.

Because practice is characteristically quite a bit more complex than theory, many mixed methods studies incorporate several of these purposes within a given set of methods. As an example, let's probe mixed methods design possibilities in a study of the barriers, facilitators, and meanings of 'inclusion' in preschool settings, where inclusion refers to the grouping of children with and without disabilities in the same classroom. In this study, structured classroom observations could be paired with a qualitative analysis of programme documents, aiming for convergence of information about programme structure, routines, and instructional philosophy (triangulation). These same structured observations could also be paired with open-ended teacher interviews, seeking a more comprehensive and complete understanding of the character of the interactions among children in the classroom setting (complementarity). And the

teacher interviews could be, in turn, paired with a structured parent questionnaire, in an effort to surface multiple and diverse perspectives on the key values of and rationales for inclusion at the preschool level (initiation). The parent questionnaire could itself be derived from analysis of observational data gathered at parent meetings and other gatherings (development). And finally, the conceptual reach of a postpositivist quantitative study could be extended with the addition of open-ended interviews with groups of children on their preschool experiences (expansion). (This example was adapted from Li et al., 2000.)

The roots of the mixed methods conversation

The early roots of mixed methods social inquiry are found partly in the construct of triangulation, which involves the use of multiple methods – each representing a different perspective or lens – to assess a given phenomenon, in order to enhance confidence in the validity of the findings. If, for example, data from a self-report instrument and data from an external observation converge, the overall results are more likely to be valid, credible, and warranted. Interestingly, triangulation has an honoured history in multiple methodological traditions (Denzin, 1978; Webb et al., 1966).

Other roots of the contemporary interest in mixing methods are embedded in the infamous qualitative–quantitative debate that raged in the social sciences during the latter quarter of the twentieth century. This debate was most often about method, but also invoked deeper questions of what philosophical paradigms, or what sets of assumptions about the social world and our knowledge of it, are appropriate for the social sciences. Proponents of quantitative methodologies advanced philosophies of realism and objectivity and privileged causal explanation and universal truth, while advocates of qualitative methodologies underscored the interpretive, value-laden, contextual and contingent nature of social knowledge. With rapprochement came a general acceptance of the legitimacy of multiple philosophical traditions for social inquiry and an opening for inquirers to eschew allegiance to one in favour of taking advantage of social science's full methodological repertoire.

Beyond method, what else is mixed in mixed methods inquiry?

Yet debate persists about the sensibility and defensibility of mixing at the philosophical level. That is, beyond method and design, what else is being mixed when we mix methods in social inquiry? The legacies of the qualitative–quantitative debate demonstrated that while social scientific methods are not tightly bound to a given philosophical tradition, methods are indeed framed by the philosophical world-view of the inquirer. Within this world-view, key assumptions include views of the social world (e.g. realism or constructivism), perspectives regarding the nature of social knowledge (e.g. objective or value-laden), and positions regarding what is most important to know (e.g. generalizable causal relationships or contextual meaningfulness). The controversial issues here are thus, when social inquirers mix methods are they also mixing philosophical assumptions, and should they?

There are currently three primary stances on this issue. First, proponents of *a-paradigmatic stances* argue that philosophical assumptions are useful conceptual tools but they should not drive practice decisions. Rather, practical decisions about design and method should be steered by the demands of the context or by the requirements of the substantive constructs being studied. Michael Patton (2002) has long been an eloquent spokesperson for this practical stance. Second, proponents of a *dialectic stance* argue in favour of intentionally mixing philosophical assumptions while mixing methods, because philosophical assumptions should and do meaningfully influence practice decisions, implicitly if not on purpose. And because all sets of philosophical assumptions are partial and limited, more comprehensive and insightful mixes are attained via the intentional inclusion of more than one philosophical framework. In this dialectic perspective, possible tensions and dissonance from different sets of assumptions are especially welcomed as generative of new insights and fresh perspectives. The work of Jennifer Greene and Valerie Caracelli (1997) well illustrates this dialectic stance. Third, proponents of *pragmatic stances* advance an alternative, inclusive philosophical framework within which multiple assumptions and diverse methods can comfortably reside. In this third stance, like the first, differences in philosophical traditions are de-emphasized and thereby not considered either particularly beneficial or problematic in mixed methods work. Various forms of contemporary realism and American pragmatism are the most popular alternative frameworks advanced within this pragmatic perspective. The work of Abbas Tashakkori and Charles Teddlie (2003; Teddlie and Tashakkori, 2009) well exemplifies a practical, pragmatic alternative paradigm stance.

Mixed methods practice

The practicalities of mixed methods inquiry are still being developed. An ever-expanding repertoire of creative mixed methods studies in various fields is helping to catalyse the development of frameworks and guidelines for mixed methods practice. An iterative and respectful relationship between theory and practice remains a hallmark of this inquiry genre.

With respect to *designing* a mixed methods study, several key dimensions of importance have been consistently identified. One is whether the methods and data sets are integrated throughout the study or rather kept separate until the end, at which point conclusions and inferences are compared or connected. In an integrated design, data from various methods can inform the design of a particular instrument or the sampling plan for another, and data of different types can be iteratively merged or blended in analysis, yielding a unique set of results and inferences in which the different data forms are possibly no longer distinct. In a component design, data retain their original form and character throughout, and conclusions and inferences seek harmony and connection rather than full blending or integration. Clearly, analysis and quality considerations are quite different in integrated versus component designs. A second important design dimension is whether the different methods involved are considered of relatively equal importance and weight or one methodology is dominant and the other less dominant. Designs with one dominant methodology tend to adhere to the traditional guidelines of that methodology, while the more practically challenging mixed methods designs are those where the different methods have relative parity in importance. Third, different methods can be implemented concurrently or sequentially, either for important conceptual reasons or for reasons of practicality.

Ideas about mixed methods *data analysis* are currently clustered by analytic phase — descriptive, relational, inferential — and will be selectively illustrated below. These ideas pertain primarily to integrated designs, because in component designs, data would be analysed according to the conventions of that data type and then 'mixed' at the point of inference.

One integrative analytic strategy (relevant to all phases of data analysis) is to transform one data set into the form of the other (words into numbers or numbers into words) for purposes of joint analysis.

Incorporating quantified observational data (originally in qualitative form) in an analysis of key dimensions of a school's educational climate can enrich the subsequent results. Data importation is a mid-stream analytic strategy, in which the interim results of the analysis of one data set are infused into the analysis of another data set to see what could be learned. Factor analytic results from a questionnaire analysis could be used to sort interview data or themes to explore additional meanings thus revealed. In this analytic strategy, the 'structure of meaning' generated in one analysis is imposed on the other data set in an open, meaning-seeking manner. An increasingly popular inferential analysis strategy in mixed methods inquiry is the use of a data matrix or display, an analytic idea anchored in the fine analytic thinking of Matthew Miles and Michael Huberman (1994). In this strategy, multiple forms of data are arrayed in the same analytic space, using some kind of order or organization. An analysis of the matrix or display can reveal substantive cross-method patterns of importance and can thus catalyse integrative insights. (See Lee and Greene, 2007, for one example of a generative analytic matrix.)

Other challenges of mixed methods practice remain in development. Criteria and procedures for judging the *quality of mixed methods social inquiry* remain problematic, particularly when the studies include stances from different methodological traditions, different methods of relatively equal importance, and efforts at integration. Setting aside traditional criteria in favour of constructs and criteria of broader relevance is a promising approach, as illustrated by Teddlie and Taskakkori's (2003) notions of 'inference quality'. And finally, some inquirers are experimenting with using *mixed representational forms to report* the results from mixed methods social inquiry. In addition to standard textual and tabular presentations, stories, poems, cartoons, and performances can all help to capture and re-present the broader, deeper and more nuanced results that are themselves the 'better understandings' of mixed methods inquiry.

Implications for inquiry design

The whole point of mixed methods social inquiry is to incorporate, intentionally and respectfully, multiple design standpoints and positions in a single study or programme of research. Thus, there is not a uniform profile of design stances that characterizes mixed

methods social inquiry. Instead, the design portrait of a mixed methods study reflects the assumptive stances of the inquirer or inquiry team *and* the character of the mix to be enacted in that study. If the inquirer is mixing at the level of method, and possibly methodology/design, but is not mixing underlying assumptions or world-views, then the character of the design would adhere to the particular mental model of the inquirer. The many other chapters of this volume profile the inquiry standpoints of different inquiry traditions and mental models. If, however, the inquirer is intentionally mixing paradigmatic assumptions and stances, then the nature of the inquiry design itself intentionally reflects such a mix.

Let's envision two studies of the character, context, and consequences of youth gang violence in selected urban areas of the northeast of the US. In the first, the inquirer adopts a mixed methods design *within* an overall constructivist paradigm. Methods include participant observation, unstructured interviews, and analysis of various data records from the police, the census, and the schools. The design stances in this study conform to the design stances of constructivist inquiry in general, even though a mix of methods is being used. To illustrate, the key questions in this study probe gang members' constructions of meaning of their actions in particular contexts. Sampling is purposeful, the inquirer co-constructs meanings with the participants, analysis is inductive, and results are presented as narratives.

In the second study, the inquirer intentionally mixes not just methods but also the world-views and assumptions of constructivism and postpositivism. The key questions in this study probe gang members' constructions of the meaning of their actions in particular contexts, in conjunction with external assessments of the nature and consequences of gang violence for both gang members and other victims. These questions probe contextualized meanings of violence among the members of gangs, alongside assessments of which socio-psychological and economic factors best account for or explain high incidences of gang violence. Sampling in this study is both representative and purposeful, the inquirer seeks meaning in both external and constructed meanings, and the analysis is both statistical and thematic. The design stances in this study, that is, intentionally and purposefully respect the varied inquiry practices of multiple traditions.

So, in a mixed methods study that is mixing on all levels – method, design, and paradigm – the design stances should reflect a respectful juxtaposition of design parameters from multiple inquiry traditions. The acknowledged tension created by such juxtaposition well reflects the generative potential of mixed methods social inquiry (Greene, 2007).

Stories from the field

Holly Kreider and Ellen Mayer

This is a story of a mixed methods analysis journey into a large and complex mixed data set. The story highlights conceptual and practical challenges of integrative mixed methods analysis and thereby adds case study data to our emerging understanding of how to productively work simultaneously with different data sources and forms.

The first few waves of data had been collected in the School Transition Study (STS),[2] when we (Kreider and Mayer) together with other researchers[3] at the Harvard Family Research Project (HFRP) began an early mixed methods analysis examining family educational involvement. The STS was a complex mixed methods investigation following approximately 400 ethnically diverse children in low-income families from kindergarten through fifth grade across three different sites in the US. The study's purpose was to understand school, community and familial influences on successful pathways through middle childhood. Data collection included both a range of quantitative instruments and assessments, such as surveys of the children's primary caregivers and teachers, and in-depth qualitative case studies of a representative sample of 23 children over their first and second grade years. Our HFRP contingent had just completed overseeing collection of the case study data. We added a quantitative researcher to our qualitative team, and embarked on our first mixed methods analysis.

Where to begin?

In hopes of broadening our understanding of the nature of educational involvement of low-income families, we first listened to our rich qualitative case study data, as qualitative data are often well suited to exploratory analysis and generative of new understanding. We deliberately followed unexpected and surprising themes as they emerged.

We don't even have a [Parent-Teacher Association] at this school ... I have often wondered if PTA will become a thing of the past, because parents are too busy just trying to make ends meet and get dinner on the table, and occasionally wash a pair of socks. (Second grade teacher)

I think every parent should have time for their kids, no matter how much work you have? ... When I want to talk to [my child's teacher], I just fax him something to school, from my job, or I call him. (Mother of a second grader)

Our case study interview protocols focused primarily on family educational involvement issues, without directly exploring parental work and its relationship to family involvement. Yet no matter whom we asked – teacher, parent or principal – and no matter what aspect of involvement we asked about – the level of parent involvement at school, parent–teacher communication, or what could help children succeed – we heard reference to parents' work in the qualitative data.

The surprising salience of this theme seemed to warrant further analysis, but we carefully thought through the mixed methods potential of this line of analysis before deciding to pursue it. First we narrowed our consideration to *maternal* work, largely because the vast majority of STS primary caregiver respondents were mothers. We then reviewed prior research, identifying only a few studies on the connections between maternal work and family involvement in education, and concluding that this limited understanding could be especially strengthened through a mixed methods analysis. Specifically, we could move beyond the existing research emphasis on negative associations between work and involvement, especially for low-income mothers, to examine in addition parental strengths and strategies. Most existing literature also lacked a strong empirical base, relying on theory, advice, anecdotal information, or singular methods, whereas our data set offered the potential of an integrated mixed methods analysis. With this reassurance, we felt ready to follow this discovery, in much the same way as other researchers have been pulled in unexpected directions (Rabinow, 1977).

To systematically explore the connection between work and family involvement, we deliberately crafted guiding research questions that required reaching into both quantitative and qualitative data sources: How does maternal work influence low-income mothers' involvement in children's education? What strategies enable low-income working mothers to become and/ or stay involved in their children's education?

How to work together?

We chose a team approach to analysis for practical reasons. Specifically, we had far too many data for one person to handle, a team structure was already in place from data collection, and the study was situated within a larger organizational culture of team-based work.

We put several structures and processes in place to create a space for qualitative and quantitative researchers to talk together. We set up clear team procedures that would support the necessary intentional reflexivity. These included regular team meetings and two sets of written logs, one to track substantive findings and another to record thoughts about our mixed methods process. Reading through the shared logs kept team members in daily touch with the work of others, and later helped us gain a more coherent understanding of the analysis journey we had taken.

Norms of extensive and respectful dialogue also were crucial to supporting our ability to work together. A stance of openness and discovery is one inherent to mixed methods, which actively seeks multiple routes to enhanced understanding (Cook, 1985). This openness to other views and perspectives includes not just rival explanatory hypotheses, but more profoundly rival ways of thinking and valuing. As qualitative and quantitative researchers we approached our work together with openness and curiosity, not only about the others' methodology and findings, but also about the others' different paradigmatic assumptions and traditions. The interdisciplinary nature of our team, which brought together the disparate disciplines of psychology, education and sociology, also made open dialogue critical.

In addition, we developed structured analytic exercises to start this new mixed methods process and generate hypotheses – exercises that honoured our different ways of thinking about and analysing empirical data. We each explored the core construct of work by scouring a particular quantitative or qualitative data source and generating a list of knowledge claims about work. Then we reconvened to discuss these claims, as well as our understandings of the strengths and weaknesses of each particular data source. This led us – as a team – to understand work as linked to a variety of supports for mothers' work and family lives. Among the familial supports we identified,

parent initiative emerged as important for mothers' strategies in balancing work and family involvement.

How to plan?

First, the team generated a rough mixed methods analysis plan. As neophytes in this enterprise, we diligently read the literature about mixed methods analysis and settled on the notion of iterative or 'cross-over tracks' analysis to guide our initial analytic planning and analysis (Li et al., 2000). In this approach, an intentional and iterative interplay exists between the separate analyses of qualitative and quantitative data sets, such that mixing and integration happen throughout the analysis.

However, we soon found ourselves in uncodified territory with our integrative mixed methods analysis – the cross-over tracks approach provided only minimal guidance. In reality, our work process was fluid and intuitive. For example, the quantitative analyst brought her factor analysis results to qualitative team members for interpretation and validation. Qualitative analysts drew on their long-time internalized stores of case study knowledge to see if the factors passed the grounded 'this makes sense' test, and whether revised factor analyses were appropriate or necessary.

These and other discussions often began by pitting objective reality and contextual nuance, numbers and words, against one another. Over time and through discussion, we found ourselves relaxing our different paradigm assumptions. For example, we took a primary caregiver survey that had always been viewed as a 'quantitative' instrument and approached it anew as a source of qualitative data. We read the survey transcripts holistically, and discovered, for example, a rich new layer of narrative in the spontaneous talk of primary caregivers, talk which occurred as the interviewer moved from one survey question to another.

How to interpret our contradictory findings?

Interesting mixed methods analyses are likely to be replete with both convergent and divergent results. In our work, we took care to be open to both, privileging neither. Our first descriptive quantitative analyses showed parental work as a perceived *barrier* to family involvement. When asked 'What barriers to parent involvement do you see among your parents?' 89.5 per cent of the kindergarten teachers surveyed named parents' work schedules as somewhat of a problem or a serious problem. Yet early case study analyses suggested that work perhaps had some *positive* connections with involvement – witness the mother who contacted her child's teacher by fax from her workplace.

We turned more systematically to our case study data, developing case portraits of the involvement patterns of the 20 mothers who worked, and conducting a cross-case analysis. We discovered that work could present opportunities and resources for involvement. Four strategies emerged that these working mothers used to become or to stay involved in their children's learning. First, they described *promoting a kith and kin network*, overseeing a complex support system of helpers, including family members and co-workers, to support their children's learning. Second, they *used their workplace as a home base* for a variety of involvement activities, such as taking their children to work for stop-gap child care or enrichment purposes. Third, they intentionally *garnered other resources from work*, such as summer camp fees, educational advice from fellow workers or clients, or homework help for their children. Finally, they described *conquering time and space challenges* by negotiating transitions and adaptively finding time to be involved in their children's education, such as by selecting jobs near or even in their children's school.

These divergent findings between quantitative and qualitative data sources led us to a more expansive and complete understanding of educational involvement among low-income working mothers. We also stayed open to divergences in later iterations of quantitative analyses. For example, quantitative findings continued to show maternal work as a barrier to family involvement, but also began to suggest its opportunities. Univariate analyses of maternal reports showed that full-time working mothers reported attending significantly fewer events at their children's schools (such as parent–teacher conferences and open houses) than those who were not employed or employed part time ($\chi^2 = 19.02$, df = 9, $N = 216$, $p < .05$). However, part-time working mothers reported the most involvement of any group, suggesting that the time demands of full-time work may interfere with involvement in school activities, but that work in general may provide opportunities for selective involvement. In this way, our quantitative findings converged with our qualitative findings to strengthen our interpretation of maternal work as a potential resource for educational involvement.

By mixing methods we had arrived at a unique, complex and nuanced understanding of low-income mothers' employment as both obstacle and opportunity for their family educational involvement. We had also arrived at an appreciation of mixing methods as a challenging but imminently worthwhile approach.[4]

Notes

1. The term 'social inquiry' is used in this chapter to refer to both research and evaluation.
2. STS, directed by Deborah Stipek and Heather Weiss, was supported by a grant from the John D. and Catherine T. MacArthur Foundation, with supplementary funds from the W.T. Grant Foundation. We thank STS ethnographers for data collection. See www.hfrp.org for a fuller description.
3. Other researchers were Heather Weiss, Margaret Vaughan, Rebecca Hencke and Kristina Pinto. We thank Jennifer Greene, STS steering committee member, for inspiration as we began this analysis.
4. More detailed accounts are available of the substantive findings (Weiss et al., 2003) and mixed methods analytic process (Weiss et al., 2005).

Annotated bibliography

Cook, T.D. (1985) 'Postpositivist critical multiplism', in R.L. Shotland and M.M. Mark (eds) *Social Science and Social Policy.* Thousand Oaks, CA: Sage. pp. 21–62.
This important statement on the fallibility of postpositivist (traditionally quantitative) approaches to applied social science anchors contemporary thinking about using multiple methods in order to enhance validity.

Creswell, J.W. and Plano Clark, V.L. (2006) *Designing and Conducting Mixed Methods Research.* Thousand Oaks, CA: Sage.
Creswell has been a steady contributor to the mixed methods conversation over the past decade. His work focuses on typologies of mixed methods design and the practicalities of implementation.

Greene, J.C. (2007) *Mixed Methods in Social Inquiry.* San Francisco: Jossey-Bass.
This book, by one of the 'founders' of mixed methods thinking, offers a multilevel framework for conceptualizing, designing and conducting defensible mixed methods empirical work. Attention to the assumptions that social inquirers

inevitably bring to their work is a signature characteristic of Greene's mixed methods way of thinking.

Greene, J.C. and Caracelli, V.J. (eds) (1997) *Advances in Mixed-Method Evaluation: The Challenges and Benefits of Integrating Diverse Paradigms: New Directions for Evaluation no. 74.* San Francisco: Jossey-Bass.

This volume engages the paradigm issue in mixed methods evaluation, offers descriptions and rationales for several different stances, and includes exemplary mixed methods evaluations illustrative of each stance.

Li, S., Marquart, J.M. and Zercher, C. (2000) 'Conceptual issues and analytic strategies in mixed-method studies of preschool inclusion', *Journal of Early Intervention, 23*: 116–32.

This study is already a classic mixed methods case example, noted especially for its creativity and reflexivity in both design and analysis.

Plano Clark, V.L. and Creswell, J.W. (eds) (2008). *The Mixed Methods Reader.* Thousand Oaks, CA: Sage.

The editors of this volume have assembled many of the critically influential early works on mixed methods conceptual thinking, along with both classic and more contemporary empirical case examples.

Tashakkori, A. and Teddlie, C. (eds) (2003) *Handbook of Mixed Methods in Social and Behavioral Research.* Thousand Oaks, CA: Sage.

This comprehensive volume incorporates multiple perspectives on mixing methods in each of several sections devoted to frameworks and rationales, purposes and designs, and analysis strategies. Chapters on mixing methods in various domains of social science are also featured.

Tashakkori, A. and Teddlie, C. (eds) (2010). *The SAGE Handbook of Mixed Methods in Social and Behavioral Research*, 2nd edn. Thousand Oaks, CA: Sage.

This Handbook will constitute a state-of-the-art contribution to the exponentially expanding literature on mixed methods social inquiry. Given the rapid development in the field, it will differ considerably from the first edition.

Teddlie, C. and Tashakkori, A. (2009) *Foundations of Mixed Methods Research: Integrating Quantitative and Qualitative Approaches in the Social and Behavioral Sciences.* Thousand Oaks, CA: Sage.

This book extends the authors' previous thoughtful contributions to broad frameworks for mixed methods inquiry. It offers a strong pragmatic statement about mixed methods work, along with detailed practical guidance about the design and implementation of mixed methods studies.

Weisner, T.S. (ed.) (2005) *Discovering Successful Pathways in Children's Development: New Methods in the Study of Childhood and Family Life.* Chicago: University of Chicago Press.

This exciting volume offers papers from a 2001 working conference on mixing methods in the study of children's development – in family, school, and community locales. The key question addressed was, what did a mixed methods approach uniquely contribute to our understanding about children's developmental pathways?

Further references

Denzin, N.K. (1978) *The Research Act: An Introduction to Sociological Methods.* New York: McGraw Hill.

Lee, Y-J. and Greene, J.C. (2007) 'The predictive validity of an ESL placement test: A mixed methods approach', *Journal of Mixed Methods Research*, 1(4): 366–89.

Miles, M.B. and Huberman, A.M. (1994) *Qualitative Data Analysis: An Expanded Sourcebook*, 2nd edn. Thousand Oaks, CA: Sage.

Rabinow, P. (1977) *Reflections on Fieldwork in Morocco.* Berkeley, CA: University of California Press.

Patton, M.Q. (2002) *Qualitative Research and Evaluation Methods*, 3rd edn. Thousand Oaks, CA: Sage.

Teddlie, C. and Tashakkori, A. (2003) 'Major issues and controversies in the use of mixed methods in the social and behavioral sciences', in A. Tashakkori and C. Teddlie (eds), *Handbook of Mixed Methods in Social and Behavioral Research.* Thousand Oaks, CA: Sage. pp. 3–50.

Webb, E.J., Campbell, D.T., Schwartz, R.D. and Sechrest, L. (1966) *Unobtrusive Measures: Nonreactive Research in the Social Sciences.* Chicago: Rand McNally.

Weiss, H., Mayer, E., Kreider, H., Vaughan, P., Dearing, E., Hencke, R., and Pinto, K. (2003) 'Making it work: Low-income working mothers' involvement in their children's education', *American Educational Research Journal*, 40: 879–901.

Weiss, H.B., Kreider, H., Mayer, E., Hencke, R. and Vaughan, M. (2005) 'Working it out: The chronicle of a mixed-method analysis', in T.S. Weisner (ed.) *Discovering Successful Pathways in Children's Development: Mixed Methods in the Study of Childhood and Family Life.* Chicago: University of Chicago Press. pp. 47–64.

Random Reflections on Modelling, Geography and Voting

Kelvyn Jones, School of Geographical Sciences, University of Bristol, UK

Stories from the field

Introduction

This short piece is about applying quantitative modelling to a dispute about the importance of area effects in understanding voting behaviour in the UK. In particular it uses multilevel modelling to assess the nature and extent of place effects and thereby challenges the familiar critique of quantification that in pursuing generality, it ignores specificity. In that context, I try to bring two general standpoints to my work:

- A realist philosophy (Sayer, 2000) which encourages both intensive (qualitative) and extensive (quantitative) empirical work, but rejects the positivist position that causation equates with regularity, and replaces this with

  outcomes = mechanism + context

  so that there are no 'universal' laws in social science that are independent of the context in which they are embedded.
- The importance of place; as a geographer I see local specificity as integral to explanations of general social processes. I see people and places existing in a recursive relationship. People create structures in the context of places; those structures then condition the making of people. This is a large claim for it means that geography matters so much that human processes cannot be under-

stood without being informed by a geographical imagination.

These standpoints influence how I undertake statistical modelling in a way, I hope, that is far removed from the anti-positivist caricature that is often given to quantification. In standard regression models, local specificity is often regarded as deviation which must be minimized during calibration. Attention is solely focused on the underlying generality and not the departures from this generality. Standard models deny geography and history in fitting an 'average' model to all places and times. However, the multilevel model (Jones, Chapter 27, this volume), in developing the random part of the model, allows relations to vary from place to place. These two standpoints and approach to modelling informed some research with colleagues that contributed to a key debate on voting behaviour (Jones et al, 1992).[1]

Voting behaviour in context?

The crux of the argument is that geography does not make a *contextual* difference, but it is merely *compositional*. Thus, the strong support for Labour in South Wales is simply due to a high percentage of that population being of a low social class who, irrespective of place, generally vote Labour. These arguments have been strongly expressed:

> contextual variables have little or nothing to add (Tate, 1974: 1662)

where a voter lives is of very little relevance (Rose and McAllister, 1990: 124)

Other researchers, however, contend that context does matter. According to a social-contact model, Conservatives get their core support from the controllers of society (employers and managers), and while few individuals belong to this 'core' class, voting is related to the local contacts with them. Others have argued that core class is an important element of the local milieu in which people are politically socialized. In a society that is spatially segregated by class, place is a continually self-reinforcing context for political socialization (Johnston, 1986).

Evaluating alternatives

To enter such debates, we need:

- *To be able to set out the empirical implications of alternative theories:* If geography is contextually unimportant, as we model composition by including individual characteristics of voters, any place effects should attenuate. If geography is important, people of similar characteristics should vote differently in different places.
- *To set out a plausible model that is a fair test of the alternative theories:* Much of the literature is rendered problematic by including attitudinal variables measuring voters' political values as an explanation of actual voting, and then claiming that there is no evidence for contextual effects. If the dependent variable is voting Conservative or not, surely it makes little sense to include right-wing ideology as an explanatory attitudinal variable and then to conclude that there is no 'residual' geography.[2] Consequently the model should include a range of individual characteristics for socio-economic and demographic position in society, but not attitudinal variables per se.
- *Good reliable empirical evidence from a range of different contexts.* Data are required on voting choice, individual and place characteristics. This is provided by the British Electoral Study, which is undertaken contemporaneously with the General Election. The survey has a multi-stage design with individuals at level 1 nested in constituencies at level 2.
- *An appropriate modelling framework:* much of the research in this area has been undertaken using traditional modelling working at a single level, but

this debate can only be addressed by recognizing that individuals and constituencies form different levels in a hierarchical structure, with multilevel modelling as the appropriate method.

Some results

We undertook an analysis of the 1987 and 1992 General Elections. For the latter we modelled 2,275 respondents nested within 218 constituencies with a binary outcome, the probability of voting Labour as opposed to Conservative. Crucially, the differences between constituencies remained substantial even when age, sex, tenure, income, qualifications and class were taken into account. The probability of voting Labour for the 'stereotypical' individual (a middle-aged woman with low qualifications, living in an owner-occupied household whose head is unskilled working class, and receiving a 'middle' annual income) ranges from 0.22 in Nottingham East to 0.70 in Renfrew West. These are not small differences.

Going beyond crude composition/contextual debates, Figure 29.1 shows results when modelling the interaction between individual and place characteristics. In each of the graphs, the vertical axis is the probability of voting Labour, while the lines on the graph portray the relation for eight 'fractions' of individual class. The horizontal axis in each graph is a different measure of constituency characteristics. In (a) there are marked individual class effects (lowest support from the petty bourgeoisie, highest from unskilled manual workers), but these do not change in relation to the tenure characteristics of the constituency. Local geography in the form of tenure is not important.

A more complex picture is found in (b) in which the horizontal axis is the percentage of the constituency labour force who are in employment. Voting Labour is related to employment levels more markedly for working-class than non-working-class individuals. While the latter are somewhat immune to the economic situation of the local area, the working class are affected by the local economic environment. Graph (c) shows a strong place effect, which takes a consensual form in that both individual and constituency class (represented by the percentage of employers and managers in an electoral constituency) are mutually reinforcing. Where this core class forms a sizeable proportion of the population, more or less everyone, irrespective of their individual class, votes Conservative.

(a) Individual class and constituency tenure

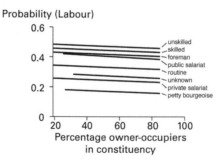

(b) Individual class and constituency employment

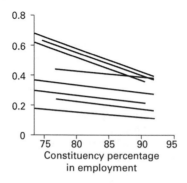

(c) Individual class and constituency elite class

Figure 29.1 Voting behaviour, people and place characteristics

Another aspect of the importance of geography is shown in Figure 29.2 where the relation between variables is allowed to vary from place to place. Underlying the graph is a three-level model of people in constituencies in regions. The outcome variable on the vertical axis is the choice between Labour and Conservative for the 1987 General Election.[3] The horizontal axis is the percentage of the constituency labour force employed as coal miners as measured by the 1981 census. The lines on the graphs show the relation between Labour voting and employment in coal mining for each region in the UK after conditioning on individual class, tenure, employment and demographic characteristics. The most marked contrast is between South Wales and the East Midlands. South Wales is a pro-Labour area, and this support

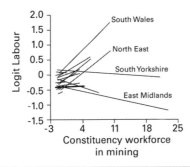

Figure 29.2 Constituency vote/mining relationships varying over region

increases, as the economy of the constituency is more involved with mining. The opposite is found in the East Midlands, the most anti-Labour areas are the coal-mining constituencies! Places that appear to be outwardly the same (they both were coal-mining areas) are shown to be quite differently when the analysis is sensitive to place differences. The East Midlands mining area known as the Dukeries has a distinct history of working traditions, cultural practices and social relations that differ from other coalfield areas to the extent of electing a Conservative MP in 1987.

These results show that any analysis of British voting that does not take place into account is at best partial. Voting depends not only on who you are (class and age), what you have (tenure and employment), but also on where you live in the context of the history and traditions of that place.

Conclusions

For me, there are several aspects of this 'tale from the field' that are important. There is a need in quantitative research work to pay *simultaneous* attention to theory ('what do we mean by a contextual effect?'), operationalization ('what are fair tests of alternative theories?'), data collection ('what is reliable and appropriate data?') and data analysis ('what is the appropriate technique that addresses the research question taking account of the structure of the data?').

Moreover, in reality of course, there is also no simple neat linear narrative which leads inexorably to a set of conclusions. Along the way we fitted a range of models, trying all the time to see if the sizeable contextual effects were simply an outcome of specifying the wrong model.

Developments in random-coefficient modelling mean that we can now address more sophisticated questions. Indeed, the complexity of the world is not ignored in the pursuit of a single universal equation (as has been done in much previous modelling), but the specifics of people and places are retained in a model which still has a capacity for generalization. Keeping contexts in the model allows the possibility of bridge-building with qualitative researchers, posing such questions as 'what is it about areas such as the East Midlands that has allowed a distinct local political culture to develop?'

Notes

1. More recent developments are reported at: http://www.ccsr.ac.uk/methods/
2. It is like saying there is no geography of death when we take account of those who are mortally ill!
3. Modelled for technical reasons in a logit form.

Further references

Johnston, R.J. (1986) 'The neighbourhood effect revisited', *Society and Space*, 4: 41–56.

Jones, K., Johnston, R.J. and Pattie, C.J. (1992) 'People, places and regions: Exploring the use of multilevel modelling in the analysis of electoral data', *British Journal of Political Science*, 22: 343–80.

Rose, R. and McAllister, I. (1990) *The Loyalties of Voters*. London: Sage.

Sayer, A. (2000) *Realism and Social Science*. London: Sage.

Tate, C.N. (1974) 'Individual and contextual variables in British voting behaviour', *American Political Science Review*, 68: 1656–62.

Methodological Issues in International Comparative Assessments of Educational Progress

W.J. Pelgrum, Department of Curriculum Technology, Faculty for Behavioural Sciences, University of Twente, The Netherlands

Stories from the field

Introduction

The history of international comparative statistical assessments of educational progress started around 1960, when the International Association for the Evaluation of Educational Achievement (IEA) ran a first study among 10,000 students from 12 education systems to explore the feasibility of conducting international comparative assessments. The results were positive (Foshay, 1962) and from then onwards a regular series of assessments has been conducted by IEA in mathematics, science, reading, writing, civics and Information and Communications Technology. Since 1999 the Organization for Economic Co-operation and Development (OECD) has also conducted international comparative assessments of student achievement in mathematics, science and reading every three years.

The interest of countries in participating in large-scale international comparative assessments has considerably increased over the past 30 years. This development illustrates that in particular among policy-makers a need exists to collect hard data on educational progress. This need may be motivated by various considerations, including economical and accountability factors or the need for educational improvement. Although in the past international comparative assessments were the domain of a relative small in-crowd of researchers, nowadays the huge data bases can also be processed with relatively small computers and are available for the educational research community at large. Based on the author's more than 25 years of experience in international comparative assessments, this chapter provides a description of a number of methodological issues related to international comparative assessments and the way that the data from these assessments can be accessed.

Conceptualization of international comparative assessments

The conceptual frameworks of the various assessments that were conducted by IEA contain generic elements such as the ones which are shown in Figure 30.1, where a distinction is made between input, process and output characteristics of education systems, and interdependencies between several components of the system are hypothesized.

In practice, the hypothesized models are much more complex than the one which is presented in

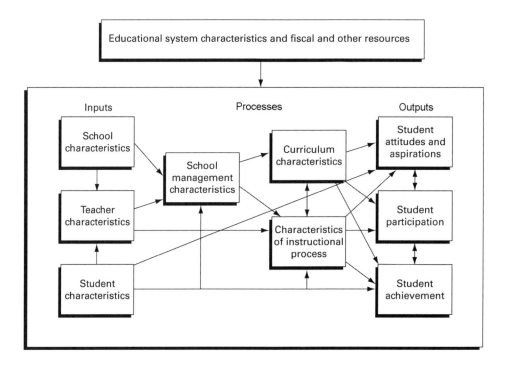

Figure 30.1   Elements of an educational monitoring system containing indicators of educational quality on different levels

Figure 30.1. The investigation of which models can be fitted to the data is particularly important for advancing our theoretical knowledge on how education systems function. In general this is realized through secondary analyses (e.g. Robitaille and Beaton, 2002), but especially through doctoral theses of which hundreds[1] have been produced over the last decade.

Design issues

One of the greatest challenges for international comparative assessments is the issue of comparability. How can instruments and samples be designed so that the international statistics are comparable? Several aspects of this comparability issue are reviewed in more detail below.

The comparability of achievement tests

The average country scores on international achievement have usually attracted the greatest attention from policy-makers and in particular the press. Quite often the criticism of international assessments is that

an attempt is made to compare the incomparable. Incomparability would stem from differences in educational contexts and national curricula. The international test designers are usually very much aware of this potential fallacy and have tried through several mechanisms to minimize this problem, by for instance:

- Conducting curriculum analyses in order to determine the overlap between intended curricula of the participating countries, as a basis for the definition of the domain and for test construction.
- Including so called Opportunity to Learn (OTL) measures in the testing programme, by letting teachers judge to what extent the items in a test cover the implemented curriculum. These measures can be used to determine post hoc to what extent comparisons between particular groups of countries are warranted or may be biased to the advantage of some countries.
- Conducting analyses of differential item-functioning (DIFF). This may be caused by the fact that

in some countries the curriculum very heavily emphasizes the content that is needed to answer some items correctly.

It may be of interest to note that quite often the potential incomparability of tests is mainly mentioned in the context of international comparative assessments. However, the lessons learnt from these international assessments may be of particular value also for national assessments, from which quite often comparisons are made between states, districts and even schools. Here also the comparability issue needs to be examined because within countries different schools (or alternatively districts or states) may implement a curriculum in substantially different ways. Although it is to be expected that such differences in particular will exist in decentralized education systems, past research has shown that also in centralized systems there may be quite huge differences between schools in terms of OTL.

The comparability of questionnaires

During international assessment-projects the participating researchers create, on the basis of a common conceptual framework, questionnaires that are meant to tap the intended concepts. These (English language) questionnaires are then translated into national languages and extensively pilot-tested in order to determine their measurement characteristics. It is obvious that translation errors can seriously affect the comparability of these measures. Therefore, translation verification is an important activity to try to minimize this risk. Translation verification can take place in several forms, such as:

- *Independent back translations*: This is a very costly activity because professional translators need to be contracted who can translate the national versions of questionnaires back to English in order to be compared with the original version. Any deviation between the original and the back-translated version may point to translation problems and, hence, these deviations need to be examined in detail in order to determine how the national translation needs to be adapted. The option of back translation is usually (because of the associated costs) only applied for the items in the achievement tests.
- *National verification*: This option consists of checking the national translations against the original

English version by a group of people who are independent of the group that was involved in the translation. Obviously the simultaneous mastery of English and the native language is crucial for recruiting people who can do this. In some countries it has proved to be quite difficult to find such people and, hence, this would be a circumstance that would need to be taken into account when interpreting the data.

- *Data-analytical techniques*: Once the data from international assessments are collected they are verified in a variety of ways. Data-checking and data-cleaning software is applied to extensively check whether potential inconsistencies exist in the data. Such inconsistencies may result from different sources of which translation error is one (other potential sources are: data-entry errors, inconsistency of the respondents). An example of a potential inconsistency is when a substantial number of respondents in a particular country indicate that they highly value the use of computers in school while at the same time saying that computers are useless for educational purposes.

The comparability of samples

International comparisons are made on the basis of estimates from data that result from national samples of students, teachers and schools. If the samples are incomparable obviously the comparability of the estimates is at stake. There are a number of aspects that need to be taken into account when national samples are defined and selected, namely:

- *The comparability of the nationally defined target population with the international definition*: As a first step to maximizing the chance of getting comparable samples from countries, in international comparative assessments, the researchers agree upon an international population definition. Such a definition may be: *all students that have reached a particular age on a particular date during the school year*. Or *all students at a particular grade level in the school system that is comparable in terms of student age composition*.
- *The accuracy of the population statistics*: Population statistics are estimated from sample data. Depending on the size of the sample these statistics have a particular accuracy (that is the confidence interval, see Lewin, Chapter 25, this volume). In international comparative assessments these confidence intervals are defined before national

sampling plans are created. This is usually done by using the criterion that the national estimates of statistics based on student data should have the same accuracy as a simple random sample of 400 students from an infinite population. Due to the fact that most countries cannot draw simple random samples, but instead need to apply more complex sampling designs (for instance first selecting schools and next selecting students within schools), in practice the sample sizes need to be much higher than 400, usually by a factor of 10. An important implication of the complex sampling designs is that statistical tests from the standard statistical program (such as SPSS or SAS) can no longer be applied, but that more sophisticated techniques for estimating sampling error need to be applied (such as jack-knifing: Gonzalez and Foy, 2000)

- *The representativeness of the sample*: A sample is representative if every element in the population has a known chance of being selected. These chances are not known if considerable non-response occurs. Therefore, currently most international assessments have strict rules for the percentage of non-response that can be accepted in order to include the data from a country in the international reports.

Reporting

The international reports that result from assessments of IEA or OECD are available at the websites of these organizations[2] where information can also be found regarding the accessibility of the data. Several types of reports are distinguished, such as: descriptive reports, secondary analyses and technical reports.

International assessment databases and their potential uses

International comparative assessments result in huge data sets (50 countries with on average 5,000 students per country is not abnormal) that are nowadays easily accessible for several purposes. Also the background documents on design and methodological issues (sampling, technical standards, psychometrics) reflect how researchers in the field apply theoretical insights from educational methodology. These data can be of value for examining and illustrating several methodological topics that have been addressed throughout this book, such as:

- *Conceptualization: concepts and indicators*: When students at universities (for instance from departments of educational sciences) are being trained in creating conceptual frameworks, the international assessments may offer them plenty of examples of concepts and indicators that have been defined to reflect these concepts.

- *Questionnaire development*: By critically examining questionnaires that have been used in international assessments, forming hypotheses about the strong and weak points and analysing the data to find evidence for these hypotheses, much can be learned about issues that concern questionnaire development.

- *Sampling*: Several issues are worth examining and discovering in the international data files, such as:
  - Is the accuracy of the population estimates comparable to theoretical expectations?
  - Do education systems where streaming occurs have higher intra-class correlations than systems where this is not the case?

- *Data collection*: International comparative assessment projects have over the past 30 years developed a whole set of tips and tricks for collecting high quality data from large samples of students, teachers and schools in a country.

- *Data-analysis*: International comparative data sets nowadays offer a wealth of opportunities to investigate how certain measures behave under different circumstances. For example, in questions like: do attitude measures from Japanese and UK data show the same underlying dimensions?

- *Substantive questions*: International comparative assessments typically cover a broad range of topics. For instance the tests for measuring student achievement may contain hundreds of questions covering a large part of the mathematics domain. Detailed examination of these items may reveal much more than the overall tests statistics which are published in the international reports.

Notes

1. At one small university in The Netherlands we have already counted 11 theses based on international assessment data over the past 15 years.

2. Access to the reports and databases of IEA and/or OECD can be acquired via, respectively: www.iea.nl and www.oecd.org

Further references

Foshay, A.W. (ed.) (1962) *Educational Achievements of Thirteen-Year-Olds in Twelve Countries*. Hamburg: UNESCO Institute for Education.

Gonzalez, E. and Foy, P. (2000) 'Estimation of sampling variance', in M.O. Martin, K.D. Gregory, K.M. O'Connor and S.E. Stemler (eds) *TIMSS 1999 Benchmarking Technical Report*. Chestnut Hill, MA: Boston College. pp. 203–22.

Robitaille, D.F. and Beaton, A.E. (eds) (2002) *Secondary Analyses of the TIMSS Data*. Dordrecht: Kluwer Academic Publishers.

Evaluating Literacy Advance in the Early Years of School

John Ainley, Australian Council for Educational Research

Stories from the field

Literacy Advance was a systemic reform of the Catholic Education Commission of Victoria that began in 1998 with the purpose of improving the literacy development of students, especially in the early years of schooling. Over a period of five years we conducted a parallel Literacy Advance Research Project using longitudinal, multilevel and multi-method approaches to evaluate the impact of the initiative on student learning. This chapter provides an outline of what we did. Our results are described in greater detail in the reports of the study (Ainley and Fleming, 2000, 2004; Ainley et al., 2002).

Background

Literacy Advance operated through the support of programmes in schools, emphasizing a whole-school approach to programme design, mandated professional development for teachers, designated blocks of time for literacy in schools, intervention programmes for students needing additional assistance and the systematic evaluation of student learning. The strategy arose out of a renewed interest in the development of literacy in primary schools and the effects of large-scale educational reform on improving learning. Each school proposed a plan for the improvement of literacy and, on the basis of these plans, schools received additional funds. Key requirements included the appointment of a literacy co-ordinator, systematic monitoring of children's progress and assessment of all Year 1 students. Each school plan nominated a focus for its literacy teaching in the early years of school. These included: Western Australian First Steps (WAFS), the Children's Literacy Success Strategy (CLaSS), and the Early Years Literacy Program (EYLP). In addition, schools could nominate an Approved School Design (ASDN) programme.

Design

The Literacy Advance Research Project began in 1998 and involved more than 150 schools in the Catholic education system of Victoria. We made a number of key design decisions at the beginning but modified details (such as particular instruments) during the course of the project, depending on our analysis at each point. We collected information at student, classroom and school level for two cohorts of students: the first entered Year 1 (following a preparatory year in school) in 1998 and the second in 2000. From the beginning our focus was on achievement growth in literacy so we chose to develop a longitudinal design in which individuals could be followed over their primary school years. For our first cohort we initially sampled students within schools but when we confronted the complexities of various transfers we realized it was more sound to include all students from the designated Year level in each school. Furthermore, since we were interested in influences that operated at individual level (such as intervention programmes), classroom level (such as approach to teaching) and school level (such as contextual influences) we planned to analyse our data using multilevel methods. Figure 31.1 outlines the overall design of

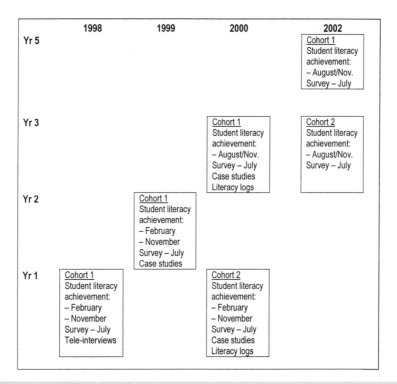

Figure 31.1   Design of the Literary Advance Research Project

our study. We didn't conduct any assessments during 2001, which means that there are no assessment data in Year 2 for the second cohort.

Measures

Student achievement was assessed at the beginning and end of Years 1 and 2, and at the end of Year 3. Teachers provided information about each student during each year. In addition, we gathered information about school and classroom organization, programmes and approaches by means of questionnaires. From the analyses of these data it was possible for us to evaluate the extent to which the factors influencing student literacy development had changed as a result of the implementation of Literacy Advance.

Student progress in literacy

In general we made use of assessment data that were being collected as part of the regular operation of Literacy Advance and supplemented these with other assessments. Assessment in Year 1 was based on the Burt Word Reading Test, Text Level and components

of the Clay Observation Schedule. In Years 3 and 5 the Burt Word Reading Test and the Reading, Writing and Spelling components of the statewide assessment programme were used to assess student literacy proficiency. At each point in the study we combined the individual assessment components to form a composite measure (using confirmatory factor analysis to establish the appropriate weights for each component).

Influences on literacy growth

We analysed student achievement in a series of multilevel analyses using student-level data (such as initial achievement, participation in individual programmes such as Reading Recovery, engagement, as well as social and language background) and school/classroom-level data (such as approach to literacy teaching, time allocation to literacy, interruptions in the literacy block, school and classroom characteristics). In the analysis we found it necessary to combine school and classroom level data because where there are multiple classrooms for each Year students often change classes from one year to the next and because many schools had just one classroom for each Year.

Results

Cohort comparison

When we compared word recognition scores over Year 1 for the 1998 cohort and the 2000 cohort we found that Year 1 students in 2000 began with higher average scores than did their counterparts in 1998: equivalent to one-quarter of a year's growth in word recognition. This initial advantage was maintained over the course of Year 1 and through to the end of Year 3. In addition Year 1 students in 2000 began Year 1 with higher text level scores than Year 1 students in 1998. We found that the sustained advantage for the second cohort was corroborated in the reading scores on the statewide assessment for the two cohorts and there was a consistent difference between the two cohorts in the ratings given by teachers for each of the skills listed in the profiles. Thus from several perspectives we were able to conclude that there had been an improvement between 1998 and 2000 that was sustained as students progressed through school.

Analysis of influences on Year 1 reading growth

In our analysis of reading growth in Year 1 we used two-level regression analysis of end-of-year literacy achievement to allow us to investigate influences at the school or classroom level at the same time as influences at the individual level.

Not surprisingly we found that the strongest influence on end-of-year achievement was achievement at the beginning of the year. This highlights the importance of what happens before Year 1, either in the preparatory year or in the pre-school years. Because we included initial achievement, the analysis of the other variables refers to achievement growth. We found several individual-level factors that influenced achievement growth. Attentiveness, as measured by a rating scale completed by teachers (Rowe and Rowe, 1999), was strongly related to progress in reading over Year 1. We also found that participation in Reading Recovery had an effect on reading development of the Year 1 students who participated in it for both cohorts, but more for the 1998 cohort.

At school and classroom level we found a significant effect for the CLaSS approach compared with other approaches but the magnitude was smaller in 2000 than in 1998. Information about characteristics of the literacy block was only available for the 2000 cohort (because we did not develop adequate measures for the first cohort). For that cohort we found a significant positive effect on reading growth of the time allocated to the literacy block and there was a negative effect of interruptions in that time.

Influences on literacy to the end of Year 3

We conducted similar analyses using the literacy outcome measures at the end of Year 3 for both cohorts of students. Our intention was to explore the extent to which the factors that influenced Year 1 reading in a beneficial way had enduring effects through to Year 3.

We found again that reading proficiency at the beginning of Year 1 strongly influenced literacy achievement at the end of Year 3. This reinforces the importance of the early years in providing a strong basis for development. We also found that student attentiveness had a lasting influence on Year 3 achievement and that engagement (measured in Year 3) had an even stronger influence. We also found that, on average, participation in Reading Recovery did not appear to have a significant influence on literacy achievement in Year 3. We concluded that the benefits of Reading Recovery in Year 1 did not endure over time.

We found that the benefits from the CLaSS approach in Year 1 endured. Other things being equal, students from CLaSS did better in Year 3 literacy than students from other Year 1 programmes. It appears that what occurs in the first year of schooling can make a difference to literacy development. When we reflected on these results we remembered that in the 1998 cohort schools that became part of the CLaSS approach were from socio-economically disadvantaged schools. They were achieving below their capacity at the beginning of Year 1 and intensive attention to literacy development resulted in substantial gains that endured.

Influences on literacy at the end of Year 5

We also analysed influences on literacy outcome measures at the end of Year 5 for the 1998 cohort of students. We found that the strongest influence on achievement at the end of Year 5 was achievement at the beginning of Year 1; the influence of attentiveness measured in Year 1 persisted through to Year 5; and engagement measured in Year 5 had an influence on literacy achievement. We found no lasting effect of participation in Reading Recovery through to the end of Year 5. We did find a significant effect for the CLaSS approach, compared with other approaches although the magnitude of that effect was less than that in Year 3.

Reflections

The assessment of school and programme influences on student learning needs to be based on measures of achievement growth rather than single static measures (Willet, 1994). In this study we successfully measured changes in literacy achievement over time using composite measures of achievement that were robust. We were able to study changes over an extended time and thereby evaluate enduring as well as immediate outcomes from different approaches to teaching. The fact that the study extended over several years meant that it was not possible to examine school and classroom level factors separately (because classes typically change each year). However, our design enabled us to compare effects at the time of and subsequent to an initiative and so provide a basis for inferences about the effects of the intervention and the main elements within the intervention (such as broad approach to teaching and individual interventions).

We were less successful in capturing more detailed aspects of classroom practice and the influence of those practices on student learning. It seems that this may be partly due to the absence of an established conceptual framework of classroom practice and partly because survey research methods based on questionnaires may not provide sufficiently sensitive measures of practice. It may also be that variable-focused analytic methods do not capture enough of the contingencies and interactions that are important aspects of classroom influences on learning. The use of classroom or person-focused analyses could help to identify clusters of factors that in combination shape student learning. In this study we made use of case studies and teacher logs to capture more detail of classroom practice but we used these for descriptive purposes. The potential of such methods is likely to be more fully realized when they are linked to quantitative analyses of the type conducted in this study and are used to interpret the broader patterns established from the survey analyses.

Further references

Ainley, J. and Fleming, M. (2000) *Learning to Read in the Early Years of School*. Melbourne: Catholic Education Commission of Victoria.

Ainley, J. and Fleming, M. (2004) *Five Years On: Literacy Advance in the Primary Years*. Melbourne: Catholic Education Commission of Victoria.

Ainley, J., Fleming, M. and McGregor, M. (2002) *Three Years On: Literacy Advance in the Early and Middle Primary Years*. Melbourne: Catholic Education Commission of Victoria.

Rowe, K.J. and Rowe, K.S. (1999) 'Investigating the relationship between students' *attentive–inattentive* behaviors in the classroom and their literacy progress', *International Journal of Educational Research*, 31(2): 1–138.

Working Backwards: The Road Less Travelled in Quantitative Methodology

Brian Doig, Faculty of Arts and Education, Deakin University, Australia

Stories from the field

Context

The context of this example of quantitative researchers in action is set in the early 1990s in Victoria, Australia. The Victorian Department of Education requested the Australian Council for Educational Research (ACER) to investigate the science achievements of Victorian school students at Year 5 (9- to 10-year-olds) and Year 9 (13- to 14-year-olds). Thus the variable of interest, science achievement, was quite clear, as was the population.

However, at that time the Department of Education did not know what the content of the school science curriculum was, especially in primary schools. Secondary school science, on the other hand, was better known, as the popular science textbooks gave some indication of what was being taught. This had come about because the Department had made a decision, in the early 1980s, to have schools develop their own curricula without central oversight from the Department.

The dilemma facing the research team was how to report on students' science achievement when it was unknown what students had been taught, nor was there time or funds available to ascertain this.

Methodology

The methodology used to achieve the desired outcomes of this research project was typical of quanti-

tative research in other contexts. Good practice in quantitative research suggests that you should start where you want to end up, and work backwards. This means that you should:

- decide how the findings can be reported most usefully for your audience; then
- select the analytic approach that will provide the results in a form suitable for this form of reporting; and finally
- prepare to collect data that can be analysed in your chosen way.

The relationship between the last two steps is never completely one-way, as there are contextual aspects of the data collection that may influence your choice of analysis. While this 'start at the end' strategy may appear simplistic, it does ensure that you finish with data that can be analysed in a way for you to report the findings usefully.

Reporting

In the example being discussed here, we turned, as one should, to the research literature on students' achievements in science to provide a context for our research and the reporting of its results. At the time, there had been a considerable amount of international investigation of student understandings of science concepts. This research has been variously characterized as 'children's science', or 'mis-conception research' because of its focus on children's mis-understandings of scientific phenomena. (For an overview, see, e.g., Driver and Easley, 1978; Osborne and Freyberg, 1985.) At the time, most of this research had been conducted through clinical (one-to-one) interviews using a variety of stimuli, and the findings provided insights into a range of understandings held by children for a range of different aspects of science. We argued, then, that we should report on students' conceptual understandings, as these are independent of the curriculum studied, and the Department agreed that this should be done.

Analysis

The literature on children's science made it obvious to us that we should report on the full range of understandings in the student population. We were interested in being able to describe the understandings of students at different points along a continuum of understandings, from the naive to the most sophisticated. Clearly, an analysis that allowed higher 'scores' for more scientifically sophisticated responses to a stimulus was needed.

The analytic approach we adopted was an Item Response Theory (IRT) model, that of Masters (Masters, 1982, 1988; Wright and Masters, 1982). Masters's Partial Credit Model (PCM) is an extension of the Rasch model (Rasch, 1960). The PCM analysis has two distinct features that make it eminently suitable for analysing data for which there is no single, correct response. First, it allows a range of responses, from the least to the most sophisticated, to be preserved: that is, it does not place all 'incorrect' responses into a single 'wrong' class, but preserves and reports all responses, and, in this case, places them in order of scientific sophistication. The second feature of the PCM is that it places student total scores and student responses on the same scale, which means that it is possible to estimate, for any given student total score, the likely response of a student with that score to any question. (See Bond and Fox (2001) for a detailed explanation of Item Response Theory and its applications.)

The intention was that students would respond to a stimulus and provide written responses that could be categorized into levels of increasing scientific understanding. The PCM analysis would then scale the students' performance, in terms of their scientific understandings, and the categories of response would

describe the development of these. At no stage would ideas of 'correct' or 'incorrect' responses be used, but instead, there was to be a continuum of increasingly sophisticated science understanding.

Data source

After much debate and reflection, we decided to create pseudo-interviews, that is, written questionnaires that would, as far as possible, emulate the clinical (one-on-one) interviews found in the literature. In this way, we believed, our results could be comparable with those found in the literature, and also add to knowledge in the field. A series of short written stories was created, based on the typical questions and results described in the 'children's science' literature. There were six of these stories in all, each assessing students' beliefs about a particular topic in science. This set of stories was entitled *Tapping Students' Science Beliefs* (TSSB). The six stories were:

- *The Day We Cooked Pancakes at School*: A cartoon story that had a focus on the structure of matter.
- *What Happened Last Night*: A short story that is a conversation between a child and an alien visitor and focuses on the Earth and Space.
- *Skateboard News*: This was a newsletter about skateboarding with a focus on force and motion.
- *Children's Week*: This was a role play, where the focus was on various aspects of light and sight.
- *Our School Garden*: A cartoon story with a focus on living things.
- *Environmental Impact Survey*: This was a role play that had a focus on living things and the environment.

(See Doig and Adams, 1993, for details of the TSSB assessment units.)

Figure 32.1 shows Question 4 from the *Our School Garden* TSSB.

The practice

The official report of the research project (Adams et al., 1991) provides details of the analysis and the findings. For this discussion it is useful to examine how the three aspects, report, analysis and data, were implemented. For the sake of clarity, the description of this is in the reverse order to the project's design: that is, it starts with the data collection and concludes with the report.

Adams, R.J., Doig, B.A. and Rosier, M. (1991) *Science Learning in Victorian Schools: 1990*, ACER Research Monograph No. 41 (ACER: Camberwell, 1991). Reproduced with the permission of the Australian Council for Educational Research.

Figure 32.1   Question 4 from the *Our School Garden* TSSB assessment unit (Adams et al., 1991: 124)

A sample of students, at Year 5 and Year 9, were administered a battery of surveys as well as the TSSB instruments. See Adams et al. (1991) for details of the sample of students involved in the project.

The design of the questions in the TSSB booklets meant that, in most cases, students at both year levels were administered the same TSSB booklets. Each student completed two booklets.

When the completed TSSB scripts were returned from schools, two of the researchers took a random sample of 100 of each booklet. Student responses were examined on a question-by-question basis, and responses that indicated 'like' responses were grouped together. Descriptions of these 'like' categories of response were made, and the two collections of scripts swapped between the researchers. Each researcher then used the other's category descriptions to categorize the same set of student responses. Whenever a response was not able to 'fit' into a category, discussion between the researchers led to either a new category being established, or the description of an existing category revised. This iterative process was continued until all student responses to the questions were categorized. The number of categories of response to any question was dependent on the range

of understandings indicated by the student responses, and there was no attempt made to force a set number of categories. The refined descriptions were used by a group of trained markers on the remaining student scripts.

Categorized student responses were analysed using Masters's Partial Credit Model, a scale established, and students' total scores placed on the scale to show levels of understanding. So that the report would show clearly how the scientific understandings developed, a continuum of understanding was constructed for each TSSB.

Figure 32.2 shows the continuum for Light and Sight (Adams et al., 1991: 25). The distribution of Year 5 and Year 9 students by total score are at the extreme left and right, respectively, while the description of levels of scientific understanding are in the central column. The highest level of understanding displayed represents the highest level of understanding displayed by the students sampled. The total score scale range (50 to 70) was selected to avoid confusion or misinterpretation with percentages, particularly, 50 per cent being taken as some sort of 'pass' score.

This continuum shows that, of the students sampled, those whose total score on the *Children's Week*

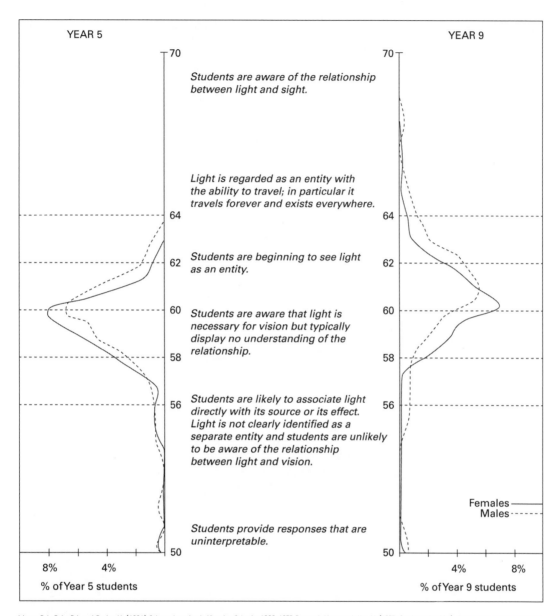

YEAR 5

70

Students are aware of the relationship between light and sight.

64

Light is regarded as an entity with the ability to travel; in particular it travels forever and exists everywhere.

62

Students are beginning to see light as an entity.

60

Students are aware that light is necessary for vision but typically display no understanding of the relationship.

58

56

Students are likely to associate light directly with its source or its effect. Light is not clearly identified as a separate entity and students are unlikely to be aware of the relationship between light and vision.

Students provide responses that are uninterpretable.

50

8%   4%

% of Year 5 students

YEAR 9

70

64

62

60

58

56

Females ———
Males - - - - -

50

4%   8%

% of Year 9 students

Adams, R.J., Doig, B.A. and Rosier, M. (1991) *Science Learning in Victorian Schools: 1990*, ACER Research Monograph No. 41 (ACER: Camberwell, 1991). Reproduced by permission of the Australian Council for Educational Research.

Figure 32.2   The *Light and Sight* continuum (Adams et al., 1991: 25)

TSSB booklet was 56 are likely to believe that light is directly associated with its source, and it is not an entity. On the other hand, those students whose total score was, say, about 64 regard light as an entity that can travel. Clearly, learning experiences provided for these two groups of students need to be very different.

Conclusion

Quantitative methodology is unforgiving, as all statistical procedures rely on you, and your data, addressing the assumptions underlying the procedures. My message is: if you don't know what you wish to say in your report when you begin, you run the risk of having data that you cannot analyse in a manner that allows you to report usefully.

As one of my students said 'I work backwards all the time. When I am cooking I know what I wish to eat before I start. Research is the same.' So, plan ahead – but work backwards!

Further references

Adams, R.J., Doig, B.A. and Rosier, M. (1991) *Science Learning in Victorian Schools: 1990*. ACER Monograph No. 41. Melbourne: Australian Council for Educational Research.

Bond, T.G. and Fox, C.M. (2001) *Applying the Rasch Model: Fundamental Measurement in the Human Sciences*. Mahwah, NJ: Lawrence Erlbaum Associates.

Doig, B. and Adams, R.J. (1993) *Tapping Students' Science Beliefs*. Hawthorn: Australian Council for Educational Research.

Driver, R. and Easley, J. (1978) 'Pupils and paradigms: A review of literature related to concept development in adolescent science students', *Studies in Science Education*, 5: 61–84.

Masters, G.N. (1982) 'A Rasch model for partial credit scoring', *Psychometrika*, 47: 149–74.

Masters, G.N. (1988) 'Partial Credit model', in K.J.P. (ed.) *Educational Research, Methodology, and Measurement*. Oxford: Pergamon Press. pp. 292–7.

Osborne, R. and Freyberg, P. (eds) (1985) *Learning in Science: The Implications of Children's Science*. Auckland: Heinemann.

Rasch, G. (1960) *Probabilistic Models for Some Intelligence and Attainment Tests*. Copenhagen: Danmarks Paedogogiske Institut.

Wright, B.D. and Masters, G.N. (1982) *Rating Scale Analysis*. Chicago, IL: MESA Press.

PART VIII

RESEARCHING IN POSTMODERN CONTEXTS

Introduction

The chapters in this Part of the book do not divide so neatly into separately demarcated methodologies and methods as those in the earlier sections; instead they overlap with one another, visiting and re-visiting a number of core themes, resisting the notion of certainties in the construction and production of research knowledge and challenging the very notion that there are clearly defined methodological territories. This is signified by three of the chapters having hybrid titles (e.g. 'From Hermeneutics to Post-structuralism') and one incorporating in the title an intentional 'strike-through' to denote that deconstruction can only be talked about as a method 'under erasure'.

All the chapters explore the implications for social science research of the linguistic theories which developed during the twentieth century, beginning with Saussure and culminating with Derrida, involving a fundamental challenge to Enlightenment rationalism through recognition that all meaning is represented by signs which are arbitrary. These theories are important in destabilizing certainty and reconstructing knowledge as partial and contingent rather than valid and reliable. They resist traditional processes of data collection, analysis and interpretation grounded in assumptions of established procedures of induction and deduction in moving between 'the field' and 'theories'. These chapters adopt a Foucauldian analysis of knowledge produced and represented in discourses emanating from the development of systems and categories which instantiate power in social groups.

Put more simply, the theories presented in this section are important because they have given social science research a means of resisting the assumption that knowledge relating to human experience and behaviour can be developed using very similar methods to those which have been so spectacularly successful in the natural sciences (e.g. in producing planes that fly, and materials that the body tolerates in hip replacements). The chapters do this in two ways – first by radically challenging much that has been presented and discussed in the earlier chapters in the book, and second by taking ideas from these earlier chapters and exploring them through a different lens. The process can perhaps best be understood through the metaphor of music organized in the form of a theme and variations. Hence, the theme presented in the chapter on semiotic engagements in Part V is re-presented in a playful variation in 'From Structuralism to Post-structuralism', and the themes presented in the chapters on feminist methodologies and queer theory in Part III are re-presented in the chapter on feminism/post-structuralism. As with music, the delight for readers may be in identifying the interplay of ideas between theme and variations.

Some of the ideas contained in these chapters are difficult to grasp on first encounter, but they are presented here with considerable clarity. Rather than being seen as 'authentic' narratives of the present, which mimic the voice of 'unwritten' texts, the Stories from the Field should be read as playful conversations with the Key Concepts sections. Part VIII as a whole might be seen as providing a critique on the book itself, destabilizing and deconstructing its categories and certainties.

Deconstruction ~~as a Method of~~ ~~Research~~

Erica Burman, Discourse Unit, Manchester Metropolitan University, UK

Maggie MacLure, Education and Social Research Institute, Manchester Metropolitan University, UK

Summary

- The world is always mediated, always written
- Sustained, philosophical interrogation of binary oppositions
- Key theorists and writers
  - Jacques Derrida
  - Patti Lather

Key concepts

Maggie MacLure

Today is, among other things, the day where we have lost our 'metaphysical comfort'. (Biesta and Egéa-Kuehne, 2001: 50)

Pre-amble: 'key concepts' in the text below are dark yet starry, thus: '**différance**'. The 'strike-through' in the title is intentional and is explained below.

Perhaps the most important proposition of deconstruction is that our dealings with the world are *unrelievedly textual*. This is in contrast to many other philosophies or theories, which dream of a 'binary' universe of fundamental things on the one hand (reality, truth, thought, identity, etc.), and the textual or sign systems that convey these on the other. For these latter kinds of theories, texts (e.g. writing, speech or pictures) are a kind of unfortunate, prag-matic necessity. They are merely *mediators* whose function is to give us access to those fundamentals, origins or first principles that, if we only could, we would access directly, without mediation. Deconstruction challenges such 'metaphysical' thinking. In a famous phrase, Derrida wrote that 'there is no outside-text'.[1] In other words, there is no vantage point external to text, or discourse, that would give us an unmediated access to truth, ethics, being etc. The world is always 'mediated', always-already textualized.[2]

Deconstruction is difficult to define further, because definitions presuppose some kind of contract between words and meanings. But as I have already hinted, deconstruction tangles with, and tangles up, pairings such as word/meaning. It provides a sustained, philosophical interrogation of this and other **binary oppositions** that have underpinned Western thought – truth/error; reality/representation; cause/effect; thought/language; essence/appearance; man/woman; presence/absence; nature/culture; mind/body; reason/emotion; universal/particular: world/text; original/copy, and so on.

There is always a hierarchy in these oppositions. One term always represents some higher principle or ideal or **presence**, while the other is always a kind of **supplement** – something lesser and subordinate. This binary logic has been deployed by many different philosophical systems in their enduring preoccupation with fundamentals and first principles. Derrida refers to this preoccupation as the 'metaphysics of presence'. He describes it as:

> the enterprise of returning 'strategically', in idealization, to an origin or to a 'priority' seen as simple, intact, normal, pure, standard, self-identical [i.e. *presence*], in order *then* to conceive of derivation, complication, deterioration, accident, etc. . . . good before evil, the positive before the negative, the pure before the impure, the simple before the imitation, etc. (1988: 236, original emphasis)

You might think the metaphysics of presence is just an arcane practice of philosophers, but it is central to the way we make sense of the world. Consider these remarks, from a former UK Chief Inspector of Schools with a beef about research journals:

> I used to try to read these journals. Life is too short. There is too much to do in the real world with real teachers in real schools to worry about methodological quarrels or to waste time decoding unintelligible, jargon-ridden prose to reach (if one is lucky) a conclusion that is often so transparently partisan as to be worthless. (Quoted in MacLure, 2003: 11–12)

Do you see the hierarchy that privileges presence? The *real* (real world, real teachers, real schools) is opposed to the *written* (i.e. the debased jargon of the academics). Another example of 'presencing' underpins the very structure of this book, whose central chapters are organized in terms of Key Concepts followed by Stories from the Field. The Key Concepts set out the general principles or the ideas – that is to say the ground of 'presence', while the Stories from the Field provide examples or particulars. That is why (if you read in a linear way) you will find yourself reading 'me' first and 'Erica' later. Deconstruction would interfere with these oppositions – as indeed Erica does in her Stories from the Field, which complicate the very notion of story, and of field.

Derrida shows how the binary law of presence always contains the seeds of its own undoing. It will always break down under pressure. Indeed deconstruction could be described as the act of bringing pressure to bear on the cherished oppositions that are woven into texts, forcing/allowing them to reveal their blind spots or **aporias** – that is to say points of impasse – where the integrity of the oppositions is

fatally compromised, and an excess of disorderly and contradictory meanings and resonances is released. Erica's examples 'below' apply just that sort of pressure to ostensibly simple texts relating to childhood and children, opening these texts up to a 'perplexing surplus of contested and conflicting meanings'.

One of Derrida's primary targets for deconstruction, which he has returned to many times, is the opposition between *speech* and *writing*, in which writing is generally the lesser partner. This ancient and persistent bias in Western philosophy is one manifestation of **logocentrism** – the belief in orders of meaning, reason or logic that exist independently of language or text. In privileging speech over writing philosophers have assumed that we are closer to thought, meaning, imagination, logic, our inner selves, other people, or external reality when we speak than when we write. Writing has been accused of many crimes. It appears derivative, lifeless and artificial, in contrast to 'living' speech with its seeming proximity to presence as thought, consciousness or intention. It stands for the 'bad' side of the nature/culture divide, as the disfiguring mark of alienated, 'civilized' societies, in contrast to the authenticity and apparent 'self-presence' of oral cultures. Lacking the supposed 'transparency' of speech, and its real-time connectivity between speaker and addressee, writing seems to offer too many chances for messages to go astray, or for meanings to be distorted, or for the stylistic vanities of writers to pervert the truth. This is the threat to presence that the Chief Inspector perceived (above). In many different ways, then, writing has been considered the pre-eminent threat to presence. It stands for secondariness, distance, non-identity, absence, exteriority and mediation. Writing seems to deflect or to *come between* us and the important stuff.

Deconstruction interferes with the hierarchy of opposition between speech and writing, to show how speech is no less troubled by distance, difference and delay than writing, and therefore no more secure a guarantor of presence. Those extralinguistic desirables such as meaning, reason and so on, are still brought to us – made present to us – via *signs*, which refer to other signs, in a chain of endless substitutions or differences. We will never arrive at the end of the chain, to claim the prize of unmediated access to reality, truth, etc. Something always intervenes or deflects. The world is always mediated. Always *written*. Thus, Derrida reverses the hierarchy of privilege, to show that speech has the same qualities of writtenness, as it were, as writing. In so doing, he invests the word **Writing** (sometimes called **arche-writing**) with a new, quasi-technical status, as the mark of all those qualities of secondariness, distance, displacement, textuality, absence that mediate the world. Writing (under deconstruction) institutes a paradoxical logic very different from the orderly economy of presence. It brings you closer to what you desire – reality, meaning, truth, origins, other people, the 'self' – by condemning you also always to be separated from it. Separated by the very words, or signs, that make the world possible.

In place of origins or essences, deconstruction thus finds **différance** – the term coined by Derrida which, in French, contains traces of both difference and deferral, and can only be distinguished from the conventional French *différence* in its written form. 'Différance' thus embodies a little joke or allusion to the priority of writing over speech, as the figure of the absence/difference/deferral that lies at the 'heart' of meaning. Sometimes also referred to as **spacing**, différance is the irreducible gap that allows meaning, reality, identity, etc, to come to definition in contrast to their opposites (words, representation, otherness). But the spacing is always uncanny – a matter of opening a space between things that cannot exist, yet must have existed, prior to the movement of opening.

Derrida says that philosophy's longing for presence arises from the desire to escape from the **play** of différance – to 'arrest', for example, the flickering relays of differences amongst signs that produce, but also endlessly defer, meaning. Why not go along with that project? Why not try to make a wobbly world more stable? Derrida's argument is that the binary hierarchies of presence are always '*violent*' (Derrida, 1972: 41). The stability that is (temporarily) achieved is always at the cost of suppression of some 'other' – of whatever is banished to the 'wrong' side of the binary. This can be seen very clearly with binaries such as white/black, man/woman, adult/child, as Erica's Stories 'below' show. There is always power, authority and violence at play in the stratagems of presence. This is not to say that we can ever entirely escape it. The 'closure' of metaphysics is too deeply wired into our ways of being. But we can continually try to glimpse the **trace** of what has been silenced, or 'othered', in order to provide us with our metaphysical 'comforts of mastery' (Johnson, 1987: 13). This is, says Derrida, an *ethical* stance of responsibility to the 'other': that is, to whatever remains silent, unthought or 'untruthed' so that presence can

come into being. *Education* is pre-eminently a scene where ethical responsibility is demanded (see Biesta and Egéa-Kuehne, 2001).

Can deconstruction be a 'method' of research?

Derrida would say No. You can see why: to call it a method or theory is to conjure another metaphysical opposition, between an external world and deconstruction, as if this were something separate, which could be 'applied'. Deconstruction is always inextricably tangled up with whatever is its object (Derrida, 1996). Moreover, to reduce it to a set of procedures ('Spot the binary, reverse the binary, displace the binary') would be to remove its capacity to engage with the unpredictable Other that is its focus. So, if we are to talk of deconstruction as a method, we need to do so **under erasure** – that is, in the acknowledgement that it is one of those impossible things that we cannot do without. The strike-through notation, as used in the title of this chapter, is the mark of something put under erasure. (In the case of the title, it is the im/possibility of deconstruction as 'a method' that is put under erasure.)

With the foregoing warnings in mind, I offer some precepts (or perhaps pretexts) for doing deconstruction. They are annoyingly gnomic. They should be read alongside instances of deconstruction such as Erica's, 'below', and the texts in the Annotated Bibliography.

- See the world, your data, and yourself, as *text*, with all that that implies. For example, that there is no direct access to reality, other people, or even one's self. Think of such things as 'the classroom', 'the child', 'the researcher' with invisible quotation marks around them: they are not 'natural', not self-evident, and *never* innocent.
- Look for the binary oppositions in texts (which might be interview transcripts, observation notes, questionnaire returns, documents, your own biases and assumptions) and worry away at them. Put pressure on them. This is what Erica does in her stories 'below'.
- Challenge the taken-for-granted – not in a destructive spirit, nor in the hope that you will reveal some deeper truth. But in order to *open up* textual spaces that seem closed or, contrariwise, to *tangle up* or confound things that seem too intent on keeping their distance.

Implications for research design

If deconstruction has implications for design, these are not so much about the paraphernalia of methods or sampling – which might look pretty conventional – as about our ways of engaging with the world and the status that we accord such things as 'data', 'analysis', 'subjects', and so on. Perhaps the primary insight that deconstruction affords is that methods are typically *devices for policing 'presence'*. Method – qualitative or quantitative – is about ensuring that we come as close as possible to truth, trustworthiness, generalizability, authenticity, justice, knowledge or ethical propriety. As we have seen, deconstruction puts all these concepts 'under erasure'. Here are a few examples of the boundaries that are policed by Method, which deconstruction would problematize.

Researcher/researched

Think of all the methods that are designed to dissolve the boundaries between the researcher and her 'subjects', or to bring their different worlds into closer proximity. This would include 'conversational' interview techniques, and narrative or life-history methods, which try to speak to subjects in their own vernacular, and thus to bridge the gap of power and alienation that has been such a trouble for social research. It would include action research, with its prioritizing of practitioners' experience over academics' theories. These examples prioritize the world of the research subjects as the ground of presence, in contrast to that of the researchers, which is external, alien, cold, unnatural. Deconstruction would not, of course, prioritize their opposites, or suggest abandoning these 'vernacular' methods (cf. MacLure, 2003: Chapter 7). But it would argue that these methods exhibit a 'drive to innocent knowing' (Lather, 1996) which can never uncomplicatedly deliver the warmth of presence that it seeks, and often leaves power and inequity intact. Researchers will always be knottily entangled with their subjects and ambiguously positioned both inside and outside various worlds and realities.

Fieldwork/theorywork

Erica will have more to say about the field below. For the moment, notice how in ethnography 'the field' generally stands for subjects' real, unmediated experience, and for the place where the researcher has her/his direct contact with that experience. While academic monographs may carry the authority (i.e. the presence) bestowed by science, or the higher-order abstractions of theoretical knowledge, that knowledge is always insufficient or incomplete without the alternative, if lesser, legitimacy granted to the researchers and their research by their Stories from the Field (Clifford, 1990). Think of the special status of field notes or snatches of conversation which, when inserted into reports, seem to bring a little piece of the real into the written. As Erica shows, 'the field' is no less a textualized, power-infused space than that of theory, though its contours are different.

Research/writing

Deconstruction denies, of course, that these are two entirely separate things. One of the more specific implications for research design is that researchers might experiment with novel, 'playful' forms of writing and reporting, with the aim of producing knowledge that is more surprising and less masterful than is often the case.

Attempting to summarize, deconstruction raises questions. What counts as analysis? How do phenomena come to be 'data'? What would be an 'ethical' stance towards the Other? What is the status of the knowledge produced by research? How are the selves of researchers and subjects fabricated – that is to say fashioned and knotted together – in research?

Stories from the field

Erica Burman

Deconstructing stories

To the deconstructionist reader/writer, 'Stories from the field' seem oddly modernist and objectivist; the agricultural metaphor suggestive of the discourse of data flourishing 'out there' (where? anywhere that is not 'here', perhaps?), awaiting collection like ripe fruit. 'Stories' – after Benjamin (1955/1973a) – evoke the oral tradition of spoken wisdom countering the dead weight of sterile information in an industrial age, at a time that has forgotten how to communicate. Here the discourse of 'what methodology books don't/can't tell you' (which is now a new niche publishing market) meets a longstanding preoccupation that links voyeurism with the intimacy of informal/illicit knowledge.

Pausing to consider the kinds of relations presumed by this discourse of stories invites consideration of who is deemed worthy to tell and to hear stories. Typically the dominant stories, or received histories, have been produced by those who have won progress's competitions (capitalism, patriarchy, colonialism . . .). In the case of stories of childhood, these are – of course – usually told by adults, i.e those who have accomplished the development story. Benjamin notes that '[t]he storyteller is the figure in which the righteous man [sic] encounters himself' (1955/1973a: 106). There is a project of implicitly masculine (self-) recognition structured into storytelling that evokes not only the Enlightenment subject of humanism but also its implicit correlate: victorious heroic struggle, whose residues can remain within more apparently 'critical' or post-Enlightenment accounts.

Meeting points/engendering the field

So telling 'stories from the field' seems a suspect activity, replete with gendered, age and colonial relations. Indeed such notions remain alive and kicking – for those with the money, gender and class status and leisure to 'play':

> THE FIELD is the world's original country and fieldsports magazine . . . For nearly 150 years, THE FIELD has been the first choice for those that love the British country sports tradition. And if you love gameshooting, flyfishing, hunting, dogs and the land, it will be your natural choice too. (Editorial statement, http://www.countrylife.co.uk/thefield/who.htm)

Indeed the genre of stories can often be a place to disclose the 'off-takes', the tales of 'not always getting it right' that the rigours of published academic research seem to demand. But here even the traditional sporting advice has pre-emptively usurped the genre to reinstate itself again. Hence, we see traditional hegemonic western masculinity get a laddish facelift in *The Field* editorial, from the man who always does his country sports right, to a less severe and more playful, and altogether more (self-) indulgent and fallible character:

> Well, we almost always do the right thing. Sometimes our labradors and spaniels forget their manners and riot, badly. Sometimes, among friends, we cannot resist shooting the high, curling bird that is rightfully theirs. Sometimes we find ourselves in Irish bars after a day's salmon fishing, drinking too much Guinness, laughing too loud,

having another cigarette when we've promised we'd given up. (Editorial statement, http://www.countrylife.co.uk/thefield/who.htm)

'Who am I to write this?' is a necessary question, but not necessarily a paralysing one. Instead of pretending the position of disembodied, omniscient (culturally masculine) knower or even its feminine/feminist autobiographical variety (which also sheds its subjectivity by virtue of, instead of denying, its reflexive status), we can attempt research stories that highlight the ambiguities and instabilities of the identities of researcher and researched, and attend to shifting convergences and contests over respective agendas that are structured within any encounter. For the deconstructionist, at issue is the impossibility of attaining that secure place of 'knowing' that characterized the modernist methodological and interpretive project. These wider debates are exemplified by researching with, or about, children.

Picturing children

Childhood is an uneven and troubled 'field', from which researchers are always partly exiled by virtue of having grown up. This field is often conceptualized as an enclosed space of domesticated nature from which 'we' (adults) originated. What do the prevailing discourses of 'innocence' or 'primitiveness' or 'development' conceal or suppress about children's experiences, and their unequal power relations with adults?

Rather than striving to close the gap between 'us' and 'them', our research 'others', we can analyse what is being covered over. What follows is an attempt to create some space to reflect upon the construction of stories of childhood, to promote moments of radical political possibility as 'brief truces . . . wrest out of history' (Rajan, 1993: 143). Precisely because of their naturalized and abstracted status, representations of childhood offer a repository of some of our most deeply held precepts. Hence these stories highlight the perplexing surplus of contested and conflicting meanings mobilized by and around children (and childhoods), and the impossibility of separating the object from the subject of the research. In terms of form, they also stretch the notion of 'story' to move from and between the 'privatized/feminized' sphere of personal account to seemingly more authoritative, public statements. Rather than proposing a specific 'moral' (or conclusion), the stories are accompanied by questions that, as Maggie introduced above, rather than cover over aim to open up the dilemmas produced by prevailing, but limited, binary polarities structuring children and their others. The questions I pose are, therefore, inevitably 'leading', but quite where they go is another matter.

Methodologically speaking, as an exemplification of the deconstructionist mode that Maggie described, in various of these accounts I deploy the following tactics:

- Displacing the high/low culture binary, in relation to the binary of expertise vs the everyday. Hence I do not 'speak as' – only – an academic psychologist, but 'as' a woman (therefore) with non/motherhood status and racialized and classed positioning (cf. Burman, 2008).
- Highlighting the materiality of the context of production of academic knowledge (personal vs academic identities and settings) and so challenging the model of knowledge and research as abstracted and disembodied.
- Displacing the privileging of specific disciplinary authority (e.g. psychological knowledge of children) – by drawing on other (e.g. anthropological) sources.
- Drawing attention to claims of presence and its relations with absence, including the temporal relations of the (narration of the) research space.
- Highlighting the identification and allocation of separate spaces: for example, us and them, and how these are constituted.
- Opening up for exploration claims to the Rights and Wrongs of childhood: childhood as a site of indulgence vs exploitation, but for which children?
- Intertextuality: how the different texts of childhood relate to each other, and each elaborate distinct subject positions for other constituencies around children.

Stories of risk

Far from being a benign space of sport and entertainment, 'the field' has become somewhere to be protected from. Discourses of 'risk' have emerged as the contemporary response to and expression of vulnerability – and the ways we position children index this.

Story I: PURITY AND DANGER

At the public swimming baths, the changing rooms are locked. Why, I ask? Because the schools are using them, when they come for lessons. But can't I use them at the same time, I

persist? The attendant says, 'We're not allowed to – child protection'. This appears to signal an absolute stopping point for that line of inquiry. So he tells me I should use the 'disabled' shower room instead. But, I say (since I have tried this already), these are kept locked too. 'Oh yes', he says, 'we have to keep them locked 'cos kids vandalize them'.[3] (February 2003)

Some questions:

(1) Am I a potential child abuser, or a victim of vandalism?
(2) What are the ambiguities about who or what is being protected?
(3) How is this coded by the opposition between 'children' and 'kids'?
(4) What concatenations of identity categories are at play, and with what effects?
(5) What institutional relations structure those identity categories?

Some reflections:

- This story is placed somewhere between commonsense and expertise.
- It might be particularly useful to challenge psychological authority which peddles received cultural norms back to parents, and educators and health professionals dressed up in jargon.
- Risk appears as the mode by which to express vulnerability – with significant consequences for the elaboration of the individual/state relationship (in terms of discourses of responsibility and scrutiny).
- Children in particular function as tokens in this cultural economy of 'risk', with consequences for 'our' positioning in relation to them.

Story II: ACCESS AND LIABILITY

The following notice appeared on the noticeboards and corridor walls of my workplace (see box overleaf):
Some questions:

(1) Who does this 'notice' address (is it 'children under 10')?
(2) Who or what is the 'speaker'?
(3) What kinds of 'concern' are being expressed?
(4) Which kinds of (gendered, classed, aged) 'staff/students/visitors' are likely to be most affected by such measures?
(5) What penalties follow from failure to comply with such prescriptions? How can it be regulated or enforced?

---

the
Manchester
Metropolitan
University

IMPORTANT NOTICE

CHILDREN

The University is concerned that small children (under 10) may be at risk from falls from height from staircases and landings in buildings that have not been designed with children's safety in mind

Therefore until further notice **children under 10 are prohibited from University buildings.**

Staff, students and visitors are expected to co-operate with the University in the interest of preventing accidents and injuries

I.W.Hallam
Personnel Director

(Typeface and emphasis following the original)

Some reflections:

- This is a story of self-regulation.
- 'Small' seems to work to conflate size with immaturity and irresponsibility.
- Children are portrayed as a distraction/obstacle to the education/work business.
- The welfare of children is assimilated to a Health & Safety issue.

Post-script: This text was subsequently replaced by a more extensive four-page poster entitled 'children onsite generic risk assessment' which is now prominently displayed on walls near all entrances and exits. Instead of 'CHILDREN' as the featured topic, this now carries the heading 'WARNING'. What are we to make of this substitution/statement of equivalence? As might be expected from the acceleration and intensification of defensive (exclusionary?) practice, the claims in big print of 'high risk of falls to children under the age of 10 years from landings, stairways and windows' and requests 'that all children under the age of 10 are supervised at all times', are accompanied by tables specifying 'risk control methods'. However, these, in smaller print, moderate the injunction that 'children (persons under 16 years old) are generally prohibited from university premises' with a series of

'exceptions' contingent on risk assessment having been undertaken by the responsible division/department such that 'there is no requirement to undertake a risk assessment for a short-term visit to low risk areas'.

Story III: CHILDHOOD LOST AND REGAINED

A 1999 Virgin Entertainment advertisement on hoardings and at bus stops announces in large blue and yellow letters: 'DELAY BECOMING YOUR PARENTS'. The small print at the bottom of the poster reads: 'www.virgin.net movies, music, travel, shopping' and on the next line: 'make the most of your free time'.

Some questions:

(1) What characteristics of parents are implied?
(2) What characteristics of children are implied?
(3) What assumptions (and psychological models) underlie the notion that 'we' will eventually 'become' our parents, and that all we can do is to 'defer' this?
(4) Who are 'we'?
(5) What age, class, gender and cultural assumptions are set in circulation?

Some reflections:
Motifs in circulation include:

- Becoming 'old' before your time?
- (Modern) childhood as the space of (freedom, irresponsibility and) play.
- Cultivating 'your' 'inner child' as the route to ward off this process.
- Consumption as the most visible measure of success in this project.

Story IV: EXPLOITATION OR EDUCATION?

'No Job Too Dirty' [accompanying picture of girl on knees, scrubbing floor] cleans quietly and efficiently

This is the kind of work Farida does 17 hours a day, 7 days a week. It could be worse. In parts of the world, children as young as 6 are being sold into prostitution or hazardous work. All because they are desperately poor and desperately vulnerable.

UNICEF is working to end the exploitation of children. With your help we can make sure they get a proper education. We can help their families to earn an income. And we can lobby governments to protect them by law.

CHILDREN LIKE FARIDA CAN'T ASK YOU FOR HELP, SO WE ARE. PLEASE, SEND AS MUCH AS YOU CAN TODAY

(UNICEF, as in the *Guardian* – 6 February 2003)

Some questions:

(1) Does this ad resist or reiterate prevailing representations of childhood?
(2) What happens when the discourses of sentiment and human rights are rubbed up against each other, is indulgence contingent upon notions of exploitation?
(3) How mandatory are the measures being advocated? And in relation to what or whom?
(4) What kind of appropriate childhoods, family and state relations are implied here?
(5) What kind of relationships between donor and recipient(s) are elaborated?

Some reflections:

- Child labour incites controversy but the ad side-steps this by the ambiguity of whether all working children are exploited.
- First/Third World relations are elaborated via polarized discourse around child labour ('1st W': 'working to play' (Mizen et al., 2000) vs '3rd W': 'working to live').
- The positioning of children as in 'desperate' (× 2), in need of 'help' (× 2) and 'protect[ion]' does not seem to allow for agency and decision-making (notwithstanding how this does not reflect young people's actual role within e.g. International Labour Organization debates).
- The girl child as the quintessential (deserving?) victim, exemplifying the elision between selective memory and cultural tourism that the term 'souvenir' encapsulated. By this, Hutnyk (2004) argues, the 'trinketization' of childhood deepens prevailing global inequities.

Notes

1. 'Il n'y a pas de hors-texte' (Derrida, 1978: 158). Frequently translated as 'There is nothing outside of the text', this aphorism has been widely misunderstood by critics of deconstruction as a statement of relativism and nihilism.
2. Such a view – that realities are mediated through text or discourse – places deconstruction within that broad strand of intellectual work known as *post-structuralism* – see Miller, Whalley and Stronach, in this volume.
3. A fuller version of this story would include how: (a) the staff indicated that there had been a design fault in the plans for the new complex by failing to include non-public showers; (b) that in lieu of this staff had arrived at an arrangement to open up the disabled shower rooms on request, which clearly posed problems with capacity, highlighted my middle-class status as having the cultural capital to have discovered this arrangement, and posed questions about how adequately they would be able to cater for disabled bathers, as well as (c) wider cultural-historical analysis of why/how most of us have come to prefer washing 'in private' (Elias, 2000).

Annotated bibliography

Reading instructions

Derrida's writing is notoriously difficult. His work assumes a familiarity with European philosophy, and is full of puns, word-plays, digressions and complications. The two texts recommended here happen to have excellent introductions. Culler also provides a good companion. There are also useful digests on the internet, from university departments of literary theory or philosophy. Typing your keywords into the Google search engine will usually throw up several useful sites.

Texts by Derrida

Derrida, J. (1981) 'Plato's pharmacy', in *Dissemination*. Trans. and introduction by Barbara Johnson. London: Athlone.
Deconstruction of speech and writing via Plato. Relatively accessible and entertaining, with a wonderful closing section where the Pharmacist becomes overwhelmed by the dissemination of meaning.

Derrida, J. (1978) 'Nature', 'Culture', 'Writing', in *Of Grammatology*. Trans. and introduction by Gayatri C. Spival. Baltimore: Johns Hopkins.

Deconstruction of speech and writing via Rousseau and Levi-Strauss. Hard-going, with a challenging introduction by Spivak; but this sets out and explains the basic terrain and concepts of deconstruction.

Commentary/introductory text

Deutscher, P. (2005) *How to Read Derrida*. London: Granta. An accessible introduction to Derrida's thought and writing.

Deconstruction and social research

Biesta, G.J.J. and Egéa-Kuehne, D. (2001) *Derrida and Education*. London: Routledge.
Edited collection by educationalists who know their Derrida.

Brown, T. and Jones, L. (2001) *Action Research and Postmodernism: Congruence and Critique*. Milton Keynes: Open University Press.
Thoughtful deconstruction of the nursery classroom and the discourses of child development, gender and action research.

Burman, E. (2008) *Developments: Child, Image, Nation*. London: Sage.
Explores how deconstruction and other critical frames can illuminate the ways representations of childhood function, both within psychology and social research and also within national and international development policies.

Lather, P. (2007) *Getting Lost: Feminist Efforts Toward a Double(d) Science*. New York: SUNY Press.
Lather's distinctive feminist-post-structuralism takes on research and praxis amongst the 'ruins' of methodology. Deeply informed by Derrida's work.

MacLure, M. (2003) *Discourse in Educational and Social Research*. Milton Keynes: Open University Press.
Methodological implications of deconstruction for social and educational research, via topics including parents' evenings, women's writing and life-history interviews.

Peters, M.A. and Biesta, G.J.J. (2009) *Derrida, Deconstruction, and the Politics of Pedagogy*. New York: Peter Lang.
An authoritative account of the implications of Derrida's work for politics and pedagogy, focusing on the humanism that the authors identify in his work.

Stronach, I. and MacLure, M. (1997) *Educational Research Undone: The Postmodern Embrace*. Milton Keynes: Open University Press.
Engagements between deconstruction and educational research, in the context of a range of research and evaluation projects with which the authors were involved.

Further references

Benjamin, W. (1955/1973a) 'The Storyteller', in *Illuminations*. London: Jonathan Cape. pp. 83–107.

Benjamin, W. (1955/1973b) 'Theses on the philosophy of history', in *Illuminations*. London: Jonathan Cape. pp. 245–55.

Clifford, J. (1990) 'Notes on field(notes)', in R. Sanjek (ed.) *Fieldnotes: The Makings of Anthropology*. Ithaca: Cornell.

Derrida, J. (1972) *Positions*. Trans. Alan Bass. Chicago: University of Chicago Press.

Derrida, J. (1988) *Limited Inc*. Evanston, IL: Northwestern University Press.

Derrida, J. (1996) 'As if I were dead: An interview with Jacques Derrida', in J. Brannigan, R. Robbins and J. Wolfreys (eds) *Applying: To Derrida*. London: Macmillan.

Elias, N. (2000) *The Civilising Process*. Oxford: Blackwell. Revised edition (trans. E. Jeffcott).

Hutnyk, J. (2004) 'Photogenic poverty: Souvenirs and infantilism', *Journal of Visual Culture*, 3(1): 77–94.

Johnson, B. (1987) *A World of Difference*. Baltimore, MD: Johns Hopkins University Press.

Lather, P. (1996) 'Methodology as subversive repetition: Practices towards a feminist double science'. Paper presented at the Annual Meeting of AERA, New York, April.

Mizen, P., Bolton, A. and Pole, C. (2000) 'School age workers: the paid employment of children in Britain', *Work, Employment & Society*, 13(3): 423–38.

Rajan, R.S. (1993) *Real and Imagined Women*. London and New York: Routledge.

From Hermeneutics to Post-Structuralism to Psychoanalysis

Tony Brown, Education and Social Research Institute, Manchester Metropolitan University, UK

Daniel Heggs, School of Health and Social Sciences, University of Wales Institute, Cardiff, UK

Summary

- Hermeneutic circle
- Four kinds of hermeneutics: conservative; moderate; critical; radical
- Distortions that are the source of self-misunderstanding
- Emancipation
- Self-identity/versions of self
- Key theorists and writers
  - Michel Foucault
  - Jürgen Habermas
  - Jacques Lacan
  - Paul Ricoeur

Key concepts

Tony Brown

The issues to be discussed in this chapter relate to the question: How does language shape the life it seeks to describe and how does life shape language? This circularity is an example of the 'hermeneutic circle', where 'hermeneutics' might be understood simply as the process of interpretation, often combined with the term 'phenomenology'; the logic of the world as experienced (see Titchen and Hobson, Chapter 14, this volume). The focus is on how people experience the world and make sense of it rather than on any notion of underlying truth. We consider these terms here in relation to how researchers experience and describe the world but also with how those descriptions impact on subsequent experience.

The chapter is guided by Gallagher (1992), who categorizes four forms of hermeneutics:[1]

Conservative hermeneutics

This early conception of hermeneutics is exemplified in the task of reading a text where the primary objective is to understand the author in the way the author intended, or within schooling, the learner's task is restricted to understanding what the teacher had in mind. As Schleiermacher puts it, this involves a 're-cognition and re-construction of a meaning (towards) prepar(ing) the individual for common participation in the state, the church, free society, and academia' (cited in Gallagher, 1992: 213).

Moderate hermeneutics

Leading exponents of twentieth-century hermeneutics were **Gadamer** and **Ricoeur** (e.g. 1981), for whom there are certain truths that orientate our way of seeing things. Moderate hermeneutics does not see tradition as fixed, but rather sees it as being transformed through an educative process, where its components are not seen as fully constituted objects to behold but rather as being in a permanent state of evolution. Hermeneutics permits a range of interpretations, some of which may be seen as being closer to the truth, yet no interpretation is ever final. Such understanding never arrives at its object directly as one's approach is always conditioned by the interpretations explored on the way. Here there is an attempt to capture the continuity of understanding in discrete forms, as explanations, which themselves then feed into and shape the continuous experience of understanding. Whilst one's own understanding may become 'fixed' in an explanation for the time being, such fixity is always contingent. Were I to act as if my explanation is correct, the world may resist my actions in a slightly unexpected way, giving rise to a new understanding, resulting in a revised explanation, providing a new context for acting and so on. This circularity between explanation and understanding is another encapsulation of the *hermeneutic circle*.

Critical hermeneutics (or critical social theory)

Here we have a conception of human behaviour understood in relation to consensual universal principles (e.g. moral perspectives, the existence of God, particular forms of common sense) that can be called upon in the event of some supposed divergence from rational behaviour. Its chief contemporary exponent, **Habermas**, aims for unconstrained language but sets out by supposing that in most societies language has become distorted as a result of the interplay of alternative forms of political power. Habermas seeks 'Ideal' communication without the hidden exercise of force resulting from supposed ideological distortion. His reflecting subject has a conception of the universal principles at work and of how any in-built contradictions to these can be overcome. This subject is thus trying to find ways of making things better from some supposed deficit position. This entails an *emancipatory* interest whereby these contradictions are confronted and action is designed to remove them.

Radical hermeneutics (or post-structuralism)

All my books … are, if you like, little tool boxes. If people want to open them, or to use this sentence or that idea as a screwdriver or spanner to short-circuit, discredit or smash systems of power, including eventually those from which my books have emerged … so much the better. (Foucault, cited in Patton and Meaghan, 1979: 115)

Foucault (e.g. Rabinow, 1991) rejects the idea of human activity being governed by universal principles and specifically rejects Habermas's notion of communication based around these.

The idea that there could exist a state of communication that would allow games of truth to circulate freely, without any constraints seems utopian to me. This is precisely a failure to see that power relations are not something that is bad in itself, that we have to break free of. I do not think a society can live without power relations, if by that one means the strategies by which individuals try to direct and control the conduct of others. (Foucault, 1997: 298)

For Foucault (1998: 448) 'no given form of rationality is actually reason'. There are no universal rules to be located beneath ideology. Habermas later suggested that with the publication of the *Birth of the Clinic* Foucault elected to abstain from dealing with texts through commentary and give up all hermeneutics, no matter how deeply it may penetrate below the surface of the text. He no longer (as he did in *Madness and Civilisation*) sought madness itself behind the discourse about madness.

Another leading writer identified with post-structuralism is **Derrida**, who has shown how our understandings of the present are conditioned by the media through which we receive depictions of it. Actuality is *made* and virtuality ('virtual images, virtual spaces, and therefore virtual outcomes') is no longer distinguishable from actual reality. 'The "reality" of "actuality" – however individual, irreducible, stubborn, painful or tragic it may be – only reaches us through fictional devices' (Derrida, 1994: 29).

And then to psychoanalysis

If phenomenology is the logic of world as it is experienced, how do we understand the 'person' 'experiencing'? Also, how do people use language in describing the world around them and by implication the way they see themselves fitting in? And how do we share ways of describing the world, which perhaps lock us into discourses that favour some more than others?

Freud is at the root of contemporary psychoanalysis. In the following extract Habermas characterizes the importance of Freud's contribution:

Freud dealt with the occurrence of systematically deformed communication in order to define the scope of specifically incomprehensible acts and utterances. He always envisaged the dream as the standard example of such phenomena, the latter including everything from harmless, everyday pseudo-communication and Freudian slips to pathological manifestations of neurosis, psychosis, and psychosomatic disturbance. In his essays on cultural theory, Freud broadened the range of phenomena which could be conceived as being part of systematically distorted communication. He employed the insights gained from clinical phenomena as the key to pseudo-normality, that is to the hidden pathology of collective behaviour and entire social systems. (Habermas, 1976: 349)

Thus Freud's work underpinned Habermas's critical quest to detect the faults in society more generally and find ways of repairing these. Freud's psychoanalytic sessions were predicated on a supposed cure achieved through 'helping the subject to overcome the distortions that are the source of self-misunderstanding' (Ricoeur, 1981: 265).

Giddens discusses this:

Self identity has to be created and recreated on a more active basis than before. This explains why therapy and counselling of all kinds have become so popular in Western countries. When he initiated modern psychoanalysis, Freud thought that he was establishing a scientific treatment for neurosis. What he was in effect doing was constructing a method for the renewal of self identity ... what happens in psychoanalysis is that the individual revisits his or her past in order to create more autonomy for the future. Much the same is true in the self-help groups that have become so common in Western societies. At Alcoholics Anonymous meetings, for instance, individuals recount their life histories, and receive support from others present in stating their desire to change. They recover from their addiction essentially through re-writing the story line of their lives. (1999: 47–8)

Perhaps this account of Freud provides a helpful metaphor for practitioner research in which the researcher is seen as a psychoanalyst's client who lies back on a couch and talks of her life, her motivations, fears and aspirations, which become more tangible as they are spoken to the analyst. The words and the way they are put together become part of her. The story that the client tells of her life shapes her actual experience by providing a framework against which she understands what she is doing. Nevertheless, this reification of lived experience can deceive as well as enlighten.

An alternative to Freud's quest for a cure, is possibly to be found in the writings of Lacan. Lacan (e.g. Homer, 2005) sees the human subject as caught in a neverending attempt to capture an understanding of his or her self in relation to the world in which he or she lives. The human subject is always incomplete and remains so, where identifications of oneself are captured in a supposed image, an image of which, Lacan insists, we should always be wary. Here the individual is forever on a quest to complete the picture she has of herself in relation to the world around her and the others who also inhabit it. She responds to the fantasy she has of the Other and the fantasy she imagines the Other having of her. The identity thus created evolves through a series of interpretations (and mis-recognitions) through interactions with others.

In the context of practitioner research, for example, reflective writing may provide a forum for building such a narrative layer, in which the researcher acts as her own analyst, as it were (Brown, 2008). The images constructed in this process provide material for the researcher to interrogate herself. In this perspective the flow of narrative is an on-going construction of a reflective/constructive/disruptive layer that feeds whilst growing alongside the life it seeks to portray.

Implications for research design

These alternative attitudes to how we relate to the language depicting our actions primarily lend themselves to practitioner research contexts centred on building analytical apparatus through which to inspect and develop practice. They are a powerful means of deepening self-understanding and building a conception of one's professional situation in terms of what one can do about it through a process that unfolds through time and experience. They relate to conceptions of action research shaped around *reflective* analysis, targeted at stimulating a process of 'professional development', that gets at how current practice is trapped in regulative, *conservative*, or merely tired models, by following a cyclical *reflexive* model in which new understandings of self emerge during the research process. The questions to be asked along the way might include: How do I understand the broader social context within which my work takes place? How do I resist/support the discourses that define my professional practice? What stories do I tell to justify my actions? Here the practitioner-researcher forges, and reflects upon, a professional trajectory within which the research situation is recognised as being a function of her evolving perspective and the discourses that shape her practice, resulting from successive encapsulations of herself created within the research process (*moderate hermeneutics*). In *critical hermeneutics* research this becomes a transformative process, primarily concerned with the 'emancipation' from the ideological structures that govern professional actions (curriculum frameworks, codes of conduct, legislative frameworks, terms of reference, etc.). *Radical hermeneutics*, meanwhile, entails a complete break with existing structures. For Foucault, each individual is responsible for her own self-mastery without reference to universal or ideological rules. The individual must harmonize any perceived antagonisms to create a 'balanced' person. Through such processes the researcher develops an understanding of her practical relation to the situation.

An analogy might be drawn between such processes and a sequence of *psychoanalytic* sessions where the researcher, in creating reflective writing, would be producing accounts of herself, revelatory of particular perspectives. That is, writing, produced as part of the research process, would be seen as providing declarations by the researcher, more or less aware, of who she was and of what she was trying to achieve. The writings would provide framings of the past and possible formats for crafting the future. Yet within a psychoanalytic framework this version of events is perhaps haunted by the bits that she chooses not to see, or is unable to see. The image might be seen as a cover story for things the researcher is finding difficult to address. At the same time the researcher has to reconcile her own image with the image others seem to have of her and also how the tasks she faces seem to be framed for her by others. But more broadly these cover stories might pertain to a wider community, specific forms of common sense or ideologies that govern ways of life (Žižek, 2008). The research might then become an attempt to address personal difficult issues or, more widely, to better delineate how ideologies shape forms of action.

Such research procedures may be shaped primarily around the researcher collecting autobiographical data, such as a reflective diary, over a period of time,

in relation to the world she occupies, perhaps shaped around some specific research questions that perhaps change as the research evolves. Such data could include the routine or mundane as well as more noticeable events. On-going discourse analysis of the data (see Lee and Petersen, Chapter 16, this volume) could provide points of reference for her in constructing an account of who she was at different points in time and in different situations. Through this later analysis the researcher could provide an account of her own evolving self as a professional and as a researcher, shaped around earlier data that now provide an historic account of earlier events and perspectives. This research approach is discussed more fully by Brown and Jones (2001). At an ideological level the research may be shaped more around discursive analysis of the structures that govern social action in specific populations, such as curriculum documents, codes of conduct etc. (Brown et al., 2006).

Stories from the field

Daniel Heggs

I have read comic books for as long as I can remember and had associated them with fleeting, simple pleasures, yet looking at them with a critical eye has changed my relationship with them. A general history of the medium might focus on humorous newspaper strips, American superheroes and children's comics and these dominate our common perceptions of what is suitable material for a comic. Here the relationship between word and image is seen as straightforward. Knowledge of the typical content then regulates understandings of the form. So, the 'silly medium, suitable only for children' (Barker, 1984: 6) is hampered by a restricted message, in spite of having 'a highly developed narrative grammar and vocabulary based on an inextricable combination of verbal and visual elements' (Witek, 1989: 3). Comics are texts in which representations are held in the blend of words and pictures, and so recognition of their hybrid form is an important first step in their analysis. This offers up a first problem. Interpretation and analysis develop from a translation of a hybrid medium into a verbal one. Simple description involves choices as to what is included, especially as intertextual knowledge can constrain what is focused upon. For instance, popular characters have a longevity that has seen them be regularly updated for new audiences and media. Batman and Superman have both moved into film, television, radio and cartoon. Our cultural knowledge of the characters and settings must be taken into consideration when looking at them critically as our preconceptions influence how a reading might progress.

The research from which this section is derived took Superman and Batman comic books as its main object of enquiry. These American superheroes have long and intriguing histories (Brooker, 2001; Wolk, 2007). They have been updated and translated for various media and are always in print in comic book form. It was important, then, to develop and employ a theoretically informed approach to the analysis of these hybrid texts that would remain sensitive to their signifying properties, that would provide a methodical and checkable approach and that would look to the function of the texts in broad cultural contexts. Concepts from narrative analysis, discourse analysis and psychoanalysis were employed in the readings of Batman and Superman texts in order that no single theoretical orientation dominated interpretation, thus allowing the logic of the world illustrated and as experienced to be shown. The role of the analyst/ interpreter is therefore central to any sense that is made of the text. I will now briefly outline what I take from these three interlocking areas of theory before offering an example reading.

Narrative analysis allows the general features of a plot to be explored and the particular narratives of the characters to be emphasized, and so I employed narrative analysis to focus on surface features of stories to be examined. Narrative also enables intertextual links to be highlighted, as narrative relates to other narratives, especially in the superhero canon. Discourse analysis was used to identify key themes beyond the salient narrative features. A Foucauldian approach allows emphasis on representation and meaning, which made its application to hybrid texts appropriate. Finally psychoanalysis was employed through the readings derived from discourse and narrative. Two broad areas, the Oedipus complex and the structure of fantasy, as described by Lacan, were focused upon. These two interlinking aspects of psychoanalytic theory enable issues of subjectivity to be explored and look to the relationship between the intersubjective and the intrasubjective. In this dimension the connections between the social and the individual are paramount, and these are grasped through an understanding of fantasy as a screen for desire. This goes beyond the internal logic of the text and includes the subjective position of the analyst/reader.

Each of these areas of theory could be employed independently, yet together they enable analyses to combine different perspectives so that meaning is not closed down through the application of a particular theoretical frame. As such the eclectic analysis I offer moves from post-structuralist, or radical, hermeneutics to psychoanalysis.

Example reading

Superman first appeared in the first issue of *Action Comics* in June 1938 and, much to the surprise of the publishers (McCue, 1992), was an instant success. Less than a year later, in issue 27 of *Detective Comics*, Batman had his debut. Although both characters have certain similarities – caped costumes and secret identities – it is the contrasts that provoke fascination. As a comic book author and illustrator put it '[t]heir primal, complementary qualities have given rise to the entire field [of superheroes] and, arguably, have defined its parameters' (Gibbons and Rude, 1992: Introduction). These can be grasped clearly through the origin stories for the characters. These stories provide a psychological backdrop for the motivations of the characters, offering accounts as to why young orphaned boys would take up the fight against crime or injustice while dressed outlandishly. Superman's origin story was told with his first appearance, and Batman's was told six issues after he debuted. Since then the stories have been repeated many times in different contexts. The retellings allow for different interpretations of the characters, yet also delimit the possible range of character representations. The origin stories might then be said to provide an immanent textual surveillance of the characters, conferring authenticity on the figures represented and so guaranteeing that a genuine Batman or Superman is illustrated.

The example reading is from *Superman and Batman: World's Finest* (Gibbons and Rude, 1992). It is a two-page spread (see Figure 34.1) that contrasts the origin stories for both heroes, and as such it highlights some of their structural similarities. Two main factors have influenced the selection of the text. First, it is not from the mainstream continuity of either character, but was from a special edition three-part series. The appearance of the characters deliberately harks back to the early Shuster and Kane versions and so recognizes the nostalgic appeal of the characters and their longevity as it pays homage to the 'team-up' titles of the 1940s and 1950s. Secondly, the juxtaposition of the two versions of the origin stories does some of the analytic work for a critical reader by illustrating the opposition of the characters in a complementary fashion.

The general approach I used is based upon Eco's semiotic reading of comic strips (Eco, 1987), but not in order to search for the meaning of the text so much as to look at the way that meaning is signified. A panel by panel description highlights relationships between verbal and visual elements in the text, which in turn enables links to be explored. The sequence of panels selected here show Batman and Superman dreaming. Following Clark Kent's and Bruce Wayne's attendance at a fund-raising event for an orphanage both sleep fitfully, recalling their origin stories in parallel. This device reminds us that both characters are orphans and that they passed through a traumatic event that makes sense of their superheroic actions. The panels are juxtaposed, with Superman's origins being shown in sepia coloured panels on the left-hand side of the page and Batman's in inky-blue on the right-hand side (in the full colour original). Reading the sequence over the two pages the breakdown of the central edge of each panel can be seen. Rather than simply offering a straight edge to the panels' contents the panels also represent meaning. Here a jagged pattern that becomes stronger through the sequence can be seen, indicating increasing agitation and disturbance on the part of the dreamers until they wake in the final two panels. As such, these origin stories are shown to be disturbing and powerful and maintaining an influence on the characters' actions.

The first panels show concerned and caring parents and the actions they take to protect the children, placing a child in a rocket to escape destruction or pushing him out of the way of a gunman. On the second page the first two panels depict the moments in which the course of the characters' lives is irrevocably altered with the launch of the rocket and the pulling of the trigger. The subsequent panels contain the consequences of the freeze-framed irreversible moments. A small child is held in the arms of a woman while a man behind her fights to put out a fire; a young boy is led away by a policeman while another searches for a pen and readies his notebook. Visible in the background of each panel is what has been lost by the characters, their biological parents. In the foreground are indications of their future roles. Such dreams are disturbing. Bruce Wayne and Clark Kent wake.

The sequence depicting the origin stories appears early in the story, once we have been introduced to the cities and main protagonists. We know that the

heroes are different, fighting different problems. The unwitting recollection of the origin stories implies a more complex relation and reaction to the orphanage than mere altruistic concern. There is an identification between the heroes and orphans in the loss of parents, and it is the circumstances of this loss that have led to the adoption of vigilante identities and distance from family life. The description of the text is the first stage of interpretation, which can be refined through the three theoretical terms to show how they can be employed in the analysis of the sequence.

The repetition of the origin stories is a key plot point showing motivation of the characters and tying them into the emotional development of the story as the heroes make an identification with the orphans – an important aspect as the orphanage plays a key role in the events of the story. The orphans need care and protection. The juxtaposition of the two stories shows them to be equivalent yet different: one a super-powered alien, the other a determined human. Further, the origin stories also tie the characters back into the superhero narratives that return to the late 1930s. Looking discursively, the importance of the family comes to the fore. Loss of biological parents is contrasted to an ideal of a caring and protective family life. A discourse on family helps to make sense of the characters' actions as they seek to protect people from social threats. Further, a discourse of the lone hero might be discerned in this as individual figures emerge from the traumatic loss of parents, showing them to be alone, even when they have the support of others. This points to the social/individual divide, whereby individual roles and actions are constructed from a social loss, that of family. This can be understood through psychoanalytic theory. The origin stories can be understood as *primal scene fantasies* as they are concerned with the origins of the superhero subject. The conflation of *primal scene* and *primal fantasy* alludes to the manner in which an important originary moment for the subject can be understood as not necessarily having taken place to be psychically effective, but that it is interpreted by the child as an act of violence by the father towards the mother. This can be grasped through Freud's elaborations of the Oedipus complex. First, the origin stories relate a crisis in the Oedipal situation in which the child is wrenched from the familial support network through an act of supreme violence. The adoption of the superhero role, then, is an attempt to resolve a crisis caused by the failure to enter into full symbolic relationship with the other. Second, Freud

Figure 34.1 *World's Finest* (Gibbons and Rude, 1992: 22/23).

argued, in *Totem and Taboo* (Freud, 1913), that the Oedipus complex was a repeat of a much earlier clan trangression that took place in pre-history. Without accepting Freud's claims, this idea of pre-history can be applied to the use of origin stories for the two heroes. The origins are re-enacted or re-imagined in their pre-history in dream-like time (Reiff, 1963). The origin stories describe two imagined and fantasized single events that took place in a pre-history and that constitute the hero identity in the present. The scene from the past becomes what it always was. As such we can see the way that origin stories can be repeated and give a coherence to the multiple versions of Superman and Batman.

The reading offered here is not unproblematic. The analysis was based on how to approach a hybrid text, with a particular concern with how the individual and social combine. Central, here, is the role of description, and not just for the way it supports interpretation. Description enables analysis to start, and so links between prior knowledge of the characters, the text and theory. As such, the description is important for the reflexive turn. Knowledge of characters and of theory influences the conclusions that are made.

From this brief analysis the hermeneutic process whereby narrative, discourse and psychoanalysis come together to show the functioning of a text has been illustrated. Narrative has highlighted how key events can be grasped and described, discourse analysis has shown how immanent features help to make sense of the narratives, and psychoanalysis has brought these two aspects together to offer an account for the importance and repetition of the origin stories as 'genuine' representations of superhero identity.

Note

1. The headings used are from his theoretical work in philosophy as a framework for discussing my own ideas which relate to a completely different field centred on practitioner research in education.

Annotated bibliography

Brown, T. and Jones, L. (2001) *Action Research and Postmodernism*. Buckingham: Open University Press.
This book offers detailed discussion of practitioner research carried out in the context of masters and doctoral degrees. It focuses in particular on hermeneutic enquiry in which reflective writing generated by the researcher builds towards an assertion of professional identity through which professional demands are mediated.

Brown, T., Atkinson, D. and England, J. (2006) *Regulatory Discourses in Education: a Lacanian Perspective*. Oxford: Peter Lang.
Here Lacanian psychoanalysis is employed to develop new ways of understanding educational domains. It analyses events, practices and policies that occur in school classrooms, teacher education and higher-degree studies including educational research. It provides an accessible introduction, description and analysis of those aspects of Lacan's work concerned with language, identity and subjectivity directly relevant to the field of education.

Gallagher, S. (1992) *Hermeneutics and Education*. Albany: State University of New York Press.
This book offers an excellent overview of theoretical perspectives. It provides an examination of how education offers a productive paradigm for work more generally in the social sciences.

Hall, S. (1997) *Representation: Cultural Representations and Signifying Practices*. Milton Keynes: The Open University.
An accessible introduction to how the language we use shapes our perception of life in the context of social science.

Harvey, D. (1992) *The Condition of Postmodernity*. Cambridge: Blackwell.
This book offers a clear exposition of postmodernity from the perspective of a geographer. It presents an interesting account of how conceptions of time and space themselves evolve through time and how this impacts on individual and social values.

Rabinow, P. (1991) *The Foucault Reader*. London: Penguin.
This edited collection gathers together a good selection of Foucault's work from different periods in his varied and influential writing.

Ricoeur, P. (1981) *Hermeneutics and the Human Sciences*. Cambridge: Cambridge University Press.
This collection provides some key writings by Ricoeur applicable in a broad range of social scientific disciplines. Centred on discussion of how understandings are processed as explanations it offers detailed examination of how language conditions the ways in which humans make sense of their world.

Further references

Barker, M. (1984) *A Haunt of Fears: The Strange History of the British Horror Comics Campaign*. London: Pluto Press.

Brooker, W. (2001) *Batman Unmasked: Analyzing a Cultural Icon*. London: Continuum Publishing.

Brown, T. (2008) 'Desire and drive in researcher subjectivity: The broken mirror of Lacan', *Qualitative Inquiry*, 14(3): 402–23.

Derrida, J. (1994) 'The Deconstruction of Actuality', *Radical Philosophy*, 68: 28–41.

Eco, U. (1987) 'A Reading of Steve Canyon', in S. Wagstaff (ed.) *Comic Iconoclasm*. London: Institute of Contemporary Arts.

Foucault, M. (1997) *Ethics*. Harmondsworth: Penguin.

Foucault, M. (1998) *Aesthetics*. Harmondsworth: Penguin.

Freud, S. (ed.) (1913) *Totem and Taboo. Penguin Freud Library 13*. London: Penguin.

Gibbons, D. and Rude, S. (1992) *Superman and Batman: World's Finest*. New York: DC Comics Inc.

Giddens, A. (1999) *Runaway World: How Globalisation is Reshaping our Lives*. London: Profile Books.

Habermas, J. (1976) 'Systematically distorted communication', in P. Connerton (ed.) *Critical Sociology*. Harmondsworth: Penguin.

Homer, S. (2005) *Jacques Lacan.* Routledge: London.

McCue, G. (1992) *Dark Knights: The New Comics in Context*. London: Pluto Press.

Patton, P. and Meaghan, M. (1979) *Michel Foucault: Power, Truth, Strategy*. Sydney: Feral Publications.

Reiff, P. (1963) 'The meaning of history and religion in Freud's thought', in B. Mazlish (ed.) *Psychoanalysis and History*. Englewood Cliffs, NJ: Prentice Hall.

Witek, J. (1989) *Comic Books as History: The Narrative Art of Jack Jackson, Art Spiegelman and Harvey Pekar*. Mississippi: University Press of Mississippi.

Wolk, D (2007) *Reading Comics: How Graphic Novels Work and What They Mean*. Cambridge, MA: Decapo Press.

Žižek, S. (2008) *Violence*. London: Verso.

From Structuralism to Post-Structuralism

Lee Miller, Faculty of Arts, University of Plymouth, UK

Joanne 'Bob' Whalley, Field of Theatre, University College Falmouth Incorporating Dartington College of Arts, UK

Ian Stronach, Faculty of Education, Community and Leisure, Liverpool John Moores University, UK

Summary

- Structural properties of a system
- Its functioning nature
- Relations and relationships
- The table is not there. It is only someone writing 'table'
- Irresolution and border-crossing
- Key theorists and writers
  - Basil Bernstein
  - Jacques Derrida
  - Michel Foucault

Key concepts

Ian Stronach

A boundary is not that at which something stops but, as the Greeks recognized, the boundary is that from which something begins its presencing. (Martin Heidegger, *Poetry, Language, Thought*, 1971: 152–3)

Think of a table. Flat top, four legs, standing there. Where? Here. In the centre of the table, there is a vase of flowers. What is the relation between the vase of flowers, the four legs and the tabletop? Do the legs and top need the vase for the table to work as 'table'? Does the vase 'perform' the table as table? Is the vase a part of the structure we call 'table', or is it merely decorative from a structural perspective?

One way of sorting out some of the preliminary complexities of vase-sits-on-table-with-four-legs-but-what-the-hell-is-going-on-epistemologically is to think of the table in terms of *structures* and *functions*. They are different. The tabletop 'needs' the legs in a way that it does not need the vase: the legs are structural necessities for the tabletop. One fewer and it wobbles. Two fewer and it falls. And with it its 'tablehood'? Yet the vase may be just as necessary for the table to be a table – rather than a stool, or something to stand on. The vase, then, defines the table as table in a quite different way. The vase is an object on the table just as knives and forks, or pens and phones might be. Their presence (culturally circumscribed as always, but we will ignore that for the moment) indicates that the object, which may or may not look structurally like the conventional range of objects that we call table, is being used *as* a table. Think of 'as' in the last sentence. It means 'in the function of'.

Where does that take us? A table is never wholly defined or undefined by its conventional structures: there is always an aspect of function that may disrupt or confirm the object-as-named object. The two notions work together either to define, disconfirm, or at least make us uncertain about, the object in its 'true' nature and 'proper' definition.

Now imagine that we all want to be 'tablologists'. One way of doing that would be to develop a line of thinking that was mostly oriented towards the structural properties of tables. A typology would soon emerge since snooker tables, for example, have very different properties and underlying dynamics from coffee tables and card tables. But in all cases we would hope to be able to find some deep, perhaps hidden properties of tables that constitute them as such. A universal theory of tables could then be derived from these commonalities. The theory might identify what essentially defines tables, moving from the descriptive to the analytical, the real to the ideal. In so doing, it would subordinate instances of variation to the status of peripheral and unimportant differences, or at least those unthreatening to the developing core epistemology of 'tablologists'.

Before we move on from this train of thought, let's take an example from Education, moving metaphorically not very far from the 'table' to the 'timetable', another object that can be held to have regular structures and definitive functions that constitute it as such.

Bernstein's famous paper 'On the classification and framing of educational knowledge' (1971) saw the curriculum as a kind of table. The timetable was compartmentalized into a number of boxes, usually containing 'subject' contents. These boxes were more or less cut off from each other. The degree to which they overlapped or were distinct encouraged Bernstein to develop concepts that expressed these features, like 'classification' and 'framing', either of which could be 'weak' or 'strong'. From these he claimed to have derived the underlying principles which shaped them and which in turn were related to broader social and political influences. We're not really concerned here with this theory as such but with its structural properties, indeed, with the theory as a carefully worked through instance of *structuralism*. Fortunately, Bernstein was explicit about his methodology and so leaves a clear trace of his thinking:

1. I shall first distinguish between two types of curricula: collection and integrated.
2. I shall build upon the basis of this distinction in order to establish a more general set of concepts: classification and frame.
3. A typology of educational codes will then be derived.
4. Sociological aspects of two very different educational codes will then be explored.
5. This will lead on to a discussion of educational codes and problems of order.
6. Finally, there will be a brief discussion of the reasons for changes in educational codes. (Bernstein, 1971: 48)

Without going into too much detail, we can see that what begins the inquiry is the inspection of surface phenomena (classes, teaching, learning, assessing, timetables, subjects, and so on). Beneath these, the theorist sees the *structural properties* of the curriculum or the pedagogical and assessment relations. He distinguishes between structural properties (like classification and framing), and those which in terms of the 'vase' analogy would be dismissed as decorative or unimportant. To the theorist, the actual content of the 'History' box doesn't matter: to the 'tabulist', it doesn't matter what kind of flowers. Both express interest only in the structural properties as 'deeper' markers that indicate hidden relations. Bernstein shows how knowledge can be 'classified' and 'framed' in different ways, either 'strongly' or 'weakly'. These concepts are not part of the surface description, although they are derived from it. Participants may not recognize them at all. He then relates those structures to still deeper and more general notions like 'code' and links the whole thing as a kind of *functioning*, where events at the broadest level (e.g. society) can be related to events at the microsocial (e.g. classroom). *By tracing the structural properties of the system, he is able to show its functional nature.* This clarification of hidden functioning by structural identification typified much of radical educational theorizing in the USA and the UK in the 1970s to 1980s. Its purpose was often expressed in terms of words like 'demystification', the unmasking of the ways in which power operated (*structures*) in educational systems to the ultimate benefit (*functions*) of economic elites.

It is of course only one example of structuralism. Bernstein was a classic theorist of this kind of approach, although there were others who took a Marxist approach. There are numerous examples of this kind of structural thinking, some of which you will already know. For example, Piaget claimed to have found some of the deep structures of learning, to have typologized stages of development (concepts like 'concrete'/'abstract').[1] Freud explored the mind in terms of its alleged structures. Similarly Marx made claims about being able to explain surface phenomena in relation to underlying stages of economic development. Each is quite different, politically, but each makes the same 'radical' move, offering to get to the root of things. As Raymond Williams points out, these are all examples of structuralism as an explanatory system:

> It is here, especially, that *structuralism* joins with particular tendencies in psychology (when Id, Ego, Superego, Libido or Death-Wish function as primary characters, which actual human beings perform in already structured ways). (1983: 306, emphasis in original).

Williams raised a problem for this kind of structuralism which it never satisfactorily resolved:

> ... it is a very fine point, in relation to any system or structure, whether emphasis is put on the *relations* between people and things, or on the relationships, which include the relations and the people and things related (1983: 306, emphasis in original).

The issue raised here concerns relations (which happen to us) and relationships (which we make). To go back to our analogy of the table, the problem was that tables don't have intentions and desires, but people do – in and out of the timetable. Thus issues of 'agency' as opposed to 'structure' grow more insistent. If relations do not wholly determine action and thought for people, then what is the role of active 'relationship' against the 'relations' in which people find themselves? This was an issue on which structuralism was apparently weaker, and which other 'isms' like phenomenology or 'social interactionism' placed in the foreground. They were, after all, primarily concerned with agency, interaction, and consciousness.

A further problem emerged. Universalist theories (e.g. of deep structures, elaborate connected systems that could explain all phenomena) developed a history of inconsistency over time, inconstancy over place, unpredictability over circumstance. Piaget, Marx, Freud all came under attack for the certainty and determinacy of their systems of thought, even by those who were sympathetic to their underlying concerns for child development, economic justice or psychic health. Worse still, such epistemologies relied

on subjects whose identities would be regular in their development, constant in their nature, and so capable of an 'authentic' expression (once whatever mystifications had been cleared up).

But before we get further into the problems of structuralism, and the solutions (or really non-solutions) of post-structuralism, let's go back to the table and think about some of the instabilities that our structural/functional thinking suppressed.

The first of these was signalled by the unexplained interjection in line 1 of this account, '... there. Where? Here.' It was an attempt to remind the reader that, (a) there *is* no table there, only the writing of 'table', and, (b) that the no-table – let's call it a *'writing-desk'* by way of a pun – is available to you only in imagination as a *'reading-desk'*, and on my say-so, though you may resist that say-so if you notice it as such, and that, (c) the time and circumstance of *'writing-desk'* is always political, pedagogically strategic, culturally coloured, quietly privileging.

So what's the problem? The table is not there. It is only someone writing 'table'.[2] The table is performed rather than represented and it is a command performance ('Think of a table'!). Writing performs the table, and positions the self who will read. The failure of the table ever to be neutrally *there* is repressed, and the impossibility of 'going back' to it is denied. The active engagement of the reader in this masquerade is demanded. The acceptance of the heuristic is imposed rather than proposed. What at first sight can seem to be an innocent attempt to recruit the reader to a new possibility in thinking can simultaneously be exposed as shot through with power-play, inauthenticity, manipulation and misrepresentation. This is what has often been called the 'linguistic turn' – an acceptance that these 'flaws' no longer seem open to correction. We have to live with the mess – there can be no recourse to a level of discourse where 'pure' structures/concepts/theories really tidy up the everyday nature of complexity and contradiction:

> What is profoundly unresolved, even erased, in the discourses of post-structuralism is that perspective of depth through which the authenticity of identity comes to be reflected in the glassy metaphorics of the mirror and its mimetic or realist perspectives. (Bhabha, 1994: 48)

Now we're thinking post-structurally, and maybe you can feel the difference. For a start *you're* here with me, as a paradox of that impossibility of which you have to be reflexively aware:

> You and I, we will never be here, and yet here we are. (Stronach, 2002: 294)

Perhaps that undermines the 'authenticity of identity', the 'easy realism' of writing, the unproblematic relation of author to reader. It makes them part of what we have to think about in the uneasy equations of writing and reading. The rest of Bhabha's claim is difficult to understand, but important. The 'glassy metaphorics' of the 'mirror' refers to Rorty's postmodernist account in 'Philosophy and the mirror of nature' (Rorty, 1980). In his account language can only pretend to 'mirror' nature. Structuralism sought a new language that would mirror the 'true' depth of things. Post-structuralism casts doubt on such projects, seriously modifies their ambitions and pretensions to clarity, challenges them as utopian, or eventually totalitarian in tendency. Here's a post-structuralist mirror to look into instead:

> The mirror takes place – try to think out the taking-place of a mirror – as something designed to be broken. (Derrida, 1981: 315)

Just as phenomenology sought out a favoured ground of 'presence', and structuralism sought insight through 'depth', so too (if any nutshell can do it) did post-structuralism draw most insistently on notions of 'difference'. With that term, a whole range of splits, disjunctions, displacements, and provisionalities, come to the surface. Post-structuralism claims they were always the hidden disasters, tragedies and crimes of the 'systems' of social and cultural thinking that preceded it, including, amongst others, structuralism. For such systems of thought, post-structuralism offers the last word, not in terms of definition, but in terms of irresolution. It is the last word for last words.

Which takes us back to the first quote. If post-structuralism *were* the last word in a definitive and arresting sense, it would be the latest paradigm. It would claim to set the boundary of what we can know, culturally, socially, educationally. But it is a different kind of boundary, which refuses to think in separate states, and insists on attending to the 'border-crossings'. It is more like the Heidegger quote with which we began, with a 'boundary' as an opening-out, a new 'presencing':

We should be done once and for all with the search for an outside, a standpoint that imagines a purity for our politics. (Hardt and Negri, 2000: 57)

Implications for research practices

Imagine a 'structuralist' at work in research. Firstly he (they mostly were) would collect data, as speech, documents, etc. Next, he might look for structural properties suggested by the data. And he would decide what sorts of theories (psychological, anthropological, linguistic, etc.) addressed his purposes in collecting such data. These would emerge, metaphorically, as 'depth' generalizations – stages of learning (Piaget) or grieving (Kubler-Ross), theories of 'Id' (Freud), types of organization (Handy). The surface would be sifted, gathered together, and analysed until it yielded its secrets. Note that the 'secret' has the property of being 'already there', awaiting discovery. And 'discovery' is a central metaphor for the structuralist in search of his hidden depths. This is not, then, a constructivist model.

Now for the post-structuralist. She will also collect data. But the process is a little different. There is a similar eye on what the subjects are saying, writing, doing. But the other eye, a cock-eye, is on what is not said, what discourses make it impossible to say, what practical or theoretical logics hide away from sight. The interest here, following Foucault, is in how power is intrinsically present in all forms of knowledge. It's a theory, therefore, that denies 'depth' its 'purity'. It says if you want to be profound, attend profoundly to the surfaces and pot-holes of discourses. And that attention implies a reflexive methodology:

> ... the formation and accumulation of knowledge – methods of observation, techniques of registration, procedures for investigation and research, apparatuses of control ... All this means that power, when it is exercised through these subtle mechanisms, cannot but evolve, organize and put into circulation a knowledge, or rather apparatuses of knowledge, which are not ideological constructs. (Foucault, 1980: 102)

Such an approach, empirically speaking, more or less demands an ethnographic approach. Ethnography collects data without first determining a focus; very often it is its surfeit or excess that turns out to be significant. Casting around in ignorance, confusion (and even despair!) is very much part of the process of coming-to-think. The relation between researcher, research object, and relevant data is much more recursive and expedient. 'Method' and 'methodology' are in a much more 'liquid' state. And their relation with 'theory' much more deconstructive. Current drives towards precise initial focus, a priori research design, are the antithesis of this approach – as Stronach (2010) is at pains to point out.

Stories from the field – 'taking the piss': notes on collaborative practice as research

Lee Miller and Joanne 'Bob' Whalley

On behalf of Roadchef, may I first of all say how thrilled we were to allow Lee and Bob permission to renew their wedding vows here at Sandbach. It's probably a landmark occasion for the motorway industry (Peter Kinder, Site Director, Roadchef Sandbach Services).

This story focuses upon a doctoral project in the domain of Performance Studies consisting of an originally devised, site-specific performance centred on Joanne 'Bob' Whalley and Lee Miller's renewing of their wedding vows. The one-off performance took place at Roadchef Sandbach Services on the M6 Motorway on 20 September 2002 in the UK.

When writing about their collaborative research, Gilles Deleuze commented on his work with Félix Guattari thus: '[s]ince each of us is several, there was already quite a crowd' (Deleuze and Guattari, 1988: 3). This sentiment accurately articulates our collaborative research and practice, because the research in which we were engaged lay in the interstices between us, a product of manifold conversations, arguments and dialogues.

Our collaborative practice as research had its origins in the chance observation of what appeared to be a bottle of urine, lying abandoned on the hard shoulder of the M6 motorway. In order to confirm our suspicions, we stopped to collect it, and having seen one bottle, we began to see them at regular intervals along the hard shoulder. Knowing that these bottles and their contents were the product of fellow travellers, Bob felt uncomfortable about simply taking them, and so it was decided that we needed to make some sort of exchange. At first we left behind

whatever we had in our pockets (coins, tissues, paid utility bills), but this developed into keeping a selection of items in the car, gifts that had been given to us, things with some provenance, things we could exchange for the bottles of urine we found on our travels.

Because of the illegality of stopping unnecessarily on the hard shoulder, a ritualized behaviour developed which performed the outward signifiers of mechanical failure. Lee would activate the car's hazard warning lights, open the bonnet, stand in front of the car and scratch his head. Throughout this, Bob would be executing the exchange, collecting the bottle and leaving the treasured item behind. Following the discovery of the first discarded bottle of urine and as a result of the many subsequent exchanges executed, we began to explore the position that the motorway occupied in current cultural perception. This found articulation in the writing of French sociologist Marc Augé, who conceptualizes spaces such as the motorway, the airport lounge and the shopping mall as 'non-places'. Augé remarks that:

> [i]f a place can be defined as relational, historical and concerned with identity, then a space which cannot be defined as relational, or historical, or concerned with identity will be a non-place. (1995: 78)

We felt that this was only a partial account of the motorway, one that ignored possible subversions of its 'normative' use, and so we sought to qualify Augé's thesis. On Friday 20 September 2002 we invited 50 family, friends and interested parties to the Roadchef Sandbach Services between junctions 16 and 17 of the M6 for the performance event *Partly Cloudy, Chance of Rain*. Between the hours of 11am and 4pm, 10 performers in wedding dresses, ten performers in morning suits, a six-strong choir, a three-piece jazz-funk band, a keyboard player and a priest occupied the site. At 12.30, we renewed our wedding vows in a ceremony that was open to all the users of the service station. After the ceremony, our guests were taken on a guided tour of the site, and users of the service station were witness to a variety of performative actions.

It might not seem appropriate, but I want to tell you a tale of heartbreak and tragedy. It is reputed that a ghost stalks this very bridge, this bridge that spans the northbound and southbound carriageways of the M6. Legend has it that Electric Suzy (a girl named for the multicoloured spiralled wire that connects the cab with the truck) walks the bridge, awaiting the day when an Eddie Stobart Lorry emblazoned with her name will set her free. It is said that she sings to pass the time and on a still day, it is possible to hear the strains of *Ave Maria* (text from *Partly Cloudy, Chance of Rain* 2002).

Within a postmodern context, the incursion into the service station provided by *Partly Cloudy, Chance of Rain* can be articulated as redundant, since the multi-accented sign already accounts for a multiplicity of readings, thus ensuring that place and non-place are given equal primacy. However, an acceptance of 'habitus' (Bourdieu, 1994) developed out of the functional need for a sedimentation of meaning, suggests that our incursion into the non-place was necessary. The project accounts for *both* a recognition of the slipperiness of language *and* a recognition of the need for a sedimentation of use, thus ensuring a dialogic both-and position is maintained.

The role of the vow renewal ceremony was to function as both parodic and sincere, to provide the audience with an experience that could not simply be reduced to the position of either/or, and thus support the creation of an exoteric/esoteric aesthetic. It was both a sincere event and a parody, and in this respect conforms to Linda Hutcheon's definition of the postmodern in which she states:

[p]ostmodernism offers precisely that 'certain use of irony and parody' … As form of ironic representation, parody is doubly coded in political terms: it both legitimizes and subverts that which it parodies. (1989: 101)

In order that our qualification of Augé's non-place might be successful, it was necessary to provide space for the wedding ceremony to function as a sincere event. However, at the same time we needed to provide space for the event to be read as parodic, to ensure that we were not simply replacing one mono-logic conception of space with another. In this way, the employing of parody can be articulated as a postmodern strategy of resistance, subverting and affirming that which is represented. By employing parody and sincerity within the same moment, we were ensuring that both the exoteric and esoteric aesthetics were accounted for.

As part of this site-specific performance work, we made tapes and CDs, which were sent to the guests who would be attending the renewal of our wedding vows. The central paradox comes from locating the aesthetic of self-hypnosis tapes to the interior landscape of the car on a motorway journey:

Close your eyes. Visualize a picture in your mind. Think of the most beautiful service station you have ever seen. Imagine a lovely service station in the sun. The car park lights are so tall and radiant. Graceful, beautiful floodlights. There are lovely golden fast-food outlets that are so completely unspoilt. There are wild and exotic plants. Some of them plastic. And the toilets are so clean, so clean, so clear, so calm.

The sun is shining from a perfect sky. It's a beautiful island. A service station that is private, belonging to you. Your own private service station.

In Augé's thesis, the motorway is a (non)place of transit: a scape to be traversed, lacking co-ordinates with the everyday world. The hypnosis text was intended to encourage the listener to recognize that, rather than the binary suggested by Augé (place/non-place), the experience of using the motorway is both dislocating and familiar at the same time. The taped narratives were thus encouraging the listener to engage in theory at the same time as experiencing that which the theory conceptualized.

The concept of 'situated cognition' (Brown et al., 1989) has been influential in shaping our approach to research and practice, allowing us to develop the concept we have termed 'operational knowledge'. 'Operational knowledge' refers to knowledges developed through intuition and experience, as much as through the objective analysis of data. Thus, *Partly Cloudy, Chance of Rain* sought to generate operational knowledge through the location of a site-specific performance within the quotidian space of the motorway service station, and was characterized by the user of the space encountering a challenge *to* the space she is using, *in* the space she is using.

Whilst the general users of the space do not necessarily have access to the vocabulary of Augé, their use of the space suggests that they are familiar with the concept, at least at an operational level. Thus, to provide a challenge without engaging solely in academic discourse, our research presented a context-specific qualification of Augé's thesis, one that would encourage the development of operational knowledge in the users of the service station. This explicit engagement with the thesis of Augé suggests that this project is both theory aware and knowledge producing, which led us to question for whom such knowledges are intended:

Interviewee One: I prefer a more traditional method myself.

Interviewee Two: What, with everybody taking tea and coffee and all that ... breakfast and dinner and ... no I don't think so. (*Granada Reports*, 6.30pm: 20 September 2002)

These two users of the Sandbach Service Station on the M6 were interviewed as part of *Granada Reports*, a regional television news bulletin for the North West. They were questioned about their experience of the location of a 'wedding ceremony' in the quotidian space of the service station.

The responses of the two interviewees, whilst not necessarily representative of all the users of the service station on that day, serve as useful markers of the position that the service station occupies in current cultural perception. The fact that both men responded negatively to the location of an explicitly anthropological event within the service station suggests that Augé's articulation of the non-place is operationally valid. The responses of the two men indicate that there is a certain sedimentation in culture of the public's attitude to the service station. Although the users of the space may not be consciously aware of the habitus of the service station, nonetheless they occupy the space according to a set of acculturated principles. Whilst it is fair to assume that the two men interviewed were unlikely to be familiar with the arguments and terminology of Augé, their responses suggest that they have an operational understanding of the habitus of the service station.

Whilst it is possible to construct an entirely written thesis to qualify the way in which Augé articulates the operation of non-places within society, this qualification would provide no account of the way in which the 'non-place' is used. The aim of *Partly Cloudy, Chance of Rain* was to go beyond a qualification of Augé within his own terms. Instead, it sought to provide an operational alternative to the habitus articulated in the responses of the two men interviewed for *Granada Reports*. Whilst we can articulate our conceptual framework and challenge Augé in an appropriately academic manner, this sort of academic discourse is not enough if the aim of our research is to affect some sort of operational shift. The location of *Partly Cloudy, Chance of Rain* at the Roadchef Sandbach Services on the M6 motorway was in part an attempt to provide a challenge to the concept of the non-place at an operational level. This strategy provided us with the opportunity to challenge a habitus of how the motorway is perceived by the users of such spaces, thus allowing the motorway to be the site of both a contestation and a generation of knowledge.

Notes

1. Those interested in education in England might like to mark the irony that school effectiveness claims no affiliation to 'theory'. It is about what works. Yet the notion of 'key stages' (structuring education around age ranges 5–7, 7–11, 11–14, and 14–16) is based on a 'common-sense' notion that relies somewhat on the spinning corpse of Piaget.
2. Note the irony: I have to use speech marks to indicate 'writing marks' – for which we have no sign.

Annotated bibliography

Atkinson, P. (1985) *Language, Structure and Reproduction. An Introduction to the Sociology of Basil Bernstein*. London: Methuen.
Paul Atkinson is a leading sociologist of education in the UK. He has long complained of the neglect accorded Bernstein's work in recent years. In Chapter 2, 'A structuralist anthropology of schooling', Atkinson outlines what he takes Bernstein's position to be. You will find that it clashes with the account implied above in that he finds Bernstein to be 'suggestive' rather than 'definitive' in his theorizing. Chapter 7 may interest you: in it Bernstein meets Foucault, or, if you like, structuralism meets post-structuralism.

Foucault, M. (1979) *Discipline and Punish: The Birth of the Prison*. Harmondsworth: Penguin.
Foucault was a prominent thinker about the nature of the 'social', whether that's about clinics and the medical gaze, the nature of knowledge down the ages, or in this case – his earliest post-structuralist work – the nature of discipline. Try reading 'The means of correct training' to get a flavour of the difference between his style, which is much more historical and genealogical, and that of Bernstein.

Hardt, M. and Negri, A. (2000) *Empire*. Cambridge, MA: Harvard University Press.

If Foucault's *Discipline and Punish* is early post-structuralism, this book travels through what it argues are the final positive achievements of post-structuralism and deconstruction, and arrives at a new revolutionary state based 'not on the basis of resemblances but on the basis of differences: a communication of singularities' (2000: 57). I have my doubts, but the first 50 pages take you through the outline of the journey.

Stronach, I., Piper, H. (2008) 'Can liberal education make a comeback? The case of "relational touch" at Summerhill School', *American Educational Research Journal*, 45(1): 6–37.

This article offers a critical case study of the famous 'free school' and 'child democracy' that is Summerhill School. The authors consider how the school works as a community and as a learning culture. They upend theorizing about schools, arguing that the school is a 'benign panopticon' that makes redundant the strictures and procedures of the audit culture, which in the guise of Ofsted tried to close the school down in 1999. The article offers an example of 'case study' critically conceived, as well as elements of 'grounded theory' and 'deconstruction'.

Stronach, I. (2010) *Globalizing Education, Educating the Local: How Method Made Us Mad*. London: Routledge.

This book offers a critical and deconstructive account of global discourses on education, arguing that these overblown 'hypernarratives' are neither economically, technically or philosophically defensible. Nor even sane. Their 'mythic economic instrumentalism' mimics rather than meets the needs of global capitalism, in ways that the Crash of 2008 brings into vivid disarray. The book offers 'local' alternatives to global discourses, exploring possibilities for methodology and theory.

Further references

Augé, M. (1995) *Non Places: An Anthology of Super-Modernity*. Trans. J. Howe. London and New York: Verso.

Bernstein, B. (1971) 'On the classification and framing of educational knowledge,' in M. Young (ed.) *Knowledge and Control. New Directions for the Sociology of Education*. London: Collier-Macmillan. pp.47–69.

Bhabha, H. (1994) *The Location of Culture*. London: Routledge.

Bourdieu, P. (1994) *Distinction: A Social Critique of the Judgement of Taste*. Trans. R. Nice, 2nd edn. London: Routledge. (1st edn, 1984.)

Brown, J.S., Collins, A. and Duguid, P. (1989) 'Situated cognition and the culture of learning', *Educational Researcher*, 18(1): 32–42.

Deleuze, G. and Guattari, F. (1988) *A Thousand Plateaus: Capitalism and Schizophrenia*. Trans. B. Massumi. London: The Athlone Press.

Derrida, J. (1981) *Dissemination*. Trans. B. Johnson, 2nd edn. London: Athlone. (1st edn, 1972.)

Foucault M. (1980) 'Power/Knowledge', in C. Gordon (ed.) *Selected Interviews and Other Writings 1972–77*. Brighton: Harvester. pp. 170–94.

Heidegger, M. (1971) *Poetry, Language, Thought*. New York: Harper & Row.

Hutcheon, L. (1989) *The Politics of Postmodernism*. London and New York: Routledge.

Rorty, R. (1980) *Philosophy and the Mirror of Nature*. Oxford: Blackwell.

Stronach, I. (2002) 'This space is not yet blank: Anthropologies for a future action research', *Educational Action Research*, 10(2): 291–307.

Williams, R. (1983) *Keywords: A Vocabulary of Culture and Society*. London: Fontana.

36

Feminism/Post-Structuralism

Bronwyn Davies, University of Melbourne, Australia

Susanne Gannon, University of Western Sydney, Australia

Summary

- Three feminisms: liberal; radical; post-structural
- Relations of power
- Gendered discursive practices
- The rational conscious subject is de-centred
- Grand narratives are challenged
- Key theorists and writers
  - Judith Butler
  - Bronwyn Davies
  - Patti Lather
  - Betty St Pierre

Key concepts

Feminist post-structuralist theory can be taken as a third feminism, historically following on from, but not replacing, liberal feminism and radical feminism (Kristeva, 1981). Whereas liberal feminism mobilizes a discourse of individual rights in order to gain access to the public domain, and radical feminism celebrates and essentializes womanhood in order to counteract the negative constructions of women and girls in masculinist discourse, feminist post-structuralism troubles the binary categories male and female, making visible the constitutive force of linguistic practices, and dismantling their apparent inevitability.

Post-structuralist analysis begins, then, with the discursive and regulatory practices in the texts of science, of literature, of philosophy and of everyday life. It calls into question the grand narratives through which the humanist/modernist individual is made into the heroic, creative origin of him- or herself, and it shows, in contrast, how individuals and their social and geographical worlds are made possible in relation to one another. Feminist post-structuralist theorizing focuses in particular on the specific processes whereby individuals are made into gendered subjects.

Feminist post-structuralism makes visible, analysable and revisable, in particular, the male/female and straight/lesbian binaries, which are, in turn, mapped on to other binaries such as adult/child, normal/abnormal, rational/irrational. Through analysis of texts and talk, it shows how relations of power are constructed and maintained by granting normality, rationality and naturalness to the dominant term in any binary, and in contrast, how the subordinated term is marked as other, as lacking, as not rational. Through examining the ways the social inscribes itself on the individual, and by calling into question the construction of the individual in the essentializing terms of humanist and modernist theories, post-structuralist theory shows how it is that power works not just to shape us as particular kinds of being, but to make those ways of being desirable such that we actively take them up as our own.

This approach troubles 'foundational ontologies, methodologies, and epistemologies' (St Pierre and Pillow, 2000: 2) and opens up the possibility of a different kind of agency. That agency is no longer the defining feature of the successful, powerful, heroic, lone individual, retracing well worn narrative trajectories, but that of the subject-in-relation who is, in Deleuzian terms, open to the not-yet-known (Deleuze, 2004). That subject-in-relation is an ethical subject, who is reflexively aware of the constitutive force of her discursive practices, and of the particular social, historical moments, and material contexts in which her ongoing differentiation (becoming other than she was before) is made possible. She is thus capable of disrupting the signifying processes through which she constitutes herself and is constituted. As Butler (1992: 13) says, the 'subject is neither a ground nor a product, but the permanent possibility of a certain resignifying process'.

In this way post-structuralist feminism breaks with theoretical frameworks in which gender and sexuality are understood as inevitable, and as determined through structures of language, social structure and cognition. The *agency* that feminist post-structuralism opens up does not presume freedom from discursive constitution and regulation of self (Davies, 2000). Rather it lies in the capacity to recognize that constitution as historically specific and socially regulated, and thus as able to be called into question. Agency is contingent on the discourses at play and on our positioning within them (Davies, 2008). Not only are we constituted through multiple and contradictory discourses, but how those discursive positionings are read opens up or closes down the possibility of agency. Through writing we can open up strategies for resisting, subverting, decomposing the discourses themselves through which we are constituted (Barthes, 1977; Davies and Gannon, 2009).

In post-structuralist analysis the rational conscious subject is decentred, and the play of desire and the unconscious are made relevant. Old ways of knowing, such as through master or grand narratives, are resisted as arbiters of meaning, even while they are recognized as having constitutive force. It is not that the grand narratives with their rational, agentic heroes no longer have force, but they are read against the grain of dominant ways of seeing.

New subjectivities may be generated through post-structuralist activities of reading and writing, not through opposition and resistance but through a series of escapes, of small slides, of plays, of crossings, of flights – that open (an other, slippery) understanding. (Cixous and Derrida, 2001). Agency in post-structuralist writing is not understood, then, in terms of an individual standing outside or against social structures and processes. Agency becomes instead a recognition of the power of discourse, a recognition of one's love of, immersion in and indebtedness to that discourse, and also a fascination with the capacity to generate life; not just the endless repetition of old habituated practices, but the generation of new life-forms, life-forms capable of disrupting old meanings of gender, even potentially overwriting or eclipsing them. We are thus subjects-in-process, subjects-in-relation, and through ongoing processes of differentiation we may eclipse the gendered discourses and regulatory practices through which we are constituted (Davies and Gannon, 2009).

While the 'discursive turn' of post-structural theory has led feminists to attend to the constitutive effects of language, and to develop powerful strategies for deconstructing gendered binaries, recent work by feminist post-structuralists turns further towards 'spatiality' and 'materiality'. In work influenced by Deleuze, for example, subjectivity can be understood as an 'assemblage' of flows of desire and affect of varying speeds and intensities, not bounded but constituted in relation to other human and non-human subjects, spaces, times, surfaces and events. The subject is thus always 'non-unitary' and 'inhabits a time that is the active tense of continuous becoming' (Braidotti, 2002: 62).

Feminist post-structuralist research is focused on the possibility of moving beyond what is already known and understood. Its task is not to document differences between those categorized as men and those categorized as women, but to multiply possibilities, to de-massify ways of thinking about 'male' and 'female' – to play with the possibility of subjectivities that are both and neither – to understand power as discursively constructed and spatially and materially located. Discourse, or more properly, discursive practices, have the power to hold the normative order in place, and the power to open up the not-yet-known. In the analysis of gendered discursive practices in texts and talk, the following summary may be a useful guide to help avoid some of the pitfalls generated by adherence to scientific principles and 'evidence-based-practice' much loved by contemporary managerialists intent on controlling academic practice:

(1) 'Data' do not stand as transparent *evidence* of that which is real. Accounts or descriptions or performances of gendered ways of being reveal not the truth of gender, but *the ways in which sense is being made of gender*, or *the way gender is being performed* in that particular text and context.

(2) The way that sense is made of gender in accounts or descriptions or performances is not of interest because it might reveal something about the individual sense-maker, or about his

or her motives or intentions. Rather, interest lies in the insight it may give us into *the processes of subjectification and the kinds of gendered subjectivities that are available within particular discourses.*

(3) Subjectification involves the simultaneous imposition and active take-up of the gendered conditions of existence (Butler, 1997). Discourses do not originate in the subject, yet each subject takes them up as her own, defends them, desires their maintenance, and understands herself in terms of them.

(4) The language that is found in texts and talk is not of interest because it reveals something other than itself. It is interesting because it may be deconstructed and broken open to show *the ways in which the real is constructed*, for example through binary categorizations, through habituated, unreflected repetitions, and through particular repeated images, storylines and modes of explanations.

(5) Researchers are not separate from their data. The complexity of the movement between knowledge, power and subjectivity *requires researchers to survey gender from within itself.* They use their own bodies, affects and relations with others (both human and not human) as texts to be read.

(6) 'Science' is the product and practice of systemic discourses that produce knowledge in ways that are, notwithstanding the fact that they are generally highly regarded, not necessarily better than others (Lather, 2007). Furthermore, scientific discourses and practices may be seen to produce the very thing they set out to measure. The psy-sciences, for example, are themselves implicated in the production of the liberal humanist gendered subject (Henriques et al., 1998).

(7) *Neither the gendered subject who produces the texts to be read, nor the researcher, is the final arbiter of meanings* in any text being read. Gendered experience is constituted through multiple discourses, which give rise to *ambivalent understandings and affects.* Understanding gendered experience (one's own, and that of others) is very often through the recognition of ambivalence and contradiction. The insistence on interpretations cleansed of doubleness, oppositions and multiplicity is a strategy through which the illusion of the rational subject is constituted.

(8) The point of a feminist post-structuralist analysis is not to expose the hidden truth of sex/gender

in all its simplicity, but to *trouble that which is taken as stable/ unquestionable truth.*

(9) Gendered subjects exist at the intersection of multiple discursive practices. *The individual is not fixed at any one of these points or locations.* Not only does the individual shift locations or positions, but what each location or position might mean changes with shifts in relation to others (both human and non-human others), and over space and time.

(10) Power is understood in terms of lines of force. It is not the property of one gender. Its *strategies, its manoeuvres, its tactics and techniques* are always contingent and unstable (Deleuze, 1988; Foucault, 1980).

(11) Feminist post-structuralist theory is interested in the folding and unfolding of history, in the movement from one configuration of feminism (Kristeva, 1981) or of gender (Davies, 2003) to another, and in the lines of flight that may open up the not-yet-known. The researcher working with post-structuralist theory may contribute to those lines of flight rather than remain simply an observer of others' lines of flight (Deleuze, 1988).

The example of feminist post-structuralist work we will draw on in this chapter is collective biography. Collective biography is a post-structuralist methodology that works with the memory stories of both researchers and research participants. It moves beyond individualized readings of the subject's remembered stories towards a sense of subjects who are constituted in common discursive, relational and material spaces. In collective biography workshops convened for the purpose of collaboratively researching a particular topic, memory stories are told, then written, then read out loud and usually re-written following careful listening to the read story by the group. Through this process, each storyteller works to express the very 'this-ness', or hæcceity, of the remembered moment. Hæcceity is integral to what Deleuze calls smooth space – the space that escapes the over-coded striations of territorialized space. In *Doing Collective Biography* (Davies and Gannon, 2006), we coined the term mo(ve)ment in order to evoke the doubled action involved in our collective storytelling and writing, of dwelling in and on particular moments of being, and of movement towards, or openness to, new possibilities both of seeing and of being. In telling, listening, questioning, writing, reading and rewriting our stories, a shift takes place such that the memories are no longer told and heard as just autobiographical (that mark one individualized person off from the next), but as openings through which each subject's specificity in its particularity and sensory detail becomes the collectively imagined detail through which we know ourselves as human, even as more human – as humans-in-relation.

Implications for research design

Post-structural ethics requires the researcher to remain open to the not-yet-known, the not-yet-understandable. Funding bodies and the apparatus of institutional ethics review are gripped by a liberal-humanist desire for control that assumes that ethical practice will be guaranteed by adherence to rules and prior modelling of the research process. They presume researchers are unable to make ethical decisions without this surveillance. Such thinking is based on universal notions of general human attributes and rights accompanied by assumptions of the irreducible alterity of the other – that other being fragile, passive and in need of protection. Post-structural ethics in contrast struggles toward a different kind of respect for the other, one which does not divide researcher from researched, but comprehends their mutual embeddedness in discourse and relations of power. The research cannot thus be totally planned in advance but maintains its openness to the other, and to the ethical demands that arise in the encounter with the other, where the researcher will become someone-she-was-not-already.

The asking of research questions in post-structurally informed research must be well-grounded not just in the substantive literature, but in the post-structuralist philosophy that may help to open up a completely new way of envisaging what it is that might become known. Once again, however, it is vital that the question itself be open to evolution through the research process, as the researcher, in relation with her research subjects, comes to think differently about what it is possible to know.

Post-structuralist theorizing does not hold with positivist conventions that rely on method as a guarantor of truth or 'validity'. Truth arises, rather, from engagement with the other, from the particularity of events that the researcher is able to apprehend in relation to the other, from a specific kind of listening to the other that stretches the ears of the listener, that requires the listener to be open to

becoming different and in that difference, to know the world differently (Badiou, 2001; Nancy, 2007).

There are many methodological approaches to feminist post-structuralist research – since the emphasis is on the process of exploration rather than the following of a method. Its instruments are not so much instruments of measurement, but equipment in Heidegger's sense (1993). The equipments of feminist post-structuralist research emerge through the research, becoming something other in their use. Although we outline the steps we have taken in conducting a collective biography (Davies and Gannon, 2006), we emphasize that the practice of collective biography will become something else each time it is used.

Ideally all the participants in the collective biography workshop will work together on the analysis of the stories to see in what way they can be used to generate new understandings desired by or imagined within the originating research question. The ways in which the stories can be used emerge both in the workshops and in the writing of the stories, as well as, finally, the writing of the collaborative paper since writing too is a method of inquiry (Richardson and St Pierre, 2005).

Stories from the field

The collective biography workshop that we draw on here was one where we set out to understand more closely the implications of feminist post-structuralist theorizing for the meaning and experience of 'being a subject'. The post-structural subject-in-process that we invoke in collective biography workshops is one who plays between a close and detailed observation of what she finds in her memories *and* one who recognizes the constitutive force of that same moment of speaking/writing such a description. The post-structural subject might be said to exist at the site of an almost intolerable contradiction, a contradiction that is necessary to comprehend subjectification. Butler says of this necessary ambivalence:

> The subject is itself a site of this ambivalence in which the subject emerges both as the *effect* of a prior power and as the *condition of possibility* for a radically conditioned form of agency. A theory of the subject should take into account the full ambivalence of the conditions of its operation. (Butler, 1997: 14–15)

In this particular workshop we re-examined the 'break' between humanism and post-structuralism, since we had noted the persistence of humanist conceptions in our own thinking and writing, despite our immersion in post-structuralist thought. During the workshop sessions we generated memories around themes that had emerged from preliminary readings and discussions on the subject in post-structuralist theory. We used these themes as triggers for memories of: 'being someone'; 'being hailed as someone in a way that felt good'; 'being mis-recognized'; and 'changing'. They enabled us to *re*-remember particular moments when we recognized ourselves (and others recognized us) as *particular* selves, as unique and unitary individuals differentiated from others – qualities that we saw as productive of humanist subjects. In the workshop sessions we each told one or two memories, in response to each trigger, to the group. We then wrote them, read them aloud and began collectively interrogating the sorts of 'selves' we produced ourselves as in these memories. After we had parted, analysis continued online as we typed up and annotated the final versions of our memory stories. Finally, we took turns with the evolving draft of an analytical text using the memories as data. We moved back and forth between personal and collective knowledge, between lived experience and theoretical understanding, and between narrative and analytic texts as we continued to struggle towards a paper to which we could all put our names.

While liberal humanism might read our stories as snapshots of progress towards a more or less stable and self-contained personhood, reading through a feminist post-structuralist lens enables us to read them as stories of (in)appropriate(d) femininity, providing instances of the ways in which subjects are constituted as these particular (sexed) subjects, at these particular moments, in these particular social contexts. We found as we wrote that though instability and slippage mark post-structuralist analyses, they do not erase or displace the humanist analyses that are always already there. The two memories analysed below demonstrate our way of working with memory texts as well as the precarious, tangled subjectivities we constructed within them.

My school report card had arrived. My parents silently read the comments written in neat careful handwriting in each of the boxes. The report card was passed over to me to read. There was a comment in relation to each school subject. Then at the bottom, in the seven or so lines of overall comments, the word 'conscientious' appeared. I'd never heard the word, or read it before. I wondered what it meant. I asked, and when my mum told me, I thought it sounded good. I had my own special word. I felt proud and important. I read it over and over to myself. I liked having that word on my report card. I savoured the word, the sound of it, the speaking of it, the meaning of it. There was no discussion about my coming first in the class. Then my father pointed out to me that I shouldn't think I was better than my big sister. She was in the B grade at her boarding school solely because of subject preference. She wanted to study art. And dressmaking was useful for a girl. She was coming near the top of her class, and she was excelling at tennis, which was very pleasing to him. She might be chosen to represent her school. I felt shamed about feeling proud, shamed that I was not good at tennis. But I liked that word, conscientious, its curious spelling, the sound of it, the virtuous feeling of it. I went around saying it to myself over and over.

This memory, generated in response to 'being hailed as someone in a way that felt good', can be understood in a liberal humanist reading as indicative of developmental progress. A school psychologist, for example, might conclude that the girl is emotionally well adjusted and from a good family. She is succeeding at school and her parents take care to ensure that she is sensitive to the needs and skills of other family members. The words on the page are taken as clues to the (real) existence of the individual subject with a particular eye to her adjustment to the social world and to any possible areas where her capacity to adjust might be flawed and in need of remediation. From a post-structuralist perspective the story might be read in terms of the process of subjection to the term *conscientious*: 'Subjection exploits the desire for existence, where existence is always conferred from elsewhere; it marks a primary vulnerability to the Other in order to be' (Butler, 1997: 20). The child experiences herself as willingly embracing the term, despite the lecture she receives from her father about not thinking she is better than her sister. She can therefore be read as the resisting subject, as well as the desiring subject. She can also be read as being taught by her father the precise and detailed embodiment of pleasure in her achievement – it will be quiet, not displaying itself as superior. She takes up these limitations in the correct form of desire and attitude and bodily comportment in the dual act of being recognized and recognizing herself. In order to be, she is vulnerable to the report-writing teacher and the father. The story shows the process as *both* an imposition *and* an act of agency in which she seeks out and lives the meaning of herself, her subjecthood, within the terms made available to her. The girl did not first experience herself as conscientious and then learn the word for it. In hearing herself described as such, her experience is constituted as such. She is constituted (subjected) as conscientious and she actively takes up the constitution of herself inside the new term that she understands as a desirable way of being. At the same time she reads herself as already that kind of person.

In the second story, told in response to the prompt of 'misrecognition', a young teacher is called into an undesired and abject naming by a student:

> She asked a question and looked across the hands thrust up into the air to Alex over by the window, up to something, as usual. 'Alex', she said, calling him back to attention, 'What do you think of blah blah blah?' Suddenly, Roslyn stood up in the centre of the room and shouted 'You only ask the boys questions,' she said, 'because they've got penises'. Everyone stared at her as she stood at the front of the class, the tears in a burning rush up behind her eyes and her throat choking. She wanted to say, 'No, you've misunderstood'. Or 'No, that is the last thing I would want to do'. But she thought she would collapse, or explode, and she couldn't speak through her horror at these words. She turned and walked out of the classroom before they could see what they'd done to her, she marched briskly up the path, heart thumping, feeling like she might throw up. She marched straight into the staff toilets where she locked the door and sat on the seat and sobbed and sobbed until the bell rang.

This story enters volatile terrain. The teacher sees herself as sensitive and responsive to the needs of students, as professional and reasonable, as equitable. Yet, in her classroom practice, she falls into an old gender trap where – for diverse reasons – teachers tend to interact more with boys than with girls in classrooms. Although the teacher has the 'power' to select this student (Alex) rather than that one (Roslyn) to participate in the discussion, her authority is tenuous and depends on the more or less willing subjection of students to the disciplinary regimes of the school and the classroom. Roslyn refuses this subjection and assumes authority in the class, bodily by 'standing up' and 'shouting' into a space where she is not authorized to stand or speak, discursively constituting the teacher as one who only attends to boys. The humanist question the teacher might ask herself in that moment is 'Am I really that person?' and she struggles to do this in the story by examining her conscience and her practice and beginning to rehearse answers to that question. But it is not possible to answer from this unspeakable place. These students are young men and women. Roslyn's accusation is that her excessive interest in the boys is because of their male genitals. She cannot debate this rationally with Roslyn/the class. It is a dangerous moment, as the violent reaction of her body reveals. In feminist post-structuralism, this embodied response is as relevant as the words that are spoken in mapping the dynamic relations and effects of power. In particular, post-structuralism questions the workings of relations of power – between the teacher and Alex, between the teacher and Roslyn, between the rest of the class and these subjects – and how they are constituted in the moment-to-moment interactions of that intense social space.

Binary categories slip and slide through this story. The teacher reads Roslyn as 'the students'. Although only one student speaks, the teacher leaves the room 'before they could see what *they* had done to her'. She positions herself in binary opposition to the whole class (whom she imagines aligned with Roslyn, though they too may be stunned into silence). Another binary fracture exists between the rational reflective teacher of her imagination and the sexist, capricious, even lascivious, woman that Roslyn names her as. In this story, she is not willing in her subjection to Roslyn's conferral of this new subject position but she lacks the resources to resist it. She *has* been favouring the boys. She *is* sexist in her practice, in effect if not in intention. And because her way of 'being' has been named in that way, so too her way of thinking (about herself, her practice, her students) is cast in that moment in terms of sex/gender rather than through any other possible categories. The binary shifts from teacher/students, to women/men. 'Woman' entails the (un)teacherly characteristics of emotionality and susceptibility to desire. But she *is* a woman as well as a teacher, and, as in other spheres of her life, these multiple subject positions are in delicate balance, fluid, and precariously achieved.

We could say much more about these stories but for now note that our analyses demonstrate the sorts of issues and approaches we are interested in as feminist post-structuralist researchers. Using lived experience as the ground for theorizing is central to feminist research, as is our particular interest in examining discourses of sex/gender. Post-structuralism enables us to attend to processes of subjectification and discursive regimes. In our analyses of the speaking subjects of these stories, traces of the self-contained liberal humanist subject remain in some readings but our subjects are called into existence in social spaces where power and knowledge circulate unpredictably and where subjects are always tenuous, in process, vulnerable and prone to decomposition.

Annotated bibliography

Braidotti, R. (2002) *Metamorphoses: Towards a Materialist Theory of Becoming*. Cambridge, UK: Polity.
Elaborates sexual difference, materiality, embodiment and technology as it reworks feminism and post-structuralism through a 'cartography of becoming'.

Butler, J. (2004) *Undoing Gender*. Abingdon and New York: Routledge.
Further develops theories of gender performativity and explores the consequences of undoing normative conceptions of sex and gender. Gender is understood as reiterative, unstable, citational and improvisational.

Davies, B. (2000) *A Body of Writing*. Walnut Creek, CA: AltaMira Press.
An engagement with feminist post-structuralist theory that defies the boundary between theory and embodied practice. Concepts of subjectivity, agency, feminism and power are elaborated through vital depictions of life experience and empirical research.

Davies, B. (ed.) (2007) *Judith Butler in Conversation: Analysing the Texts and Talk of Everyday Life*. New York: Routledge.
Implications of Butler's theorizing are taken up in a range of interdisciplinary contexts that are placed in conversation both with each other and with Butler herself. Notions of subjectivity, performativity, desire, melancholia and intelligibility are worked through social sites including kindergartens, theatre, academia and politics.

Davies, B. and Gannon, S. (eds) (2006) *Doing Collective Biography: Investigating the Production of Subjectivity*.

Maidenhead, Berkshire: Open University Press/McGraw Hill.
Elaborates the methodology of collective biography and puts it to work in relation to post-structural concepts including knowledge/power and subjectivity.

Hyle, A., Ewing, M., Kaufman, J. and Montgomery, D. (eds) (2008) *Dissecting the Mundane: International Perspectives on Memory-Work*. Lanham, MD: University Press of America.
Demonstrates the breadth of epistemological approaches to collective memory-work taken up by feminist researchers across diverse disciplines and paradigms including post-structuralism.

Lather, P. (2007) *Getting Lost: Feminist Efforts toward a Double(d) Science*. New York: SUNY Press.
Resituates and interrogates earlier articulations of post-structuralism and feminist praxis within a context of paradigm proliferation and demands for 'scientificity' in educational and social research.

Mazzei, L. and Jackson, A.Y. (eds) (2009) *Voice in Qualitative Inquiry: Challenging Conventional, Interpretive, and Critical Conceptions in Qualitative Research*. Abingdon and New York: Routledge.
Aims to strain the notion of 'voice', and to push it to its limits, by deconstructing notions of presence, authenticity and reflexivity. It exemplifies the methodological instabilities and the transgressive possibilities of feminist post-structuralist approaches to research.

St Pierre, E.A. and Pillow, W. (eds) (2000) *Working the Ruins: Feminist Post-structural Theory and Methods in Education*. New York: Routledge.
Demonstrates the creativity and breadth of research undertaken by feminist post-structuralist educators.

Wilson, E.A. (2004) *Psychosomatic: Feminism and the Neurological Body*. Durham, NC: Duke University Press.
Shows the limiting effects of the prevailing tendencies in science and in feminist studies to marginalize, and even to repudiate, the material body and the biological dimensions of the human subject. It asks instead how science can contribute to contemporary accounts of embodiment in the humanities and social sciences.

Further references

Badiou, A. (2001) *Ethics: An Essay on the Understanding of Evil*. Trans. P. Hallward. London: Verso.
Barthes, R. (1977) *Roland Barthes*. Berkeley, CA: University of California Press.

Butler, J. (1992) 'Contingent foundations', in J. Butler and Scott, J.W. (eds) *Feminists Theorize the Political*. New York: Routledge. pp.3–21.

Butler, J. (1997) *The Psychic Life of Power*. Stanford: Stanford University Press.

Cixous, H. and Derrida, J. (2001) *Veils: Cultural Memory in the Present*. Stanford: Stanford University Press.

Davies, B. (2003) *Shards of Glass. Children Reading and Writing Beyond Gendered Identities*, 2nd edn. Cresskill, NJ: Hampton Press. [1st edn, 1993.]

Davies, B. (2008) 'Re-thinking "behaviour" in terms of positioning and the ethics of responsibility', in A.M. Phelan and J. Sumsion (eds) *Critical Readings in Teacher Education. Provoking Absences*. Netherlands: Sense Publishers. pp. 173–86.

Davies, B. and Gannon, S. (2009) *Pedagogical Encounters*. New York: Peter Lang.

Deleuze, G. (1988) *Foucault*. London: The Athlone Press.

Deleuze, G. (2004) *Difference and Repetition*. London: Continuum.

Foucault, M. (1980) *Power/Knowledge*. Brighton: The Harvester Press.

Heidegger, M. (1993) *Basic Writings*, 2nd edn. Ed. D. Farrell Krell. New York: Harper Collins.

Henriques, J., Hollway, W., Urwin, C., Venn, C. and Walkerdine, V. (1998) *Changing the Subject: Psychology, Social Regulation and Subjectivity*, 2nd edn. London: Methuen. [1st edn 1984.]

Kristeva, J. (1981) 'Women's time'. Trans. A. Jardine, *Signs*, 7(1): 13–35.

Nancy, J-L. (2007) *Listening*. Trans. C. Mandell. New York: Fordham University Press.

Richardson, L. and St Pierre, E.A. (2005) 'Writing: A method of inquiry', in N.K. Denzin and Y.S. Lincoln (eds) *Handbook of Qualitative Research*, 3rd edn. Thousand Oaks CA: Sage. pp. 959–78.

Glossary

We would like to thank Harry Torrance, Professor of Education at Manchester Metropolitan University UK, for providing us with critical feedback on the draft of this glossary.

The aim of this glossary is to give an indication of the breadth of meaning attaching to a number of terms in common usage amongst different groups of social science researchers, rather than simply to give dictionary definitions. Where terms have been used only once and glossed at the point of use they are not included in the glossary. Some terms are defined fully in specific chapters and readers are recommended to use the index to locate the actual page(s) where the term is described.

As it has not been possible to go into any real depth, readers are recommended to use a reference book such as the *Fontana Dictionary of Modern Thought* (Bullock and Trombley, 2000) in addition to this glossary. Numerous definitions can also be found on the internet through (www.google.com) by searching on: define: (term)

Affordances refers to the physical properties of an object (in Vygotskian terms, a 'tool') which determine how it can be used. The affordances of a tool offer human beings possibilities for developing ways of using it, but do not, in themselves, determine human behaviour.

Agency refers to the capacity of a human being to take action and exercise control in formal or informal social groups. Whether or not individuals have agency is sometimes disputed on the grounds that their actions are determined by the social structures within which they live. This is known as the 'structure and agency debate' (see **Structure and agency**).

Anthropological refers to a tradition of research which focuses on human beings (the original meaning of anthropology was 'the study of mankind'). It is used to refer to research methods which give importance to spending long periods of time collecting data 'in the field' (the site of study), often using participant observation and/or interviewing.

Artefacts are constructed objects which may be tools or texts or any products of human beings. In post-Vygotskian theory they have a special significance because tools or cognitive frameworks/procedures mediate all human activity. (See **Mediation**)

Assessment means determination of relative worth. Assessment can refer to individuals, groups or organizations, and can be done both quantitatively and qualitatively. In quantitative research it will involve measurement against a standard.

Authentic (authenticity) is used in qualitative research to describe data that genuinely represent the views and values of individual participants. Data might not be authentic if they are collected under conditions that are likely to have shaped responses. In quantitative research authentic data relate to the respondents' interests in order to elicit reliable responses.

Axiology refers to philosophical questions relating to the nature of values.

Behaviourist psychology emphasizes the importance of stimulus and response in human behaviour, which translates into practice in terms of giving material or psychological rewards to subjects who exhibit desired behaviours.

Belief is a conviction of the truth of something which is based on faith rather than evidence.

Bias means an in-built tendency to see the world – and hence to interpret data – in a particular way. Researchers either need to eradicate bias or understand it through a process of reflexivity and account for it in reporting their work.

Binary oppositions are categories which are paired, so that their difference is emphasized. For example, embedded in the 'mind/body' binary pair is the notion of their separation. Western philosophy, going back to the ancient Greeks, has had a tendency to create binary oppositions and make it more difficult to perceive things holistically. In post-structuralist theory and deconstruction binary opposites are seen as forcing oppositions and indicating hidden mechanisms of power and control embedded within language.

Categories are types of data. When employing quantitative methods the researcher makes decisions at an early stage about what categories of data to collect. When using a grounded theory approach the categories are drawn out from the data as part of the process of analysis.

Cause and effect (causal, causation) refers to the process of establishing a causal link between a 'treatment' and a research outcome. It requires a particular kind of research design which makes it possible to measure the impact on the dependent variable of changing one of the independent variables. To demonstrate causality three conditions need to be present:

1. The causal variable needs to precede the effect variable in time.
2. The causal and effect variables need to be correlated with one another.
3. No third variable can be the cause of the relationship demonstrated under 2.

Correlations which establish strong associations between variables are insufficient to prove cause and effect. (See **Variables**, below.)

Classification is the process of organizing data into types (classes) and naming them.

Clinical is the term used, particularly in the field of health, to describe research in practice settings such as hospitals or health centres.

Co-construction is used to describe the process whereby interaction (dialogue, working together) between two or more people leads to constructing knowledge, or identity, and so forth.

Cognitive refers to the inner processes of the mind by which knowledge is constructed and organized, such as awareness, perception, reasoning and judgement.

Composite measure in quantitative research means that several measures have been combined to produce one overarching measure that incorporates them all.

Concepts are internal representations of ideas and/or phenomena which are key component parts in human understanding. In quantitative research a concept will need to be operationalized, that is represented by a number of measurable/observable indicators.

Conceptual framework in quantitative research is the set of concepts and indicators that provide an overall description of the field of study. The research can then be designed to collect data that cover all aspects of the framework.

Confidentiality is a term that means that data have been given to the researchers on the understanding that they will not be made public without specific prior permission, and that the identity of participants in the research will remain concealed.

Constructivism is the term used to describe a theory of knowledge which stresses the active process involved in building knowledge rather than assuming that knowledge is a set of unchanging propositions which merely need to be understood and memorized.

Contingent means dependent upon circumstances, events, and so forth.

Correlation is the term used in quantitative research to describe the relationships between two variables. They are correlated with one another if they are associated with one another more frequently than would be expected randomly.

Correspondence theory of truth assumes that truth corresponds to a fact or facts, that it is established in relation to an observable reality in the world.

Critical is used to describe engagement with and interrogation of assumptions and meanings that are not immediately obvious. It does not have the straightforward negative connotations that it has in common usage. However, it often denotes an oppositional stance to assumptions of authority and normality.

Critical incidents are occurrences of human behaviour that have been observed, or described in interview, and are selected by the researcher as the focus for further investigation. They are 'critical' in the sense that they seem to be particularly significant and are likely to be worth analysing in depth.

Critical theory started with a group of philosophers in Germany (in the late nineteenth/early twentieth century), known as the 'Frankfurt School', who emphasized the importance of analysing the unspoken and implicit power relations governing actions and understandings. It incorporates from the work of Marx the notion of 'false consciousness' to describe how individuals are disempowered by the social structures which shape how they think as well as how they act.

Cultural capital is the term used for the cultural assets that children acquire in the home and from their social milieu; because educational processes are congruent with particular (middle class) cultural backgrounds, cultural capital can in turn influence subsequent academic performance. (See **Habitus**, below.)

Cultural norms refer to the expected social practices, value assumptions and so forth which social groups develop and impose on their members and mutually enforce.

Culture, as used in social science research, means the whole range of social practices, artefacts, value assumptions and daily routines which are associated with a social group. The social group can be of any kind, from the people who live in a particular community, to members of a professional group such as nurses, to those with a particular religious or national background, and so forth.

Cyberspace is the location of internet surfing, email interactions, online chat and interactive web-based games. People enter cyberspace when they go online.

Data saturation is used to describe the point in qualitative research when the issues contained in data are repetitive of those contained in data collected previously. It indicates that sufficient data have been collected, for example that it is not necessary to carry out any more interviews.

Deductive (deduction) refers to the process of using established theories as a framework to interpret empirical data in contrast to inductive/induction (see below).

Demographic data are data relating to the population, such as age range, socio-economic status, ethnicity. They are nearly always collected in surveys in order to enable a judgement to be made about the representativeness of the respondents in terms of the larger population.

Dialectics is a method of argument and refers to the shaping of ideas through considering oppositional points of view, challenging one with the other and reaching conclusions through a process of recognising the competing claims made by each. Its modern form derives from Hegel and assumes progress in ideas through the development of thesis, antithesis, synthesis.

Dialogic strategies (dialogue) are research methods which involve discussion between participants and genuine sharing of ideas on the basis of equality.

Dichotomy refers to two sharply divided types or groups (see **Binary oppositions**).

Discursive constitution (discursive colonization, discursive practices) refers to the process whereby individuals are constructed into particular roles or performances by the assumptions and values embedded in the verbal utterances and texts dominant in their social group.

Disrupt is a word used in feminist and post-structuralist theory for the creative agency which disturbs and unsettles assumptions that would otherwise be oppressive (see also **Transgressive**).

Distributed cognition refers to the creative process whereby ideas and knowledge are developed through social interactions (between individuals, artefacts and the environment) rather than by individual minds.

Dogmatism is used to indicate fixed adherence to a set of principles or beliefs. It always indicates inflexibility.

Emancipation literally means 'setting free'. It is an important concept in post-Marxist theory where it has come to mean the process whereby individuals can be freed from ideological constraints imposed by society, including their own false consciousness, by learning to analyse their social context and experiences critically to uncover hidden mechanisms of power and control (see also **Critical theory**).

Empiricism (empirical) describes an approach to research which assumes that all concepts are derived from experience. Empiricism, therefore, gives high priority to the collection of data by observation (using the five senses: sight, hearing, touch, smell and taste). It is often used to criticize quantitative research, but qualitative research that involves interviewing, observing, or capturing images in the field of study, is also empirical and can drift into empiricism if such data is not interpreted and theorized appropriately.

Enculturation refers to the process whereby human beings become imbued with the social practices, value assumptions and routines of the social group in which they live and work (see **Culture**).

Enlightenment (the Enlightenment project) is the name given to the intellectual and cultural renaissance that began in Europe in the second half of the seventeenth century and dominated approaches to philosophy and research until well into the twentieth century. It emphasized the importance of scientific progress over belief. It assumed that knowledge and truth could be established, and develop over time, in the service of human emancipation, through observation, experimentation and the exercise of reason. It is criticized by postmodern and post-structuralist researchers as failing to bring the promised progress and as just one more belief system which ignores the complexity, ambiguity and emotionality of human experience.

Epistemology (epistemological) refers to philosophical questions relating to the nature of knowledge and truth.

Essentialize refers to the process of identifying the fundamental qualities or essence of a set of practices, ideas or group of people (for example women). In the politics of identity, essentializing is seen as a means whereby constraints are imposed on individual freedoms.

Ethnomethodology refers to a research approach which adopts the methods of ethnography but may not strictly be classifiable as ethnography. It tends to be used loosely to define research which gives priority to collecting data about people using methods such as interviewing and unstructured observation, and using description and narrative in reporting.

Evolutionist (social Darwinism) refers to the notion that economic, social and political organization evolves in accordance with very similar rules to those that govern the development of species in Darwin's Theory of Evolution. It emphasises the extent to which particular forms of human and social organization are adaptations to the environment in which humans find themselves.

Existential refers to a body of theory that sees human existence as radically different from other objects. Human behaviour is shaped by experience rather than being pre-determined. Existentialism therefore places emphasis on understanding the inner world of experiences of human beings and to the individual acting to give meaning to their own life.

Experimentalism (experiment) is an approach to research which involves setting up an experiment, running it and measuring the outcomes. In its pure form, experiments must be set up in such a way that all the variables are controlled except the one that is to be measured, making it possible to prove causality (see **Randomized controlled trials**).

Factor analysis (factors) in quantitative research is a technique that identifies the general dimensions or concepts within a set of responses to questions, bringing together a range of correlated variables into a smaller number of factors which can be interpreted more easily. It is also used in scale development and to reduce data.

Falsifiability is the term used in Popperian philosophy of science to replace verifiability. Popper argued that it would never be possible to prove the truth of any proposition because of the limitations of human experience. It was, therefore, preferable to seek to falsify a proposition, so that if this proved impossible the proposition could be said to have been established as true until such time as evidence was found to disprove it.

Field/the field (field work) is the place in which research data are collected. The use of this term reveals the origins of much qualitative research in anthropological studies in which the researcher left home and went to live with a community which was often located in a rural area. However, the term 'field of study' is also used across all disciplines.

Functionalist refers to designing research to be 'fit for purpose' with a particular emphasis on outcomes which can be easily applied to policy and practice.

Gender is the term for the socioculturally constructed characteristics of masculinity and femininity. It normally refers to social or cultural differences rather than biological ones.

Generalizable (generalization, generalizability, generalizable laws) is the term used to claim that knowledge generated by research in a specific context will also hold true in other contexts. Claims to generalizability turn on the research sample adequately representing the population to which the generalization refers, but the concept is regarded as highly problematic by many social science researchers who argue that knowledge is always context-dependent (see also discussion in the chapter on Case Study).

Genre refers to a type or style of text, which can either be a written text or an image-based text such as a movie or a radio soap opera. Genres are socioculturally constructed and become part of even young children's experience very early: for example, 'Once upon a time …' is easily recognizable as the opening of a fairy story.

Globalization refers to the growing economic interdependence of countries across the world. In social science research it is seen as the process whereby the concerns of individuals and nation states are becoming increasingly dependent upon international economic trends, flows of capital, the activities of multi-national companies, and policy borrowing across countries and continents. Globalization has increased rapidly since 1990 as a result of the internet and digital communications.

Grand narratives is a term used in postmodern and post-structuralist theory for the explanatory stories – or theories – which impose an all-encompassing framework on the complexity of human experience. Grand narratives capture human imagination because they give us a sense of order and control, but post-structuralists believe they distort human understanding and are fundamentally oppressive.

Habitus refers to the whole sociocultural environment in which individuals or groups live and by which their social persona are constructed. Habitus envelops the whole person, incorporating gestures, discourse, clothes, intellectual assets, social class, gender and so forth, all of which are constructed by learned behaviours and interactions within the family group, school and community (see **Cultural capital**).

Halo effects are distortions in the data resulting from the research process itself producing inflated outcomes (children working harder, workers making more effort, and so forth).

Hegemony is the process by which power is allocated and exercised in social groups. It often refers to the exercise of power through the control of ideas.

Heterogeneous is applied to individuals or things which are different from one another.

Heteronormativity refers to the societal assumptions that give authority to heterosexual relations and assume that other sexual orientations are abnormal.

Heuristic refers to the process of discovery or problem-solving that is central to the research process. It involves informed judgement grounded in experience rather than systematic analysis of data. It is the creative, heuristic process that takes researchers beyond the data to deeper insights.

Holistic refers to a research process which does not fragment or categorize data prior to analysis but, instead, looks at all the data in relation to one another, and makes judgements on the basis of the big picture.

Homogeneous is applied to individuals or things which are similar to one another.

Humanism is a philosophical system which gives priority to human values, actions and the products of the mind. It is associated with the Enlightenment and places emphasis on the importance of rationality as well as human creativity.

Hypothesis is the term used for a proposition that will be tested in subsequent research. Alternatively, hypotheses emerge during the early stages of data analysis and are tested in later rounds of data collection and analysis. In this case, emerging hypotheses can be seen as the first step in theory development.

Ideal types are created by researchers as a way of organizing data during analysis. Since individual informants are all unique they are not easy to categorize, but three or four 'ideal types' may be developed from holistic analysis of data and these can be presented, drawing on examples from actual responses of selected individuals to illustrate particular features.

Identity (identity formation) is the socioculturally constructed sense of self which is centrally important in terms of human agency. Identity either empowers or constrains individuals depending on its social formation (see also, **Positioning**).

Ideology is the term for a body of beliefs that is shared by a social group, nation or political party and provides the basis for action.

Illuminate (illuminative) is used in qualitative research to mean that light is being shed on things which would otherwise be hidden. It often refers to the process of uncovering, and challenging, previously unquestioned assumptions.

Immersion refers to the process whereby researchers engage totally in the field of research, quite the opposite of trying to maintain distance.

Indicators are standards or other measures specified in advance, against which performance can be evaluated.

Inductive (induction) refers to the process of constructing theories from empirical data by searching for themes and seeking to make meanings from the evidence, in contrast to deductive/deduction (see above).

Informant (key informant) is the term for someone who provides the researchers with data, often through giving an interview or responding to a questionnaire. A key informant is the term used in participatory research (originally ethnography) for an individual who, through local knowledge and social status, is able to give the researchers access to the community under study.

Instruments is the term for materials developed by researchers for data collection and analysis. They include interview schedules/protocols, questionnaires, pro-forma for observations, record sheets for coding, and so forth.

Intelligence refers to the mental capacity to acquire and use knowledge. Whether or not intelligence is inherited and can be measured has been the source of considerable disagreement among social science researchers. It is now generally recognized to be constructed from a combination of inherited capacities and sociocultural nurturing.

Interdisciplinary refers to the process of bringing two or more disciplines (such as economics, psychology, politics) together.

Inter-observer (inter-rater) reliability is a technical term for making sure that when several researchers work together and conduct observations in different settings they are, as far as possible, observing the same things, applying the same analytic criteria in the same way, and able to reach valid (because comparable) judgements.

Interpretivist is the term given to research in the hermeneutic tradition which seeks to uncover meaning and understand the deeper implications revealed in data about people. Interpretivist is a broad category which encompasses a wide range of research approaches including ethnography and case study.

Intersubjective refers to the process of interaction between self and other, which may be actual or used as a metaphor for the relationship between self and the expectations of the social group.

Intervention refers to the process whereby researchers introduce a change and observe its impact, for example on group behaviour. In some research methodologies the researchers invite the participants in a social group to introduce a change and work with them to explore the outcomes. In both these cases the research focuses upon the impact of the change and its implications for future development.

Intrasubjective refers to the internal reflexive process of self awareness and self-discovery (see also **Reflexivity**).

Legitimation is the process of establishing the validity of someone or something and recognizing its rights.

Logical positivism was the original form of positivism (see below) which established logic and the principle of verification as essential elements in the search for knowledge and truth.

Longitudinal study refers to research which takes place over time in order to track changes and development. The length varies: at one extreme a longitudinal study might track a sample of individuals over their life time; at the other extreme, a longitudinal study may only span four or five years. Shorter studies cannot really be called longitudinal.

Managerialism is used to describe an approach to organization which emphasizes monitoring of performance and the application of standards. It is often used with much the same meaning as the term 'audit culture'.

Marxism refers to the social, economic and political theories developed by Karl Marx through a process of historical analysis; it focuses particularly on who controls the means of production and the inequalities inherent in capitalism between capital and labour (see **Critical theory**).

Measurement is the term used in quantitative research to describe the production of outcomes that are precise, quantified and reliable.

Mediation (Distributed Cognition, Zone of Proximal Development) is used in post-Vygotskian psychology to refer to the process whereby tools (including language), artefacts and social organization are an integral part of human activity. Human activity is dependent on the mediating context in which it takes place so that agent and tool, together, are the unit of analysis for research. Mediation of the knowledge-building process by groups working together is known as 'distributed cognition'. Mediation by a knowledgeable other (often an adult working with a child) is the process which supports individuals in achieving what they could not otherwise achieve (in their 'zone of proximal development').

Meta-discourse (meta-narrative, grand narrative) is used in postmodern theory to mean a set of ideas or theories which have been constructed and imposed on the complexity of human experience and constitute a manipulative and oppressive act of control.

Metaphysical refers to the process of developing ideas, concepts and philosophical positions without any direct reference to human experience. It develops theories from what are called 'first principles' (abstract notions of worth and value) rather than empirical data.

Methodology in its narrowest sense is the collection of methods or rules by which a particular piece of research is undertaken and judged to be valid.

However, it can be used in a broader sense to mean the whole system of principles, theories and values that underpin a particular approach to research.

Mind refers to consciousness, the inner mental processes of a human being. In Cartesian philosophy it was seen as separate from body and this mind/body dichotomy still persists in 'western' culture. The development of mind (learning) has been and remains a major focus of study in educational psychology.

Models (modelling) (1) are diagrammatic representations used to assist in understanding complex theories, practices, systems, and so forth. Their strength lies in their simplicity which provides an organizational framework for planning or analysing research or any other activity. Models may not literally be represented in diagrammatic form but they always provide a conceptual framework in which each aspect of a complex system has a place in relation to other aspects.

Models (modelling) (2) in quantitative research is the term for a framework that displays the relationships among a number of factors. This may either be set up in advance to guide data collection, or more than one model may be applied during the analysis stage to find the 'best fit'.

Modernity (or modernism) refers to the system of thought and broad cultural movement (involving art, architecture, poetry and the like) which developed at the end of the nineteenth and during the first half of the twentieth century. It is often used by postmodernists to signal connotations of unwarranted certainty and structural solidity which attempt to impose control by means of rationality.

Neo-liberalism refers to a set of political beliefs that see deregulation and a free market as the means of ensuring economic growth and hence prosperity for all.

Normalization refers to the hidden processes whereby individuals are socially conditioned to conform to normative standards and practices.

Normative is a term that denotes conformity to an authoritative standard. It is used to describe the values and ideals of a society, but can have connotations of oppression for those who celebrate identity differences.

Objectivity (objectivist, objective) refers to the removal of the persona (emotions, knowledge, experience, values, and so forth) of the researcher from the research process. It is seen as central to the quality of research based on epistemological

assumptions that truth can be determined as something distinct from particular contexts or participants (see also **Correspondence theory of truth**).

Ontological (ontology, ontologically) refers to philosophical questions relating to the nature of being and the reality, or otherwise, of existence.

Open coding is a term used to describe a procedure for analysing qualitative data. During a detailed reading of a text (e.g. interview transcript), the researcher writes 'concept' descriptors in the margin to indicate the contents of each paragraph (or short extract). If the concept descriptor uses words from the text itself, it is called an 'in vivo' concept. The concept descriptors for the whole text then become the basis for deriving a small number of 'categories' which become the framework for analysis.

Organic is a term used to mean living and capable of developing.

Outcomes is used as an alternative to 'findings' or 'results' to describe the knowledge that is generated by research. The choice of the word 'outcome' often indicates that epistemologically the research is not concerned with producing measurable, generalizable truths.

Paradigm is a term used to describe an approach to research which provides a unifying framework of understandings of knowledge, truth, values and the nature of being. There are a number of different paradigms (e.g. interpretivism, positivism).

Participant researcher refers to a researcher who is a participant in the community or activity that is the object of research. Participant researchers do not seek to remain objective, but instead acknowledge their subjectivity and employ reflexivity (see below) to ensure quality.

Performativity in post-structuralist theory denotes the pressures on individuals to conform and perform in accordance with cultural norms. It has an oppressive effect.

Phenomenography is a research methodology which seeks to identify and understand how human beings apprehend phenomena. It assumes that human awareness is organized in terms of a central core, surrounding field and outer fringe, and that different individuals will develop different patterns of awareness of phenemona. Through interview and other forms of data collection, the phenomenographic researcher seeks to identify the four or five typical patterns of awareness among a group about particular phenomena. *Note*: phenomenography is quite separate from phenomenology.

Phenomenon (plural: phenomena) refers to anything which can be observed or experienced by human beings.

Philosophy is the study of knowledge and wisdom – how can we decide what it is that we know? It has been hugely influential in the development of western thought, going back to the time of the Ancient Greeks in the fourth century BC. Other notable early contributions to Western philosophy came from Arab, Christian and Jewish scholars during the early Middle Ages.

Photo-elicitation is a method whereby photographs are used to stimulate the memory of an interviewee. It is a way of focusing an interview on specific activities without asking leading questions. It is particularly useful in interviewing children.

Policy is the body of official documents, official statements, guidelines and so forth that together make up a programme for action. National governments, state governments, health services, schools and other such bodies all develop policies.

Political (politics) is used (with a small 'p') to mean social processes which involve manoeuvring for power; it is often referred to as 'micro-politics' in studies of institutions and organizations.

Population refers to all the people or phenomena under study, from whom a sample will be selected for research.

Positioning in feminist theory, critical race theory, queer theory, and so forth is the process whereby individuals are pushed to adopt specific roles because of group expectations that they will conform to cultural norms. It is an oppressive process. On the other hand, self-positioning can also be a process whereby an individual adopts a role in order to gain greater agency.

Positivist (positivism) is used to describe an approach to research based on the assumption that knowledge can be discovered by collecting data through observation, measurement and experimentation to establish truth. The huge advances in the natural sciences during the twentieth century resulted from research of this kind. In social science research positivism has proved problematic because human behaviour and social interaction are unpredictable and not easily susceptible to control and measurement. For this reason, the term positivism has come to be used by some social science researchers with strongly negative connotations.

Post-colonialism refers to a social movement – and a research approach – which seeks to oppose the racist and oppressive features which self-perpetuate in societies that were formally colonies of European empires.

Power is an important concept in qualitative research and what exactly constitutes power has been the source of considerable debate. Power is seen to be a factor in all organizations and human groups, and is the means by which some have greater autonomy than others and are able to control others. The exercise of power in an organization takes place through micro-political processes as well as through formal authority. Power is not necessarily oppressive, but can be seen to be a productive force created and sustained by the norms of the group and amenable to cooption.

Praxis refers to the process of embedding the development of theory in practical action. Theory and practice are seen as reciprocal rather than hierarchical or sequential.

Progressive focusing is a method whereby initial data collection is followed by preliminary analysis in order to select an issue or issues which will be the focus for the next round of data collection . . . and so on. By this means the research starts broad and narrows to a much more specific focus by the third round of data collection.

Proposition is the term for a statement that could provide the focus for research to try to prove or disprove it.

Protocol is the term used for the outline framework which will be used in data collection (see **Instruments**).

Qualitative refers to research approaches which involve the collection and analysis of data such as field notes, interviews, documents and images (see the chapters in Parts II–V and VIII in this volume).

Quantitative refers to research approaches which involve the collection and analysis of numerical data, often using statistical methods (see the chapters in Parts VI and VII in this volume).

Random sample (random sampling) is a selection from a population in which each item has an equal chance of being selected and the selection of one does not affect the selection of any other. In other words, the selection is made by 'chance', for example by allocating number to each item and using a random number generator on a computer.

Randomized controlled trials are used in experimental research and comprise: selecting a random sample representative of the total population being studied; randomly dividing this into two component parts (treatment group and control group); administering a pre-test to the whole cohort and subsequently a 'treatment' (some kind of change) to the treatment group only; and following up with a post-test to establish the differences in the changes that have taken place over time between the two groups in order to identify those changes which have resulted from the treatment.

Rationality is the process of establishing concepts and theories by rational means, using logical reasoning (see **Enlightenment**).

Realism (real, realist, reality) is based on the epistemological assumption that truth can be determined as something distinct from the processes of mind (see **Correspondence theory of truth**). It assumes that there is a reality 'out there' which can be investigated and understood on the basis of collecting data and identifying supportive evidence.

Reductionist refers to the process of 'data reduction' by which complex data sets are organized and presented in briefer, more coherent forms, often by means of coding responses. This process is an important step in data analysis, but care needs to be taken not to oversimplify when coding open-ended data since this can lead to superficial analysis.

Reflection is used in qualitative research to describe the process of mentally reviewing and evaluating practice. It can take place both during and after an event.

Reflexivity (reflexive) combines the process of reflection with self-critical analysis. It is seen as a means whereby social science researchers are able to explore their own subjectivity, be more aware of the impact they necessarily have on the research data they collect and increase the sensitivity of their analysis and interpretations of data (see **Subjectivity**).

Regulatory practices are ways of doing things within a social group which are considered as norms, with which members are expected to comply.

Relativism is a philosophical position that holds that truth is not constant but varies in relation to context, time, circumstances, and so forth.

Reliability is the term used to mean that the truth of the findings has been established by ensuring that they are supported by sufficient and compelling evidence. In quantitative research, it refers specifically to a measurement repeatedly giving the same

result or to a research instrument being internally consistent.

Representation (1) (representative, representativeness) is used in relation to the selection of a research sample, for example those selected for interview. It may be important to select individuals who, together, are representative of the larger group (for example if there are 30 men and 10 women a sample of 6 men and 2 women might be said to be representative).

Representation (2) is used in semiotics to describe the process whereby human beings make meaning through creating a range of written texts, images and visual designs. Once created, texts require interpretation to understand how they socioculturally construct meaning.

Representation (3) is used in deconstruction and post-structuralism to describe the way in which concepts like childhood or marriage are constructed and positioned to give them particular cultural meanings, which enforce particular kinds of behaviour.

Researcher bias refers to the process whereby data collection and analysis may be strongly influenced by the assumptions and values of the researcher. Some social scientists argue that bias should be addressed by discussing such assumptions and their potential impact on research design and analysis, rather than simply attempting to bracket them out.

Respondent is the term for someone who completes a questionnaire or gives an interview.

Response rate refers to the proportion of a sample in survey research from whom usable data is collected (for example the number of people surveyed who return completed questionnaires).

Rigorous is the term used to indicate that research has used tried and tested methods and procedures which will lead to reliable results. It is often used in relation to quantitative and experimental methods, but can be applied to all research approaches that require systematic data collection and analysis. It is sometimes treated by politicians and the media as co-terminous with an experimental approach.

Rituals are routinized activities (performances) that are carried out in a specified way and often repeated, giving them established cultural meanings.

Sample refers to the individuals who are included in data collection, selected from the whole population.

Scale is the reference standard against which measurements are recorded on a graph. When two variables are plotted there will be two scales. The representation of scale on a graph is important in making the spread of data clear to readers: for example, if the scale is 100 and the representation shows only up to the 60th percentile this must be clearly indicated. It is never acceptable to show two graphs side by side which display different scales or the same scale showing different percentiles.

Sexuality refers to the physical and genetic characteristics which distinguish men from women. (See Filax et al., Chapter 10 in this volume, for more detailed discussion of the implications of such categorization.)

Significant effect (positive/negative) (significance) is the technical term in quantitative research meaning that a relationship or difference found in the sample is unlikely to have occurred purely by chance or due to some peculiarity of the sample. A significant relationship is therefore likely (but not certain) to be the result of the existence of a real relationship in the population rather than coincidence. 'Significant' is used with a less precise meaning in qualitative research. Mixed-methods researchers must ensure that they only use it with its technical meaning to avoid confusion.

Social constructivism refers to the process by which phenomena in the social world are formed and sustained by social structures and interactions rather than being constants that conform to natural laws. Researchers who adopt this approach are likely to use mainly qualitative rather than quantitative methods.

Sociology of knowledge is the study of how knowledge is affected by social contexts, in particular by the social processes through which power and status are differentially allocated (e.g. to ethnic groups, academic disciplines).

Stakeholders are all those people who have an interest in the outcome of an enterprise, for example in social research this would include the sponsors, future audiences for any report, and all the participants in the research field.

Standardized is the term in quantitative research for a research instrument (usually a test to be administered to individuals) that has been piloted extensively to establish the normal distribution of results in a very large population. Test papers can, therefore, be administered to a small cohort and the scoring, using the standardized instructions, will produce reliable results.

Standpoint is the position adopted by a researcher who recognizes the need to be an advocate for a particular point of view. It embodies the assumption that the researcher is working in a context which is oppressive and in which certain groups are routinely denied social justice.

Statistical analysis involves the use of mathematical methods to describe and compare data, and distinguish between them in order to establish results.

Structure and agency refers to the long-standing debate about the degree to which individuals have free will or are constrained by circumstances. Structure refers in particular to the social norms and organizational/administrative structures within which individuals live (see also **Agency**).

Subjectivity (subjectivist) refers to the human persona (emotions, knowledge, experience, values, and so forth). Psychoanalytic theory focuses attention on subjectivity as a key area of inquiry. From a different point of view, the subjectivity of the researcher – the self as a research instrument – is seen as central to the quality of certain types of research based on epistemological assumptions that truth is not something that can be 'found' separately from the particular contexts or participants in the area of study.

Subjects is a technical term used in some social science research to refer to the people who are the objects of study. Some researchers prefer to use words such as 'participants' or 'informants', because the word 'subjects' has connotations of subjection and seems to accord a dominant position to the researcher.

Surveys are a form of research which seeks information from a large number of people by means of questionnaires, which may be administered online or postally, and in some cases are collected through face-to-face interaction.

Symbolic interactionism refers to a set of theories concerning the way that individuals form and maintain their identity in relation to others. It is based on the notion that social interaction is made up of patterned (and often habitual) behaviours or utterances which have easily recognizable symbolic meanings which invite responses of similarly patterned behaviours from others.

Synthesizing is an important step in the process of generating knowledge. After data have been analysed which often involves breaking them up and examining parts or groups in detail, synthesis is the process of bringing together the outcomes of the analyses and generating overall meanings.

Systematic review refers to a particular approach to reviewing research literature in order to establish evidence that should be put into practice (evidence-based practice). It begins by establishing the criteria by which published research will be selected for, or excluded from, the review. It tends to pay little attention to the contextual differences between research sites (e.g. the country where it was carried out).

Teleological refers to the process of explaining or evaluating events and phenomena in terms of their outcomes. The concept is often used by social science researchers to indicate a mechanistic process.

Temporal means with reference to a specific time.

Text (textual, textualized, textuality) is used in linguistics and related fields of the social sciences to denote anything that can be 'read' and interpreted, whether it is written, comprises images, or is enacted. Its meaning derives from the values of those who construct it. In post-structuralism and deconstruction it is seen as the fundamental component of human experience. There is no possibility of experience outside text since language constructs all experience. We can't get through or beyond language.

Theoretical framework is the term used to describe the body of theory which governs all the decisions made in carrying out research (from methods of data collection and analysis to the nature of the knowledge outcomes).

Theories are explanations or propositions. In the natural sciences they are generally regarded as guiding truths, until proved false by new data or experimentation. In the social sciences they are more open to challenge, especially if the methodology is grounded in epistemological assumptions that truth and reality are socioculturally constructed. Social science research normally starts with a theoretical framework and develops new theories (or variations of existing theories) as research outcomes.

Transformative is one of those words that has very specific (but different) meanings in different methodologies. Its most basic – and most common – meaning relates to the process of change, growth, radical improvement. A claim that transformation has occurred, for example, as a result of a new teaching method, is seen by most researchers to be difficult to support with evidence. However, in semiotics 'transformation' refers to the process involved in creating any text or image or utterance, drawing upon sociocultural models and genres but nevertheless in every case creating a unique production. Others would argue that all learning involves a process of transformation.

Transgressive is a term that literally means overstepping the limits. It tends to be used to denote intentional non-conformity in methodologies such as queer theory or feminism (see **Disrupt**).

Triangulation is a method whereby data from at least three different perspectives (for example, teacher, students and observer) are collected on the same issue/event so that they can be cross-validated. Alternatively, three or more different kinds of data (for example video, interview and questionnaire) are collected on the same issue/event and used to shed light on one another.

Typology is the term used for a list or table which organizes phenomena into categories and hierarchies. Typologies are often used as an organizing framework in research, or the development of a typology may be an outcome of the research.

Utilitarian refers to practices, including research practices, which place high priority on the usefulness of outcomes.

Utopian comes from Thomas Moore's book, *Utopia*, written in the sixteenth century, and refers to a place or a set of ideas which verge on perfection and are, therefore, probably unobtainable.

Validity is the term used to claim that the research has investigated and demonstrated what it set out to investigate – i.e. the methods and results have addressed the research questions. In quantitative research validity refers specifically to the extent that research instruments are measuring what they set out to measure.

Value literally means 'merit, worth, significance' but in social science research the term 'values' (value systems) has much wider significance, denoting the entire set of beliefs and principles which underpin a set of judgements or a particular endeavour.

Variable(s) (independent variables, dependent variables) is the term that refers to the features of a situation which can be counted or measured in quantitative research. The independent variables are the features which the researchers decide to include in order to give a range of information about the object of study and which they organize and manipulate to design an effective test. The dependent variable is the feature which is expected to change as a result of manipulating the independent variables in order to test its functioning or behaviour in some way.

Verification (verificationist) refers to the process of collecting evidence to prove the truth of a proposition. It is the opposite approach to falsification (see **Falsifiability**).

Reference

Bullock, A. and Trombley, S. (eds) (2000) *New Fontana Dictionary of Modern Thought*. London: Harper Collins.

Index

Added to a page number 'f' denotes a figure, 't' denotes a table and 'g' denotes glossary.

black-box model building 208
bloggers/blogging 148, 149
blogs 45, 46
Bonferroni correction 234
border-crossings 307
boundaries, case studies 53, 54
boundary objects 176
Bourdieu, P. 7, 9, 62, 192
bourgeois ideology 184
British Journal of Statistical Psychology 6
brokers 176
Bruner, J. 8–9
burden of proof 213
Burt, C. 6
business studies, principles of research 12–13
Butler, J. 4, 70, 88, 313

capitalism 3, 13, 80, 89, 290
care, ethic of 27, 71, 72, 107
Cartesian philosophy 214, 325
case studies
  annotated bibliography 59
  evaluative 55, 105
  key concepts 53–5
  in psychology 6
  research designs 55–6
  stories from the field 56–9
case-control designs 207
categorical data 227
categories 114–15, 116
  challenge to notion of 4
  CHAT as a science of 183
  defined 321g
  in feminist research 71
  intersectionality 73
  open-ended questions 225
  social semiotics 167
categorization
  practitioner research 96
  queer theory 87–8
category development 151
category maintenance 136
category saturation 116
causal inferences 204, 221, 222, 246
causal mechanisms 208
causality 207, 209, 221, 222
causation 239
cause and effect 239, 241, 321g
CDA *see* critical discourse analysis
census 222
central tendency 227, 230
certainty 137, 139, 214, 306
change, action research 13, 97
charts 226
CHAT *see* Cultural-Historical Activity Theory
chi-square 237–8
Chicago School of Sociology 55, 157
citation practices 16
citizenship 5

civil rights, participatory action research 96
class discrimination 80
classical action research 13
classical theory 13
classification 205, 321g
classification diagrams 250, 251f
classrooms
  ethnographic research 37–40
  practitioner research 135–7
clinical 321g
Clinical Academic Training Pathway for Nurses, Midwives and Allied Health Professions 10–11
'closed interview' format 62
closed questions 133, 225
closed systems 203–4
Closely Observed Children 43
cluster sampling 223
CMO configurations 209
co-construction 117, 321g
co-production 63
co-researchers 4, 95–6, 126
Cochrane Collaboration 10
codes of practice 27, 96, 134
coding 114, 133
  see also open coding
coding frame 226
cognition 175
  see also distributed cognition; situated cognition
cognitive 321g
cognitive functions 183
cognitive knowing 122
cognitive patterns 12
coherence 46
collaboration
  action research 13, 94, 97
  life history and narrative research 160, 162
  with participants 94
  research diaries 45–6
collaborative practice, as research 308–10
collective biography 314–15
  story from the field 315–17
colonial evolutionism 184
colour, in questionnaires 225
colour-blindness 78, 79, 80
The Coming Crisis of Western Sociology 7
commitment, to clear vision 48–50
communication
  Habermas on 296
  semiotics 167
  systematically deformed 297
  see also dialogue; language; speech
Communities of Practice: Learning, Meaning and Identity 175
communities of practice
  affinity spaces as an alternative construct to 149
  annotated bibliography 180–1
  health research 10

key concepts 174–7
research designs 177
stories from the field 177–80
community
  CoP model 174
  CRT and sensitivity to 81
comparability 272–4
comparisons 64, 115
complementarity 260
The Complexities of an Urban Classroom 43
complexity, statistical 251–2
complexity social science 207
complicitous critique 88
composite measure 277, 321g
computer-based techniques 8, 226
Comte, A. 212
concept descriptors 326
concept identification 116
concepts 114–16, 321g
conceptual frameworks 213, 271–2, 274, 321g
conclusion validity 247
condensed fieldwork 55
conditioning, regression modelling 242–5
conditions of possibility 88
confessional technologies 88
Confessions 44
confidence intervals 223, 273–4
confidence level 223
confidentiality 26, 226, 321g
confirmation 205
conflict theories 7
confounders 207
conjectural knowledge 214
connective inquiry 147, 148–9
consensual process, policy as 191
consent 26, 134
conservative hermeneutics 295
constant comparative method 64
constructionism 7, 35, 203, 262
  see also social constructionism
constructionist ontology 71–2
constructivism 261, 262, 321g
  see also social constructivism
content, affinity spaces 150
content analysis 73
context/contextuality 3, 6, 10, 26, 54, 94, 115, 122, 160, 209, 215, 253
contingency table *see* crosstabulation
contingency theorists 12
contingent 205, 321g
continuity 44, 159
continuous data 227
contract research 193
contradictory findings, interpretation 264–5
contrastive demi-regularities 206
control 58, 96, 191, 315
convenience sampling 63, 224
convergence 260
conversation analysis 73, 140, 141